Doo-Wop

The forgotten
third of
Rock 'n Roll

by Dr. Anthony J. Gribin & Dr. Matthew M. Schiff

Published by

 **krause
publications**

700 East State St.   Iola, WI 54990-0001

**Library of Congress Catalog Number: 91-77560
ISBN: 0-87341-197-8**

Printed in the United States of America

Table of Contents

Dedication

To our parents, wives and children.

About The Authors

Tony Gribin and Matt Schiff have led parallel lives. Both grew up and attended high school during the doo-wop era. Both graduated the City College of New York before going on to attain their professional degrees. Both settled in the same part of Central New Jersey, each with exactly 1.0 wives and 2.0 children.

They met for the first time in 1975 and, roughly 15 years later, decided to write a book on a subject they both always loved: doo-wop music.

Dr. Gribin is a Clinical Psychologist who has a private practice and consults, and Dr. Schiff is a Child and Adolescent Psychiatrist who enjoys writing for local newspapers as well as national publications.

Preface

Looking back, we had it pretty easy growing up. We were both only children of doting parents, and the New York City that surrounded us (Queens for Tony, the Bronx for Matt) didn't seem as threatening as it does now. The late 1950s, those years during which we achieved teenagehood, were innocent and sheltered for us and rather unremarkable. And all the while, the music that we grew to love, doo-wop, was being created by kids only slightly older than we were, but who were, as a rule, less fortunate and sheltered. We wouldn't have thought that they were less fortunate at the time, and we would have envied the prospect of not being as sheltered as we were. But we were young then.

In early adolescence we were still playing stickball, punchball and basketball, the main sports of the cement school yards of New York City. Although blessed with above average intellect, we weren't bright enough to realize that we should be actually using our minds for purposes other than calculating and remembering baseball statistics and committing the lyrics of the top forty songs to memory. We both seemed to fall in with groups of kids who were similarly disposed, and we gravitated to that music, doo-wop, which echoed the emotions and feelings of our teenage years.

Doo-wop music wasn't square, and it belonged to us rather than to our parents. What our parents liked we hated, and what they didn't like we felt almost an obligation to defend. We might have been too shy to ask girls out, too well brought up to become "juvenile delinquents," too young to drag race in souped-up cars, but we sure could fantasize with the help of our music. Doo-wop represented the few tough guys in our academically progressive high schools, it stood for the guys who got the girls (it sure wasn't us!), and it epitomized male bonding. It symbolized all the things that we wished we could be or have but could never attain.

Although nowadays kids seem to have friends of both sexes (and travel in packs), back then, for us, it was just half a dozen guys "hangin' out." Once in a while we'd see a movie, play pool or go bowling, but the backbone of the Friday night activity schedule was just standing on the avenue or outside the candy store making comments about the girls that slinked past or "ranking" on one another about anything that provided apt material. When all this fun subsided we walked home. We were too cool to stay home, but not cool enough to actually have something to do.

We suspect that we aren't the only ones out there whose hearts still lie with doo-wop. Both of us still staunchly defend the honor of this music despite its melodic repetitiveness and lyrical simplicity. Other musics say the same thing more eloquently, but none says it with more heart. Actually, we got into this project because we started to think about the music rather than just listen to it. We noticed, for example, that the doo-wop music created in the early fifties was allied strongly with down-and-dirty rhythm and blues, but the music created later had more of an innocent quality. We also noticed differences between doo-wops created after 1960 and those recorded in the fifties. The more we thought things through and talked them out, the more curious we grew. This book is the result of that curiosity.

We've made a good team for this type of enterprise. Matt likes the ballads and Tony prefers the uptempo numbers. Matt knows more of the songs than

Tony does (after all, he's three years older and thus has had more time to study them), and Tony's better at organizing things (he owns the computer). At first we thought the songography, at least, would be a straightforward task. We soon learned, however, that there were more street corners in the 1950s than we had anticipated and that each one had five or so guys trying to harmonize. We were often tantalized by one bit of information, say the name of a group, and then went crazy trying to find out whether or not it was truly a doo-wop group, what songs they sang, which label deigned to release their output and when. We've done the best we could under the circumstances. The reader will note many blank spaces in the songography. Anyone who can help us to fill in those blanks will be met with gratitude.

This has not been an easy project. It took us two years to get it done, although to be fair, we do have other jobs. The publication of *Doo-Wop* has redeemed us. In the eyes of our families, we've gone from a couple of middle-aged men trying to recapture our youths to a couple of respectable authors, in one fell swoop. As for our friends, we can finally look them in the eye after two years of saying "we're still working on it."

We had to have a lot of assistance along the way. Nina Meissler provided invaluable help by typing, copying, collating and searching out information for us. Nina always believed in our project, which is either testimony to the book or a comment on her naivete. Andy Rosetta and Marc Feldman encouraged us, fed us information and taught us some things. Lillian Brown, proprietor of the Music Exchange, a famous repository for sheet music and other printed material related to music (in New York City), convinced us that our project was worthwhile and helped us make some contacts within the industry.

Tom Goodell, an oldies aficionado from Houston, Texas, provided us with yearly "Top Oldies" surveys from all over the country, in effect helping us to prove that doo-wop music is still in demand. Thanks to Bill Himmelman, who helped us track down the rock 'n' roll collectors cards that he published, and then graciously allowed their use as illustrations in this book. Thanks to Eliot Zolin, Hal Lesser and Harvey Nash who sent us other material that we digested and incorporated into our book. Jeff Kreiter, himself a discographer, helped us fill in the blanks in our own data base, and discussed doo-wop philosophy with us. And thanks to Marvin Magalaner, an English professor who learned a lot about doo-wop while helping us to correct our lousy grammar.

Finally, thanks to people who helped us get the manuscript published. Thanks to Robin Kaigh for teaching us something about the book business, about which we knew zip. Thanks to Rob Cohen, our agent, for being patient with our impatience. Thanks to Pat Klug and Mary Sieber, of Krause Publications, for making our first experience with the world of publishing a pleasant one. And thanks to our content editor, Bob Pruter, for his perseverance, knowledge and willingness to share that knowledge. Bob made us make the book better than it was, and made us wiser in the process.

Chapter 1

A Doo-Wop In The Bucket

Most of us look back fondly on our teenage years, even if they weren't so hot when we were actually living them. The humiliations we suffered then now conjure up laughter rather than anguish, and the exciting and fun times seem better than real life allows. The teenage years are special to us because that is when we began to run our own lives. Preferences and beliefs emerged in us that were uniquely our own (so we thought), and that were certainly different from what our parents espoused. We thought we were adults, and wanted to be treated as such, even if we didn't know our proverbial asses from our elbows.

We can never go back to those times, but we can catch glimpses of who we were and what we were about. Old clothes, old friends, television shows, movies, and snapshots can bring us back to those memories, but the medium that allows a recapturing of the past most easily is the music of our teenage generation. OUR music is always readily available on the radio, on (almost antique) 45 RPM records, albums, tapes, concerts and, for those of us who have mastered the new-fangled technology, compact discs. And, of course, OUR music was and is the very best.

For those of us who were teenagers in the 1950s and the early part of the 1960s, OUR music often equates, at least in part, to doo-wop music. The group sound of doo-wop reminds us of our friends and our exploits, the male- and female-bonding activities of our generation: the practical jokes, ball-playing, drag racing, the candy store or malt shop hangout, the cliquishness, the insecurities, the pool halls and bowling alleys, the poker games, the school hallways. The innocence of the lyrics of doo-wop songs recall our first feelings of romance and lust. We grew up with doo-wop and now, thirty-odd years later, doo-wop helps us retrace that journey from childhood to adulthood.

Since the "oldies" phenomenon was born during the doo-wop years (roughly 1960), even our younger brothers and sisters know OUR music. Through this oldies phenomenon, doo-wop, as well as other types of rock 'n' roll, have been passed down from teen generation to teen generation. Fifties and sixties dance clubs, with names like "At The Hop" and "Yakety Yak Cafe," cater to young adult singles, testimony to this "hand-me-down" effect. Most of the denizens of these clubs weren't even close to life at the time that doo-wop flourished. It may not be THEIR music, but young people apparently have enough sense to know it and appreciate it.

Considering that so many people, aged 55 and on down, recognize and identify with doo-wop music, one would think it would be easy to find a book on the subject. A "book," by the way, is a tool often used by older folk to either overcome insomnia or to set good examples for their children. In the New York metropolitan area there are no fewer than six radio stations that play oldies (including doo-wop), so if you want to give your ears a treat you are in luck. Keeping your eyes occupied will be significantly more difficult because it is very hard to find a book on doo-wop music. We tried to find one and it started us on an odyssey, the result of which is this opus. The more we searched, the clearer it became that (a) doo-wop music has been consistently overlooked and underrated, and (b) the social and cultural history of doo-wop demands that this music be considered as an entity separate from (but related to) the larger body of rock 'n' roll. The reasons for these statements should become clear as the story unfolds.

As stated above, doo-wop music has received little attention in the mainstream media. John Rockwell, a contributor to the *New Grove Dictionary of American Music* describes doo-wop as "a style of vocal rock-and-roll popular in the 1950s and early 1960s. It was essentially an unaccompanied type of close-harmony singing by groups of four or five members; if an accompaniment was added it functioned as a restrained background, largely obscured by the voices. The beginnings of the style can be detected in 19th-century barbershop singing and in the music of such black vocal groups as the Ink Spots in the 1930s and the Orioles in the late 1940s." Rockwell goes on to list some of the derivative groups and cites some of the more important songs of the era. Unfortunately, he chose "There's A Moon Out Again" by the Capris as an example. This song was recorded by the Capris, but not until 1981, as the "B" side of their hit "Morse Code Of Love." The correct citation should have been "There's A Moon Out *Tonight*" (which was released in 1960). The *New Grove Dictionary* is a well-respected, often referred-to work in four huge volumes containing thousands of pages. The amount of space allotted to doo-wop music is roughly one-quarter of one page. Something is drastically wrong!

When we first decided to look into the possibility of writing a book on doo-wop, it was anticipated that either so much had already been written that we could add little to the field, or that at minimum the volume of the documented material might just overwhelm us. We were overwhelmed, but not in the manner expected. In fact, very little had been written on doo-wop music. The overwhelming part came in trying to assemble and organize materials from literally hundreds of sources, including (a) many small citations in books written about fifties music, rock 'n' roll or rhythm and blues, (b) catalogs and discographies itemizing records in general categories, (c) numerous historical articles on individual groups and record companies found in a number of periodicals, and (d) liner notes from innumerable albums. The material was so well buried that we became white-collar archaeologists.

Attempting to start with the biggest and best, we visited the Library of Congress Recorded Sound Section in Washington, D.C. This national institution houses one of the country's largest collection of musical recordings and literature. Aside from giving us a funny look or two when we announced our topic, the librarians there did everything within their power to be of assistance. They entered "doo-wop" and its variations into their computer and only came up with a few in-stock record albums and films. It seems that most of the bigger record stores that specialize in oldies have more extensive collections than the Library of Congress. They also scurried about and were able to find a few gems in print, ones like that from the *New Grove Dictionary*. We left with very little besides Xerox copies of the backs of several record albums, an appreciation for the enthusiasm of those librarians, and a new-found respect for our subject matter.

Robert Santelli, music critic for the *Asbury Park Press*, wrote, "Page through any rock history book and, chances are, doo-wop is given scant attention. There is no good reason why this offshoot of '50s rock 'n' roll that featured intricate rhythm and blues-flavored harmonies and urban street corner sensibility gets shortchanged, other that its rather short-lived popularity (it was all but dead as a pop vocal form by 1963) and its limited influence on future rock 'n' roll." While Santelli may be premature in burying doo-wop, he is accurate about the dearth of material to be found in the print media.

Another rock critic with a slightly larger audience, Dave Marsh, ex-writer for *Rolling Stone* magazine and author of *The Heart Of Rock and Soul: The 1001 Greatest Singles Ever Made*, agrees. He writes, "Some of the most beautiful records ever made (though you'd be hard-pressed to find it out in previous histories) are the sound of willful young men learning to unify themselves in three- and four- or five-part harmony: That is the special glory of doo-wop, and restoring that music to its central place in the early chapters of the story provides one of the great lost truths of rock and soul." Apparently, bookstores have not yet run out of room on their doo-wop shelves.

There are plenty of *musical* tributes to doo-wop, issued today by a handful of labels, including Relic (Hackensack, New Jersey), Rhino (San Francisco, California), Collectables (Narberth, Pennsylvania), Crystal Ball (Flushing, New York), Classic Artists (Los Angeles, California) and Ace (London, England). While the ears of doo-wop aficionados are still keen and functional, the part of the brain governing the writing of books seems to have atrophied. There are three exceptions. Phil Groia wrote a fascinating book titled *They All Sang On The Corner*, which chronicled the successes and failures of many of the New York doo-wop groups. Johnny Keyes, lead singer of the erstwhile Magnificents ("Up On The Mountain"), in a book entitled *Du-Wop*, told the story of the rehearsals, performances and traveling involved in being a group singer during the doo-wop era. Lynn McCutcheon's *Rhythm And Blues* was an interesting attempt to clarify the dimensions involved in rockabilly, rhythm and blues and soul music, and looking at the similarities among them. Unfortunately, all three of these works have had limited circulation and are fairly hard to come by. There have also been over a dozen periodicals which are outside the mainstream media, have small circulations and are geared to dedicated doo-wop buffs. Examples are *Bim Bam Boom*, which published 14 issues between 1971 and 1974 (Bronx, New York), the *Record Exchanger*, which put out 31 issues between 1969 and 1983 (Anaheim, California) and *Record Collector's Monthly*, with 50 issues since 1982 (Mendham, New Jersey). One mainstream magazine, *Goldmine*, does regularly focus on doo-wop as a subject. A list of magazines that are devoted to doo-wop can be found in Appendix II. The articles in these magazines, however, are almost always historical treatises; that is, they trace the origins, career and fate of group members. What is missing, and what is needed, is analytical treatment of the subject. Very little had been done to place doo-wop in a sociological, psychological or even musical perspective. In any event there seems to be enough people out there that like doo-wop music for at least one more book on it to be written.

Statistics which describe the popularity of doo-wop music are confusing and/or misleading. The perceived importance of the music depends not only upon the source of the information, but also upon the breadth of one's perspective. As the reader will note in the sections that follow, the penetration of doo-wop music ranges from 2-4 percent all the way to more than 30 percent, depending upon how the data are viewed and analyzed.

The Popularity of Doo-Wop in the Rock 'n' Roll Era (1955-1987)

The *Billboard* charts of the most popular songs of the rock 'n' roll era provide interesting data. Of the top 100 records (1955-1988), only two (2 percent) were doo-wop songs, and of the top 100 artists, only three (3 percent) sang in doo-wop style during some time in their careers. Of *Billboard's* top 1000 singles between the years 1955 and 1987, only 38 (3.8 percent) were recorded doo-wop songs. Of records which cracked the "Top 40" during these same years, only 375 of 8800 (4.4 percent) were doo-wop songs. As a generalization, it is safe to say that doo-wop made up roughly 4 percent of the music that made the national charts since the dawn of the rock 'n' roll era. These figures imply that doo-wop had but a small impact.

The Popularity of Doo-Wop in its Heyday (1954-1963)

Other data yield different conclusions. Looking more specifically at the years during which doo-wop flourished yields a more realistic figure. Of the *Billboard* number one hits between 1955 and 1963, 29 of 169 (15.4 percent) were done in doo-wop style. The *Norm N. Nite Almanac*, which used national charts, airplay lists and an undescribed computer program to yield its data, listed 354 doo-wop songs among 1800 (19.7 percent) of the most popular songs between the years 1954 and 1963. Averaging these two figures, doo-wop accounted for roughly seventeen percent of the hit songs during the years that it was popular.

The Popularity of Doo-Wop in Retrospect

Data gathered from many areas of the country support the notion that although doo-wop was mainly an urban phenomenon, it was appreciated just about everywhere. The information gathered in surveys performed by oldies stations (in either 1989 or 1990) broadcasting from 10 large metropolitan areas are presented in Table I, below. These surveys are retrospective; that is, in most cases listeners were asked to write to the station and vote for (as an example) their favorite three "oldies." After being tallied, the results yield the Top 500 (or 400 or 300) records of the past, as viewed by current listeners.

Table 1:

CITY	STATION	TOTAL # OF HITS	PERCENT IN THE TOP							
			10	25	50	100	200	300	400	500
Boston	WODS-FM	500	20	16	26	23	21.5	20.7	19.3	18
Chicago	WJMK-FM	500	20	8	12	17	17	13.7	12.5	12.2
Cincinnati	WGRR-FM	500	0	4	8	16	21.5	19	16	13.8
Houston	KNUZ-AM	300	30	20	32	31	29	25.7		
Kansas City	95-FM	500	10	16	14	13	15	11	10.5	11.2
Los Angeles	KRLA-AM	300	30	20	28	27	25.5	22		
New York	WCBS-FM	500	70	60	56	47	41	36.3	34.3	31.8
Philadelphia	WOGL-FM	500	30	28	30	30	28.5	24.7	23.5	22.8
St. Louis	KLOU-FM	400	0	12	16	18	17.5	16.7	14.5	
Tampa	WYUU-FM	500	10	8	14	15	15	13.7	11.8	11.2

Aside from New York, the other northeast urban areas, namely Philadelphia and Boston, show a large penetration of doo-wop music in their surveys, as does Los Angeles. While these results were to be expected, the surprisingly high numbers from Houston were not. The numbers from both Chicago (because it was a hotbed of independent labels that recorded doo-wop) and Cincinnati (because Alan Freed started his pilgrimage in Ohio) were disappointingly low. Penetrations of doo-wop in Kansas City, St. Louis and Tampa, not central to the doo-wop movement, were low as expected. All in all, the numbers range from a low of 11 percent to a high of almost 32 percent (see Table I). The "average" penetration over cities, if such a number exists, is pegged at roughly 18 percent. Thus almost one of every five songs remembered fondly by oldies aficionados was performed in doo-wop style. Not bad for a music that gained little respect in its heyday, and which competed with Elvis, the Beatles, Stones, Supremes, Beach Boys, Michael Jackson, etc. for the hearts of the reminiscing public. It must be noted that the sampling procedures of the individual radio stations cited above is not known and, in all likelihood, vary quite a bit. The stations also vary in their popularity within their listening areas. For these and other reasons, the conclusions drawn are not statistically rigorous.

The Popularity of Doo-Wop When the Perspective is Narrowed

Even this average figure of 18 percent can be misleading. Doo-wop blossomed and thrived primarily in the larger urban areas. While people in Nashville and Memphis were listening to rockabilly and country rhythm and blues, those in urban areas such as New York, Philadelphia and Los Angeles focused on doo-wop. In these urban areas, doo-wop accounted for a greater percentage of the local hits. Further, the statistics presented above represent a variety of listeners and record buyers. If the focus of examination were even more narrow, so that only adults who grew up in the doo-wop era (from these urban areas) were polled, an even greater percentage of the hit songs would be doo-wop in style. From Table I, the New York survey of urban teens and young adults that have grown up, namely the WCBS-FM "Top 500 for 1989," paints a radically different statistical picture. In this survey, doo-wop songs represented seven of the top 10 (70 percent), 28 of the top 50 (56 percent), 47 of the top 100 (47 percent) and 159 of the top 500 (31.8 percent). The aforementioned WCBS-FM, which is exclusively an oldies station, is far and away the most listened to among New Yorkers in the 29-54 year-old population. Most people in this age span grew up during part of the doo-wop era. It may be that doo-wop music is better appreciated today, at least among certain populations, than it was in its prime.

There are other reasons for writing this book. According to legend, the rock 'n' roll explosion did not occur until 1955. The doo-wop seed was not planted in 1955; it had already blossomed. It certainly antedated what we call rock 'n' roll, and in fact may have helped to create it. The Orioles hit the charts in 1948 with "It's Too Soon To Know" and "Tell Me So," and in 1949 with "What Are You Doing New Year's Eve?" The Ravens made the charts in 1950 with "Count Every Star." The Five Keys ("Glory of Love") and the Clovers ("Fool, Fool, Fool") hit the charts in 1951; the Vocaleers ("Be True") and the Clovers ("One Mint Julep") in 1952; the Harptones ("Sunday Kind Of Love") and the Spaniels ("Baby It's You") in 1953; the Chords ("Sh-Boom") and the Diablos ("The Wind") in 1954 (among other examples). Some of the most significant contributions to the body of doo-wop music were made before rock 'n' roll was popularized. Too often, books on rock 'n' roll treat these years 1951-1954 as harbinger years, with the result that doo-wop gets overlooked. If doo-wop preceded the rock 'n' roll explosion, then it ought to be viewed as an integral and important category within rhythm and blues. This is not the case either, for most books treating rhythm and blues gloss over doo-wop, going from Wynonie Harris and Louis Jordan straight to Ray Charles. It seems rhythm and blues fans would prefer to leave doo-wop to the rock 'n' roll generation, which brings us back to where we started. Doo-wop fell through the cracks in a most undeserved and undignified manner.

The Chords

The Clovers

An example of the confusion surrounding the provenance of doo-wop can be found in modern price guides to 45 RPM records. Doo-wop has been classified as either rhythm and blues or rock 'n' roll depending upon the race of the singing group! Osborne Enterprises published one book entitled *The Blues, R&B and Soul Price Guide* and another called *Rockin' Records: Buyers-Sellers Reference Book And Price Guide*. The former lists black doo-wop groups almost exclusively, and the latter lists only white doo-wop groups. Similarly, Goldmine's *Rock 'n Roll 45 RPM Record Price Guide* lists only white groups and *Honkers and Shouters: the Golden Years of Rhythm & Blues*, by Arnold Shaw, omits almost all white groups. The implication is that if you are white you can't sing rhythm and blues and if you are black you can't

The Five Keys

sing rock 'n' roll. There are more than a few artists, not to mention their audiences, who would take issue with that classification scheme.

The way out of this rather ridiculous situation is to use the music as a point of reference rather than the skin color of the artists performing it. The song "Gloria" is doo-wop music, whether recorded by the Cadillacs or Channels

The Harptones

(both black), Passions or Vito & the Salutations (both white). The Belmonts, with Dion DiMucci out front, certainly have more in common with their black doo-wop counterparts than they do with Elvis Presley or other white rock 'n' rollers. The umbrella for the music should be doo-wop, not rhythm and blues, and not rock 'n' roll (although there are interrelations which will be discussed in a later chapter). That doo-wop should be separate and distinct from both rhythm and blues and rock 'n' roll is a major tenet of this book.

To add insult to injury, doo-wop groups never received their fair share of hero-worship. Until the arrival of Elvis Presley, the conventional wisdom held that songs were more important than artists. As a result, it was not uncommon to be able to buy three or four renditions of the same popular song at local record stores. As an example, in August 1953, "Crying In The Chapel" was available in six versions (the Orioles on Jubilee, June Valli on RCA, Darrell Glenn on Valley, Rex Allen, Ella Fitzgerald and Sister Rosetta Tharpe on Decca), four of which placed in the Top 10 on the pop charts at the same time! Jukeboxes featured multiple versions as well. Apparently teens did not as yet know that they were supposed to have idols, a fact that might shock members of today's Pepsi generation. In truth, young Frank Sinatra and Benny Goodman had earlier been the focus of teen adulation, but they were exceptions and not the rule. Worship became the rage with the advent of rock 'n' roll, and it was lavished not on groups, most of whom were doo-wopists, but on individuals such as Presley, Jerry Lee Lewis, Gene Vincent, Little Richard, Fats Domino, Chuck Berry, Carl Perkins and Ray Charles. Doo-wop groups were "Out In The Cold Again," as Frankie Lymon once lamented. Kids did not wake up to the notion that groups deserved deification until the Beatles forced their hands. By this time, the doo-wop formula had grown old.

Statistics from the Rock And Roll Hall Of Fame clearly show the disrespect for groups. Of 25 inductees in 1986 and 1987 (the first two years of its existence), 23 were individual artists, one was a duo (the Everly Brothers) and only one, the Coasters, was a doo-wop group. From 1986 through 1992, only three of 57 artists inductees have been groups, namely the Coasters, Drifters and Platters. Frankie Lymon & the Teenagers and the Moonglows, more "hard-core" doo-wop groups, were nominated but were denied admission. To add insult in injury, Dion was inducted without either the Belmonts or Del

Satins, and Clyde McPhatter and Jackie Wilson were taken in without the group in which they both began their careers (i.e., the Dominoes).

Another reason doo-wop was not adequately chronicled is that it didn't have a name until its popularity had already waned. It was never considered as a separate entity in its heyday, being subsumed under the general categories of rock 'n' roll, rhythm and blues, '50s music or oldies (after 1960). *The Oxford English Dictionary*, Second Edition (1989) defines doo-wop thusly: "A variety of (originally American) vocal group music, usually performed a capella or with little instrumental accompaniment, so called from the use of nonsense phrases accompanying the vocal lead." It then goes on to cite occurrences of the word in print. The first attribution is not until 1969! The genre was spelled doo-wap in 1969, doo-wop in 1972, do-wop in 1973, doowhop in 1974, doowop in 1977 and doo-wop thereafter. It must have been difficult to muster the enthusiasm necessary to write about something that you had no name for and/or didn't know how to spell. One can only speculate on what course events might have taken if Alan Freed or someone of his stature had coined the term in the early 1950s. In actuality, the term was in use much earlier, in 1961, in the *Chicago Defender*. Referring to "Blue Moon" by the Marcels, an article by Chuck Davis told of "a real doo-wop, like those of many years ago, is making the scene but big in Chi-town...." It just took the *Oxford* eight years to catch up. By the way, doo-wop is pure unmitigated onomatopoeia, a word we were sure we'd never need or see again. Our English teachers get the last laugh. The sound of the word describes what it defines. Yielding to this unfortunate truth will hopefully not diminish the reader's appreciation for the music.

The love of doo-wop music has never died, apparently because its fans won't let it. As early as 1960, the "classical" period of doo-wop was revived with the issue of Art Laboe's *Oldies But Goodies* albums, and the *Golden Oldies* album series on the Original Sound and Roulette labels respectively. These albums became so popular that many of the songs on them went on to receive more national attention than they had when first released in the mid-1950s. "In The Still Of The Night" (Five Satins), and "Earth Angel" (Penguins) both attained widespread popularity and, to this day, usually place in the top 25 (of 500!) in countdowns run at year's end by oldies stations and oldies record stores. New doo-wop songs, possessed of the classical sound, such as "There's A Moon Out Tonight" (Capris), "Angel Baby" (Rosie and the Originals) and "A Thousand Stars" (Kathy Young and the Innocents' remake of the original by Gene Pearson and the Rivileers) helped fuel the revival. In 1961, summary records such as "Those Oldies But Goodies" (Little Caesar and the Romans) and "Jukebox Saturday Night" (Nino and the Ebbtides) not only supported classical doo-wop efforts, but helped spawn the baroque doo-wop sounds of groups such as the Marcels, Regents, Vito and the Salutations and Earls.

In 1969 Richard Nader produced the first wave of rock 'n' roll revival shows which featured many doo-wop groups. By the early 1970s oldies stations began to punctuate the radio dial, and shows specializing in the doo-wop sound emerged. Norm N. Nite's "Nite Train Show" on WCBS-FM, New York (probably the most influential oldies station in the country) was one of the forerunners of this trend. His successor, Don K. Reed, is still going strong after 15 years with his own "Doo-Wop Shop." Throughout the 1970s, oldies revival concerts appeared often and have continued to prosper. In fact, most of the groups are working more and some are doing better financially than they did when their records rode the charts. A majority of the groups taking part in these concerts are doo-wop groups such as Earl Lewis and the Channels, the

Earls, the Cadillacs, the Skyliners, the Chantels, and Lee Andrews and the Hearts. Even though it is rare to find more than one original member in each group, the vocals remain true to form.

There's plenty for doo-wop fans to listen to; they need more to read. If these loyal fans can read some more about doo-wop, if they can lend an air of mental inquisitiveness to their gut-level affinity to the music, they will have more strength to counter arguments that listening to doo-wop is a sure sign of intellectual vacuousness. If this book paves the way for one bedraggled and beleaguered overweight middle-aged man or woman to earn the right to listen to "The Doo-Wop Shop" on Sunday night, on the way back from grandma's house, over the protests of spouse and children, it will have been well worth the effort.

Chapter 2

What is Doo-wop Music?

Although the term "doo-wop" has been bandied about at least since the early 1970s, definitions of it are either assumed (by disc jockeys and annotators of record albums) or stated in general and broad terms in books on rock 'n' roll, dictionaries and musical encyclopedias. Yet doo-wop has its own characteristics, many of which are hard to miss and are rarely found outside the genre. If doo-wop is to be taken seriously as a musical style, a more rigorous approach to defining its qualities needs to be taken.

It must be noted that doo-wop is a style of music, more specifically a style of vocal music. Although we and other authors refer to "doo-wop groups" and "doo-wop songs," these phrases really miss the point. A song, by itself, is neither doo-wop nor non-doo-wop. It can, however, be rendered in doo-wop style by a group of vocalists. Similarly, a group is neither doo-wop nor non-doo-wop. A group can sing in doo-wop style or some other style (e.g., soul). A doo-wop record is created only when a group sings a song in doo-wop style.

Further, although songs performed in doo-wop style have been called "vocal group harmony," this phrase is not specific enough. The Beatles, the (Curtis Mayfield) Impressions, the Ink Spots and the Four Preps offer vocal group harmony, but not the doo-wop style. Doo-wop music is therefore a subcategory of vocal group harmony, one that contains certain musical qualities, namely group harmony, a wide range of voice parts, nonsense syllables, simple beat, light instrumentation, and simple music and lyrics.

One feature of doo-wop music not included in the list of characteristics (because it is so obvious) is that doo-wop is first and last group music. The presence of a group of vocalists is an integral and unavoidable characteristic of the style. Single artists are only included for consideration when they are backed by a group, regardless of whether or not the group is mentioned on the record itself. Together, the single artist and his/her backup group must meet the same criteria as more conventional groups. Examples of this are Dion, Bobby Day, Thurston Harris and Nathaniel Mayer backed by the Del Satins, Satellites, Sharps and Fabulous Twilights, respectively. Most often there are few differences between "single artist doo-wops" and the more standard fare. The most common difference is that in single artist doo-wops the relative volume of the singer to his/her background group is usually greater. That is, the lead singer stands out more. Although the narcissistic tendency to use one's name alone flies in the face of the theoretical and philosophical underpinnings of the doo-wop credo (i.e., the specter of groups huddled on the street corner), we have chosen to overlook these transgressions in the interest of completeness. Aside from the "group-ness" of the music, we have identified five requisite categories of characteristics which set doo-wop apart from its contemporaries. These characteristics are outlined in Figure I.

Figure I.

DOO-WOP MUSIC IS COMPOSED OF:				
VOCAL GROUP HARMONY	WIDE RANGE OF VOICES LEAD FIRST TENOR (FALSETTO) SECOND TENOR BARITONE BASS	NONSENSE SYLLABLES	SIMPLE BEAT & LIGHT INSTRU-MENTATION	SIMPLE MUSIC & LYRICS

I. Group Harmony

Wide ranging voices (usually from bass to high tenor or falsetto) must combine in vocal harmony to echo or more commonly run underneath the lead vocalist. Usually the second tenor and baritone blend together as one sound, with the high tenor or falsetto running over the lead and the bass resounding underneath. This group harmony is *always* found in doo-wop renditions. It is a necessary (though not sufficient) condition for a given sample of music to be classified as doo-wop. Single artists without back-up groups are excluded from the doo-wop category. Group harmony does not lead throughout very often (as is the case in barbershop style), though on occasion it may alternate with a tenor as lead voice (as in many of the offerings of Earl Lewis and the Channels). In the early 1950s, with the Ravens and Five Keys in the forefront, harmonies turned the corner from rhythm and blues to doo-wop with the invocation of "blow harmonies," so-called because emergent sounds like "ha-oo" or "ah-hoo" were the result of blowing air out of the mouth. They replaced humming as the predominant background support. Harmonies in doo-wop are more complicated than the call-and-response technique found in gospel arrangements, yet do not offer the musical complexity (through the use of minor keys) that is found in much of the later works of the Beach Boys.

A device occasionally employed is that of progressive entrances by the different voices. The bass will usually begin, followed by the other voices, entering one at a time, until full harmony is achieved. Examples of this technique can be found in "Bermuda Shorts" by the Delroys, "Memories of Love" by Lenny Dean & the Rockin' Chairs, and "Bong, Bong (I Love You Madly)" by Vince Castro backed by the Tonettes. The presence of this technique is a sure sign of doo-wop style.

II. Wide Range of Voice Parts

A. Lead Voice   The lead voice is usually a tenor, sometimes a high tenor ("castrato") as in the efforts of Frankie Lymon (of the Teenagers), Leslie Martin (of the Schoolboys) and Little Bobby Rivera (of the Hemlocks). Infrequently, but notably, a bass will lead for part of the song, as in "Bim Bam Boom" by the El Dorados, and "Zing Went The Strings Of My Heart" by the Coasters. Bass leads are more common in uptempo songs, while falsetto leads are more often found in ballads. As mentioned previously, the group harmony part may alternate with a tenor as leading voice. Melisma, a gospel-derived vocal technique in which syllables are elongated to fit the meter of the song (e.g., "O-o-only You" instead of "Only You" in the Platters' song) was employed with some regularity by the lead voice in early doo-wop ballads.

B. Bass   Almost always there is a distinct (and sometimes distinctive) bass part. This bass part frequently provides the introduction to the song (e.g., "Fine, Fine Frame" by the Continentals) and/or punctuates the song between choruses (e.g., "Dorothy" by the Hi-Fives). The bass also commonly runs under the lead voice, either as part of the background harmony or as a voice separate from both lead and harmony. The better and deeper the bass, the more likely he is to be given free rein to run under the song (e.g., "All Night Long" by the Du Mauriers, "Never Let You Go" by the Five Discs and "I Wonder Why" by Dion and the Belmonts). Occasionally, the bass will provide a "talking bridge" in the middle of the song (during which the lyrics are recited, not sung), as in "Little Darling" by the Diamonds (which covered the Gladiolas' version). The bass may also provide a percussive beat to the song, as if taking the place of a stand-up bass instrument. The first of the great bassmen was Jimmy Ricks of the Ravens, who would frequently sing lead, especially on jump tunes. He is more important as an influence on the doo-wop style than as a contributor, however, because only a few of the Ravens' songs were done in doo-wop style.

A problem arises with the consideration of all-female groups. These groups, for reasons of nature, have trouble providing a true bass part. This issue was dealt with by allowing the presence of a contrasting lower voice to substitute for a bass voice. By bending the rules but slightly, groups like the Angels, Chiffons, Chantels, Tonettes and Bobbettes have no trouble meeting our criteria. Though some would argue that all-female groups do not belong in the category of doo-wop style (was there a little-known law in the 1950s banning women from street corners?), we felt that many distaff groups were able to contribute to doo-wop style well enough to warrant inclusion.

C. Falsetto   Falsetto parts are often found in doo-wop renditions, most commonly at the end of the song, as part of the lead voice's dramatic fade-out (e.g., "Tell Me Why?" by Norman Fox and the Rob Roys and "Since I Don't Have You" by the Skyliners). Especially in ballads, the falsetto will echo the lead voice, be part of the background harmony or "run above" the background harmony. Sometimes the lead singer will move in and out of a falsetto voice (Earl Lewis on "The Closer You Are"), or use it throughout the song ("Florence" and" Twilight" by the Paragons, and "Dee I" by the Rocketones). The prototype for falsetto leads is Maithe Marshall of the Ravens, although he usually did not sing in doo-wop style.

Falsetto is used only by male groups because distaff voices are naturally higher to begin with. A high-pitched female voice will take the place of falsetto on some recordings made by mixed-sex groups (e.g., "To Know Him Is To Love Him" by the Teddy Bears).

Figure II diagrams a typical doo-wop arrangement from opening through the end of the first chorus. Note that the bass introduces the song and punctuates the chorus at its end. When not operating alone, the bass will typically join the harmonizers, as will the first tenor when not singing in falsetto.

Figure II.

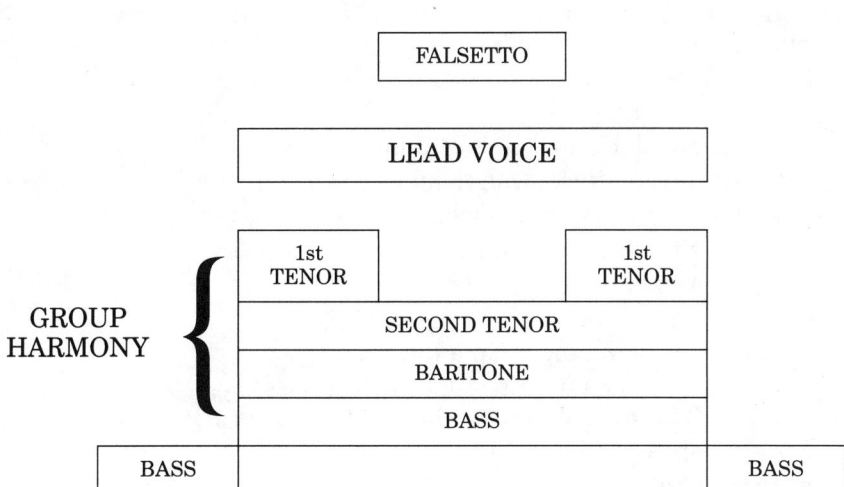

III. Nonsense Syllables

There is a liberal and frequent employment of "nonsense syllables" (syllables that have no meaning for English-speaking peoples) such as "doo-wop," "bum-buh-buh-bum-bum," "dit-lit-lit-lit-lit," etc. Bass and harmony parts commonly use this device; its presence makes it almost certain that the song in question can be classified as doo-wop. These nonsense syllables tend to be more restrained, simple and somber when employed in ballads (e.g., "doh-doh-doh," "doo-wah," or even "doo-wop"). In uptempo numbers the range of syllables is greater, the mood more festive and the bass given more freedom to "run" under the song.

Depending on one's perspective, the provenance of nonsense syllables can be traced back to bop and jazz styles of the 20th century or further back to centuries-old West African chants. Nonsense syllables were used in earlier scat singing, but their use in the doo-wop style differs in that the syllables form a regular pattern that is repeated throughout the song. Perhaps the most likely explanation as to how they found their way into doo-wop is that they were originally used, in a capella street corner singing, to replace the instrumental bass (just as finger-snapping and hand-clapping replaced drums). Once used, they appealed to the ear of both performer and listener, and caught on. Nonsense syllables first appeared in doo-wop-styled songs in "Count Every Star" by the Ravens in 1950 and "Harbor Lights" by the Dominoes in 1951. They began to abound by 1954, in efforts by the Crows ("Gee"), Spaniels ("Goodnight, Sweetheart, Goodnight"), Jewels ("Hearts Of Stone") and Shirley Gunter & the Queens ("Oop-Shoop"). Their use soon became an integral part of the doo-wop signature.

The *ne plus ultra* among examples of the creative use of nonsense syllables was provided by the Chips in the uptempo "Rubber Biscuit," recorded in 1956. According to Phil Groia in *They All Sang On The Corner*, the lyrics were inspired by neighborhood "callin' cades" and were refined by lead singer Charles "Kenrod" Johnson while marching around the campus of the Warwick School for Delinquents in upstate New York (he was probably there for reasons other than lyrical inspiration). The tune was later "covered" by the Blues Brothers (Dan Aykroyd and John Belushi) in 1979. Lyrics are presented below to allow those so disposed to sing along, but please do not hold the authors responsible for their accuracy. In the first two stanzas, "Kenrod" ejaculated:

Gow gow hoo-oo,
Gow gow wanna dib-a-doo,
Chick'n hon-a-chick-a-chick hole-a-hubba,
Hell fried chuck-a-lucka wanna jubba,
Hi-low 'n-ay wanna dubba hubba,
Day down sum wanna jigga-wah,
Dell rown ay wanna lubba hubba,
Mull an a mound chicka lubba hubba,
Fay down ah wanna dip-a-zip-a-dip-a,
Mm-mh, do that again! (interjected by the bass)
    [Note: "Kenrod" couldn't, so what he replied was:]
Gow gow lubba 'n a-blubba lubba,
Ow rown hibb'n 'n a-hibba-lu,
How low lubbin 'n a-blubba-lubba,
Hell fried ricky ticky hubba lubba,
Dull ow de moun' chicky hubba lubba
Wen down trucka lucka wanna do-uh,
How low a zippin 'n a-hubba-lu,
Hell fried ricky ticky blubba-lu,
How low duh woody woody pecka pecka. *

* "Rubber Biscuit," Nat Epps, Charles Johnson, Shedreck Lincoln, Samuel Strain
(Adam R. Levy & Father Enterprises, 1956), BMI.

"Rubber Biscuit," in 1956, was way ahead of its time, and may be seen as the forerunner of the way nonsense syllables were used beginning in 1960. At that time, perhaps as a result of a doo-wop revival during 1960-1962 (or because background singers became more creative or restless), nonsense lyrics became more complicated, bordering on the baroque. The Earls' "oop shoop, jing-a-ling-a chop-chop" in "Never" and the Five Discs (indescribable) in "Never Let You Go" are examples. Often these lyrical contortions became the main focus, intentionally or not, of the song, as in the 1961 (second) release of "Rama Lama Ding Dong" by the Edsels, "Imagination" by the Quotations and the thunderous bass parts of "Blue Moon" and "Heartaches" by the Marcels.

The equivalent of "Rubber Biscuit" among ballads was provided by the Ramblers with the "Vadunt-Un-Va-Da Song" in 1954. The lyrics of the song are almost completely described by the title, the harmonizers crooning them throughout. There are several other lines in the lyrics which are intelligible, but they seem to blend in with the background chant, producing an almost hypnotic "mantra" effect. It's a great ditty with which to meditate, if one is disposed towards that sort of thing.

IV. Beat and Instrumentation

A. Beat   Doo-wop music started on street corners and the rhythm was originally provided by the snapping of fingers or clapping of hands. Perhaps as a result, background beats in doo-wop songs are simple and heavy (with the emphasis on the second and fourth beats), and the drumming structure is uncomplicated and anything but subtle.

B. Instrumentation   Vocal gymnastics are the main contributors to the musical quality of the song. No instruments were to be found outside the candy store, and when the music moved to recording studios, instrumental accompaniment played little part. This is a major difference between doo-wop and other contemporaneous forms of rock 'n' roll that relied heavily on the sound of their instruments (e.g., rockabilly and the "honking" type of rhythm and blues). Piano, guitar, saxophone and drums are often found as doo-wop accompaniments, but are very much in the background. Almost invariably, an instrumental "break" or "bridge" or "channel" is provided in the middle of the song. In fact, Earl Lewis and the Channels took their name from this middle part of the song. It probably sounded better than "Earl Lewis and the Breaks."

The break is most often dominated by a saxophone, as in the magical accomplishments of Jimmy Wright as the "house musician" for the Gee/Rama group or King Curtis on Atlantic. The provenance of these solos dates back to the swing bands of Duke Ellington and Count Basie in the 1930s. Guitars were the second most common break instrument. An exception to the rule can be found in "Desirie" by the Charts where the same choruses are repeated throughout the song (i.e. no break occurs). According to Phil Groia, this resulted in the group being booed at the Apollo. Apparently fans became ill-disposed when the unspoken rules of the doo-wop credo were arbitrarily broken.

V. Simple Music and Lyrics

Most doo-wop songs are composed with simple melodies. Very often basic four-chord progressions are used. Even uptempo renditions of old "standards," such as "Over the Rainbow," "Stormy Weather" and "A Sunday Kind Of Love" tend to flatten out the melody line, in effect simplifying it. Ed Ward, in an off-handed compliment to doo-woppers, comments, "'In The Still Of The Nite' had been one of the first of this genre [rockaballad with four-chord melody], but hundreds-perhaps even a thousand- were to follow, and it is a real testimony to the inventiveness of the harmony group singers that those changes could be rung so many ways and so successfully so much of the time."

Lyrics written for doo-wop songs tend to be repetitive, simple, dialectical, hackneyed and occasionally ungrammatical, yet are still able to transcend the banalities to convey genuine feelings of tenderness and love. When Vernon Green (of the Medallions) sang the phrase "sweet words of pismotality" in "The Letter," we sense tenderness, despite having no idea of what Vernon really meant. "Don't hurt me" and "Don't desert me" are often paired, "I'll never let you go" often follows "I love you so," and "Kiss you" and "Miss you" are rarely found apart. In fact, the last two couplets just alluded to can be found in one song, namely "Darling (You Know I Love You)" by the Vocaltones (1956). This song is, by itself, a dictionary of the trite, although somehow "By my side, to be my guide (or bride)" was unexplicably omitted. Taken together, the lyrics and melodies of doo-wop songs reach the hormones and emotions but do not offer much in the way of intellectual stimulation. Some of the few exceptions to the rule are found in those same "standards," referred to above, which were doo-wopped up repeatedly to suit a new generation. There are more than 25 versions each of "Over The Rainbow" and "Sunday Kind Of Love" included in the songography part of the book!

To be classified as doo-wop, a song must fit into all five of the above categories, with minor exceptions. These exceptions are permitted because it is recognized that some groups, considered by most to sing in doo-wop style, never used falsetto as a technique. Others had bassi that blended with harmony so that the bass part was in no way distinct. Still others had voices echoing the lead without resorting to nonsense syllables.

A problem arises in categorizing groups (as opposed to songs) as doo-wop or non-doo-wop because some groups only fulfill our requirements part of the time. While some groups such as the Paragons, Bop Chords and Earls were exclusively doo-wop groups (i.e., they sang in doo-wop style virtually all the time), other well-known groups such as the Drifters, Little Anthony and the Imperials and the Clovers recorded some songs in doo-wop style and some songs that are better characterized as rhythm and blues, soft rock or popular music. Related to this is the common occurrence of groups growing into, through, and out of a doo-wop phase. The Drifters started in a rhythm and blues era, grew through a doo-wop stage and evolved into a group turning out popular music. The Four Lovers were predominantly a doo-wop group, but their progeny, the Four Seasons, abandoned most doo-wop characteristics to become one of the most successful soft-rock, pop music groups.

Scale of Doo-wop-ishness

We have developed a scale of "Doo-Wop-ishness" that allows the reader to assess the degree to which a given song fits into our five categories. The scale emphasizes those qualities that seem to discriminate best between doo-wop and other styles. One point is assigned for each of the following qualities if they are found in the song under scrutiny. Neither the reliability nor the validity of the scale has been assessed. It is included more for its conceptual usefulness than anything else. If it also allows the reader to rate his/her own favorite doo-wop songs, so much the better.

1) Bass introduction to the song

2) Bass contributes between choruses

3) Bass running with harmony part

4) Bass running under the lead but separate from the harmony part

5) Bass lead

6) Melismas used by lead

7) Falsetto trail-off at end of song

8) Falsetto running with harmony part

9) Falsetto running over the lead but separate from the harmony part

10) Falsetto lead

11) Castrato lead

12) Nonsense syllables in name of song

13) Nonsense syllables frequently used

14) Blow harmonies present

15) Nonsense syllables used throughout the song by the bass or harmony part

16) Group harmony running under the lead

17) Group harmony echoing the lead

18) Group harmony leading at times

19) Progressive entrances technique employed

20) Back beat simple and heavy

Chapter 3

The Evolution of Doo-Wop

Previous authors have viewed doo-wop as either a part of rhythm and blues or rock 'n' roll, or in some cases as a part of both. Hence, before tracing the evolution of doo-wop music, it is worthwhile to clarify the interrelationships among its predecessors and contemporaries. When Alan Freed coined the phrase "rock 'n' roll" in 1952, he was referring to rhythm and blues and group "street corner" music, or doo-wop (which had just come into existence). It was not until 1955 that "rockabilly," a combination of country rhythm and blues and country and western music, blossomed and was added under the rock 'n' roll umbrella. From that point on, rock 'n' roll comprised a combination of three separate musics - rhythm and blues, rockabilly and doo-wop. The interrelationships among these musical styles is diagramed below in Figure III. Doo-wop both evolved from rhythm and blues (among other styles) and ran concurrent with it. Doo-wop preceded, ran concurrent with and did not influence rockabilly. Doo-wop music was merely subsumed by rock 'n' roll. Thus, in order to look into the roots of doo-wop, we must start with rhythm and blues, itself a panoply of sounds.

Figure III.

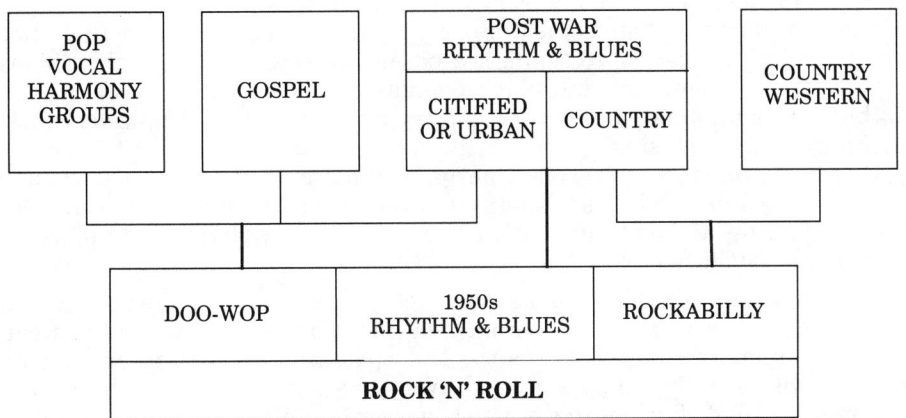

Charlie Gillett, author of *The Sound Of The City: The Rise Of Rock 'n' Roll,* sees things slightly differently. He asserts that rock 'n' roll was comprised of five different styles of music that "developed almost completely independently of one another." The identified styles were (1) northern band rock 'n' roll (as exemplified by Bill Haley), (2) the New Orleans dance blues (Fats Domino and Little Richard), (3) Memphis country rock, or rockabilly (Elvis Presley, Carl Perkins, Jerry Lee Lewis and Roy Orbison), (4) Chicago rhythm and blues (Chuck Berry and Bo Diddley), and (5) vocal group rock 'n' roll (what we call doo-wop). Gillett's treatment is interesting, especially regarding the geographical identity of the music, but his focus is more on the broader field of rock 'n' roll than is ours. Further, the present authors view the components of rock 'n' roll as more interrelated than does Gillett.

Lynn McCutcheon, in *Rhythm and Blues*, also takes a different view. He defines three eras of rhythm and blues: the Pioneer Era, which spanned the years 1946-1955, the Rock 'n' Roll Era, which covered 1956-1963, and the Soul Era, which began in 1963 and continued until the book was written in 1971. McCutcheon goes on to explain, for example, the role of instrumentation in the three eras (it increased from Pioneer to Rock 'n' Roll to Soul) and "feeling" (it was high in both the Pioneer and Soul Eras, lower in the Rock 'n' Roll Era because whites became involved). While interesting, seeing doo-wop music as only part of rhythm and blues is a situation that this book has tried to veer away from. We feel that the doo-wop songs recorded in 1953, 1957 and 1961 have more in common with each other than they do with some representatives of McCutcheon's Pioneer and Rock 'n' Roll Eras. That is, doo-wop needs to be seen as an entity in its own right.

The term "rhythm and blues" was originally a catchall phrase, used by *Billboard* starting in 1949 as a new way of describing "race" or "sepia" music. The idea was to find a term that was less offensive to blacks and that at the same time appealed to a larger percentage of the white population. When initially used, the only thing meant by "rhythm and blues" was music made by blacks aimed at predominantly black audiences. Within a few years, however, rhythm and blues began to connote something more specific, namely bluesy music to which rhythm had been added. As with the term "rock 'n' roll," it appears that coining the phrase "rhythm and blues" helped shape the music it described.

Rhythm and blues never represented a single sound. In the late 1940s the rhythm and blues music emanating from large urban centers was slightly different from rhythm and blues music played in rural areas. In the cities, rhythm and blues was more sophisticated, itself growing out of urban blues, gospel, swing, bebop, jazz and black popular music. In the country, rhythm and blues was an amalgamation of country blues, gospel and hillbilly music. Shouting, a style of singing in which the lead seemed to shout over and between instrumental background parts, was more prevalent in the country version of rhythm and blues. Examples of country rhythm and bluesers were Arthur "Big Boy" Crudup, and Rufus Thomas. Country rhythm and blues led to rockabilly music and Memphis soul.

In urban areas, the instrumentation, melodies and arrangements found in rhythm and blues were more complicated, being influenced by the intricate vocal harmonies of groups such as the Ink Spots and Mills Brothers, the big band sounds of Ellington, Basie and Webb, and jazz greats Gillespie and Hampton. Citified rhythm and bluesers were more often crooners than were their rural counterparts. Examples of the latter are Cecil Gant and Ivory Joe Hunter.

In the rural areas, when country rhythm and blues began to attract the white teenage and young adult populations as both audience and performers, rockabilly was born. The early artists (Elvis Presley, Gene Vincent, Carl Perkins, Bill Haley and Eddie Cochran) continued the country r&b traditions of the shouting style of singing, heavy instrumentation and simple arrangements. In the cities, something entirely different evolved. Beginning around the time of World War I and continuing into the 1950s, there was a tremendous migration of (mostly) blacks from the rural areas to mid-size and larger cities, especially to those along the northeastern seaboard, the West Coast and the industrial belt that ran from New York through Philadelphia, Pittsburgh and Cleveland to Chicago. While the intent of these refugees was to find work, the result of it was black ghettos populated by uprooted and often broken families living below the poverty level.

In general, the teenagers in these ghettos were unemployed, uninterested in school, and poor. Music was a large part of their lives. Many were trained in gospel with its religious themes, organ backgrounds, call-and-response patterns, group harmonies and falsettos. Most also heard the sophisticated urban rhythm and blues, which because of its cadences and spicy lyrics had natural appeal to youngsters. Further, they were exposed to the blending of voices, talking bridges and high-tenor leads that were present in popular black vocal group music, which provided them with examples of blacks who had "made it" in a white world (i.e., the Ink Spots and Mills Brothers).

These teens, with little else to do, took to the streets and sang. Hanging out on the streets represented their independence from their parents and kept them out of the overcrowded apartments where they resided. Most could wield no other instrument than their own voices, so that is what they used. When a group of these teens, usually friends, sang together, they sang group music. And if no instruments were available, they used their voices to replace them, covering the vocal range from falsetto to bass, clapping their hands to provide a beat, and punctuating choruses with harmonized vocal improvisations rather than brass sections. The doo-wop style of vocal music was born in these ghettos from (a) citified rhythm and blues, (b) gospel, and (c) popular black vocal group music. As a starting point for debate, we propose that the contributions of these musics were roughly 40 percent (a), 40 percent (b) and 20 percent (c), respectively. Socioculturally, doo-wop was born out of wish fulfillment, male bonding, directionlessness and ingenuity. Unlike rockabilly, the performers of the first wave of doo-wop music were overwhelmingly black, and their audience, as measured by the meager penetration of their music onto the white pop charts, was mostly black as well.

The "Paleo-Doo-Wop" Era (approximately 1952-1954)

Doo-wop music evolved slowly, unlike rockabilly which seemed to explode onto the scene in the 1955-1956 period. Between 1948 and 1951 the doo-wop characteristics of nonsense syllables and falsetto began to emerge in songs such as "It's Too Soon To Know" by the Orioles, "Count Every Star" by the Ravens, "Harbor Lights" by the Dominoes, and even in the immensely popular "Sixty-Minute Man," also by the Dominoes. That is not to say that these songs were even mostly doo-wop in style; their backgrounds show that they are still oriented to jazz (Ravens) or rhythm and blues (Dominoes). By the period 1952-1954, however, a significant number of doo-wop characteristics can be discerned in slow songs by the Five Keys, Feathers, Orioles and Vocaleers, and in fast songs by the Chords, Crows, Drifters and Shirley Gunter & the Queens. We have labeled the style of this era "paleo-doo-wop," since the prefix "paleo-" means ancient, early or primitive.

We place the birth of paleo-doo-wop in the year 1952, although we realize that this choice is somewhat arbitrary. Our conceptual model for viewing the birth of doo-wop is the first half of the normal curve, or ogive, which is illustrated below in Figure IV. Years are shown on the x-axis and the number of doo-wop characteristics present in the "average" vocal group record (as might be counted using the "Scale of Doo-wop-ishness" presented earlier) is displayed on the y-axis. According to this model, the number of doo-wop characteristics increased gradually, beginning in late 1948. Since the model does not permit a quantum leap in the number of characteristics in any given year, the choice of birth year is arbitrary.

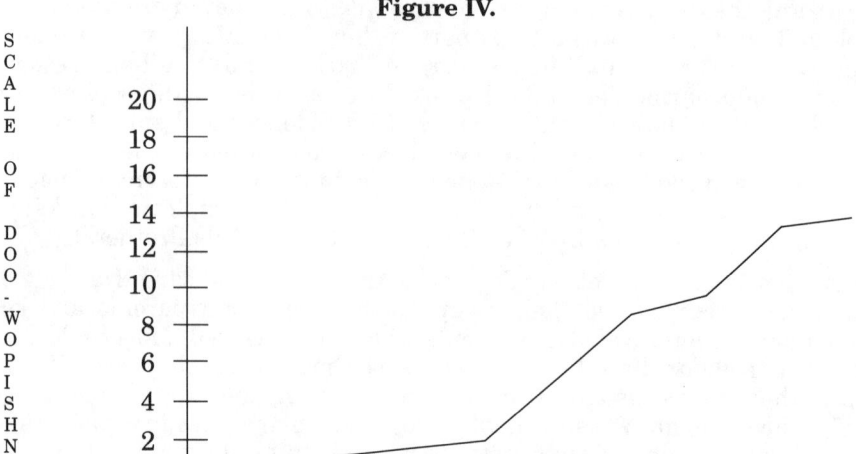

Figure IV.

Instrumentation, vocal arrangement and overall "feel" of paleo-doo-wop was still based in r&b and other progenitors. For example, the influence of r&b can be heard in "Hey, Baby Doll" by the Clovers and "Money Honey" by the Drifters. Gospel techniques are heard in such songs as "Heavenly Father" by the Castelles and "The Bells Of St. Mary's" by Lee Andrews and the Hearts, and the influence of black popular vocal group harmony is found in "Foolishly" by the Three Chuckles and "Only You" by the Platters.

The changes that signaled the dawn of the doo-wop era were the appearances of blow harmonies and nonsense syllables, the use of falsetto to "run over" the

The Crows

The Penguins

The Magnificents

lead (especially in ballads), and the punctuation of choruses by bassi (especially in jump tunes). Lead singers in paleo-doo-wop were cut from the silky tenor mold of Clyde McPhatter of the Drifters and Rudy West of the Five Keys. Melisma was employed frequently, especially in ballads. Subject matter was at times suggestive in uptempo numbers, as it had been in rhythm and blues. The primary theme of classical doo-wop, namely innocent love, began to emerge here (as in such songs as "Gee" by the Crows and "Be True" by the Vocaleers). Many of the girls addressed by paleo-doo-woppers had already "done it," while those glorified in later stages were waiting for the church bells to ring.

The Wrens

Prominent Examples of the Paleo-Doo-Wop Era:

Group	Song	Tempo	Year
Cadillacs	Gloria	slow	54
Charms	Gumdrop	fast	56
Chords	Sh-Boom	fast	54
Clovers	One Mint Julep	medium	52
Crows	Gee	fast	54
Diablos	The Wind	slow	54
Drifters	Honey Love	fast	54
Five Keys	Out Of Sight, Out Of Mind	slow	56
Harptones	A Sunday Kind Of Love	slow	53
Hearts (Lee Andrews & the)	Long Lonely Nights	slow	57
Jewels	Hearts Of Stone	fast	54
Magnificents	Up One The Mountain	fast	56
Meadowlarks (Don Julian & the)	Heaven And Paradise	slow	55
Medallions (Vernon Green & the)	Buick '59	fast	54

Group	Song	Tempo	Year
Moonglows	In My Diary	slow	55
Orioles	Crying In The Chapel	slow	53
Penguins	Earth Angel	slow	54
Rivileers	A Thousand Stars	slow	54
Robins	Smoky Joe's Cafe	medium	55
Wrens	Come Back My Love	fast	55

The songs listed above are taken from our appendix of the best 500 doo-wop songs. From this list, we chose 20 songs for each doo-wop period which we felt were representative of the doo-wop music of the time. The 20 are roughly equally divided between slow and fast tempos, although occasionally medium tempo songs are found. These examples are not necessarily what we consider the best of the 500; they were chosen for their representativeness.

The "Classical Doo-Wop Era" (1955-1959)

By 1954, the trade magazines remarked on the preponderance of groups on the rhythm and blues charts, at the expense of single artists. Apparently the boys hanging out in the street, who watched the street corner singers, figured out that singing was not only fun, but commanded respect in the neighborhood, attracted girls and offered the dream of economic solvency as well. Those with the requisite talent took up the art of doo-wop themselves, leading to an explosion of groups and serious competition for unused corners. These new entrants were influenced by little other than the existing groups through the medium of their live or recorded performances. Rhythm and blues, gospel, black pop music, swing and jazz ceased to be much of a factor although many of the emerging harmonizers had experience with gospel music as youths.

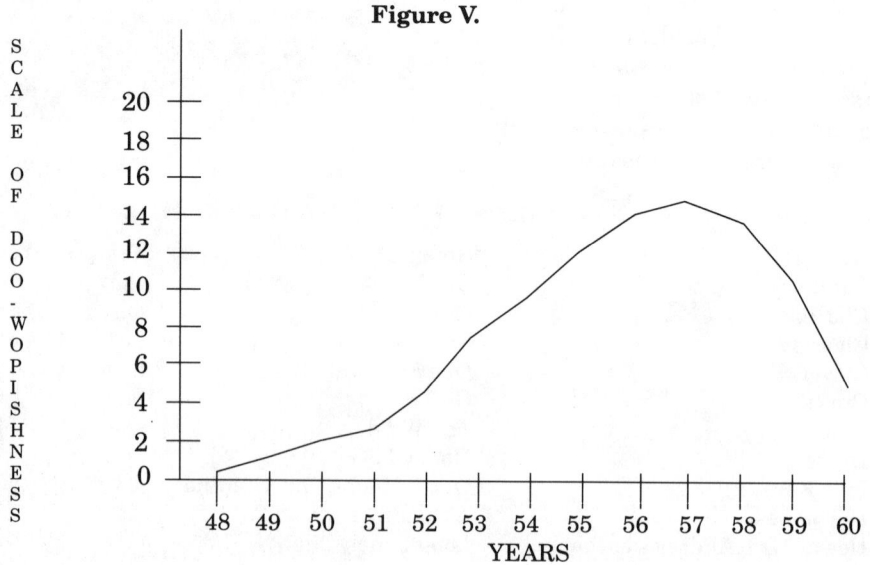

Figure V.

Thus, roughly in 1955, a new stage of doo-wop music, which we have termed "classical doo-wop," emerged, and lasted (again roughly) until 1959. Our conceptual model for the evolution of doo-wop, namely the normal curve, is extended through the classical period in Figure V. The number of doo-wop characteristics (on average) increased markedly around 1955, and this represents the beginning of the classical period.

Harmonies were tight and sweet, but lead singers lost much of their smoothness found so often in paleo-doo-wop. Leads began to alternate between tenor and falsetto and the latter was frequently used to "run above" the song in ballads and became almost *de rigeur* as a trail-off in jump tunes. Bass singers were less often merely part of the background harmony. They were given more "voice" and were usually found bum-bum-bumming around between choruses. Nonsense syllables were used in almost every song, and were more subdued in ballads than they were in uptempo numbers.

These syllables, strung together, became pure poetry in the hands (actually throat) of a competent bass. For example, in "I Wonder Why" by Dion and the Belmonts:

"Dun Dun Dun,
Duh Dun Duh Dun Dun,
Duh Duh Dun Dun Dun,
Duh Dun Duh Duh Duh, Duh Duh, Duh Duh....." *

* *"I Wonder Why," Ricardo Weeks, Melvin Anderson (Schwartz Music Co. Inc., 1958), BMI.*

Even the distaff group, the Shirelles, got into the act in "I Met Him On A Sunday":

"Doo Ron,
Day Ron Day Ron Day, Bop A Doo Ron,
Day Ron Day Ron Day, Bop A Doo Ron,
Day Ron Day Ron Day, Bop A Doo,
Oo-oo-oo-oo....." *

* *"I Met Him On A Sunday," Doris Coley, Addie Hawis, Beverly Lee, Shirley Owens (Ludlow Music, 1958), BMI.*

The Cleftones

The Shirelles

As a final example, the Cleftones in "Little Girl Of Mine" proudly announced:

"Dit Lit Lit Lit Lit, Yeah,

Dit Lit Lit Lit Lit, Yeah,

Dit Lit Lit, Lit Lit Lit Lit, Lit Lit Lit Lit Lit Lit....." *

* "Little Girl Of Mine," Herbert Cox, George Goldner (Kahl Music Inc., 1956), BMI.

Simple and elegant, yet profound.

Performers who emerged in the classical doo-wop era were virtually all young, and the lyrics of their songs spoke almost exclusively to the topic of young, idealistic love. Suggestive lyrics, a staple of the paleo-doo-wop stage, were rarely heard. Groups that had been around for a while and who had cut their teeth in the rhythm and blues or paleo-doo-wop eras, put out "story" records (e.g. the Coasters, Clovers and Robins), but added classical doo-wop overtones. Melody lines tended to be simplistic and formulaic, as in the "rockaballad" and four-chord uptempo numbers. Backbeats were heavy, but instrumentation remained in the background.

Those unsympathetic to the cause have traditionally criticized classical doo-wop music on the grounds that they could not tell one song from another. While this rap may, in fact, be a commentary on their "ear" for good music, it is accurate to some degree. Starting in the classical period, many doo-wop efforts adhered to the "rockaballad" or four-chord uptempo format, almost as if they were searching for one perfect song. We have used the term "formula doo-wop" to describe these efforts. Examples range from "Coney Island Baby" by the Excellents, to "The Closer You Are" by the Channels, to "I'm So Happy" by Lewis Lymon and the Teenchords. Groups showed creativity within that rather strictly defined set of musical parameters, which is testimony to their

The Del Vikings

The Five Satins

The Dubs

The El Dorados

inventiveness. It also proves that great minds think alike.

Evolution of the music within the classical era and newly devised marketing strategies led to music aimed at particular audiences such as young teens (the same age group that would later respond to the Bay City Rollers and the New Kids On The Block), older and tougher teens, and crossover white teens. Within classical doo-wop, sub-styles began to emerge, namely: schoolboy doo-wop, gang doo-wop, pop doo-wop and italo doo-wop. With the exception of italo doo-wop groups (which covers other white groups of the era), several integrated groups (the Del Vikings and the Crests), and a handful of female doo-woppers, the groups consisted of all young black males.

The Willows

Prominent Examples of the Classical Doo-Wop Era:

Group	Song	Tempo	Year
Aquatones	You	slow	58
Cleftones	Little Girl Of Mine	fast	56
Del Vikings	Come Go With Me	fast	57
Du Mauriers	All Night Long	fast	57
Dubs	Could This Be Magic	slow	57
El Dorados	At My Front Door	fast	55
Five Satins	In The Still Of The Night	slow	56
Flamingos	I Only Have Eyes For You	slow	59
Heartbeats	A Thousand Miles Away	slow	56
Mello Kings	Tonight Tonight	slow	57
Monotones	Book Of Love	fast	58
Nutmegs	Story Untold	slow	55
Passions	I Only Want You	fast	60
Rays	Silhouettes	slow	57
Rob Roys (Norman Fox & the)	Tell Me Why	fast	57
Shells	Baby Oh Baby	slow	60
Silhouettes	Get A Job	fast	57
Time-Tones	Here In My Heart	fast	61
Tune Weavers	Happy Happy Birthday Baby	slow	57
Willows	Church Bells May Ring	fast	56

The Heartbeats

The Flamingos

The Mellokings

The "Schoolboy Doo-Wop" Subcategory

One of the first subclassifications to emerge in the classical doo-wop stage was "schoolboy doo-wop." Thirteen-year-old boys, having the 16 to 18-year-old singers as their role models, naturally thought they could do the job as well or better, and formed their own groups. The cardinal feature of this subcategory was the ultra-high tenor, or "castrato," usually offered by a male in his early teenage years (Pearl McKinnon of the Kodaks, being female, was a notable exception) who tried to get his licks in before his voice changed. Frankie Lymon (fronting the Teenagers) was the definitive voice in this subcategory, in terms of

The Schoolboys

Lewis Lymon & The Teenchords

Frankie Lymon & The Teenagers

Little Anthony & The Imperials

popularity, commercial success, and in respect to voice quality. Lyrics and music were even more simple and formulaic than the average classical doo-wop effort, especially among those that followed Frankie, such as Lewis Lymon and the Teenchords (an obvious attempt to corner the market) and the Kodaks.

Prominent Examples of Schoolboy Doo-Wop:

Group	Song	Tempo	Year
Desires	I Wanna Rendezvous With You	fast	60
Elchords	Peppermint Stick	fast	57
Hemlocks (Little Bobby Rivera & the)	Cora Lee	fast	57
Imperials (Little Anthony & the)	Two People In The World	slow	58
Kodaks	Teenager's Dream	slow	57
Schoolboys	Please Say You Want Me	slow	57
Students	I'm So Young	slow	58
Teenagers (Frankie Lymon & the)	Share	slow	56
Teenchords (Louis Lymon & the)	I'm So Happy	fast	57
Tops (Little Jimmy Rivers & the)	Puppy Love	fast	61

The "Gang Doo-Wop" Subcategory:

In the competitive and tough urban neighborhoods where classical doo-wop flourished there were plenty of rival gangs and clubs. Groups often faced off against one another in "singing rumbles" held at local parks or community centers. The atmosphere at these events was similar to that of high school basketball games, where each team (in this case each singing group) had its partisan fans. The nice part about the sing-offs was that each partisan crowd could return home thinking that their guys had won. These contests

The Channels

The Paragons

eventually found their way onto record albums, the prototype of which was *The Paragons Meet The Jesters*. On the cover of this album are two young men aptly dressed in full gang regalia. These groups most often came from New York City. Phil Groia's book further narrows down the stomping grounds of many of these groups to Manhattan between 115th and 119th streets, and between Fifth and Eighth Avenues (e.g., the Matadors, Jesters, Bop Chords and Love Notes), although gang doo-wop also found adherents in Brooklyn and the Bronx.

Even if the average teenager did not fight often, he had to talk tough and appear cocky. Some of this posturing and braggadocio found its way into song. We have called this "gang doo-wop," a second subcategory within the classical stage. Lead singers in gang doo-wop were miles away from being smooth and seemed to swagger as they sang. These men in boy's clothing were street smart, and implied that high school was a place for "L7s" (squares, aka nerds; to form the square, one makes an "L" with the forefinger and thumb of the left hand, then a "7" with the same two fingers of the right, then brings them together) if you were male and girls if you were pretty. They told their girls what they expected of them and put them up on much-truncated pedestals compared to other classical doo-wop leads. Lyrics taken from "Oh Baby" by the Jesters and "Hey, Little Schoolgirl" by the Paragons are typical:

(Oh Baby)
"Oh-oh-oh baby, don't try to get away from me, (repeat)
I'm yours pretty baby, and I guess I'll always be...
Oh-oh-oh baby, I have got to make love to you, (repeat)
If you leave me baby, all I got's eternity....." *
* "Oh Baby," Harlan Jackson, Paul Winley (Ninny-Ethel-Byrd, 1958), BMI.

(Hey, Little Schoolgirl)
"Hey, pretty little girl walkin' down the street,
Looks so fine, dressed so neat,
Hey-ey, little girl, will you be mine,
I'm gonna love you all the time....." *

* *"Hey, Little Schoolgirl," Reese Palmer, Paul Winley (Cranford Music Corp., 1957), BMI.*

One can almost picture a street scene in which a strutting male targeted a passing girl and told her that she was going to be his and his alone. How he knew that she was unattached was rarely dealt with, but these guys appeared to be too sure of themselves to let a little rejection get in the way. Latent sensitivity is implied, but never shown. Harmonies in gang doo-wop were intricate yet rough. The product was frequently softened by the liberal use of falsetto, either as lead voice or as a fairly constant background presence.

Prominent Examples of Gang Doo-Wop:

Group	Song	Tempo	Year
Bop Chords	When I Woke Up This Morning	fast	57
Channels	That's My Desire	slow	57
Charts	Desiree	slow	57
Collegians	Zoom Zoom Zoom	fast	57
Continentals	Picture Of Love	fast	56
Jesters	I'm Falling In Love	fast	57
Kuf-Linx	So Tough	fast	58
Love Notes	United	slow	57
Matadors	Vengeance	slow	58
Paragons	Let's Start All Over Again	slow	57

The "Italo-Doo-Wop" Subcategory:

Through the paleo- and early classical doo-wop stages, white performers were rarely in evidence. Some of the reasons for their invisibility were (A) white teens on average were more protected and allowed to hang out on the streets less than their black counterparts, (B) whites and blacks, for the most part, lived separately so that there was slower cross-fertilization between blacks and whites than there was among blacks, (C) though there is evidence through reports of concert attendance that whites appreciated black music, it is likely that they initially gravitated to the rockabilly subcategory of rock 'n' roll because many of its stars were white, and (D) again on average, music was more a part of a black teenager's childhood (especially through the church) than it was of a white teenager's.

Aside from blacks, the ethnic group for whom music was most important in their upbringing (again through the church) was Italian. Although isolated white groups such as the Bay Bops, Neons and Three Friends were around since the mid-fifties, in 1958 the first significant wave of white doo-wop groups, led by Dion and the Belmonts, the Elegants and the Five Discs began to emerge. We have called their style "Italo-doo-wop" in their honor, although representatives of other ethnic groups soon jumped on the bandwagon. Members of these early white groups, like their gang doo-wop counterparts, grew up in tough urban neighborhoods. The sound differed from that of the black groups that preceded them only slightly. Italo-doo-wop was distinguished by offering even tighter group harmonies and rough-edged tenors singing at the top of their ranges to produce a "sweet" sound (e.g., Dion DiMucci of the Belmonts and Vito Piccone of the Elegants). The prominence of

The Mystics

The Elegants

bass singers in Italo-doo-wop renditions presaged the neo-doo-wop style which arose circa 1960. Prototypes Carlo Mastrangelo of the Belmonts and Charles DiBella of the Five Discs sounded as if they were born with machine guns in their vocal chords.

Prominent Examples of Italo-Doo-Wop:

Group	Song	Tempo	Year
Belmonts (Dion & the)	I Wonder Why	fast	58
Capris	There's A Moon Out Tonight	slow	58
Chaperones	Cruise To The Moon	slow	60
Chimes	Once In A While	slow	60
Classics	Till Then	slow	63
Earls	I Believe	slow	64
Elegants	Little Star	medium	58
Five Discs	I Remember	fast	58
Mystics	Hushabye	medium	59
Selections	Guardian Angel	fast	58

Also evident in the classical doo-wop stage was a flood of songs that were recorded with substandard equipment. We have called these amateurish productions "garage band doo-wop," which we use as a descriptor rather than a subcategory within the classical stage. The term "garage band," which was not coined until the rock era, is used to describe music created with meager resources. A group that sounded good performing a capella on the street corner would often be recorded without the benefit of accomplished background musicians or record producers because of lack of money. Bobby Jay (Robert Jeffers), a disc-jockey for WCBS-FM (New York), and bass singer for the still-active doo-wop group the Laddins, described the conditions under which his group and others would record. A two-hour block of recording time would be paid for by the owner of a small independent record company (Central Records for the Laddins) and the expectations were that four to six sides would be turned out. Compared to the recording practices of today, those sessions were primitive, as were the products that emanated from them. The enthusiastic but amateurish young singers wouldn't complain because they had no say in the matter and were thrilled merely to be given the chance to record. Examples of garage band doo-wop are "Did It" by the Laddins and "The Clock" by the Contenders. It must be noted that we are not referring to the quality of either the songs or the talent of the artists who recorded those songs, only to the production practices used in recording. A further discussion of these practices can be found in Chapter 8, entitled "The Street Corner Singers."

Another useful descriptor for doo-wop songs is "novelty doo-wop." Sometimes these songs represent flights into fantasy as in "Rockin' In The Jungle" by the Eternals, "Stranded In The Jungle" by the Cadets (jungles were big in the fifties), and "Love Potion Number 9" by the Clovers. At other times novelty doo-wops depict rebelliousness, as in "Charlie Brown" and "Yakety Yak" by the Coasters; fads, as in "Bermuda Shorts" by the Delroys or "Short Shorts" by the Royal Teens; or even comic book or cult figures, as in "The Lone Teen Ranger" by Jerry Landis and group (aka Paul Simon) or "Alley Oop" by Dante & the Evergreens. These novelty songs are invariably uptempo. Apparently songsters could not keep a straight face while attempting a slow arrangement.

A third descriptor is "pseudo-doo-wop" which as the name implies, is not really doo-wop at all. The term is offered to cover single-artist and dual-artist recordings that, aside from the unfortunate fact that they contain no group, are rendered in the doo-wop style. "Angel Baby" by Rosie & the Originals and "Love You So" by Ron Holden & the Thunderbirds are single artist recordings. The names of these groups are deceptive because most combinations of a person's name and the name of a group, that were released during the doo-wop era, were in fact doo-wop in style. The lyrics, melody and beat of these songs are done in doo-wop mode; they are both rockaballads. Yet for each the group, and thus group harmony, is absent. Songs by duos such as Marvin & Johnny, Johnny & Joe, Robert & Johnny, and Don and Juan warrant similar treatment. These duos commonly mimic the style, but they are "duo-wop," not doo-wop.

The "Pop Doo-Wop" Subcategory:

Most doo-wop singers have very little knowledge of either business principles or the practices of the recording industry. The style in which they sang, the material they recorded and the degree to which they gained financially from their efforts depended in large part on the label owners and record producers with whom they connected. Many of the industry moguls, aside from liking a smooth doo-wop sound, also had fiscal savvy and/or the

The Coasters

The Royal Teens

foresight to judge which songs and styles would appeal to the broadest audience. Often they wanted to stick with a proven formula which, in the case of group vocals, meant the "prep" music of such groups as the Four Lads, the Four Preps, the Four Aces and the Crew Cuts. Those that sang in pure prep style tended to be white, go to college, wear pinstripe shirts, sport short hair and be polite. Influenced by the Ink Spots, Mills Brothers, barbershop quartets and their junior high school elocution teachers, these groups offered tight harmony, but little else in the way of typical doo-wop traits.

The efforts of record producers to sell more records involved the amalgamation of this prep sound with traditional doo-wop style. The strategies that evolved to broaden the market included (a) "cover" records, (b) softening the doo-wop sound so that it would appeal to a wider range of age groups, and (c) jazzing up tried and true adult-oriented songs so that they would appeal to youngsters. We have called the results of these collective strategies "pop doo-wop."

Most commonly, the doo-wop signature was smoothed over so that the result would be acceptable to adults as well as teenagers. Songs in this category often ended up being somewhere between doo-wop and prep styles. Falsetto was used only as a trail-off if at all, the bass part blended with the harmony rather than standing alone to punctuate choruses, and the nonsense syllables were minimized and softened. For example, the Fleetwoods in "Come Softly To Me," took the nonsense syllables "Dom Dom, Dom Doo Dom, Doo Doo Bee Doo (repeat ad infinitum)" from the bass part and gave it to a tenor. The result was a top 10 pop doo-wop song. The general sound was more melodic, less formulaic and softer than traditional doo-wop fare. Other groups singing in this pop doo-wop style were the Skyliners ("This I Swear"), Duprees ("You Belong To Me") and Temptations ("Barbara"). All of them hit the charts repeatedly.

Another variety of pop doo-wop occurred as doo-wop groups revived old "standards" by adding doo-wop overtones. Examples are "Pennies From Heaven" and "I'll Be Seeing You" by the Skyliners, "Have You Heard" by the Duprees and "I'm In The Mood For Love" by the Chimes. It should be noted that not all remakes were done in pop doo-wop style. Records such as "Over The Rainbow" by David Campanella and the Delchords, "Them There Eyes" by Lewis Lymon and the Teenchords and "That's My Desire" by the Channels were done in straight classical doo-wop style. Music and lyrics in this subcategory share no particular theme, but on a percentage basis the groups were more "white" than average. The common thread was merely a smoother and more manufactured doo-wop sound.

Prominent Examples of Pop Doo-Wop:

Group	Song	Tempo	Year
Castells	So This Is Love	slow	62
Duprees	You Belong To Me	slow	62
Echoes	Baby Blue	medium	61
Fleetwoods	Come Softly To Me	medium	59
Jaguars	The Way You Look Tonight	slow	56
Platters	The Great Pretender	slow	55
Royal Teens	Believe Me	medium	59
Skyliners	It Happened Today	fast	59
Temptations	Barbara	fast	60
Tymes	So Much In Love	slow	63

The Platters   **The Skyliners**

The "Neo-Doo-Wop" Era (1960-1963)

Beginning roughly in 1960, classical doo-wop gave way to a "neo-doo-wop" stage. This changeover occurred in large part because of the oldies (really doo-wop) revival that started in 1959, which forever "framed" the sound of the classical doo-wop groups in the minds of fans. Groups that kept evolving the doo-wop sound became "neo-" groups; those that were enamored of the sound represented by the revival kept on with the classical formula. Our conceptual model pinpoints the birth of neo-doo-wop as somewhere between 1959 and 1960, its height of popularity as 1962 and its fall from grace as beginning in 1963. Figure VI, below, portrays a bimodal (meaning two "bumps") distribution of doo-wop characteristics. The first bump in the curve represents the paleo- and classical eras, the second curve defines the neo-doo-wop years.

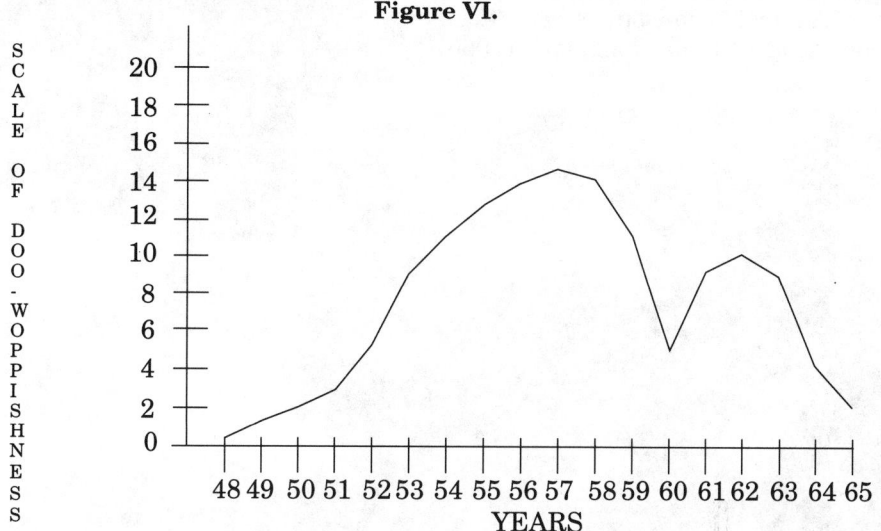

Figure VI.

Although neo-doo-wop maintained the simple melody lines and young love-oriented lyrics of the classical phase, the signature qualities of doo-wop were exaggerated. Songs were more frequently led by falsettos. The philosophy seemed to become "more is better" (or "go for baroque"). Instruments also played a more important role.

The bass parts became heavier and more prominent, proffering more complicated patterns of nonsense syllables that often took over the song. For example, examine the two bass riffs below:

(1) Bon Bon Bon, *

    Buh Bon Buh Bon Bon,

    Buh Buh Bon Bon Bon,

    Buh Bon Buh Bon Bon Bon....." *

* *"Zoom Zoom Zoom," Donald Hayes, Harlan Jackson (Selma Music, 1957), BMI.*

(2) Bon Buh Buh Bon,

    Buh Bon Buh Bon Bon,

    Buh Buh Bon Bon Bon,

    Ka Dang A Dang Dang,

    Ka Ding A Dong Ding....." *

* *"Blue Moon," Lorenz Hart, Richard Rodgers (Robbins Music Corp., 1934), ASCAP.*

By the way, the pronunciation of the nonsense syllable "Bon" is difficult to convey. It is NOT pronounced like bon bon, the ice cream treat. It sounds more like "Bawn" except the "n" is not pronounced, accomplished by not letting the tongue touch the palate. The best approximation is found in the French word "bon," meaning good. It is possible that those bassi choosing to use this syllable had at least one semester of French.

The first of the two samples is from the classical doo-wop effort "Zoom Zoom Zoom" by the Collegians (1956),

The Marcels

The Regents

in which it was used to punctuate choruses. Astute readers will note its similarity to the bass riff in "I Wonder Why," presented earlier in the chapter. The second sample is extracted from "Blue Moon", a 1935 melodic ballad converted to uptempo format by the Marcels (1961), who used it to introduce and end their song as well as to embellish their choruses. Aside from the base (or is it bass?) plagiarism involved, the gratuitous and sudden shift from "Buh-Bons" to "Ka-Dangs" is typical of neo-doo-wop nonsense syllable riffs. Those knowing both "Zoom" and "Blue Moon" will also note the difference in delivery. The former is delivered in a laid-back manner, while the latter conveys stridency and resoluteness. This too, is typical of the advances made in the neo-doo-wop era.

The Marcels follow-up to "Blue Moon," namely "Heartaches," provides a lesson.

"Yip Yip Yip Yip,
Werp Wuh Werp Werp,
Bum Muh Mum Mum,
Bon Buh Bon Bon,
Dum Duh Dum Dum Dum,
Mum Muh Mum Mum Mum Mum....." *

* "Heartaches," John Klenner, A. C. Hoffman (Leids Music Corp., 1931), ASCAP.

Notice the rapid shifts from "Yips" to "Werps" to "Bum-Mums" to "Buh-Bons" to "Dums" and "Mums." Purists see this as too ornate and artificial, but one has to admit it is heady stuff and does make a statement.

Prominent Examples of the Neo-Doo-Wop Era:

Group	Song	Tempo	Year
Blue Jays	Lover's Island	slow	61
Chandler, Gene (with the Dukays)	Duke Of Earl	medium	61
Crests	My Juanita	fast	57
Demensions	Over The Rainbow	slow	62
Devotions	Rip Van Winkle	fast	61
DiMucci, Dion (with the Del Satins)	Runaround Sue	fast	61
Dreamlovers	When We Get Married	slow	61
Drifters	This Magic Moment	medium	60
Excellents	Coney Island Baby	slow	62
Impressions (Jerry Butler & the)	For Your Precious Love	slow	58
Jive Five	My True Story	slow	61
Lee, Curtis (with the Halos)	Pretty Little Angel Eyes	fast	61
Marcels	Blue Moon	fast	61
Vacels (Ricky & the)	Lorraine	slow	62
Paradons	Diamonds And Pearls	slow	60
Quotations	Imagination	fast	61
Reflections	(Just Like) Romeo & Juliet	fast	64
Regents	Barbara Ann	fast	61
Roomate (Cathy Jean & the)	Please Love Me Forever	slow	61
Stereos	I Really Love You	fast	61

The "Tin Pan Alley Doo-Wop" Subcategory

The dawn of neo-doo-wop witnessed the infiltration of new young talented men and women. The result was what we have called "Tin Pan Alley doo-wop." "Tin Pan Alley" was a term previously reserved for an agglomeration of composers, lyricists and record producers (centered around the Brill building in New York City) that turned out mainstream popular music aimed at white audiences. There was little overlap between this ASCAP-allied crowd and the inner city, BMI-allied group of young black artists and maverick white businessmen that created doo-wop music. Though the product of the BMI-allied groups was considered musically and lyrically inferior, those that created doo-wop often had ability, but lacked musical education and sophistication.

By the late 1950s, a new, talented group of young adults began to enter the job market. Exposed to paleo- and classical doo-wop for a number of years, but also trained in musical theory and practice, these newcomers soon developed their own ideas about what music should sound like. The songwriting teams of Gerry Goffin and Carole King, Barry Mann and Cynthia Weil and Jeff Barry and Ellie Greenwich and producers like Phil Spector and the Tokens became the new superstars. The songs and records they wrote and produced blended mainstay doo-wop features of tight harmony, bass and nonsense syllables with more complex melodies, more instrumentation (e.g., Spector's "Wall of Sound") and painstaking production practices. These efforts helped bring to a close the period of classical doo-wop and, through groups such as the Chiffons, Crystals, Blossoms, Ronettes and Bobb B. Soxx & the Bluejeans, put female groups on the map.

The Tokens

The Angels

Prominent Examples of Tin Pan Alley Doo-Wop

Group	Song	Tempo	Year
Angels	Til	slow	61
Blue Jeans (Bobb B. Soxx & the)	Why Do Lovers Break Each Others Hearts	fast	63
Chiffons	He's So Fine	fast	63
Crystals	Da Doo Ron Ron	fast	63
Jelly Beans	I Wanna Love Him So Bad	fast	64
Oxfords (Darryl & the)	Picture In My Wallet	slow	59
Rainbows (Randy & the)	Denise	fast	63
Raindrops	The Kind Of Boy You Can't Forget	fast	63
Teddy Bears	To Know Him Is To Love Him	slow	58
Tokens	Tonight I Fell In Love	fast	61

The "Distaff Doo-Wop" Subcategory

We have used the term "distaff doo-wop" to refer to the contribution of female groups to the body of doo-wop works. Earlier contributions to this category were made by Shirley Gunter and the Queens, the Bobbettes, the Tonettes, and of course the Chantels and Shirelles. On occasion, women lead singers fronted male groups, as in Zola Taylor with the Platters, Pat Spann with the Cleftones and Barbara Lee with the Aquatones. With these few exceptions, women did not play a prominent part in the doo-wop movement until the 1962-1963 neo-doo-wop-Tin Pan Alley sound grew in favor.

The songs that are used here to illustrate this category, as mentioned above, came from our list of best doo-wop songs. Unfortunately, not many of the best paleo- and classical doo-wop songs were recorded by all-female groups. We do not think this represents a bias on our part; in fact both authors admitted privately to an inclination to include these groups.

Prominent Examples of Distaff Doo-Wop:

Group	Song	Tempo	Year
Blue Belles (Patti LaBelle & the)	You'll Never Walk Alone	slow	63
Bobbettes	Mr. Lee	fast	57
Chantels	Maybe	slow	58
Cookies	Don't Say Nothin' Bad	fast	63
Delrons (Reperata & the)	Whenever A Teenager Cries	medium	64
Ponitails	Born Too Late	slow	58
Queens (Shirley Gunter & the)	Oop-Shoop	fast	54
Rosebuds	Dearest Darling	slow	57
Shirelles	Will You Still Love Me Tomorrow	medium	60
Tonettes	Oh What A Baby	fast	58

The same evolutionary process that created the doo-wop style also led to its disappearance. Beginning in 1963, the doo-wop sound was heard less and less often. The audience moved on to other sounds, and the artists did likewise, with mixed success.

As a summary, and for the sake of clarity, Table II, which follows, offers a synopsis of the most important characteristics of the doo-wop style by period. While the entries in the Table are generalizations, it should be possible for the reader to trace the evolution of, for example, nonsense syllables before, through and after the doo-wop era.

The Chantels

The Bobbettes

Table II:

	PRE DOO-WOP 1945-1951	PALEO- DOO-WOP 1952-1954	CLASSICAL DOO-WOP 1955-1959	NEO- DOO-WOP 1960-1963	POST- DOO-WOP >1964
NONSENSE SYLLABLES	not present	emergence of blow harmonies & simple patterns of non. sylls.	more complex patterns in almost every song	subdued in some cases and more complex patterns in others	words replace non. sylls. as background responses
HARMONY PART	humming, very much in background	given more voice	given even more voice, may alternate with lead	same as classical	recedes into background
FALSETTO	occasionally present, almost never leads, operatic quality	present more often, occasionally leads, operatic quality	almost always present, frequently leads, almost always used as trail-off	not always present, but more frequently leads when present, used less as trail-off	diminished presence, almost never leads or used as trail-off
BASS	frequent bass leads and talking bridges, but not between stanzas, not distinct from harmony under lead	begins to separate from harmony, begins to punctuate stanzas	frequently introduces song, almost always separate from harmony, almost always punctuates stanzas	same as classical	used less as a separate voice throughout
BEAT	allied with jazz &/or r&b	very little jazz influence, more allied with r&b	beat heavy & distinct (on 2nd & 4th beats), allied with rock 'n' roll	same as classical except for pop doo-wop where beat is softer	remains heavy in most new musics
INSTRUMEN TATION	heavier than standard doo-wop fare	less present than before, honky-tonk piano or organ typical	instruments unimportant except during break in middle of song	instruments re-emerging	instruments much more important
MELODY	blues or jazz progressions	melodies begin to simplify	simple melodies & four chord structures common	more variation than in classical	significantly more variation in melodies
LYRICS	often lascivious	still lascivious but innocent love themes begin to take over	almost exclusively innocent love, almost no politicizing or social commentary	lyrics remain innocent	most lyrics still deal with love but social commentary & politicizing appears

Chapter 4

The Teen Subculture

The evolution of doo-wop music was guided by two complementary forces: supply and demand. Although (paleo-)doo-wop was around in the early 1950s, it grew in popularity through the decade only because of the growth of a new teen subculture that demanded it. As demand rose, the music industry found ways to supply the product. The advent of this teen subculture will be discussed in the present chapter and the accommodations of the music industry in subsequent ones.

A teenager growing up in the mid-to-late 1940s was forced to take life fairly seriously. The country was just emerging from a period of war, and teens were expected to do their share of the fighting if their country ever needed them. Some used enlistment as a way of delaying a career choice (the same way that college was used later), or as a way to follow in their fathers' footsteps. Even without the looming specter of the armed services, a young male was still expected to go out and earn a living immediately after graduation from high school to help support his family of origin or his new bride. Concomitantly, women in their late teens were often expected to meet a man, marry and have children shortly after, and sometimes before, graduation from high school. College was a choice reserved for a select few. Teens had limited freedom, not much economic power, and were little able to influence the decisions made by the generations that preceded them. They accepted responsibility without demanding freedom as payment.

By the late 1960s, the age of the flower child, the landscape looked much different. For many reasons (the necessity of having a college education, the greater affluence of society as a whole, more indulgent parenting techniques) teens did not have to join the adult (rat) race until their early twenties. Those skilled in manipulating the system in general or their parents in particular could postpone growing up even longer. They had freedom to the point of parental concern and had an inordinate (by earlier standards) amount of money to spend. This generation of teens demanded freedom and equality with adults and accepted responsibility only grudgingly, in comparison with their forebears. They strongly influenced and sometimes determined decisions made by their elders, especially in the fields of fashion, music and cars. Between these two eras, immense, complex and irreversible changes occurred within the teen subculture. The seeds of these changes were sewn in the 1950s.

In the 1950s, an era blessed with peace (after the Korean War) and prosperity, the expectations for teenagers began to change. With the economy booming, parents could afford to help their children achieve more than they themselves had. In greater numbers parents insisted that their children finish high school and paid for them to go to college. Further, a whole generation of parents suffered through a wartime era filled with hardship that left few families untouched. When people come face to face with death and despair they realize what is important in their lives; namely, the people they love the most and their happiness. Parents began to prefer that their children not enter the armed forces and, in general, exhibited more indulgence for their whims. If their own lives were too far along to make significant changes for the better (because of family constraints, financial necessity or just plain inertia), they could try to help their children to have better lives.

As a result, youngsters received (and occasionally earned) allowances, and had free time after school when they weren't forced to work to earn money or help with the family chores. They had more time to "hang out," be social, form peer group bonds and notice pimples than ever before. Teens began to have fun and be less serious about life in ways that past generations would have envied. Episodes involving college pranks such as stuffing people into Volkswagons or telephone booths, goldfish swallowing, fraternity hazing and panty raids were just some of the more outrageous examples of how much less serious life was for the new generation of young people. Even at Princeton University, students let down their hair briefly on May 17, 1955. They inexplicably and repeatedly blared "Rock Around The Clock" from many dormitory rooms at once, producing a cacophony that continued until the wee hours of the morning, and which was quelled only by the appearance of a dean, who apparently inspired fears of academic suicide.

The new liberalized culture also allowed teenagers, for better or worse, to make more decisions for themselves, decisions often at odds with what their parents would have chosen. Music was one of the first realms in which unorthodox choices became readily apparent (mode of dress being another). Before World War II, musical input to teens was limited and controlled. For white teens, radio and the occasional record purchase for the most part defined the limit of their exposure to music. The choice of music entering the home was made almost exclusively by parents, teens given little choice in the matter. And what was chosen by most white parents was "white" music, as in the products of Tin Pan Alley, or melting-pot black music that had been adapted to white tastes, as had swing and blues. Parents were neither exhibiting ornery behavior nor intentionally trying to protect their children from rebellion. They were simply seeking out and choosing music which was consistent with tastes bred in them during their own adolescence.

In the 1950s, teens began to own their own radios or turned to the family television for their entertainment. These proclivities seemed harmless at first, and were relatively unmonitorable by parents (except those willing to confiscate earplugs and batteries). Disc jockeys and radio stations, encouraged by their growing audience, became emboldened and played more of the new music. Jukebox operators and record store owners, similarly influenced, increased their supply of the sought-after tunes. Record companies found talent and pressed records to accommodate the tastes of the young. The choices made by teens individually to turn to a new kind of music soon began to be felt by the society as a whole. A new subculture was in the process of being formed, one catering to, geared for, and run by teenagers. Somewhere along the way the "generation gap" emerged as a concern of parents (teens saw nothing particularly wrong with it). More than ever before the dress, beliefs, pastimes, social mores, speech patterns and music of teens differed from those of their parents' generation.

When Alan Freed coined the label "rock 'n' roll" (of which doo-wop was a significant part in 1952) and it caught on, he gave teens a focus for their interest and made the music more acceptable. This helped doo-wop, as a part of rock 'n' roll, to become part of a teen's identity. We now take this "labeling effect" for granted; labels such as heavy metal, thrash metal and death metal help a teen to specifically carve out his own turf. Back then styles of music such as "blues," "jazz" and "rhythm and blues" tended to last for decades and belong to adults. Nelson George, in *The Death of Rhythm-and Blues*, noted that coining the term rock 'n' roll "disguised the blackness" of the music, which allowed white teenagers to feel more comfortable with it. While rhythm and blues was seen as music for blacks, rock 'n' roll became popular as a "universal music," acceptable to all races. In effect, under the new rubric, white teenagers became the focus of marketing strategies, supplanting blacks.

The origins of the term "rock 'n' roll" were quite raunchy, as Wes Smith notes. "Since the 1920s, when blues singers like Trixie Smith, who sang 'My Man Rocks Me (with a Steady Roll)' wailed about their urgent need 'to rock' or 'to roll' and 'to rock 'n' roll', it had been clear they weren't talking about gymnastics.... Such explicitness was all the better to feed raging teen hormones." A paleo-doo-wop group called the Blenders (aka Sparrows) had even recorded a song called "Don't F... Around With Love" in 1953. Perhaps in deference to the cardiovascular systems of parents, it was not released until 1971. In retrospect, it is interesting that most white parents never did seem to catch on to the meaning behind the euphemism. (As an experiment, the reader might ask a group of 40-to-50-year-olds, "What is the meaning of the phrase rock 'n' roll? The odds are that they will give some answer relating to music.)

With their new-found freedom, white teens now, in addition to black, were opting for music that they found more interesting. Songs such as "How Much Is That Doggie in the Window?" and "Que Sera, Sera" somehow paled in comparison to the danceable and romanceable rhythm and blues played by "cool" black cats. So many white teens were drawn to the music that the word "cats" soon came to describe white kids who gravitated to black music. Ed Ward, writing about the early stages of rock 'n' roll in *Rock Of Ages; The Rolling Stone History Of Rock 'n' Roll*, describes them as "poor white kids who lived in slum neighborhoods with blacks and worked side by side with them at various bottom-of-the-barrel jobs. Although few of them thought of the blacks as their equals and most were happy to be segregated from them in movie theaters and at school, the cats somehow related more to black culture than to hillbilly culture, yearning for the sophistication they heard in rhythm and blues songs. Being cats meant they could stand out in a world that offered them precious little in the way of a chance to be somebody." Interestingly, Jerry Lieber and Mike Stoller, probably the most noteworthy songwriting team of the 1950s rock 'n' roll era, were "cats" themselves. Both grew up (independent of one another) with and around blacks, which allowed them an understanding of the black perspective not often seen in whites.

These white teens with money to spend increased the ability of the stations to attract advertisers, and the clout of the stations (and deejays) playing rhythm and blues grew. As Wes Smith reported: "The jocks may have loved it, but if rhythm and blues on the radio had failed to sell baby chicks or Bibles or Royal Crown hair dressing, the deejays would have been playing something that did: gospel, jazz, bebop, country-and-western, whatever worked. They played to their listeners' taste." Following suit, other more conservative stations changed their formats to accommodate this new audience. Teenagers had accomplished something their counterparts in other generations had not been able to do; they had voted for and obtained their own music, made it an integral part of the new teen subculture, and on the way very nearly overthrew the music establishment.

Thus far we have treated the teen subculture that arose in the 1950s as though its members were a homogeneous group. In fact, there were differences within that group, along the dimensions of urban-rural, black-white and rich-poor, most of which had to do with the style of music that was most favored. For example, poor blacks were exposed to purer strains of music, ones that were not yet subject to homogenization by the larger white society. This happened because poor families were more likely to listen to local radio stations, eschewing the nationally syndicated shows. Historians generally agree on the importance of the link between local black radio and black culture. Often they were one and the same. Some, without radios at all, would depend on family members "jamming" on the porch or church affiliation for their musical input. The poorer one was, the more likely one was to grow up liking the as-yet uncross-fertilized local or regional music. Poor black teenagers, who grew up in urban areas, made doo-wop a part of their lives because it was already a part of the culture of the neighborhood. It was a participatory activity for many, and idols were neighborhood residents rather than national heroes. Phil Groia in *They All Sang On The Corner* describes the idolatry accorded New York groups such as the Vocaleers, the Bop Chords and the Teenagers. For example, "The Vocaleers rivalled Jackie Robinson and Willie Mays as Harlem folk heroes," no minor league accomplishment.

Whites, both teens and adults, had historically taken to a black musical style only after white performers got in on the act, literally and figuratively. Rockabilly followed in the footsteps of swing, bebop and jazz when white performers like Elvis Presley and Jerry Lee Lewis came on the scene. Rural white teens then chose rockabilly as a part of their new-found identities.

Despite these differences among members of the teen generation in choice of music, the historical, economic, sociocultural and psychological effects on teenagers were almost identical. It is interesting that many white

The Belmonts

The Falcons

and black performers who went on to make a name for themselves as single artists in the broader field of rock 'n' roll started their careers as members of doo-wop groups in the paleo- or classical period (usually as lead singers). This list includes Wilson Pickett and Eddie Floyd (Falcons), Neil Sedaka (Tokens), Dion DiMucci (Belmonts), Carole King (Palisades), Gene Pitney (Embers), Bobby Darin (Rinky Dinks and Ding Dongs), Diana Ross (Primettes), Ben E. King (Five Crowns and Drifters), Clyde McPhatter (Drifters), Phil Spector (Teddy Bears and Spector's Three), Dee Clark (Kool Gents), Marvin Gaye (Moonglows and Rainbows), Billy Stewart (Rainbows), Paul Simon (Tico & the Triumphs), Bobby Freeman (Romancers), Ernie K-Doe (Blue Diamonds) and Brook Benton (Sandmen).

Teens heard the music on their radios, were exposed to it on television and danced to it at parties. This generation was not old enough to appreciate the dance bands of the swing era; their music was rhythm and blues, it was doo-wop, and it was rockabilly. Teen dances or "sock hops," which had always been around since George Washington went to school, served as a delivery system for their favorite music. The new music was easy to dance to, a feature which had historically attracted the younger generations. The fast numbers allowed more brazen teens to get some of the energy out of their systems and prove their athletic prowess to their dates. Fast dances were usually some variation of the lindy or jitterbug. Since a fair percentage of the teen male population did not have the coordination or guts to dance fast, slow numbers, most of them doo-wop, were included in the program. The ballads did not require lessons at an Arthur Murray studio; all that was necessary was that a guy could lean on his girl as hard as, but no harder, than she could lean on him (that way they would not fall over). As for the feet, if you moved one once in a while you met the demands of social acceptability. "Dirty dancing," a term not even on the drawing board in the 1950s, nonetheless described what replaced the fox trot as the preferred method of slow terpsichorean intercourse. Through the medium of the new music, teens were playing at sex. Their own newly emerging culture, however, would not let them actually have sex until the 1960s.

Speaking of the "S" word, the formation of this subculture generated fears in parents that were reasonable, when viewed with the benefit of hindsight. The behavioral changes that parents witnessed in their own offspring were unlike anything they had known from their own childhood. Psychologically, members of the teen generation of the fifties isolated themselves from their parents. They became private, secretive, clannish, oppositional, sullen, defensive and even disrespectful at times. Though not new, this set of traits had measurably increased in this generation of teens. The generation gap, which formed as a result of postwar affluence and indulgence of children was not recognized as causative of these behaviors until later. The music that teens adored, though merely a symptom of the growing differences between parents and children, was easy to focus on and blame. The occasional public disturbance at a concert, the fanatical adherence to the music, its stars and the media for their distribution (e.g., radio, records, TV) stood out like a sore thumb. Today we have become resigned to these teen behaviors as a normal part of their upbringing. We also take comfort in knowing that for the most part, teens eventually come out of it; that is, they shed their rebelliousness by their early twenties in favor of more conventional beliefs. Back then parents did not have this reassuring knowledge, and it was scary.

Some of their misgivings were warranted, if misdirected. Juvenile delinquency WAS on the rise and integration of the races WAS under way. Delinquency and integration foretold real changes in the structure of both the family and the greater society, changes of a magnitude not seen for many generations. People as old as parents found even changes of lesser import agonizing. And although any given child did not run out and rob stores or come under the influence of so-called "inferior" races, the media were telling parents that love of rock 'n' roll (which included doo-wop music) was the first step on the road to damnation. When parents saw their children being drawn into the culture of a music that was foreign to them, it was easy to think that the worst was right around the corner. Unfortunately for them, their disapproval unintentionally helped the music to become even more popular. The best way to assure rebelliousness, as parents, teachers and opponents of democracy now know, is to absolutely forbid someone to do something. The more authority figures representative of their parents' generation derogated their music, the more teens espoused it.

For a while, there was a good deal of flak emanating from more conservative members of the recording industry. Peter Potter, a KLAC (Los Angeles) disc jockey and host of the CBS-TV show "Juke Box Jury" was quoted as saying, "The artist and repertoire men [talent developers for record companies] are responsible for inculcating poor listening tastes of today's teen-agers." About rhythm and blues (which included paleo-doo-wop music), Potter averred that much of it was "obscene and of lewd intonation, and certainly not fit for radio broadcast." Stan Freberg, a popular satirist appearing on Potter's show, concurred, stating, "I hope this puts an end to rhythm and blues." Freberg later made nice (again on Potter's show) with the Chords ("Sh-Boom"), who were one of his favorite targets, saying that his attacks on the music were in jest.

Additionally, in early 1954, a group of rhythm and blues disc jockeys set up the "Metropolitan Disc Jockeys Club" in New York to discourage records that dealt with sex in a suggestive manner. The idea was that if one of the members received a disk that was dirty, he would advise other deejays and ask them not to play the disk. Separate letters would be sent to the record company and artist detailing the complaint and asking them not to continue making such recordings. Members of the club included such notables as Hal Jackson (WLIB), Jack Walker (WOV) and Tommy "Dr. Jive" Smalls (WWRL). "Such A Night" by the Drifters (and covers by Johnny Ray and Bunny Paul) exemplifies the type of record which attracted their ire. In fact, this tune was banned from WDIA in Memphis and from the top rhythm and blues station in Detroit. The bans had little effect on teens, who continued to call the stations with requests that it be played. "Such A Night," a paleo-doo-wop song, was suggestive, but as mentioned in the previous chapter, this suggestivity vanished from the doo-wop genre with the dawning of the classical period in 1955. Industry leaders Billboard and Cash Box, railing strongly against the lewd lyrics of some rhythm and blues offerings, helped in the cleanup. Many record companies, radio stations and distributors agreed that suggestive material should not be aired or even produced, but most could not agree on a method of policing. It should be noted that these types of lyrics had always been a part of rhythm and blues, and became generally unacceptable (not coincidentally) when the white teenage population became consumers.

The news media, run by and responsive to the establishment, fed parental fears and coordinated the backlash against doo-wop and rock 'n' roll.

Sometimes reporting practices were accurate but sensationalistic. An example was the banner in the *Miami Herald* (May 1959) entitled "Booze, Broads and Bribes" on the morning following the third annual deejays convention in Miami. The headline, by itself, described the schedule of activities at the conference and marked the beginning of the end of the personality deejays. The Harris congressional subcommittee began its enquiry into the practice of accepting "payola" in the fall of 1959. Payola, or the practice of paying deejays to play particular records, was not considered illegal at the time, but obviously raised many ethical issues. The investigation gave numerous congressmen a stage for teeing off, not only on the jockeys who happened merely to be messengers bearing the bad news, but the evil force of teenage music as well.

At other times reporting practices were downright subjective and venomous. Wes Smith reports on a story appearing in the *New York Times* the day after one of Freed's concerts at the Brooklyn Paramount in February 1957: "...[mental health professionals] queried by the *Times* said that the rock'n'roll craze seemed to have its roots in 'rhythmic behavior patterns' dating back to the Middle Ages. One... described the Paramount frenzy as 'spontaneous lunacy'. The *Times* quoted a 1949 study that found that as many as 20 percent of children rock 'n' roll in their beds as a natural instinct, but another study found the new music and dance craze similar to the disease St. Vitus's Dance, also known as chorea major, a mass, dance-like, whirling dervish frenzy that struck Germany and then the rest of Europe in the 14th century. Victims would start dancing and then be unable to stop. The Italians attributed the behavior to the bite of a tarantula, and called it 'Tarantism'....According to Dr. Joost Meerlo...jukebox rhythms inspired young people to throw themselves into 'prehistoric rhythmic trances', the good doctor said, until their dancing progressed beyond accepted forms of cultural expression." It was apparent that Dr. Meerlo did not have any adolescents (or adolescence) of his own. Fortunately, the response of most mental health professionals was more empathic and reasonable.

At various times, the backlash by the news media, religious leaders, educators, politicians, music nabobs and other recalcitrants was effective, but not very, and not for long. In the sphere of television, Ed Sullivan, host of the "Toast of the Town" (the top-rated Sunday night television show), at first bowed to pressure from the establishment to keep Elvis Presley's waistline (or thereabouts) off TV. He bowed, that is, until Steve Allen (host of a competing show) soundly thrashed him in the ratings when he allowed Presley to perform. Sullivan somehow amended his position, in a manner to be envied by many politicians, and signed Presley to a $50,000, three-show deal. Concerts were attacked as well. Alan Freed's wing-ding, held in Boston in May 1958, incited a riot according to the media. The strong reaction to this report did have the effect of stopping concert tours, but only for a year or so. And in the realm of radio, where the payola scandal all but eviscerated the powerful deejays of the era, the backlash affected the messengers (the deejays) more than the bad news (the music). The establishment reaction would plug one hole in the dike, only to find two more streams of water aimed at them. The net result of establishment censure was to slow the spread of doo-wop and of rock 'n' roll, not stop it entirely.

Did doo-wop music actually spur teens to mug and have sex with each other? Were parental fears justified? Steve Propes in *Those Oldies But Goodies: A Guide To 50's Record Collecting* identifies themes in fifties rock 'n' roll that he perceives as integral to the teen experience. The themes seem to support the parental view, and include (1) sex and virility (e.g., "Sixty Minute Man" by the Dominoes, "Toy Bell" by the Bees and "Work with Me Annie" by the Midnighters); (2) partying and night life ("Let the Good Times Roll" by Shirley & Lee and "Rip It Up" by Little Richard); (3) fast cars ("Maybelline" by Chuck Berry and "Buick '59" by the Medallions); (4) drinking (approached boastfully) ("One Mint Julep" by the Clovers and "WPLJ" by the Four Deuces); (5) money problems ("Money Honey" by the Drifters and "Your Cash Ain't Nothin' But Trash" by the Clovers); (6) crime and punishment ("Smokey Joe's Cafe" by the Robins and "Stagger Lee" by Lloyd Price); (7) appeals for religious help ("The Bells" by the Dominoes and "Crying in the Chapel" by the Orioles); and (8) adolescent problems ("Yakety Yak" by the Coasters). Although the subjects identified by Propes were accurate for the rhythm and blues and paleo-doo-wop eras, the main subject of songs became innocent, idealistic and often unrequited love as doo-wop evolved into its classical stage. In fact, of the three subcategories of rock 'n' roll, doo-wop (rhythm and blues and rockabilly being the other two) was by far the least sensationalistic and bawdy. Love became the almost exclusive theme of doo-wop within and after this classical period of 1955-1959. Also, the major proponents of rhythm and blues in the late 1940s and early 1950s were older, more sexually experienced (and jaded) men. The doo-wop performers that emerged in the early to mid-1950s were almost invariably young men in their teen years or early twenties. They were neither cynical nor experienced enough to sing persuasively about sex or drinking. The most they could achieve was braggadocio.

Further, if these subjects were a reflection of the things that were important to teens, they were important mostly in a sensationalistic sense. *Peyton Place*, *Lady Chatterley's Lover* and *Playboy* magazine were read by many teens of that era, but they were not necessarily representative of what teens were reading. The racy and rebellious songs merely titillated and attracted them. Singing about love was not new, did not make headlines and did not deserve to evince a backlash. Singing about sex was new, shocking and to some, reprehensible.

The lyrics of doo-wop songs tell us a lot about the real morality and fantasies of the teen subculture of the 1950s. In the "classical" doo-wop period, for every song that can be placed comfortably in one of Propes' categories, at least 10 dwell on one or more of the various stages of first love. The torturous process of this first love is illustrated in "The Book Of Love," which follows in Figure VII.

A slice of the story of a boy falling in love with a girl (sometimes vice versa) is THE theme, almost to the point of exclusivity, of slower doo-wop songs. Uptempo doo-wop songs also deal with this issue, but lack the tenderness and seriousness that inhere to the slower songs. There is more braggadocio ("Daddy Cool" by the Rays) and cockiness ("Speedoo" by the Cadillacs) in the approach to love, and many fast songs vary the theme to include humor ("Along Came Jones" by the Coasters), lasciviousness ("Honey Love" by the Drifters), chauvinism ("Hot Dog Dooly Wah" by the Pyramids) and mild rebelliousness ("Charlie Brown" by the Coasters).

FIGURE VII

THE BOOK OF LOVE

Our musical protagonist dreams of a girl	"Girl In My Dreams" by the Cliques,
Loves her from afar	"Image Of A Girl" by the Safaris,
Is afraid to approach her but dares to	"Please Say You Want Me" by the Schoolboys,
Thinks she's fine	"So Fine" by the Fiestas,
Dates her	"Saturday Night At The Movies" by the Drifters,
Proclaims his undying adulation of her	"Sunday Kind Of Love" by the Harptones,
Revels in her beauty	"Love Doll" by the Scarlets,
Asserts that she meets every need that he has	"The Way You Look Tonight" by the Jaguars,
Anticipates graduation day so they may wed	"When We Get Married" by the Dreamlovers,
Disdains parental warnings that they're young	"Not Too Young To Fall In Love" by Teenchords,
A break-up occurs	"Tears On My Pillow" by Little Anthony & the Imperials,
Because he was cruel to her	"Sorry, I Ran All The Way Home" by the Impalas
Or cheated on her	"Little Darlin" by the Gladiolas,
Or took her for granted or deceived her	"Come Back My Love" by the Wrens,
He begs abjectly for forgiveness	"Down On My Knees" by the Heartbeats,
And promises atonement.................................	"I'm Sorry" by the Platters,
Occasionally she dumps him permanently	"I Met Him On A Sunday" by the Shirelles,
He then mourns his loss but keeps hoping	"Long Lonely Nights" by Lee Andrews & Hearts,
That if he waits long enough she will return.	"In My Lonely Room" by the 4 Haven Knights,
And the story of their love replays in his mind	"The Book Of Love" by the Monotones.

Frequently, the starstruck supplicant would name his inamorata outright. There were probably almost as many girls named Gloria walking around in the fifties as there were renditions of the song by the same name. Mary (Schoolboys), Mary Lou (Robins), Marianne (Fireflies), MaryAnn (Lendells), Mary Ann (Young Ones), Annie Mae (Arrows), Flossie Mae (Saucers), Lillie Mae (Cupids), Lilly Maebelle (Valentines), Lula Mae (Barons), Molly Mae (Crests), Sally Mae (Corvairs), Verdie Mae (Twilights), Annabelle Lee (Coeds), Barbra Lee (Orioles), Carol Lee (Martels), Coralee (Hemlocks), Donna Lee (Demilles), Jerri Lee (Flamingos), Lola Lee (Five Trojans), Mary Lee (Rainbows), Wanna Lee (Vocal Tones), among hundreds of others, were all glorified (gloria-fied) by doo-wop music. One can't help wondering whether this was a marketing ploy designed to carve out a share of the market. A boyfriend would be foolish to miss a chance to score points with his sweetie by not buying her a record that bore her name. And for those Charlenes (Aladdins) and Estelles (Belltones) that were between beaus, a record bearing their name would exert an irresistible pull on their baby-sitting wages (girls bought more records than boys).

Female groups in turn sang about their guys. Apparently girls in those days had less exotic tastes in boys, because the guys they sang about were most often named Johnny Darling (Feathers), Billy (Bobbettes), Tommy (Reperata & the Delrons) or Bobby (Desires).

The Chiffons

The Charms

Other doo-wop groups aimed their plaints of love at a more general audience. "Honey Baby" (Blue Diamonds), "Honey Bun" (Colts), "Honey Love" (Drifters), "My Love" (Arcades), "Oh My Love" (Chiffons), "Love Doll" (Scarlets), "Doll Baby" (Paragons), "Angel Baby" (Rosie & the Originals), "My Baby Dearest Darling" (Charms), "Dearest Darling" (Castroes), "My Darling" (Aquatones), "Oh My Darling" (Capris), and "Always My Darling" (Cadillacs) are all titles of doo-wop songs. These were more pragmatic efforts, at least in a financial sense, because any young Brenda (Cupids), Juanita (Crests) or Florabelle (Calvanes) might, upon thinking the song was directed at them, go out and buy the record.

The theme of innocence that permeated the music of the 1950s was a reflection of the teen subculture. "Bad boys" back then didn't do crack, have a rap sheet a mile long or commit suicide. They spiked the punch at the high school hop, drag-raced their cars, and called the English teacher "Daddio" (from "Charlie Brown" by the Coasters). They had gang wars or "rumbles," but the most likely intent was to injure and discourage others from invading their "turf," not to kill and take over the local trade in drugs. Bad girls back then were girls who got pregnant and/or dropped out of high school to marry. Most innocent when seen in light of today's standards. The music is relatively free of financial pressures, the prospect of divorce, mid-life crisis or children. The lyrics speak of unrealistic love, born of infatuation and allied with fantasy. Existential issues, realism, political causes and statements, drugs, racial themes and alienation are not found in this music; they would have to await the coming of another teen subculture.

Looking at those who produced the music gives us another view of the teen generation of the 1950s. Doo-wop music was created by relatively innocent bad boys. These weren't the guys that were home studying or doing their chores, these were the ones hanging out on the corner outside the candy store, or at the local pool hall or bowling alley. If your parents were wealthy enough to own a garage (regardless of whether a house was attached), you could develop "garage band" music. If your parents didn't own a garage, and your one- or two-bedroom apartment was crowded with younger siblings, you met on the corner to create your music.

Doo-wop blossomed in an age when video arcades, shopping malls and dens with VCRs were not even on the drawing board. The hangouts were pool halls, bowling alleys (not especially conducive to group singing) and candy stores. The street corners, back stairwells and boys' rooms of the high school (not only to relieve physical discomfort and boredom, but to provide echo) were the studios "au naturel" of the 1950s.

Singing became an expression of the male (and female) bonding process which is a necessary part of healthy maturation. It joined playing (stick-, punch-, base-, basket-, foot-) ball, playing cards and drag racing as a way of having fun with the guys. The lyrics of "Heart Of My Heart" (by the Four Aces, who were a preppy group) convey the emotional impact of that bonding process:

"Heart of my heart, I love that melody
Heart of my heart, brings back a memory
When we were kids on the corner of the street
We were rough and ready guys
But Oh!, how we could harmonize
Heart of my heart, men friends were dearer then

58

Too bad we had to part
I know a tear would glisten
If once more I could listen
To that gang that sang heart of my heart." *

* "(The Gang That Sang) Heart Of My Heart," Ben Ryan (EMI Music Publishing, 1926), ASCAP.

While singing in the school glee club or musical was "faggy" (read "nerdy"), singing in a doo-wop group had status. It was a pastime legitimized by the now full-blown teenage addiction to music; those that could actually create that music were well-respected. They might not be the greatest athletes or care about their schoolwork, but they had found their own niche. And as with today's rock groups, it had the added benefit of attracting the attention of girls, never a factor to be taken lightly.

Further, it was a way for kids with little formal musical training and a bare minimum of vocal talent to "make it," to become well-known, if only on a neighborhood or local basis. No instruments were needed, you just had to be able to carry a tune and get a hall pass so you could meet your friends in the boys' room or back stairwell, smoke a butt and harmonize. The atmosphere of those times may be best conveyed by the lyrics of a tune by Kenny Vance (formerly a member of the Harbor Lights and Jay & the Americans) called "Looking For An Echo":

"At Erasmus Hall High School, we used to harmonize
Me and Denny and Ara, and two Italian guys
We were singing oldies, but they were newies then
And today when I play my old 45s I remember when
We practiced in a subway, in a lobby or a hall
Crowded in a doorway, singing doo-wops to the wall
And if we went to a party and they wouldn't let us sing
We'd lock ourselves in the bathroom and nobody could get in
'Cause we were looking for an echo
An answer to our sound
A place to be in harmony
A place we almost found
And the girls would gather round us, and our heads would really swell
We'd sing songs by the Moonglows, the Harptones and the Dells
And when we sang 'Sincerely', we'd really sing it high
Even though it was falsetto, we almost reached the sky
We sang a lot of changes since 1955
And a lot of bad arrangements, we tried to harmonize
Now we've turned into oldies, but we were newies then
And today when I play my old 45s I remember when
We were looking for an echo
An answer to our sound
A place to be in harmony
A place we almost found. *

* "Looking For An Echo," Kenny Vance (Warner Brothers Music Corp., 1975), ASCAP.

Doo-wop music was created mainly in urban areas by poor blacks and secondarily by poor whites. There was no money for music lessons and most of these "bad boys" did not have enough trust in authority or perseverance to utilize the music departments in their high schools. Creating this music was a natural for those who were poor and disaffected with the establishment, but who were still young, innocent and idealistic enough to dream about love. It also provided the dream of making it BIG; that is, making lots of money and earning adulation. Blacks began to be integrated into the music business (though certainly not on an equal basis) around the time they were integrated into professional sports, so it stands to reason that the lure of a career as a professional in music easily became fantasy for the average poor teenager. In fact, in 1954 Jubilee Records put out an album by the Four Tunes to encourage these fantasies. On this album there were separate tracks for "bass," "tenor," "alto" and "baritone," so that aspirants could sing along with a famous professional group.

The teen generation of the fifties broke the ice for their younger brothers. Given license by postwar affluence and parental indulgence, they set precedents for succeeding generations. They established the rules, which revolved around music, dress and slang, and this set them apart from their parents. Once freedom was theirs, not many opted to give it back.

Chapter 5

The Technology of the Doo-Wop Era

The American private-enterprise economy is based both on meeting needs and creating them. It is fair in an economic sense (i.e., survival of the fittest) though not necessarily in a moral or political sense. This fairness makes it efficient, often to the point of ruthlessness. The teen subculture of the 1950s engaged the mechanisms of this kind of economy to meet its demands for music.

There were three noteworthy avenues through which supply matched teenage demand. The first had to do with the explosion in postwar technology, some of which was channeled through the music and recording industry and which helped catalyze the spread of doo-wop and rock 'n' roll. The second involved the evolution of "personality deejays" who not only helped deliver doo-wop to its potential consumers, but who also stimulated the growth of even greater demand for the music. Last was the remarkable growth of small independent record companies that challenged the establishment in a race to deliver the product.

Just as Americans (believe it or not) made do with one car and one television set at earlier points in history, the prewar norm was for each family to have but one radio. The old Stromberg-Carlson or Motorola had its place in the living room and the family had to reach a single decision, usually made by parents, about which program would be tuned in. After the war, smaller but not yet portable (or independent of vacuum tubes) radios became available.

Transistors, tiny electronic gizmos made of silicone, were invented in 1947 by three Americans, William Shockley, John Bardeen and Walter H. Brattain, and soon made bigger and bulkier vacuum tubes obsolete. The triumverate received the Nobel Prize in 1956, no doubt as a result of a write-in campaign by teenagers. Transistors were used in the production of small portable radios beginning in the mid-fifties just as the classical doo-wop period was beginning to unfold. As the decade progressed, these radios (as with all technological advances except taxes) came down in price, became more powerful and delivered better and clearer sound. As a result, more teens could purchase these appliances directly because of their growing affluence, or became heir to the family console when Mom and Dad bought the new-fangled ones. Also of enormous importance was the concurrent proliferation of television sets. Many parents opted to continue their tyrannical rule of the airwaves with that instrument, bequeathing the family radio to their elder children.

Aside from delivering transistor radios into the hot little hands of eager teens, the postwar explosion in media technology unintentionally conspired to spread the music that was coming up over the horizon. As television invaded more and more homes in the early 1950s, network radio suffered. Then as now, network radio catered primarily to adults, carrying news programs, farming reports, talk shows, comedies, serials and music for the undeniably mature. Radio station owners needed to find an audience to replace the one they were losing to the television networks, and in many cases this new audience consisted of individuals from the teen and young adult generations. This was especially true in the early evening hours, when parents would turn on their television sets, leaving teens with an unsupervised assignation with the household radio. These young people did not choose the same programming that their parents did, so that there was pressure on most stations to convert to a new, younger sound. In the cities the sound that attracted these new consumers was rhythm and blues and group doo-wop music. The disc jockeys who chose, for whatever reasons, to program the new music became popular. Since they were catering to a younger audience, they resorted to a tried-and-true method of garnering the attention of teens: outlandishness. This led to an increasing number of "personality deejays" and their acceptance by teens, and accounts for the saintly tolerance of program directors for their often flamboyant antics.

It was not only radio and television which indirectly contributed to the spread of doo-wop and rock 'n' roll. By World War I, an invention by a fellow by the name of Emile Berliner, the phonograph record (which played at 78 revolutions per minute), had won out over the Edison wax cylinder and became the standard for musical transcription. The 78 format remained unchallenged until the late 1940s when Columbia Records unveiled its slower 33rpm record (the LP, or long playing record), which offered better sound and provided roughly 10 times the amount of recording space as the old 78s. The grooves on these new records were much thinner and the needle much smaller, producing a clearer sound and wider spectrum of sounds. Shortly thereafter (early 1949), RCA Corporation produced the 45rpm record, which while only containing as much music as the old 78s, offered even better sound than the 78s. In addition, the availability of light, portable record players that would play up to 10 records on a spindle made 45s honored guests at teen parties and dances. As of July 1954, most record companies shipped only 45s to disc jockeys as promotional copies, replacing 78s. By the mid-1950s, 45s were the main conveyance of doo-wop and rock 'n' roll, although by 1960 albums began their dominance of the market. Doo-wop music was heard on 45s almost exclusively because many of the groups did not have enough "cuts" to make an album; the standard recording session for doo-wop groups only included two ballads and two jumps. Albums came to the fore only with the "oldies revival" of 1960 (*Oldies But Goodies* series). Cutting an album and releasing singles from it, a common practice today, was unheard of in the 1950s. Albums were usually made up of previously released singles.

Recordings on tape were becoming more widely used as well. Magnetic tape recording was invented in 1935 but was first widely used by Germany during World War II for propaganda broadcasts. Tape recording soon replaced the older method of recording on wire as a means of duplicating sound. By the 1950s tape recordings replaced 16-inch records as the primary means of distributing network broadcasts to affiliate members. Tapes produced better sound quality and were less fragile when transported. The public, however, would have to await the 1960s to benefit from the commercialization of tape recordings through the use of eight-track cartridges and cassettes.

Finally, the dimensions of sound within the home grew tremendously during the 1950s. Many families rushed out to replace their tinny, small-sounding 78 players with the latest in "Hi-Fidelity" equipment only to learn that a new sound distribution system, "Stereophonic Sound," was just around the corner. Soon teens would be able to annoy their parents with two speakers rather than just one. All this technology eased the way for these ungrateful and disloyal young folk to become, with little fanfare, consumers of music. They could now choose, virtually unbeknownst to their elders, anything on the radio dial that appealed to them. A minor coup de grace was administered when earphones were regularly included with the purchase of a radio, further removing teens from accountability to their parents and lending an air of secrecy to their listening habits. And conspiring with teenagers was a new breed of radio stars: the "personality deejay."

Chapter 6

The Personality Deejays

Unaware of the current or impending technological advances, the deejays on second tier radio stations had been sending rhythm and blues over the ether regularly since the mid 1940s. At first, this music was exclusively black music aimed at black audiences. Regardless of their natural pigmentation, most of these deejays sounded black in order to establish and maintain credibility with their audience and not coincidentally to be able to represent adequately the products being hawked by their stations. As described by Wes Smith in his book *The Pied Pipers of Rock 'n' Roll: Radio DeeJays of the 50's and 60's*, some of these men were upstanding members of the community, serving as role models and teachers for teens and adults alike. Others were simply hucksters.

The type of music that deejays played for their teenage audience depended on what part of the country they hailed from. Those in rural areas pushed country rhythm and blues and later rockabilly. Those who broadcast from the larger urban areas played sophisticated rhythm and blues and the group sound of doo-wop. Alan Freed led the way, carrying the doo-wop sound with him on an odyssey that took him from obscurity to stardom. Concerts introduced teens to their newly emerging deejay idols "up close and personal." Freed was clearly in the forefront. On March 21, 1952 he hosted "Moon Dog's Coronation Ball" (a combination concert and dance) in the Cleveland Arena. The facility held 10,000 people and it was sold out. Somehow, roughly twice that number managed to get inside, and fire and police officials called off the concert midway through. A stabbing (over a girl or a seat), a little public drunkenness and a lot of dancing in the aisles prompted vicious reviews in the next day's newspapers, a reaction that soon became a tradition wherever Freed took his show. The publicity attendant to the "riot" in Cleveland only served to broaden Freed's appeal as a cult hero and to focus the attention of as-yet unconverted teens on the music from which parents were trying to shield them. Of course the concerts, as forbidden fruit, now held even greater appeal for teenagers. Similar endeavors in Akron (July 1952) and Cleveland (July 1953) were sold out, as was Freed's first foray into the East, at the Newark Armory (May 1954) which drew 10,000 avid youngsters.

Alan Freed, though "rock 'n' roll's" self-proclaimed king, was nonetheless as important to the evolution of doo-wop as he was to the broader field of rock 'n' roll. Freed introduced and helped establish such groups as the Platters, Moonglows, Flamingos, Frankie Lymon & the Teenagers and the Three Chuckles. He was the first to promote concerts, make rock 'n' roll movies, and showcase the music on television. He was also one of the first to claim composer rights to songs (predominantly) written by others. According to John Jackson in *Big Beat Heat*, Freed put his name on "Sincerely" by the Moonglows and "Nadine" by the Coronets (he managed both groups), supposedly to make the songs more visible.

In Freed's music-promotion activities, a large percentage of the acts were doo-wop groups. His telephone-book banging, "Moon Dog" howling, love-driven song dedications, and enthusiastic shouts of "Go! Go! Go!" above the music made him the prototype of the personality deejay and earned him the adulation and respect of teenagers far more than anyone else of that era. According to the *New York Times* in May 1960: "Going to one of Alan Freed's musicales has always been something like having an aisle seat for the San

Francisco earthquake. His favorite art form has caused riots in Boston, been banned in New Haven and broken all marks for drawing customers to the Brooklyn Paramount." Later in the same article, "Soon after his arrival [from Cleveland] the dial setting for radio station WINS became one of the things that was not to be touched in a home that housed a teen-ager."

The concerts began to grow in numbers and spread geographically like an untreated disease. Reserved seating was now required as a concession to safety. Further, audiences which initially were almost exclusively black shifted gradually but inexorably to being largely white. Even Freed's first three concerts, held in 1952 and 1953, attracted audiences that were roughly one-third white. Exceptions to this trend occurred only when the concerts were held at "chitlin circuit" locales, such as the Apollo in New York, the Howard in Washington, D.C., the Uptown in Philadelphia and the Royal in Baltimore. However, the general shift in audience from black to white was an unerring testimony to the rapid spread of doo-wop and rock 'n' roll through the white teenage middle-class population. John Jackson (*Big Beat Heat*) reported that in 1952, a rhythm and blues record which hit the top of the *Billboard* charts would sell 250,000 copies, on average. By 1953, a top rhythm and blues hit would sell 1,000,000 disks, implying that white teens got into the action.

Jeff Greenfield, in *No Peace, No Place*, described what one saw at one of these concerts: "Four or five singers, outlandishly dressed, in flaming red tux jackets, purple pants, yellow shirts with velvet ties — this in a time when charcoal gray was a bit daring. There are always two mikes — one for the lead singer, one for the rest of the group, including (always) a bass singer who supplies the doo-bobba, doo-bobba doo line, one falsetto to surround the reedy lead voice with logistical support in the form of descants.

The steps. They defy description. In a tribute to symmetry, the guy on the left puts out his left hand, the guy on the right puts out his right hand, and the guy in the middle puts out both hands. Fingers snap and wave, legs flash out and up, in mirror-image perfection. Now the hands switch, the feet shuffle in tempo. The tenor sax break begins. The singers spin completely around; they do splits. They gesture with the words.

'You know' — (the singers) point out

'In my heart' — point to the heart

'I pray' — hands together in prayer

'We'll never part' — hands separate, heads shake no.'"

In September 1954, Freed migrated to WINS in New York City, lured by the highest salary ever paid to that point in time to a personality disc jockey ($75,000 per annum and a share of future syndication revenues). He began by broadcasting in the 11 p.m. to 2 a.m. time slot (six days per week) and soon added a show between 7 p.m. and 9 p.m. New York offered not only bigger salaries, but bigger arenas and a larger listening audience. His first concert in New York was called the "Rock 'n' Roll Jubilee Ball" (featuring the Clovers, Drifters, Harptones and Moonglows) and was presented before 16,000 fans at the St. Nicholas Arena on Jan. 14th and 15th, 1955. Reviewers enthused about the "...solid mass that stood for five hours to see the spectacular r&b show put on by Freed and company. Seen from above, the enthusiastic teeners seemed to be jelled into one swaying body with thousands of heads. That they adored Freed was evident from the uproarious welcome with which they greeted his appearance. The enthusiasm of the audience was transferred to the performers, who reacted to the frenzy with tremendous performances. A finale that lasted about half an hour was rocked in the atmosphere of a revival meeting." And eventually "...the entire troupe returned to the stage for a closing that was without parallel. Singers and instrumentalists danced, dancers and singers grabbed instruments and instrumentalists and dancers sang. Alan Freed and his lovely wife, Jackie, jitterbugged and the kids went wild."

Freed's second New York concert, in early 1955, featuring Chuck Berry, Tony Bennett, the Moonglows and the Harptones, netted over $100,000, an enormous sum for that time. Dick Clark, an emerging TV-deejay and entrepreneur, went on the road with his "Caravan of Stars" in 1957, and Freed continued to sell out the Brooklyn Paramount and any other place he chose to book. One of the most ambitious of tours was an 80-day extravaganza appropriately called

The Three Chuckles

the "Biggest Show of Stars for 1957." Featuring Fats Domino, Clyde McPhatter, Frankie Lymon (sans Teenagers), Paul Anka, the Everly Brothers, Spaniels, Bobbettes, Johnnie and Joe, the Drifters, Eddie Cochran, Buddy Knox and Jimmy Bowen and the Rhythm Orchids, it was the first tour to be integrated. Despite some setbacks (e.g., when Freed's May 1958 show in Boston set off another "riot" and resulted in his being fired from WINS) concerts continued to spread the gospel. In fact, it soon became easier to book rhythm and blues acts than pop acts, owing to the larger number of establishments catering to rhythm and blues. These public displays represented the front lines in the war between the doo-wop and rock 'n' roll movement and the outraged establishment.

The Moonglows

Less controversial but more effective in terms of the number of teens reached were the movies that served as a showcase for the new heroes. Two Freed productions, *Rock Around the Clock* (featuring the Platters, Bill Haley & the Comets and Freed) and *Rock, Rock, Rock* (with Frankie Lymon & the Teenagers, the Moonglows, the Flamingos, Chuck Berry, the Three Chuckles, Cirino and the Bowties, and the Johnny Burnette Trio) were released in 1956. *The Girl Can't Help It* also debuted that same year and featured some real actors (Edmund O'Brien, Tom Ewell and Jayne Mansfield) with a real script that allowed for incidental appearances by Little Richard, Fats Domino, Gene Vincent, Eddie Cochran and the Platters. And then there was Elvis, making his film debut in *Love Me Tender* in September 1956. The critics said he couldn't act, but his fans seemed to feel differently.

There were also more serious films that dealt with the general topic of teen rebellion. In 1953 *The Wild One* starring Marlon Brando appeared, and forever doomed nice teenagers to only riding their motorcycles over their parents' dead bodies. Then, in the spring of 1955, *The Blackboard Jungle* (MGM studios) sent Bill Haley's theme song and incipient teen anthem, "Rock Around the Clock" (on Decca Records), to the top of the charts (after a mediocre reception upon its first release in 1954). The enormous impact of this record, combined with a controversial film about juvenile delinquency, heightened parental concerns about their interrelation. *Rebel Without A Cause*, also released in 1955, confirmed parents' fears that teens could become thankless, unfeeling ingrates. These serious movies were well-attended by teens and parents alike, so that the movie industry had the distinction of fueling both teenage rebellion and the backlash against it.

Finally, television hit the teen generation where they lived, literally. After school, an easy segue away from the Mickey Mouse Club, and on Saturdays, when parents were too busy to monitor their children's watching habits, doo-wop as well as rock 'n' roll were on television. Not only could teens watch their favorite stars perform, but they could learn vicariously from the real-life youngsters who were fortunate enough to be picked for the show. Fantasies were born by watching more glamorous, outgoing and better-dancing peers careening across the screen.

Again, Freed was in the forefront, although he proved, after several efforts, that he should have stuck with radio. He bombed with a record review show ("Request Review") in Cleveland in 1950, then tried again in 1957 with a dance show that featured mainly black artists and doo-wop groups. Unfortunately, according to Wes Smith, one of the show's first guests, Frankie Lymon, had the audacity to dance with a white girl on camera. John Jackson (*Big Beat Heat*) reports on the pressure exerted by sponsors and the Southern white audience which resulted in the show being cancelled after four outings. The paragon of teen music shows was and is "American Bandstand," hosted by Dick Clark. "Bandstand," which hosted many doo-wop acts, made its national debut in August 1957, after ABC picked it up from its Philadelphia affiliate. Within a year, it became far and away the most popular show of its ilk and the only one that was national. The only rivals to "Bandstand" were local shows hosted by Freed, Clay Cole and "Jocko" Henderson.

While competition between and among doo-wop deejays occurred in all urban centers, it was perhaps the most fierce in New York, the "hotbed" of the doo-wop sound. Because of the size of the market and the media coverage offered by the New York-based trade publications such as *Billboard and Cash Box*, many of these New York deejays became household names. Despite being the "King" in New York, Freed vied with Tommy "Dr. Jive" Smalls on WWRL, Phil "Dr. Jive" Gordon on WLIB, Willie "The Mayor Of Harlem" Bryant and Ray Carroll on WHOM, Jack "The Pear Shaped Talker" Walker on WOV (who did public relations for Atlantic Records on the side), Peter Tripp on WMGM, Hal Jackson on WLIB, Joe Bostic on WBNX and slightly later, Douglas "Jocko" Henderson on WLIB and WADO. WLIB was the most popular station in the black market in the doo-wop era, outdistancing its nearest competitor by 20 percent in some surveys taken in the mid-fifties. WOV offered the unusual combination of rhythm and blues and Italian music (in roughly equal proportions) which may account in part for the black influence on Italian youth who emerged as "italo-doo-woppers" in the late 1950s. Italian programming was mostly during the day with rhythm and blues programming at night after 8 p.m.

One of Freed's competitors, Willie Bryant, had a bad case of sour grapes, most of which had nothing to do with Freed. Bryant was a fair-skinned, "white"-haired well-rounded entertainer who had been a legitimate actor, orchestra leader, dancer and comic before he turned to broadcasting rhythm and blues and doo-wop and emceeing shows at the Apollo. Broadcasting from the Birdland Club with Ray Carroll on WHOM, Willie featured the Top 20 r&b hits every Saturday night at midnight. Ted Fox, in *Showtime At The Apollo*, interviewed Leonard Reed, one of Bryant's dance partners, who stated: 'He was a great showman... He could do it all... He was on the ball, but bitter, and he had a right to be. Willie was as good as, if not better than, [a major white comic] ever dared to be. But they knew he was part Negro, and downtown they wouldn't let him work. Willie was made to stay in Harlem. ...But Willie was Negro, and he never did get the chance. The white man only lets a few Negroes through. At the time there was no room for five; maybe one or two.' Bryant, installed as Harlem's locality mayor in 1952 (an honorary position) by then Mayor Vincent Impellitteri, tried to use his clout by calling a protest meeting in a Harlem auditorium with the intent of censuring Freed for, in effect, sounding black when he wasn't. Bryant also objected to the syndication of Freed's shows, believing that it would take jobs away from blacks. It all came to naught and Willie had to settle for being "the Mayor" instead of "the King." Bryant did make important contributions to the doo-wop movement, however, emceeing not only numerous shows at the Apollo, but two 1955 feature films, *The Rock 'n' Roll Revue* and *The Rhythm & Blues Revue*, which showcased all-black talent.

The strongest competitors among deejays who played doo-wop in the New York arena were Tommy "Dr. Jive" Smalls who brought a rhythm and blues (and doo-wop) review to the Ed Sullivan "Toast of the Town" show, Peter Tripp, who popularized the Top 40 format in New York, and "Jocko" Henderson (who also broadcast in Philadelphia on WHAT). "Dr. Jive" bought Small's Paradise, a landmark Harlem night club previously owned by one Edwin Smalls, and capitalized on the name to bring premier doo-wop and rhythm and blues acts before the public. Smalls was also the most popular of the Apollo emcees, and was second only to Freed in the presentation of concerts in New York City. Peter Tripp, "the curly-headed kid in the third row," offered the first (and only for a while) record countdown based on actual record sales (Freed presented a "Top 25" but it was subjective, based on his own tastes and listener requests), and often inserted doo-wop songs in his survey show as "extras." "Jocko" Henderson, whose rhyming patter (e.g., great gugga mugga shugga bugga) was the forerunner of modern rap music, was also the first to put gang doo-wop before the public, and even had a doo-wop song dedicated to him ("Jocko Sent Me" by Ben White & the Darchaes).

The competition was in outlandishness and popularity on the surface, but ultimately it was audience share that was at stake. It got fierce at times. Jocko Henderson, Tommy Smalls and Freed vied in the promotion of live shows at New York's numerous theaters (e.g., Brooklyn Fox, Brooklyn Paramount and THE Apollo) and on television. Freed usually outgrossed the others (in the monetary sense), except at the Apollo (where "Dr. Jive" reigned), because he was able to attract more of the white teen audience. In addition to competing for money and fame, these deejays also tried to be the first to play the latest and best records for their audiences. In New York that meant doo-wop music. Songs by all of the great and not-so-great groups were filtered through the capitalistic system run by this crew of deejays. The teen public voted with their radio dials.

Syndication was another Freed first. While still at WJW in Cleveland, his show was sold to 10 other stations, and after his move to WINS in New York, upwards of 50 stations carried his patter and taste in music to eager teens. Other rhythm and blues disc jockeys such as Hunter Hancock of Los Angeles, Zenas "Daddy" Sears of Atlanta and Tommy Smalls also syndicated their shows as early as 1954. The success of these syndications was surprising at the time because earlier attempts by pop-music disc jockeys to syndicate had failed. The success of the rhythm and blues jocks lay in their charisma, the fanaticism of their audience, and the fact that the shows were sold to independent radio stations, which catered more to teens than the network stations (which were geared to adult tastes).

Whatever their demeanor when not performing, these early deejays had two things in common: they loved rhythm and blues, doo-wop and/or rock 'n' roll, and they had strong personalities while on the air. Often it was the language they used or the way it was delivered. Most were up on (or created) the latest slang and delivered it in a humorous fashion. Frequently they displayed a cynicism for the establishment that young audiences found irresistible. Occasionally they would be naughty, bawdy, or downright lewd. Wes Smith gives examples of rhythm and blues deejay Gene Nobles' (WLAC, Nashville) licentious handling of commercials: "He got away with some fairly risqué lines for the times, including a few twisted around commercials for Gruen (rhymes with screwin') wristwatches: 'If your girlfriend is mad at you, why don't you give her a good Gruen?' He had particular fun with commercials for White Rose Petroleum Jelly, which he advised his young listeners to keep in the glove compartments of their cars 'for whatever might come up.'" Not surprisingly, the audience most drawn to these titillating shenanigans were the teenagers. Just as generations since have gravitated to the likes of Steve Allen, Soupy Sales, the Saturday Night Live crew, Howard Stern and Don Imus, the teens of the 1950s were drawn to these "personality deejays," and for the same reasons. Give teens music they could dance to, with a little humor, lasciviousness and sarcasm thrown in, and you had (and still have) a sure winner. The stations promoting these deejays began to have larger and more enthusiastic audiences which knew no bounds of color.

Unfortunately for the deejays, their high-flying life styles and on-air shenanigans only lasted until the late 1950s. Payola came under the scrutiny of the Harris commission in 1959. Aside from emotional backlash generated in the political establishment, there was also sentiment within the music industry for eliminating the practice because station owners did not get a slice of the pie, because they wanted to be seen as upstanding members of the community they served and because record companies got fed up with paying out all that money. The personality deejays, who attracted a large share of the money because they were so popular, were ferreted out, creating new standards for the industry in the process. Those who tried to "tough it out," such as Alan Freed and Tommy "Dr. Jive" Smalls, got hit hard while those who chose to cooperate, such as Dick Clark, lived to fight other battles. More subtle ways of getting records played, such as promotions, giving away free records and three-martini lunches, became part of the new ethos of the industry. Choice of programming, more and more, was given over to program directors that were more allied to the station owner than the deejays. The spontaneity was taken out of playing the hits and the old-time deejays knuckled under, withered away or left the business. Yet these deejays had accomplished their task. Millions of members of the teen generation of the 1950s had been converted to the cause. Other deejays, perhaps a little less controversial after the payola debacle, continued to spread the word. As Danny & the Juniors might have sung if they had had more foresight, "Doo-Wop and Roll Is Here To Stay"!

Chapter 7

Indies Versus the Establishment

The major record companies (or majors) in the late 1940s were RCA, Columbia, Decca, Capitol, Mercury and MGM. They dominated record sales, whether measured by actual number of records sold or by gross dollar revenues. Their orientation was to be clearly biased toward white tastes in music. By and large, they ignored minority music without much discrimination (sic): Latin, Polish, Yiddish, country, and "race" or "sepia" music were all given short shrift. Executives of these companies first thought, then hoped, that doo-wop and other forms of rock 'n' roll would go away. Their token ventures into rhythm and blues were often done through subsidiary labels, such as Bluebird (RCA) and Okeh (Columbia). The latter, although a distinguished outlet for black music from the 1920s through the early 1940s, had to be resuscitated in the early 1950s so that its parent could try to jump on the doo-wop and rock 'n' roll bandwagon. In the same period, RCA introduced both the "X" and Groove labels in 1954 which were aimed at the rhythm and blues market segment. Almost concurrently Capitol, Mercury and Decca (which hired Lieber and Stoller) also stepped up efforts in the rhythm and blues field under their own imprints.

The reasons for initially overlooking black ethnic music were simple. There was little money to be made because blacks, in comparison to white consumers, could not afford to buy very many records. There was also high overhead involved in paying the expenses of corporate talent scouts, who had little knowledge of black tastes and even less expertise in the field of black music, so that they could scour the country in search of a hit. Further, the majors were corporate giants, beset with the same philosophical conservatism and bureaucratic inertia as large businesses are today. And no matter how it is couched, racial bias played a part. In the late 1940s schools were segregated, as were stages; it was the way things were. The majors sold their records to the white public, and black artists were valued only if whites liked their music (e.g., Mahalia Jackson on Columbia, Nat "King" Cole on Capitol and the Mills Brothers and Ink Spots on Decca).

The major record companies were closely allied with the American Society of Composers, Authors, and Publishers (ASCAP), which was established in 1914 to provide an income for those who wrote music that others enjoyed. ASCAP instituted and administered the process of collecting royalties, so that each time a song was played on the air or a record (or sheet music) sold, its composers and publishers would be paid an appropriate sum. Unfortunately, whether through economic malice or sociocultural inertia, for many years ASCAP functioned as an exclusive fraternity, keeping out blues and hillbilly songwriters. The needs of these small-timers were provided for by the formation of Broadcast Music, Inc. (BMI) in 1940. BMI developed close ties to the radio industry and serviced composers shunned by ASCAP. This put BMI in the catbird seat when the demand for doo-wop and other forms of rock 'n' roll rose sharply. The ASCAP establishment had clearly misread the tastes of the "silent majority" and, at least in an economic sense, had cut off its nose to spite its face.

The focus on the major (white) segment of the market left a gap that was historically filled by small, independent record companies (or indies). In an entrepreneurial style typical of our country's economic growth, the indies were

70

often a one- or two-person operation; this person or pair of persons handled the talent, production and business ends of the company. The indies, focusing on doo-wop and other forms of rock 'n' roll, were owned and operated by people who were ambitious and hard-working, and who frequently had a more than economic interest in the music and talent they purveyed. An inordinate percentage of these owners were women (e.g., Vivian Bracken of Vee Jay and Bess Berman of Apollo), blacks (Bobby Robinson of Whirlin' Disc and Paul Winley of Winley Records) and Jews (George Goldner of Gee and Leonard and Philip Chess of Chess). The disenfranchised found, through the medium of doo-wop music, a way to "make it" in society.

Meager financing was a double-edged sword for these companies. Not having high overheads or salaries to pay allowed these men an independence and freedom of movement unmatched by the corporate behemoths. Not having much money to spend meant that their "corporate offices" (often no more than a room) were located in poorer neighborhoods, putting them closer to the culture that they needed to know in order to spot talent. Once in a while, an avid and gutsy group would gather below the window or in the office of a label owner, and filibuster in vocal harmony until they were auditioned. Patience and indefatigability had to substitute for fat expense accounts, and allowed many would-be moguls to develop personal relationships within the black communities that they farmed.

On the down side, the necessity of feeding one's family and paying studio expenses put enormous pressure on a label to come up with a hit. The costs of producing and pressing even a single record put a financial strain on fledgling companies. Too many misses in a row meant extinction. Ironically, as Ed Ward points out, even having a major hit could spell doom for a poorly capitalized indie. "The whole economic structure of a record company is based on distributor payments, and in order to get major distributors ...a label had to offer them attractive terms, such as allowing them to return unsold records for credit and letting them hold on to wares for up to 90 days without paying a cent. Meanwhile, the label would need money to keep pressing and shipping records, and if a record got hot, that could mean a huge sum. Of course, many distributors were less than honest about sales figures, and during the 1950s, some even pressed and sold bootleg or counterfeit copies, sending the legitimate records back, especially but not solely to indies. By the time the big profits started rolling in, a label owner could very well have sold everything he owned to amass the capital to keep pressing— literally starving his company to death with success."

Monetary pressure and/or poor judgment occasionally forced indie owners to make desperate moves. Sometimes the rights to a proven hit would be sold to a major or a more financially secure indie (e.g., Imperial, Roulette, ABC-Paramount or Dot). Other times money could be raised by peddling master tapes of a particular artist or group if he, she or it got "hot," especially if the performer was no longer under contract to the original label. Sometimes the entire company would be sold outright to cover debts. And occasionally the rights to a promising but as yet undeveloped talent would be sold, as in the case of the sale of Elvis Presley to RCA by Sam Philips (of Sun Records) for $40,000 in 1955. In comparison to Sam, the Native Americans did well in selling Manhattan.

Indie labels sprang up anywhere talent could be found, which usually meant the urban centers of Chicago, Los Angeles and New York. Groups often switched their allegiance from one label to another because of personnel changes within the group, disadvantageous contracts, record company buyouts or bankruptcies. Johnny Keyes, author of *Du-Wop* and lead singer of the Magnificents, described the powerlessness of the groups in relation to their managers, producers and other business types. Groups were too often robbed of writing credits and thus royalties, overcharged for production costs, sent on tours for which they were paid next to nothing, and invariably there was no recourse. Perhaps because of these kinds of situations, the Harptones, not letting any grass grow under their feet, were already on their sixth label when they recorded for George Goldner on Gee in 1957! Discussed below are some of the main independent labels that focused on doo-wop music. Note that owners often used more than one label to distribute their products, often because of the realization that disc jockeys would not play too many records from one label, to allow the formation of partnerships among different people, or to provide a niche for a new employee or family member (much the same way as each mutual fund within a family of such funds is managed by a different individual and is aimed at a particular market segment).

While not all of the independent labels that were around in the fifties contributed to the body of doo-wop works in an important way, many of them did. The histories of these doo-wop labels are often intertwined through the lives of their owners. In some ways, it was as if these doo-wop label owners belonged to the same fraternity, sharing the success and the glory, but also the failures.

Chicago

Chess/Checker/Argo

These labels were owned by Phil and Leonard Chess. The Chess brothers came to the United States from Poland in 1928, and began their careers by owning and running a high-class black nightclub in Chicago (the Macamba), by which they established ties within the black music community. Their first record label, Aristocrat, did not do well, and its name was changed to Chess in 1948. In the late 1940s through the mid-1950s, they specialized in blues and rhythm and blues. They entered the doo-wop arena in 1953, and in 1955 had a big hit with "Sincerely" by the Moonglows which, though covered by the McGuire sisters, benefited their publishing interests. Chess had a close relationship with Alan Freed who supposedly "co-authored" "Sincerely" and Chuck Berry's "Maybelline." In 1956 Chess produced the first rock 'n' roll sound track album for *Rock Rock Rock* (a Freed film), which featured doo-wop songs by the Flamingos and the Moonglows. By the late 1950s they were one of the largest and most successful of the indies, owning Arc Publishing (in partnership with Gene and Harry Goodman and George Dalin), several radio stations and the rights to the masters of Chicago disc jockey Al Benson's Parrot and Blue Lake labels, Joe Liebowitz' Monarch and Lee Egalnick's Premium labels. Chess also leased many of their doo-wop releases from East Coast companies. Through the doo-wop era they featured 30 doo-wop groups, including Lee Andrews & the Hearts, the Flamingos, Moonglows, Monotones, Students and Tuneweavers. Chess was sold to the GRT conglomerate in the 1969, and went out of business in 1975.

The Tune Weavers   Lee Andrews & The Hearts

Vee Jay/Falcon/Abner

Vee Jay and its subsidiaries were owned by Vivian Carter Bracken, James Bracken and Calvin Carter. Vee Jay Records was founded in 1953 in Gary, Indiana, but within a few months moved to Chicago. Bracken and Vivian Carter owned a record store ("Vivian's Record Shop"), Vivian Carter was a local disc jockey (after winning a contest run by Chicago deejay Al Benson) and Calvin Carter, Vivian's brother, was an established musician. Before Vee Jay, they advised the Chess brothers on the commercial viability of their recordings, establishing a long-standing friendship. Shortly *after* the formation of Vee Jay, Vivian Carter made an honest man out of James Bracken, heretofore merely her business partner, in nuptials conducted on Dec. 16, 1953. Vee Jay was the first large independent record company owned by blacks, and this allowed them easy access to local black communities and the talent that existed within them. Unlike Atlantic and Chess, which built their reputations on blues and rhythm and blues, Vee Jay made most of its fortune with the doo-wop sound (Jimmy Reed and John Lee Hooker were exceptions). The Spaniels, El Dorados, Magnificents, Dukays, Dells and Sheppards all had multiple hits for the label. "Goodnight, Sweetheart, Goodnight" by the Spaniels had the unfortunate distinction of being the first rhythm and blues record to be successfully covered by a white group (the McGuire Sisters). In all, 26 doo-wop groups passed through their doors. By 1957, Vee Jay had acquired the catalogs of Chance and Sabre Records (Chicago) from Art Sheridan and Steve Chandler, and Ping Records (Chicago) from Frank Evans. They owned their own publishing company, under the name Conrad. Falcon Records was started in 1957, but its name was changed to Abner to avoid a copyright infringement. Poor financial management led to bankruptcy in 1966 despite having a wealth of talent including the Dells (who started as the El Rays at Chess), Four Seasons and Jerry Butler and the Impressions.

Cincinnati

King/Federal/Queen/DeLuxe/Rockin'

Syd Nathan founded King Records in 1945 as a sort of hobby when his physician advised him to leave the business world for health reasons. He was autocratic, canny and unpredictable. According to legend, Nathan took full advantage of an intended joke by a West Coast deejay who told his listeners that if they liked "Work With Me Annie" by the Midnighters, they would love the sequel titled "Annie Had A Baby." When orders for the nonexistent record began to pour in, Syd, not missing a beat, wrote, recorded and released a song by that name in 1954. If he could not find talent, he bought it, acquiring the DeLuxe label from David and Jules Braun in 1949, and the catalogs of Rockin' (from Andy Razaf and Henry Stone) in 1953 and Bethlehem (from Gus Wildi) in 1961. Although most of King's success came from hillbilly, blues and rhythm and blues, through the years 58 doo-wop groups passed through Syd's doors, most notably the Platters, Swallows, Midnighters and Otis Williams & the Charms. When Henry Stone amicably severed his partnership with Nathan in DeLuxe Records in December 1955, he got the Charms as part of the settlement. Unfortunately for him, however, he left behind their lead singer Otis Williams, who went on to have more hits as "Otis Williams & His New Group." In 1967, King merged with Starday, and the following year Nathan died.

New York

Apollo/Doe/Lloyds/Timely

Apollo and its subsidiaries were owned be Bess and Ike Berman, Hy Siegel and Sam Schneider, but were really run by Bess Berman, Ike's talented and imperious wife. The Bermans eventually bought out Siegel (who went on to start Timely Records in 1953) and Schneider in 1948. Apollo was started as a gospel label in the mid-1940s. In fact Bess Berman was Mahalia Jackson's manager and close personal friend. Apollo turned to doo-wop recordings in the early 1950s, listing the Cellos, Chesters (with "Little" Anthony Gourdine), the Larks and Opals among 17 such groups. Lloyds was launched in June 1954 as a pop and r&b label, with the Larks as the first to record. By 1955 the Bermans acquired the catalogs of Luna Records (New York) from Charles Lopez and Ray Santos (in 1954), the Timely label (New York) from Hy Siegel (also in 1954), and operated a publishing company called Bess Music.

Jubilee/Josie/Todd/Chex/Le Cam/Whirlin' Disc/Port

Jerry Blaine joined with Herb Abramson (later a co-founder of Atlantic) who had been running Quality Records out of Washington, D.C. Together they formed Jubilee in New York in 1947. Blaine, a former bandleader, became a big name in the record distributing business (Cosnat Distributors), formed the Josie label (originally called Jo-Z) as a companion to Jubilee in 1954, bought the Dana label from Walter Dana, acquired the catalog of National Records from Sid Demay, and co-formed Whirlin' Disc with Bobby Robinson. Eighty-seven doo-wop groups appeared on his array of labels, most notably the Cadillacs, Channels, Continentals, Orioles (according to some, the first true doo-wop group) and the Volumes. Blaine had a stormy relationship with Esther Navarro, the plucky composer for the Cadillacs (a Josie act), to the point where each combatant had a separate group of Cadillacs. For trivia

74

The Volumes

The Cadillacs

buffs, Blaine's daughter, Enid, married Jack Braverman's (of Herald Records) son, Teddy, on June 19, 1954.

Atlantic/Atco/East West/Cat/Plaza/Trey

The primary owners of the Atlantic conglomerate were Ahmet Ertegun, Herb Abramson and Jerry Wexler. The Atlantic label was created in 1947 by Ertegun, the son of a Turkish diplomat, and Herb Abramson, the Artist & Repertoire (A&R) man for National Records (and incidentally a dentist). Both were avid jazz buffs and easily translated their knowledge of music to blues, rhythm and blues and doo-wop. In 1954 Atlantic, by now financially secure and established as a quality label, had to weather the storm of an attack by major record companies, in

The Drifters

The Cardinals

the form of "cover" records. Over the summer of 1954, seven of Atlantic's hits, including "Sh-Boom" by the Chords and "Honey Love" and "Such A Night" by the Drifters, were covered by a total of 18 different artists. Fortunately, five of the seven songs were published by Progressive Music, Atlantic's publishing arm, so that the firm made out okay in the end. Undaunted despite the absence of legal recourse to these tactics, the brain trust at Atlantic continued to unearth new artists, many of whom were doo-wop groups. For example, Ertegun, upon learning that Clyde McPhatter had left the Dominoes after a rift with the tyrannical Billy Ward, signed him up and blended him with an ex-gospel group called the Thrasher Wonders. The newly formed group was called the Drifters and they continued to produce hits for Atlantic well into the 1960s, despite several changes in lead singers and replacement of the group en masse (with the erstwhile Five Crowns). Ertegun, Abramson and Jerry Wexler (who joined Atlantic in 1953) were extremely knowledgeable and perfectionistic about the kind of product they turned out. They provided the best available backup musicians (e.g., King Curtis on sax) and producers (e.g., Jesse Stone) for recording sessions, and supported their artists financially, and emotionally if necessary. As a result their products were top-notch. Their instincts for ferreting out artists and their caring approach to them attracted many talented men and women to their labels. The Cat label was launched in April 1954, named after the "cat" phenomenon (i.e., white teens drawn to black r&b). In July 1955, the Atlas subsidiary was launched, but was quickly changed to Atco because "Atlas" was already an existing label. The Spark label, which employed Lester Sill as national sales manager and Jerry Lieber and Mike Stoller as "A&R" men, was added to the Atlantic team in 1955 through catalog acquisition (from A.L. Stoller of Los Angeles). In this acquisition, Atlantic got not only Lieber and Stoller, but the Robins, who they quickly reorganized and called the Coasters. The famous "playlet" records such as "Along Came Jones" and "Yakety Yak" resulted. Through the years 58 doo-wop groups recorded for Atlantic and/or its subsidiaries, among them such famous groups as the Bobbettes, Cardinals, Chords, Clovers, Coasters, Drifters and Sensations.

Gee/Rama/Tico/Gone/End/Roulette/Red Bird/Mark-X/Cindy/Goldisc/ Juanita/Tee-Gee

George Goldner began his career in the music business in the early 1950s by forming Tico Records, an outlet for Latin music. Building on the success of Tico, he started a series of rhythm and blues labels, beginning with Rama in 1953. On Rama, he had the first crossover (r&b to popular) smash with "Gee" by the Crows (who were signed after winning in the finals of the amateur show at the Apollo Theatre). He soon founded Gee Records in their honor, followed by Gone, End, Juanita, Mark-X, Goldisc, Roulette, and a host of others. The reason for the multi-label format was that disc jockeys would only play so many records from one label in a given time period. So, Goldner began a label each time a new niche emerged in the market. Goldner had a good feel for teenage preferences and had the good sense to hire Richard Barrett (of the Valentines) as a talent scout and producer. Together they

The Dixie Cups

established such groups as the Chantels, Cleftones, Crows, Dubs, Flamingos, Harptones, Heartbeats, Little Anthony & the Imperials, Frankie Lymon & the Teenagers, Valentines and Wrens. In all, 93 doo-wop groups recorded for his panoply of labels, an incredible figure. Roulette, formed in partnership with Morris Levy, eventually bought out Goldner's interest in the doo-wop labels and Goldner went on to form the short-lived Red Bird label with Jerry Lieber and Mike Stoller. Though successful in the promotion of groups such as the Dixie Cups, Shangri-Las and Ad Libs, it folded prematurely owing to personality differences. Goldner died in 1970 at the age of 52.

The Valentines

Rainbow/Derby/Riviera/Central

Larry Newton, the central figure in the above labels between 1949 and 1956, was affiliated with Lee Magid (ex-Savoy executive for Herman Lubinsky) for Riviera and Central Records, and Eddie and Herb Heller for Rainbow Records. Central was the rhythm and blues affiliate of Derby Records, which went bust in October 1954. Later, Newton was instrumental in helping to establish ABC-Paramount as a major force in the recording industry. With Eddie Heller on Rainbow, he first recorded the Clovers, Lee Andrews & the Hearts, and the Five Crowns with Ben E. King (the group that was transmogrified in the Drifters when Clyde McPhatter left the group). Other prominent doo-wop groups, among the 23 recorded on Newton's labels were the Bonnie Sisters, the Charmers and the Laddins (with Robert Jeffers, or Bobby Jay, a popular contemporary oldies deejay).

Robin (Red Robin)/Fire/Fury/Enjoy/Whirlin' Disc/Everlast/Cee Jay/ Vest/Holiday

Bobby Robinson opened a record store in Harlem after World War II. As the rhythm and blues market opened up, A&R men would come to Bobby, who was black, for advice on what would sell. After giving free advice to the likes of the brothers Bihari, Chess and the Mesners, Robinson decided that if money could be made from his taste and expertise, he may as well be the one who made it. In partnership with his brother Danny Robinson, he formed Robin Records (soon changed to Red Robin because of a copyright infringement), which released its first record in 1951. Bobby went on to form the Fire, Fury, Enjoy, Fling and Whirlin' Disc labels (the last with Jerry Blaine). Danny left Red Robin and founded Everlast, Cee Jay, Vest and Holiday. Bobby's talent included Earl Lewis & the Channels, the Continentals, the Kodaks and Lewis Lymon & the Teenchords. Among Danny's groups were the Bop Chords, Charts and Lovenotes. Together they unearthed the Scarlets, Velvets and Vocaleers on Red Robin. In sum, the brothers recorded 30 doo-wop groups, most of whom sang in gang doo-wop (such as Paul Winley's groups) or schoolboy doo-wop style.

Herald/Ember/Natural

Al Silver got his education about the music industry by starting the Silver Record Pressing Company in lower Manhattan with his brother-in-law Jack Braverman in 1947. He became partners with Fred Mendelsohn (who started his career as a jukebox serviceman) in Herald Records in 1953 and soon bought him out. He repeated the process with Jack Angel and the Ember label shortly thereafter. Natural was launched as a pop-subsidiary of Herald in March 1955. Silver had good business sense

The Silhouettes

The Nutmegs

in addition to an ear for the doo-wop sound and released "Paradise Hill" by the Embers, "Story Untold" and "Ship Of Love" by the Nutmegs, and "In the Still Of The Nite" by the Five Satins within the period 1955-1956. The Herald-Ember banner represented 60 doo-wop groups at one time or another, including the Embers, Five Satins, Mello Kings, Nutmegs, Silhouettes, Turbans and Maurice Williams & the Zodiacs. Many of the top hits of all time emanated from Silver's legions. When the payola scandal hit, Silver was dunned for taxes he should have paid on money spent promoting records. Herald-Ember and his Angel Publishing Company went under in 1962 and he leased his song catalog to Flashback records.

Laurie/Mohawk/Rust/Andie/Emge

This conglomerate was owned by a complicated network of individuals, including Allen Sussel, Gene Schwartz, Bob Schwartz, Elliot Greenberg and Ernie Maresca. Sussel, formerly in the music publishing end of the business, was prominent among them, naming Laurie and Andie Records for two of his children. Lest his third child get a complex, he formed Philadelphia-based Jamie Records with Harold Lipsius and Harry Finfer (who were not part of the Laurie network). As far as we know, Mohawk, Rust and Emge were NOT names of Sussel's progeny. Ernie Maresca was another prominent owner, himself a performer ("Shout! Shout!" with the Del Satins), songwriter ("Runaround Sue," "The Wanderer" for Dion), publisher and record producer (for Dion & the Belmonts and the Five Discs). Thirty-one doo-wop groups came under their auspices, including Dion & the Belmonts, the Chiffons, Dion (backed by the Del Satins), the Five Discs, the Jarmels, Randy & the Rainbows, Vito & the Salutations and the Mystics. The Sussel-Maresca group was far and away the most prolific purveyor of the Italo- (and other white) doo-wop sound in both the classical and neo- eras.

Old Town/Paradise/Whiz/Munich

Sam Weiss left the record distributing business to form Old Town Records with his brother, Hy, in 1954. In September 1955 Sam resigned from Cosnat (record) Distributors, where he had worked with Jerry Blaine, to devote his energies to making records. They recorded 17 doo-wop groups, including the Solitaires, Fiestas and Keytones. Sam returned to distributing records in the late 1950s and Hy sold out to MGM in 1965.

The Fiestas

The Solitaires

Winley/Porwin/Cyclone

Paul Winley was a jack-of-all-trades, being a singer (Paul Winley & the Rockets), composer and manager of groups. Paul's brother Harold was a bass singer with the Clovers (who, after many years with Atlantic, recorded on Porwin and Winley). In 1955 Paul started the Winley label in order to get his own compositions on wax. On a shoestring he built a small but extremely important stable of 10 doo-wop groups. Winley began with the Duponts (with "Little" Anthony Gourdine), and added the Collegians, Jesters, Paragons and Quinns. His trademark was the ability to unearth local New York street corner groups and, working closely with Dave "Baby" Cortez, produce the gang doo-wop sound from them. In part, this style owed a large debt to the lyrics of the songs Winley wrote for them. Working with these street kids was not easy. Of Julius McMichael, talented lead singer for the Bed-Sty Paragons, Winley said, "(He) could never sing the same thing twice and if he did, he couldn't remember what he was saying. The people could never understand what he was saying." And yet, despite these kinds of obstacles, Winley's minions turned out some of the best classical doo-wop ever put to wax.

Los Angeles

Modern/RPM/Flair/Crown/Kent/Meteor/Rhythm & Blues

The Bihari brothers (Jules, Joe, Lester and Saul) were part of a Lebanese business family that had their hands in many different parts of the recording industry. They not only owned 10 record labels (of which Modern and RPM were the most successful ones), but a publishing company, a record pressing plant (Cadet) and a jukebox business (started in 1935 by Jules). Modern Records was started in 1945 and initially focused on rhythm and blues, using talent indigenous to the local Watts (Los Angeles) community. They recorded

24 doo-wop groups through the years, including prominent ones such as the Cadets, Jacks, Shirley Gunter & the Queens, the Teen Queens and Arthur Lee Maye & the Crowns. Maye, who was signed at 17, was at the same time a "bonus baby" for the Milwaukee Braves. As Lee Maye, he later went on to have a successful career in professional baseball. Lester Sill, at one time the national sales manager for Modern, gave Jerry Lieber and Mike Stoller, as well as Phil Spector, their starts in the record business. Sill later became Spector's partner in trend-setting Philles Records ("Phil-" for Phil Spector and "-les" for Lester Sill).

Aladdin/Score/7-11/Lamp

The Mesners (Eddie, Leo and Ida) started Philo Records in 1945, but quickly changed its name to Aladdin. Their initial successes came from the rhythm and blues field, but they gained entry to the doo-wop arena in a big way when they spotted and signed the Five Keys (from Newport News, Va.) after a gig at the Apollo Theatre in New York. Their Lamp subsidiary was launched in 1954, with Jesse Stone, formerly of Atlantic, at the helm. They recorded 17 doo-wop groups in all, including Thurston Harris & the Sharps, the Robins, the Jayhawks and, of course, the Five Keys. Their catalogs were bought out by Lew Chudd's Imperial Records in 1958.

Dootone/Dooto/Authentic

Dootone was founded in 1954 by Dootsie Williams who, as a black man, had close ties with Los Angeles' Watts community. He immediately had a monster hit with "Earth Angel" by the Penguins, but its commercial success was muted somewhat by a successful cover by the Crew Cuts on Mercury. Also among 12 recorded doo-wop groups were the Cuff Links, Don Julian & the Meadowlarks and Vernon Green & the Medallions. Dootsie's groups did not achieve much commercial success for him at the time but, as a consolation, did win critical acclaim in later years.

Although indies dominated the *Billboard* rhythm and blues and pop charts by the mid-1950s, they were involved in an economic dance of survival of the fittest. The process was quite similar to what happened in the field of computers in the early to mid-eighties; that is, many brands and operating systems distilled down to just two, IBM and Apple. Independent record companies competitively attempted to put new talent in front of the public for its evaluation (which helped to accelerate the rate at which doo-wop and rock 'n' roll developed and the course that it took). In the process, those indies whose proteges gained public regard survived and flourished, as in the case of Atlantic Records. Owners of labels who lacked instinct, or who had trouble discerning the taste of the buying public, or who were beaten to the punch by savvier competitors, soon found another line of work.

The first assault by the majors took the form of "cover" records, which exploded in number between the years 1954 and 1957. The usual scenario involved a major record company hiring a white vocal group to reproduce, as faithfully as possible, a record recently released by a black vocal group. If the cover record intentionally reproduced the entire arrangement note for note, it was referred to as a "copy." Not only did copies dilute the pot for the original artist and record company through competition, but conceivably a record buyer could buy a copy version by mistake. With enormous resources at its disposal, a large record company could effect this process quickly, and within a week or two be competing on the pop charts with the original version. Sound quality of the covers was usually superior to that of the original, which gave them an advantage. Further, they did not have to expend money in finding and developing talent. By choosing to cover only up and coming records, the covering label would be virtually assured of having a hit. Example of this are "Sh-Boom" by the Chords covered by the Crew Cuts on Mercury, "Sincerely" by the Moonglows covered by the McGuire Sisters for Coral Records (a subsidiary of Decca), and "Walkin' Along" by the Solitaires and "Little Darling" by the Gladiolas, both covered by the Diamonds on Mercury. The McGuire Sisters' version of "Sincerely" was so popular that it won the record industry's rare "Triple Crown Award" when it placed first on the national charts of dealers, deejays and jukebox operators simultaneously in February 1955. One record company, Dot, virtually became a major by dint of this strategy. Dot's Fontaine Sisters covered "Adorable" by the Drifters (who in turn, covered the original version by the Colts on Vita Records), and Pat Boone covered "Gee Whitakers" by the Five Keys, "At My Front Door" by the El Dorados, "I'll Be Home" by the Flamingos and "Two Hearts" by Otis Williams and the Charms. Even Frank Sinatra and Doris Day got into the action, both covering "Two Hearts" in early 1955. While many of the covers were perpetrated by single and/or preppy artists, black groups often covered one another as in Frankie Lymon and the Teenagers covering "I Promise To Remember" by Jimmy Castor and the Juniors, the Charms covering the Jewels' "Hearts Of Stone" and "Ling Ting Tong" by the Five Keys, and the Cadets' cover version of the Jayhawks' "Stranded In The Jungle." Black groups also borrowed from white artists in the early fifties by changing the style of the record. Thus the Moonglows came out with a doo-wop version of Doris Day's "Secret Love" and the Orioles produced a national hit out of "Crying In The Chapel," originally a country and western hit for Darrell Glenn. This is not quite "covering" because the differing versions were really not in competition with each other.

Before doo-wop records (and other rhythm and blues forms) commonly crossed over onto the pop charts, any pop cover versions released by the

The Jayhawks/Vibrations/Marathons

The Cadets/Jacks

majors added to the coffers of the publishers. When doo-wop songs began to appear directly on the pop charts in the 1954-1955 period, cover versions became direct competitors of the originals and ate into the money to be made by the original record company. Inroads against "copy" records were made when WINS-NY (Alan Freed's station) banned them from play on their station. Other stations soon followed suit. The impetus for this action came not only from the independent record companies, but from the artists as well. Lavern Baker made headlines in March 1955 by raising the "copy" issue with her congressman in full view of the media. In a prior suit (1951), the courts had upheld the Copyright Act of 1909, which protected the song but not the arrangement. Baker argued that the act needed revision because she had personally lost an estimated $15,000 in royalties to exact copies of her hit record "Tweedle Dee" made by Georgia Gibbs and Vicki Young. The noise made by record companies, publishers, artists and radio stations helped to reduce drastically the practice of "copying," though "covering" was still considered ethical.

Covering became a profitable pastime for the major record companies at the expense of not only the original artist and label, but the publisher as well. When selling their cover versions, record companies often gave away (for example) one disc for every three or four sold. Under the copyright laws, royalties (usually two cents per disc) were due only on the number sold, and not on the number given away. The publishing company would therefore lose a significant percentage of expected royalties and, because more records were in circulation, fewer copies of the original would be sold. In retaliation, Syd Nathan (head of King Records) and Herman Lubinsky (head of Savoy) refused to license his songs to other record companies in 1955, forcing them to file a "Notice Of User" application with the copyright office before releasing their version. This procedure legally obligated them to pay royalties on the number of records manufactured rather than the number sold (effectively eliminating the giveaways) and also required that they pay royalties every 30 days rather than quarterly, which was industry practice.

An interesting anecdote about covers deals with the song "Hound Dog," written by Lieber and Stoller and recorded by Willie Mae Thornton on Peacock in March 1953. A Sun label answer record, called "Bear Cat" by Rufus Thomas Jr. appeared less than two weeks thereafter, containing different lyrics but the same melody. Up to this point in time, it was assumed that rhythm and blues music was in the public domain, and thus not subject to the copyright laws. However, Peacock successfully sued Sun, and since then answer records could not be covers (i.e., both melody and lyrics had to be different).

Cover records should not be confused with remakes. If the original version has already faded from the charts (so that there is no competition), any attempt to copy the song, faithfully or not, is defined as a remake. Remakes can only help the original version, by better engraving it in the minds of fans, or by making money for the composers and publishers. Remakes are nice, covers are nasty. A few examples of remakes (among thousands) are Gabriel and the Angels' 1961 version of "Zing Went The Strings Of My Heart" originally sung in doo-wop style by the Coasters in 1958; and the Dreamlovers (1962), Craftys (1962) and Enchords (1961) versions of "Zoom Zoom Zoom" originally performed by the Collegians in 1956.

Additionally, by 1955, the major record companies yielded to growing economic pressure and stepped up their efforts in the doo-wop, rhythm and blues and rock 'n' roll arenas. In 1954 for example, Atlantic owned 11 of the year's Top 30 r&b hits, and other indies such as Chess/Checker, Vee Jay and Rama did well also. Of the majors, only Mercury and Columbia (on their Okeh and Epic subsidiaries) placed songs in that same Top 30. Since gross sales in the r&b field were increasing steadily (25 million in 1954), and since the indies had begun to make inroads on the pop charts (historically owned by the majors) with discs such as "White Christmas" (by the Drifters on Atlantic), "Sincerely" (by the Moonglows on Chess), "Earth Angel" (Penguins on Dootone) and "Hearts Of Stone" (Charms on DeLuxe), the majors had plenty of motivation to fight back. Their first efforts were "covers," discussed earlier, but they soon unearthed their own talent. For example, Capitol hit both the pop and r&b charts in early 1955 with "Ling Ting Tong" by the Five Keys, the first time this record company saw the r&b charts since 1953 (with the Du Droppers).

The success of these efforts by major record companies depends upon which form of rock 'n' roll one is talking about. In rockabilly, RCA (with Elvis Presley), Decca/Coral (with Bill Haley) and Capitol (with Gene Vincent) made significant inroads in terms of market share. In doo-wop and rhythm and blues, however, their impact was not great. For example, of the records listed in the songography in the back of this book, only 8.95 percent of the songs were released by a major record company (Columbia, RCA, Decca, Mercury, Capitol & MGM) or any of their subsidiaries. The remainder, or 91.05 percent were released by the independent labels. In fact, the three most prolific indies alone, Gee/Rama, King/Federal and Atlantic, released more records than all the majors combined (10.89 percent). While the indies continued to dominate in the doo-wop and rhythm and blues fields, the entry of the majors into the fray resulted in more competition and meant that the pie was being sliced into smaller pieces. This unfortunately spelled doom for many of the less successful indies.

Technological advances during the 1950s provided the teen generation with portable radios, television, and better-recorded sound and record-playing equipment. The deejays of the era used these media to reach their young audiences through radio, TV, concerts and movies. The independent record companies kept pace by unearthing and promoting those performers, which most pleased the teen generation. In these ways, supply met demand. Demand was also met, in a much different way, throughout the careers of young performers. It is to the careers of these young street corner singers that we now turn our attention.

Chapter 8

The Street Corner Singers

In The Beginning

Contrary to legend, most doo-wop groups did not start singing on the street corners, but they did end up singing there eventually. Most singers, in interviews, report their first experience with music was either through the church or at home, and usually before the onset of adolescence. At best, there was an uneasy truce between the church and the group music produced when youthful enthusiasm and rebelliousness was appended to gospel training. Sometimes there was no truce at all. Hank Ballard (of the Midnighters) recalled "'...I was a runaway at 14, man... That part of the family was heavy into religion. They used to beat me if they caught me humming the blues in the house. They couldn't understand. I was not allowed to sing anything but gospel. I had to get out of that.' After the eighth grade he dropped out of school and returned to Detroit to live with another set of relatives."

The family of Eugene Pitt (lead singer of the Jive Five), as related by Wayne Stierle, was a lot more supportive: "Pitt came from a family of nine girls and five boys, and, as he says, 'We had two complete gospel groups right there.' In fact, they did have two gospel units, and the kids were trained very seriously by Eugene's father, who would see to it that everybody practiced. Pitt's father did not approve of Eugene singing anything other than gospel, but naturally,

The Impalas

The Larks

Eugene was listening to the radio, and could not miss what was going on in '50s music. Pitt's father, who had been a member of a gospel group, no doubt understood what his talented son was feeling, and when Eugene finally sang in an r&b group, his father provided important help." Another Eugene, Eugene Mumford, lead singer of the Larks, also began his singing career in a family gospel group called the Mumford Brothers.

These group singers were teenagers, and often young ones at that. Schoolboy doo-woppers with high tenor leads started notoriously young; Richard Lanham recorded with the Tempo-Tones at age 12; the Schoolboys, Desires and Bobbettes formed and were active in junior high school. Frankie Lymon of the Teenagers was 13 when his group first recorded, and Cathy Jean (of the Roomates) was 14. Other classical doo-wop artists such as Gaynel Hodge of the Turks was 16 when he recorded, as was Joe "Speedo" Frazier of the Impalas; Herb Cox of the Cleftones was a mature 17. It was the norm for groups to form in high school (or before), and many of those that eventually recorded did so during their high school years. While many of the paleo-doo-wop artists were "old men" of 20-30 by the mid-1950s, the classical doo-wop explosion was fueled, driven and supported by high schoolers.

Bruce Pollock, author of *When Rock Was Young*, sets the scene well. "Those four chords would usher in an age of harmony. In almost any ethnic neighborhood in the early 1950s, especially in the East, in housing project and candy store and school yard, wherever baseball cards were being flipped or traded and pennies pitched, there was that sound — caterwauling in courtyards, cascading down the sides of buildings from the rooftop, sinuously drifting out of open basement windows. It was to be heard on the street corners under lamplight or moonlight, or under boardwalks or elevated train lines in the summer, or inside hallways and under stairwells in the winter- an urban, rattling, reckless sound, blending with the sirens and the traffic. In threes and fours and fives, hardly ever twos, they gathered — minigangs, basketball teams, sidewalk social clubs — their heads close together, hands behind their backs, the odd finger sings bass, to serenade the urban passing throng, city girls, and the very moon of love. Most of these serenades would never be preserved. Most of these singers would never leave the street. But in their dreaming voices, their ceaseless quest for harmony, lay the seeds of the future."

In many ways the kids who created the doo-wop genre were very similar to teens of any era. They were carefree, hedonistic and sometimes irresponsible. They were naive and gullible and ignorant of the larger world around them. They knew it all, felt invincible, yet lived with a whole host of secretly held insecurities. They hung out with the guys or gals, told white lies to their parents and laughed about the furtive pranks and adventures they got away with. They thought incessantly about the opposite gender, learned about love and sex by trial and error, and were usually awkward and shy in social situations because they were deathly afraid of humiliation.

By the time these young people were ready to sing on the corner, they had already formed groups. Each of the between four and six members knew their voice part and their roles within the group, just as they would know their position on a softball field. Singing on the streets was meant to impress; it was a social thing that helped establish a group's turf, to pull rank on friends not in the group, and to show off for the ladies. At night, outdoor locales were often used as the apartments and hallways were off limits because of sleeping younger sibs. More serious practices were often held at indoor locales geared to deliver echo, nirvana for the doo-wop singer. According to Johnny Keyes, lead singer of the Magnificents, in *Du-Wop*: "...The men's room of any office building had the best echo in the world, as far as the 50s Du-Wop Group was concerned. And, the boy's bathroom in high school was used for something other than smoking cigarettes and washing your hands. This area furnished the best echo chamber for singing slow songs with 'woooo' in the background. All of that tile and porcelain was tailor-made for singing." Subway stations and the back stairwells of schools were coveted for similar reasons.

Most of the time the doo-wop group was synonymous with the peer group; they were really one and the same. Charlie Horner and Steve Applebaum, in a story about the Castelles, wrote: "Picture five young boys, not yet in their teens, living in the same neighborhood, playing basketball together, fighting together, going to school together, and raising hell together. On summer evenings, they would sit on the steps... and harmonize." Fred Parris, of the Five Satins, adds: "We were just ordinary chums in school. We went to Hillhouse High School together." Groups were formed gradually, starting with a dream in one guy's head. As people were enlisted, they formed or became a new peer group and soon were tight friends. If a member couldn't or didn't get along, he left or was asked to leave. The group that remained became even tighter.

In Watts, a black section of Los Angeles that was to become famous (or infamous) in another generation for different reasons, friendships and singing groups were one and the same. "We used to sit around [Alex and Gaynel Hodge's] living room and harmonize. Back then I wanted to be a part of the music, part of the fun at parties. It wasn't about being a star," explained Al Frazier (of the Lamplighters and Rivingtons). Harry Weinger, writing about the early days of the Platters, continues: "The Hodge house on East 56th Street was a favorite hangout. Gaynel was sweet on Zola Taylor, then a student at Jordan Junior High. She [Ms. Taylor] reminisced, 'Jesse Belvin and Gaynel used to fight over me but my boyfriend was Carl Gardner. He's the one mama approved of. I had a piano but the Hodges lived closer to everyone else, so we'd all go to there to sing — Richard Berry, Etta James, the Hollywood Flames, the Robins, Bobby Day, the Queens. And when the recording companies signed us up we all sang on each other's records.' " What an unbelievable collection of talented young people gathered in that house. They had it all; they had youth, they had friends and they had doo-wop. It doesn't get much better than that!

Almost all of the groups were formed in industrial urban areas, particularly in the big cities. The cornfields of Nebraska didn't give good echo. In urban neighborhoods, doo-wop groups were often formed from within street gangs. Johnny Keyes (*Du-Wop*) reports about his experience in Chicago in the early 1950s: "There were very little gang problems in the 50s, by today's standards. Gangs seldom killed anything but time. One reason may be the fact that street kids competed on more than one level. It's true that there was a lot of fighting over territorial rights, or the capital offense of talking to the wrong girl. That one would get you hurt seriously, sometimes mortally. But, in addition to the combat, they would compete on the softball diamond or the street corner. Every gang had within its ranks a softball team and a singing Group, made up of six or seven cats. It was similar to belonging to a club within a club, a fraternity within a fraternity."

(Little) Anthony Gourdine (of the Imperials) had no choice but to join a gang. "They weren't social clubs," Anthony says, "they were real gangs. If you were hanging out with the guys on the street, you automatically were part of the gang. I was in the Chaplains. I was what you call a part-time Chaplain. I didn't give my all to it. I was the type of guy that was too busy singing, too interested in that. But when I need it, like in school, when I needed the protection of a gang, I did cling close to them....I didn't want to be in any gang. But where I lived it was a thing you fell right into."

And, like gangs and fraternities, doo-wop singers had codes of ethics that were uniquely their own. "There were several unwritten laws for vocal groups of the '50s, and among these was the understandable, although strange, practice of contributors to 'style' or background being listed as co-writers of the tune itself. Another law was that the writer of a song became the lead singer on that song," wrote Wayne Stierle in an article on the Monotones.

Another unwritten part of the code was that singers were allowed to traverse hostile territory with impunity. Keyes explains that "a group singer, who for some reason found himself 'visiting' out of his neighborhood, was seldom attacked by the gangs that inevitably surrounded him as he was leaving the girl's house. Escaping is hard to do, so you're trapped. A Group singer would be allowed to go on his way if he identified himself and was believed, or was recognized as belonging to another gang....the gang would invite the alleged Group singer to 'hit a tune' with a couple of the fellas ...to weed out impostors. ...if they called a tune and you were not a Group singer or

The Dominoes

The Swallows

were no good at improvisation, you better be good at running because there was going to be trouble. It was either 'hit a tune' or get hit in the head."

Sometimes you didn't get a chance to explain yourself. William "Pete" Johnson, a member of a group called the Romancers from Philadelphia, was talking to another guy's girl at a party. The jealous boyfriend "called him out" and shot him five times in front of witnesses. The rest of the Romancers drafted another lead singer and, out of respect for Will, changed their name to the Dreamlovers ("When We Get Married").

The singing groups formed almost as naturally as non-singing peer groups did. Once formed, the group became the most important influence in the life of any of the members. Singing in a group was similar to being a gifted athlete; it was accorded respect and status on the block, in the neighborhood and the school. Girls were even more attracted to the singers than they were to the jocks because the singers were a lot more romantic. The following interchange took place between Larry Chance of the Earls (LC) and Don K. Reed (DKR) on the latter's show of May 19, 1991:

LC: "It was an easy way to get girls. I'll tell you, we just sang on the street corner and had all the ladies..."

DKR: "You're not the first person who said that."

LC: "You're a teenager. What's important in life? The girls. The girls came easy when you sang."

As did competence in sports, singing offered the dream of escape from the poverty, prejudice and a lack of education that many doo-wop singers had to endure. In an article about the Crows, Jeff Beckman and Hank Feigenbaum report that "...[they] were just five ordinary black kids growing up on 142nd Street between 7th and Lenox Avenues facing the harsh realities of life in the Harlem of the late 1940s and early 1950s. The expectations and aspirations of people born in this ghetto were few. Whether through faults of their own or through the influences of their environment, education was usually neglected, probably in many instances because it was no guarantee that the door would not be closed in their face when the time came to look for a job. Whatever the reason, without an education the vicious circle was unbroken, and most blacks found themselves relegated to occupations that required long hours, many of them spent at hard, manual labor." Candice Van Ellison, in *Harlem On My Mind*, presents shocking statistics about the problems in education of the teenage population from which doo-wop singers emerged: "In [Harlem's] one high school, Benjamin Franklin, the 1966 senior class contained approximately 2,000 seniors, 1,000 June graduates, and 38 graduating academic diplomas." And Little Anthony Gourdine, of the Imperials, was also "...a kid who never had anything and never went anywhere, and I was used to it. I didn't have the kind of education I wanted because I didn't finish high school. I really didn't know where I was going, all I could do was sing."

Singing doo-wop was a clear-cut way to emulate one's idols. Homer Dunn, lead singer of the Rivieras, was "captivated... by singing combos with names like the Swallows and the Dominoes and he'd breathe in every note. He listened for songs by his favorite group, Sonny Til and the Orioles. Sonny was not yet getting the lead singer recognition but Homer Dunn knew his name." Paleo-doo-wop singers were the idols of the younger and as yet unrecorded classical doo-wop generation.

Bobby Jay (actually Robert Jeffers of the Laddins) told a similar story of idol-worship to Don K. Reed in an interview on Reed's radio show of June 24, 1990:

BJ: "I started singing in 1955 and in 1956, in the month of January, when I heard a record called "Why Do Fools Fall In Love." I decided from then on that I was going to be a singer and aspire to a professional career as a singer."

DKR: "When you heard the song "Why Do Fools Fall In Love," did you envision yourself as the next Frankie Lymon?"

BJ: "No, I envisioned myself as the next Sherman Garnes."

DKR: "At that point, you knew you were a bass?"

BJ: "When I heard Sherman, because at the time that the Teenagers were starting and that record came out, my voice was in the transitional stage. Prior to that I was a first tenor. I'm still a frustrated first tenor. I still break out into falsetto every chance I get but when I heard [sings the opening bass part to "Why Do Fools Fall In Love"]. I said I got to be a bass singer. I lived vicariously through Sherman Garnes, followed everything Sherman did. I achieved a lot of what Sherman did except his height. I never got tall."

DKR: "When the hormones cut loose you were a bass?"

BJ: "Absolutely!"

Getting the same people together repeatedly for practice was often close to impossible and sometimes even comical. Carl Hatton, in letters to Will Anderson, described the instability in membership endured by the ("Long Tall Girl") Carnations: "'As the years went by, things were a little rough on some of the guys, living in the ghetto. As a result, in 1957, Harvey, Arthur and I joined the Army. While in the Army we sang with several members of the Eldorados. When our two year enlistment was up, in 1959, Harvey and I got out, but Arthur liked it so much he stayed in. By 1959 Arthur's younger brother, Tommy Blackwell, was old enough to "hang out," and since he had a good bass voice, took his brother's place in the group. Also, while we were in the service, Allen had joined another group, so we needed an additional voice. That's when Edward Kennedy [not the future senator] joined us. At this time, with several personnel changes, we decided to change our name to 'The Teardrops.' "

The changes within the Solitaires, however, makes changes within the Carnations pale by comparison. Paraphrasing an article by Marv Goldberg and Mike Redmond, the original members in 1954 were Winston "Buzzy" Willis (second tenor), Pat Gaston (bass), Eddie "California" Jones (lead), Rudy "Angel" Morgan (baritone) and Nick Anderson (first tenor). Alvin "Bobby" Baylor came over from the Hi-Lites to replace "California" when the Solitaires got a recording contract. Bobby "Schubie" Williams and Monte Owens (both from the Mello-Moods) replaced Rudy and Nick, who didn't show up for rehearsals. Herman Curtis (aka Herman Dunham of the Vocaleers) joined as lead to make a sextet. In 1955, Curtis joined the Air Force, and Milton Love (from the Concords) took his place as lead. In 1956, Pat Gaston joined the Air Force and was replaced by Freddy Barksdale (although Wally Roker from the Heartbeats sometimes stood in for him). Bobby Williams left to do some jazz singing with Charlie Mingus and subsequently died in 1961. In 1960, Buzzy Willis and Bobby Baylor both went into the Army and were replaced by Cecil Holmes and Reggie Barnes (both from the Fi-Tones). Roland Martinez (of the Cadillacs) joined the group for appearances occasionally. Milton Love went into the Army in 1961, and Harriet "Toni" Williams (who sung with the Harptones and married Reggie Barnes) joined. Cathy Miller eventually replaced Williams, Cecil Holmes (from the Cavaliers Quartet and Fi-Tones) joined, and Herman Curtis rejoined briefly before going on to the Vocaleers. Got all that? Phil Groia, in *They All Sang On The Corner*, does a yeoman's job of sorting out the complex patterns of seemingly interchangeable membership that plagued many of the early groups.

Once the group members stabilized they refined their repertoire. Often there would be standard songs that they "had" to sing, such as "Gloria" or "Lily Maebelle" (each city, borough or neighborhood probably had different requisite numbers), but a good portion of any group's material was original and written by group members. Most of the guys would have a contribution to make to each new song, especially when it involved the voice part they themselves sang. With repeated practice the groups would improve, the amount of improvement depending on their cohesiveness, work ethic and talent. They would enter "battle of the groups" contests held at local schools, churches and parks. The best groups would end up singing on the stage of the Apollo and other chitlin circuit locales. Eventually, the cream rose to the top.

Some were fortunate to hook up with musically talented people like Raoul Cita, Phil Spector or Al Browne ("Mr. New York Sound"), who would help them refine their talent. Browne, who worked with groups like the Crests, Crescents, Gaytunes and Eddie & the Starlights, in an interview with Don K. Reed (July 29, 1990), describes how he would try to help a group: "Well, when you're arranging, you have to think of the group you're working with. Sometimes you have a good group and sometimes not so good. You have to work it out. If the tenor isn't doin' right you give it to the baritone....You try to get the voices as close as possible....And sometimes when they can't harmonize, then you let the instruments do something in the background." Phil Spector backed the Ducanes on the four-chord "I'm So Happy" with 15 musicians (which is almost four musicians per chord) and a professional screamer for the bridge, according to member Eddie Brian.

Once established and with repertoire, a group was ripe for discovery. For some, it was easy because someone in the music business tripped over them, as when Bobby Robinson found the Mello-Moods singing on a stoop in the Harlem River Projects, or when the engineer at a recording studio liked the sound of the (Lenny Cocco) Chimes so much he had them wait until he returned with an executive from Tag records. Others had the tubes greased for them because a group member knew someone of importance in the music business. Goldberg and Redmond describe the way the Solitaires hit paydirt: "Fortunately, Buzzy [Willis, of the Solitaires] knew the great dj, promoter, and manager, Hal Jackson. Buzz and Hal's son, Jackie, had grown up together, and Buzzy worked as unofficial program librarian for Hal's show at WLIB in Harlem's Hotel Teresa. Hal made arrangements for Buzzy to meet Hy Weiss of Old Town Records."

For most groups it was much more difficult, sometimes requiring that some member of the group, literally or figuratively, pursue someone in the music business. Fred Parris and his buddies "used to stand around singing on the street corners and I wanted to make a record. So, I decided to go to New York and pound the pavement. I really didn't know where to go and was unaware that the downtown area was the place to go to make a record. So, I went to Harlem because that was the only section of New York City that I knew at the time. I met Bobby Robinson from Red Robin Records, and we recorded our first record..." In Philadelphia, Marcia Vance reports that Danny (Rapp) and the Juniors "used to sing outside [Johnny Madera's] window, hoping to attract his attention (a la The Teenagers and Richie Barrett). They got his ear but the wrong way for he used to yell at them to 'shut up- you're waking my kids.' The boys didn't give up and apparently Johnny listened to them because one day he came downstairs and said that they were pretty good. He took them to see a local disc jockey named Larry Brown and Larry's partner, Artie Singer of Singular Records."

Lee Andrews and the Hearts were persistent and cunning. According to Andrews, "We went down to [Kae Williams'] radio show after school one day [in 1954]. He allowed kids to come in and dance in another studio, while listening to the music he was playing. We had contrived an idea, where all of us would go down, under the guise of dancing. When he came in to talk to the kids, as he always did, we would tell him what great singers we were. We were very persistent and he said, 'Well, after I get off the air, I'd like to hear you.' When he finished his show we went into yet another studio and we sang for him." Williams liked their sound enough to both manage and record the group.

Even persistence was sometimes not enough. According to Paul Albano (member of the Five Discs) as told to Richard Dunne, the talent of the Five Discs was appreciated by record companies but they were denied contracts in the beginning of their career because they were an integrated group. All-white or all-black was all right, but interracial was a no-no, probably because the label figured that no one would book them on a tour. They finally were signed on Emge and went on to record for other labels, but their concert tours were relegated to the northeast portion of the country. A great many other groups, not being resourceful or lucky, not having contacts and not possessed of great talent, retained their amateur status until the time when they eventually broke up.

Making The Big Time

Hooking up with someone in the music business, which most of the time meant that the group would eventually record, must have been an unbelievable event for those teenagers. And they were, for the most part, teenagers with all the naivete and idealism and all the feelings of cockiness and indestructibility that goes along with that time of life. For most, what they imagined was in store for them had to be infinitely better than what really lay ahead.

As mentioned earlier, recording practices were often primitive by today's standards. Bobby Robinson, referring to the Mello-Moods, recounts that he "...had them come down to rehearse in the record shop. I didn't have anyplace else. They'd come down at night at about eleven, and we'd lock the doors and rehearse right in there. We worked out the whole idea right there in the record shop. We worked until about one, two or three nights a week until I got it just the way I wanted it. No musicians had ever heard it and when we got to the studio they just listened to the group put it down. I said just accompany what you hear. The musicians got their instruments together and the group got in the middle of the floor and started singing just the way we had worked it out." Head arrangements, unthinkable today in an era of layering tracks and digitalized sound, were the order of the day. They were more the rule than the exception with the doo-wop sound and lent a wonderful air of spontaneity to the product.

Bobby Jay, as told to Jeff Tamarkin, described the Laddins' record "Did It" as having "a certain street charm but it was crudely done, recorded in a store in Harlem under the crudest of circumstances." Herb Cox, of the Cleftones, recalls the situation in more detail. "A hallmark of the early days of the rock era was its uninhibited spontaneity, but a recording session with Jimmy Wright's hard-honking band was downright unabashed disorganization. There was almost no structure to the session, except for our vocals, which we had practiced and refined. There was nothing in the way of written charts or arrangements. A lead sheet would be developed right on the spot to identify the changes and chord progressions for the musicians. The band members had a sixth sense to 'feel' the music, as well as the other musicians.

The studio had all the ambiance of a production line. Groups would queue up as if they were in a dentist's waiting room. Any night you might find four or five acts lined up awaiting their turn to record. The emphasis was on getting out the best product in the shortest possible period of time. Time was money, and the independent labels such as Gee just didn't have the resources the major labels had. Therefore, creativity and productivity were the order of the day. The sessions were usually all-night affairs... ."

After recording and releasing a record, a group would walk on air. Odds are that the group members, their girlfriends and friends would be calling all the local disc jockeys with requests for their song. Eddie Brian, of the Ducanes, recalled that so many fans of theirs called Murray "the K" to request "Little Did I Know," which was the B-side of their hit "I'm So Happy," that it became Kaufman's record of the week. Sometimes the group's manager or label owner would invest money in his proteges to hire a choreographer, as when Esther Navarro hired "Cholly" Atkins (from the well-known dance team of Coles & Atkins) to devise dance routines for her Cadillacs. Her investment paid off well because fans went wild over the group's elegant footwork. Atkins later worked with the Solitaires and the Motown Temptations.

Dancing, rather than harmonizing, was sometimes the strong point of a group. Robert Pruter quotes Reggie Smith, of the Five Chances, on their practices. "We used to rehearse eight hours a day dancing and the next day would rehearse singing eight hours a day. We learned a lot of dance steps from different shows we were on...." Later in the same article, Wesley Spraggins from the (Chicago West Side) Ideals commented that "the Five Chances... were one of the first to have great choreography." This is high praise for a group that did not have professional coaching. The Laddins of New York were another group known for their self-taught dance routines.

Sometimes the label owner would see that they got an advance to buy outfits so they would look impressive on stage. They were professionals now. Usually the duds were tuxedos of varying color and style that gave each group a different look. "Nolan Strong and the Diablos wore purple satin jackets with yellow shirts, ties and pants... the Moroccos [wore] red tuxedos with gold cummerbunds, black shirts and white ties.... Bobby Charles wore a white suit, red shirt and white tie..." reported Peter Grendysa about a 1956 concert in Detroit. Take a hike, Pierre Cardin.

Novelty groups such as Little Caesar & the Romans needed no haberdasher; they sported togas, sandals and wreaths around their heads. David Ceasar Johnson (Little Caesar) reported that once an overstimulated bunch of followers "jumped up and ripped our nightgowns right off." Fortunately, the group was given to wearing undergarments.

The groups that recorded became heroes in their neighborhoods, schools, families and, most notably, with the ladies. Johnny Keyes describes the motivations behind singing against other groups to a hometown audience: "You sing two of the five songs you know and you're not setting the world on

The Diablos

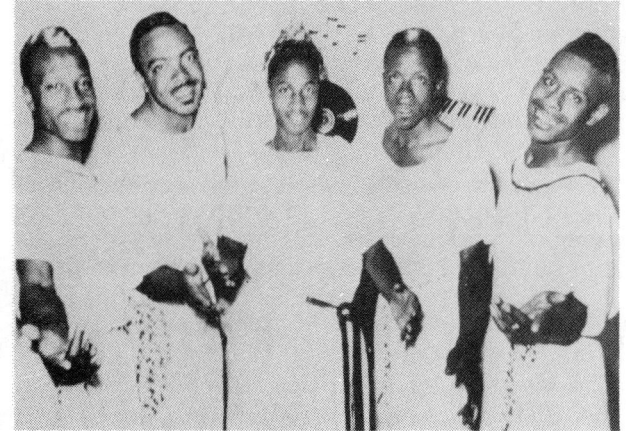

Little Ceasar & The Romans

fire. But everybody's there in the audience, friends from school, a couple of buddies from the neighborhood and, most importantly, girls are there. They're right in front and poised, ready to scream hysterically. Screaming girls motivated Du-Wop Groups at this stage of the game, because money hasn't entered into it yet. There had to be certain inducements besides sounding better than the other singing Groups on the show or who could win the trophies. Screaming girls were the main inducement. If they liked what you were doing, they would scream and pull on your clothes, organize fan clubs, invite you to dinners (at their homes), buy your record when and if you record one and pay to see you perform if your record is hot enough to get you booked. These girls made a guy pay for the ticket to see you, bought your autographed souvenir programs at the big concerts and would occasionally visit your hotel room to inspire you to put on a better show the next time you step on stage. Yes, they were in the front, paying attention. And that was enough to keep some serious adrenaline flowing."

Joey Dee, of the Starlighters, commented on the between-show activity while doing the "Murray the K Christmas Show" at the Brooklyn Fox. "You'd hang out in the dressing room playing cards or trying to talk to some pretty chicks out the window. There was heavy security at the theater, but we'd be yelling out the window to them and they'd be yelling to us, and we'd get a phone number or something. There were a lot of parties."

Singing professionally was hard and sometimes anxiety-provoking. Herb Cox, lead of the Cleftones, in an interview on the Don K. Reed Show (July 8, 1990) recalled: "[Our] first big show was Alan Freed at the Paramount. The very first time we were very scared to see the amount of people coming out to see the show. After overcoming that, it was the nine to eleven shows a day....That was the norm for the Apollo Theatre too."

"You try to remain calm, but are soon tapping your feet nervously... The make-up people dust you off, which causes the hairs on your neck to stiffen. There are dance steps and words to remember... the studio floor was covered with masking tape, leaving little chance for error... What if the record skips?...To tell the truth, I was in a state of panic, not so much for the performance itself because we were lip-synching, but because of the interview [Dick] Clark would do afterward." Those are some of the anxiety-ridden thoughts of Jeff Leonard, Johnny Smith and Fred Gerace, members of Little Joey & the Flips, immediately prior to their appearance on "American Bandstand."

In addition to stage fright, another hazard of the trade was a restive or disappointed audience. Ted Weems, of Lee Andrews & the Hearts, once recounted a story about playing the Royal Theater in Baltimore. "If they didn't like you they threw these little miniature whiskey bottles at you,"said Weems. "Frankie Lymon got bottles! He'd be singing and the bottles were whistling through the air! That was a hard place." Luckily for the Hearts, they pleased the audience and avoided the barrage, and luckily for Frankie the audience preferred their libations in small packages. Herb Cox, of the Cleftones, supports this view of Baltimore audiences. "There was only one place in the world that we wanted to be less than Korea in 1956; that was the Royal Theater. The crowds in Baltimore were absolutely aggressive and antagonistic toward their guests. Among other expressions of ugly deportment, the Royal audiences often threw bottles at the performers on stage." As with Lee Andrews & the Hearts, the Cleftones were greeted warmly so that no incoming missiles were reported. Apparently, the groups upon whom the bottles were bestowed were either too embarrassed or too concussed to tell about the incident.

Additionally, the black groups of the fifties had to endure segregation and openly expressed prejudice, especially in the South. "Traveling in the South during the 1950s presented problems for black entertainers," wrote Charlie Horner. "Since much of the South was segregated, it was often difficult to get food or lodging. [Lee Andrews &] The Hearts would often stock up on crackers and sodas from gas station vending machines, since they didn't know when they'd find a restaurant that served blacks on the open road. Once at their destination they had to find a hotel or boarding house in the black section of town.

"While the entire Jackie Wilson Tour was black, many whites attended the concerts. Inside the concert arenas, the audiences were segregated: The blacks were on one side and the whites on the other. Even being cautious, black entertainers were at risk. In Birmingham, Curry and Calhoun [members of Lee Andrews & the Hearts] were walking across the street when a white policeman threw them against the wall and pointed a gun at their heads for jaywalking."

The Bobbettes, just teenagers and young ones at that, experienced things on a southern tour that no kids should have to face. Reather Turner, an original member, recalled, "One night, the Ku Klux Klan was outside the bus. We had no experience with the Ku Klux Klan. We were five girls from Spanish Harlem....We were on this bus, and we were being noisy, as usual. They were pushing our heads down so we wouldn't make so much noise. We were yelling, 'What's wrong? Why do they have those masks on, what's happening?' And everybody was saying 'Shhh! Be quiet, be quiet!' The tour manager was outside, telling them that we were entertainers. And that was the first time I ever saw a KKK, or knew anything about them.

"We didn't know anything about [segregation], and you don't know unless you really experience it. I tell my kids now that they don't really understand. All they know is what they read in books, and they don't really believe that. We experienced seeing dogs set loose on black people....We even saw a guy hanging from a tree once. We were on the tour bus and we stopped to go to the bathroom. And the guy was out there in the field hanging from the tree."

For many groups, the adulation was the only positive reinforcement they ever got. This was because many of the singers made little money out of what they did. The label owners, concert promoters and agents sometimes soaked up what money there was to be had. The singers were led down the proverbial garden path. Not that they could be blamed, for they were really just kids with no understanding of business practices. For example, Nate Nelson, lead of the Flamingos, argued that he should have gotten a good part of the credit for composing "I'll Be Home," a solid hit for the group. Instead, the writing credits were given to disc jockey Fats Washington and a record distributor named Stan Lewis. "Leonard Chess came to me," said Nelson, and "all he had was the first line and the first line melody. I took the thing home and worked on it... I wrote the entire second verse, the bridge, the melody for the bridge, and the third verse. But I didn't know anything about copyrighting."

Groups trusted their contact in the music business. After all, didn't their contact find them and/or give them the break the group needed? Why would he try to help and then take them to the cleaners? There was very little reason to be suspicious of motives. If a label owner told a group that his own name would be listed as composer (instead of theirs) so that the disc jockeys would recognize the name (and therefore hold the record in higher regard), they believed it. If the group was told that it was standard practice to pay the talent by the session, rather than by the number of records sold (e.g., royalties), they believed it. When the group was told that their money would come from the tours they would be sent on until their names became well-known, they believed it. And signed on the dotted line when asked.

Peter Grendysa, in an article for *Record Collector's Monthly*, pointed out that the groups, especially those without professional representation, could sign contracts that allowed the record company to pay studio and promotional costs out of the *artist's* share of royalties. This gave the record company close to a free ride. The contract could also cede to the owner of the record company the rights to an artist's original songs. If a group signed without looking, they were assuring financial suicide. Grendysa does note, however, that many record companies, such as Atlantic records, were more ethical, and were quite fair with their artists.

Hank Ballard (of the Midnighters) was deceived by his record company when it came to "...maintaining a piece of the publishing rights. 'The company I was with said there's no such thing,' he laughs today. 'King Records, ...if you asked for publishing rights, they'd give you your contract back. I didn't know there was so much money involved in publishing....On my early tunes I didn't even have a BMI contract. I got it later, but they didn't even tell me I had to apply for it.' "

Hank's manager did him dirty too. "...He tied us up in a contract where he was getting 50 percent of our money. We didn't know a ... thing about it. When we found out we took him to court and got out of that contract.... In those days, the manager's job seemed more secretarial than anything else. If the caller on the other end of the line was willing to pay the price, the manager would accept the date, take his cut, and let the chips fall where they might. Such niceties as career-planning and longevity, routing, and proper accommodations were unheard of. Besides, what did it matter if the next gig was five hundred or seven hundred miles away?...Thus were the acts encouraged to spend their nights on the road. This attitude toward black performers prevailed until Berry Gordy, at Motown, put some structure and guidance into the business and made the artists feel a bit more secure, esteemed as human beings with a life-span of more than six months to a year."

These rip-offs happened to a large percentage of doo-wop groups. It happened to the Willows: "Although 'Church Bells' was a million seller for The Willows (selling even bigger than The Diamonds' version), the guys never got paid for it (writer royalties) because Morty Craft claimed bankruptcy. The Willows took him to court- won their case — but were only awarded $200.00! Split between the five of them! And on a million seller!" This was confirmed with Tony Middleton, lead singer of the Willows, in a phone interview conducted on Feb. 24, 1992. It happened to the Pipes (as told by group member Louis Candys to Rick Whitesell): "Although 'Be Fair' did well locally, the Pipes received only a few dollars (and no songwriting royalties) for their effort. Most of the money was lavished on 'sessions and traveling.' "

It happened to the Quin-Tones, according to member Phyllis Carr. "People may not believe this but we've yet to receive royalties on that record ['Down The Aisle Of Love']. Never, not ever, did we get anything! I don't know what 800,000 copies would bring. I didn't even know till recently that many were sold. It's all so frustrating, so, so frustrating. We were just kids, too young, didn't know nothin'. We didn't know we had any recourse."

Ralph Newman reports on a whole host of shady practices experienced by Tony Passalacqua and his group, the Fascinators. "Tony maintains that out of all the records, he received a statement for only one of them, in the amount of $6.00; that was for one of the records of himself as a single artist, and the Fascinators never received a dime. He also recalls that the lack of royalties did not extend merely to recordings, and that most of the acts were doing the big rock shows for free to push their records. In addition, he feels that payola was very much a reality and an overwhelming factor in determining whether or not you had a hit. Apparently, for instance, it was standard practice for a group to have to pay to appear on the major television shows, instead of the reverse! During the later days, when the rules were tightened and it was mandatory for checks to be issued to acts per union scale, the acts had to surrender a check before the performance which was larger than the one which they would receive after!" This kind of transaction was substantiated by Mike Zero of Randy and the Rainbows. "We did the 'Clay Cole Show' in New York about four times. They'd give you the check. You'd sign it. Thank you. And back to them. You want to be on TV, so you did what you had to do." The Bay Bops (according to group members) and Little Joey & the Flips (according to their co-manager Sy Kaplan) had the same experience on "American

Bandstand" in 1958 and 1962, respectively. Apparently that was standard operating procedure back then.

As a matter of fact, most doo-wop groups interviewed on radio or in print report similar treatment. The record men were greedy, the singers naive, and the rules of the game loose. Some groups did make money, especially those with real talent, such as the Moonglows, and those associated with the larger (and in some ways more legitimate) record companies. It is sadly ironic that many of the small independent record companies, which practically gave birth to the whole genre of doo-wop music, ended up being the villains by legally shortchanging the singers.

Another part of this irony is that many more of the groups could have survived and even prospered if they could have avoided the unfair deals into which they entered. Those that should have made the most money were the singers that were also the composers of the songs their group sang. Examples of these prototype singer-songwriters were Curtis Williams of the Penguins, who co-wrote "Earth Angel," Fred Parris of the Five Satins who wrote "In The Still Of The Nite," and James Sheppard of the Heartbeats who wrote "A Thousand Miles Away." These people would have received so-called "mechanical rights" royalties as a performer and "performance rights" royalties as a composer. They would have been paid for the number of records that were sold (roughly one million in the case of the above three examples), for the number of albums sold which contained their song (for example, all three songs were on the *Oldies But Goodies* album series), and for radio plays both at the time the song was popular, for years thereafter for replays on "oldies" stations and for plays of versions by other artists over the years. We have tried to come up with a conservative estimate for how much money should have been made on a million seller by a singer-songwriter on the number of records sold. Please note that these are only estimates.

For the sale of the 45:
   (a) (1,000,000 records sold) - 10 percent giveaways/returns =900,000 records
   (b) 900,000 records X $.98/record = $882,000 gross sales
   (c) $882,000 X .02 royalty rate = $17,640
   (d) $17,640 - $5,000 (production/distribution costs) = $12,640
   (e) $12,640/four group members = $3,160 per man

For album sales:
   (a) (500,000 albums sold) - 10 percent giveaways/returns = 450,000 albums
   (b) 450,000 albums X $3.98/album = $1,791,000 gross sales
   (c) $1,791,000 X .03 royalty rate = $53,730
   (d) $53,730 - $6,000 (production/distribution costs) = $47,730
   (e) $47,730/12 cuts per "Oldies But Goodies" album = $3,978
   (f) $3,978/four group members = $994 per man

By our calculations, $4,154 was due each member of a four member group for records sold. Thirty-five years ago, $4,154 was a year's salary for the average person. In today's dollars, an equivalent sum might be more than $40,000. The figures for composer's royalties for radio plays, both at the time the song was popular, and throughout the years as an "oldie but goodie" are much more elusive. For the really popular songs such as "In The Still Of The Nite," there would be dozens of versions recorded over the years and released both as singles and as album cuts. All of these versions would have added to the coffers of the composers and, of course, the publishers as well. The royalties over the 30 or so years since the doo-wop era would have meant a small fortune for the composers of a really popular doo-wop song.

For example, in a phone interview a BMI representative reported that "In The Still Of The Nite" was played 1,307,815 times between the time it came out in 1956 and the end of 1991. This figure is for the United States and Canada and includes both radio and television "plays" for all versions of the song. If we conservatively estimate $.08 per play as an average rate of remuneration over the years (it was less in the 1950s and more in recent years), the revenue would equate to 1,307,815 plays multiplied by $.08/play, or $104,625. Of this amount, one-half goes to the publisher and the remaining half to the composer(s). In the case of "In The Still Of The Nite" that would mean over $52,000 to Fred Parris over the years (he was the lone composer). This figure does not include royalties for foreign plays, jukeboxes plays, live performances, bonuses for frequent plays or premiums for multiple hits by one composer. The actual bottom line is likely to be a great deal higher than $52,000. Writing and recording a hit record paid well — that is, if you could arrange to get paid what was due you!

Of those who did make money and achieve fame, some just couldn't handle it. Timmy Lymon said that his talented brother Frankie "made a lot of money (probably not a million dollars by the age of 13 as the legend goes) which went in part for a Saratoga Springs home for his mother. Frankie never complained of being ripped off by companies, managers, or lawyers." Frankie, unfortunately, was one of the ones who couldn't handle success, and he started using heroin. In the aforementioned article, Timmy Lymon believes Frankie's drug problem stemmed from "a combination of the urban ghetto struggle, plus some personal hang-ups." Louie Lymon, in the same article, blames "super-stardom, attained before maturity" and "Frankie's desire to please and be accepted by the adults he was exposed to." Frankie died in 1968 in a friend's apartment in Harlem. He was 26. Clyde McPhatter, one of the few singers of that era with talent greater than Frankie's, ended up on a similar road. He drank himself to death at the age of 40, according to Hank Ballard in an interview with Bruce Pollock. Jimi Hendrix, Janice Joplin, Jim Morrison, move over.

Sometimes the sudden fame led group members to make decisions, such as quitting school, which they would regret in later life. Vito Piccone (of the Elegants) recalled, "The next thing we knew we were on top of the world. I was in my last year of high school at the time, so I left to go on [tour]. Frankie left, he was a junior; Jimmy had graduated, Carmen had quit. We never really thought about any kind of financial situation at that point. We were just enjoying ourselves."

The road to glory taken by these youngsters had a lot of potholes. Most of the groups were little fish in a big pond. The best part was the adulation and notoriety they received after having recorded. Seeing the name of their group on the marquee of the Apollo or Brooklyn Paramount had to be a thrill. They were also given the illusion of wealth in the form of fancy clothes and fancier talk. The money didn't come through for most, and those that made money often had problems as a result of it. A group was seen and treated as special as long as their records were on the charts; when their run was over and they were no longer seen as a meal ticket by their managers, they were discarded.

The End Of The Dream

The way the members of a group handled the end of their career probably paralleled a general paradigm of grieving for any significant loss. In the beginning, when news of their records not charting and their labels not being overeager to record them again began to come in, there was probably a good deal of "denial." That is, the group members refused to or couldn't see that the end was in sight and continued to have dreams of stardom. They pretended the bad news wasn't there. When it was no longer possible to hold onto these dreams, i.e. denial was no longer possible, anger and frustration set in. Group members may have looked to blame their label, their manager or even each other for the lack of success. There may have been a "bargaining" stage, in which the members hoped for just one more hit, so they could go out as winners. When this didn't work, depression set in. Group members saw things as hopeless, both in terms of their careers in music and in terms of other parts of their lives. They also might see themselves as helpless to do anything about it. The final stage of grief was reaching "acceptance," wherein they were at peace with what happened to them, they accepted the bad times with the good, and got on with the rest of their lives. Unfortunately, not everyone made it through to the last stage. Some got stuck in the stage of anger and walked around with a chip on their shoulder. Others became stuck in depression and couldn't get themselves started on the rest of their lives. Alcohol and drugs were easy paths to follow for those that were bitter or hopeless. Luckily, it seems from the articles written about the doo-wop groups that most members eventually reached the stage of acceptance and went on to lead productive lives in other spheres.

The bottom-line reason for abandoning a career as a doo-wop singer was financial. As a rule, the 16-year-olds that started singing weren't very materialistic. They didn't have to be because, as minors, their parents provided food, clothing and shelter. After graduation from high school (or quitting it), however, the situation changed. Parents might be willing to provide for a short time while the singer had a go at his career, but they became impatient quickly if progress was not in evidence. Eventually they ran out of patience and the singer had to get a "real" job.

Love also had a way of sobering a fellow. A 16-year-old girlfriend tolerated a lack of ambition, very rarely even thought about it. A 21-year-old wife had a lot less tolerance, and the infant son or daughter you helped bring into the world provided a strong motivation to get a legitimate job with a predictable income. Emil Stucchio, lead singer of the Classics, put it this way: "We stayed together but that was our last record. From then [1966] on we went under different agents and tried different styles....The group never really broke up but when nothing is happening there is no need to get together. We went for three years with nothing happening and, when you have a family you have to look elsewhere for money. I became a cop."

Sometimes, egos got in the way. Danny Zipfel, talented lead singer of the Bay Bops practically forced the group's demise by telling them he wanted to claim songwriting credits on a collection of material written by all members of the group. This came at a time when the group was beginning to experience success. "Joanie" was a local hit for them and they made numerous appearances on national television shows, including those of Dick Clark and Steve Allen. According to the group's founder, Barney Zarzana, it was as much the feeling of betrayal as it was the issue of royalties which led the group to, in effect, tell Danny to get lost.

Lucius McGill, an original member of the El Rays (soon to become the Dells), dropped out of the group in favor of a job with the U.S. Postal Service. McGill said "I just didn't have that feeling for show business. The thrill and excitement of having a lot of young people screaming at you, it just wasn't for me. I needed a job, we all did."

Sometimes a shift in priorities prematurely ended the career of a group. According to Margo Sylvia of the Tune Weavers, "My son was eight months old when we went on the road. By the time we came back, he was about a year-and-a-half, and he didn't know who I was. That hurt me to my heart. You know, it became very detrimental to our home life. The money was not really worth it when I thought about going home to kids who saw me and thought, 'Who is that lady over there?' " For the (Chicago) Pastels their manager, Leona Lee (who was a teacher at one member's school), quit because her husband complained that he didn't see enough of her. The group, having lost their contact in "the business," never recorded again.

Unfortunately, not many of the doo-wop groups were able to make a living out of singing. Either because of the monetary practices by which the singers were shortchanged or because of the lack of demand for their product in the years 1959-1960 and again after 1963, the pickings were slim. Most groups were one-hit (or no-hit) wonders, and when the hits stopped, they would be dropped from their label. The more successful groups followed a hit immediately with another release. If there was too much of a gap between records, the group would be forgotten by the disc jockeys and the public. That was exactly the problem that befell the Elegants. "That much touring was probably our downfall. We were on the road so long we didn't know we should have come back to New York and recorded the follow-up to 'Little Star' We never really prepared for a second hit. We had a manager, but he wasn't really experienced either, to say the least. He was on the road making money, we were making money, and that's what he thought we should be doing. Nobody remembered that it all started in the studio."

Release decisions, however, were out of the hands of the group itself and squarely in the lap of a sometimes inept label owner. With talent, good material and rapid-fire releases, groups like the Platters and Drifters enjoyed relatively long careers. Some, such as the Dells and Little Anthony & the Imperials, were even able to make the transition to other styles of music, but most groups just disbanded.

Sometimes the monetary aspects of singing created rifts that destroyed the sound of a group or the group itself. Peter Grendysa reports that the Del Vikings were split into two groups when their manager had group members, who were under 18 when they signed with the Fee Bee label, sign with Mercury (because as minors their old contract was null and void). This left the rest of the group still on Fee Bee. The rift occurred in May 1957, just after "Come Go With Me" had a successful run on the charts. Grendysa continues, "Attempting to unravel the tangled web of personnel changes and comings and goings of the Del Vikings from this point on could break the heart of the corporate lawyer. Suffice to say the Del Vikings as a discrete entity ceased to exist with this initial breakup. Clarence Quick and Kripp Johnson orbited around each other for the next 30 years, occasionally even singing together."

The reason the Hurricanes broke up was financial but the story is rather unique. As told by Marv Goldberg, "...In 1959 the group got to do a year-long tour of Canada with a troupe that contained country singers and a belly dancer. All they received was enough weekly allowance to pay the hotel bills and eat. They were told that the rest of the money was being held back, to be paid at the end of the tour in one lump sum. However, before the tour ended, the promoter ran off with the belly dancer leaving the rest of the acts stranded. This was the last straw, and the group disbanded."

As it became clear that the group members couldn't make a living through singing, some of the groups parted amicably, and some burst apart from dissention. When things go wrong it's easy to look for someone to blame for the lack of success. "People just don't get along. They used to fight like cats and dogs. They were just too close to each other," said Buck Ram, manager of the Platters. The (West Coast) Pearls were a group that parted amicably. "By early 1961, various forces were tugging at the group. The members had families," Elsie Pierre admitted. "This was a pretty unhappy time for us because we'd been together for four years and we were very close friends, and we felt that we had a good sound. But I guess we were just in the wrong place at the wrong time." So the groups broke up, and the members went their separate ways to live their lives as adults. But that's not the end of the story.

Recidivism For Fun And Profit

Time was kind to some of the singers and hard on others. Over the years almost all had jobs outside of the music business to support themselves and their families. Many died over the years; the articles written on the groups describe more losses than one would expect considering their ages. Joey Hall, of Little Joey & the Flips, was a diabetic and had a reputation for not eating right and forgetting his medicine. The co-manager of the group, Sy Kaplan, said that he died from insulin shock in 1974, at the age of 32. Nolan Strong of the Diablos died of unknown causes at the age of 43. Jesse Belvin was killed at the age of 27 in a head-on car crash caused by, it is thought, a heroin-addicted chauffeur who was driving recklessly. Jannie Pought, a member of the Bobbettes, was 35 when she was stabbed to death while walking down the street in Jersey City, New Jersey.

Even putting aside these early deaths, many of the people from the doo-wop era are still dying too young. A singer who was 18 in the very beginning of the era, say 1950, was born in 1932, making him or her 60 years of age in 1992. One who was 18 in 1963 was born in 1945 and would be 47 years old in 1992. People between 47 and 60 shouldn't be dying as often, and yet the losses mount; Kripp Johnson (lead, Del Vikings at 57), Bobby Day (fronting the Satellites and other groups, at 56), Margo Sylvia (lead, Tuneweavers, at 55) and Richard Blandon (lead, Dubs, at 57) have all died during 1990-1991. One can only speculate on the reasons for these premature deaths. Alcohol and drugs are often associated with the entertainment industry. Success as a youth followed by anonymity thereafter may have been hard to countenance for some, and may have led them to substance abuse. Perhaps poverty during the formative years with concomitant poor health care may have played a part.

Some of the singers never left the music business or, if they did, didn't leave it for long. Lenny Cocco has been particularly persistent. He's had a "Chimes" group from 1957 to 1965, then again from 1970 to 1973, and yet again from the early 1980s to the present. Many members of the Chicago groups like the

El Dorados, Kool Gents and Moroccos have managed to keep their hands in the business, if only on a sporadic basis. Richard Lanham (who fronted the Tempo-Tones) has worked with jazz artists and new and reconstituted doo-wop groups, and has done off-Broadway theater in the United States and abroad. Bobby Jay (bass for the Laddins) has spent almost 30 years as a disc jockey, and has put doo-wop groups such as the Laddins and Desires back together. He sings bass and dances with and for these groups, does repertory theater and helps produce record albums in his spare time.

It seems that most others that left the business jump at any reasonable chance to reenter. Many who are interviewed describe singing as being in their blood and look back fondly on the years in which they sang, despite the financial hardships. Considering that most of the original singers are at least in their late 40s, they have probably reached the age when their children are grown and on their own. They have time on their hands, especially in the evenings after their day jobs and don't have to be asked a second time to rejoin their old group or even a new one. Even for the groups of lesser stature, there seems to be enough work at local clubs to keep most groups' calendars pretty full.

These men came back to singing for the music and for the thrill of performing, but the prospect of renewed male bonding may be the strongest motivation of all. On Don K. Reed's "Doo-Wop Shop" on CBS-FM, New York, on Sunday evenings, the 11 p.m. to 12 a.m. slot is usually reserved for interviews with doo-wop groups that are currently performing. Regardless of their ages, the interaction among the group members is almost always the same. These grown men kid each other and even demean each other in a playful way. The interactions are full of gallows humor and pot shots at one another that (one can tell) have been repeated a hundred times. This banter is the verbal equivalent of giving a friend a punch in the arm. It conveys the apparent attempt to injure while saying "just kidding." This type of male-male exchange was once the fodder of the search for identity when these men were boys. Now the exchanges are fun because the venom is gone and there's no longer anything to prove.

Even men who love their wives and children cannot have this kind of relationship with them. Nor can their wives easily understand what lies behind the apparent cruelty of the verbal sparring. In truth it is not cruel. It conveys loyalty (without intimacy) and understanding (without verbalization), things that men generally have a much more difficult time putting into words than do women. Mock ridicule is the perfect medium for men to be able to show caring to other men, receive it in return, and yet not seem to do so. It feels good and it's fun. That's why these guys keep coming back to singing. They get the same feelings as adults in poker games or bowling leagues, but singing allows more nights out, a fairly strong sense of accomplishment, and the chance to make a few bucks as well.

Although the oldies revival is usually pegged at 1969, the year of the first of Richard Nader's oldies concerts, the revival in doo-wop — at least on the East Coast — still seems to be heading towards a crescendo in the 1990s. An oldies concert in July 1990 put on by Nader featured 15 doo-wop groups, attracted 15,000 people and went on for six hours. DeLauro and Lanz's Annual Royal New York Doo-Wop Show put on at the famous Radio City Music Hall in New York City regularly attracts thousands of people. The services of doo-wop groups are more in demand than ever. Some of the groups ironically make more money than they did during the doo-wop era. It's not a totally rosy picture though. Tony Middleton noted that he couldn't get rich through concert appearances although he enjoyed doing them. The group might get paid $1500-2000, which seems like a lot. However, after getting suits cleaned, arranging for transportation and paying your backup musicians $100 apiece for the evening, there isn't that much left to split among five guys.

For many of the singers, there are other perquisites, such as being able to relive their youth for a short while. A 30-year perspective makes the good times better and the bad times easier to take. It is also nice for group members to see each other again and catch up on old times. In many ways the concerts serve the function of high school reunions for the group singers. And, at roughly fifty years of age, it must be nice to see that your talent and the efforts that you made are recognized and appreciated by so many people, even if this recognition comes a few years late.

Things aren't perfect in doo-wop land. Group conflicts still occur, just as they did during the months and years that the groups were forming. Guys drop out, others replace them, the rest of the group gets closer. In 1990, Randy & the Rainbows split into two factions, each group purporting to be the real thing. Vito Balsamo, personable ex-lead singer of Vito & the Salutations, has to call his act "The Vito Balsamo Group" because somehow, someway, sometime and for some reason he legally lost the right to use the group's original name. Fortunately, there are groups that still get along, and better represent the group bonding that originally was so much a part of the doo-wop genre. 'A difference between the Bobbettes and their contemporaries is their close togetherness.' Turner [Reather Turner, group member then and now] explains, 'We aren't just business partners, we're friends. Everybody knows that the rest of us are there for them, no matter what. Even though there were hard times, we stuck together. Most groups are just in it for the money, just business partners. They don't see each other when they're not singing. Our kids all call us 'Aunt Emma,' 'Aunt Laura' and 'Aunt Reather.'

Another reason we stuck together is that we were never 'Emma and the Bobbettes' or 'Laura and the Bobbettes' or 'Reather and the Bobbettes.' Whoever sounded best singing a song, sang it. We were never a leader and a group. That's why a lot of groups broke up. Someone will take that leader and leave the rest of the group behind. That couldn't happen with us. We've always been very loyal to each other. Nobody could ever break us up."

In other words, doo-wop was about friendship, about loyalty and about caring. And that's why so many people still love it.

Chapter 9

The Death Knell(s)

Doo-wop music had the unique distinction of fading from the public eye not once, but twice. It enjoyed two lives, and suffered through the same number of deaths. Initially, the popularity of doo-wop stemmed from its appeal to a newly emerging teenage generation in the early to mid-1950s. During these years, doo-wop music was fresh and different, a perfect medium to enable teens to carve out identities that differed from those of the generations that preceded them. Individually, teens needed and used their own music, along with the latest modes of dress and speech, to figure out who they were in relation to their peers and the rest of the world. But as fate would have it, each succeeding generation of teens has had the same need.

The First Demise

Concurrent with the fickleness of teenagers was the growth and evolution of the music itself and the artists who created it. Just as young listeners gave enormous weight to the newness of the sound, young artists have always attempted to expand or extend the sounds they grew up with. The identity of these artists was better defined by their own creations than it was by imitating the works of others. Thus paleo-doo-wop was created in the early 1950s with the addition of youthful idealism to its predecessor, rhythm and blues.

Classical doo-wop evolved with the wholesale entry of the teenage generation to the market in 1955. Artists in this period were young, enthusiastic and musically unsophisticated. They worked, it seems in retrospect, along parallel lines to develop the "perfect" doo-wop song. The result was the musically and lyrically simple, love-oriented and emotional "rockaballad" or four-chord doo-wop song, in all possible variations. These songs were the fruit of the classical period. However, by 1960, classical doo-wop had run its course. Doo-woppers apparently had said just about all they had to say. The new generation of teens, three to five years younger than classical doo-wop aficionados, were ready for their own, new music. Classical doo-wop faded from the pop music charts, apparently relegated to the history books.

As the music changed, so did the dances. While the classical doo-wop generation gyrated to the lindy, stroll and grind, the teenage feet of the early 1960s turned cold to these offerings. Rather, they moved to the beat of the twist (Chubby Checker, Joey Dee & the Starlighters), the pony and hucklebuck (Chubby Checker), the swim (Bobby Freeman), the mashed potatoes (Dee Dee Sharp) and the monkey (Smokey Robinson & the Miracles, Major Lance). As a point of interest, these new dances demanded that partners NOT be in physical contact with one another. Each to his/her own.

There were other reasons for the demise of classical doo-wop. The notorious convention of deejays, held in Miami in May 1959, brought the excesses of the industry to the attention of the public. The Harris subcommittee, convened in the fall of the same year, made the term "payola" a household word, and subsequently led to the convictions of numerous deejays, including doo-wop proselytizers Alan Freed, Tommy "Dr. Jive" Smalls, Jack Walker and Peter Tripp. Freed's fate was particularly tragic. His popularity made him a target for attempts by members of the establishment to find a scapegoat for the increasing, as they saw it, corruption of youth. Always a staunch and eloquent defender of the innocence of the music and the teenagers that espoused it,

Freed was (it seemed gleefully) accused of taking payola (which was not illegal at the time) and subsequently of tax evasion (which was and is). According to Wes Smith, the legal battles that ensued eroded the fortune he had amassed and helped to worsen his affinity for the bottle. He died in poverty from complications relating to alcoholism in 1965 at the age of 43.

As the personality deejays disappeared from the airwaves, their replacements played the "Top 40" or "countdown" format. This programming technique, inaugurated in the Midwest by Todd Storz several years before, had the unintended effect of shutting out small timers. Struggling small independent record companies, without public relations departments, had a difficult time getting their products on the air. Doo-wop groups especially, because they were not household names, fell prey to the new regime.

Additionally, around 1959, a second wave of single artists (Presley, Vincent, Berry, etc. representing the first wave) flooded the market, ushering the group sound into disfavor on their road to stardom. Frankie Avalon (January 1958), Fabian (January 1959), Bobby Rydell (April 1959) (collectively known as the Philadelphia Pretty Boy School), Bobby Darin (May 1958), Freddie "Boom Boom" Cannon (May 1959), Bobby Vee (September 1959) and Bobby Vinton (May 1962) all made the big time. Clyde McPhatter (November 1955), Neil Sedaka (November 1958), Dion DiMucci (October 1960) and Johnny Maestro (January, 1961) all left doo-wop-oriented groups to try (and succeed) to make it on their own. The new idols were manufactured and/or supported by record companies, and were sold as clean-cut products in an attempt to mollify adults. Parents might still hold that their offspring's taste in music was puerile and misguided, but they were hard pressed to identify the new idols with marauding and pillaging delinquents. The group sound, and the (mostly) black artists who were easily identified with gang rumbles, delinquency and poverty, were left out.

The music delivered by the new wave of idols, who were mostly white, was geared to engender idolatry in the teen generation, especially the white teen generation. For the most part, these attempts were successful. This was made possible in part by the increasing importance of the visual media (i.e., television) in the life of the average teenager. In the early 1950s, teens inherited radios as their parents moved on to better things. By 1960, teens were inheriting first generation TVs as their parents bought new ones. Also, because they were predominantly black, doo-wop artists were much less of a drawing card to (in 1960) an overwhelmingly white teenage television audience.

As classical doo-wop was heard less and less over the ether, the small record companies that were the backbone of the doo-wop era went under or sold out. With several exceptions, Atlantic and Vee Jay among them, the Indies died as classical doo-wop waned around 1960. Additionally, many of the youngsters who sang classical doo-wop were by now in their 20s. The majority had never received more than token remuneration for their efforts and were forced to get jobs outside of the music industry to support themselves or their incipient families. A doo-wop group could have sold several hundred thousand copies of a record and yet have received nothing because they signed off on their rights to royalties on the "good advice" of a record mogul, because the label went under, because the composer's name was changed, because the record was covered, or because of a combination of the preceding events. Most doo-wop groups died from attrition as their members sought financial security in fields other than music. Only a select few individuals were able to make a living in the field of music (e.g., Harvey Fuqua, lead singer of the Moonglows, who became a record producer for Motown, and Teddy Randazzo, who became involved in producing records for United Artists).

Resuscitation

Then fate intervened to give doo-wop a second life. The "oldies" revival of 1960-1962 kicked off the process of resuscitation. Led by men such as Art Laboe, who issued a series of *Oldies But Goodies* albums, classical doo-wop songs like "Earth Angel," "In The Still Of The Night," "Tonite, Tonite" and "Heaven And Paradise" received as much or more attention than when originally issued. Albums were the hot new medium (supplanting 45s) and doo-wop, for the first time, benefited from this trend. Irving "Slim" Rose, owner of the Times Square record store (housed in the 42nd Street subway station in New York) issued or reissued classical doo-wop songs on five labels (Times Square, Candlelight, Victory, Romantic Rhythm and Shield). He also sponsored radio shows which featured old (meaning paleo- and classical) and rare doo-wop recordings. Some of the groups whose records emanated from Slim's stable included the Timetones, the Five Satins, the Nutmegs, the Volumes, the Flamingos, the Paragons and the Moonglows. Through a second generation of personality deejays like "Cousin" Bruce Morrow, Murray "the K" Kaufman and Alan Fredericks, a second generation of youngsters came to appreciate classical doo-wop and also responded favorably to the neo-doo-wop efforts of the Marcels, Earls, Tokens, Ronettes and Chiffons between the years 1960-1963. Further, musically talented people, who had cut their teeth on classical doo-wop, entered the arena. Creative songwriting teams and producers introduced more complicated melodies, more sophisticated lyrics and placed greater emphasis on instrumentation. Tin Pan Alley doo-wop was the result in the early 1960s.

Attempts to add to what had come before resulted in the neo-doo-wop period and also helped to hasten the demise of the genre. On one hand, neo-doo-wop groups added to classical doo-wop by employing more falsetto and bass, and by the exaggerated use of nonsense syllables. This produced pastiche songs such as "Papa-Oom-Mow-Mow" by the Rivingtons, "Surfer Bird" by the Trashmen and "Mr. Bassman" by Johnny Cymbal. Paradoxically, the neo-doo-wop period also brought about a diminution of these same classical doo-wop characteristics of falsetto, bass and nonsense syllable through cross-fertilization with other styles of music (e.g., the pop doo-wop sounds of the Duprees and Chimes).

The Second Demise

Evolution has a way of not wanting to stop, and by 1963 neo-doo-wop went from the current events file to the history books. This process was a fairly slow one, beginning around 1962 and ending by 1965. Group by group, song by song, and year by year, the halcyon traits of falsetto, bass and nonsense syllables were left behind. The wide range of voice parts that were so much a part of the doo-wop style were replaced by instruments such as lead guitar and violin (replacing falsetto) and bass guitar (replacing the bass vocalist). In some cases (e.g., Dixie Cups and Essex) group harmony was reduced to "Ooh Ooh" or some variation thereof. It was almost as if a regression to paleo-doo-wop blow harmonies occurred. In most other cases, group harmony and bass, when present, echoed the lead singer's assertions with words rather than nonsense syllables. In "Sherry," by the Four Seasons, for example, after Frankie Valli wails "Sheh-eh-eh-eh-eh-er-ree Bay-yay-bee," all that his harmonizing cohorts could return was "Sherry Baby." Doo-woppers would have blithely responded with "bum-bums" instead of resorting to grammatically correct twaddle. Background response in words became the rule in most subsequent musics, including those emanating from Detroit, Philadelphia, California and Liverpool. Nonsense syllables became anathema to the new generation of lyricists.

The Tokens, Crests (later the Brooklyn Bridge), Marvelettes and Gene Chandler followed interesting paths. Their earlier work was clearly performed in doo-wop style (e.g., "Tonight I Fell In Love" by the Tokens) but their later efforts left doo-wop qualities behind in favor of heavier instrumentation and different vocal patterns. Some neo-doo-wop groups gravitated to the Motown and other soul sounds, others entered the mainstream of popular music, and still others disappeared from sight. "Surfin'," one of the earliest releases by the Beach Boys, with its thunderous bass line (bon bon dit dit it dit it, bon bon dit dit it) is clearly "surf doo-wop" music, a category which has few other entries. Both the Four Tops (as the Four Aims) and the Supremes (as the Primettes), stalwart Motown groups, began their careers ululating in doo-wop style. Jerry Butler & the Impressions had a soulful doo-wop-style hit in 1958 with "For Your Precious Love." As their careers progressed, Butler became a successful pop/soul singer and Curtis Mayfield led the Impressions as they became one of the top groups in the field of soul music.

In some cases (e.g., the British Invasion and Surf music) the changes can simply be ascribed to musical evolution. In the case of Motown in particular, soul music in general and folk music, the evolution was as much of a political as a musical nature. The early 1960s witnessed increasing education, sophistication and willingness to stand up for their beliefs on the part of blacks and vocal support for these causes on the part of liberal whites. It was a time of John F. Kennedy, liberalism and peaceful racial protest ("sit-ins"), creating a culture markedly different from that of the Dwight Eisenhower years (1952-1960). The new culture, as is the norm, gave birth to and supported a new music. Black pride, peace and protest all found their way into song. Philosophy and politics became part of a lyricist's armamentarium, subjects that were foreign to doo-wop composers. The sound of soul was different. Voice register was much higher (with frequent falsetto leads and melismas), bass was employed less, nonsense syllables virtually absent. The music went back towards its gospel roots.

The British Invasion, Motown and surf music administered the coup de grace to the neo-doo-wop sound. This time, after its second coming, the doo-wop era went down for the count. Part of the reason for the de-evolution of doo-wop lay with the advent of Marshall amplification systems, which allowed better sound volume and distribution and lent more emphasis to the guitar and other instruments. Stereophonic sound, by allowing the separation of instruments and voices, also lent importance to the former. The triumph of instruments continued as the Beatles, one of the first popular self-contained groups (i.e., they played their own instruments, thus obviating the need to hire musicians), set the trend for the future. Most members of doo-wop groups were not musicians and were at a disadvantage. Club owners, if hiring a doo-wop group, would also need to retain the services of a band (unless they expected their patrons to dance to a capella). Also of enormous importance was the freshness of the musical styles just coming up over the horizon. The new generation of 13-year-olds had a marvelous plethora of sounds to choose from, and on which they could base their own culture: the British music of the

Beatles and Stones, the surf sound of the Beach Boys and Jan & Dean, the Philadelphia sound of the Orlons and Patti LaBelle & the Blue Belles, or the Motown groups like the Supremes, Temptations, Four Tops and Miracles. Each succeeding generation of teens has had a need to reinvent its own musical wheel.

Another reason for the popularity of the new musics was that the vacuum, created when doo-wop, rockabilly and rhythm and blues (i.e., rock 'n' roll) withered away, needed to be filled. Isolated doo-wop efforts achieved popularity after 1963-1964, as in songs by Reperata and the Delrons ("Whenever A Teenager Cries"), Bill Deal and the Rondells ("May I"), Exodus ("M & M") the Capris ("Morse Code of Love") and even Billy Joel with a backup group ("For The Longest Time"), but by and large the age of doo-wop had come and gone. "Here today, gone tomorrow," as the evolutionists like to remind us.

Figure VIII

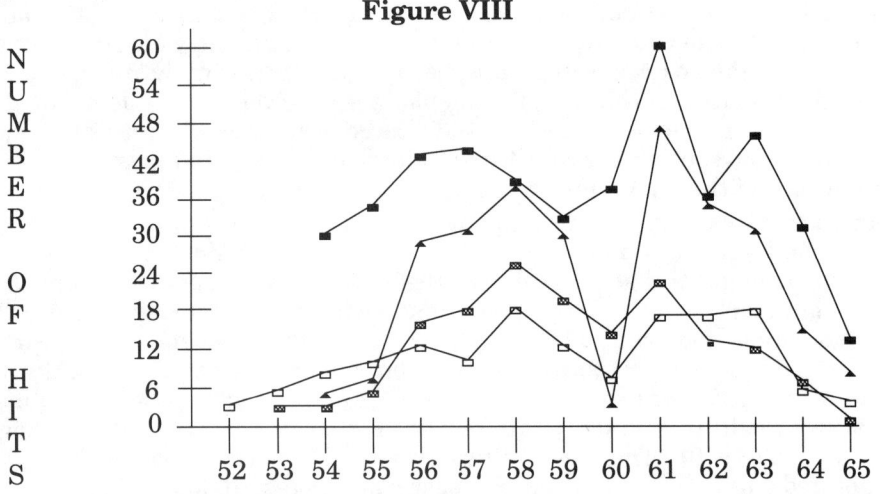

▲ TOP 40   ■ NNN ALMANAC □ DAVE MARSH ⊠ WCBS-FM 500

Evidence for the two lives and deaths of doo-wop is presented below in Figure VIII. To arrive at the data for Figure VIII, every doo-wop song listed in (a) the *Billboard Book of Top 40 Hits* (375 total), (b) *Norm N. Nite's Almanac* (354 total), (c) Dave Marsh's *Heart Of Rock and Soul* (139 total), and (d) the WCBS-FM Top 500 Oldies for 1989 (156 total) were tallied according to the year in which they became popular. Each of the four curves viewed separately presents a bimodal distribution, with the first peak occurring between 1957 and 1958, and the second somewhere between 1961 and 1963. The first peak represents the classical doo-wop stage and second peak demarcates neo-doo-wop. The year 1960 (or 1959, depending upon the source) was an "off" year, indicating the time at which classical doo-wop was on the wane, and neo-doo-wop had yet to come on strong. This period delineates the first "death" of doo-wop. In the years 1964-1965, all four of the plotted curves drop off precipitously, heralding the occurrence of the second demise of (neo-) doo-wop.

While the doo-wop era has come and gone, doo-wop music has never really gone away. Oldies radio programs and stations are an ever present and popular part of radio fare. In 1990, WCBS-FM (New York), the station that hosts Don K. Reed's "Doo-Wop Shop" on Sunday nights and that plays generalized oldies the rest of the time, is overall the number one radio station in the New York area. It is traditionally the number one station in the 25-54 age group (the people with money to spend), and is the most profitable of the CBS-owned stations (according to an article in *New York Magazine*, Aug. 6, 1990). The continued devotion to fifties music in general and doo-wop in particular accounts for their success. "Brand name" groups that filled the airwaves 35 years ago still perform on a regular basis to packed houses, even though the group members are different and often younger. New doo-wop and a capella (which itself seems to have evolved to an art form) groups seem to be springing up all over the place, often led by artists that were not born when the seeds of their music were sewn.

Enthusiast/businessman types, following in the tradition of struggling Indie record company "moguls" (such as Irving "Slim" Rose of Times Square Records) continue to supply the music. Examples of this type of person include Ronnie Italiano of Clifton Music, Eddie Gries and Donn Fileti of Relic Records, and Bill Himmelman of the Music Nostalgia Company. Italiano ("Ronnie I") almost single-handedly put together an organization called the UGHA (United in Group Harmony Association), which sponsors concerts, puts out a newsletter, helps many of the old groups get back together and perform, and has recently helped organize a "United In Group Harmony" Hall of Fame for doo-wop stars. So far, in two years of existence, the Hall of Fame has enshrined 14 doo-wop groups. Those accepted in 1991 were the Cadillacs, Clovers, Harptones, Heartbeats, Shep & the Limelites, Orioles, Ravens and Frankie Lymon & the Teenagers. In 1992, admittees were the Channels, Five Keys, Flamingos, Moonglows, Solitaires and Spaniels. Greis and Fileti run Relic Records, which has put out an enormous (approximately 100 vinyl albums!) and varied collection of doo-wops, many of which were not previously available to the general public. The liner notes to these albums are fascinating, providing detailed information of what went on in the record industry during the doo-wop era. And finally, there is Bill Himmelman who, as a labor of love, put together a series of 280 (so far) collectors cards (like baseball cards), over half of which portray doo-wop groups.

Aside from these professional enthusiasts, amateur "oldies" like the present reader and authors continue to listen to the music with which they grew up. Apparently the doo-wop sound is not ready to die. Not until the people that grew up with it do, in any case.

"Close your eyes baby,
Follow my heart,
Call on the memories,
Here in the dark,
We'll let the magic take us away,
Back to the feelings we shared when they played...
'In The Still Of The Night,'
Hold me darling,
Hold me tight,
Oh, Oh,
Shoo-doop shoo-bee-doo,
Shoo-doop doo,
So real, so right,
Lost in the fifties tonight...." *

* *"Lost In The Fifties Tonight," Ronnie Milsap (Lodge Hill Corporation., 1985), ASCAP.*

Chapter 10

Some Idiosyncrasies of Doo-Wop

The bands called "Strawberry Alarm Clock," "Moby Grape," "Electric Prunes" and "Iron Butterfly" hail from the late 1960s and early 1970s, the psychedelic era of rock. Putting together words that have nothing to do with one another is a signpost of Woodstock Generation music makers. In a similar way, the doo-wop era produced a whole slew of idiosyncrasies, some dealing with the choice of group name, others with songs chosen to record, and still others with the subject matter and titles of those songs.

As an example, doo-wop groups had a penchant for telling us, in their names, how many members they had. The Five Discs, the Four Fellows and the Three Friends are examples. In the songography, there are 119 different "Five" groups, 142 different "Fours" and 28 different "Threes." If all groups are included, that is Four Fellows (1) is counted separately from Four Fellows (2), there are 134 "Fives, 175 "Fours" and 30 "Threes."

Another general quirk of doo-wop is that groups incorporated the suffix "-tones" or the word "Tones" in their name whenever they could. A staggering 228 groups did this and the figure burgeons to 272 when all groups with different numbers, such as Mello-Tones (1) and Mello-Tones (2), are included.

A third general characteristic is the use of the adjectives "Original" and "Fabulous" as introductions to the group name, as in the "Original Drifters" and the "Fabulous Flames." The careers of most doo-wop groups were short. "Fabulous" would often be used if and when the group tried to make a comeback well after the demand for its services had waned. "Original" was often used to distinguish a group from other groups which had taken the identical name, or from splinter groups started by a departing group member (e.g., Original Cadillacs, Original Drifters). It is no wonder that confusion surrounds group identity when there are so many groups going by identical names (e.g., there are 11 groups calling themselves the "Dreamers," nine groups going by the name "Accents," etc.).

The Choice Of Group Name

Doo-wop groups had an affinity for birds. This trend no doubt started with the Ravens in the mid-1940s and the Orioles in the late 1940s. For these groups, the names made sense. Birds sing, ravens are black, the "Ravens" is an excellent choice for a black singing group (as was the "Ink Spots"). The Oriole is the state bird of Maryland, and Sonny Til and his friends came from Baltimore. Again, good choice. After them, however, many groups just jumped on the bandwagon and the logic behind their choice of avian names was for the birds. By our count, more than 40 additional groups chose a fine feathered friend to represent them. That's enough for a decent size aviary. The group names follow, in order of the first year they recorded.

Group Name	Year First Recorded
Ravens	1946
Orioles	1948
Bluebirds (The Four)	1949
Robins	1949
Cardinals	1951

Group Name	Year First Recorded
Larks	1951
Skylarks	1951
Swallows	1951
Blue Jays	1953
Crows	1953
Flamingos	1953
Parrots	1953
Sparrows	1953
Swans	1953
Whipoorwills	1953
Buzzards (Big John & the)	1954
Eagles	1954
Hawks	1954
Parakeets	1954
Peacocks	1954
Pelicans	1954
Penguins	1954
Quails	1954
Starlings	1954
Wrens	1954
Birdies (Robert Byrd & His)	1956
Jay Birds	1956
Jayhawks	1956
Night Owls	1956
Drakes	1957
Ospreys	1957
Bobolinks	1958
Nighthawks	1958
Jays	1959
Doves	1960
Birds (Don Mikkelsen & the)	1961
Nightingales	1961
Hummingbirds	1962
Pheasants	1963
Ladybirds	1964
Warblers	1973
Owls	N/A
Whooping Cranes	N/A

A second passion was precious stones and gems. Here, the first groups to emerge were the Diamonds in 1952, and the Rubies, Crystals and Jewels in 1953. As the trend continued, 16 gem-type names were used, representing over 60 doo-wop groups when all were counted — that is, Rubies (1) and Rubies (2), etc.. These sparkling monikers were:

Group Name	Year First Recorded
Diamonds	1952
Crystals	1953
Jewels	1953

Group Name	Year First Recorded
Rubies	1953
Blue Diamonds	1954
Emeralds	1954
Gems	1954
Opals	1954
Ivories	1956
Pearls	1956
Garnets	1957
Zircons	1957
Jades	1958
Sapphires	1958
Blue Crystals	1959
Fabulous Pearls	1959
Ivorys	1962

Similarly, many groups went floral, after the Carnations in 1952, and the Blue Belles and Orchids in 1953. (Were the session producers for these groups called "floral arrangers"?) A list of groups follows.

Group Name	Year First Recorded
Carnations	1952
Blue Belles	1953
Orchids	1953
Daffodils	1955
Laurels	1955
Marigolds	1955
Blossoms	1957
Dahlias	1957
Gladiolas	1957
Hollyhocks	1957
Rosebuds	1957
Roses	1958
Goldenrods	1959
Tigre Lillies	1959
Lavenders	1960
Bouquets	1963
Daisies	1964
Astors	1965

The tendency to name a group after the name of a car or car model was more than a trend; it became practically an obsession. Although there were several groups with car names before 1954, it was more by accident than intention. For example, although Checker was the name of a car company, the singing group called the "Checkers" was named after the game, to take advantage of the success of another "game" group, the Dominoes. In 1954 the Cadillacs began recording and, as the list below demonstrates, many other groups followed in their dust. Esther Navarro, manager of the Cadillacs, said that the name was chosen because all the good bird names were already taken and a member of the group suggested "Cadillacs" after seeing one pass by the window. Cadillacs' member Charles Brooks had another version, stating that they named the group as they did to impress the ladies. There have been worse reasons. Cars were always an expression and reflection of the male ego, so the idea to name your group after a car that you had or desired was compelling. As the first important car group, the Cadillacs took the most prestigious name available at the time. In the early to mid-1950s, the Cadillac was considered the best car around. Lincolns and Chrysler Imperials were not as popular, the company that produced Packards was in decline, and the foreign showboats such as Jaguars, Mercedes and BMWs had not as yet made significant penetrations into the American market. This was in an age when American-made products were considered the best and anything "made in Japan" was met with derision. Paralleling the state of affairs in the marketplace, doo-wop groups chose to use the names of General Motors cars more frequently than either Chrysler or Ford products. Among cars produced abroad, British vehicles were the most popular and were also chosen most often as names for doo-wop groups. A complete listing follows.

Category	Name Of Car	Group Name
General Motors	Chevrolet	Belairs/Chevelles/Chevies/Corvairs/Corvettes/El Caminos/Impalas/Stingrays
	Pontiac	Bonnevilles/Catalinas/Tempests
	Oldsmobile	Deltas/Holidays/Starfires
	Buick	Centurys/Electras/Invictas/Rivieras/Skylarks/Specials/Wildcats
	Cadillac	Caddys/Cadillacs/De Villes/El Dorados/Fleetwoods
Chrysler	Plymouth	Belvederes/Furys/Satellites/Savoys/Valiants
	Dodge	Coronets/Rams/Royals
	Chrysler	Chryslers/Imperials/New Yorkers/Newports/Windsors
Ford	Ford	Fairlanes/Falcons/Galaxies/Mustangs/Thunderbirds/T-Birds
	Mercury	Mercurys/Meteors/Monarchs/Montereys
	Lincoln	Continentals/Lincolns
	Edsel	Edsels
American Motors	Nash	Metropolitans
	Rambler	Ambassadors/Ramblers/Rebels/Matadors
Misc. American	Studebaker	Avantis/Hawks/Studebaker "7"
	Packard	Packards
	Checker	Checkers
	Jeep	Cherokees
	Shelby	Cobras
Foreign	(British)	Bentleys/Healeys/Jaguars/Phaetons/Rovers/Sunbeams/Triumphs
	(French)	Renaults
	(German)	Merceedees (misspelled)
	(Italian)	Fiats/Spiders

While there is no doubt that doo-wop groups often took their names from car models, it is conceivable that the reverse is also true. This is because car models introduced *after* the doo-wop era quite frequently have names that were used earlier in time by doo-wop groups. Astros (van), Blazers (all-purpose), Cavaliers, Celebrities, Citations and Suburbans (all-purpose) are all newer model Chevrolets *and* names of doo-wop groups. Challengers, Chargers, Darts, Diplomats, Lancers and Shadows are all names of more recent Dodge models *and* names of doo-wop groups. Escorts, Explorers (all-purpose), Fiestas and Tempos are newer Fords *and* names of doo-wop groups. Were marketing executives from Detroit hanging around on the street corners or is this phenomenon just a coincidence?

Another possibility presents itself when we examine the names of professional baseball teams. Exactly half of them, or 13 out of 26, share names with doo-wop groups. There were doo-wop groups called the Angels, Astros, Blue Jays, Cardinals, Cubs, Dodgers, Mariners, Orioles, (Swinging) Phillies, Pirates, Royals, Tigers and (Hong Kong) White Sox. It just may be that some names are testosterone-friendly, that is, they attract men. Since baseball, cars and doo-wop form a cluster of interests that appeal especially to males, it is not surprising that these activities share labels.

Doo-Wop Songs That Were Recorded Most Often

As part of the rock 'n' roll explosion, doo-wop groups recorded music that was lyrically and melodically quite different from what had come before. It is ironic, therefore, that the three songs most recorded by doo-wop groups had their roots in earlier eras. These three are "Over The Rainbow" written by Harold Arlen and E. Y. Harburg in 1931, "A Sunday Kind Of Love" written by Barbara Belle, Louis Prima, Anita Leonard and Stan Rhodes in 1946, and "Gloria," the provenance of which is discussed below.

"Somewhere Over The Rainbow" was first recorded by Judy Garland for the movie "The Wizard Of Oz" in 1939. It was first recorded by doo-wop groups in 1954 (Castelles and Checkers) and then repeatedly throughout the doo-wop era. Most of the time the title was shortened to "Over The Rainbow," the lyrics simplified to fit the doo-wop style, and it was rendered as a ballad most of the time. The most well-known doo-wop versions are by David Campanella (son of Roy Campanella, MVP catcher for the erstwhile Brooklyn Dodgers) & the Delchords in 1959 and by the Demensions in 1960. The latter spent nine weeks on the *Billboard* charts, reaching number 16 in August 1960. Thirty-five versions are listed below.

Group Name	Year	Label
Castelles	1954	Grand 118
Checkers	1954	King 4719
Moroccos ("Somewhere...")	1956	United 193/B&F 193 (1960)
Del Vikings ("Somewhere...")	1957	Luniverse 106
Echoes	1957	Specialty 601
Mondellos (Yul McClay & the)	1957	Rhythm 105
Satisfiers	1957	Coral 61788
Chanters (Bud Johnson & the)	1958	DeLuxe 6177
Buddies (Little Butchie Saunders & the)	1959	Angle Tone 535
Delchords (David Campanella & the) ("Somewhere...")	1959	Kane 25593
Emjays	1959	Paris 538

Group Name	Year	Label
Imperials (Little Anthony & the)	1959	End LP 303/End EP 204 (1959)
Baysiders	1960	Everest 19366
Demensions	1960	Mohawk 116/Coral 65559 (1966)
Delrons	1961	Forum 700
Guys (Little Sammy Rozzi & the)	1962	Pelham 722
Original Checkers	1962	King 5592
Tones (Little Sammy & the)	1962	Jaclyn 1161
Vibrations	1962	Checker 1002
Darchaes (Nicky Addeo & the)	1964	Selsom 104
Lytations (a capella)	1964	Times Square 107
Young Ones (a capella)	1964	Times Square 104
Aztecs (Billy Thorpe & the)	1965	GNP Crescendo 34
Blue Belles (Patti LaBelle & the)	1965	Atlantic 2318
Five Fashions	1965	Catamount 103
Mustangs	1965	Vest 8005
Hamiltons (Alexander & the)	1966	Warner Bros. 5844
Portraits	1968	Sidewalk 935
Admirations	1972	Kelway 108
Kac-Ties (a capella)	1975	Relic LP 108
Marcels	N/A	Monogram 113
Monarchs	N/A	Reegal 512
Mystics	N/A	Collectables LP 5043
Remainders	N/A	Vico 1
Ricquettes (Danny Skeene & the)	N/A	Valex 105/106

"A Sunday Kind Of Love" was first recorded by Jo Stafford for Capitol records in 1947. Paleo-doo-wop ballad versions were released in 1953; the great Harptones' rendition on Bruce and one by Bobby Hall & the Kings on the Jax label. In 1957, the Del Vikings put out an up-tempo arrangement that caught on and made the song a doo-wop standard (especially for a capella groups) even though no rendition has ever charted in *Billboard*. Since then, renditions have been roughly equally divided into slow and up-tempo numbers. Twenty-six versions are listed.

Group Name	Year	Label
Harptones	1953	Bruce 101/Raven 8001 (1962)
Kings (Bobby Hall & the)	1953	Jax 320
Del Vikings	1957	Mercury 30112
Highlanders	1957	Ray's 36
Sentimentals	1957	Mint 802
Lambert, Rudy (with the Lyrics)	1958	Rhythm 128
Gothics	1959	Dynamic 101
Winters, David (& group)	1959	Addison 15004
High Seas	1960	D-M-G 1001/D-M-G 4000
Heard, Lonnie (& group)	1961	Arliss 1008
Marcels	1961	Colpix LP 416
Mystics	1961	Laurie 3104

116

Group Name	Year	Label
Persians	1962	RTO 100
Rapid-Tones (Willie Winfield & the)	1962	Rapid 1002
Roommates	1962	Cameo 233
Camelots	1963	AAnko 1004
El Sierros	1963	Yussels 7702
Timetones	1963	Times Square 26
Devotions	1964	Roulette 4556
Excellons	1964	Bobby 601/Old Timer 601 (1964)
Five Shadows	1965	Mellomood 011/012
Bees (Honey & the)	1968	Arctic 158
Blue Moons	N/A	Jaguar 1001
Earls	N/A	Harvey 100
Statics (Lynn & the)	N/A	Mantis 101
Themes	N/A	Ideal

"Gloria" has the most interesting history of the three. Ferdie Gonzalez and Art Turco, in an article for the *Record Exchanger* (June 1973), help to make sense of the events. "Gloria" was first penned by Leon Rene in the late 40s and was first recorded by Johnny Moore's Three Blazers for Rene's Exclusive record label. Next, the Mills Brothers had a charted hit with it on Decca in November 1948. The song told the story of a guy (the singer) who used to toy with women's affections until he met our protagonist Gloria. He duly fell in love with her, but she wasn't buying. The lyrics, as recorded in Gonzales and Turco, were:

"Gloria, it's not Marie, it's Gloria
It's not Cherie, it's Gloria
She's in your every dream

You like to play the game of kiss and runaway
But now you find it's not that way
Somehow you've changed it seems

Wasn't Madeline your first love
It was just hello goodbye
Wasn't Caroline your last love
It's a shame you made her cry

What a fool you are
You gave your heart to Gloria
You're not so smart cause Gloria
Is not in love with you

What a fool you are
She's not in love with you"*

* "Gloria," Leon Rene (Rene Leon Publications, 1946), ASCAP.

Skip to 1954, when the Cadillacs put out the first doo-wop version of "Gloria," written ostensibly by Esther Navarro, the group's manager. Navarro wrote the song after one of her proteges, a singer named Gloria "Little Miss Muffet" Smith. Somehow, Navarro took elements of the older song and blended them into a doo-wop format to resurrect the belle Gloria. Navarro's lyrics were:

"Gloria, it's not Marie
Gloria, it's not Cherie
Gloria, but she's not in love with me

Can't you see, it's not Marie
It's Gloria, it's not Cherie
It's Gloria, but she's not in love with me

Yes, maybe she loves me, but who am I to know
And, maybe she loves me, but who am I to know

Gloria, it's not Marie
It's Gloria, it's not Cherie
It's Gloria, but she's not in love with me"*

* "Gloria," Esther Navarro (Benell Music, 1954), BMI.

The commonalities between the two versions are (1) the story line, i.e., Gloria not returning the love of a suitor, and (2) three lines, namely "It's not Marie," "It's not Cherie" and "She's not in love with me (you)." The melodies differ and Rene's lyrics are much more sophisticated, as befitting a song geared for adult audiences. Navarro's lyrics are simpler and more repetitive. Additionally, Rene's tale is recounted in second person (e.g., "What a fool you are") while Navarro's is told in first person (e.g., "Who am I to know"). Whether the "borrowing" that Navarro did was accidental or purposeful will never be truly known. Gonzalez and Turco sense that she knew what she was doing because her name did not appear on the first pressing but did on subsequent ones. Apparently when no one raised a fuss, she figured it was all right to take credit.

Whether by design or not, Navarro and the Cadillacs left the legacy of a doo-wop masterpiece, one that quickly became a street corner "standard." "Gloria," along with "Sunday Kind Of Love," became fodder for would-be doo-woppers to strut their stuff. You had to be able to sing these two songs to get respect on the street.

"Gloria," despite being a name that is difficult to rhyme with (except perhaps with "eu-" and "dysphoria," "trattoria" and "I wanna see more a ya"), has attracted songwriters like flies. Other doo-wop groups such as the Five Thrills, the Five Chances, the Chariots and Arthur Lee Maye & the Crowns put out entirely different songs by the same name. The Frankie Grier Quartet put out "Oh Gloria," the Windsors recorded "My Gloria" and the New Yorkers Five produced "Gloria, My Darling." Van Morrison wrote the G-L-O-R-I-A "Gloria" in 1965 (not a doo-wop version) for his group Them, and the Shadows Of Knight had an eight-week run on the Billboard charts with a garage band version of it in 1966. Finally, Laura Branigan visited the charts for 22 weeks (three of them at number two) with a neurotic, manipulative "Gloria" in 1982 (again, not doo-wop). A list of "Gloria" songs follows.

118

Group Name	Year	Label
Johnny Moore's Three Blazers	1946	Exclusive 703
Four Gabriels	1948	World 2505
Mills Brothers	1948	Decca 24509
Cadillacs	1954	Josie 765/Lana 119 (1964)
Five Thrills	1954	Parrot 800
New Yorkers 5 ("... My Darling")	1955	Danice 801
Crowns (Arthur Lee Maye & the)	1956	Specialty 573
Five Chances	1956	States 156
Wallace, Jerry (& group)	1956	Mercury 70812
Clark, Dee (with the Kool Gents)	1957	Falcon 1002/Vee Jay 355 (1960)
Grier Quartet (The Frankie Grier Quartet) ("Oh...")	1958	Swan 4019
Windsors (Lee Scott & the) ("My...")	1958	Back Beat 506
Chariots	1959	Time 1006/Brent
Passions	1960	Audicon 106
Chapelaires	1961	Hac 102
Blue Knights (Steve Colt & the)	1962	Fleetwood 4550
Escorts	1962	Coral 62302
Hi-Lites	1962	Julia 1105
Love Notes	1962	Wilshire 203
Parrish, Troy (& group)	1962	Baronet 10
Salutations (Vito & the)	1962	Rayna 5009/Red Boy 5009 (1962)
Youngones (a capella)	1962	Times Square 28
Darchaes (Nicky Addeo & the)	1963	Savoy 200/Earls 1533
Del-Lourds	1963	Solar 1003
Vandells (Johnny Greco & the)	1963	Far-Mel 1
Five Sharks (a capella)	1964	Old Timer 604/Siamese 404 (1965)
Ubans	1964	Radiant 102
Good Guys (Doug Robertson & the)	1965	Jerden 767
Savoys (a capella)	1965	Catamount 105
Sultans	1965	Ascot 2228
DiMucci, Dion (& group)	1969	Warner Bros. ?????
Channels (Earl Lewis & the)	1971	Channel 1000 (recorded in 1956)
Lanterns (a capella)	1973	Baron 110
Clefftones	N/A	Old Town/Murray Hill LP 000083

The practice of "borrowing" parts of a song, exemplified by the Rene-Navarro story, became a common, if not quite accepted, practice among doo-wop practitioners. "I Wonder Why," the song that established Dion & the Belmonts in 1958, was partly borrowed from "Now I'm Telling You" by the Legends, also in 1958. The songs start out almost identically before diverging. "I Do Love You" by Tex & the Chex in 1961 was more closely "borrowed" from "My Darling To You" by the Bop Chords in 1957, and "Dreams Come True" by the Earls in 1974 is an exact, though up-tempo, replica of "Teenager's Dream" by the Kodaks in 1957.

Incidentally, other "standards" popularized in previous eras were also favorites with the doo-wop set. The songography contains 16 versions of "The White Cliffs Of Dover" (written by Nat Burton and Walter Kent in 1941) emanating from World War II, and 17 versions each of "Blue Moon" (written by Richard Rogers and Lorenz Hart in 1934) and "Stormy Weather" (Harold Arlen and Ted Koehler in 1933).

The Subject Matter Of Doo-Wop Songs

Detectives glean information from clues, garbologists deduce much about the way a family lives by examining their refuse, and much can be inferred about the doo-wop generation by examining the subjects of their songs. To begin, doo-woppers were wild about jungles. This trend is easily traced to the novelty song "Stranded In The Jungle," which was released in 1956 by the Jayhawks, Cadets and Gadabouts. Edgar Rice Burroughs' Tarzan, played in movies by fine specimens of manhood Buster Crabbe and Johnny Weissmuller, enjoyed widespread popularity, and television shows such as "Ramar Of The Jungle" entertained the adolescents of the 1950s. Songs with "Jungle" in the title soon proliferated. Songs without the word "Jungle" but conveying similar messages also were heard, as in "Dancin' In The Congo" (by the Chandeliers in 1958) and "Tarzan's Date" (by the Chuck-A-Lucks in 1961), "The Lion Sleeps Tonight" (by the Tokens in 1961) "Bongo Stomp" (by Little Joey & the Flips in 1962), "(Native Girl) Elephant Walk" (by Donald Jenkins & the Delighters in 1963) and "Ubangi Stomp" (by the Velaires in 1963). Three "Jungle" songs made our Top 500, namely "Stranded In The Jungle" (Jayhawks' version), "Rockin' In The Jungle" (Eternals) and "Bongo Stomp" (Little Joey & the Flips). The complete list of "Jungle" songs includes:

Group Name	Song	Year	Label
Cadets	Stranded In The Jungle	1956	Modern 994
Gadabouts	Stranded In The Jungle	1956	Mercury 70898
Jayhawks	Stranded In The Jungle	1956	Flash 109
Five Quails	Jungle Baby	1957	Mercury 71154
Flips	Jungle Hop	1958	Challenge 59008
(Kip Tyler & the)			
Raiders	Walking Through The Jungle	1958	Brunswick 55090
Shadows	Jungle Fever	1958	Del-Fi 4109
Starlettes	Jungle Love	1958	Checker 895
Channels	Jungle Lights	1959	Mercury 71501
Eternals	Rockin' In The Jungle	1959	Hollywood 68/ Musictone 1111 (1961)
Fabulous Pearls	Jungle Bunny	1959	Dooto 448
Individuals	Jungle Superman	1959	Show Time 595/ Show Time 598 (1959)/Red Fox 105
Playboys	Jungle Fever	1959	Rik 572
Dyna-Sores	Jungle Walk	1960	Rendezvous 120
Passions	Jungle Drums	1960	Audicon 106
Romancers	Jumpin' Jungle	1960	Palette 5067

Group Name	Song	Year	Label
Vibrations	Stranded In The Jungle	1960	Checker 982
Concepts	Jungle	1961	Apache 1515/ Musictone 1109 (1961)
Five Cashmeres	Walkin' Through The Jungle	1961	Golden Leaf 108
Cap-Tans (Wailing Bethea & the)	Rockin' In The Jungle	1962	Hawkeye 0430
Legends	Jungle Lullabye	1962	Caldwell 410
Mystics (Ed Gates & the)	In The Jungle	1962	Robins Nest 2
Grand Prees	Jungle Fever	1963	Candi 1020
Velvet Angels	Jungle Fever (a capella)	1972	Relic LP 5004
Apostles	Stranded In The Jungle	N/A	A-Square 401
Starlites	Bop Diddlie In The Jungle	N/A	Claremont 959

Another passion of the doo-wop generation was exotic women. The foreign women who were celebrated most often in song were Spanish-speaking. They were addressed as "senorita" if the swain did not know her, and usually had the name "Juanita" if he did. She was almost invariably from south of the border, down Mexico way. Other Spanish-speaking countries are rarely visited. The Mexican senorita represented well the idealized version of love so prominent in songs of the doo-wop era. Infatuation and chauvanism are common themes in these songs. A selected list of songs of this type follows.

Group Name	Song	Year	Label
Bell Notes	Old Spanish Town	1959	Time 1010
Belvin, Jesse (& group)	Senorita	1957	Modern 1013
Blue Chips	Adios, Adios	1961	RCA 7935
Caronators	Senorita	1960	Clock 1045/Clock 227
Catalinas	Hey Senorita	1961	Zebra 101
Champions	Mexico Bound	1956	Chart 611
Coasters	Down In Mexico	1956	Atco 6064
Crests	My Juanita	1957	Joyce 103/Musictone 1106 (1962)
Delighters (Donald & the)	Adios My Secret Love	1963	Cortland 112
Diablos	Adios My Desert Love	1954	Fortune 509/510
Dootones	Ay, Si, Si	1955	Dootone 366
Drifters	Mexican Divorce	1962	Atlantic 2134
Echoes	Aye Senorita	1956	Combo 128
Five Discs	Adios	1958	Callo 202
Four Wheels	Adios, My Pretty Baby	1956	Spin-It 108
Heartspinners (Dino & the)	Hey Senorita	1973	Bim Bam Boom 119
Holidays	Never Go To Mexico	1958	Music City 818
Hollywood Flames	Dance Senorita	1965	Symbol 211
Impressions	Senorita I Love You	1959	Abner 1025
Kappas	Sweet Juanita	1959	Wonder 1012

Group Name	Song	Year	Label
Locomotions	Adios My Love	1962	Gone 5142
Magic Tones	Spanish Love Song	1957	Howfum 101
Nutmegs	Down In Mexico	1963	Times Square 27
Penguins	Hey Senorita	1954	Dootone 348/ Power 7023 (1954)
Rivileers (Gene Pearson & the)	Hey, Chiquita	1954	Baton 200
Robins	Smokey Joe's Cafe	1955	Spark 122/Atco 6059 (1956)
Rocketones	Mexico	1957	Melba 113
Royaltones	Latin Love	1956	Old Town 1028
Schoolboys (Professor Hamilton & the)	Juanita Of Mexico	1961	Contour 0001
Serenaders	Adios My Love	1963	Riverside 4549
Tokays	Hey Senorita	1967	Brute 001
Travelers	Spanish Moon	1963	Princess 52/Vault 911
Visuals	My Juanita	1963	Poplar 117
Wanderers	Run Run Senorita	1962	United Artists 570
Wonders	Hey Senorita	1959	Ember 1051

A second group of exotic women that were exalted by the doo-wop generation came from the Orient. Most often the maiden spoke Chinese, frequently called Hong Kong home and was duly servile and subservient. Sometimes, the damsel can be heard speaking "Chinese" in the background, except it really sounded like a male in falsetto muttering gibberish (e.g., "Hong Kong" by the Quinns and "My Chinese Girl" by the Five Discs). These efforts symbolized the ultimate in male-domination fantasies. Males in these Oriental odysseys were often wise or had special powers, as in "Ling Ting Tong" by the Five Keys or "Rang Tang Ding Dong" by the Cellos. A selected list follows.

Group Name	Song	Year	Label
Five Keys	Ling Ting Tong	1954	Capitol 2945
Rovers	Ichi-Bon Tami Dachi	1954	Music City 750/ Capitol 3078 (1955)
Charms	Ling Ting Tong	1955	DeLuxe 6076
Rays	Moo Goo Gai Pan	1955	Chess 1613
Blue Jays	Ling Ting Tong	1956	Dig EP 778
Downbeats	China Doll	1956	Gee 1019
El Dorados	Chop Ling Soon	1956	Vee Jay 197
Hi-Fives	Hong Kong	1956	Flair-X 3000
Ray-O-Vacs	Hong Kong	1956	Kaiser 389
Cellos	Rang Tang Ding Dong	1957	Apollo 510
Glad Rags	My China Doll	1957	Excello 2121
Three Friends	Chinese Tea Room	1957	Lido 504
Columbus Pharaohs	China Girl	1958	Esta 290/Ransom 101 (1958)/Paradise 109 (1958)

Group Name	Song	Year	Label
Hy-Tones	Chinese Boogie	1958	Hy-Tone 120
Peppers	Yoko Hoko Homa	1958	Jane 105
Premiers	China Doll	1958	Cindy 3008
Quinns	Hong Kong	1958	Cyclone 111
Five Discs	My Chinese Girl	1959	Dwain 6072/Dwain 803 (1959)/Mello Mood 1002 (1964)
Quarter Notes	Suki-Yaki-Rocki	1959	Whizz 715
Revels	Foo Man Choo	1959	Norgolde 104
Lincolns	Sukiyaki Rocki	1961	Bud 113
Masquins (Tony & the)	Fuji Womma	1961	Ruthie 1000
Tellers (Artie Banks & the)	Oriental Baby	1961	Imperial 5788
Tabbys	Hong Kong Baby	1963	Metro 2
Bermudas	Chu Sen Ling	1964	Era 3125
Q's (Bruce Clark & the)	Went To Chinatown	1964	Hull 762
Channels	Old Chinatown	1965	Groove 0061
Pixies	Geisha Girl	1965	Autumn 12
Royaltones	Hong Kong Jelly Wong	1985	Murray Hill LP 000083
Fabulous Persians	Ling Ting Tong	N/A	Bobby-O 3123
Master Four	Love From The Far East	N/A	Tay-Ster 6012

Although the country was at peace for most of the doo-wop era, the Korean War and World War II were not yet forgotten. Phil Groia's book on the New York doo-wop groups notes that many group members left their singing careers in midstream to join the service, voluntarily or involuntarily. Being before Vietnam, the 1950s were years of unabashed patriotism. The songs written by and for doo-wop groups often reflected this patriotism by addressing soldiers and sailors in song as buddies or loved ones. Ironically, one of the best records of this ilk is "Good Goodbye" by the Bob Knight Four (1961 on Laurel 1020/Taurus 100), despite the fact that it doesn't mention a soldier or sailor in the title. A partial list of soldier/sailor songs follows. Roughly three-quarters address soldiers, the remaining quarter address sailors, and an inordinate number of these songs are rendered by distaff groups.

Group Name	Song	Year	Label
Marshalls (Bill Cook & the)	A Soldier's Prayer	1951	Savoy 828
Question Marks	Another Soldier Gone	1954	Swing Time 346
Violinaires	Another Soldier Gone	1954	Drummond 4000
Four Fellows	Soldier Boy	1955	Glory 234
Williams, Mel (& group)	Soldier Boy	1955	Federal 12236
Five Echoes	Soldier Boy	1956	Vee Jay 190
Stags	Sailor Boy	1958	M&S 502

Group Name	Song	Year	Label
Tassels	To A Soldier Boy	1959	Madison 117/Amy 946 (1966)
Interludes	White Sailor Hat	1960	Valley 107
Cavaliers (Little Bernie & the)	Lonely Soldier	1962	Jove 100
Debelaires	So Long, My Sailor	1962	Lectra 502
Dootones	Sailor Boy	1962	Dooto 471
Hallmarks	My Little Sailor Boy	1962	Dot 16418
Illusions	Lonely Soldier	1962	Mali 104/ Sheraton 104/ Northeast 801
Shirelles	Soldier Boy	1962	Scepter 1228
Shondelles	Don't Cry My Soldier Boy	1962	King 5597
Soldier Boys	I'm Your Soldier Boy	1962	Scepter 1230
Montells	Soldier Boy, I'm Sorry	1963	Golden Crest 582
Chiffons	Sailor Boy	1964	Laurie 3262
Kisses (Candy & the)	Soldier Baby (Of Mine)	1965	Cameo 355
Shirelles	(Mama) My Soldier Boy Is Coming Home	1965	Scepter 12123
Chantels	Soul Of A Soldier	1966	Verve 10387
Echoes	Soldier Boy	N/A	4 Hits EP 11
Marie, Elena (& group)	Soldier Boy	N/A	Gee Bee 01

Few people realize that doo-woppers were also amateur campanologists; that is, they loved bells of any sort. Especially favored in titles of songs were chapel bells, church bells, wedding bells (do we detect a trend?) and school bells. There are "The Bells Of St. Mary's" (by the Drifters, Lee Andrews & the Hearts and Tokens), "The Bells Of Rosa Rita" (Admirations), "The Bells Of Love" (Pearls, Mint Juleps, Terri & the Velveteens), "The Bells Of My Heart" (Fascinators), and "The Bells Of Joy" (Angelo & the Initials). The bells whisper (so say the Del Vikings and a slew of others), ring out (L'Cap-Tans and Van Dykes) and even whistle (School Belles). There are well over 100 songs with "Bells" in the title contained in the songography, and six appear in our Top 500 ("The Bells Of Rosa Rita" by the Admirations, "Whispering Bells" by the Del Vikings, "Lullaby Of The Bells" by the Deltairs, "Chapel Bells" by the Fascinators, "Wedding Bells" by Tiny Tim & the Hits and "Church Bells May Ring" by the Willows).

The doo-wop generation had a serious side as well. Many songs were written and sung about characters, real and fabled. Those who gravitated to doo-wop evidently had quite an interest in both American history and American literature. "Christopher Columbus" was recorded by the Paramounts, "George Washington" by the Toppers, "The Ballad Of Betsy Ross" by the Batchelors, "Paul Revere" and "The Ride Of Paul Revere" by the Furness Brothers and Terracetones, respectively (the American Revolution must have been a particular favorite), "Pony Express Riders" by Shadoe & the Highbrows and "A Prayer at Gettysburg" by the Velvitones. The works of the American novelist Washington Irving were celebrated by no less than five groups in "Rip Van Winkle" (Devotions, Nutmegs and Adventurers), and in "The Legend Of

Sleepy Hollow" (Monotones and Carnations). Herman Melville's "Billy Budd" was offered by the Montereys.

Other doo-wop groups took us on a tour of "recorded" history. "Adam And Eve" was offered by the Mystics, "The King Tut Rock" by Kenny & the Socialites, "Romeo And Juliet" by the Reflections and Starlets, "Cleopatra" by Bobby Sanders & the Performers, Precisions and Bobby Capri & the Velvet Satins, "Caesar Haircut" by Tammy James & group (the aforementioned six records may also imply a latent interest in Shakespeare), "Casanova" by Erlene & the Girlfriends and "Napoleon Bonaparte" by the Top Notes.

Detectives of the era were celebrated, as in "Mr. Moto" by Nino & the Ebbtides, "Charlie Chan" by the Eventuals and "Dick Tracy" by the Chants. Television shows and personalities were regaled in "Our Miss Brooks" by the Goofers, "Mr. Dillon, Mr. Dillon" by the Fiestas (the show was "Gunsmoke"), "Steve Allen" by the Emperors, "Clarabel" by Vince Anthony & the Bluenotes ("The Howdy Doody Show") and "Mister Magoo" by the Kodoks.

Teens of the fifties loved cowboys, monsters and comic strips, and all of these interests were well-reflected in song. There was "The Masked Man (Hi-Yo Silver)" by Eddy Bell & the Bell-Aires, "The Lone Stranger" by the Majestics and Del Counts, "Dodge City" and "Western Movies" by the Olympics, "Wyatt Earp" by the Marquees and "Billy The Kid" by the Raves. Monsters crept into "Dead Man's Stroll" by the Revels, "Frankenstein's Den" by the Hollywood Flames, "Frankenstein's Party" by the Swinging Phillies, "Miss Frankenstein" by George Jackson & the Uniques, "You Can Get Him-Frankenstein" by the Castle Kings, "The Mummy's Ball" by the Verdicts and "Screamin' At Dracula's Ball" by the Duponts. "Popeye" was performed by the Dreams and Enchantments and "Popeye The Sailor Man" by the Gaylads. "Superman Lover" was released by Andy & the Marglows, "Jungle Superman" by the Individuals and "He's My Superman" by the Sweethearts. The story of "Alley Oop" was recounted by Dante & the Evergreens, the Hollywood Argyles and the Dyna-Sores.

Perhaps reflecting the innocence of the times, nursery rhymes were also accorded inordinate attention by doo-wop lyricists. Old MacDonald, Humpty Dumpty, Mary Had A Little Lamb and Hickory Dickory Dock were favored subjects. Other songs that had nursery rhyme subjects, but not titles (such as "Little Star" by the Elegants, which is related to "Twinkle Twinkle Little Star" and "Great Big Eyes" by the Rivieras, which is derived from "Goldilocks") are not included in the following list.

Group Name	Song	Year	Label
Five Keys	Old MacDonald Had A Farm	1952	Aladdin 3118
Bradford Boys	Little Boy Blue	1955	Rainbow 307
Bonnie Sisters	Little Bo Peep	1956	Rainbow 336
Errico, Ray (with the Honeytones)	Humpty Dumpty Rock	1956	Masquerade 56003
Five Stars	Humpty Dumpty	1956	Atco 6065
Jumpin' Jacks (Danny Lamego & the)	Hickory Dickory Rock	1956	Andrea 101
Shaweez (Big Boy Myles & the)	Hickory Dickory Dock	1956	Specialty 590
Orlandos	Old MacDonald	1957	Cindy 3006
Chargers	Old MacDonald	1958	RCA 7301

Group Name	Song	Year	Label
Emperors	Nursery Rhyme	1958	3-J 121
Gems	Nursery Rhymes	1958	Win 701
Ricardos	Mary's Little Lamb	1958	Star-X 512
Schoolmates (Colleen & the)	Mairzy Doats	1958	Coral 62024
Bluedots	Mary Had A Rock 'N' Roll Lamb	1959	Hurricane 104
Elegants	Little Boy Blue	1959	Hull 732
Five Sparks	Little Bo Peep	1959	Jimbo 1
Ideals (Johnny Brantley & the)	Mary's Lamb	1959	Checker 920/Checker 979 (1961)
Isley Brothers	Rockin' MacDonald	1959	Mark-X 8000
Troupers	Peter, Peter, Pumpkin Eater	1959	Red Top 118
Lions	Hickory Dickory	1960	Imperial 5678
Magnatones	MacDonald's Rock	1960	Cedargrove 313/Time 108 (1960)
Emblems	Poor Humpty Dumpty	1962	Bay Front 107
Rock-A-Byes (Baby Jane & the)	Hickory Dickory Dock	1962	Spokane 4001
Selectones (Jay Jay & the)	Humpty Dumpty	1962	Guest 6201/6202
Aladdins	Simple Simon	1963	Witch 111
La Donna, Marie (& group)	Georgie Porgie	1963	Gateway 730
Nobletones	Rock And Roll Nursery Rhymes	1973	Vintage 1014
Kingsmen	Humpty Dumpty	N/A	Arnold 2106

Titles Made Up Of Nonsense Syllables

As discussed in an earlier chapter, nonsense syllables are central to the definition of doo-wop music. They usually occur in the background, serving to accentuate or punctuate the lyrics. Occasionally they become the focus of the song, as in "Mope-Itty Mope" by the Bossmen, "Rang Tang Ding Dong" by the Cellos or "Ala-Men-Sa-Aye" by the Quotations. They rarely *are* the lyrics, although exceptions can be found ("Rubber Biscuit" by the Chips and the "Vadunt-Un-Va-Da Song" by the Ramblers). One would think it noteworthy then, when nonsense syllables are chosen as the title of a song. And yet, in doo-wop, it happens so often that it is almost not remarkable, except for the fact that it *does* occur so often. By our count, there are roughly 400 doo-wop songs whose titles are composed of nonsense syllables alone. And that is not counting songs where there are real words anywhere in the title like "Oo-Wee Baby" by the Ivy-Tones or "Bong Bong (I Love You Madly)" by Vince Castro (with the Tonettes).

The tendency for titles to be made up entirely of nonsense syllables is not found to any degree in other musical eras; it is idiosyncratic to doo-wop. One can only speculate as to the motivation behind this practice. The popularity of songs like "Gee" by the Crows in 1953 (although the title is more exclamation than nonsense syllable) and "Sh-Boom" by the Chords in 1954 may have served as models. Groups may have hoped to imitate the success of these songs by using nonsensical titles. Also, since most of the titles consisting of nonsense syllables were up-tempo numbers, they may have been "throwaways," issued as the B-sides of ballads. In other cases advertising nonsense syllables was better than promoting the lyrics, which may have had little to recommend them. "Rama Lama Ding Dong" and "Zoom Zoom Zoom" were great songs, but certainly not because of their lyrics or any message they contained. The nonsense syllables overshadowed the lyrics and dominated the songs. Titles may also have been chosen this way to give a message such as "this music is for teenagers" or "if you are a teen, you'll like this record," thus helping to reach a certain market segment. These titles were also a fairly reliable predictor of the lyrics of a song, almost like "what you see is what you get."

To discuss the use of nonsense syllables in titles, we have grouped then into "families," the first of which is the "Ding Dong" family. These syllables may recall the discussion of bells earlier in this chapter. No fewer than 11 groups chose to put out records with the reductionist "Ding Dong" as a title. The most well-known of these was by the Echoes in 1957. It should be noted that wherever a "Ding" appears, a "Dong" is not far behind. The only exceptions that we could find were in "Ring A Ling A Ding" by Richie Thompson & the Jesters, "Ding-A-Ling-A-Ling" by the Troys and "Sha-Bee-Dah-Ah-Ding" by the Four Vanns.

The most successful record emanating from this family was "Rama Lama Ding Dong," a big hit for the Edsels in 1961. The song was released three years earlier as "Lama Rama Ding Dong" but it met with little success, perhaps implying that a slight change in the order of the nonsense syllables had a profound effect on its appeal. Another popular song from this group was "Ka Ding Dong" by the G-Clefs in 1956 (and covered by the Diamonds). A number of songs from this family have colorful titles: "Shang Lang A Ding Dong" by the Charades, "Shanga Langa Ding Dong" by the Cameos (note the subtle differences between the two titles), "Giddy-Up And Ding Dong" by the Continentals, "Giddy-Up-A-Ding-Dong" by the Playmates, "Ding Ding Dong" by the Jivetones (the extra "Ding" was no doubt for emphasis), "Ding Dong Doo" by the Frontiers and the infamous "Ding-A-Ling-Ling Ding Dong" by Dicky Dell & the Bing Bongs.

The second family is made up of a couple of "Ch-" sounds, namely "Ching" and "Chop." There is one song that does contain both, "Chop, Chop, Ching-A-Ling" by the Roamers, but as a rule they are found separately. There is "Ching Ching" by Gloria Wood & the Afterbeats, "Ching Chong" by the Pips, "Ching-A-Ling" by the Accents, "Ching-A-Ling Baby" by the Rocky Fellers and "Ching Bam Bah" by the Velveteens (which sounds as if it should taste good). As for the "Chops," there is "Chop Chop" by Ferris & the Wheels and the Chimes, "Chop Chop Chop" by the Candy Makers, "Chop Chop Boom" by the Dandeliers and the Savoys and "Chickie Chop Chop" by the Flints and the Newports.

Led by "Sh-Boom," the "Boom" family is a colorful one. The names of the songs just kind of roll off the tongue. Besides "Sh-Boom," others to achieve notoriety were "Bim Bam Boom" by the El Dorados in 1956 and "Shtiggy Boom" by Patti Anne (Mesner with the Flames) in 1955. A more complete list, alphabetized by title, follows.

Group Name	Song	Year	Label
El Dorados	Bim Bam Boom	1956	Vee Jay 211
Cardinals	Bim Bam Boom	N/A	Atlantic EP only
Hearts	Boom	1959	United Artists 162
(Lee Andrews & the)			
Fascinations	Boom Bada Boom	1960	Sure 106
Barons	Boom Boom	1955	Imperial 5343
Five Keys	Boom Boom	1957	Capitol 3786
Jiveleers	Boom Chic-A-Boom	1960	Cousins 1/2
Starlites	Boom Chica Boom	1957	Ember 1021
(Kenny Esquire & the)			
Creslyns	Boom Chip-A-Boom	1963	Beltone 2036
Pastels	Boom De De Boom	1956	United 196
El Dorados	Boom Diddle Boom	1957	Vee Jay 263
Charms	Boom Diddy Boom Boom	1956	Chart 623
Love Bugs	Boom Diddy Wawa Baby	1955	Federal 12216
Cashmeres	Boom Mag-Azeno Vip Vay	1955	Mercury 70617
Astro Jets	Boom-A-Lay	1961	Imperial 5760
Tidal Waves	Booma Shooma Rock	1961	Tide 0020
Storey Sisters	Cha Cha Boom	1958	Baton 255
Del-Rhythmetts	Chic-A-Boomer	1958	J-V-B 5000
Danderliers	Chop Chop Boom	1955	States 147/B&F 1344 (61)
Savoys	Chop Chop Boom	1955	Combo 90
Tokays	Fatty-Boom Bi Laddy	1952	Bonnie 102
Gadabouts	Go Boom Boom	1955	Mercury 70581
Jaye Sisters	Pitter Patter Boom Boom	1958	Atlantic 1171
Four Blues	Re Bop-De-Boom	1950	Apollo 1145
Thunderbirds	Rock Boom Boom	1955	G.G. 518
Chords	Sh-Boom	1954	Cat 104
Sh-Booms	Sh-Boom	1961	Atco 6213
Popular Five	Sh-Boom	1967	Rae-Cox 1001
Crowns	Sh-Boom	N/A	Dig 149 (unreleased)
(Arthur Lee Maye & the)			
Sapphires	Sh-Boom	N/A	Ravin' 100
Decades	Sha-Boom Bang	1962	Ramco 3725
(Brother Zee & the)			
Creators	Shoom Ba Boom	1963	Philips 40060
Houston, Joe	Shtiggy Boom	1955	RPM 426
(& group)			
Nuggets	Shtiggy Boom	1955	Capitol 3052
Patti Anne	Shtiggy Boom	1955	Aladdin 3280
(Mesner with the Flames)			
Castells	Stiki De Boom Boom	1961	Era 3064
Dories	Stompin' Sh-Boom	1962	Dore 629
Savoys	Yacka Hoom Boom	1955	Combo 75
Supremes	Zip Boom	1985	Murray Hill LP 000083
Cadillacs	Zoom Boom Zing	1959	Jubilee LP 1089

One can find the syllable "La" present in a title anywhere from two to five times. There are two "La's" in "La La" by the Cobras (a minor hit and on our Top 500) and the Five Knights, "Ooh-La-La" by Skip & the Echotones and the Hollywood Flames, "Oo La La" by Dave Joseph (& group), "Ooh La La" by Bobby Long & His Cherrios, "Tra-La-La" by the Majors and "Sha La La" by the Prophets and the Shirelles. There are three in "La La La" by the Co-Eds and the Deltones, four in "Tra La La La La" by the Viriations and five in "La La La La La" by the Blendells.

Several other families of nonsense syllables, namely the "Z" and "Y" families, tend to be alliterative. The "Z" family is quite prolific because of all the "Zooms," either singly ("Zoom" by the Cadillacs, et al.) or in triplets ("Zoom Zoom Zoom" by the Collegians et al.). A complete list, alphabetized by title follows.

Group Name	Song	Year	Label
Diamond, Ronnie (& group)	Zig Zag	1958	Imperial 5554
Counts (Bobby Comstock & the)	Zig Zag	1959	Triumph 602
Del-Rays (Detroit Jr. & the)	Zig Zag	1964	CJ 636
G-Clefs	Zing Zang Zoo	1957	Paris 506
Dells	Zing Zing Zing	1955	Vee Jay 166
Pitch Pikes	Zing Zong	1957	Mercury 71099
Commodores (Darrell Glenn & the)	Zinga-Zingo	1957	RPM 488
Diamonds	Zip Zip	1957	Mercury 71165
Jivetones	Zip Zip	N/A	Apt (unreleased)
Empires	Zippety Zip	1957	Amp-3 132
Pearls	Zippety Zippety Zoom	1956	Onyx 503
Chords	Zippety Zum	1954	Cat 109
Cadillacs	Zoom	1956	Josie 792
Historians (Barbaroso & the)	Zoom	1957	Jade 110
Cuff Linx	Zoom	1958	Dooto 438
Starlighters	Zoom	1960	Hi-Q 5016
Unique Echos	Zoom	1961	Southern Sound 108
Crescents	Zoom	1985	Relic LP 5053
Heartspinners (Dino & the)	Zoom	N/A	Robin Hood 141
Cadillacs	Zoom Boom Zing	1954	Josie 759 (unreleased)
Collegians	Zoom Zoom Zoom	1957	Winley 224
Dreamlovers	Zoom Zoom Zoom	1961	Heritage 107
Enchords	Zoom Zoom Zoom	1961	Laurie 3089
Craftys	Zoom Zoom Zoom	1962	Elmor 310
Schaefer, Freddy (& group)	Zoom Zoom Zoom	1962	King 5621
Reminiscents	Zoom Zoom Zoom	1963	Day 1000
Charts	Zoop	1957	Everlast 5001/ Everlast 5026 (63)/ Lost Nite 173 (1981)
Delstars	Zoop Bop	1964	Mellomood 1001
Keynotes	Zup Zup	1956	Apollo 498

If the question "Y" is asked, the answer is "Ya Ya" by Frankie Gee (& group), the Revlons, Shepherd Sisters and Videls, "Yum Yum" by the La Salles, Lamplighters and Swinging Earls, "Yum Yummy" by the Pearls, "Yo Yo Yo Yo Yo" by Little Caesar & the Romans, "Yibby-Yah" by the Caprisians, "Yodee Yakee" by the Drifters, "Yadi-Yadi-Yum-Dum" by the Rivingtons and, of course, "Yakity Yak" by the Coasters and Markeys.

The "Ting-A-Ling" family recalls the "Ding Dong" family, with bells coming to mind again. And just as "Ding" begets "Dong," so does "Ting" beget "A-Ling" in some form or other. The only exception extant was "Ting Tang Tagalu" by Jerry McCain (& group). Basic members of this group include "Ting-A-Ling" by the Clovers, Poka-Dotts and Nicky & the Nobles. Suffixes were added to arrive at "Ting Aling Ting Toy" by Lenny Dell & the Demensions (take note of the absence of hyphens), and "Ting-A-Ling-Ling" by the Sweethearts. Prefixes were appended to get "Ring-A-Ting-A-Ling" by the Creations, "Ring Ting-A-Ling" by the Dials, "A-Ting-A-Ling" by the Metrotones and the mellifluous "Ring Dang Doo Ting A Ling" by the Bell Hops.

Oddly enough, there aren't many titles related to the name of the genre, i.e. doo-wop. There is a "Du Wap" by the Chimes, a "Du Whop" by the Chessmen, a "Do Whop-A-Do" by the Five Daps and a "Shu-Wop" (originally called "New Way") by the Dandeliers. Close, but no cigar. "Doo-Wop" is, however, one of the most commonly used nonsense syllables (it is really bi-syllabic), even if it does not appear in song titles. If the title alone was the criterion, the name "Ding Dong Music" or "Boom Zoom Music" might have been more appropriate.

There are hundreds of other titles that are composed entirely of nonsense syllables that were not included in our discussion. The way groups chose their titles, as well as the way that they chose their names, songs and the subjects of these songs make doo-wop music fascinating to study and very easy to enjoy.

Appendix I

The Best 500 Doo-Wop Songs

The list that follows represents our choices of the 500 best songs of the doo-wop era. Note that there are several qualifications. First, songs released after 1965 are excluded from the list. This leaves out well-known songs such as "Morse Code Of Love" by the Capris and "ForThe Longest Time" by Billy Joel (and group), as well as some less well-known ones such as "I'm In Love" by Arthur Lee Maye & the Crowns and "She's An Angel" by the Dahills. These later songs (recidivist doo-wop?) will be reviewed for a subsequent edition. Also excluded are songs that were released on albums only, such as "Double Dealin' Baby" by the Souvenirs, "Pretty Face" by the Hi-Lites and "House Of Love" by Henry Hall & the 5 Bell Aires.

Only one version of any given song is included, and usually the one included is by the group that released it first. Thus cover, copy and even remake versions of songs are not on this list. Some exceptions are that there are two versions of "Sunday Kind Of Love" (one slow and one fast), and the Velvetones version of "Glory Of Love" was preferred over the one done by the Five Keys because the former became a doo-wop "standard."

Abbreviations:

C= Classical Doo-Wop Era	N= Neo-Doo-Wop Era	P= Paleo-Doo-Wop Era
S= Slow Tempo	M= Medium Tempo	F= Fast Tempo
D= Distaff Doo-Wop	I= Italo-Doo-Wop	G= Gang Doo-Wop
SB= Schoolboy Doo-Wop	POP= Pop Doo-Wop	TPA= Tin Pan Alley Doo-Wop
NOV= Novelty Song		

Patti LaBelle & The Blue Belles

The Blue Notes

GROUP	SONG	ERA	T	SUB	YR
Admirations	The Bells Of Rosa Rita	C	S		59
Alaimo, Chuck (Chuck Alaimo Quart.)	How I Love You	C	S		57
Angels	Til	N	S	D/TPA	61
Angels	My Boyfriend's Back	N	F	D	63
Angels (Gabriel & the)	Zing Went The Strings Of My Heart	N	F		61
Aquatones	You	C	S		58
Astros (Pepe & the)	Judy My Love (Judy Mi Amor)	N	F		61
Avons	Baby	C	S		57
Baltineers	Moments Like This	P	S		56
Bel-Larks	A Million And One Dreams	N	S		63
Bell Notes	I've Had It	C	F	I	59
Belmonts	Diddle-De-Dum	N	F	I	62
Belmonts (Dion & the)	I Wonder Why	C	F	I	58
Belmonts (Dion & the)	No One Knows	C	S	I	58
Belmonts (Dion & the)	Don't Pity Me	C	S	I	58
Belmonts (Dion & the)	A Teenager In Love	C	F	I	59
Belmonts (Dion & the)	Where Or When	C	S	I	60
Belvin, Jesse (& group)	Goodnight My Love	C	S		56
Blue Belles (Patti LaBelle & the)	You'll Never Walk Alone	N	S	D	63
Blue Jays	Lover's Island	N	S		61
Blue Jays	Let's Make Love	N	S		61
Blue Jeans (Bob B. Soxx & the)	Why Do Lovers Break Each Others Hearts	N	F	D/TPA	63
Blue Notes	If You Love Me	N	S		56
Blue Notes	My Hero	N	S		60
Blue Notes	Blue Star	N	S		61
Bobbettes	Mr. Lee	C	F	D	57
Bonnevilles	Lorraine	C	S		60
Bonnevilles	Zu Zu	C	S		60
Bop Chords	I Really Love You	C	F	G	57
Bop Chords	Castle In The Sky	C	F	G	57
Bop Chords	So Why	C	F	G	57
Bop Chords	When I Woke Up This Morning	C	F	G	57
Bosstones	Mope-Itty Mope	N	F	NOV	59
C-Notes (aka C-Tones)	On Your Mark	C	F		57
Cadillacs	Gloria	P	S		54
Cadillacs	Speedoo	P	F		55
Cadillacs	Down The Road	P	F		55
Cadillacs	Zoom	P	F		56
Cadillacs	You Are	P	S		56
Cadillacs	My Girl Friend	P	F		57
Camelots (aka Cupids/aka Harps)	Don't Leave Me Baby	C	F		64
Candles (Rochell & the)	Once Upon A Time	N	S		60
Capris	There's A Moon Out Tonight	N	S	I	58
Carallons (Lonnie & the)	Chapel Of Tears	N	S		60
Carnations (aka Startones)	Long Tall Girl	C	F		61

GROUP	SONG	ERA	T	SUB	YR
Carousels	You Can Come (If You Want To)	N	S		61
Caslons	Anniversary Of Love	N	F		61
Castelles	My Girl Awaits Me	P	S		53
Castelles	Do You Remember	P	S		54
Castelles	Over A Cup Of Coffee	P	S		54
Castells	So This Is Love	N	S	POP	62
Castro, Vince (with the Tonettes)	Bong Bong (I Love You Madly)	C	F		58
Castroes	Dearest Darling	C	S		59
Cavaliers	Dance Dance Dance	C	F		58
Cavaliers	The Magic Age Of Sixteen	N	S		63
Cellos	Rang Tang Ding Dong	C	F	NOV	57
Chalets	Fat Fat Fat Mommio	C	F		61
Chandeliers (aka Chandeliers Quintet)	Blueberry Sweet	C	F		58
Chandler, Gene (with the Dukays)	Duke Of Earl	N	M		61
Channels (Earl Lewis & the)	The Closer You Are	C	S	G	56
Channels (Earl Lewis & the)	The Gleam In Your Eyes	C	S	G	56
Channels (Earl Lewis & the)	That's My Desire	C	S	G	57
Channels (Earl Lewis & the)	Bye Bye Baby	C	F	G	57
Channels (Earl Lewis & the)	My Love Will Never Die	C	S	G	57
Chantels	He's Gone	C	S	D	57
Chantels	Maybe	C	S	D	58
Chantels	Look In My Eyes	C	S		61
Chanters	No No No	C	F	SB	58
Chaperones	Cruise To The Moon	N	S	I	60
Chariots	Gloria	C	S		59
Charles, Jimmy (with the Revelettes)	A Million To One	N	S		60
Charts	Dance Girl	C	F	G	57
Charts	Zoop	C	F	G	57
Charts	Desiree	C	S	G	57
Chesters	The Fires Burn No More	C	S		58
Chestnuts	Love Is True	C	S		56
Chevrons	Lullabye	C	F		59
Chex (Tex & the)	I Do Love You	N	S		61
Chiffons	He's So Fine	N	F	D/TPA	63
Chiffons	One Fine Day	N	F	D/TPA	63
Chiffons	I Have A Boyfriend	N	F	D/TPA	63
Chimes	Once In A While	N	S	POP/I	60
Chimes	I'm In The Mood For Love	N	S	POP/I	61
Chips	Rubber Biscuit	C	F		56
Chords	Sh-Boom	P	F		54
Classics	Till Then	N	S	I	63
Cleftones	Can't We Be Sweethearts?	C	F		56
Cleftones	Little Girl Of Mine	C	F		56
Cleftones	You Baby You	C	F		56
Cleftones	Why You Do Me Like You Do	C	F		57
Cleftones	See You Next Year	C	S		57

GROUP	SONG	ERA	T	SUB	YR
Cleftones	Heart And Soul	N	M		61
Click-Ettes	Lover's Prayer	N	S		60
Cliques	Girl In My Dreams	C	S		56
Clovers	One Mint Julep	P	F		52
Clovers	Blue Velvet	P	S		55
Clovers	Devil Or Angel	P	S		56
Clovers	Love Potion No. 9	C	F	NOV	59
Clusters	Darling Can't You Tell	C	F		58
Coasters	Searchin'	C	M		57
Coasters	Yakety Yak	C	F	NOV	58
Coasters	Charlie Brown	C	F	NOV	59
Cobras	La La	N	F		64
Collegians	Zoom Zoom Zoom	C	F	G	57
Collegians	Let's Go For A Ride	C	F	G	58
Contenders	The Clock	N	F		63
Continentals	Fine Fine Frame	C	F	G	56
Continentals	Picture of Love	C	F	G	56
Continentals	Dear Lord	C	S	G	56

The Corsairs

The Crests

GROUP	SONG	ERA	T	SUB	YR
Cookies	Chains	N	F	D	62
Cookies	Don't Say Nothin' Bad (About My Baby)	N	F	D	63
Cordovans	Come On Baby	C	F	SB	60
Corsairs	Smoky Places	N	M		61
Corvairs	True True Love	N	F		62
Crescendos	Oh Julie	C	S		57
Crescents	Everybody Knew But Me	C	S		57
Crests	No One To Love	C	S		57
Crests	Sweetest One	C	S		57
Crests	My Juanita	N	F		57
Crests	Sixteen Candles	C	S		58
Crests	The Angels Listened In	C	F		59
Crests	Step By Step	N	F		60
Criterions (Tygh & the)	To Be Mine	C	S		63
Crows	Gee	P	F		54
Crows	I Love You So	P	S		54
Crystals	There's No Other (Like My Baby)	N	S	D/TPA	61
Crystals	Da Doo Ron Ron	N	F	D/TPA	63
Cuff Links	Guided Missles	C	S		57
Cupids	Brenda	N	S		63
Danleers	One Summer Night	C	S		58
Darchaes (Ray & the)	Carol	N	S		62
Debonaires	Darling	C	F		57
Debonaires	We'll Wait	N	S		60
Del Vikings	Come Go With Me	C	F		57
Del Vikings	Whispering Bells	C	F		57
Del Vikings	Sunday Kind Of Love	C	F		57
Dells	Oh What A Night	C	S		56
Delrons (Reperata & the)	Whenever A Teenager Cries	N	S	D	64
Delroys	Bermuda Shorts	C	F	NOV	57
Deltairs	Lullabye Of The Bells	C	S		57
Deltas	Lamplight	C	F		57
Demensions	Over The Rainbow	N	S		62
Demilles (feat. Carlo Mastrangelo)	Donna Lee	N	F	I	64
Desires	Hey, Lena	C	F	SB	59
Desires	Let It Please Be You	C	S	SB	59
Desires	I Wanna Rendezvous With You	C	F	SB	60
Devotions	Rip Van Winkle	N	F	NOV	61
Diablos	The Wind	P	S		54
Dimples (Eddie Cooley & the)	Priscilla	C	F		56
DiMucci, Dion (with the Del Satins)	Runaround Sue	N	F	I	61
DiMucci, Dion (with the Del Satins)	Lovers Who Wander	N	F	I	62
Dorn, Jerry (with the Hurricanes)	Wishing Well	P	S		56
Dovers (Miriam Grate & the)	Sweet As A Flower	C	S		59

GROUP	SONG	ERA	T	SUB	YR
Dreamlovers	When We Get Married	N	S		61
Drifters	Money Honey	P	F		53
Drifters	Honey Love	P	F		54
Drifters	Adorable	P	S		55
Drifters	Ruby Baby	P	F		56
Drifters	There Goes My Baby	N	M		59
Drifters	This Magic Moment	N	M		60
Drifters	Save The Last Dance For Me	N	M	TPA	60
Du Mauriers	All Night Long	C	F		57
Dubs	Don't Ask Me To Be Lonely	C	S		57
Dubs	Could This Be Magic	C	S		57
Dubs	Chapel Of Dreams	C	S		59
Duprees	My Own True Love	N	S	POP	62
Duprees	You Belong To Me	N	S	POP	62
Duprees	Why Don't You Believe Me	N	S	POP	63
Earls	Life Is But A Dream	N	F	I	61

The Echoes

The Edsels

GROUP	SONG	ERA	T	SUB	YR
Earls	Lookin' For My Baby	N	F	I	61
Earls	Remember Then	N	F	I	62
Earls	Eyes	N	F	I	63
Earls	I Believe	N	S	I	64
Ebb Tides (Nino &)	Jukebox Saturday Night	N	F	I	61
Echoes	Baby Blue	N	F	POP	61
Edsels	What Brought Us Together	N	S		60
Edsels	Rama Lama Ding Dong	C	F		61
Edsels	Shake Shake Sherry	N	F		61
El Domingoes	Lucky Me, I'm In Love	N	F		62
El Dorados	At My Front Door	C	F		55
El Dorados	I'll Be Forever Loving You	C	F		55
El Dorados	Bim Bam Boom	C	F		56
Elchords	Peppermint Stick	C	F	SB	57
Elegants	Little Star	C	M	I	58
Emotions	Echo	N	M	I	62
Encounters	Don't Stop Now	N	F		64
Essentials (Billy & the)	Maybe You'll Be There	N	F		62
Eternals	Babalu's Wedding Day	C	F	NOV	59
Eternals	Rockin' In The Jungle	C	F	NOV	59
Evergreens (Dante &)	Alley Oop	N	F	NOV	60
Excellents	Coney Island Baby	N	S		62
Extremes	Come Next Spring	C	S		58
Fabulaires	While Walking	C	F		57
Fabulous Twilights (N. Mayer & the)	Village Of Love	N	F		62
Falcons	You're So Fine	C	F		59
Fascinators	Chapel Bells	C	S	I	58
Fascinators	Oh Rose Marie	C	F	I	59
Feathers	Johnny Darling	P	S		54
Fi-Dells	What Is Love	N	S		61
Fi-Tones	My Faith	C	S		57
Fidelitys	The Things I Love	C	S		58
Fiestas	So Fine	C	F		58
Fireflies	You Were Mine	N	S		59
Fireflies	I Can't Say Goodbye	C	S		59
Five Discs	I Remember	C	F	I	58
Five Discs	Never Let You Go	N	F	I	61
Five Keys	Glory Of Love	P	S		51
Five Keys	Ling Ting Tong	P	F		54
Five Keys	Out Of Sight, Out Of Mind	P	S		56
Five Keys	Wisdom Of A Fool	P	S		56
Five Satins	In The Still Of The Night	C	S		56
Five Satins	Wonderful Girl	C	S		56
Five Satins	To The Aisle	C	S		57
Five Satins	Oh Happy Day	C	S		57
Five Sharps	Stormy Weather	P	S		52
Flamingos	Golden Teardrops	P	S		53
Flamingos	I'll Be Home	P	S		56
Flamingos	A Kiss From Your Lips	P	S		56

GROUP	SONG	ERA	T	SUB	YR
Flamingos	Lovers Never Say Goodbye	C	S		58
Flamingos	I Only Have Eyes For You	C	S		59
Fleetwoods	Mr. Blue	N	M	POP	59
Fleetwoods	Come Softly To Me	N	M	POP	59
Flips (Little Joey & the)	Bongo Stomp	N	F		62
Four Dots (Jerry Stone & the)	Pleading For Your Love	C	S		59
Four Fellows	Soldier Boy	P	S		55
Four Haven Knights	In My Lonely Room	C	F		56
Four J's	Here I Am Broken Hearted	N	F		64
G-Clefs	'Cause You're Mine	C	F		56
G-Clefs	Ka Ding Dong	C	F		56
G-Clefs	Symbol Of Love	C	S		57
Gaytunes	I Love You	C	S		57
Gaytunes	Plea In The Moonlight	C	F		58
Genies	Who's That Knockin'	C	F		59
Gladiolas	Little Darlin'	C	F		57
Halos	Nag	N	F		61
Harmonaires	Lorraine	C	S		57
Harptones	Sunday Kind Of Love	P	S		53
Harptones	Life Is But A Dream	P	S		54
Harptones	My Memories Of You	P	S		54
Harptones	On Sunday Afternoon	P	S		56
Harptones	Three Wishes	P	S		56
Harptones	That's The Way It Goes	P	S		56
Harris, Thurston (with the Sharps)	Little Bitty Pretty One	C	F		57
Heartbeats	A Thousand Miles Away	C	S		56

The G-Clefs

The Hollywood Flames

GROUP	SONG	ERA	T	SUB	YR
Heartbeats	Crazy For You	C	S		56
Heartbeats	People Are Talking	C	S		56
Heartbeats	Your Way	C	S		56
Heartbeats	Darling How Long	C	S		56
Hearts (Lee Andrews & the)	Long Lonely Nights	P	S		57
Hearts (Lee Andrews & the)	Teardrops	P	S		57
Hearts (Lee Andrews & the)	Why Do I	P	S		58
Hearts (Lee Andrews & the)	Try The Impossible	P	S		58
Hearts (Lee Andrews & the)	I'm Sorry Pillow	P	S		63
Hemlocks (Little Bobby Rivera & the)	Cora Lee	C	F	SB	57
Hi-Fives	Dorothy	C	F		58
Hi-Lites (Ronnie & the)	I Wish That We Were Married	N	S		62
Hide-A-Ways	Can't Help Loving That Girl Of Mine	P	S		54
Highlands	I Laughed	N	F		61
Hits (Tiny Tim & the)	Wedding Bells	C	S		58
Hollywood Flames	Buzz Buzz Buzz	C	F		57
Imaginations	Hey You	N	S		61
Impalas	Sorry, I Ran All The Way Home	C	F		59
Imperials (Little Anthony & the)	Two People In The World	C	S	SB	58

Danny & The Juniors

The Kac-Ties

GROUP	SONG	ERA	T	SUB	YR
Imperials (Little Anthony & the)	Tears On My Pillow	C	S	SB	58
Imperials (Little Anthony & the)	When You Wish Upon A Star	C	S		59
Imperials (Little Anthony & the)	Traveling Stranger	C	F		61
Impressions (Jerry Butler & the)	For Your Precious Love	N	S		58
Ivy-Tones	Oo-Wee Baby	C	F		58
Jacks	Why Don't You Write Me	P	S		55
Jaguars	The Way You Look Tonight	P	S	POP	56
Jamies	Summertime	C	F		58
Jayhawks	Stranded In the Jungle	C	F	NOV	56
Jaytones	Oh Darling	C	F		58
Jelly Beans	I Wanna Love Him So Bad	N	F	D/TPA	64
Jesters	I'm Falling In Love	C	F	G	57
Jesters	So Strange	C	S	G	57
Jesters	Please Let Me Love You	C	S	G	57
Jesters	I Laughed	C	F	G	58
Jesters	Oh Baby	C	F	G	58
Jewels	Hearts Of Stone	P	F		54
Jive Five	My True Story	N	S		61
Jive Five	What Time Is It	N	S		62
Juniors (Danny & the)	Sometimes When I'm All Alone	C	S		57
Juniors (Danny & the)	At The Hop	C	F	I	57
Juniors (Danny & the)	Rock and Roll Is Here To Stay	C	F	I	57
Kac-Ties	Happy Birthday	C	S		65

The Kodoks (Kodaks)

The Laddins

GROUP	SONG	ERA	T	SUB	YR
Keytones	Seven Wonders Of The World	C	S		57
Knight, Bob (The Bob Knight Four)	Good Goodbye	C	S		61
Knockouts	Darling Lorraine	C	S		59
Kodaks (aka Kodoks)	Little Boy and Girl	C	F	SB	57
Kodaks (aka Kodoks)	Oh Gee Oh Gosh	C	F	SB	57
Kodaks (aka Kodoks)	Teenager's Dream	C	S	SB	57
Kodaks (aka Kodoks)	Runaround Baby	C	F	SB	60
Kuf-Linx	So Tough	C	F	G	58
Ladders	Counting The Stars	C	F		57
Laddins	Did It	C	F		57
Laddins	Yes, Oh Baby Yes	C	F		59
Larks	Darlin'	P	S		52
Larks (with Don Julian)	There Is A Girl	N	F		61
Lee, Curtis (with the Halos)	Pretty Little Angel Eyes	N	F		61
Legends	I'll Never Fall In Love Again	C	F		57
Limelites (Shep & the)	Daddy's Home	C	S		61
Limelites (Shep & the)	Three Steps To The Altar	C	S		62
Love Notes	Tonight	C	F		57
Love Notes	United	C	S	G	57
Ly-Dells	Wizard of Love	N	F		61
Lyrics	Let's Be Sweethearts Again	N	S		61
Magnificent Four	The Closer You Are	N	F		61
Magnificents	Up On The Mountain	P	F		56
Magnificents	Don't Leave Me	C	F		58
Majors	A Wonderful Dream	N	F		62
Marcels	Blue Moon	N	F		61
Marcels	Heartaches	N	F		61
Marcels	Goodbye To Love	N	S		61
Marquis	Bohemian Daddy	C	F		56
Marvelettes	Forever	N	S	D	63
Matadors	Vengeance (Will Be Mine)	C	S	G	58
Meadowlarks (Don Julian & the)	Heaven And Paradise	P	S		55
Meadowlarks (Don Julian & the)	Always And Always	P	S		55
Meadowlarks (Don Julian & the)	This Must Be Paradise	C	S		55
Medallions (Vernon Green & the)	Buick '59	P	F		54
Mello-Kings	Tonight Tonight	C	S		57
Mello-Moods	How Could You	P	S		52
Mellows (Lillian Leach & the)	Smoke From Your Cigarette	P	S		55
Metronomes	I Love My Girl	C	S		57
Monarchs	Always Be Faithful	C	F		56
Monarchs	Pretty Little Girl	C	F		56
Moniques	I'm With You All The Way	C	F		63
Monotones	Book Of Love	C	F		58
Moonglows	Secret Love	P	S		54
Moonglows	Sincerely	P	S		54
Moonglows	Most Of All	P	S		55
Moonglows	In My Diary	P	S		55
Moonglows	Seesaw	P	F		56
Moonglows	We Go Together	P	S		56

GROUP	SONG	ERA	T	SUB	YR
Moonglows (Harvey & the)	Ten Commandments Of Love	C	S		58
Mystics	Hushabye	C	M	I	59
Mystics	White Cliffs Of Dover	C	F	I	60
Native Boys	Strange Love	C	F		56
Nobles (Nicky & the)	Poor Rock & Roll	C	F	I	58
Nutmegs	Story Untold	C	S		55
Nutmegs	Ship Of Love	C	S		55
Nutmegs	Shifting Sands	C	F		57
Nutmegs	Let Me Tell You	C	F		63
Olympics	Dance By the Light Of The Moon	N	F	POP	60
Opals	Come To Me Darling	P	S		54
Orients	Queen Of The Angels	N	S	SB	64
Orioles	It's Too Soon To Know	P	S		48
Orioles	What Are You Doing New Year's Eve	P	S		49
Orioles	Crying In The Chapel	P	S		53

The Monotones

The Passions

142

GROUP	SONG	ERA	T	SUB	YR
Oxfords (Darryl & the)	Picture In My Wallet	N	S	TPA	59
Paradons	Diamonds And Pearls	N	S		60
Paragons	Hey, Little School Girl	C	F	G	57
Paragons	Stick With Me Baby	C	F	G	57
Paragons	Florence	C	S	G	57
Paragons	Let's Start All Over Again	C	S	G	57
Passions	Just To Be With You	C	S	I	59
Passions	I Only Want You	C	F	I	60
Pastels	Been So Long	P	58		58
Pearls	Let's You And I Go Steady	C	F		56
Penguins	Hey Senorita	P	F		54
Penguins	Earth Angel	P	S		54
Pentagons	To Be Loved (Forever)	N	S		60
Perfections	Hey Girl	C	F		59
Personalities	Woe Woe Baby	C	F		57
Phillips, Phil (with the Twilights)	Sea Of Love	N	S		59
Pixies Three	Birthday Party	N	F	D	63
Pixies Three	442 Glenwood Avenue	N	F	D	63
Platters	Only You (And You Alone)	P	S	POP	55
Platters	The Great Pretender	P	S	POP	55
Platters	My Prayer	P	S	POP	56
Platters	My Dream	P	S	POP	57
Platters	Smoke Gets In Your Eyes	P	S	POP	58
Platters	Twilight Time	P	S	POP	58
Ponitails	Born Too Late	C	S	D	58
Precisions	Eight Reasons Why (I Love You)	N	S		62
Pyramids	Hot Dog Dooly Wah	C	F		58

Randy & The Rainbows

The Rays

GROUP	SONG	ERA	T	SUB	YR
Pyramids	Ankle Bracelet	C	S		58
Queens (Shirley Gunter & the)	Oop-Shoop	P	F	D	54
Queens (Shirley Gunter & the)	You're Mine	P	F	D	55
Quin-Tones	Down The Aisle Of Love	C	S		58
Quinns	Hong Kong	C	F		58
Quinns	Oh Starlight	C	S		58
Quotations	Imagination	N	F		61
Quotations	Ala-Men-Sa-Aye	N	F		61
Rainbows (Randy & the)	Denise	N	F	I/TPA	63
Raindrops	The Kind Of Boy You Can't Forget	N	F	TPA	63
Ramblers	Vadunt-Un-Va-Da Song	P	S		54
Rays	Silhouettes	C	S		57
Re-Vels	False Alarm	C	F		58
Reflections	(Just Like) Romeo & Juliet	N	F		64
Regents	Barbara Ann	N	F	I	61
Regents	Runaround	N	F	I	61
Rivera, Lucy (& group)	Make Me Queen Again	N	S		59
Rivieras	Count Every Star	N	S		58
Rivileers	A Thousand Stars	P	S		54
Rivingtons	Papa Oom-Mow-Mow	N	F	NOV	62
Rob Roys (Norman Fox & the)	Tell Me Why	C	F		57
Rob Roys (Norman Fox & the)	Dream Girl	C	S		58
Rob Roys (Norman Fox & the)	Dance Girl Dance	C	F		58
Robins	Smoky Joe's Cafe	P	F	NOV	55
Rocketones	Mexico	C	F		57
Rockin' Chairs (Lenny Dean & the)	A Kiss Is A Kiss	C	F		59
Rockin' Chairs (Lenny Dean & the)	Memories Of Love	C	F		59
Romans (Little Caesar & the)	Those Oldies But Goodies	N	S		61
Roomates	Band Of Gold	N	S		61
Roomates (Cathy Jean & the)	Please Love Me Forever	N	S		60
Rosebuds	Dearest Darling	C	S	D	57
Roulettes	I See A Star	C	S		58
Royal Teens	Believe Me	C	F	I/POP	59
Safaris	Image Of A Girl	C	S	I	60
Salutations (Vito & the)	Unchained Melody	N	F	I	63
Scarlets	Dear One	P	S		54
Scarlets	Love Doll	C	S		55
Schoolboys	Shirley	C	F	SB	57
Schoolboys	Please Say You Want Me	C	S	SB	57
Schoolboys	Angel Of Love	C	S	SB	58
Selections	Guardian Angel	C	F	I	58
Senors	May I Have This Dance	N	M	SB	62
Sensations	Please Mr. Disc Jockey	P	S		56
Sensations	My Debut To Love	P	S		57
Sensations	Let Me In	N	F		61
Shells	Baby Oh Baby	C	S		60
Sheppards	Island Of Love	C	S		59

144

GROUP	SONG	ERA	T	SUB	YR
Shields	You Cheated	C	S		58
Shirelles	I Met Him On A Sunday	C	F	D	58
Shirelles	Dedicated To The One I Love	N	S	D	59
Shirelles	Will You Still Love Me Tomorrow?	N	M	D	60
Shirelles	Tonight's The Night	N	M	D	60
Shirelles	Baby It's You	N	S	D	61
Shirelles	Soldier Boy	N	S	D	62
Showmen	It Will Stand	N	F		61
Silhouettes	Get A Job	C	F		57
Silhouettes	Bing Bong	C	F		58
Silva-Tones	Chi Wa Wa (That's All I Want From You)	C	S		57
Six Teens	A Casual Look	C	S		56
Skyliners	It Happened Today	C	F	POP	59
Skyliners	Since I Don't Have You	N	S	POP	59
Skyliners	This I Swear	N	S	POP	59

The Shields

The Shells

GROUP	SONG	ERA	T	SUB	YR
Skyliners	Pennies From Heaven	C	F	POP	60
Solitaires	The Angels Sang	P	S		56
Solitaires	Walkin' Along	C	F		57
Sophomores (Anthony & the)	Embraceable You	C	S		61
Spaniels	Goodnight Sweetheart Goodnight	P	S		54
Spinners (Claudine Clark & the)	Party Lights	N	F		62
Squires	Dreamy Eyes	C	S		57
Stereos	I Really Love You	N	F		61
Students	Every Day Of The Week	C	F	SB	58
Students	I'm So Young	C	S	SB	58
Superiors	Lost Love	C	S		57
Supremes (Ruth McFadden & the)	Darling, Listen To The Words Of This Son	P	S		56
Techniques	Hey! Little Girl	C	S	POP	57
Teddy Bears	To Know Him Is To Love Him	C	S	TPA	58
Teenagers (Frankie Lymon & the)	I Want You To Be My Girl	C	F	SB	56
Teenagers (Frankie Lymon & the)	Why Do Fools Fall In Love	C	F	SB	56
Teenagers (Frankie Lymon & the)	Share	C	S	SB	56
Teenagers (Frankie Lymon & the)	I Promise To Remember	C	F	SB	56
Teenagers (Frankie Lymon & the)	Teenage Love	C	F	SB	57
Teenchords (Lewis Lymon & the)	I'm So Happy	C	F	SB	57
Teenchords (Lewis Lymon & the)	I'm Not Too Young To Fall In Love	C	F	SB	57
Teenchords (Lewis Lymon & the)	Please Tell The Angels	C	S	SB	57
Teenchords (Lewis Lymon & the)	Honey Honey	C	F	SB	57
Tempo-Tones (Nancy Lee & the)	So They Say	C	S		57
Tempo-Tones (with Richard Lanham)	Get Yourself Another Fool	C	S		57
Temptations	Barbara	C	F	POP	60
Three Chuckles (with Teddy Randazzo)	Runaround	P	S	POP	54
Three Chuckles (with Teddy Randazzo)	Foolishly	P	S	POP	55
Three Friends	Blanche	C	S	I/POP	56
Thrillers (Little Joe & the)	Peanuts	C	F	SB	57
Time-Tones (aka Timetones)	Here In My Heart	C	F		61
Timetones (aka Time-Tones)	Pretty Pretty Girl	C	F		61
Tokens	Tonight I Fell In Love	N	F	TPA	61
Tokens	The Lion Sleeps Tonight	N	M	TPA	61
Tonettes	Oh What A Baby	C	F	D	58
Tops (Little Jimmy Rivers & the)	Puppy Love	C	F	SB	61
Treble Chords	Theresa	C	F		59

GROUP	SONG	ERA	T	SUB	YR
Tremaines	Jingle Jingle	C	F		58
Tuneweavers	Happy Happy Birthday Baby	C	S		57
Turbans	When You Dance	C	F		55
Turbans	Congratulations	C	S		57
Tymes	So Much In Love	N	M	POP	63
Uniques	Do You Remember	N	S		59
Uniques	I'm So Unhappy	N	S		60
Universals	Again	C	S		57
Vacels (Ricky & the)	Lorraine	N	S		62
Val-Chords	Candy Store Love	C	F		57
Valentines	Woo Woo Train	C	F		55
Valentines	Nature's Creation	C	S		56
Vel-Tones	Now	C	F		60
Velours	Can I Come Over Tonight	C	S		57
Velvets	Tonight (Could Be The Night)	N	F		61
Videos	Trickle Trickle	C	F		58
Vocaleers	Be True	P	S		52
Vocaleers	Is It A Dream	P	S		52
Volumes	I Love You	N	F		62
Wheels	My Heart's Desire	C	S		56
Whirlers	Magic Mirror	C	S	G	56
Willows	Church Bells May Ring	C	F		56
Wrens	Come Back My Love	P	F		55
Zodiacs (Maurice Williams & the)	Stay	C	F		60

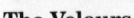

The Velours

The Wheels/Federals

Appendix II

Selected Non-mainstream Periodicals
That Deal With Doo-Wop
(courtesy of Robert Pruter)

Primarily Doo-Wop:

Name of Periodical	Location	Years Published	#Issues
Record Exchanger	Anaheim, CA	1969-1983	31
Stormy Weather	Brooklyn, NY later Oakland, CA	1970-1976	10
Bim Bam Boom	Bronx, NY	1971-1974	14
Big Town Review	Flushing, NY	1972	3
50s Revisited	Brooklyn, NY	1973	2
Remember Then	Brooklyn, NY	1974	2
Time Barrier Express	White Plains, NY later Yonkers, NY	1974-1980	27
Yesterday's Memories	New York, NY	1975-1977	12
Echoes Of The Past	New York, NY	1976-1977	4
Story Untold	Jackson Heights, NY later Maitland, FL	1977-1986	10
Harmony Tymes	Clifton, NJ	1980-1987	3
Record Collector's Monthly	Mendham, NJ	1982-	50
Echoes Of The Past	Agawam, MA	1987-	20

Not Primarily Doo-Wop, But With Good Coverage:

Name of Periodical	Location	Years Published	#Issues
Paul's Record Magazine	Hartford, CT	1975-1978	16
Goldmine	Frazier, MI later Iola, WI	1974-	310
Now Dig This	Tyne & Wear, England	1983-	107

Introduction to the Songography

One of the most difficult tasks in assembling a songography of doo-wop music, as we have defined it, lay in deciding which groups to include and which to leave out. These decisions were especially troublesome for groups singing at the beginning of the doo-wop era and for those singing at its end. Since we conceptualize the "doo-wop-ishness" of a song as on a continuum, we had to make some hard choices that are, in truth, arbitrary and open to question. Among the more prominent groups omitted from paleo-doo-wop, and thus from the songography, were the Five Royales. We judged them as being too allied with pure rhythm-and-blues. For similar reasons we eliminated much of the works of both the Dominoes and Ravens, although songs that are clearly doo-wop by these groups are included. For other paleo-doo-wop groups like the Five Keys and Orioles, all songs were included because enough of them contained enough doo-wop characteristics to sway us. We were able to acquire and listen to the songs of most of the groups from the paleo-doo-wop era and classify them experientially as "in" or "out". Occasionally, we made educated guesses to include/exclude, based on the song title, the record label or even the name of the group itself (e.g., if the name of the group ends in -tones, it is likely a doo-wop group). For example, the Five Echos (aka Five Echoes) were included without having heard them, primarily because they recorded for Vee Jay, a stalwart doo-wop label.

The same problem confronted us for the neo-doo-wop era. Groups excluded from our lists include the Four Seasons, Huey "Piano" Smith & the Clowns, Ruby & the Romantics and the Ronettes. The Four Seasons certainly demonstrated falsetto, the Clowns displayed traces of nonsense syllables, and the Romantics and Ronettes offer group harmony, but we felt that there was not enough doo-wop in enough of their works to warrant inclusion. On the other hand, a few songs of the Isley Brothers, the Miracles and the (Diana Ross) Supremes were included because they are doo-wop in character.

For the purposes of this songography, we have done the following. For groups that sang almost exclusively in doo-wop style we have listed all of their works. For those that were precursors of the doo-wop style (e.g., Ravens and Dominoes), or those that only recorded a few songs in doo-wop style before making their name in another genre (e.g., Miracles and Supremes), we have included only doo-wop-styled versions. For groups that made significant contributions to both doo-wop and other genres (e.g., Dells and Little Anthony & the Imperials) we have listed only their doo-wop works.

The songography that follows is the most complete in existence, primarily because we had so many excellent sources to rely on. Our most important sources are listed below, with the works by Robert Ferlingere, Fernando Gonzales and Jeff Kreiter being of greatest help. Aside from its completeness, ours differs from its predecessors primarily on being exclusively a doo-wop songography, while others have focused on the broader field of rhythm-and-blues. Further, many other lists, especially those published by Jerry Osborne, dwell on record prices while ours does not. Our primary sources were:

Clee, Ken. The Directory of American 45 R.P.M. Records (4 Vols). Philadelphia: Stak-O-Wax, 1989.

Ferlingere, Robert. A Discography Of Rhythm & Blues And Rock 'N Roll Vocal Groups, 1945 To1965. Hayward, CA: California Trade School, 1976.

Gart, Galen. American Record Label Directory And Dating Guide (4th ed.). Milford, NH: Big Nickel Publications, 1990.

Gonzales, Fernando L. Disco-File (2nd ed.). Flushing, N.Y.: Fernando L. Gonzales, 1977.

Hill, Randall C. The Official Price Guide To Collectible Rock Records, 2nd ed. House Of Collectibles, 1980.

Kreiter, Jeff. 45 R.P.M. Group Collector's Record Guide, 4th ed. Bridgeport, OH: Boyd Press, 1992.

Mawhinney, Paul C. The Music Master: The 45 RPM Record Directory By Artist (V. I) Pittsburgh, PA: Record-Rama Sound Archives, 1983.

Mawhinney, Paul C. The Music Master: The 45 RPM Record Directory By Title (V. II) Pittsburgh, PA: Record-Rama Sound Archives, 1983.

Nite, Norm N. Rock On, Vol. I. New York: Thomas Y. Crowell Co., 1974.

Osborne, Jerry. Record Collector's Price Guide, 1st ed. O'Sullivan, Wardside, 1976.

Osborne, Jerry. Blues, R&B And Soul Price Guide, 1st ed. O'Sullivan, Wardside, 1980.

Osborne, Jerry. The Complete Library Of Amer. Phonograph Recordings, 1959. Tempe, AR: Osborne Enterprises, 1987.

Osborne, Jerry. The Complete Library Of Amer. Phonograph Recordings, 1960. Tempe, AR: Osborne Enterprises, 1987.

Osborne, Jerry. The Complete Library Of Amer. Phonograph Recordings, 1961. Tempe, AR Osborne Enterprises, 1987.

Osborne, Jerry. Rockin' Records: Buyers & Sellers Ref. Book And Price Guide. Port Townsend, WA: Osborne Enterprises, 1989.

Propes, Steve. Those Oldies But Goodies: A Guide To 50s Record Collecting. New York: MacMillan, 1973.

Propes, Steve. Golden Oldies: A Guide To 60s Record Collecting. New York: Chilton, 1974.

Whitburn, Joel. The Billboard Book Of Top 41 Hits: 1955-1987. New York: Billboard Books,1989.

Unfortunately, two sources occasionally presented conflicting information about the titles, flip sides, year, and even record number and label. Many of the sources we relied on often had incomplete information about a record, for example the year was missing, and we often could not fill in the blank. Especially troublesome was the confusion surrounding groups singing under the same name. For example, one source may have presented a (hypothetical) group called the Ostriches recording on the A, B and C labels and a second group of Ostriches singing on D and E. A second source may have reported the first Ostrich group as being on labels A, D and E. A third source may have recommended that three separate Ostrich groups recorded for labels A through E. We have done our best to sort out these puzzles.

Our goal was to give the reader as many song titles as we could find. We have concentrated our efforts in the years that define the doo-wop era, namely 1952 to 1963. While recordings outside of these years are listed, the information is less complete. The overwhelming majority of titles have complete information (i.e., flip side, year, record label and record number), and were recorded as singles. In some cases however, songs appear in the songography that are missing a flip side, a year and a record label. Most often, when this occurs, the song was recorded for an LP or EP. A single may exist somewhere, but we could not unearth it. We would welcome help from our readers in filling in the blanks.

How To Read The Songography

Group Name: Most entries in this column are the names of groups, listed in alphabetical order. A group with the moniker "Tiny Tony & the Tots" is listed as "Tots (Tiny Tony & the)". Occasionally, individual names are listed, e.g., "Mouse, Matthew (& group)". The presence of a group is certain, but the name of this group is unknown.

If other information is known, it is given in parenthesis. "Tots (with Tiny Tony)" or "Tots (featuring Tiny Tony)" means that Tiny Tony's name appeared on the recording. Other information is supplied (because it may be of interest to the reader) using the following abbreviations in parenthesis: "fb" is fronted by, "bb" is backed by, and "gm" is group member. Where these three abbreviations are used, the information that follows them is not on the recording itself.

Often, groups with identical (or nearly so) members sang under more than one group name. In these cases, one name is referenced by another using the phrase "also known as" or "aka". For example, "Tots (aka Toddlers/aka Kid-Tones)" means that the three groups had identical (or nearly so) membership. If the groups are not identical, but are related to one another "ref" (standing for "refer to") is used, e.g., Oldsters (ref Seniors).

Numbers in parenthesis following the name of a group (e.g., "Tots (1)" or "Tots (2)") are used to differentiate between different groups of singers that sang under the same group name. Decisions about whether groups were identical or separate, as mentioned earlier, were not always easy to make. Often, these decisions were made on little but the labels recorded on and the years of release. Again, any help from our readers is welcome.

Song Titles: In most cases, "A" sides are listed first, "B" sides second, when this distinction could be made. Flip sides are separated by the slash symbol ("/"). In some instances the flip side is unknown, but some information is included such as "flip is instrumental" or "flip has no group". If the flip side was recorded by a different group, its name appears in parenthesis after the title of the flip side.

Year: The year refers to the first known release date for the record. If a date is given for an unreleased song, it refers to the recording date for the song.

Label: Label and label numbers are given for each song when known. If a label name is followed by a number, a "/", and another number, e.g., "Superlabel 1001/1002", the two numbers refer to the two sides of the record. If the same record was released by two different labels (or the same label at two different points in time), both names appear, the first release coming first, and they are separated by a "/" (e.g., "Goodlabel 104/Betterlabel 5003"). If release dates are known for the second, third, etc. labels, they are included in parenthesis.

Label listings imply that the record was released as a single, most often a "45", occasionally a "78". In the interest of completeness, songs released only on albums are included in the songography. Information about the album (LP) or extended play (EP) are given, if known, as for example, "Goodlabel LP only" or "Goodlabel LP 1011".

ARTIST/SONG	YEAR	LABEL
A-Tones (Roger & the) (Roger Bailon)		
Why/Look A Who	N/A	Nike 002
Academics		
At My Front Door/Darla, My Darling	56	Ancho 100/Relic 509 (64)
Heavenly Love/Too Good To Be True	57	Ancho 101/Relic 510 (64)
Girl That I Love/I Often Wonder	58	Ancho 104 (unreleased)
Drive-In Movie/Something Cool	58	Elmont 1001/1002
Accents (1)		
Baby Blue/Don't Expect A Miracle	55	Blue Mill 111
Where Will You Be/Voice Of The Bayous	56	Accent 1036
Name Song/This Ole Body	56	Accent 1037
22 Del Rio Avenue/Red Light	59	Jubilee 5353
Till You Bring Your Love Back/Cassius Clay	62	Joker 200
Accents (1) (featuring Robert Draper Jr.)		
Wiggle Wiggle/Dreamin' And Schemin'	58	Brunswick 55100
I Give My Heart To You/Ching A Ling	59	Brunswick 55123
Anything You Want Me To Be/Autumn Leaves	59	Brunswick 55151/
(Les Ferrilles Mortes)		Coral 62151 (59)
Accents (1) (Jackie Allen & the)		
Don't Go/Cool-A-Roo	55	Accent 1025
Forever Yours/Yes, Yes	55	Accent 1031
Accents (2) (Jim Murphy & the)		
I'm Gone Mama	57	Rev 3508
Accents (3)		
Jo-Baby/Lovin' At Night	58	Robbins 108
Accents (4)		
Our Wonderful Love/A Hundred Wailin' Cats	62	Jive 888/Vee Jay 484 (62)
Little Boy Blue/Movin' Along	62	Matt 0001
Where Can I Go/Rags To Riches	63	Sultan 5500
Accents (4) (Scott English & the)		
High On A Hill/When (by the Dedications)	63	Sultan 4003/Spokane 4003 (63)
Accents (5)		
Enchanted Garden/Tell Me Now	63	Mercury 72154
Where Can She Be	N/A	N/A
Accents (6) (featuring Sandi)		
I've Got Better Things To Do/Then He Starts To Cry	64	Charter 1017
Better Watch Out Boy/Tell Me (What's On Your Mind)	64	Commerce 5012/Challenge 1112
		(64)/Challenge 59254 (64)
He's The One/On The Run	64	Karate 529
Tell Me/Sweet Talk	65	Challenge 9294
Friendly Stranger/People Are Funny	N/A	Gazzari 90391
Accents (7) (Danny & the)		
Her Diary/She Can't Be Real	65	Valli 307
Accents (8) (Ron Peterson & the)		
Sticky/Linda Lou	65	Jerden 728
Acey, Johnny (& group)		
Why/Please Don't Go (Back To Baltimore)	60	Fire 1015
Acorns		
Angel/I'm Going To Stick To You	58	Unart 2006

ARTIST/SONG	YEAR	LABEL
Actors		
Cool Water/Peanut Brittle	62	Laurie 3135
Ad Libs		
The Boy From New York City/Kicked Around	65	Blue Cat 102
He Ain't No Angel/Ask Anybody	65	Blue Cat 114
On The Corner/Oo-Wee Oh Me Oh My	65	Blue Cat 119
Just A Down Home Girl/Johnny My Boy	65	Blue Cat 123
Adams, Link (& group)		
Angel Or Not/Lonely Teen	61	A Okay 111
Adapters		
Believe Me	N/A	Richie 65
Addictions		
Daddy's Home/When We Get Married (a capella)	72	Kelway 102
Adelphis		
Darling It's You/Kathleen	58	Rim 2020
Kiss-A-Kiss/(The Sun Will) Shine Again	58	Rim 2022
Admiral Tones		
Hey Hey Pretty Baby/Rocksville, Pa.	59	Felsted 8563
Admirals		
Oh Yes/Left With A Broken Heart	55	King 4772
Close Your Eyes/Give Me Your Love	55	King 4782
It's A Sad, Sad Feeling/Ow (with Cathy Ryan)	55	King 4792
Admirals (with Cathy Ryan)		
Twenty Four Hours A Day/With You	55	King 1495
Admirations (1)		
Just Like A Baby/My Baby	61	Apollo 753
Admirations (1) (featuring Joseph Lorello)		
The Bells Of Rosa Rita/Little Bo Peep	59	Mercury 71521
To The Aisle/Hey Senorita	61	Mercury 71883
Over The Rainbow/In My Younger Days	72	Kelway 108
A Kiss And A Rose	N/A	N/A
Memories Are Here To Stay/Dear Lady	N/A	Atomic 12871
It All Happened So Fast	N/A	Mercury (unreleased)
Remember The Day	N/A	Mercury (unreleased)
Admirations (2) (aka Bel Mars)		
Coo Coo Cuddle Coo/Down To Earth (by the Nutmegs)	63	Times Square 19
Mixture Of Love/I've Searched (by the Heartspinners)	63	Times Square 20/Relic 537 (65)
Admirations (2) (Norveen Baskerville & the) (aka Bel Mars)		
Gonna Find My Pretty Baby/Li'l Li'l Lulu (by the Bel Mars)	60	X-Tra 100/Candlelite 414 (74)
Admirations (3)		
Moonlight/Ain't It Funny	64	Hull 1202
Adolescents (Little Willie & the)		
Get Out Of My Life	N/A	Tener 1009
Adorables		
Our Love Song	N/A	N/A
Adorables (Ginger & the)		
He's Gone (a capella)	75	Relic LP 104

ARTIST/SONG	YEAR	LABEL

Adorations

Linda · N/A Dreamtone 200

Adrian, Lee (bb the Chaperones)

Barbara, Let's Go Steady/I'm So Lonely · · · 59 Richcraft 5006/SMC 1385 (62)
School Is Over/A In Love · · · · · · · · · · · · · · · · · 62 SMC 1386

Adventurers

Rip Van Winkle/Trail Blazer · · · · · · · · · · · · · · 59 Capitol 4292
Little Genie/Excelsior · 59 Jerden 105
Shaggin'/Two O'Clock Express · · · · · · · · · · · 59 Mecca 11
Peppermint Stick · 61 Columbia
Rock And Roll Uprising/My Mama Done Tole Me · · · 61 Columbia 42227
Baby, Baby, My Heart/Lover Doll · · · · · · · · · · 66 Reading 602

Affections (Judy & the)

Dum Dum De Dip/Marie, Give Him Back · · · · N/A Dode

Afterbeats (Gloria Wood & the)

Ching Ching/Doo Dee Doo Doop · · · · · · · · · · · 60 Buena Vista 361

Agee, Ray (& female group)

I Need You/Without A Friend · · · · · · · · · · · · · · 55 R&B 1311

Agee, Ray (& group)

These Things Are True · · · · · · · · · · · · · · · · · · · N/A Marjan 001

Agents

The Love I Hold/Trouble · · · · · · · · · · · · · · · · · · N/A Liberty Bell 3260

Aire-Dales (Rocky Roberts & the)

Buzz Buzz Buzz/Too Much · · · · · · · · · · · · · · · · 65 Brunswick 55357

Aktones (Will Wendel & the)

Lonely Blue Boy/Lover · · · · · · · · · · · · · · · · · · · 62 Trans America 10000

Aladdin, Johnny (bb the Passions)

Why Did You Go/Happy Together · · · · · · · · · · N/A Chip 1001

Aladdins (1)

Cry, Cry Baby/Remember · · · · · · · · · · · · · · · · · 55 Aladdin 3275
Get Off My Feet/I Had A Dream Last Nite · · 55 Aladdin 3298
All Of My Life/So Long, Farewell, Bye-Bye · · 56 Aladdin 3314
Help Me/Lord Show Me · · · · · · · · · · · · · · · · · · · 57 Aladdin 3358

Aladdins (2)

Dot, My Love/My Charlene · · · · · · · · · · · · · · · · 58 Frankie 6

Aladdins (3)

Gee/Then · 62 Prism 6001
Please Love Me/Munch · · · · · · · · · · · · · · · · · · · 62 Witch 109
Our Love Will Be/Simple Simon · · · · · · · · · · · 63 Witch 111

Aladdins (4)

Magic Carpet · N/A Duplex 9012

Alaimo, Chuck (Chuck Alaimo Quartet)

That's My Desire/Leap Frog (instrumental) · · 57 MGM 12449
How I Love You/Local 66 (instrumental) · · · · 57 MGM 12508

Alam-Keys

Please Come Back To Me · · · · · · · · · · · · · · · · · · N/A Kiski 2056

Alamos

Donkey Walk/Pork Chops · · · · · · · · · · · · · · · · · 57 Hi-Q 5030

ARTIST/SONG	YEAR	LABEL
Alamos (Sammy Houston & the)		
Summer Souvenir/Hey Swamper	60	Cleveland 104
Alamos (Tony Valla & the)		
Jane Why Did You Do It/La Bamba	61	Fortune 858
Love, Boy (Made A Fool Out Of You)/Maria Christina	61	Fortune 859
Alcoves		
Heaven/The Ballad Of Cassius Clay	64	Carlton 602
Aldenaires (Paul Alden & the)		
Crazy Memories	N/A	Glolite 106
Alexander, Jeff (the Jeff Alexander Quartet)		
I'll Pay As I Go/Dr. Geek	55	Aardell 0001
Algers (Skip & Fruit & the)		
Heavenly Father/Oh Baby	60	Northern 3730
Aliens		
Wild Love	N/A	Stilt 66801
All Americans (Joey Rogers & the)		
Jeannine/They Didn't Believe Me	58	Nu-Clear (no number)
All Nighters		
You Talk Too Much/Summertime Blues	64	GMA 1
Allan, Johnny (bb the Krazy Kats)		
Unfaithful One/Rubber Dolly	62	Viking 1016
Allen Trio		
That's What I Like/Teach Me Tonight (by the Five Dips)	55	Original 1005
Allen, Charlie (& group)		
Sweetie Pie/Wheelin' And Dealin'	62	Portrait 107
Allen, George (& group)		
I Must Be Crazy	61	Sotoplay 0031
Allen, Mimi (& group)		
Do You Miss Me/Whoopee (Love's A Wonderful Thing)	61	Three Speed 711
Allen, Rich (bb the Ebonistics)		
Echoes Of November/Fanarri	68	Groovey Grooves 160
Allen, Sue (& group)		
I Dedicate My Heart/Don't Leave Me Here To Cry	54	Groove 0037
Allen, Tony (bb the Wonders)		
Dreamin'/Be My Love, Be My Love	61	Kent 364
Alley Cats		
This Thing Called Love/Spang-A-Lang	56	Whippet 202
Last Night/Snap, Crackle And Pop	57	Whippet 209
Puddin' 'N Tain' (Ask Me Again, I'll Tell You The Same)/ Feel So Good	62	Philles 108
I Should Have Stayed At Home Tonight/Lily Of The West	65	Epic 9778
Alleycats		
I Cried Enough	58	Jalo 201
I Want To Thrill You	58	Jalo 202
Allie Oop's Group (fb Gerry Granahan)		
Bloop, Bloop/Dinosaur	60	Caprice 102

ARTIST/SONG	YEAR	LABEL
Allison, Gene (& group)		
You're My Baby/Somebody Somewhere	56	Calvert 106/Decca 30185 (56)
Hey, Hey, I Love You/You Can Make It If You Try	57	Vee Jay 256
Let's Sit And Talk/I Don't Know Why	58	Vee Jay 286
Allisons		
Lessons In Love/Oh, My Love	62	Smash 1749
Money/Surfer Street	63	Tip 1011
Allures		
King Love	63	Melron 5009
Alston, Henry (& group)		
Once In A Beautiful Lifetime/I Dare You Baby	59	Skyline 500
Alston, Jo Ann (& group)		
He Left Me Crying/Looking Like A Fool	63	Vest 8001
Alston, Walter (& group)		
Gypsy Lady/Hey Baby	61	Gamut 101
Altairs (gm George Benson)		
If You Love Me/Groovie Time	60	Amy 803
Altecs		
Easy/Recess	61	Felsted 8618
Yok Yok Yok/Tweeda	N/A	Cloister 6201
Alteers		
Words Can't Explain/Keep Laughin'	61	Laurie 3097
This Lovely Night/No End	64	G-Clef 705
Altones		
Summer Love	61	Archer 104
Love Me Love Me/Eileen	61	Gardena 121
Alvans		
Love Is A Game/What Can It Be	61	May 102
Amaker, Donald (& group)		
Don't Let Me Shed Any More Tears/Pleasing	59	Raines 418
Amato, Jerry (& group)		
Dream On Little Fool/When I Met You	N/A	Tacit 109
Ambassadors (1)		
Darling I'm Sorry (I Made You Cry)/Willa-Bea	54	Timely 1001
Lorraine/Come On And Dance	63	Playbox 202
Calling For Love	87	Relic LP 5071
Moanin'	87	Relic LP 5071
Ambassadors (2) (Vern Young & the)		
Cindy Lou/One Last Look At My Darling	60	Chords 101
Ambassadors (3)		
Keep On Trying/The Switch	56	Air 5065
I Wonder Why/The Power Of Love	62	Bon 001/Reel 117 (62)
Ambassadors (4)		
Oh Nancy/Ambassador Blues	6363	Bay210
Amber, Kenny (& group)		
Tears In My Eyes	N/A	Zenette

ARTIST/SONG	YEAR	LABEL
Ambers (1)		
Listen To Your Heart (Caroline)/Loving Tree	59	Greezie 501
Ambers (1) (gm Ralph Mathis) (Johnny's brother)		
Never Let You Go/I'll Make A Bet	58	Ebb 142
All Of My Darling/So Glad	60	Todd 1042
Ambers (2) (Joey & the)		
Treasure In My Heart/Sweet, Sweet Memory	60	Big Top 3052
Ambertones		
Charlena/Bandido	64	GNP Crescendo 329
One Summer Night	N/A	Dottie 1129
I Need Some/If I Do	N/A	Dottie 1130
I Only Have Eyes For You	N/A	Rayjack 1002
Ambitions		
Traveling Stranger	62	Cross 1005
Ambrose, Kenny (& group)		
Don't Be A Fool For Love/Come On And Marry Me	58	Hamilton 50019
American Beetles		
She's Mine/Them Of American Beetles	64	BYP 1001
Amorettes (Armond Adams & the)		
The Storm/Diamond Pins And Broken Beads	64	Fortune 572
Anastasia (& group)		
Every Road I Walk Along/Bicycle Hop	N/A	Stasi 1000
Seven Days A Week/Nothing Beats My Girl	N/A	Stasi 1001
Anders, Bernie (& group)		
My Heart Believes/Too Late I Learned	55	King 4833
Anders, Terri (& group)		
Come Back My Love/All In My Mind	60	Chief 7027
Anderson, Bubba (& group)		
Where Has My Lover Gone/Please Don't Leave Me	62	Ace 662
Andrews, Gene (& group)		
Linda Linda/Lonely Room	63	Rust 5054
Andrews, Lee (bb the Hearts)		
I've Got A Right To Cry/I Miss You So	60	Swan 4965
Angel, Gary (& group)		
Judy	N/A	Kama 501
Angel, Johnny (& group)		
Starlight/The Story Of Love	58	Power 250
Doubt/Falling Teardrops	60	Imperial 5673
Angelenos		
As Long As I Have You/Don't Cry Baby	N/A	Peepers 2824
As Long As I Have You/On An Island	N/A	Peepers 2824
Come On Baby/Hully Gully Fever	N/A	Peepers 2827
Angelettes		
You And Only You/Mine And Mine Alone	57	Josie 813
Angelones		
Praying For A Miracle	N/A	Relic LP 5044

ARTIST/SONG	YEAR	LABEL
Angels (1) (with Sonny Gordon)		
Leaving You Baby/Sha-Wa-Wa	56	Irma 105
Angels (1) (with Sonny Gordon) (male)		
Wedding Bells (Are Ringing In My Ears)/Times Have Changed	54	Grand 115
A Lovely Way To Spend An Evening/You're Still My Baby	55	Grand 121
Glory Of Love/It's You I Love Best	56	Gee 1024
Angels (2) (Little Bobby Bell & the)		
Came, Saw, Conquered/Whole Wide World	57	Demon 1501
Angels (3) (ref Safaris)		
A Lover's Poem (To Her)/A Lover's Poem (To Him)	59	Tawny 101
Angels (4) (Gabriel & the)		
That's Life (That's Tough)/Don't Wanna Twist	59	Casino 107/Swan 4118 (62)/ Itzy 7 (62)
Hey/Chumba	60	Amy 802
Zing Went The Strings Of My Heart/The Rooster	61	Amy 823
I'm Gabriel/Ginza	61	Norman 506
All Work, No Play/Peanut Butter Song	63	Swan 4133
Angels (5) (female) (aka Starlets)		
P. S. I Love You/Where Is My Love Tonight	60	Astro AS202-1
Til/A Moment Ago (with Linda Jansen)	61	Caprice 107
Cry Baby Cry/That's All I Ask Of You (with Linda Jansen)	62	Caprice 112
Everybody Loves A Lover/Blow, Joe	62	Caprice 116
I'd Be Good For You/You Should Have Told Me	62	Caprice 118
A Moment Ago/Cotton Fields	62	Caprice 121
Cotton Fields/Irresistible	63	Ascot 2139
My Boyfriend's Back/(Love Me) Now	63	Smash 1834
I Adore Him/Thank You And Goodnight	63	Smash 1854
Wow Wow Wee (He's The Boy For Me)/Snowflakes And Teardrops	64	Smash 1870
Little Beatle Boy/Java	64	Smash 1885
Dream Boy/Jamaica Joe	64	Smash 1915
The Boy From 'Cross Town/A World Without Love	64	Smash 1931
What To Do/I Had A Dream I Lost You	67	RCA 9129
You'll Never Get To Heaven/Go Out And Play	67	RCA 9246
With Love/You're The Cause Of It	67	RCA 9404
The Modley/If I Didn't Love You	68	RCA 9541
The Boy With The Green Eyes/But For Love	68	RCA 9612
Merry Go Round/So Nice	68	RCA 9681
Papa's Side Of The Bed/You're All I Need To Get By	74	Polydor 14222
Angels (6)		
I'm Saying Goodbye/A Real Sensation	60	Audio 203/Milestone
Angels (7) (Hannibal & the)		
Please Take A Chance On Me/Love Is Funny	60	Pan World 517
Angels (8) (Lonny & the)		
Before I Saw You Smile/Bargain Love	61	Pledge 102
Angels (9) (Little Betty & the)		
Why Did You Do It/I May Be Wrong	61	Savoy 1603
Angels (10) (fb Joel Katz)		
Dearest Little Angel	64	N/A
Angletones		
Darling	85	Relic LP 5051
Angloes (Julie Gibson & the)		
I Got News For You/You've Been Cheatin' On Me	62	Herald 575

ARTIST/SONG	YEAR	LABEL
Anglos (Linda Martell & the)		
A Little Tear/The Things I Do For You	62	Fire 512
Annuals		
Hungry, I'm Hungry/Once In A Lifetime	59	Marconn CR1
Answers		
Have No Fear/Keeps Me Worried All The Time	57	United 212
Anteaters (Chuck Harrod & the)		
Sandy/They Wanna Fight	59	Champion 1013
Antell, Pete (& group)		
Keep It Up/You In Disguise	63	Cameo 264
Antennas		
Thirty Minutes To Go	62	United (unreleased)
Ubangi Baby	62	United (unreleased)
Anthony, Mike (& group)		
Little Linda/My Secret Heartache	61	Imperial 5813
Anthony, Paul (& group)		
My Promise To You/Bop Bop Bop	58	Roulette 4099
Step Up/Look At Me Now	N/A	Metro International 1003
Antlers		
Just In Case You	52	Artists 1260
Antones		
Jeanette/You Are The One	N/A	Black Crest 106
Antones (Joey Pfarr & the)		
All My Life/Time For Love	N/A	Black Crest 107
Antwinetts (female)		
Johnny/Kill It	58	RCA 7398
Apollo Brothers		
My Beloved One/Riot	60	Cleveland 108
Apolloes		
Summertime Blues	64	Look 001
Apollos (1)		
I Love You Darling/Bandstand Baby	59	Harvard 803
I Can't Believe It/Sometimes I Feel	61	Galaxy 707
Apollos (2)		
Just Dreaming/Rockin' Horses	60	Mercury 71614
Apollos (3) (Paul Stefen & the)		
You/Cry Angel Cry	62	Cite 5008
Hey Lonely One	63	Citation 5007
Apollos (4) (B. Charles & the)		
No Money/Forget	62	Tide 1084/1085
Apostles		
Stranded In The Jungle/Tired Of Waiting	66	A-Square 401
Apparitions		
Part Of Our Love (a capella)	75	Relic LP 103
Autumn Leaves (a capella)	75	Relic LP 105
Don't Leave Me Baby (a capella)	75	Relic LP 105

ARTIST/SONG	YEAR	LABEL
Forgotten Spring (a capella)	75	Relic LP 105
Image Of A Girl (a capella)	75	Relic LP 108
Since I Fell For You (a capella)	75	Relic LP 108
Valerie (a capella)	75	Relic LP 109

Aqua-Nites

Carioca/Lover Don't You Weep	65	Astra 1000/Astra 2003 (65)
Christy/Lover Don't You Weep	65	Astra 2001

Aqualads (Anthony & the)

The Heart That's True/I Remember	N/A	Gold Bee 1650

Aquatones

You/She's The One For Me	58	Fargo 1001
Say You'll Be Mine/So Fine	58	Fargo 1002
Our First Kiss/The Drive-In	58	Fargo 1003
My One Desire/My Treasure	59	Fargo 1005
Every Time/There's A Long Long Trail	59	Fargo 1015
Crazy For You/Wanted (A Solid Gold Cadillac)	60	Fargo 1016
My Darling/For You, For You	60	Fargo 1111
My Treasure/Say You'll Be Mine	62	Fargo 1022
Light Up The Sky	N/A	Fargo LP 5033X

Arabian Knights (Haji Baba & the)

Early One Morning/Don't Put Me Down Baby	56	Gotham 313

Arabian Knights (Ray Gant & the)

I Need A True Love/Don't Leave Me, Baby	71	Jay Walking 014

Arabians (1)

Heaven Sent You/The Shack	60	Jam 3738/Twin Star 1018 (60)
My Heart Beats Over And Over Again/Crazy Little Fever	60	Magnificent 102/ Magnificant 102 (60)
Teardrops In The Night/Take Me	60	Magnificent 114

Arabians (2)

You Upset Me Baby/Please Take A Chance On Me	64	Le Mans 001

Arabians (3)

Condition Your Heart/Bouncing Ball	64	Teek 4824-1/4824-2

Arabians (4)

My One Possession/Somebody Tell Me	61	Carrie 1516

Arabians (5)

I Love You So/Now You Have To Cry Alone	60	Lanrod 1605
Tell Me/School Is Cool	N/A	Mary Jane 1006

Arabians (5) (Edward Hamilton & the)

Thank You Mother/Thank You Mother (instrumental)	N/A	Mary Jane 1007/1008

Arabians (6) (Lawrence & the)

I'll Try Harder	N/A	Hem

Arc-Angels

Little Wheel/Goddess	61	Lan-Cet 142

Arcades

Blackmail/June Was The End Of August	59	Guyden 2015
Fine Little Girl (w. King Curtis)/My Love	59	Johnson 116/Johnson 320 (62)
Our Love/The Pal	60	Julia 1100

Arcados

When You Walked Out/Sugar Sweet	63	Fam 502

ARTIST/SONG	YEAR	LABEL
Archiads		
I Told You So	N/A	Ro-Cal
Arcs (J. Lambert & the)		
Alone/Rockin' Strings	58	K&C 100
Ardees (Phil Alan & the)		
Four Leaf Clover	N/A	Ko Co Bo 1010
Ardells (fb Johnny Maestro)		
Every Day Of The Week/Roll On	61	Marco 102
Eefenanny/Lonely Valley	63	Epic 9621
Seven Lonely Nights/You Can Fall In Love	63	Selma 4001
Argyles (1)		
Everytime You Smile/Moonbeam	57	Bally 1030
Argyles (2) (aka Hollywood Argyles)		
Vacation Days Are Over/It Takes Time	59	Brent 7004
Arist-O-Kats		
I Don't See Me In Your Eyes Anymore/Chasin' The Blues	57	Vita 168
Aristocats		
So In Love With You/Lawdy When She Kissed Me	58	Sue 714
Aristocats (Bobby Blue & the)		
You're Mine	58	N/A
Aristocrats (1)		
Believe Me/I'm Waiting For Ships	54	Essex 366
Aristocrats (1) (Murray Schott & the)		
Ooh How I Love Ya/The Unfinished Rock	55	Josie 788
Aristocrats (2)		
Don't Go/Squeeze Me	62	Home Of The Blues 237
Aristocrats (2) (Jackie Leonard & the)		
Another Love	63	Lesley 1926
Ark Angels (Little Caesar & the)		
The Ghost Of Mary Meade	60	Jack Bee 1008
Arlington, Bruce (& group)		
You Made Me Cry/How Could You Know	64	King 5918
Armen, Mickey (& group)		
Cheating On Me	65	Peek-A-Boo 1001
Armpits (Snake & the)		
Can't We Be Sweethearts/My Son	N/A	Explo 013
Arnells		
Take A Look/Heart Repair Shop	63	Roulette 4519
Arondies		
All My Love/Sixty-Nine (69)	N/A	Sherry 69
Arpeggios		
Mary/I'll Be Singing	63	Aries 001
Arribins (Duke Savage & the)		
Your Love/Hey Baby!	59	Argo 5346

ARTIST/SONG	YEAR	LABEL
Arrogants (fb Ray Morrow)		
Tom Boy/Make Up Your Mind	60	Big A 12184/12185
Take Life Easy/Stone Broke	62	Vanessa 200
Mirror Mirror/Canadian Sunset	63	Lute 6226
Arrows (1) (Joe Lyons & the)		
Honey Chile/What's New With You	56	Hollywood 1065
No End To True Love/One Too Many Times	56	Hollywood 1071
Shim Sham Shufflin' Jive/Bop-A-Loop	59	Hit Maker 600
Arrows (2)		
Annie Mae/Indian Bop Hop	58	Flash 132
I'm Checking On You Baby/No Other Arms	64	Hugo 1174
Arrows (3)		
Run Like The Wind/When You Were Sweet 16	60	Cupid 105
Arrows (4) (Big Bo & the)		
A Thousand Miles Away/I Done Got Over It	64	Checker 1068
Artis, Ray (& group)		
Art Of Love/That's All I Want From You	61	A 111
Artistics		
Life Begins At Sixteen/One Way	62	S&G 302
Arvettes (female)		
At A School Dance/Lovely Emotions	61	Hac 104
Pledge Of Love/Stolen Hours	66	Ideal 100
Ascots (1)		
What Love Can Do/Everything Will Be All Right	56	J&S 1628/1629
Ascots (2)		
It It Really You/Easier Said Than Done	59	Arrow 736
Ascots (3)		
Perfect Love/I'm Touched	62	Ace 650
She Did/Hip Talk	62	Bethlehem 3046
(Darling I'll See You) Tonight/I Don't Care One Bit	62	King 5679
Acapulco Run/The Gladiator	63	Dual-Tone 1120
Ascots (4)		
Miss Heartbreaker/This Old Heartache	65	M.B.S. 106
Ascots (5)		
Sometimes I Wonder/Anytime	65	Mir-A-Don 1001
Mother Said/Yes It's All Right	65	Mir-A-Don 1002
Another Day	65	Mir-A-Don 1004
Ashley, John (& group)		
Seriously In Love/I Want To Hear It From You	60	Silver 1002
Astors		
What Can It Be/Just Enough To Hurt Me	63	Stax 139
I Found Out/Candy	65	Stax 170
Astra-Lites		
Space Hop/Lonely	62	Tribute 101
Astro Jets		
Boom-A-Lay/Hide And Seek	61	Imperial 5760
Astronauts (1)		
Come Along Baby/Tryin' To Get To You	61	Palladium 610

ARTIST/SONG	YEAR	LABEL
Astronauts (2)		
Farewell/Chili Charlie	N/A	Trial 3521
Astros (Pepe & the)		
Judy My Love (Judy Mi Amor)/Now Ain't That A Shame	61	Swami 553/554
Atlantics		
Boo-Hoo-Hoo/Everything Is Gonna Be All Right	61	Linda 103
Remember The Night/Flame Of Love	62	Linda 107
Fine, Fine, Fine/Beaver Shot	65	Rampart 643
Atlantics (Barry White & the)		
Flame Of Love/Tracy	63	Faro 613
Atomics (Dennis Brown & the)		
Hiding My Tears With A Smile/Show Me The Rose	57	Atomic 57-101
Attitudes		
That Old Black Magic/Mama's Doin' The Jerk	67	Times Square 110
Attractions (J.R. & the) (aka Duprees?)		
I'm Yours/Bristol Stomp	65	Hunch 928
Audios (Cell Foster & the)		
Honest I Do/I Prayed For You	56	Ultra 105
Austin, Little Augie (bb the Chromatics)		
My Love For You/I Thank My Lucky Star	60	Pontiac 101
Autumns		
Maureen/Dearest Little Angel	62	Medieval 208
Never/Exodus (a capella)	66	Amber 856/Power
Avalons (1)		
Chains Around My Heart/Ooh! She Flew	56	Groove 0141
It's Funny But It's True/Sugar Sugar	56	Groove 0174
My Heart's Desire/Ebb Tide	58	Unart 2007
You Do Something To Me/You Can Count On Me	59	Casino 108
Begin The Beguine/Malanese	63	Olimpic 240/NPC 302 (64)
What's Wrong	N/A	Collectables LP 5037
I Follow The Stars	N/A	Groove (unreleased)
Little Cutie	N/A	Groove (unreleased)
You Do Something To Me	N/A	Groove (unreleased)
Avalons (2)		
I Miss You/Love Me	56	Aladdin (unreleased)
Louella/You Broke Our Hearts	58	Dice 90/91
Avalons (3)		
Is It The End/Many Things From Your Window	64	Roulette 4568
Avalons (4)		
A Star	87	Relic LP 5072
I Don't Know	87	Relic LP 5072
Suddenly	87	Relic LP 5072
Baby Looka Here	88	Relic LP 5075
Do Something For Me	88	Relic LP 5075
Love Me Or Let Me Go	88	Relic LP 5075
Avantis		
Keep On Dancing/I Wanna Dance	63	Argo 5436
Averones (Bob & the)		
Please Say You Want Me/Patti	64	Brent 7054

ARTIST/SONG	YEAR	LABEL
Avons (1)		
Our Love Will Never End/I'm Sending S.O.S.	56	Hull 717
Baby/Bonnie	57	Hull 722
You Are So Close To Me/Gonna Catch You Nappin'	58	Hull 726
What Will I Do (If You Go Away)/Please Come Back To Me	58	Hull 728
What Love Can Do/On The Island	59	Hull 731
Fairy Tales	60	Hull LP 1000
Once Upon A Time	60	Hull LP 1000
Someone For Everybody	60	Hull LP 1000
Baby/Whisper (Softly)	63	Astra 1023
A Girl To Call My Own/The Grass Is Greener On The Other Side	63	Hull 754
Avons (1) (with the Miller Sisters)		
Whisper (Softly)/If I Just (Had My Way) (with the Miller Sisters)	61	Hull 744
Avons (2) (female)		
We Fell In Love/Pickin' Petals	60	Mercury 71618
Avons (3) (female)		
Push A Little Harder/Oh, Gee Baby	63	Groove 0022
Rolling Stone/Words Written On Water	63	Groove 0033
Tonight Kiss Your Baby Goodbye/Whatever Happened To Our Love	63	Groove 0039
Avons (4) (female)		
Talk To Me/Got To Get Used To You	67	A-Bet 9419
Aztecs (1)		
Teenage Hall Of Fame/Traffic Jam	64	Card 901
Da Doo Ron Ron/Hi-Heel Sneakers	64	World Artists 1029
Aztecs (2) (Billy Thorpe & the)		
Over The Rainbow/That I Love	65	GNP Crescendo 340
Summertime Blues/What'Cha Gonna Do About It	65	GNP Crescendo 346
Twilight Time/My Girl Josephine	65	GNP Crescendo 359
Baby Dolls (1)		
Cause I'm In Love/Tutti Frutti (Pop-Pi)	58	RCA 7296
Go Away Baby/I'm Lonely	59	Maske 103
Hey Baby/Quiet	59	Warner Bros. 5086
Thanks, Mr. Dee-Jay/What A Wonderful Love	61	Maske 701
I Will Do It (Cause He Wants Me To)/Now That I've Lost You	66	Boom 60002
Baby Dolls (1) (fb Bill Baker)		
Is This The End?/Boy Friend	59	Elgin 021
Baby Dolls (2)		
Why Can't I Make Him Like You/Got To Get You In My Life	61	Hollywood 1111
Baby Dolls (3) (Rosie's)		
In Between (Wishing I Was Sweet Sixteen)/I Should Have Known	61	Fargo 1017
Bachelor Three		
Lover Man/Enchanted Summer	61	Vi-Way 288
Mary Mary/Head Bo Thread Bo	61	Vi-Way 289
Bachelors (1) (Dean Barlow & the)		
Is This Goodbye/Weekend Blues	51	International 777
Baby/Tell Me Now	55	Earl 102
In A Little Inn In Italy/Bachelor Mambo	55	Excel 105
I'm Lost/Texas	55	Excel 106
Bachelors (1) (fb Dean Barlow)		
Delores/I Want To Know About Love	55	Earl 101

ARTIST/SONG	YEAR	LABEL
Bachelors (2) (aka Jets)		
Can't Help Loving You/Pretty Baby	53	Aladdin 3210
You've Lied/I Found Love	56	Royal Roost 620
After/You Know! You Know! (I Love You)	57	Poplar 101
Bachelors (3)		
Selfish	55	Palace 140
From Your Heart/A Million Teardrops	57	National 104
Sometimes/Teenage Memory	58	MGM 12668
I Want A Girl/Today, Tomorrow, Forever	58	National 115
Bachelor's Club/Do The Madison	60	Epic 9369
The Day I Met You/Hey Little Girl	61	Smash 1723
Bad Boys		
What Do You Want With Me/It's More Like Voodoo	64	Herald 592
Bailey, Don (& group)		
Be My Own/Wedding	62	USA 723
Bailey, Herb (& group)		
Precious Lilly/Someway Somehow	64	Movin' 126
Bailey, Jimmy (& group)		
Constantly/Let Your Conscience Be Your Guide	58	Wynne 103
Baker, Bill (& group)		
Just To Be Near You/To The Aisle	62	Audicon 118/ Musictone 1108 (62)
Teenage Triangle/Why Did Summer Have To End	62	Musicnote 119
Another Sleepless Night/It Shouldn't Happen In A Dream	N/A	Parnaso 110
Baker, Bill (bb the Del Satins)		
Is It A Dream/I Wanna Know	61	Audicon 115
Baker, Charlie (& group)		
Star Of Wonder/You Crack Me Up	59	Liberty 55226
Baker, Roy Boy (& group)		
Bridge Of Love/I Thought I Heard You Call My Name	57	Dess 7011
Balladeers		
Goodbye Little Girl/I Wish I Was Single Again	52	RCA 4612
Balladiers		
What Will I Tell My Heart?/Forget Me Not	52	Aladdin 3123
Balladiers (Billy Matthews & the)		
Dance The Rhythm And Blues/My Love For You (by the Rockets (2))	56	Wrimus
Ballads (1)		
Before You Fall In Love/Broke	56	Franwil 5028
Somehow/Knee Bop	60	Ron-Cris 1003
Ballads (2)		
A Fool/That's My Baby	72	Klik 1021
Ballads (3)		
We Know/This Is Magic	64	Tina 102
Ballards		
I Hope I Never Fall In Love/Do It Now	N/A	Veltone 1738
Ballards (Billy Brown & the)		
I See A Girl/Why, Baby, Why	63	El Tone 439

ARTIST/SONG	YEAR	LABEL
Baltineers		
Moments Like This/New Love	56	Teenage 1000
Tears In My Eyes/Joe's Calypso	56	Teenage 1002
Ban Lons		
I Like It/Hey Good Lookin'	59	Fidelity 4056
Bandits		
Nothing Can Change My Love For You/This Love Of Ours	63	Emjay 1935
(by the Dynamics)		
Bandmasters (Lou Rall & the)		
Never Let Me Go/Party At Lesters	64	Way Out (no number)
Banks, Otis (& group)		
She's My Baby/Sazarac	57	Bow 304
Banlons		
Hey Baby/Highest Mountain	73	Baron 108
Banners		
Fortune Tellers/Sales Talk	60	MGM 12862
Bards		
Easy Going Baby/I'm A Wine Drinker	54	Dawn 208
Avalon/Gravy	55	Dawn 209
Baritones		
After School Rock/Sentimental Baby	58	Dore 501
Barlow, Dean (& group)		
Baby Doll/Third Window From The Right	61	Lescay 3004
Love, Is That You?/Little Sister	61	Seven Arts 704
Barnes, Johnny (& group)		
(There Is) No Love For Me/Tell Me Why	61	Flippin' 105
(That's What I Want To Know)		
Barnes, Othea (& group)		
Your Picture On The Wall/Same As Before	63	ABC 10434
Barnette, Billy (& group)		
Marlene/Two Brothers	61	Parkway 826
Baron, Nancy (& group)		
Oh Yeah	62	Chelsea 102
Baronaires		
I Have A Father Who Cares	60	Carrie
Barons (1) (aka Mel Williams & the Montclairs)		
Exactly Like You/Forget About Me	54	Decca 29293
A Year And A Day/My Baby's Gone	54	Decca 48323
Barons (2)		
Cryin' For You Baby/So Long, My Darling	54	Imperial 5283
Eternally Yours/Boom Boom	55	Imperial 5343
My Dream, My Love/I Know I Was Wrong	55	Imperial 5359
Searching For Love/Cold Kisses	55	Imperial 5370
Don't Walk Out/Once In A Lifetime	56	Imperial 5397
Hold Me Baby/Shake The Dice	N/A	Imperial (unreleased)
My Secret/I Love You Baby	N/A	Imperial (unreleased)
Barons (3) (Walter Miller & the)		
My Last Mile/Standing On The Highway	56	Meteor 5037

ARTIST/SONG	YEAR	LABEL
Barons (4) (formerly the Peppermints)		
Gravel Gert/The Fight	59	Demon 1520
If You Want A Little Lovin'/Jay Walk	59	Key 1001
Dog Eat Dog/Money Don't Grow On Trees	61	Soul 837
Willow Weep For Me/I've Been Hurt	61	Spartan 400
I Miss You So/Money Don't Grow On Trees	61	Spartan 402
Barons (5)		
Song Of Songs/Bridgitte	59	Whitehall 30008
Barons (6) (gm Larry Chance)		
Lula Mae/Lovely Loretta	60	Dart 126
The Bandit/Wanderin'	63	Bellaire 103
Perfect Love/Until The 13th Chime	63	Dart 134
Pledge Of A Fool/Don't Go Away (Pretty Little Girl)	63	Epic 9586/Epic 10093 (66)
Remember Rita/Lucky Star	64	Epic 9747
(I Just Go) Wild Inside/Silence	64	Imperial 66057
Drawbridge	58	Tender 511
Barons (7)		
When You Dance (a capella)	75	Relic LP 101
Barons (8)		
Come To Me	N/A	Blue Jay 154
Barrett, Richard (& group)		
Remember Me/Smoke Gets In Your Eyes	58	MGM 12616
Barries		
Why Don't You Write Me/Mary-Ann	62	Vernon 102
Tonight Tonight/Mary-Ann	63	Ember 1101
When You're out Of School/Loneliest Man In Town	64	Di-Nan 101
Bartley, Chris (& group)		
Love Me Baby/The Sweetest Thing This Side Of Heaven	67	Vando 101
Basics		
Basic Surf/Jailer Bring Me Water	N/A	Lavender 1851
Oh Lonely Me/Time	N/A	Lavender 2002
Basin St. Boys (Charles Brown & the)		
I Sold My Heart To The Junkman/Lost In The Night	56	Exclusive 39/Cash 1052 (56)
Batchelors		
Mountain Dew/The Ballad Of Betsy Ross	55	Rama 176
Baum, Allen (bb the Larks)		
My Kinda Woman/Too Much Competition	54	Red Robin 124
Baxter, Ronnie (bb the Chantels)		
Is It Because/I Finally Found You	59	Gone 5050
Bay Bops		
Joanie/Follow The Rock	58	Coral 61975
To The Party/My Darling My Sweet	58	Coral 62004
Bay City 5 (Luigi Martini & the)		
Please Don't Talk About Me/Basin Street Blues	54	Jaguar 3001
Oh Marie/I'm Sorry I Made You Cry	54	Jaguar 3002
Baysiders		
Over The Rainbow/My Bonnie	60	Everest 19366
Look For The Silver Lining/Trees	60	Everest 19386
The Bell's Of St. Mary's/Comin' Through The Rye	60	Everest 19393

ARTIST/SONG	YEAR	LABEL
Bear Cats		
Rama Lama Ding Dong	N/A	Bravo EP 70-2
Beard, Dean (& group)		
Little Lover/Holding On To A Memory	59	Challenge 59048
Bears		
A Pledge Of A Fool	N/A	N/A
Beasley, Billy (& group)		
A Million Teardrops/Too Long	N/A	Dee Cal 500
Beasley, Jimmy (& group)		
My Happiness/Jambalaya	56	Modern 1009
Beatnicks		
Blue Angel/Shakey Mae	N/A	Key-Lock 913
Beatniks (Charles Walker & the)		
Just Me And You/My Eyes On The World	58	Rhythm 116
Beau Belles (female)		
Wonderful You/Honky Tonk Hop	58	Arrow 729
Beau Jives		
Dip Dip/Don't Put All Your Onions In One Basket	61	Vision 111
Dip Dip/Don't Put All Your Eggs In One Basket	N/A	Lord Bingo 111
Beau-Jives		
I'll Never Be The Same/What Would You Do	62	Shepherd 2202
Brightest Star In The Sky/But I Love You	N/A	Lord Bingo 102
Brightest Star In The Sky/Mr. Sandman	N/A	Lord Bingo 107
Beau-Marks		
Clap Your Hands/Daddy Said	60	Shad 5017/Mainstream 688 (68)
'Cause We're In Love/Jimmy Went Walkin'	60	Shad 5021
Classmate/School Is Out	61	Rust 5035
Rockin' Blues/Oh Joan	61	Time 1032
Lovely Little Lady/Little Miss Twist	62	Quality 1370/Port 70029 (62)
Tender Years/I'll Never Be The Same	62	Rust 5050
Beaus (Bobbie & the)		
Losing Game/Melvin	59	Unart 2009
Beavers		
Rockin' At The Drive In/Sack Dress	58	Capitol 3956
Low As I Can Be/Road To Happiness	58	Capitol 4015
Beck, Carlton (& group)		
The Girl I Left Behind/You'll Be Coming Home Soon	63	Troy 100
Bee Hives		
Beatnik Baby/I Just Can't	61	Fleetwood 215
Bee Jay (& group)		
I'll Go On/There's No One For Me	61	Clock 1743
Bee Jays (Buddy Johnson & the) (Ella Johnson with)		
Bring It On Home To Me/Rock On (no group)	56	Mercury 70912
Beechwoods		
I'm Not A Kid Anymore/Place	63	Smash 1843

ARTIST/SONG	YEAR	LABEL
Bees (1) (Honey & the)		
Sunday Kind Of Love/Baby Do That Thing	68	Arctic 158
Almost Eighteen/Please Go Away	N/A	Pentagon 500
Bees (2)		
So Jealous/Tough Enough	N/A	Finch 506
Beginners		
I'm So Lonely Over You/Someday You'll Be My Girl	64	Dot 16629
Bel Mars (aka Admirations (2))		
Lil' Lil' Lulu/Gonna Find My Pretty Baby (by the Admirations)	74	Candlelite 414
Bel Raves (Lou Berry & the)		
Hot Rod/What A Dolly	59	Dreem 1001
Bel-Aires (1)		
Tick-Tock/Cherry Pie	54	Crown 126
Bel-Aires (2)		
My Yearbook/Rockin' And Strollin'	58	Decca 30631
Bel-Aires (3) (Donald Woods & the) (aka Donald Woods & the Vel-Aires)		
This Paradise/Let's Party Awhile	55	Flip 303 (first pressing, second is by Vel-Aires)
White Port Lemon Juice/This Is Goodbye	55	Flip 304
Bel-Aires (4) (fb Larry Lee)		
Hope And Pray/Space Walk	59	Arc 4451
Bel-Aires (5) (Eddy Bell & the)		
Anytime/The Masked Man (Hi-Yo Silver)	60	Mercury 71677
The Great, Great Pumpkin/I'm Still In Love With You	61	Lucky Four 1012
Knock, Knock, Knock (Knocking On My Door)/ Wear My Class Ring On A Ribbon	61	Mercury 71763
Bel-Aires (6) (Little D & the)		
Are You My Girl/Scratch	62	Raft 604
Bel-Airs Five		
Bring Back My Baby/The Time Has Come	64	USA 764
Bel-Larks		
Getting Married In June/A Million And One Dreams	63	Hammer 6313
A Million And One Dreams/Satisfied	63	Ransom 5001
Belairs (1)		
You'll Never Be Mine Again/Hoppin' & Boppin'	55	GG 521
Belairs (2)		
Sweet Sixteen/Louisiana Rug Roll	56	Coral 61605
Belairs (3) (aka Decoys (1)/aka Four Bel-Aires)		
Tell Me Why/Where Are You?	58	X-Tra 113/Times Square 23 (63)/ Relic 536 (65)
It's Going To Be Allright/Oh Baby (Decoys)	63	Times Square 8
Bells	N/A	Relic LP 5029
Rosa	N/A	Relic LP 5029
Belairs (4) (Barry Petricoin & the)		
Pretty Little Angel/Come Back To Sorrento	58	Al-Stan 103
Belairs (5) (Mike & the)		
She's Mine/Buscando (Searchin')	N/A	Cobra 6666

ARTIST/SONG	YEAR	LABEL
Belgianettes (female)		
My Blue Heaven/The Train	63	Okeh 7172
Belgianetts (female)		
You're Far From Home/Do The Crank	63	USA 731
Belgians		
Pray Tell Me/Changed	64	Teek 4824-3/4824-4
Bell Boys		
Are You For Me/I Love Thee	60	Era 3026
Bell Hops		
Please Don't Say No To Me/Merchant St. Blues	56	Tin Pan Alley 153
Angela/Ring Dang Doo Ting A Ling	58	Barb 100
Teenage Years/Carmella	58	Barb 101/102
Bell Notes		
I've Had It/Be Mine	59	Time 1004
Old Spanish Town/She Went That-A-Way	59	Time 1010
That's Right/Betty Dear	59	Time 1013
You're A Big Girl Now/Don't Ask Me Why	59	Time 1015
White Buckskin Sneakers And Checkerboard Socks/No Dice	59	Time 1017
Little Girl In Blue/Too Young Or Too Old	60	Autograph 204
Shortnin' Bread/To Each His Own	60	Madison 136
Friendly Star/Wild Child	60	Madison 141
A Sad Guitar	59	Time EP 100
Dream Street	59	Time EP 100
Bell Tones (1)		
Heart To Heart/The Wedding	55	Rama 170
Bell Tones (2)		
My Pledge To You/There She Goes	61	Clock 71889/Mercury 71889 (61)
Bell, Johnny (& group)		
Ev'ry Day/I'm So Glad	59	Fleetwood 1001
Bell, Tony (& group)		
My Girl	N/A	N/A
Bell-Aires (gm Billy Ford)		
I'd Never Forgive Myself/I'm Looking For A Lover	55	Ruby 103
Bella Tones (Eulis Mason & the)		
Carol Lee/Rockin' Santa Claus	59	Bella 20
Bellatones		
Forgotten Spring	59	Bella 21
Belles (1) (Terry & the)		
I'm Alone Because I Love You/Keep That Beat	58	Hanover 4505
I'll Always Be Nearby/I'd Want You	59	Ducky 711
Belles (2)		
Hear The Word/Trouble In My Soul	61	Choice 18
Everyday, Everyday/Wonderful Is His Name	62	Choice 29
Belles (2) (Glorius Wilson & the)		
Try Me And You'll See/I Hear Bells Ding Dong	56	Fairbanks 2002
Belles (3)		
Melvin/Come Back	N/A	Tiara 100

ARTIST/SONG	YEAR	LABEL

Bells
What Can I Tell Her Now/Let Me Love You, Love You | 55 | Rama 166

Belltones (1)
Carol	53	Grand 100
Estelle/Promise Love	54	Grand 102
The Merengue/I Love You, Darling	56	Scatt 1609/1610/J&S 1609/ 1610 (58)

Belltones (2) (aka Ronnie Baker & the Deltones)
I Want To Be Loved/You've Got What It Takes | 62 | Jell 188

Belltones (2) (Ronnie Baker & the)(aka Ronnie Baker & the Deltones)
Glory Be/This Big Wide World | 63 | Jell 200

Belltones (3) (Lacille Watkins & the)
His Hand In Mine/Maybe You'll Be There | 56 | Kapp 145

Belltones (4) (Johnny & the)
Ev'ry Day/My Little Baby | 57 | Cecil 5050

Belltones (5) (Tony Morra & the)
Claire/My Baby Scares Me | 59 | Arcade 152

Belltones (6)
My Pledge To You/There She Goes | 61 | Mercury 71889

Belltones (7) (Ronnie Dove & the) (aka Beltones)
No Greater Love/Saddest Hour | 62 | Jalo 1406

Belltones (8)
(Please Try) To Understand Me/Swinging Little Chickie | 62 | Olimpic 1068/Itzy 1 (62)

Belltones (9) (Kirk Taylor & the)
Been So Long/My Rosemarie | 58 | Tek 2634

Belmonts
I Need Someone/That American Dance	61	Sabina 502
Don't Get Around Much Anymore/Searching for A New Love	61	Sabrina 501
Tell Me Why/Smoke From Your Cigarette	61	Surprise 1000/Sabrina 500 (61)
I Confess/Hombre	62	Sabina 503
Come On Little Angel/How About Me?	62	Sabina 505
Diddle-De-Dum/Farewell	62	Sabina 507
Ann-Marie/Accentuate The Positive	63	Sabina 509
Walk On By/Let's Call It A Day	63	Sabina 513
More Important Things To Do/Let's Call It A Day	64	Sabina 517
C'Mon Everybody/Why	64	Sabina 519
Nothing In Return/Summertime	64	Sabina 521
I Don't Know Why/Summertime	65	United Artists 809
(Then) I Walked Away/Today My Love Has Gone Away	65	United Artists 904
I Got A Feeling/To Be With You	65	United Artists 966
Come With Me/You're Like a Mystery	66	United Artists 5007
She Only Wants To Do Her Own Thing/Reminiscences	68	Dot 17173
Have You Heard/Answer Me, My Love	69	Dot 17257
The Worst That Could Happen/Answer Me, My Love	69	Dot 17257
Cheek To Cheek/The Voyager	76	Strawberry 106

Belmonts (Bob Thomas & the)
My Day/Believe Me My Darling | 59 | Abel 232

Belmonts (Dion & the)
Teenage Clementine/Santa Margarita	57	Mohawk 106
We Went Away/Tag Along	57	Mohawk 107
I Wonder Why/Teen Angel	58	Laurie 3013
No One Knows/I Can't Go On (Rosalie)	58	Laurie 3015

ARTIST/SONG	YEAR	LABEL
Don't Pity Me/Just You	58	Laurie 3021
A Teenager In Love/I've Cried Before	59	Laurie 3027
Every Little Thing I Do/A Lover's Prayer	59	Laurie 3035
Where Or When/That's My Desire	60	Laurie 3044
When You Wish Upon A Star/Wonderful Girl	60	Laurie 3052
In The Still Of The Night/A Funny Feeling	60	Laurie 3059
All The Things You Are	60	Laurie LP 2006
I'm Through With Love	60	Laurie LP 2006
In Other Words	60	Laurie LP 2006
It's Only A Paper Moon	60	Laurie LP 2006
My Day	60	Laurie LP 2006
My Private Joy	60	Laurie LP 2006
September Song	60	Laurie LP 2006
Swinging On A Star	60	Laurie LP 2006
When The Red, Red Robin Comes Bob, Bob, Bobbin' Along	60	Laurie LP 2006
We Belong Together/Such A Long Way	61	Laurie 3080
My Girl, The Month Of May/Berimbau	66	ABC 10868
Movin' Man/For Bobby	67	ABC 10896
Come Take A Walk With Me	N/A	Ace LP 155
That's How I Need You	N/A	Ace LP 155
Will You Love Me Still	N/A	Ace LP 155
I Got The Blues	N/A	Collectables LP 5025
You Better Not Do That	N/A	Collectables LP 5025

Belmonts (fb Pete Barin)

So Wrong/Broken Heart	62	Sabina 504
Loneliest Guy In The World/Look For Cindy	63	Sabina 512

Belmonts (Freddy Cannon & the)

Mama Ain't Always Right	81	Mia Sound 1002

Beltones

I Talk To My Echo/Oof Goof	57	Hull 721
Yes Darling I'll Be Around/Party Doll	61	Decca 31288

Beltones (L. Farr & the)

Mary Lisa/Too Much Ain't Enough	64	N-Joy 1001

Belvaderes

Don't Leave Me To Cry/I Love You	56	Hudson 4

Belvederes

Come To Me Baby/Dear Angels Above (by Jimmy Morris)	55	Baton 214
We Too/Pepper-Hot Baby	55	Baton 217
Suzanne/Hey Honey	58	Dot 15852
Let's Get Married/Wow Wow Mary Mary	58	Trend 2595
Walkin' In The Garden/Buena Sera	59	Jopz 1771
Why Do You Treat Me This Way/Lost Love	62	Poplar 114
From Out Of Nowhere/Tormented	N/A	Count
The McCoy/Tired Out	N/A	Rhapsody 5163

Belvin, Andy (& group)

With All My Heart/You Were Meant To Be	N/A	Cal State 3200

Belvin, Jesse (& group)

Dream Girl/Hang Your Tears Out To Dry	51	Hollywood 120
Love Comes Tumbling Down (aka Love Song)	51	Hollywood 412
All That Wine Is Gone/Don't Cry Baby	51	Imperial 5115
Confusin' Blues/Baby Don't Go	52	Specialty 435
I'm Only A Fool/Trouble And Misery	55	Money 208
Beware/Dry Your Eyes	56	Cash 1056
Dear Heart/Betty My Darling	56	Hollywood 1059
Goodnight My Love/I Want You With Me Christmas	56	Modern 1005
Goodnight My Love/Let Me Love You Tonight	56	Modern 1005
Senorita/I Need You So	57	Modern 1013

ARTIST/SONG	YEAR	LABEL
Don't Close The Door/By My Side	57	Modern 1015
Sad And Lonesome/I'm Not Free	57	Modern 1020
You Send Me/Summertime	57	Modern 1025
Just To Say Hello/My Satellite	57	Modern 1027
Sentimental Reasons/Senorita	58	Kent 326
Little Darling/Deacon Dan Tucker	58	Knight 2012
Ever Since We Met/Volare	58	RCA 7310
Funny/Pledging My Love	58	RCA 7387
Deep In My Heart/I'm Confessin'	59	Class 267
Goodnight My Love/My Desire	59	Jamie 1145
Guess Who/My Girl Is Just Enough Woman For Me	59	RCA 7469
It Could've Been Worse/Here's A Heart	59	RCA 7543
Give Me Love/I'll Never Be Lonely Again	59	RCA 7596
Something Happens To Me/The Door Is Always Open	60	RCA 7675
Let's Make Up	N/A	Crown LP 5187

Belvin, Jesse (bb the Feathers)

Gone/One Little Blessing	55	Specialty 550
Where's My Girl/The Love Of My Life	55	Specialty 559
Sugar Doll/Let Me Dream	58	Aladdin 3431

Bengals (Bobby & the)

No Parking	N/A	BW 45

Bennet, Ron (& group)

Dingle Dangle Doll/My Only Girl	61	Ta-Rah 1

Bennett, Buddy (bb the Margilators)

Our Love Can Never Be/Baby Don't Go	59	Blue Moon 412

Bennett, Chuck (& group)

Seven Days/I Went To Your House	62	Bonnie 101

Bennetts

One Love/All My Loving	64	Amcan 401

Bentleys

Why Didn't I Listen To Mother/Did Anybody Lose A Tear	65	Smash 1988

Bermudas (fb Rickie Page)

Donnie/Chu Sen Ling	64	Era 3125
Blue Dreamer/Seeing Is Believing	64	Era 3133

Bernard, Rod (& group)

These Were Our Songs/Just Another Lie	66	Arbee 105

Berry Cups (Terry Clinton & the)

Dolores Darlin'/Hurt By A Letter	59	Khoury's 710

Berry Kids

Love Me, Love/Go, Go, Go Right Into Town	56	MGM 12379
You're My Teenage Baby/Rootie Tootie	57	MGM 12496
Suzie	N/A	Soo 12

Berry, Richard (& group)

Walk Right In/It's All Right	60	Warner Bros. 5164
I'm Your Fool/In A Real Big Way	61	K&G 1004

Berry, Richard (bb the Dreamers)

Wait For Me/Good Love	56	RPM 477
Besame Mucho/Do I Do I	58	Flip 339

Berry, Richard (bb the Flairs)

I'm Still In Love With You/One Little Prayer	53	Flair 1016

ARTIST/SONG	YEAR	LABEL
Betty Jean (& group)		
I Want To Be Your Girl	N/A	JR 5001
Bey Sisters (female)		
Patience/Wake Up	56	Jaguar 3016
Sentimental Journey/Sugar Cookie	56	Jaguar 3018/Flip 328 (57)
Bi-Langos (Donny & the)		
I'm Not A Know-It-All/I	N/A	Colton 101
Bi-Tones		
Beatnik Girl/Oh How I Love You So	N/A	Bluejay 1000
Bifield, Lenore (& group)		
Lies	64	Sketch 217
Big 5		
Blue Eyes/Stardust In Her Eyes	60	Shad 5019
Baby I Miss You/Wob-Ding-A-Ling	N/A	Junior 5000
Big Boys		
If I Had My Chance/Rock Rock Rock A Bye Baby	64	Melmar 113
Big Dog (& group)		
Doris	N/A	N/A
Big Tops		
I'm In Love/The Dance They Did	58	Warner 1017
Big Town Girls (Shirley Matthews & the) (female)		
(You Can) Count On That/Big Town Boy	63	Atlantic 2210
Billboards		
With All My Heart/Around The World	61	Vistone 2023
Billie & Lillie (bb the Thunderbirds)		
Love Me Sincerely/Whip It To Me Baby	63	ABC 10421
Binders		
Save The Last Dance For Me	N/A	Anka 7772
You Don't Have To Cry Any More/When We Were Young	N/A	Sara 7772
Bing Bongs (Dicky Dell & the)		
Ding-A-Ling-A-Ling Ding Dong/The Cling	58	Dragon 10205
Birdies (Robert Byrd & His)		
Bippin' & Boppin' (Over You)/Strawberry Stomp	56	Spark 501/Jamie 1039 (57)
Birds (1) (Bobby Byrd & the)		
The Truth Hurts/Let's Live Together As One	56	Cash 1031
Birds (2) (Don Mikkelsen & the)		
Chapel Of Love/Where I Came In	61	Deck 600
Biscaynes (aka Viscaynes)		
Uncle Sam Needs You/Yellow Moon	61	VPM 1006
Bishops		
Masquerade Ball/Open Up Your Heart	61	Lute 6010
Bishops (with the Mellow-Tones)		
The Wedding/Pretty	61	Bridges 1105
Bitter Sweets		
Another Chance/In The Night	67	Original Sound 70

ARTIST/SONG	YEAR	LABEL
Blackwells		
Here's The Question/Please Don't Come Crying	59	G&G 126
Oh My Love/Holy Sombrero	59	G&G 131/Guyden 2020 (59)
You Are Free, I'm Alone/Depot	59	Jamie 1141
Always It's You/Honey, Honey	60	Jamie 1150
Mansion On The Hill/Unchained Melody	60	Jamie 1157
Christmas Holiday/Little Match Girl	60	Jamie 1173
Love Or Money/Big Daddy And The Cat	61	Jamie 1179
You Took Advantage Of Me/I	61	Jamie 1199
Blades, Carol (with the Harptones)		
When Will I Know/What Did She Do Wrong	57	Gee 1029
Blair, Ronnie (& group)		
A Tear In My Eye/Twenty One	61	Crest 1084
Blair, Sandy (& group)		
When The Bells Stop Ringing/The Clock Says	N/A	Bobby 111
Blake, Cicero (& group)		
Don't Do This To Me/See What Tomorrow Brings	63	Success 107
Blakely, Cornel (& group)		
Don't Touch The Moon/Promise To Be True	57	Fulton 2543
Blanders		
Desert Sands/Jitterbug	65	Smash 2005
Blasers (1) (aka Four Blasers)		
She Needs To Be Loved/Done Got Over	56	United 191
Blasers (2)		
You Are The Only One	61	Lyons 108
Blasters		
Day Train/I Do (by the Youngtones)	64	Times Square 31
Blaze, Johnny (& group)		
Oh Lovin' Baby/Lolita Cha Cha	59	Apon 2142
Blazers (1) (Johnny Moore's)		
Why Johnny Why/Johnny Ace's Last Letter	55	Hollywood 1031
Christmas Eve Baby/Christmas Every Day	55	Hollywood 1045
I Send My Love/Next Time We Meet	56	Hollywood 1056
Blazers (2) (Rodney & the)		
Teenage Cinderella/Rolling Stone	60	Dore 572
Teenage Cinderella/Summertime	60	Kampus 100
Snow White/Tell Me Baby	61	Dore 588
Blazers (2) (Rodney Lay & the)		
All Over But The Crying/Little Orphan Annie	56	Chan 110
Blazers (3) (John Buck & His)		
Forbidden City/Chi Chi	58	Cadence 1359
Blazers (4) (with Dave "Baby" Cortez)		
So Nice	61	Winley 1001
Blazers (5) (Jimmy Feagans & the)		
No Matter/Saturday Night	61	Howard 501
Blazers (6) (Little Bernie & the)		
My Love, I Have You/By The Light Of The Silvery Moon	62	Josie 884

ARTIST/SONG	YEAR	LABEL
Blazers (7)		
I Don't Need You	63	Brass 306
Blazons		
Magic Lamp/Little Girl	N/A	Fanfare 5901/Bravura 5001
Bleaters		
I'm Gonna Be A Wheel Some Day/Come And Get Your Baby	63	Guyden 2100
Blen-Dells		
Say You're Mine/Forever	62	Bella 608
Blend Aires		
Sweet Sue	76	Arcade 104
Blend Tones		
She's Gone/Lights Please	61	Chic-Car 100/Don-El 106 (61)/ Imperial 5758 (61)
Blendaires		
Guaranteed/I Got It Bad And That Ain't Good	59	Decca 30938
Blendaires (Bobby Carle & the)		
Walk With Me/Anytime, Any Place, Anywhere	58	Decca 30605
I Couldn't Stand It/A Time To Love And A Time To Lie	58	Decca 30699
Blendairs		
My Love Is Just For You/Repetition	58	Tin Pan Alley 252
Blendells		
La La La La La/Huggie's Bunnies	64	Rampart 641/Reprise 0291 (64)
Blenders (1) (aka Sparrows (1))		
Don't Play Around With Love/You'll Never Be Mine Again	53	Jay-Dee 780
I Don't Miss You Anymore/If That's The Way You Want It, Baby	53	MGM 11488
Please Take Me Back/Isn't It A Shame?	53	MGM 11531
Don't Fuck Around With Love (alternate take of Jay Dee 780)	71	Kelway 101 (unreleased)
Blenders (2)		
Darline	87	Relic LP 5069
Blenders (2) (Earl Curry & the)		
Late Rising Moon/I Want To Be With You	54	R&B 1304
Dream Dream/Try And Get Me	56	R&B 1313
Blenders (2) (Ray Frazier & the)		
King Of Lovers	87	Relic LP 5069
Blenders (3)		
My Heart's Desire/Little Rose	58	Class 236
I Won't Tell The World/But I Know	59	Paradise 111
Blenders (4)		
Soda Shop/Two Loves	59	Aladdin 3449
Angel/Old MacDonald	59	Wanger 189
Craving Your Love	N/A	Wonder 722
Blenders (5) (aka Candles (2))		
I Asked For Your Hand/Dance In The Night	57	Vision 1000
Everybody's Got A Right/What Have You Got	62	Cortland 103
Daughter/Everybody's Got A Right	63	Witch 114
Boys Think (Every Girl's The Same)/Squat And Squirm	63	Witch 117
One Time/One Time	63	Witch 122
Love Is A Good Thing Going/Your Love Has Got Me Down	66	Mar-V-Lous 6010

ARTIST/SONG	YEAR	LABEL
Blenders (5) (Baby Jane & the) (aka Candles (2))		
You Trimmed My Christmas Tree	63	Witch 112
Blenders (5) (Goldie Coates & the) (aka Candles (2))		
Love Is A Treasure/Fisherman	62	Cortland 102
Blenders (6)		
It Takes Time/Graveyard	62	Afo 305
Blendors		
Tell Me What's On Your Mind/When I'm Walkin' With My Baby	61	Decca 31284
Blends		
A Thousand Miles Away/Music, Maestro, Please	60	Casa Grande 5000
Hey! Little Fool/Baby You're Wrong, Dead Wrong	60	Casa Grande 5001
Someone To Care/Now It's Your Turn	60	Casa Grande 5037
Tell Me/The Way I Want You	60	Talent 110/Skylark 108 (61)
Blends (Glenn Wells & the)		
Write Me A Letter/Lesson	60	Jin 122
Written In The Stars/You're Mine Tonight	60	Jin 133/United Artists 244 (60)
As My Tears Fall/In Memory Of Our Love	60	Jin 139
Blendtones		
Lovers/Dear Diary	63	Success 101
The Slide/Come On Home	63	Success 105
Blentones		
Lilly/Military Kick	59	MGM 12782
Blisters		
Shortnin' Bread/Cookie Rockin' In Her Stockings	63	Liberty 55577
Blossoms (Bobby Day & the)		
My Blue Heaven/I Don't Want To	58	Class 232/Class 263 (59)
Blossoms (female)		
Move On/He Promised Me	57	Capitol 3822
Little Louie/Have Faith In Me	58	Capitol 3878
No Other Love/Baby Daddy-O	58	Capitol 4072
I'll Wait/Son-In-Law	61	Challenge 9109
Write Me A Letter/Hard To Get	61	Challenge 9122
Big Talkin' Jim/The Search Is Over	62	Challenge 9138
I'm In Love/What Makes Love	63	Okeh 7162
Things Are Changing/Things Are Changing	65	EEOC-8472
(instrumental with Brian Wilson on piano)		
Blue Angels		
In The Sun/Sobbin'	59	Palette 5038
Desirie/Like Heaven	61	Edsel 781
My May/Cottage In The Country	61	Palette 5077
Blue Beards		
Romance/Crawlin'	58	Guide 1002
Blue Belles (1) (female)		
Cancel The Call/The Story Of A Fool	53	Atlantic 987
Blue Belles (2) (female)		
A Place Called Happiness/Snow White And The Three Stooges	61	20th Fox 249
I Sold My Heart To The Junkman/I've Got To Let Him Know	62	Newtown 5000
I Sold My Heart To The Junkman/Itty Bitty Twist	62	Newtown 5000
I Found A New Love/Pitter Patter	62	Newtown 5006 (1st printing)
I Found A New Love/Go On	62	Newtown 5006 (2nd printing)
When Johnny Comes Marching Home/Cool Water	62	Newtown 5009

ARTIST/SONG	YEAR	LABEL
Where Are You/You'll Never Walk Alone	63	Nicetown 5020

Blue Belles (2) (Patti LaBelle & the)
You're Just Fooling Yourself	64	Rainbow 1903

Blue Belles (2) (Patti LaBelle & the) (female)
Go On (This Is Goodbye)/Tear After Tear	62	Newtown 5007
Decatur Street/Academy Award	62	Newtown 5019
Down The Aisle/C'Est La Vie	63	Newtown 5777/King 5777 (63)
You'll Never Walk Alone/Decatur Street	63	Nicetown 5020/ Parkway 896 (63)
One Phone Call/You Will Fill My Eyes No More	64	Parkway 913
Danny Boy/I Believe	64	Parkway 935
You Better Move On/You're Just Fooling Yourself	64	Rainbow 1900
All Or Nothing/You Forgot How To Love	65	Atlantic 2311
Over The Rainbow/Groovy Kind Of Love	65	Atlantic 2318
Ebb Tide/Patti's Prayer	66	Atlantic 2333
I'm Still Waiting/Family Man	66	Atlantic 2347
Take Me For A Little While/I Don't Want To Go On Without You	66	Atlantic 2373
Tender Words/There's Always Something There To Remind Me	66	Atlantic 2390
Unchained Melody/Dreamer	66	Atlantic 2408
Oh My Love/I Need Your Love	67	Atlantic 2446
He's My Man/Wonderful	68	Atlantic 2548
Dance To The Rhythm Of Love/He's Gone	69	Atlantic 2610
Pride's No Match For Love/Loving Rules	69	Atlantic 2629
Suffer/Trustin' In You	70	Atlantic 2712

Blue Boys (Mr. Bo & the)
Lost Love Affair	N/A	Diamond 852

Blue Chips (1) (Carlron Lankford & the)
Appointment With Love/Come Back	56	DeLuxe 6100

Blue Chips (2)
I'm So In Love With You/Try My Arms	59	Wren 302
The New Year's In/Double Dutch Twist	61	Laurel 1026
Puddles Of Tears/The Contest	61	RCA 7923
Let It Ride/Adios, Adios	61	RCA 7935
Promise/One Hen	62	Groove 0006
Wishing Well/Deep Freeze	62	Sparta 001

Blue Chords
So Far Away	N/A	Reverb 6745

Blue Counts (Mike Lanzo & the)
At The Fair/Ghost Town	64	Debra 2006

Blue Crystals
Broke Up/Queen Of All The Girls	59	Mercury 71455

Blue Denims (Wild Bill & the)
Mona My Love/The Chase	60	Gone 5082

Blue Diamonds (1) (fb Ernie "K-Doe" Kador)
Honey Baby/No Money	54	Savoy 1134

Blue Diamonds (2)
Ramona/All Of Me	60	London 1954
Little Ship/Carmen My Love	62	London 10006

Blue Diamonds (3) (Don & the)
Too Late To Love/How About That	61	Skylark 113

Blue Dots (1)
Don't Do That, Baby/You've Got To Live For Yourself	54	DeLuxe 6052

ARTIST/SONG	YEAR	LABEL
Don't Hold It/Street Of Sorrow	54	DeLuxe 6055
God Loves You, Child/Save All Your Love For Me	54	DeLuxe 6061
Hold Me Tight/Let Me Know Tonight	54	DeLuxe 6067
Please Don't Tell 'Em/Saturday Night Fish Fry	57	Ace 526

Blue Dots (2)

I Wanna Know/Looking For My Baby	58	Zynn 511

Blue Echoes

It's Witchcraft	N/A	Bon 2112

Blue Flamers

Driving Down The Highway/Watch On	54	Excello 2026

Blue Flames (1)

Skylark	54	Grand 113

Blue Flames (1) (fb Chris Powell)

Uh Uh Baby/Sweet Sue Mambo	54	Grand 108

Blue Flames (2) (Buddy Love & the)

I Love You/I'm Leaving	62	Thunder 1A

Blue Flames (3)

Just A Stranger	N/A	Flame 1102

Blue Jays (1)

White Cliffs Of Dover/Hey, Pappa	53	Checker 782

Blue Jays (2)

Sweet Georgia Brown/J. J.'s Blues	59	Laurie 3037
Barbara/Practical Joker	59	Roulette 4169
Cave Man Love/Kum Ba Yah	60	Roulette 4264

Blue Jays (3)

Lover's Island/You're Gonna Cry	61	Milestone 2008
Tears Are Falling/Tree Top Len	61	Milestone 2009
Let's Make Love/Rock Rock Rock	61	Milestone 2010
The Right To Love/Rock Rock Rock	62	Milestone 2012
Venus My Love/Tall Len	62	Milestone 2014
Rock Rock Rock/The Right To Love	63	Milestone 2021
A Casual Kiss	87	Relic LP 5064
A Magic Island	87	Relic LP 5064
Cottonhead Joe	87	Relic LP 5064
Darlene	87	Relic LP 5064
So Long, Lover's Island	87	Relic LP 5064
That's All It Took	87	Relic LP 5064
The Heart You Break May Be Your Own	87	Relic LP 5064
Woe Is Me	87	Relic LP 5064
Could I Adore You/Sweet Pauline	N/A	Roadhouse 113472

Blue Jays (4) (aka Squires (3))

Earth Angel	56	Dig EP 777
Hearts Of Stone	56	Dig EP 777
Pledge Of Love	56	Dig EP 777
Sincerely	56	Dig EP 777
Ling Ting Tong	56	Dig EP 778
Shoo Do Be Do	56	Dig EP 780
Write A Letter/I Really Love You	61	Blujay 1002

Blue Jeans (Bob B. Soxx & the)

Zip-A-Dee Doo Dah/Flip & Nitty (instrumental)	62	Philles 107
Why Do Lovers Break Each Others Hearts/Dr. Kaplan's Office (instrumental)	63	Philles 110
Not Too Young To Get Married/Annette	63	Philles 113

ARTIST/SONG	YEAR	LABEL
The Bells Of St. Mary's	63	Philles EP X-EP
Baby	63	Philles LP 4002
Jimmy Baby	63	Philles LP 4002
White Cliffs Of Dover	63	Philles LP 4002

Blue Kings (Andy Charles & the)
Love Come Back/Baby Don't Go	59	D 1061

Blue Knights (Steve Colt & the)
Gloria/Train Of No Return	62	Fleetwood 4550

Blue Moons
A Sunday Kind Of Love/Peace Of Mind	N/A	Jaguar 1001

Blue Nighthawks
Two People In Love	N/A	Duplex

Blue Notes (1)
Never Never Land/I Waited	58	Colonial 9999
Darling Of Mine/I Love Her So	58	TNT 150/Dot 15720 (58)
Rufus/Your Tender Lips	61	Accent 1069
My Heart Cries For You/Shrimp Boats Are Coming	61	Gamut 100

Blue Notes (1) (Harold Melvin & the)
She Is Mine/Letter	60	Lost 105
My Hero/A Good Woman	60	Val-Ue 213/Red Top 135 (63)
Oh Holy Night/Winter Wonderland	60	Val-Ue 215
Blue Star/Pucker Your Lips	61	20th Century 1213
Get Out/You May Not Love Me	62	Landa 703

Blue Notes (1) (Todd Randall & the)
Charlotte Amalie/Make A Box	55	Tico 1083
If You Love Me/There's Something In Your Eyes, Eloise	56	Josie 800/Port 70021 (61)
With This Pen/Letters	57	Josie 814
The Retribution Blues/Wagon Wheels	57	Josie 823
W-P-L-J/While I'm Away	62	3 Sons 103

Blue Notes (1) (with Joe Loco & Quintette)
If You'll Be Mine/Too Hot To Handle	53	Rama 25

Blue Notes (2) (Joe Weaver & His)
Soft Pillow/15-40 Special	53	DeLuxe 6006
J.B. Boogie/Baby I'm In Love With You	53	DeLuxe 6021
I'm On My Merry Way/Loose Caboose	55	Fortune 820
All I Do Is Cry/Too Hot To Trot (instrumental)	60	Fortune 852

Blue Notes (2) (Joe Weaver & the)
Do You Wanna Work Now/The Lazy Susan	55	Jaguar 3011

Blue Notes (3) (Little Bill & the)
Bye Bye Baby/I Love An Angel	59	Dolton 4
Little Angel/The Next Time You See Me	61	Bolo 725
Sweet Cucumber/Why Was I Ever Born	N/A	Topaz 1302
Louie, Louie/Boy Next Door	N/A	Topaz 1305

Blue Notes (4)
I Don't Know What It Is/Summer Love	59	Brooke 111
I'm Gonna Find Out/Forever On My Mind	60	Brooke 116
Summer Love/It Had To Be You	60	Brooke 119

Blue Notes (5) (Bernard Williams & the)
It's Needless To Say/Focused On You	N/A	Harthon

Blue Rays (1) (Joe Hammond & the)
Kiss Me My Love	58	Bee 1102

ARTIST/SONG	YEAR	LABEL
Blue Rays (2)		
Come On Baby/Who (Will It Be Today)	64	Philips 40186
Blue Rockers		
Calling All Cows/Johnny Mae	55	Excello 2062
Blue Sonnets		
Thank You Mr. Moon/It's Never Too Late	63	Columbia 42793
Blue Stars		
Erlene/My Love Will Never Die	76	Arcade 101
I Only Have Eyes For You/Hey Pretty Baby	76	Arcade 102
Blue Tones		
Shake, Shake/Oh Yeah!	57	King 5088
Bluedots		
My Very Own/Mary Had A Rock N' Roll Lamb	59	Hurricane 104
Bluenotes (1) (Ivan Gregory & the)		
Kathy/Elvis Presley Blues	56	G&G 110
Bluenotes (2) (aka Blue Notes (1))		
Page One/Mighty Low	57	Colonial 434
Let Her Know/Christmas Chimes	58	Colonial 7779
Bluenotes (2) (Harold Melvin & the) (aka Blue Notes (1))		
What A Man Can Do/Go Away	66	Arctic 135
Bluenotes (3) (Henry Wilson & the)		
My Steady Girl/Mighty Lou	58	Dot 15692
Bluenotes (4)		
Winter Wonderland/Oh Holy Night	60	Valve 115
Bluenotes (5) (Donnie Williams & the)		
Cry Your Heart Out/Is Your Love	59	Viking 1005
Bluenotes (5) (James Easterling & the)		
Angel Of Mine	N/A	Reno 133
Bluenotes (5) (Phil Cay & the)		
Meet Me In The Barnyard/If They Ask Me	59	Hart 1001
Bluenotes (5) (Vince Anthony & the)		
Clarabel/All Over Again	63	Viking 1018
Blues Busters		
Tell Me Why/Behold	62	Capitol 4895
Boardwalkers (Ronnie & the)		
She Won't Go Steady	N/A	Rex 103
Bob-O-Links		
I Promise/Mr. Frog	62	Hi-Ho 101
Bob-Wheels		
She's Gone/Love Me	63	Tarx 1008
Bobbettes (female)		
Mr. Lee/Look At The Stars	57	Atlantic 1144
Come-A Come-A/Speedy	57	Atlantic 1159

ARTIST/SONG	YEAR	LABEL
Zoomy/Rock And Ree-Ah-Zole	58	Atlantic 1181
The Dream/Um Bow Wow	58	Atlantic 1194
You Are My Sweetheart/Don't Say Goodnight	59	Atlantic 2027
I Shot Mr. Lee/Untrue Love	60	Atlantic 2069
I Cried/Oh My Papa	60	Galliant 1006
I Shot Mr. Lee/Billy	60	Triple-X 104
Have Mercy Baby/Dance With Me Georgie	60	Triple-X 106
Teach Me Tonight/Mr. Johnny Q	61	End 1093
I Don't Like It Like That Pt. 1/I Don't Like It Like That Pt. 2	61	End 1095
I Don't Like It Like That/Mr. Johnny Q	61	Gone 5112
Oh Mein Papa/Dance With Me Georgie	61	King 5490
Looking For A Lover/Are You Satisfied (With Your Love)?	61	King 5551
Over There (Stands My Baby)/Loneliness	62	Jubilee 5427
The Broken Heart/Mama Papa	62	Jubilee 5442
My Dearest/I'm Stepping Out Tonight	62	King 5623
Teddy/Row, Row, Row	63	Diamond 133
Close Your Eyes/Somebody Bad Stole De Wedding Bell	63	Diamond 142
My Mama Said/Sandman	64	Diamond 156
In Paradise/I Am Climbing A Mountain	64	Diamond 166
You Ain't Seen Nothing Yet/I'm Climbing A Mountain	65	Diamond 181
Love Is Blind/Teddy	65	Diamond 189
I've Gotta Face The World/Having Fun	66	RCA 8832
It's All Over/Happy-Go-Lucky Me	66	RCA 8983
That's A Bad Thing To Know/All In Your Mind	71	Mayhew 712297/712298
Tighten Up Your Own Thing/Looking For A New Love (Bad Thing To Know)	72	Mayhew 37
It Won't Work Out/Good Man	74	Mayhew 861/862

Bobbettes 1981 (female)

Love Rhythm/I'll Keep Coming Back	81	QIT

Bobbinaires

Just Another Way To Break A Heart	N/A	Jen-D

Bobby & Jimmy (& group)

Day And Night/Down The Road And Over The Hill	63	King 5757

Bobby-Pins

Darling Don't Leave Me Now/I Want You	59	Okeh 7110
Why Did You Go/I Wanna Love	63	Mercury 72193

Bobolinks

Elvis Presley's Sergeant/Your Cotton Pickin' Heart	58	Key 573
Chocolate Ice Cream/Mechanical Man	58	Key 575
Lonesome Wind/Message From Me	61	Tune 226

Bohemians

Some Happy Day/Say Sweet Things	62	Chex 1007

Boleros (Carmen Taylor & the)

Freddie/Ooh I	54	Atlantic 1041
Teen-Age Ball/Oh Please	56	Apollo 489

Bombers

Malena/I'll Never Tire Of You	55	Orpheus 1101
Two-Time Heart/Sentence Of Love	56	Orpheus 1105

Bon Bons

Three Teens/A Girl Without A Fella	56	Columbia 40800
The Kiss In Your Eyes/Love Me Or I'll Die	57	Columbia 40887

Bon-Aires (1)

Bermuda/Stop The World	56	King 4975

ARTIST/SONG	YEAR	LABEL
Bon-Aires (2)		
Blue Beat/Driving Along	62	Rust TR3
Bye Bye/My Love My Love	64	Rust 5077
The Shrine Of St. Cecilia/Jeanie Baby	64	Rust 5097
My Heart's Desire/New Me	71	Catamount 130
Cherry/At Night (a capella)	76	Flamingo 1000
Out Of Sight, Out Of Mind/I Love You (a capella)	76	Flamingo 1001
Bon-Bons (1)		
Pass It Along/Momma Llama, Poppa Llama	55	London International 1585
Listen My Heart/Lovin' Up A Storm Tonight	64	Sampson 1003
Bon-Bons (2) (female)		
Come On Baby/What's Wrong With Ringo	64	Coral 62402
Each Time/Everybody Wants My Boyfriend	64	Coral 62435
Bonaires		
Lolita/Evergreen	60	Shasta 126
Bonairs		
It's Christmas Time/I'm Alone Tonight (by the Ernie Tavares Trio)	53	Dootone 325
Bond, Dave (& group)		
Tell Me/Rocking Good Feeling	61	Khoury's 723
Bonnets		
Ya Gotta Take A Chance/Ya Gotta Take A Chance (instrumental)	63	Unical 3010
Bonnevilles		
Give Me Your Love/Until You Say We're Through	59	Capri 102
My Love	59	Ka-Hi 121
I Do/Make Believe Lovin'	59	Whitehall 30002
Lorraine/Zu Zu	60	Munich 103/Barry 104 (62)
I Love You So	N/A	N/A
Bonnie Sisters (female)		
Cry Baby/I Saw Mommy Cha Cha Cha With You Know Who	56	Rainbow 328
Track That Cat/Wandering Heart	56	Rainbow 333
Do You Know/Little Bo Peep	56	Rainbow 336
Boogie Ramblers		
Cindy Lou/Such Is Love	57	Goldband 1030
Bop Chords		
My Darling To You/Castle In The Sky	57	Holiday 2601
When I Woke Up This Morning/I Really Love Her So	57	Holiday 2603
So Why/Baby	57	Holiday 2608
Bop Shop		
Don't Say Goodnight/Seven Wonders Of The World	72	Kelway 105
The Stars/That's How I Feel	N/A	Horizon Ent. Ltd.
Nuts 'N' Sprinkles/Cry Baby Cry	N/A	Larric 7301
Boppers (Alonzo & the)		
I'm On My Way/Juicy Melon	63	Rojac 8127
Boptones		
Be My Pussy Cat/I Had A Love	58	Ember 1043
Boss Men		
Self Pity	64	Score 1003
Bossmen		
Fever Of Love/Good Lookin' Woman	64	Busy Bee 1001
You And I/Baby Boy	66	Lucky Eleven 231

ARTIST/SONG	YEAR	LABEL
Bosstones (aka Boss-Tones)		
Mope-itty Mope/Wings Of An Angel	59	Boss 401/V-Tone 208 (60)
Boulevards		
Delores/Chop Chop Hole In The Wall	59	Everest 19316
Bouquets		
Welcome To My Heart/Ain't That Love	65	Blue Cat 115
Bouquets (Tootie & the)		
You Done Me Wrong/The Conqueror	63	Parkway 887
Bowery Boys		
Sometimes	85	N/A
Bowman, Priscilla (& group)		
Why Must I Cry/Like A Baby	59	Abner 1033
Bowman, Priscilla (bb the Spaniels)		
I Ain't Givin' Up Nothin'/A Rockin' Good Way	58	Abner 1018
Bowties (Cirino & the)		
My Rosemarie/My Baby's In Love With Me	55	Royal Roost 614
This Must Be The Place/Again	56	Royal Roost 619
Snap Jack/After Love	56	Royal Roost 622
Ever Since I Can Remember/Rock, Pretty Baby	56	Royal Roost 624
(with Ivy Schulman)		
Boy Friends (1) (Jeanie & the)		
It's Me Knocking/Baby	59	Warwick 508
Boy Friends (2) (Terry Corin & the)		
Dream Date/Sick Sick Sick	60	Colony 110
Boy Friends (3)		
Shy Boy/Snake In The Grass	61	Glasser 1000
Boyce, Tommy (& group)		
I'll Remember Carol/Too Late For Tears	62	RCA 8074
Boyd, Eddie (with His Chess Men)		
I Love You/Save Her Doctor	57	J.O.B. 1114
Boyfriends (1) (Wini Brown & the)		
Here In My Heart/Your Happiness In Mine	52	Mercury 5870
Heaven Knows Why/Be Anything, Be Mine	52	Mercury 8270
Boyfriends (2) (Janis & Her)		
Please Be My Love/Bang Bang	58	RCA 7318
Boyfriends (3) (aka Five Discs)		
Let's Fall In Love/Oh Lana	64	Kapp 569
Boys (1) (Barbara & the)		
Hooty Sapperticker/Cobra	58	Dot 15798
Boys (2)		
Angel Of Mine/I Wanna Know	N/A	SVR 1001
It's Hopeless/How Do You Do With Me	N/A	SVR 1002
Boys Next Door		
We Got Together/Now You're Talking Baby	56	Rainbow 349
Sweet Love Of Mine/You Talk Too Much	56	Vik 0207

ARTIST/SONG	YEAR	LABEL
Bracelets		
I'll Play Along/Waddle, Waddle	62	Congress 104
You're Just Fooling Yourself/You Better Move On	64	20th Century Fox 539
Bradford Boys		
That Feeling/Little Boy Blue	55	Rainbow 307
Bradford, Chuck (& group)		
You Can't Hurt Me Anymore/Wherever You Are	62	Fire 511
Bradford, Sylvester (& group)		
I Like Girls/Live Just To Love You	58	Atco 6130
Bravadoes (Little Mac & the)		
Cinderella/Dance Baby (With Me)	61	Little Mac 101
Breakaways		
He Doesn't Love Me/That's How It Goes	64	Cameo 323
Breakers		
Balboa Memories/Long Way Home	63	Marsh 206
Brentwoods		
Midnight Star/As I Live From Day To Day	60	Dore 559
Gee, But I Miss Him/Oh, Dear, What Can The Matter Be	63	Talent 1003
Brewer, Mike (& group)		
The Most Important Thing/I'm Counting On You	63	Lesley 1929
Bridges, Curley (& group)		
A Prayer Of Love (flip has no group)	60	DC 0436
Brightones		
Rumors/Swim Swim Swim	64	Warner Bros. 5472
Broadways		
Are You Telling Me Goodbye/Goin', Goin', Gone	66	MGM 13486
Brochures		
They Lied/My In-Laws Are Outlaws	61	Apollo 757
Broken Hearts		
Shining Star/Ten Lonely Guys	62	Diamond 123
Crying Over You/Thrill Upon A Hill	N/A	Rosina 147
Brooklyn Boys		
If She Should Call/Every Night	56	Ferris 902
Brooktones		
There Must Be A Reason/Cute Collegiate	58	Coed 502
Brothers		
My True Love/One Lonely Heart	61	Checker 995
Brothers (Little Toni & the)		
Princess/I Love You	60	Top Rank 2090
Brown, Billy (& group)		
Lost Weekend/Just Out Of Reach	60	Republic 2007
Brown, Bobby (& group)		
Falling From Paradise/Dreamer	62	Pak 1313
Brown, Charles (& group)		
Angel Baby/Baby Oh Baby	61	King 5439

ARTIST/SONG	YEAR	LABEL
Brown, Ruth (& group)		
Oh What A Dream I Had Last Night/Please Don't Freeze	55	Atlantic 1036
Brown, Sammy (& group)		
I'm In Love/Let's Leave It Like It Is	64	Bee Bee 701
Browne, Doris (bb the Capris)		
Oh Baby/Please Believe Me	53	Gotham 290
Until The End Of Time/Why Don't You Love Me Now, Now, Now	53	Gotham 296
My Cherie/The Game Of Love	53	Gotham 298
Browns (Barbara & the)		
Big Party/You Belong To Her	64	Stax 150
In My Heart/Please Be Honest With Me	64	Stax 158
Bruno, Bruce (& group)		
Dear Joanne/Venus In Blue Jeans	62	Roulette 4427
Bryant, Helen (& group)		
That's A Promise/I've Learned My Lesson	61	Fury 1042
Bua, Gene (& group)		
Well Honey/Golly Gee	58	Safari 1007/ABC 9928 (58)
Buccaneers (1)		
The Stars Will Remember/Come Back My Love	53	Rama 21
In The Mission Of St. Augustine/You Did Me Wrong	53	Rama 24
Dear Ruth/Fine Brown Frame	53	Southern 101/Rainbow 211 (53)
Buccaneers (2)		
Over And Over Again/Let's Drink To Happiness	54	Tiffany 1308
Buccaneers (3)		
Who Are You Foolin' Now/Blonde Hair, Blue Eyes And Ruby Lips	58	Crystalette 718
Buckeyes		
Since I Fell For You/Be Only You	57	DeLuxe 6110
Dottie Baby/Begging You, Please	57	DeLuxe 6126
Buddies (1) (Billy Bunn & the)		
I'm Afraid/I Need A Shoulder To Cry On	51	RCA 4483
That's When Your Heartaches Began/	52	RCA 4657
Until The Real Thing Comes Along		
Buddies (2)		
I Stole Your Heart/I Waited	55	Glory 230
Buddies (3) (Little Butchie Saunders & His)		
Lindy Lou/Rock And Roll Indian Dance	56	Herald 485
Great Big Heart/I Wanna Holler	56	Herald 491
Over The Rainbow/Sometimes Little Girl	59	Angle Tone 535
(by Little Butchie & the Vells)		
Buddies (4)		
A Prom And A Promise/Lottery	57	Decca 30355
Buddies (5) (Carl Ell & the)		
Bobby, My Love/Sunshine	59	Combo 154
Buddies (6)		
Castle Of Love/Give Me Your Love	59	Okeh 7123
Heartless/She's A Loser	59	Tiara 6121
Buddies (7)		
Must Be True Love/Hully Gully Mama	61	Comet 2143

ARTIST/SONG	YEAR	LABEL
Lebone Delada/Spooky Spider	61	Swan 4073
The Beatle/Pulsebeat	64	Swan 4170

Buddies (8) (aka Tokens (2))
On The Go/My Only Friend	64	Swing 102

Bumble Bees
A Girl Called Love/Echo Boogie	63	Joey 6220
Please Let It Be/Please Don't Go	N/A	Relic LP 5043

Burrage, Harold (& group)
Crying For My Baby/What You Don't Know	59	Vee Jay 318

Burt, Wanda (bb the Crescendos)
Your True Love Is Standing Here/Scheming	61	Music City 840

Bussy, Terry (& group)
How Could You/Calypso Peacock	56	Jazzmar 103

Butanes
That's My Desire/Don't Forget I Love You	61	Enrica 1007

Butler, B. B. (& group)
I Hope I Don't Cry/As Long As You Love Me	64	Barry 111

Butler, Cliff (& group)
That's How I Go For You/Devoted To You	58	Nasco 6010

Butlers (1)
Lovable Girl/When I Grow Older	63	Guyden 2081
She Tried To Kiss Me/The Sun's Message	64	Liberty Bell 1024

Butlers (2) (Frankie Beverly & the)
She Kissed Me/Don't Cry Little Boy Sad	67	Fairmount 1012

Butterballs
Butterball/Give Me A Chance (by the Chanells)	63	Times Square 24

Butterflys (female)
Goodnight Baby/The Swim	64	Red Bird 10-009
Gee Baby Gee/I Wonder	64	Red Bird 10-016

Buzzards (Big John & the)
Mean Woman/Hey, Little Girl	54	Columbia 40345
Oop Shoop/Your Cash Ain't Nothin' But Trash	54	Okeh 7045

Bye Byes
Do You/Blond Hair, Blue Eyes, Ruby Lips	59	Mercury 71530

Byrd, Bobby (& group)
Please Don't Hurt Me/Delicious Are Your Kisses	55	Sage & Sand 203
If We Should Meet Again/Looby Loo	57	Zephyr 70-018

Bystanders
Power Of A Prayer/Yellow Mellow Hardtop	57	Demon 1502

Bystanders (fb Ray Johnson)
Love A La Mode/No Stone Unturned	56	Dot 15512

C & C Boys
Hey Marvin/You Stole My Heart	62	Duke 358
It's All Over Now/My Life	64	Duke 379

C-Larks
Time/Please Write Me A Letter	56	Nova 106

ARTIST/SONG	YEAR	LABEL
C-Notes (1) (aka C-Tones)		
On Your Mark/From Now On	57	Everlast 5005
We Were Meant For Each Other/Last Saturday Night	59	Arc 4447
C-Notes (1) (Frankie & the)		
Forever And Ever/Union Hall (by the Montels)	63	Times Square 10/Richie 2
C-Notes (2) (Ron Jones & the)		
Goodbye Linda/Why	62	Mobie 3419
C-Quents		
Merry Christmas Baby/All I Want For Christmas Is You	N/A	Captown 4027
Dearest One/It's You And Me	N/A	Essica 004
C-Quins		
My Only Love/You've Been Crying	62	Ditto 501/Chess 1815 (62)
C-Tones (aka C-Notes)		
On Your Mark/From Now On	57	Everlast 5005
Cabarettes		
There Must Be A Way/Times Is Tough	63	Saxony 1002
Cabot, Johnny (& group)		
On My Own Again/Night And Day	62	Columbia 42283
Caddell, Shirley (& group)		
The Big Bounce/Don't Hurt A Good Thing	63	Lesley 1927
Caddy's (Jesse Powell & the)		
Ain't You Gonna/Turnpike (instrumental)	58	Josie 834
Cadets (1) (Aaron Collins & the) (aka Jacks)		
Pretty Evey (Evelyn)/Rum Jamaica Rum	57	Modern 1019
Cadets (1) (aka Jacks)		
Don't Be Angry/I Cry	55	Modern 956
Rollin' Stone/Fine Lookin' Baby	55	Modern 960
Fine Lookin' Baby/I Cry	55	Modern 963
Ay La Ba/My Man (Dolly Cooper)	55	Modern 965
I Got Loaded/Dancin' Dan (Sixty Minute Man)	56	Modern 1000
Fools Rush In/I'll Be Spinning	56	Modern 1006
Annie Met Henry/So Will I	56	Modern 969
Do You Wanna Rock (Hey Little Girl)/If It Is Wrong	56	Modern 971
Church Bells May Ring/Heartbreak Hotel	56	Modern 985
Stranded In The Jungle/I Want You	56	Modern 994
Love Bandit/Heaven Help Me	57	Modern 1012
You Belong To Me/Heaven Help Me	57	Modern 1017
You Belong To Me/Wiggie Waggie Woo	57	Modern 1017
Ring Chimes/Baby Ya Know	57	Modern 1026
Car Crash/Don't	60	Jan-Lar 102
I Had Fifty Cents	63	Crown LP 5370
John Henry	63	Crown LP 5370
Marie My Love	63	Crown LP 5370
The Riddle	63	Crown LP 5370
Stranded In The Jungle/Rollin' Stone	75	Relic 1032
Smack Dab In The Middle	N/A	Modern LP 1215
Let's Rock And Roll	N/A	Relic LP 5025
Memories Of You	N/A	Relic LP 5025
Cadets (1) (Bennie Bunn & the) (aka Jacks)		
One More Chance/I'm Looking For A Job	57	Sherwood 211
Cadets (1) (Will Jones & the) (aka Jacks)		
Hands Across The Table/Love Can Do Most Anything	57	Modern 1024

ARTIST/SONG	YEAR	LABEL
Cadets (2) (Kenny & the)		
Barbie/What Is A Young Girl Made Of	60	Randy 422
Cadillacs		
Gloria/I Wonder Why	54	Josie 765
Wishing Well/I Want To Know About Love	54	Josie 769
Corn Whiskey	54	unreleased
Party For Two	54	unreleased
No Chance/Sympathy	55	Josie 773
Down The Road/Window Lady	55	Josie 778
Speedoo/Let Me Explain	55	Josie 785
Zoom/You Are	56	Josie 792
Betty My Love/Woe Is Me	56	Josie 798
(That's) All I Need/The Girl I Love	56	Josie 805
Shock-A-Doo/Rudolph The Red-Nosed Reindeer	56	Josie 807
Don't Take Your Love From Me	56	unreleased
Oh! Whatcha Do	56	unreleased
Sugar, Sugar/About That Girl Named Lou	57	Josie 812
My Girl Friend/Broken Heart	57	Josie 820
If You Want To Be A Woman Of Mine	57	unreleased
Peek-A-Boo/Oh, Oh, Lolita	58	Jo-Z 846 (first pressing)/ Josie 846 (58) (second pressing)
Speedo Is Back/A Looka Here	58	Josie 836
Holy Smoke Baby/I Want To Know	58	Josie 842
Great Googly Moo	58	unreleased
It's Spring	58	unreleased
Jelly Bean	58	unreleased
Jay Walker/Copy Cat	59	Josie 857
Please, Mr. Johnson/Cool It Fool	59	Josie 861
Romeo/Always My Darling	59	Josie 866
Bad Dan McGoon/Dumbell	59	Josie 870
Baby's Coming Home To Me	59	Jubilee LP 1089
Carelessly	59	Jubilee LP 1089
Don't Be Mad With My Heart	59	Jubilee LP 1089
Why, Why	59	Jubilee LP 1089
Zoom Boom Zing	59	Jubilee LP 1089
Frankenstein	59	unreleased
I Want To Be Loved	59	unreleased
The Vow	59	unreleased
You're Not in Love With Me	59	unreleased
Your Heart Is So Blind	59	unreleased
That's Why/The Boogie Man	60	Josie 883
I'm In Love	60	unreleased
Louise	60	unreleased
Rock 'n' Roll Is Here To Stay	60	unreleased
C'mon Home Baby	61	Jubilee LP 1117
Let Me Down Easy	61	Jubilee LP 1117
Buzz Buzz Buzz	61	Jubilee LP 1117/ Jubilee LP 5009 (62)
It's Love	61	Jubilee LP 1117/ Jubilee LP 5009 (62)
Dum De Dum Dum	62	Jubilee LP 5009
Still You Left Me Baby	62	Jubilee LP 5009
Speedo/Baby It's All Right	64	Lana 118
Gloria/Hay Bob E Re Bob	64	Lana 119
I'll Never Let You Go	N/A	Josie (unreleased)
Cadillacs (Bobby Ray & the)		
I'm Willing/Thrill Me So	61	Mercury 71738
I Saw You/La Bomba	63	Capitol 4935
Cadillacs (Ray Brewster & the) (aka Solitaires)		
Fool/The Right Kind Of Lovin'	63	Arctic 101

ARTIST/SONG	YEAR	LABEL
Cadillacs (Speedo & the)		
Tell Me Today/It's Love	60	Josie 876
Cadillacs (The Original Cadillacs)		
Hurry Home/Lucy	57	Josie 821
What You Bet/You Are To Blame	61	Smash 1712
White Gardenia/Groovy Groovy Love	62	Capitol 4825
Deep In The Heart Of The Ghetto Pt. 1/Pt. 2	72	Polydor 14031
Cahperones (aka Chaperones (1)		
Cruise To The Moon/Dance With Me	60	Josie 880 (first pressing, second is by the Chaperones)
Caine, Gladys (& group)		
Please Mr. D.J.	63	Togo 602
Caiton, Richard (& group)		
You Look Like A Flower/Listen To The Drums	64	GNP Crescendo 327
Cal-Cons		
Daddy Cool	62	Allrite 621
Caldwell, Joe (& group)		
Rollin' Tears/Rowdy Mae	59	Esta 100
Calendars (1)		
I'm Gonna Laugh At You/You're Too Fast	61	Coed 564
One Week Romance/Roasted Peanuts (by the Milestones)	61	Swingin' 649
If I Could Hold Your Hand	74	Relic LP 5019
What Are You Gonna Be	74	Relic LP 5019
Calendars (1) (Shell Dupont & the)		
Share My Love/Stop Driving Me Crazy	N/A	Tribune 1001
Calendars (2) (Freddy Meade & the)		
Just Give Her My Love/Mepri Stomp	61	20th Fox 287
Calendars (3) (Roberta Watson & the)		
Dear Donnie/You Insulted Me	63	Corsican 111
Calhoun, Lena (bb the Emotions (2))		
I Can Tell/Been Lookin' Your Way	62	Flip 358
Calhoun, Millie (& group)		
This Love Will Last Forever/I Go For You	N/A	Lo Lace 708
Californians		
My Angel/Heavenly Ruby	55	Federal 12231
Caliphs		
Darling If I Had You/Mother Dear	58	Scatt 111
I Need You/Party Time	73	Vintage 1008
Callender, Bob (& group)		
Baby I'm Ready/All With You	64	Gold 102
Callenders		
If I Could Hold Your Hand/What Are You Gonna Be	59	Cyclone 5012
Calvaes		
Fine Girl/Mambo Fiesta	56	Cobra 5003
Born With Rhythm/Lonely, Lonely Village	57	Cobra 5014
Calvaes (Oscar Boyd & the)		
Anna Macora/So Bad	59	Checker 928

ARTIST/SONG	YEAR	LABEL
Calvanes		
They Call Me Foot	55	Dooto EP 205
Crazy Over You/Don't Take Your Love From Me	55	Dootone 371
Florabelle/One More Kiss	56	Dootone 380
Dreamworld/5, 7 Or 9	58	Deck 579
My Love Song/Horror Pictures	58	Deck 580
Fleeoowee	N/A	Collectables LP 5048
Calveys		
The Wind/I Need Love	61	Comma 84349/Comma 445
Camelots (1)		
Never Been In Love Before/Lulu	61	Nix 101
Camelots (2) (aka Cupids (6)/aka Harps (2))		
Don't Leave Me Baby (a capella)/The Letter	61	Crimson 1001
Your Way/Don't Leave Me Baby	63	AAnko 1001
Sunday Kind Of Love/My Imagination	63	AAnko 1004
Pocahontas/Searching For My Baby	63	Ember 1108
Don't Leave Me Baby (a capella)/Love Call (by the Ebonaires)	64	Cameo 334
Dance Girl/That's My Baby (by the Suns)	64	Times Square 32/Relic 541 (65)
Chain Of Broken Hearts/Rat Race	65	Relic 530
Your Way/I Wonder	67	Dream 1001
Camelots (3)		
Scratch/Charge	62	Comet 930
Cameos (1)		
Craving/Only For You	55	Dootone 365
Cameos (2)		
Merry Christmas/New Year's Eve	57	Cameo 123
Best Of The Can Can Pt. 1/Best Of The Can Can Pt. 2	59	Cameo 176
Please Love Me/Shanga Langa Ding Dong	59	Flagship 115
Wait Up/Lost Lover	60	Dean 504/Johnson 108 (60)
We'll Still Be Together/I Remember When	60	Matador 1808
Canadian Sunset/Never Before	60	Matador 1813
He/Can You Remember?	63	Gigi 100
Cameos (3) (Ty Taylor & the)		
The Beginning Of Love/Big Pearl	59	Design 834
Cameos (4) (Little Willie Brown & the)		
Gonna Make It On Back/Cut It Out	61	Do-Ra-Mi 1404
Cameos (5)		
Comin' On Down	N/A	Relic LP 5028
Cameron, Ken (& group)		
Don't Forget/The Prisoner's Song	61	Zynn 500
Camerons (1)		
Cheryl/Boom Chic-A-Boom (by the Jiveleers)	60	Cousins 1/2
Baby Don't You Know/She's Got It	60	Cousins (unreleased)
Lonely Teenager/Cheryl	60	Cousins (unreleased)
Camerons (2) (aka Demilles)		
Guardian Angel/A Girl I Marry	61	Cousins 1003/Felsted 8638 (61)
Campanions (aka Del Satins)		
I Want A Yul Brenner Haircut/Dorothy, My Monster	N/A	Dee-Dee 1047
Campbell, Charlotte (& group)		
True Lover/Where Did My Dreamboat Go	59	Wanger 194

ARTIST/SONG	YEAR	LABEL
Campbell, Jo Ann (bb the Dubs)		
Jim Dandy/Five Minutes More	62	Rori 711
Canadian Meteors (Buddy Burke & the)		
Street Of Sorrow/That Big Old Moon	57	Bullseye 1002
Canaries		
I'm Sorry Baby/Runaround Ronnie	64	Dimension 1047
Candies (1) (Ace Kennedy & the)		
Arms Around You/You Promise	60	XYZ 609
As Time Goes By/Never, Never, Never	63	Philips 40111
Candies (2)		
I'm Only Making It Easier For You/Yes I Love You	62	Ember 1092
If You Wanna Do A Smart Thing/Stop	63	Fleetwood 7003
Candles (1) (Rochell & the)		
Once Upon A Time/When My Baby Is Gone	60	Swingin' 623
Goodnight	61	Swingin'
Hey, Pretty Baby/So Far Away	61	Swingin' 634
Peg Of My Heart/Squat With Me Baby	61	Swingin' 640
Big Boy Pete/A Long Time Ago	61	Swingin' 652
Each Night/Turn Her Down	62	Challenge 9158
Let's Run Away And Get Married/	62	Challenge 9191
Annie's Not An Orphan Anymore		
One Night With You	85	Relic LP 5060
Candles (2) (aka Blenders (5))		
Junior/Down On My Knees (by the Starr Brothers)	64	Nike 1016
Candlettes		
Wrapped Up In A Dream/Moments To Remember	63	Rhonda 1001
Candletts		
Angel Love/Everybody Loves To Rock And Roll	58	Vita 179
My Only Love/It's Misery	59	Vita 182
Candy Canes (Jimmy James & the)		
Teen-Age Beauty/Marjolaine	58	Columbia 41192
Candy Girls		
Tomorrow My Love/Run	64	Rotate 5001
Runaround/Run	64	Rotate 5005
Candy Makers		
And So Tomorrow/Chop Chop Chop	N/A	Urban 124
Comin' Through The Rye/Chapel In My Memory	N/A	Urban 125
Cap-Tans		
Asking/Who Can I Turn To	51	Coral 65071
I'm So Crazy For Love/With All My Love	53	Dot 15114
Tight Skirts And Crazy Sweaters/I'm Afraid	60	Anna 1122
Cap-Tans (Bethea & the)		
Crazy About A Woman	N/A	Loop 100
Cap-Tans (Wailing Bethea & the)		
Rockin' In The Jungle/Annie Penguin	62	Hawkeye 0430
Capers (female)		
Miss You, My Dear/Early One Morning	58	Vee Jay 297
High School Diploma/Candy Store Blues	59	Vee Jay 315

ARTIST/SONG	YEAR	LABEL

Capes
| The Vow | N/A | Chat 5005 |

Capistranos (John Littleton & the) (with James Brown)
| Now Darling/Po' Mary | 58 | Duke 179 |

Capitols (1)
| Angel Of Love/Cause I Love You | 58 | Pet 807 |

Capitols (1) (Mickey Toliver & the)
| Rose-Marie/Millie | 57 | Cindy 3002 |
| Day By Day/Little Things | 58 | Gateway 721 |

Capitols (2) (Johnny Houston & the)
| But It's Too Late/Hula Hands | 57 | East West 100 |

Capitols (3)
| I Let Her Go | 58 | Carlton 461 |

Capitols (4)
| Write Me A Love Letter/Three O'Clock Rock | 59 | Triumph 601 |

Capitols (5)
| I'll Drink A Toast/Fine Momma's Daughter | 62 | Portrait 109 |

Capitols (6)
| Honey, Honey/ Alone In The Night (by the Jones Boys) | 73 | Baron 103 |

Capri Sisters (female)
After School Rock 'N' Roll/The Occarina Roll	56	Jubilee 5244
Run-A-Round/Hawaiian Sway	58	Dot 15851
In Between/It's All Over	59	Hanover 4531
I'm Gonna Wish For You/There But For Her Go I	60	ABC 10158
Poco Loco/The Blues Came Tumbling Down	61	Warwick 673
I Want You To Be My Boy/Fairy Tales	62	Newtown 5002

Capri, Bobby (& group)
| One-Sided Love/Charm Bracelet | 61 | Artiste 101 |

Capri, John (bb the Fabulous Four)
| When I'm Lonely/Love For Me | 59 | Bomarc 306 |

Capri, Johnny (& group)
| Don't Say Goodbye | 61 | Master 13 |

Capri, Mike (& group)
| She's My Baby/Dontcha Keep Me Wanting | N/A | Cecil 4450 |

Capri, Tony (& group)
| Sandy/Why Do You Do Me | 61 | Liban 1001 |
| Counting Wishes/That's The Way | 61 | Liban 1005 |

Capris (1)
God Only Knows/That's What You're Doing To Me	54	Gotham 7304/ 20th Century 7304 (57)
It Was Moonglow/Too Poor To Love	55	Gotham 7306
My Weakness/Yes, My Baby Please	56	20th Century 1201
It's A Miracle/Let's Linger Awhile	56	Gotham 7308
Oh, My Darling/Rock Pretty Baby	58	Lifetime 1001/1002
Bless You	N/A	Collectables LP 5000
He Still Loves Me	N/A	Collectables LP 5000
How Long	N/A	Collectables LP 5000
I Miss Your Love	N/A	Collectables LP 5000

ARTIST/SONG	YEAR	LABEL

Capris (1)

Just A Fool	N/A	Collectables LP 5000
Please Believe Me	N/A	Collectables LP 5000
She Still Loves Me	N/A	Collectables LP 5000
Yes My Baby Please	N/A	Collectables LP 5000
You're Mine Again	N/A	Collectables LP 5000

Capris (2) (aka Jesse Belvin & studio group)

Endless Love (slow version)/Endless Love (fast version)	59	Impact 34
Endless Love/Beware	59	Tender 518

Capris (3)

Can't Get Over You/This Is Goodbye	59	Fable 665
My Promise To You/Bop! Bop! Bop!	59	Sabre 201/202

The Capris

Capris (4)

There's A Moon Out Tonight/Indian Girl	58	Planet 1010/1011/Old Town 1094 (60)/Lost Nite 101 (60)/ Trommer
Little Girl	60	Lost Nite 148
Where I Fell In Love/Some People Think	61	Old Town 1099
Tears In My Eyes/Why Do I Cry	61	Old Town 1103
Girl In My Dreams/My Island In The Sun	61	Old Town 1107
Limbo/From The Vine Came The Grape	62	Mr. Peacock 118/Mr. Peeke 118 (63)
Morse Code Of Love/There's A Moon Out Again	82	Ambient Sound 02697
A Hum Diddily Dee Do	N/A	Collectables LP 5016
Stars In The Sky	N/A	Collectables LP 5016

Capris (5) (aka Mel Williams & the Montclairs)

Ooh Wah/Fools Fall In Love	55	Rage 101

Caprisians

A Lovely Way To Spend An Evening/Yibby-Yah	60	Indigo 109
Oh What A Night/Why Do You Have To Go	61	Lavender 004

Captans (Jerry Holland & the)

A Big Bite Of The Blues/Ain't No Big Thing (instrumental)	59	DC 0433

Carallons (Lonnie & the)

Chapel Of Tears/My Heart	63	Mohawk 108/ Streetcorner 101 (73)
Trudy/Hold Me Close	60	Mohawk 111

ARTIST/SONG	YEAR	LABEL
You Say/Backyard Rock	60	Mohawk 112
The Gang All Knows/Ike Hammer	60	Mohawk 113
Chapel Of Tears/Wild Weekend (by the Barons)	N/A	Mohawk 902

Caraman, Art (& group)
Falling For You/Eternity Of Love	62	Dasa 101

Caravelles
Angry Angel/Pink Lips	61	Star Maker 1925
Falling For You/Shake Baby	62	Joey 301
One Little Kiss/Twistin' Marie	62	Joey 6208

Carbo, Chuck (& group)
Times/I Miss You	57	Imperial 5479

Carbo, Leonard (& group)
So Tired/Pigtails And Blue Jeans	58	Vee Jay 291

Cardell, Nick (& group)
How Can I Help It/Arlene	63	Liberty 55556
I Stand Alone/Everybody Jump	64	Amcan 405

Cardells
Helen/Lovely Girl	56	Middle-Tone 011

Cardigans (1)
Your Graduation Means Goodbye/Boll Weevil On The Mountain Top	58	Mercury 71251
Make Up Your Mind/Half Breed	59	Spann 431

Cardigans (2) (Dave & the)
My Falling Star/Cha Cha Baby	63	Bay 216

Cardinals (1)
Shouldn't I Know/Please Don't Leave Me	51	Atlantic 938
Pretty Baby Blues/I'll Always Love	51	Atlantic 952
Wheel Of Fortune/Kiss Me Baby	52	Atlantic 958
She Rocks/The Bump	52	Atlantic 972
Lovie Darling/You Are My Only Love	53	Atlantic 995
Please Baby/Under A Blanket Of Blue	54	Atlantic 1025
The Door Is Still Open/Misirlou	55	Atlantic 1054
Come Back My Love/Two Things I Love	55	Atlantic 1067
Lovely Girl/There Goes My Heart To You	55	Atlantic 1079
Off Shore/Choo-Choo	56	Atlantic 1090
I Won't Make You Cry Anymore/The End Of The Story	56	Atlantic 1103
One Love/Near You	57	Atlantic 1126
Bim Bam Boom	N/A	Atlantic EP only
Have I Been Gone Too Long	N/A	Atlantic EP only
Love Me	N/A	Atlantic EP only
Sure Enough	N/A	Atlantic EP only

Cardinals (2) (Bobby Gregory & the)
Just Waiting/Precious One	59	Kip 403

Cardinals (3) (Claudia & the)
Much Too Much Too Soon	N/A	Teltone

Careless Five
I'm Lonely/The Question Mark Twist	N/A	Careful 1010
Summertime/Tell Me Right Now	N/A	Vitose 101

Cari, Eddie (& group)
Wishing Time/This Love Of Mine	63	Mermaid 104

Carians
She's Gone/Snooty Friends	61	Indigo 136
Only A Dream/Girls	61	Magenta 04

ARTIST/SONG	YEAR	LABEL
Caribbeans		
Keep Her By My Side/I Knew	58	20th Fox 112
Caribbeans (George Torrence & the)		
Too Soon/Sweet Little Thing	58	Galliant 1003
Carlo (aka Carlo Mastrangelo) (& group)		
Write Me A Letter/Baby Doll	63	Laurie 3151
Little Orphan Doll/Mairzy Doats	63	Laurie 3157
Story Of My Love/Five Minutes More	63	Laurie 3175
Ring-A-Ling/Stranger In My Arms	64	Laurie 3227
Claudine/Fever	70	Raftis 110
Let There Be Love	70	Raftis 112
Carlos Brothers		
Under Stars Of Love	59	Cascade-Drop LP 1008
Tonight/Come On, Let's Dance	59	Del-Fi 4112
It's Time To Go/Little Cupid	59	Del-Fi 4118
La Bamba/It's Time To Go	60	Del-Fi 4145
Carlton, Chick (& group)		
Tomorrow Never Comes/Give Me Courage	62	Imperial 5873
Carmacks		
With All My Heart/I've Got To Know	60	Autograph 205
Carmelettes (female)		
My Foolish Heart/Promise Me A Rose	59	Alpine 53
Aching For You/Something Tells Me I'm In Love	60	Alpine 61
Carmen, Jerry (& group)		
Cherry Pie/Could This Be Love	N/A	Barrish 500
Carnations (1)		
Tree In The Meadow/Clown Of The Masquerade	52	Derby 789
The Angels Sent You To Me/Night Time Is The Right Time	55	Savoy 1172
Carnations (2)		
Gimme, Gimme, Gimme/Love, Open Up My Heart	59	Enrica 1001
Casual/Red Wing	60	Fraternity 863
Sleepy Hollow/Barbary Coast	60	Terry Tone 199
Carnations (3) (Ray Allen & the)		
A Fool In Love/Betty Jo	59	Ace 130
Carnations (4)		
I'm Sorry/Oh Yeah	59	Checker 914
A Wing And A Prayer/Leap Year	60	University 606
Carnations (5) (aka Startones)		
Long Tall Girl/Is There Such A World	61	Lescay 3002
Carnations (6)		
Scorpion/Fireball Mail	61	Tilt 780
Funny Time/Punctuation	63	Laurie 3163
Carnations (7)		
You Gave Me Peace Of Mind	N/A	Music City
Carnegies (Alphonso Jones & the)		
Goodbye/Tell Her You Love Her	63	Brunswick 55230
Carole, Nancy (& group)		
The Memories We Share/My Joey	64	Luxor 1029

ARTIST/SONG	YEAR	LABEL
Carolons		
Let It Please Be You/Let's Make Love Tonight	64	Mellomood 1003
Caronators		
Senorita/Long Hot Summer	60	Clock 1045/Clock 227
Lonely Street/Fairy Tales	60	Clock 1047
This Is The Time/Casanova	60	Clock 1049
Carousels (1)		
Rendezvous/Drive-In Movie	59	Jaguar 3029
Fading Away/Solitude	60	G&C 201
Carousels (2) (female)		
I've Cried Enough/Lotsa Lotsa Lovin'	59	Spry 116
Symptoms Of Love/Hush Of Love	61	ABC 10233
You Can Come/Pretty Little Thing	61	Gone 5118 (first pressing)
If You Want To/Pretty Little Thing	61	Gone 5118 (second pressing)
Never Let Him Go/Dirty Tricks	62	Gone 5131
I Wanna Fly/Something Else	64	Guyden 2102
Beneath The Willow/Sail Away	65	Autumn 13
Just For Your Love/Goodbye	73	Vintage 1012
Carpenter, Freddie (& group)		
Money Money Money/Take Me Back Lover	58	East West 112
Carpets		
Why Do I?/Let Her Go	56	Federal 12257
Lonely Me/Chicken Backs	56	Federal 12269
Carr, Wynonie (& group)		
What Do You Know About Love/Heartbreak Melody	57	Specialty 600
Carribeans		
Wonderful Girl/Oh My Love	63	Amy 871
Carribians		
Wonderland	61	Brooks 2000/Johnson
Carrol, Eddie (& group)		
Rules Of Love/Gone From Me	61	Guyden 2046
Carroll, Cathy (bb the Earls)		
Jimmy Love/Deep In A Young Boy's Heart	61	Triodex 11
Poor Little Puppet/Love And Learn	62	Warner Bros. 5284
Carroll, Eddie (& group)		
Wait Eternally/I'm Sorry	62	Santo 504
Carroll, Yvonne (& group)		
Gee What A Guy/Stuck On You	63	Domain 1018
My Sad Love/Earth Angel	63	Domain 1020
Carter Quartet, Eddie		
Don't Turn Your Back On Me/Eat 'Em Up	53	MGM 11405
Take Everything But You/Cool Wailin' Papa	54	Grand 107 (first pressing)
Carter Rays (aka Carterays)		
My Secret Love/Ding Dong Daddy	57	Lyric 2001/Gone 5006 (57)
Bless You/Keep Listening To Your Heart	61	Mala 433
Carter Rays (aka Carterays) (Eddie Carter & the)		
Take Everything But You/Cool Wailin' Papa	54	Grand 107 (second pressing)
Carter Rays (aka Carterays) (Gloria Mann & the)		
Goodnight, Sweetheart, Goodnight/Love-Me-Boy	54	SLS 102/Jubilee 5142 (54)

ARTIST/SONG	YEAR	LABEL
Carter, Martha (& group)		
Nobody Knows/I'm Through Crying	61	Ron 336
Carter, Sonny (& group)		
Crying Over You/My Lonely Life	59	Dot 15921
Carterays (Eddie Carter & the) (aka Carter Rays)		
Ooh Baby/These Are The Things That Matter	54	Sound 105
Carthays		
Betty-Jo/So Bad	61	Tag 446
Caruso, Dick (& group)		
Blue Denim/I'll Tell You In This Song	59	MGM 12811
Teenage Blues/Playing The Field	59	MGM 12827
If I/Dee Dee Dum	60	MGM 12852
Carvels		
It's You, It's You I Love/I Love You So	85	Relic LP 5050
Carver, Bobby (& group)		
Never Leave Me/Roller Coaster	62	Coral 62337
Carvettes (female)		
A Lover's Prayer/Never Gonna Leave Me	59	Copa 200-1/200-2
Caryl, Naomi (& group)		
Before You Say Goodbye/If You Want To Be My Baby	56	Ember 1006
Casals		
Eight O'Clock Scene/Teacher Crush	61	Seville 105
Casanovas (1)		
That's All/Are You For Real?	55	Apollo 471
It's Been A Long Time/Hush-A-Meca	55	Apollo 474
I Don't Want You To Go/Please Be My Love	55	Apollo 477
My Baby's Love/Sleepy Head Mama	55	Apollo 483
Please Be Mine/For You And You Alone	57	Apollo 519
You Are My Queen/(I Got A) Good Lookin' Baby	58	Apollo 523
Pleading From My Heart To You	89	Relic LP 5081
Listen To The Bells	N/A	Apollo LP 1004/ Relic LP 5073 (87)
Love Me Baby	N/A	Apollo LP 1004/ Relic LP 5073 (87)
My Love For You	N/A	Apollo LP 1004/ Relic LP 5073 (87)
Night Rider	N/A	Apollo LP 1004/ Relic LP 5073 (87)/ Relic LP 5075 (88)
Casanovas (2)		
In My Land Of Dreams	62	Planet 1027
Casanovas (3) (Little Romeo & the)		
Remember Lori/That's How Little Girls Get Boys	65	Ascot 2192
Cascades		
She Was Never Mine (To Lose)/My Best Girl	64	Charter 1018
Casher, Billy (& group)		
Give Her Back/No Matter What I Do	61	Epic 9478
Cashiers (Eddie Cash & the)		
Doing All Right/Land Of Promises	58	Peak 1001

ARTIST/SONG	YEAR	LABEL
Cashmeres (1)		
Yes Yes Yes/My Sentimental Heart	54	Mercury 70501
Don't Let It Happen Again/Boom Mag-Azeno Vip Vay	55	Mercury 70617
There's A Rumor/Second Hand Heart	55	Mercury 70679
Little Dream Girl/Do I Upset You?	56	Herald 474
Cashmeres (2)		
Stairsteps To Heaven/Nag-Nag	59	ACA 1216/1217
Everything's Gonna Be Alright/Four Lonely Nights	60	Lake 703
Satisfied (Pt. 1)/Satisfied (Pt. 2)	60	Lake 705/Relic 1005 (65)
Life-Line/Where Have You Been	61	Josie 894
A Very Special Birthday/I Believe In St. Nick	61	Laurie 3078
I Gotta Go/Singing Waters	61	Laurie 3088
Baby Come On Home/Life Line	61	Laurie 3105
Cashmeres (3) (Dale & the)		
Last Night/Pete The Mongoose	61	Matt 161
Cashmeres (4)		
This Moment/Darling You Send Me	N/A	Rubbertown 103
Casinos (1)		
My Love For You/Why Am I A Fool	60	Casino 111
Casinos (2)		
I Like It Like That/Baby Don't Do It	61	Alto 2002
Casinos (3)		
Gee Whiz/Lovely One	64	Terry 115
Too Good To Be True/That's The Way	64	Terry 116/Airtown 886
Casinos (4)		
Do You Recall/Swim	63	Itzy 404/Olimpic 251 (65)
Casinos (5)		
I'm Falling/Speedy	59	Maske 803
Casinos (6)		
Please Let Her/When Love Was Born	62	S&G 301
Caslons		
Anniversary Of Love/The Quiet One	61	Seeco 6078
For All We Know/Settle Me Down	62	Amy 836
Castaleers		
Come Back/Hi Fi Baby	58	Felsted 8504
Lonely Boy/My Bull Fightin' Baby	58	Felsted 8512
You're My Dream/I'll Be Around	59	Felsted 8585
That's Why I Cry/My Baby's All Right	60	Planet 44/Donna 1349 (61)
Castanets (female)		
I Love Him	64	TCF 1
Castanets (Yolanda & the)		
Meet Me After School/What About Me	61	Tandem 7002
Castaways (1)		
Teasin'/I Wish	54	Excello 2038
Castaways (2) (Tony Rivers & the)		
I Love You/I Love The Way You Walk	64	Constellation 128
Castelles		
My Girl Awaits Me/Sweetness	53	Grand 101
This Silver Ring/Wonder Why	54	Grand 103

ARTIST/SONG	YEAR	LABEL
Do You Remember/If You Were The Only Girl	54	Grand 105
Over A Cup Of Coffee/Baby Can't You See	54	Grand 109
Marcella/I'm A Fool To Care	54	Grand 114
It's Christmas Time/Over The Rainbow	54	Grand 118
Heavenly Father/My Wedding Day	55	Grand 122
Happy And Gay/Hey, Baby, Baby	56	Atco 6069
Cheree	N/A	Atco (unreleased)
The Joke's On Me	N/A	Atco (unreleased)

Castells

Little Sad Eyes/Romeo	61	Era 3038
Sacred/I Get Dreamy	61	Era 3048
Make Believe Wedding/My Miracle	61	Era 3057
The Vision Of You/Stiki De Boom Boom	61	Era 3064
So This Is Love/On The Street Of Tears	62	Era 3073
Oh What It Seemed To Be/Stand There Mountain	62	Era 3083
Echoes In The Night/Only One	62	Era 3089
Eternal Love, Eternal Spring/Clown Prince	62	Era 3098
Initials/Little Sad Eyes	63	Era 3102
What Do Little Girls Dream Of?/Some Enchanted Evening	63	Era 3107
I Do/Teardrops	64	Warner Bros. 5421
Could This Be You/Shinny Up Your Own Side	64	Warner Bros. 5445
Love Finds A Way/Tell Her If I Could	64	Warner Bros. 5486
An Angel Cried/Just Walk Away	65	Decca 31834
Life Goes On/I Thought You'd Like That	66	Decca 31967
Rock Ridges/I'd Like To Know	68	Laurie 3444
Some Enchanted Evening/Jerusalem	68	United Artists 50324
Two Lovers/Jerusalem	68	United Artists 50324
Save A Chance	N/A	Black Gold 306
In A Letter To Me/We Better Slow Down	67	Solomon 1351

Castle Kings

Loch Lomond/You Can Get Him-Frankenstein	61	Atlantic 2107
Jeanette/The Caissons Go Rolling Along	62	Atlantic 2158

Castle Sisters

Will You Love Me Tomorrow/Thirteen	60	Roulette 4220
Goodbye Dad/Wishing Star	62	Terrace 7506

Castle-Tones

Goodnight/No Pork In The Beans	59	Rift 502
We Met At A Dance/At The Hot Dog Stand	60	Fire Fly 321/Rift 504

Caston, Bobby (& group)

Call Me Darling/Why Wasn't I Told	57	Atlas 1103

Castro, Vince (bb the Tonettes)

'Cause I Love You/Too Proud To Cry	58	Apt 25025
Bong Bong (I Love You Madly)/You're My Girl	58	Doe 102/Apt 25007 (58)
You're My Girl/Bongo Twist	60	Apt 25047

Castroes

Dearest Darling/Dance With Me	59	Grand 2002

Castros

Lucky Me/Darling, I Fell For You	59	Lasso 501
In My Dreams/Is It Right?	59	Lasso 502

Casual Crescendos

Wish That You Were Here/Uncle Ben's Concentrated Blueberry Jam	63	MRC 12001

Casual Teens

Need You So/She's Swinging	58	Felsted 8529

Casual Three

Some Other Fellow/The Invisible Thing	57	Luniverse 109

ARTIST/SONG	YEAR	LABEL
Casual Three (aka Casual 3)		
Candy Store Blues/Be-Bop Way Marie	57	Mark-X 7009
Casual-Aires		
Candy/Thunderbird	58	Brunswick 55064
Casualairs		
Cruising/Bossa Nova Twist	61	Craig 5001
Satisfied/At The Dance	61	Mona Lee 136
Casuals (1) (aka Original Casuals)		
Till You Come Back To Me/Hello Love	57	Dot 15671
My Love Song For You/Somebody Help Me	57	Nu-Sound 801/Dot 15557 (57)
So Tough/I Love My Darling	58	Back Beat 503 (first pressing, second is by Original Casuals)
Someday/Siboney (instrumental)	63	Moonbeam 71613
We Go Together/Pardners	N/A	Black Hawk 500
Casuals (2) (Gary & the)		
My One Desire/Someone Like You	62	Vandan 609
Casuals (3) (fb Sue Kenny)		
Look/Fool In Love	63	Tribute 118
Casuals (4) (Harold & the)		
Darling Do You Love Me/You Can Shake A Tail Feather	59	Scotty 628
Casuals (5) (Skip Mahoney & the)		
Wher Ever You Go/And It's Love	76	Abet 9465
Casualtones		
Summer School/The Very End	63	Success 102
Catalina 6		
Would You Believe It/Moon 2000	62	Flagship 126
It Had To Rain/Baby Please Come Home	62	Flagship 127
It Had To Rain/Baby Please Come Home	74	Candlelite 413
Catalinas (1)		
Castle Of Love/Give Me Your Love	58	Little 811/812/Jayne 502
Catalinas (2)		
Long Walk/Destruction	59	Fortune 535
Catalinas (3) (aka Inventions)		
Marlene/With Your Girl	58	Glory 285
Peanuts/Row Boat	60	Up
Catalinas (4)		
Speechless/Flying Formation With You	58	Back Beat 513
Ring Of Stars/Wooly Wooly Willie	60	Rita 107/Rita 1006 (60)
Catalinas (5)		
Unchained Melody/Sweetheart	61	20th Fox 286
Hey Little Girl/Hey Senorita	61	Zebra 101
Safari/Pretty Little Nashville Girl	63	20th Fox 299
Bail Out/Bulletin	63	Dee Jay 1010/Sims 134 (63)
Stormy Weather/Whole Lot Of Lovin' To Do	63	Million 77
Banzai Washout/Beach Walkin'	63	Ric 113
Your Tender Lips/Gonna Tell	64	Original Sound 48
Surfer Boy/Boss Barracuda	66	Ric 164
You Haven't The Right/Tick Tock	67	Scepter 12188
Why Oh Why	N/A	Wonder 14

ARTIST/SONG	YEAR	LABEL

Catalinas (6) (Billy Huhn & the)
Baltimore/Freshman Queen — 62 Lesley 1923

Catalinas (7) (Phil & the)
Our Love Is So True/Clementine — N/A Olimpic (no number)

Cates, Ronnie (bb the Travelers)
For My Very Own/Long Time — 62 Terrace 7508

Cavaliers (1)
Honor Bright/Somewhere, Sometime, Someday — 55 Decca 29556
Nobodys Business If I Do — 58 Gilt-Edge 3935
I Wanna Dance/Messed Up — 59 Tel 1006
I Wanna Know/Put Your Trust In Me — 62 Gum 1002
The Right Time/The Quiver — 62 Gum 1004
The Magic Age Of Sixteen/So Young, So Warm, So Beautiful — 63 Music World 101
Merry Christmas My Love — N/A Herald (unreleased)

Cavaliers (1) (fb Scott Stevens)
Dance, Dance, Dance/Play By The Rules Of Love — 58 Apt 25004
Sunday In May/Why Why Why — 59 Apt 25031/ABC

Cavaliers (1) (Tommy Rocco & the)
Let There Be Love/Midnight Train — 60 F-M 3264

Cavaliers (2) (Jerry Cox & the)
Sherry/Debbie Jean — 59 Frantic 751

Cavaliers (3) (Little Bernie & the)
Lonely Soldier/The Waddle — 62 Jove 100

Caverliers Quartet (fb Art Shelton) (aka Fi-Tones/aka Chances (2))
You Thrill Me So/Dynaflow — 54 Atlas 1031

Celebrities (1)
Goodnight/You Didn't Tell The Truth — 59 Boss 502

Celebrities (2)
I Want You/Mambo Daddy — 61 Music Makers 101

Celebritys
We Made Romance/Absent Minded — 56 Caroline 2302

Celestials (Bobby Gee & the)
Blue Jean/Julie Is Mine — 59 Stacy 922
Little Miss Fantasy/Sealed With A Kiss — 60 XYZ 611

Celestrals
Alone/Alone — 63 Don-El 125
Alone/Checkerboard Love — 63 Don-El 125

Cellos
Rang Tang Ding Dong (I Am Japanese)/You Took My Love — 57 Apollo 510
Juicy Crocodile/Under Your Spell — 57 Apollo 515
The Be-Bop Mouse/Girlie That I Love — 57 Apollo 516
I Beg For Your Love/What's The Matter For You? — 58 Apollo 524
Buffalo Bill — 88 Relic LP 5074 (88)
Doo Doo Wah — 88 Relic LP 5074 (88)
Love That Girl — 88 Relic LP 5074 (88)

ARTIST/SONG   YEAR LABEL

The Cellos

Cellos (Dolly Lyon & the)
Don't Wait   N/A   N/A

Celtics (1)
Can You Remember/Send Me Someone To Love   62   Al Jacks 2
Darlene Darling/Only The Lonely   62   War Conn 2216

Celtics (1) (Bobby Lanz & the)
Let Them Talk   73   Bridges 5003

Celtics (2)
Wondering Why   N/A   Coronado

Centennials
My Dear One/The Wayward Wind   61   Dot 16180

Centurians
We Mean More To Each Other/Since You Left My World   59   Tiger 1001

Centuries (1)
In This Whole World/Mine, All Mine   61   Life 501

Centuries (2) (Ronnie & the)
I Don't Care/Mister Mirror   62   Luna 3076

Centuries (3) (aka Jaytones/aka Revlons (3))
Betty/Ride Away (by the Revlons (3))   63   Times Square 15
Crying For You/Oh Darling (by the Jaytones)   63   Times Square 5
Crying For You/Betty   N/A   Klik

Centuries (4)
Just Today/Don't Let It Fade Away   N/A   Rich 112

Centuries (5)
Please Don't Go   85   Relic LP 5053
Time After Time   85   Relic LP 5053
When I'm With You   85   Relic LP 5053
Willette   85   Relic LP 5053

Centurys
Take My Hand/Oh Joe, Joe   59   Fortune 533
Strollin' Time/Paradiddle   60   Veltone 104

ARTIST/SONG	YEAR	LABEL
Cezannes		
Pardon Me/All At Once	63	Markay 108
Chadons		
Let's Start All Over Again/It's A Crying Shame	64	Chattahoochie 664
Chains		
I Can Learn/It Happens This Way	63	Peacock 1922
Chalets		
Fat-Fat-Fat! Mom-Mi-O/Who's Laughing Who's Crying	61	Tru-Lite 1001/Dart 1026 (61)/ Musicnote 1115 (61)
Challengers (1) (Walter Ward & the) (aka Olympics)		
I Can Tell/The Mambo Beat	57	Melatone 1002
Challengers (2) (aka Executives (2))		
Honey, Honey, Honey/Stay	62	Tri-Phi 1012
The Butterfly/Who Shot The Hole In My Sombrero	62	Tri-Phi 1015/ Challenge 1105 (62)
Why/Come On Baby	63	Explosive 3621-10
Challengers III (aka Challengers)		
Every Day/I Hear An Echo	62	Tri-Phi 1020
Chalons		
Oh You/Leave Me Baby	58	Dice 89
Champ, Billy (& group)		
Hush-A-Bye/Believe Me	64	ABC 10518
Champagnes		
Crazy/Cash	63	Skymac 1002/Laurie 3189 (63)
Champions		
Annie Met Henry/Keep-A-Rockin'	54	Chart 602
It's Love, It's Love/Mexico Bound	56	Chart 611
The Same Old Story/Pay Me Some Attention	56	Chart 620
Come On/Big Bad Beulah	56	Chart 631
I'm So Blue/Cute Little Baby	58	Ace 541 (duplicate # IS correct!)
I Do/My Heart	58	Ace 541 (duplicate # IS correct)
Champlains (fb Fred Parris)		
Ding Dong/Have You Changed Your Mind?	61	United Artists 346
Champs (Tony Allen & the)		
Nite Owl/I	55	Specialty 560
Chancellors (1) (aka Five Chancellors)		
Too Many Memories/Everything Has Its Place	56	Unique 341
There Goes My Girl/Tell Me You Love Me	57	Port 5000
I'm Coming Home/Gotta Little Baby	57	XYZ 104/XYZ 601 (59)
I Really Really Do/My Thoughts To You	59	Storm 503
Seaport At Sunset/Chalypso Train	59	XYZ 105
Chancellors (2)		
Sad Avenue/All The Way From Heaven	59	Capacity 61023
Yo Yo/Little Latin Lupe Lu	65	Soma 1421
So Fine	65	Soma 1435
My Girl/Jenny Jenny	65	USA 783
Once In A Million/Journey	66	Fenton 2066
Dear John/5 Minus 3	66	Fenton 2072
Chancers		
Shirley Ann/My One	58	Dot 15870

ARTIST/SONG	YEAR	LABEL
Chances (1) (female)		
One More Chance/It Takes More Than A Loan	61	Bea & Baby 130
Chances (2) (aka Caverliers Quartet/aka Fi-Tones)		
Through A Long And Sleepless Night/What Would You Say?	64	Roulette 4549
Chances (3) (Chuck Corby & the)		
Happy Go Lucky	N/A	Sound 717
Chandeliers (1) (aka Chandeliers Quintet)		
Wild Cherry	58	Angle Tone
Blueberry Sweet/One More Step	58	Angle Tone 521
Dolly/Dancin' In The Congo	58	Angle Tone 529
Tender Love	73	Relic LP 5012
Chandeliers (2)		
Give Me Your Love/She's A Heartbreaker	62	Sue 761
Chandeliers (3)		
Once More/Bicycle Hop	62	Du-Well 102
Chandeliers (4)		
It's A Good Thought/Double Love	64	Loadstone 1601
Chandler, Gene (bb the Dukays)		
Duke Of Earl/Kissin' In The Kitchen	61	Vee Jay 416/Nat 4003 (62)
Chandler, Lenny (& group)		
Wait For Me/Heart	63	Laurie 3158
Chanells		
Give Me A Chance/Butterball (by the Butterballs)	63	Times Square 24
Chanels (aka Five Chanels) (female)		
The Reason/Skidilly Doo	58	Deb 500
Channells (aka Channels (2))		
In My Arms To Stay/You Hurt Me	63	Hit Record 700
Channels (1) (Earl Lewis & the)		
The Closer You Are/Now You Know (I Love You So)	56	Whirlin' Disc 100/ Port 70014 (59)
The Gleam In Your Eyes/Stars In The Sky	56	Whirlin' Disc 102/ Port 70017 (60)
I Really Love You/What Do You Do?	56	Whirlin' Disc 107/ Port 70023 (60)
My Love Will Never Die/Bye Bye Baby	57	Fury 1021/Fury 1071 (58)
That's My Desire/Stay As You Are	57	Gone 5012
Flames In My Heart/My Loving Baby	57	Whirlin' Disc 109
Altar Of Love/All Alone	58	Gone 5019
My Heart Is Sad/The Girl Next Door	59	Fire 1001
Gloria (recorded in 1956)/You Said You Loved Me	71	Channel 1000
She Blew My Mind/Breaking Up Is Hard To Do	71	Rare Bird 5017
We Belong Together/Hey Girl, I'm In Love With You	72	Channel 1001
You Got What It Takes/Crazy Mixed Up World	72	Channel 1002
Close Your Eyes/Work With Me Annie	73	Channel 1003
Over Again/In My Arms To Stay	73	Channel 1004
A Thousand Miles Away/Don't Let The Green Grass Fool You	74	Channel 1006
What Do You Do (Fast Ver.)	N/A	Collectables LP 5012
Channels (2) (aka Channells)		
My Love/Sad Song	63	Enjoy 2001
Anything You Do/I've Got My Eyes On You	64	Groove 0046
You Can Count On Me/Old Chinatown	65	Groove 0061

ARTIST/SONG	YEAR	LABEL
Channels (2) (Eddie & the)		
Did I Hear You Right/Love's Burning Fire	63	Ember 584/Herald 584 (63)
Channels (3)		
Lonely	59	Mercury
Earthquake/Jungle Lights	59	Mercury 71501
Chansonaires		
If You Were Here Tonight/Love Always Finds The Way	58	Hamilton 50012
Chanteclairs		
Baby Please/Someday My Love Will Come My Way	54	Dot 1227
Believe Me My Beloved/I've Never Been There	55	Dot 15404
Chanteers		
She's Coming Home/Mr. Zebra	62	Mercury 71979
I Waited/Just A Little Boy	62	Mercury 72037
Chantels (female)		
He's Gone/The Plea	57	End 1001
Tasty Kisses	57	unreleased
Maybe/Come, My Little Baby	58	End 1005
Every Night (I Pray)/Whoever You Are	58	End 1015
I Love You So/How Could You Call It Off	58	End 1020
Prayee/Sure Of Love	58	End 1026
Congratulations/If You Try	58	End 1030
I Can't Take It (There's Our Song Again)/Never Let Me Go	58	End 1037
C'est Si Bon	58	End EP 202/End LP 312 (61)
I'll Walk Alone	58	End EP 202/End LP 312 (61)
Memories Of You	58	End EP 202/End LP 312 (61)
I've Cried	58	unreleased
I'm Confessin'/Goodbye To Love	59	End 1048
Chantel Rock	59	unreleased
Miracle Of Love	59	unreleased
Two Loving Hearts	59	unreleased
Whoever You Are/How Could You Call It Off	60	End 1069
Love, Love, Love/He Knows I Love Him Too Much	61	Big Top 3073
Look In My Eyes/Glad To Be Back	61	Carlton 555
Well I Told You/I Still	61	Carlton 564
Here It Comes Again/Summertime	61	Carlton 569
There's Our Song Again/I'm The Girl	61	End 1105
My Darlin'	61	End LP 312
Ific	61	End LP 312/
		Murray Hill LP 000385 (87)
Cotton Fields	61	unreleased
You'll Never Know	62	Carlton LP 144
Eternally/Swamp Water	63	Ludix 101
Some Tears Fall Dry/That's Why You're Happy	63	Ludix 106
Everything/Good Girls	63	Spectorious 150
Take Me As I Am/There's No Forgetting You	65	TCF-Arrawak 123
From This Moment On	66	unreleased
Lonely Am I	66	unreleased
Lover's Chant	66	unreleased
Soul Of A Soldier/You're Welcome To My Heart	66	Verve 10387
It's Just Me/Indian Giver	66	Verve 10435
Maybe/He's Gone	69	Roulette 7064
I'm Gonna Win Him Back/	70	RCA 0347
Love Makes All The Difference In The World		
Peruvian Wedding Song	87	Murray Hill LP 000385
So Real	87	Murray Hill LP 000385
Chantels (female) (actually the Veneers)		
Believe Me (My Angel)/I	60	Princeton 102/End 1103 (61)

ARTIST/SONG	YEAR	LABEL
Chantels (Richard Barrett & the)		
Come Softly To Me/Walking Through Dreamland	59	Gone 5056
Summer's Love/All Is Forgiven	59	Gone 5060
Chanters (1)		
Tell Me, Thrill Me/She Wants To Mambo	54	RPM 415
Lonesome Me/Golden Apple	55	Kem 2740
Do You Remember	88	Relic LP 5076
Chanters (1) (Brother Woodman & the)		
Why?/Watts	55	Combo 78
Chanters (1) (Gene Ford & the)		
I Love You/Hot Mamma	55	Combo 92
Chanters (2)		
My My Darling/I Need Your Tenderness (I Love You Darling)	58	DeLuxe 6162
Row Your Boat/Stars In The Skies	58	DeLuxe 6166
Five Little Kisses/Angel Darling	58	DeLuxe 6172
I Make This Pledge (To You)/No, No, No	61	DeLuxe 6191
At My Door/My My Darling	61	DeLuxe 6194
Row Your Boat/No, No, No	63	DeLuxe 6200
Heavenly You/What Are You Doing	N/A	SSP
Chanters (2) (Bud Johnson & the)		
No, No, No/Over The Rainbow	58	DeLuxe 6177
Chanteurs (1)		
New Rockin' Baby/Wishin' Well	61	La Salle 501
You've Got A Great Love/The Grizzly Bear	63	Renee/Vee Jay 519 (63)
Chanteurs (2)		
No Doubt About It/Mr. Jones	63	Bolo 745
Chanticleers		
To Keep Your Love/Daddy Must Be	58	Lyric 103
Necklace Of Roses/Green Satin	63	Old Town 1137
Chantiers		
Peppermint/Dear Mr. Clock	64	DJB 112
Chantiers (Rodney Baker & the)		
Teenage Wedding Song/Graduation	61	Jan Ell 8
Chantones		
Dear Diary/Cocoanuts And Palm Trees	59	TNT 167
It's Just A Summer Love/Five Little Numbers	58	Carlton 485
Tangerock/Don't Open That Door	60	Top Rank 2066
Stormy Weather/Sweet Georgia Brown	61	Capitol 4661
Chants (1)		
Close Friends/Lost And Found	58	Capitol 3949
Respectable/Kiss Me Goodbye	61	Tru Eko 3567/UWR 4243 (61)MGM 13008 (61)
Dick Tracy/Choo-Choo	61	Verve 10244
Surfside/Chicken 'N Gravy	68	Checker 1209
Chants (1) (Jimmy Soul & the)		
Respectable/I Wish I Could Dance (no group)	63	20th Fox 413
Chants (2) (Little Jerry & the)		
Ooh Wee Baby/The Shape You Left Me In	60	Ace 606

ARTIST/SONG	YEAR	LABEL

Chants (3)

Heaven And Paradise/When I'm With You	60	Nite Owl 40
Come Go With Me/I Don't Care	63	Cameo 277
A Thousand Stars/I Could Write A Book	64	Cameo 297/Pye 15591
She's Mine/Then I'll Be Home	64	Interphon 7703

Chants (4) (Casanova & the)

Geraldine/I Know You	N/A	Sapphire 2254

Chapelaires

I'm Still In Love With You/Not Good Enough	61	Hac 101
Gloria/Under Hawaiian Skies	61	Hac 102
It's Impossible, Why Try/Vacation Time	65	Gateway 746

Chapelaires (Joni Kay & the)

Lonely Star/Happy Memories	64	Gateway 744

Chaperones (1)

Cruise To The Moon/Dance With Me	60	Josie 880 (second pressing, first is by the Cahperones)/Port
Shining Star/My Shadow And Me	62	Josie 885
The Man From The Moon/Blueberry Sweet	63	Josie 891

Chaperones (2) (Maria Mae & the)

Teenage Love/Till The End Of Our Days	61	Phantom 986

Chapman, Grady (bb the Suedes)

I Need You So/Don't Blooper	55	Money 204
Say You Will Be Mine/Starlight Starbright	58	Knight 2003
Let's Talk About Us/Come Away	59	Imperial 5611

Chappies

Suddenly There Were Tears	N/A	Chelton 750

Chaps

They'll Never Be/Heaven Must Have Run Out Of Angels	59	Matador 1814
One Lovely Yesterday/Perfect Night For Love	60	Brent 7016

Chapters

Goodbye My Love/Love You, Love You	53	Republic 7038

Chapters (Helen Foster & the)

They Tell Me/Somebody, Somewhere	53	Republic 7037

Charades

Make Me Happy Baby/Shang Lang A Ding Dong	58	United Artists 132
Let Me Love You/Bright Red Skinny Pants	59	United Artists 183
For You/Sophia	62	Northridge 1002
Please Be My Love Tonight/Turn Him Down	63	Ava 154
Surf 'N' Stomp/Christina	64	Impact 32
Close To Me/Take A Chance	64	Original Sound 47
Flamingo/Someone's In The Kitchen With Dinah	64	Skylark 502
Hey, Operator/He's Not Your Boyfriend	64	Warner Bros. 5415

Chargers (1)

Large Charge	59	B.E.A.T. 1006

Chargers (2)

Old MacDonald/Dandelion	58	RCA 7301
Who Baby Who	N/A	N/A

Chargers (2) (fb Jesse Belvin)

Here In My Heart/The Counterfeiter	58	RCA 7417

ARTIST/SONG	YEAR	LABEL
Chariots		
Gloria/A Sunday Morning Love	59	Time 1006/Brent
Open House/A Tiger In Your Tank	64	RSVP 1105
Charles, Jimmy (with the Reveletts)		
A Million To One/Hop Scotch Hop	60	Promo 1002
The Age For Love/Follow The Swallow	60	Promo 1003
Charles, Nick (& group)		
For You/I Wonder	61	Guyden 2049
Charlettes (Larry & the)		
Love Notes	63	Sapien 1004
Charlie & Don (& group)		
Young Man's Fancy/Hush Little Baby	62	Duel 513
Charmaines		
If You Were Mine/Rockin' Old Man	61	Fraternity 873
What Kind Of Girl (Do You Think I Am)/All You Gotta Do	61	Fraternity 880
Where Is The Boy Tonight/On The Wagon	62	Dot 16351
Charmers (1)		
The Beating Of My Heart/Why Does It Have To Be Me	54	Central 1002
Tony, My Darling/In The Rain	54	Central 1006
I Was Wrong/The Mambo	54	Timely 1009
The Church On The Hill/Battle Axe	54	Timely 1011
Charmers (2)		
All Alone/Johnny My Dear	56	Aladdin 3337
He's Gone/Oh! Yes	56	Aladdin 3341
Charmers (3)		
Letters Don't Have Arms/Rock R And B	57	Silhouette 522
Charmers (4)		
Little Fool/Hard To Get	61	Jaf 2021
The Letter/Watch What You Do	63	Co-Rec 101
Charmers (5) (Prince Charles & the)		
Good Luck Charm/Twistin' At The Pool	62	Class 301
Charmers (6)		
Visiting Day/Whatever Happened To Baby Jane?	62	Terrace 7512
Charmers (6) (Mark Stevens & the)		
Magic Rose/Come Back To My Heart	62	Allison 921
Charmers (7)		
Johnny/My Kind Of Love	62	Laurie 3142
I Cried/Shy Guy	63	Laurie 3173
Sweet Talk/Work It Out	63	Laurie 3203
Looking For Trouble/After You Walk Me Home	64	Pip 8000
It's A Funny Way We Met/Where's The Boy	65	Louis 6806
Charmers (8) (Janice Christian & Johnny & the)		
Promises/Just A Bad Thing	64	Swan 4174
Charmers (9)		
For Sentimental Reasons	85	Relic LP 5051
Charmers (10)		
Lesson From The Stars/My Love	63	Sure Play 104

ARTIST/SONG	YEAR	LABEL

Charmettes (female)

Skating In The Blue Light/My Love	58	Hi 2003
School Letter/Johnny, Johnny	59	Federal 12345
I Love You To The Nth Degree/Deeds To My Heart	60	Mona 553
Donnie/Too Much True Lovin'	62	Markay 101
One More Time/Surrender My Love	62	Marlin 16001
On A Night Like Tonight/Why Oh Why	62	Tri Disc 103
Please Don't Kiss Me Again/What Is A Tear	63	Kapp 547
0021-0021-Ooh/He's A Wise Guy	64	Kapp 570
My Lover Is A Boy Scout/Mailbox	64	Mala 491
Sugar Boy/Stop The Wedding	65	World Artists 1053

Charms (1)

Love's Our Inspiration/Love Love Stick Stov	55	Chart 608
Heart Of A Rose/I Offer You	56	Chart 613
I'll Be True/Boom Diddy Boom Boom	56	Chart 623

Charms (1) (Otis Williams & His)

Rollin' Home/Do Be You	56	DeLuxe 6092
Ivory Tower/In Paradise	56	DeLuxe 6093
It's All Over/One Night Only	56	DeLuxe 6095
Whirlwind/I'd Like To Thank You Mr. D.J.	56	DeLuxe 6097
Gypsy Lady/I'll Remember You	56	DeLuxe 6098
Pardon Me/Blues Stay Away From Me	57	DeLuxe 6105
Walkin' After Midnight/I'm Waiting Just For You	57	DeLuxe 6115
Nowhere On Earth/No Got De Woman	57	DeLuxe 6130
One Kind Word From You/Talking To Myself	57	DeLuxe 6137
United/Don't Deny Me	57	DeLuxe 6138
Well Oh Well/Dynamite Darling	57	DeLuxe 6149
Could This Be Magic/Oh Julie	58	DeLuxe 6158
Let Some Love In Your Heart/Baby-O	58	DeLuxe 6160
Burnin' Lips/Red Hot Love (Oo This Love)	58	DeLuxe 6165
You'll Remain Forever/Don't Wake Up The Kids	58	DeLuxe 6174
My Prayer Tonight/Watch Dog	59	DeLuxe 6183
I Knew It All The Time/Tears Of Happiness	59	DeLuxe 6185

Charms (1) (Otis Williams & the)

Happy Are We/What Do You Know About That	53	DeLuxe 6014
Heaven Only Knows/Loving Baby	53	Rockin' 516/DeLuxe 6000 (53)
Please Believe In Me/Bye Bye Baby	54	DeLuxe 6034
Quiet Please/Fifty-Five Seconds	54	DeLuxe 6050
My Baby Dearest Darling/Come To Me Baby	54	DeLuxe 6056
Hearts Of Stone/Who Knows?	54	DeLuxe 6062
Two Hearts/The First Time We Met	54	DeLuxe 6065
Crazy, Crazy Love/Mambo Sh-Mambo	54	DeLuxe 6072
Ling, Ting, Tong/Bazoom (I Need Your Lovin')	55	DeLuxe 6076
Ko Ko Mo (I Love You So)/Whadaya Want	55	DeLuxe 6080
Crazy, Crazy Love/Whadaya Want	55	DeLuxe 6082
When We Get Together/Let The Happening Happen	55	DeLuxe 6087
One Fine Day/It's You, Yes You	55	DeLuxe 6089
That's Your Mistake/Too Late I Learned (by O.W. & His New Group)	56	DeLuxe 6091
My Friends/Secret	58	DeLuxe 6178
Welcome Home/Pretty Little Things Called Girls	59	DeLuxe 6181
In Paradise/Who Knows	59	DeLuxe 6186
Blues Stay Away From Me/Funny What True Love Can Do	59	DeLuxe 6187
It's A Treat/Chief Um	60	King 5323
Silver Star/Rickety Rickshaw Man	60	King 5332
Image Of A Girl/Wait A Minute Baby	60	King 5372
So Be It/First Sign Of Love	60	King 5389
Wait/And Take My Love	60	King 5421
Little Turtle Dove/So Can I	61	King 5455
You Know I Care/Just Forget About Me	61	King 5497
Panic/Pardon Me	61	King 5527
The Secret/Two Hearts	61	King 5558
When We Get Together/Only Young Once	61	King 5682

ARTIST/SONG	YEAR	LABEL
Baby, You Turn Me On/Love Don't Grow On Trees	65	Okeh 7225
I Fall To Pieces/Gotta Get Myself Together	66	Okeh 7235
Welcome Home/I Got Loving	66	Okeh 7248
Your Sweet Love/Ain't Gonna Walk Your Dog No More	66	Okeh 7261

Charms (1) (Tiny Topsy & the)

Come On, Come On, Come On/Ring Around My Finger	57	Federal 12309

Charms (2) (Tommy G & the)

I Want You So Bad/I Know What I Want	61	Hollywood 1109

Chartbusters

She's The One/Slippin' Through Your Fingers	64	Mutual 502

Charters (1)

I Lost You/My Little Girl	63	Alva 1001
Lost In A Dream/This Makes Me Mad	63	Merry-Go-Round 103

Charters (2)

My Rose/El Merengue	62	Tarx 1003

Charts

Desirie/Zoop	57	Everlast 5001/Everlast 5026 (63)/Lost Nite 173 (81)
Dance Girl/Why Do You Cry	57	Everlast 5002/Lost Nite 180 (81)
You're The Reason/I've Been Wondering	57	Everlast 5006/Lost Nite 186 (81)
All Because Of Love/I Told You So	57	Everlast 5008
My Diane/Baby Be Mine	57	Everlast 5010
Ooba-Gooba/For The Birds	59	Guyden 2021
Desiree/Fell In Love With You Baby	67	Wand 1112
Livin' The Night Life/Nobody Made You Love Me	67	Wand 1124

Chase, Bobby (& group)

Missing Someone/Knowing It Was Heartbreak	65	Ascot 2195

Chase, Eddie (& group)

If You Only Knew/Ginger	59	Viscount 529

Chateaus (1)

Let Me Tell You, Baby/Darling Je Vous Aime Beaucoup	56	Epic 9163
Brown Eyes/Satisfied	58	Warner Bros. 5023
The Masquerade Is Over/If I Didn't Care	59	Warner Bros. 5043
Ladder Of Love/You'll Reap What You Sow	59	Warner Bros. 5071

Chateaus (2)

Honest I Will/Summer's Here	63	Coral 62364

Chatters

My Darling One/Teenage Love Affair	59	Viking 1001

Chauntes

Bohemian Love	N/A	Tonix 15

Chavelles (aka Untouchables/aka Sabers)

Valley Of Love/Red Tape	56	Vita 127

Chavis Brothers (aka Five Chavis Brothers)

Baby Don't Leave Me/Old Time Rock And Roll	61	Coral 62270
So Tired/I Love You	62	Clock 1025

Cheaters

You're Mine/Barefootin'	64	Raynard 1056
Suzanne	65	Wax 213
Please Come Home	N/A	JBJ

ARTIST/SONG	YEAR	LABEL

Check Mates
| Hey Mrs. Jones, Pt. 1/Hey Mrs. Jones, Pt. 2 | 61 | Arvee 5030 |

Checker Dots
| Alpha Omega/All I Hear | 59 | Peacock 1688 |

Checker, Chubby (bb the Dreamlovers)
| The Twist/Toot (no group) | 60 | Parkway 811 |

Checkers
Flame In My Heart/Oh Oh Oh Baby	52	King 4558
Night Curtains/Let Me Come Back	52	King 4581
My Prayer Tonite/Love Wasn't There	53	King 4596
Ghost Of My Baby/I Wanna Know	53	King 4626
You Never Had It So Good/I Promise You	54	King 4673
White Cliffs Of Dover/Without A Song	54	King 4675
House With No Windows/Don't Stop Dan	54	King 4710
Over The Rainbow/You've Been Fooling Around	54	King 4719
I Wasn't Thinkin', I Was Drinkin'/Mama's Daughter	54	King 4751
Can't Find My Sadie/Tryin' To Hold My Gal	55	King 4764
Heaven Only Knows/Nine More Miles	58	King 5156
So Fine/Sentimental Heart	59	Federal 12355
Teardrops Are Falling/Rocka Locka (by the Five Wings)	59	King 5199/King 4781 (55) (as the Five Wings)
White Cliffs Of Dover/Let Me Come Back	60	Federal 12375

Checkmates (1) (Emil Ford & the)
| What Do You Want...Me For?/Don't Tell Me Your Troubles | 59 | Andie 5018/Cub 9063 (60) |

Checkmates (2)
| What Do You Do | N/A | Regency 26 |

Cheerettes (female)
| Lullabye My Love/Told The Sunshine | 56 | Vita 145 |

Cheerios (1)
| Ding Dong Honeymoon/Where Are You Tonight | 61 | Infinity 11/Golden Oldies 1 (61) |

Cheerios (2) (Bobby Long & the)
| Flip Flop/Station Hurt | 63 | Cub 9120 |

Cheertones
| Rose Anna/I'll Come To You | 61 | ABC 10277 |

Chell-Mars (aka Chelmars)
| Roamin' Heart/Feel All Right | 63 | Jamie 1266 |

Chellos
| Have You Heard/Fatso | 61 | Columbia 42044 |

Chellows
I Want To Be A Part Of You/Be My Baby	61	Poncello 713
Rag Doll/A Hard Day's Night (by the Jalopy Five)	66	Hit 134
Candy Girl/Hello Muddah, Hello Faddah (by Dick Martin)	64	Hit 77

Chelmars (aka Chell-Mars)
| Confess/Jigsaw Puzzle | 62 | Select 712 |
| You Know | N/A | N/A |

Cheques
| A Thousand Miles Away/Go On, Girl | 69 | Sur-Speed 214 |

Cherlos
Tell It Like It Is/99 1/2 Won't Do	56	Ultra (no number)
Cry Fool	N/A	Relic LP 5022
Little Little	N/A	Relic LP 5022

ARTIST/SONG	YEAR	LABEL
Cherokees (1)		
Rainbow Of Love/I Had A Thrill	54	Grand 106
Please Tell Me So/Remember When?	54	Grand 110
Is She Real?/Drip, Drip, The Coffee Grinder	55	Peacock 1656
Cherokees (2) (fb Fred Parris)		
My Heavenly Angel/Bed Bug	61	United Artists 367
Cherokees (3)		
Brenda	N/A	Grand
Cherokees (4)		
It's Gonna Work Out Fine	N/A	Gary
Cherubs		
Julie, Julie (16 & 23)/They Go Ape	60	Dore 545
Cheryl Ann (& group)		
Goodbye Baby/I Can't Let Him	N/A	Patty 52
Chessmen (1)		
Du-Whop/I Live For You	58	Mirasonic 1002/Mirasonic 1868
Keeper Of My Love/Why	59	Safari 1011
Mr. Cupid/What's To Become Of Me	62	AMC 101/Don-Dee 101 (62)/
		Mercury 72559 (65)
Stormy Dreams/Pick It Up	62	Amy 841
Voyage/Sorry	64	G-Clef 707
I Apologize (a capella)/Dance (a capella)	65	Relic 1015
Ways Of Romance (a capella)/Heavenly Father (a capella)	65	Relic 1016
Stars Fell (a capella)/That's My Desire	65	Relic 1017
Don't Have To Shop Around (a capella)/	65	Relic 1020
Love Is What The World Is Made Of (a capella)		
Two Kinds Of People (a capella)	75	Relic LP 101
All Nite Long (a capella)	75	Relic LP 101/Relic LP 106 (75)
For All We Know (a capella)	75	Relic LP 101/Relic LP 106 (75)
A Teardrop (a capella)	75	Relic LP 102
Let Me Come Back (a capella)	75	Relic LP 102
Sentimental Reasons (a capella)	75	Relic LP 102
I Want To Dance (a capella)	75	Relic LP 102/Relic LP 106 (75)
Is Everybody Happy (a capella)	75	Relic LP 102/Relic LP 106 (75)
Danny Boy (a capella)	75	Relic LP 105
Ooh Baby Baby (a capella)	75	Relic LP 105
A Teardrop Fell From My Eyes (a capella)	75	Relic LP 106
Dance Gypsy (a capella)	75	Relic LP 106
Flowers On The Wall (a capella)	75	Relic LP 106
I've Been Good To You (a capella)	75	Relic LP 106
The One Love Forgot (a capella)	75	Relic LP 106
There Goes My Baby (a capella)	75	Relic LP 106
When We Were So In Love (a capella)	75	Relic LP 106
You Know My Heart Is Yours (a capella)	75	Relic LP 106
Chessmen (2)		
Mustang/Mr. Meadowlands	64	Jerden 743
Chessmen (3)		
It'll Be Me	59	Salem 001
Chessmen (4)		
I Believe/Lola	61	Pac 100
Chessmen (5) (Barbara McBride & the)		
The Only Reason (flip by Woody Carr)	N/A	Mari 451
Chessmen (6)		
Bells Bells/Prayer Of Love	59	Golden Crest 2661

ARTIST/SONG	YEAR	LABEL
Chesterfields (1)		
I'm In Heaven/All Messed Up	54	Chess 1559
Chesterfields (2) (fb Al Reno)		
I Got Fired/Meet Me At The Candy Store	58	Cub 9008
Chesterfields (3)		
A Dream Is But A Dream/You Walked Away	63	Philips 40083
Chesters (ref Little Anthony & the Imperials)		
The Fires Burn No More/Lift Up Your Head	58	Apollo 521
Tears On My Pillow/Two People In The World	58	End 1027
Chestnuts (1)		
Don't Go/I Wanna Come Home	54	Mercury 70489
Chestnuts (2)		
Love Is True/It's You I Love	56	Davis 447
Forever I Vow/Brother Ben	56	Davis 452
Who Knows Better Than I?/I Feel So Blue	57	Eldorado 511
Who Knows Better Than I?/Mary, Hear Those Love Bells	57	Standord 100
This Is My Love/Wiggle Wiggle	58	Aladdin 3444
Chestnuts (2) (Bill Baker & the)		
Won't You Tell Me, My Heart?/Tell Me Little Darling	59	Elgin 007/008
Wonderful Girl/Chit Chat	59	Elgin 013/014
Chestnuts (3)		
Endless Love/Wobble Shank	60	Coral 62176
Chestnuts (4)		
Rock 'N Roll Tragedy/I'm So Blue	N/A	Night Train 906
Chev-Rons		
The Defense Rests/It's Saturday Night	62	Gait 100
Chevelles (1)		
I'm Sorry	64	Infinity 029
Chevelles (2) (female)		
It's Goodbye/Another Tear Must Fall	63	Butane 777
Chevelles (3) (Marvin Nash & the)		
Dina/Happiness	63	Courier 111
Chevelles (4) (G.W. & the)		
Walking With My New Love	68	Flaming Arrow 37
Chevelles (5) (Art Barron & the)		
One Kiss/My Lucy Lou	64	Golden 101
Chevelles (6)		
Red Tape	73	Relic LP 5007
Valley Of Love (Fast & Slow Versions)	73	Relic LP 5007
Chevells (Don & the)		
The Only Girl	64	Speedway 1000
Chevieres		
Last Nite I Dreamed (a capella)	75	Relic LP 109
Uncle Sam (a capella)	75	Relic LP 109
Chevies		
I Love That Girl So/Come On And Love Me	N/A	Dove 1033

ARTIST/SONG	YEAR	LABEL

Chevrons

That Comes With Love/Don't Be Heartless	59	Brent 7000
Lullabye/Day After Forever	59	Brent 7007
Little Darlin'/Little Star	60	Brent 7015
Come Go With Me/I'm In Love Again-All Shook Up	60	Time 1
For Your Love/Good Good Lovin'	61	Cuca 6381
Please Don't Make Me Cry/Still In Love With You	62	Sara 6462
Mine Forever More/In The Depths Of My Soul	68	Independence 94

Chex (Tex & the) (aka Lyrics)

I Do Love You/My Love	61	Atlantic 2116
Love Me Now/Beach Party	63	20th Fox 411
Be On The Lookout For My Love/Watching Willie Wobble	63	Newtown 5010

Chic-Chocs

Them There Eyes/Sugar	61	Broadway 103

Chicklettes (Angie & the) (female)

Tommy/Treat Him Tender, Maureen (Now That Ringo Belongs To You)	65	Apt 25080

Chicks (Kell Osborne & the)

Little Chick-A-Dee/Do You Mind	62	Class 302

Chiclets

I Want You To Be My Boyfriend/Don't Goof On Me	64	Josie 919

Chiffons (1) (female) (aka Five Pennies)

Tonight's The Night/Do You Know?	60	Big Deal 6003
No More Tomorrows/Never Never	61	Wildcat 601
After Last Night/Doctor Of Hearts	62	Reprise 20103
He's So Fine/Oh My Lover	63	Laurie 3152
A Love So Fine/Only My Friend	63	Laurie 3159
Why Am I So Shy?/Lucky Me	63	Laurie 3166
One Fine Day/Why Am I So Shy?	63	Laurie 3179
A Love So Fine/Only My Friend	63	Laurie 3195
I Have A Boyfriend/I'm Gonna Dry My Eyes	63	Laurie 3212
Tonight I Met An Angel/Easy To Love	63	Laurie 3224
My Boyfriend's Back/I Got Plenty O Nuttin'	63	Laurie 3364
Sailor Boy/When Summer Is Through	64	Laurie 3262
What Am I Gonna Do With You, Baby/Strange Strange Feeling	65	Laurie 3275
Nobody Knows What's Goin' On/Did You Ever Go Steady?	65	Laurie 3301
Nobody Knows What's Going On/The Real Thing	65	Laurie 3301
Tonight I'm Gonna Dream/Heavenly Place	65	Laurie 3318
Sweet Talkin' Guy/Did You Ever Go Steady	66	Laurie 3340
Out Of This World/Just A Boy	66	Laurie 3350
Stop Look And Listen/March	66	Laurie 3357
Keep The Boy Happy/If I Knew Then	67	Laurie 3377
Just For Tonight/Teach Me How	67	Laurie 3423
My Secret Love/Strange Strange Feeling	68	B.T. Puppy 558
Up On The Bridge/March	68	Laurie 3460
Love Me Like You're Gonna Lose Me/Three Dips Of Ice Cream	69	Laurie 3497
So Much In Love/Strange Strange Feeling	70	Buddah 171
My Sweet Lord/Main Nerve	75	Laurie 3630
Dream Dream Dream/Oh My Lover	76	Laurie 3648
Da Doo Ron Ron	N/A	Collectables LP 5042
Dry Your Eyes	N/A	Collectables LP 5042
It's My Party	N/A	Collectables LP 5042
My Block	N/A	Collectables LP 5042
The Locomotion	N/A	Collectables LP 5042
When I Go To Sleep At Night	N/A	Collectables LP 5042
Will You Still Love Me Tomorrow?	N/A	Collectables LP 5042

Chiffons (2) (Ginger & the) (female)

Where Were You Last Night/She	62	Groove 0003

ARTIST/SONG	YEAR	LABEL
Chimes (1) (aka Flairs (1))		
Love Me, Love Me, Love Me/My Heart's Crying For You	54	Flair 1051
Chimes (2)		
Dearest Darling/A Fool Was I	54	Royal Roost 577
Chimes (3)		
The Chimes Ring Out/I'm Leaving Baby	55	Specialty 549
Tears On My Pillow/Zindy Lou	55	Specialty 555
Pretty Little Girl/Chop Chop	56	Specialty 574
Jonelle/I Found An Angel	N/A	Dig 148 (unreleased)
Chimes (3) (Gene Moore & the)		
Only A Dream/Reap What You Sow	55	Combo 63
Chimes (3) (Tony Allen & the)		
Check Yourself, Baby/Especially	56	Specialty 570
Chimes (4) (fb Freddie Scott)		
Please Call/The Letter Came This Morning	57	Arrow 724
Lovin' Baby/A Faded Memory	57	Arrow 726
Chimes (5) (fb Lenny Cocco)		
Angel Child/Cry Cry Baby	57	Limelight 3000
Nervous Heart/When School Starts Again	57	Reserve 120
Du Wap/Stop Look And Listen	58	Limelight 3002
Once In A While/Oh How I Love You	60	Tag 444
Once In A While/Summer Night	60	Tag 444
I'm In The Mood For Love/Only Love	61	Tag 445
Let's Fall In Love/Dream Girl	61	Tag 447
Whose Heart Are You Breakin' Now/Baby's Coming Home	63	Metro 1/Laurie 3211 (63)
New York City Lady/Why Is Love So Bad	86	Freedom 223
Chimes (5) (Lenny & the)		
Paradise/My Love	62	Tag 450
Two Times Two/Only Forever	64	Vee Jay 605
Chimes (6)		
Coming Back To You	59	Storm 501
Chimes (7) (Dave Burgess & the)		
Lulu/I Don't Want To Know	59	Challenge 59037
Just For Me/Everlovin'	59	Challenge 59045
Chimes (8)		
Tears From An Angels Eyes	59	House Of Beauty 3
Chimes (9) (Leigh Bell & the)		
Terry/Eternity	61	Rust 5031
Chimes (10)		
Losing You Baby/Swanee River Rock	N/A	Jay-Tee 1000
Chipettes (Chip Allan & the)		
Tell Me Today/Summertime	63	Corsican 100
Chippendales		
What A Night/Drip Drop	59	Andie 5013
Voodoo/Day Will Come	60	Rust 5023
Chips (1)		
Rubber Biscuit/Oh, My Darlin'	56	Josie 803/Jozie 803 (56)

ARTIST/SONG	YEAR	LABEL
Chips (2) (Billy Bobbs & the)		
Shim Sham/Tweedle De Dum Dum	58	Edison International 400/ Edison International 416 (59)
Chips (3)		
As You Can See/You Make Me Feel So Good	60	Satellite 105
Chips (4) (fb Joe South)		
Bye Bye My Love/What A Lie	61	Ember 1077
Darling I Need Your Love/You're On My Mind	61	Venice 101/Strand 25027 (61)
Party People/Long Lonely Winter	65	Tollie 9042
Chips (5)		
When I'm With You/Everyone's Laughing	N/A	Clifton 54
Chirps (Marvin & the)		
I'll Miss You This Christmas/Sixteen Tons	58	Tip Top 202
Choraletters		
Hear My Prayer/I've Got To Run On	57	Duke 214
Choralettes		
I Destroyed Your Letters/Won't You Call Me	64	Fargo 1063
Chorals		
In My Dream/Rock And Roll Baby	56	Decca 29914
Chord Spinners		
Call Me/Love Is A Many Splendored Thing	61	Liberty 55368
Chord'R Notes		
Livin' The Life/How Still The Night	64	Fargo 1061
Chord-A-Roys (Bobby Roy & the)		
Little Girl Lost/Girls Were Made For Boys	60	JDS 5001
Chordcats (aka Chords)		
A Girl To Love/Hold Me, Baby	54	Cat 112
Chordells (1)		
Here's A Heart For You/I Started Out	56	Onyx 504/Relic 523 (64)
Chordells (2)		
At Last/September Song	59	Jaro 77005
Chordells (2) (Little Chip & the)		
Little More Love/Amazon Girl	61	Hull 746
Chordells (3) (Willie Howard & the)		
Letters Of Love/Louise	61	Mascot 127
Chordones (Leon D. Tarver & the)		
Oo-Ee What's Wrong With Me/I'm A Young Rooster	54	Checker 791
Chords (1)		
Daddy Loves Mommy/In The Woods	53	Gem 211
Sh-Boom/Cross Over The Bridge	54	Cat 104 (first pressing)
Sh-Boom/Little Maiden	54	Cat 104 (second pressing)
Zippety Zum/Bless You	54	Cat 109
Tears In Your Eyes/Don't Be A Jumpin' Jack	58	Casino 451
Pretty Face/Elephant Walk	59	Metro 20015
Chords (2)		
Cool, Cool Daddy/I'll Never Fool My Heart (by the Arrows)	73	Baron 107

ARTIST/SONG	YEAR	LABEL
Chris-Tones (Tommy Christy & the)		
Teen-Age Jive/Choo-Choo-Choo-Choo-Cha-Cha-Cha	58	Scot 19999
Christie, Charles (bb the Crystals)		
In The Arms Of A Girl/Young And Beautiful	66	HBR 473
Christie, Dean (& group)		
I'm A Loser/Heart Breaker	62	Select 715
Chromatics		
Wild, Man, Wild/Devil Blues	56	Crest 1011
Don't Know Why I Cry/Here In The Darkness	56	Million 2014
My Conscience/Got To Keep Her Down On The Farm	60	Ducky 716
Chromatics (Augie Austin & the)		
Too Late/My Heart Let Me Be Free	58	Brunswick 55080
Chromatics (Bob Williams & the)		
Believe Me/Who's Fooling Who (with the Tornados)	55	Blend 1005
I'll Never Change/Rockin' Beat	55	Blend 1006
Chromatics (Eddie Singleton & the)		
Too Late/Kiss-A-Kiss, Hug-A-Hug	58	Amasco 3701
Chromatics (Sherry Washington & the)		
Here In The Darkness/La De Do De Do	55	Million 2010
Honey Bug/Wabble Loo	56	Million 2016
Chryslers (Little Nate & the)		
Cry Baby Cry/Someone Up There	59	Johnson 318
Chrystalights		
The Bells	N/A	Sunset
Chuck-A-Lucks		
Heaven Knows/Chuck-A-Luck	57	Bow 305
Disc Jockey Fever/The Magic Of First Love	58	Lin 5014
Unconditional Surrender/Tarzan's Date	61	Jubilee 5415
Pick Up And Deliver/Long John	61	Warner Bros. 5198
Cotton Pickin' Love/I'm Hospitalized Over You	61	Warner Bros. 5234
Chuckles (1) (Chuck & the)		
Bury The Hatchet/One Hundred Baby	59	Shad 5015
Chuckles (2) (aka Consorts/aka 4 Clefs)		
On The Street Where You Live/I'll Wait	64	West Side 1019
Churchill, Savannah (& group)		
My Memories Of You/I Cried	54	Decca 29194
Chymes		
If I Give My Heart To You/On The Street Where You Live	64	Musictone 6125
Cincinnatians		
Magic Genie/Do What You Want To Do	N/A	Roosevelt Lee 16115/ Emerald 16116
Cincos (Ben Harper & the)		
Here Goes My Girl/Drive Away Blues	60	Talent 106
Cinderellas		
Yum Yum Yum/Mister Dee-Jay	59	Decca 30830
I Was Only Fifteen/You Never Shoulda Gone Away	59	Decca 30925
Baby, Baby (I Still Love You)/Please Don't Wake Me	64	Dimension 1026
More Than Yesterday	64	Tamara 763
Fairy Tale/Mr. Happy Love Joy	65	Mercury 72394

ARTIST/SONG	YEAR	LABEL
Cinders		
Cinnamon Cinder/C'mon Wobble	63	Warner Bros. 5326
I'll Follow You/The Story	64	Original Sound 43
Poison Ivy/Good Lovin's Hard To Find	65	Ric 156
Cineemas		
Never Gonna Cry/A Crush On You	63	Dave 911
Cineramas		
Life Can Be Beautiful/It Must Be Love	59	Champ 103
Crying For You/I'm Sorry, Baby	60	Rhapsody 71963/71964
Playing For Keeps	60	Rhapsody 71984
Is This All Mine/Crying For You	74	Clifton 4
Citadels		
New Love Tomorrow (a capella)	75	Relic LP 102
When I Fall In Love (a capella)	75	Relic LP 102
When I Woke Up This Morning (a capella)	75	Relic LP 102
Dream World (a capella)	75	Relic LP 103
Pennies From Heaven (a capella)	75	Relic LP 103
Tonite I Fell In Love (a capella)	75	Relic LP 103
I'll Never Let You Go (a capella)	75	Relic LP 104
Castle In The Sky (a capella)	75	Relic LP 105
Earth Angel (a capella)	75	Relic LP 109
Citations (1)		
It Hurts Me/Kiss In The Night	61	Don-El 113
Citations (2) (fb Nicki North)		
Magic Eyes/Mystery Of Love	62	Canadian American 136
Citations (3)		
Just For You	62	Sara 101
Slippin' And Slidin'/Moon Race (instrumental)	62	Sara 3301/Epic 9603 (63)
The Stomp/Chicago	64	Mercury 72286
I Will Stand By You/To Win The Race	67	Ballad 101
Citations (4)		
The Girl Next Door/Ten Miles From Nowhere	63	Vangee 301/Fraternity 910 (63)/Fraternity 992 (67)
Citations (5) (Buddy & the)		
Juvenile Delinquent/Don't Let Her Have Her Way	N/A	IRC 6918
Citations (6)		
Take Me	59	University 101
Citrones (Freddy Powell & the)		
Faded Pictures/Flip To The Twist	62	Sheraton 105
Ciufo, Jerry (& group)		
Fools Fall In Love/Don't Cry	65	Jeree 65
Clantones		
May I Never Love Again/If You Were Mine	59	Ebony 1021
Claremonts (aka Clairmonts/aka Tonettes))		
Why Keep Me Dreaming?/Angel Of Romance	57	Apollo 517/Apollo 751 (63)
Clarendons (Lee & the)		
Night Owl	N/A	H.S.
Clark, Dee (bb the Kool Gents)		
Gloria/Kangaroo Hop	57	Falcon 1002
Gloria/You're Lookin' Good (Dee Clark)	57	Falcon 1002/Vee Jay 355 (60)

ARTIST/SONG	YEAR	LABEL
When I Call On You/Nobody But You	58	Abner 1019
All Alone In My Lonely Room/As Long As You're In Love With Me	63	Atco 6266
I Just Can't Help Myself	60	Vee Jay LP 1019/ Charly LP 1113
Just Like A Fool	60	Vee Jay LP 1019/Charly LP 1113/Solid Smoke LP 8026

Class Cutters (Herbie & the)

Just A Summer Kick/Like Those Ivy Walls	59	RCA 7649

Class-Aires

My Tears Start To Fall/Too Old To Cry	N/A	Honey Bee 1

Class-Notes (1)

You Inspire Me/Goodness Gracious	58	Dot 15786

Class-Notes (2)

Take It Back/Bessie's House	58	Hamilton 50011

Classic IV (Four)

Early Christmas/Limbo Under The Christmas Tree	62	Algonquin 1650
Island Of Paradise/Heavenly Bliss	62	Twist 1001

Classics (1)

If Only The Sky Was A Mirror/Gosh But This Is Love	58	Class 219

Classics (2)

You're The Prettiest One/Let Me Dream	59	Crest 1063

Classics (3)

You're Everything/Burning Love	60	Top Rank 2061

Classics (3) (fb Emil Stuccio)

Cinderella/So In Love	59	Dart 1015/Musictone 1114 (63)
Angel Angela/Eenie, Meenie, Minie And Mo	60	Dart 1032
Life Is But A Dream Sweetheart/That's The Way	61	Dart 1038/Mercury 71829 (61)
Life's But A Dream/Nuttin In The Noggun	61	Streamline 1028
Till Then/Eenie, Meenie, Minie And Mo	63	Musicnote 1116
P.S. I Love You/Wrap Your Troubles In Dreams (And Dream Your Troubles Away)	63	Musicnote 118
Too Young/Who's Laughing, Who's Crying	64	Musictone 6131
You'll Never Know/Dancing With You	65	Stork 2
Over The Weekend/Dancing With You	66	Josie 939
I Apologize/Love For Today	67	Piccollo 500
Wind/Vagabond	71	Sire 353
Again/The Way You Look Tonight	N/A	Bed-Stuy 222

Classics (3) (Jimmy Ringo & the)

Full Race Cam	59	Dart

Classics (4) (fb Lou Christie)

Close Your Eyes/Funny Thing	60	Starr 508/Alcar 207 (63)

Classics (4) (Lou Christie & the)

Tomorrow Will Come/You're With It	63	Alcar 208

Classics (5) (Herb Lance & the)

Blue Moon/Little Boy Lost	61	Promo 1010

Classics (6)

The Wheel Of Love	N/A	Karen

Classics (7)

Christmas Is Here	60	MV 1000

ARTIST/SONG	YEAR	LABEL
Classics (8) (Mike Sabeh & the)		
So Fine	N/A	Empress 1001
Classics Four (Bob Gerardi & the)		
Nobody Wants You Anymore/You're Everything To Me	60	Recorte 441
Classinettes (female)		
To The Church	62	Markay 107
Classmates (1) (aka Four Classmates)		
What Am I Gonna Do/A Kiss Is Not A Kiss	55	King 1487
Return My Heart/Who's Gonna Take You To The Prom	56	Dot 15460
Break Down And Love Me/Two Straws In The Wind	56	Dot 15464
Friends/I Want My Love Close By	56	Dot 15504
You Do Something To Me/You Aren't The Only One	57	Dot 15589
High School/Don't Make Me Cry	60	Marquee 101
Until Then/Pretty Little Pet	60	Marquee 102
Homework/Here Comes Suzy	61	Seg-Way 104
All I Want Is To Love You	62	Radar 3962
Did You Ever/Will You Love Me Tomorrow	62	Stacy 935
Graduation/Teenage Twister	63	Radar 2624
Classmates (2)		
Gotta Go And See My Baby/Washed My Heart Of Love	56	Silhouette 509/510
Classmates (3) (Ronnie Jones & the)		
Little Girl Next Door/Teenage Rock	57	End 1002
Lonely Boy/My Baby Cries	58	End 1014
Lonely Boy/Teenage Rock	63	End 1125
Classmates (4) (Marc Cavell & the)		
I Didn't Lie/I See It	61	Candix 329
Classmen (1)		
True Love/Silver Medal	63	Gateway 712
Love Is Gone/My Special Angel	63	Limelight 3012
All Time Fool/Do You Wanna Dance	64	Limelight 3016
Classmen (2)		
I'm Warning You/I Won't Cry	63	CM 8464
Classmen (3)		
Why Did You Put Me On/Why Does Everybody	64	JR 5006
Clean Cut Clan (Dan & the)		
The Perfect Example/Broken Hip Party	64	Accent 1116
Cleartones		
Lost In A Dream	N/A	Announcing
Clearwater, Eddie (& group)		
Twist Like This/I Was Gone	62	Federal 12446
Cleeshays (Sonny Knight & the)		
Lipstick Kisses/Eat Your Mush And Hush	59	Eastman 787
Clef Dwellers		
Redheaded Woman/The Way You Gotta Swing Today	58	Singular 713
Clefftones (aka Whirlpools)		
My Dearest Darling/The Masquerade Is Over	55	Old Town 1011
Gloria	55	Old Town/Murray Hill LP 000083
Guess Who	55	Old Town/Murray Hill LP 000083

ARTIST/SONG	YEAR	LABEL
Little Girl	55	Old Town/Murray Hill LP 000083

Clefs (1) (fb Scotty Mann)

We Three/Ride On	52	Chess 1521
I'll Be Waiting/Please Don't Leave Me	54	Peacock 1643

Clefs (2)

Sorry/I Really Had A Ball (by the Ontarios)	73	Baron 104

Cleftones

You Baby You/I Was Dreaming	56	Gee 1000
Little Girl Of Mine/You're Driving Me Mad	56	Gee 1011
Can't We Be Sweethearts/Neki-Hokey	56	Gee 1016
String Around My Heart/Happy Memories	56	Gee 1025
Why Do You Do Me Like You Do/I Like Your Style Of Making Love	57	Gee 1031
See You Next Year/Ten Pairs Of Shoes	57	Gee 1038
Hey Baby/What Did I Do That Was Wrong	57	Gee 1041
Since We Fell In Love	57	Roulette LP 25021
Honey Bun	57	unreleased
Lover Boy/Beginners At Love	58	Gee 1048
After The Dance	59	Roulette LP 25059
Cool It, Fool	59	unreleased
Heart And Soul/How Do You Feel	61	Gee 1064
I Love You For Sentimental Reasons/Deed I Do	61	Gee 1067
Earth Angel/Blues In The Night	61	Gee 1074
Do You/Again	61	Gee 1077
Lover Come Back To Me/There She Goes	61	Gee 1079
How Deep Is The Ocean/Some Kind Of Blue	61	Gee 1080
One Hundred Pounds Of Clay	61	Gee LP 705
The Glory Of Love	61	Gee LP 705
Time Is Running Out On Our Love	61	Gee LP 705
You And I Can Climb	61	Gee LP 705
My Babe	62	Gee LP 707
Red Sails In The Sunset	62	Gee LP 707
Blue Skies	63	unreleased
Slippin' And Slidin'	63	unreleased
Sweet And Lovely	63	unreleased
My Angel Lover/You Lost The Game Of Love	90	CAR 121
She's So Fine/Trudy	58	Roulette 4094
Cuzin' Casanova/Mish Mash Baby	59	Roulette 4161
She's Gone/Shadows On The Very Last Row	60	Roulette 4302
She's Forgotten You/Right From The Git Go	64	Ware 6001

Cleftones (featuring Pat Spann)

Heavenly Father	61	Gee LP 705
Please Say You Want Me	61	Gee LP 705

Clefts

Dreaming/Come On	60	V-Tone 212

Cliches

What's Your Name/Little Egypt	59	Maar C 1530
Dream	N/A	N/A

Click-Clacks

Is It Wrong/A Kiss Goodbye	58	Algonquin 714
Rocket Roll/Kiss Goodbye	58	Algonquin 715/Apt 25032 (59)
Pretty Little Pearly/Roma Rocka-Rolla	58	Apt 25010

Click-Ettes (aka Clickettes) (female)

A Teenager's First Love/Jive Time Turkey	58	Dice 83/84
But Not For Me/I Love You I Swear	60	Dice 100
To Be A Part Of You/Because Of My Best Friend	60	Dice 92/93
Warm, Soft And Lovely/Why Oh Why	60	Dice 94/95

ARTIST/SONG	YEAR	LABEL
Lover's Prayer/Grateful	60	Dice 96/97
I Just Can't Help It/I Just Can't Help It (instrumental)	63	Checker 1060
I Understand Him/I Understand Him (instrumental)	63	Tuff 373

Clickettes (aka Click-Ettes) (female)
Where Is He/Lone Lover	60	Guyden 2043

Clicks
Come Back To Me/Peace And Contentment	55	Josie 780
You Ran Away From My Heart	63	Rush 2004

Clientells
Church Bells May Ring/My Love	62	M.B.S. 7

Clifford, Buzz (bb the Teenagers)
Three Little Fishes/Simply Because	62	Columbia 41979

Climates
Breaking Up Again/No You For Me	67	Sun 404

Climatics
All Alone/Help, There Is A Burglar	59	Request 3007/3008
My Gift From Heaven/Light Finger Willie	62	Re-No 1000

Climbers
My Darlin' Dear/Angels In Heaven Know I Love You	57	J&S 1652
I Love You/Trains, Cars, Boats	57	J&S 1658

Clinton, Buddy (& group)
How My Prayers Have Changed/ Across The Street From Your House	59	Time 1016

Clintonian Cubs (fb Jimmy Castor)
Confusion/She's Just My Size	60	My Brothers 508

Clippers (1) (Big Mike Gordon & the)
Careless Lover/The Clipper	56	Baton 233

Clippers (2) (Johnny Blake & the)
Bella-Marie/I'm Yours	57	Gee 1027

Clippers (3)
Rain/You Can't Trust A Woman	57	Fox 961

Clippers (4)
Goodnight, Irene/Beanie	60	Beacon 210
Now And Always/Forgotten Love	61	Tri 211

Clips
Wish I Didn't Love You So/Your Lovin' Moves Me	54	Republic 7102
Kiss Away/Let Me Get Close To You Baby	56	Calvert 105

Cliques (aka Jesse Belvin)
Why Oh Why/Don't Stop Loving Me	56	Modern 967 (unreleased)
Girl In My Dreams/I Wanna Know Why	56	Modern 987
My Desire/I'm In Love With A Gal	56	Modern 995

Clocks & Classmen
It's Written/Think You're Smart	58	Mail Call 1011

Clouds (1)
I Do/Rock And Roll Boogie	56	Cobra 5001
Say You Love Me	90	Relic LP 5088

Clouds (2)
Darling I Love You/T.V. Mix Up	59	Round 1008

ARTIST/SONG	YEAR	LABEL
Clouds (3) (Little Sunny Day & the)		
Lou Ann/Baby Doll	61	Tandem 7001
Clouds (4) (Donna Dee & the)		
Can't You See (Oo-Wee)/The More I See Him	61	Ramada 501
Clouds (5)		
All I Do Is Worry/Baby It's Me	61	Skylark 116
Clouds (6) (fb Bill Medley)		
My Tears Will Go Away/Night Owl	64	Medley 1001
Clouds (7)		
A Lovely Way To Spend An Evening/Say Hey Hey	N/A	Vous 1000
Clovermen (Tippie & the) (aka Tippie & the Clovers)		
Please Mr. Sun/I Like It Like That	62	Stenton 7001
Clovers		
Yes Sir, That's My Baby/When You Come Back To Me	50	Rainbow 11-122
Skylark/Don't You Know I Love You	51	Atlantic 934
Fool, Fool, Fool/Needless	51	Atlantic 944
One Mint Julep/Middle Of The Night	52	Atlantic 963
Ting-A-Ling/Wonder Where My Baby's Gone	52	Atlantic 969
I Played The Fool/Hey, Miss Fannie	52	Atlantic 977
Good Lovin'/Here Goes A Fool	53	Atlantic 1000
Comin' On/The Feeling Is So Good	53	Atlantic 1010
Crawlin'/Yes, It's You	53	Atlantic 989
Lovey Dovey/Little Mama	54	Atlantic 1022
I've Got My Eyes On You/Your Cash Ain't Nothin' But Trash	54	Atlantic 1035
I Confess/Alrighty, Oh Sweetie	54	Atlantic 1046
Blue Velvet/If You Love Me	55	Atlantic 1052
In The Morning Time/Lovebug	55	Atlantic 1060
Nip Sip/If I Could Be Loved By You	55	Atlantic 1073
Devil Or Angel/Hey, Doll Baby	56	Atlantic 1083
Your Tender Lips/Love, Love, Love	56	Atlantic 1094
From The Bottom Of My Heart/Bring Me Love	56	Atlantic 1107
Baby Baby, Oh My Darling/A Lonely Fool	56	Atlantic 1118
You Good-Looking Woman/Here Comes Romance	57	Atlantic 1129
So Young/I-I-I Love You	57	Atlantic 1139
Down In The Valley/There's No Tomorrow	57	Atlantic 1152
Wishing For Your Love/All About You	58	Atlantic 1175
Please Come On To Me/The Gossip Wheel	58	Poplar 110/Poplar 139 (59)
The Good Old Summertime/Idaho	58	Poplar 111
Old Black Magic/Rock And Roll Tango	59	United Artists 174
Love Potion No. 9/Stay Awhile	59	United Artists 180
Jamaica Farewell	59	United Artists LP 3033
Kentucky Babe	59	United Artists LP 3033
My Mother's Eyes	59	United Artists LP 3033
Pennies From Heaven	59	United Artists LP 3033
To Each His Own	59	United Artists LP 3033
Vaya Con Dios	59	United Artists LP 3033
What Is This Thing Called Love	59	United Artists LP 3033
One Mint Julep/Lovey	60	United Artists 209
Easy Lovin'/I'm Confessin' That I Love You	60	United Artists 227
Yes It's You/Burning Fire	60	United Artists 263
The Bootie Green/Drive It Home	61	Atlantic 2129
The Honeydripper/Have Gun	61	United Artists 307
Wrapped Up In A Dream/Let Me Hold You	61	Winley 255
I Need You Now/Gotta Quit You	61	Winley 265
Love Love Love/The Kickapoo	63	Brunswick 55249
He Sure Could Hypnotize/Poor Baby	65	Port 3004
Too Long Without Some Loving/For Days	68	Josie 992
Try My Lovin' On You/Sweet Side Of A Soulful Woman	68	Josie 997

ARTIST/SONG	YEAR	LABEL
Clovers (Buddy Bailey & the)		
Stop Pretending/One More Time	63	Porwin 1001
It's All In The Game/That's What I Will Be	63	Porwin 1004
Clovers (Tippie & the)		
Bossa Nova Baby/Bossa Nova (My Heart Said)	63	Tiger 201
Clusters		
Darling Can't You Tell/Pardon My Heart	58	Tee Gee 102/End 1115 (62)
Long Legged Maggie/Forecast Of Our Love	59	Epic 9330
Longing	N/A	unreleased
Zoom	N/A	unreleased
Sunday Kind Of Love	N/A	unreleased
Clusters (Gus Coletti & the)		
Hold My Hand/Without Your Love	57	Tin Pan Alley 206
Sample Kiss/My Darling Wait For Me	57	Tin Pan Alley 207
Co-Eds (1) (fb Gwen Edwards)		
Love You Baby All The Time/I Beg Your Forgiveness	56	Old Town 1027
I Love An Angel/I'm In Love	57	Old Town 1033
Co-Eds (2)		
Juke Box/Big Chief	58	Cameo 129
La La La/Juke Box	58	Cameo 134
With All My Heart/A Man	59	Dwain 802
When It's Over/Annabelle Lee	61	Cha Cha 715/Checker 996 (61)
Time After Time	61	Sheryl 337
The Magic Of Your Love/Heartthrob	62	USA 724
Co-Eds (3) (aka Blossoms)		
Son-In-Law/I'll Wait	61	Challenge 9109
Co-Hearts		
My Love/Cry Baby	58	Vee Jay 289
Co-Ops		
Your Love/Shame, Shame, Shame	59	Versailles 100
Coachmen		
Caring/Fame And Fortune	54	X 0044
Coachmen Five		
Oh Joan/This I Know	N/A	Janson 100
Coanjos		
Dance The Boomerang/Speaking Of Love	61	Dapt 208
Coasters		
Down In Mexico/Turtle Dovin'	56	Atco 6064
One Kiss Led To Another/Brazil	56	Atco 6073
Searchin'/Young Blood	57	Atco 6087
Idol With The Golden Head/(When She Wants Good Lovin') My Baby Comes To Me	57	Atco 6098
What's The Secret Of Your Success/Sweet Georgia Brown	57	Atco 6104
Dance/Gee Golly	58	Atco 6111
Yakety Yak/ Zing Went The Strings Of My Heart	58	Atco 6116
The Shadow Knows/Sorry But I'm Gonna Have To Pass	58	Atco 6126
Riot In Cell Block #9	58	Atco LP 101
Charlie Brown/Three Cool Cats	59	Atco 6132
Along Came Jones/That Is Rock 'n' Roll	59	Atco 6141
Poison Ivy/I'm A Hog For You	59	Atco 6146
Run Red Run/What About Us	59	Atco 6153
Besame Mucho Pt. 1/Besame Mucho Pt. 11	60	Atco 6163
Wake Me, Shake Me/Stewball	60	Atco 6168

ARTIST/SONG	YEAR	LABEL
Shoppin' For Clothes/Snake And The Bookworm	60	Atco 6178
Wait A Minute/Thumbin' A Ride	61	Atco 6186
Little Egypt/Keep On Rolling	61	Atco 6192
Girls, Girls, Girls Pt. 1/Girls, Girls, Girls Pt. 2	61	Atco 6204
Just Like Me (Ain't That)/Bad Blood	61	Atco 6210
Ridin' Hood/Teach Me How To Shimmy	62	Atco 6219
The Climb/The Climb	62	Atco 6234
My Babe	62	Atco LP 135
The P.T.A./Bull Tick Waltz	63	Atco 6251
T'ain't Nothin' To Me/Speedoo's Back In Town	64	Atco 6287
Bad Detective/Lovey Dovey	64	Atco 6300
Wild One/I Must Be Dreaming	64	Atco 6321
Hongry/Lady Like	65	Atco 6341
Let's Go Get Stoned/Money Honey	65	Atco 6356
Bell Bottom Slacks/Crazy Baby	66	Atco 6379
She's A Yum Yum/Saturday Night Fish Fry	66	Atco 6407
Love Potion No. 9/D.W. Washburn	71	King 6385
The Angels Listened In	N/A	Coast 187

Coasters Two Plus Two (aka Coasters)
Searchin' 75/Young Blood	75	Chelan 2000

Coastliners
Wonderful You/Alright	60	Back Beat 554
She's My Girl/I'll Be Home	60	Back Beat 566
I See Me/California On My Mind	67	Dear 1300

Cobanas (Roy Hines & the)
We Have Love/I Can Live	N/A	Solitaire 1001

Cobras (1)
Cindy (or Sindy)/I Will Return	55	Modern 964

Cobras (2)
Thumpin'/Don't Even Know Your Name	64	Monogram 519
La La/Goodbye Molly	64	Swan 4176/Casino 1309 (64)

Cocoas
Flip Your Daddy/Ooooo! Ooooo!	55	Chesterfield 364

Codas (Charles Gully & the)
Hey Little Baby	63	C.J. 641

Coeds (with the Tokens)
Mark My Words/You're My First Love	64	Swing 101

Cognacs
Charlena/Heaven Only Knows	61	Roulette 4340

Coins (1) (aka Colonials (1))
Blue, Can't Get No Place With You/Cheatin' Baby	54	Gee 10
Look At Me Girl/S.R. Blues	54	Gee 11
Look At Me Girl/Two Loves Have I (by the Colonials)	56	Gee 1007

Coins (2)
Loretta/Please	55	Model 2001

Cole, Ann (bb the Suburbans (1))
Are You Satisfied/Darling Don't Hurt Me	55	Baton 218
New Love/Easy Easy Baby	56	Baton 224

ARTIST/SONG	YEAR	LABEL
Cole, Clay (bb the Capris)		
Twist Around The Clock/Don't Twist	61	Imperial 5804
Cole, Freddy (& group)		
Don't Be Mad	N/A	Titantic 100
Coleman, Lenny (bb Nino & the Ebbtides)		
Four Seasons/Shake It Easy	65	Laurie 3290
Colleagues		
A Tear Fell/I Want You I Need You	N/A	Glodus 1651
Collegians (1) (Jackie Roy & the)		
The Leaf/You Made A Fool Of Me	53	Okeh 6970
Devil Eyes/My Heart Knows	53	Okeh 6987
Collegians (2)		
Rickety Tickety Melody/The Sackbut,	54	Cat 110
The Psaltery And The Dulcimer		
Blue Solitude/Please Let Me Be The One	56	Groove 0163
Collegians (3)		
Zoom Zoom Zoom/On Your Merry Way	57	Winley 224
Let's Go For A Ride/Heavenly Night	58	X-Tra 108/Times Square 11 (63)
Tonite Oh Tonite/Oh I Need Your Love	61	Winley 261
Right Around The Corner/Teenie Weenie Little Bit	61	Winley 263
He Will Break Your Heart	N/A	N/A
Rockin' Time	N/A	N/A
Collegians (4)		
Happy Parakeet/Cookin'	61	Hilltop 1868
I'm Ready/Grandma Told Me So	62	Post 10002
Collegians (5) (Professor Marcell & the)		
My College Girl, Pt. 1/My College Girl, Pt. 2	67	Mayhams 212
Collegiates (1) (Dicky Lee & the)		
Good Lovin'/Memories Never Grow Old	57	Sun 280
Dream Boy/Stay True Baby	57	Tampa 131
Fool, Fool, Fool/Dreamy Nights	58	Sun 297
Collegiates (2)		
Restless Lover/Brief Romance	59	Capo 001
Heartaches Don't Care/The Effigy	61	Campus 123
I Had A Dream/Growing Up	61	Heritage 105
Collegiates (3) (Harold Teen & the)		
The Genevieve Jump/Moon Over Miami	60	Goldisc 3014
Collegiates (4)		
Teenage Plea/A Kid In His Teens	60	RD Globe 009
Colognes		
A River Flows/A Bird And A Bee	59	Lummtone 102
Colonairs		
Sandy/Can't Stand To Lose You	57	Ember 1017
Do-Pop-Si/Little Miss Muffet	64	Tru-Lite 127
Colonials (1) (aka Coins (1))		
Two Loves Have I/Look At Me Girl (by the Coins)	56	Gee 1007
Colonials (1) (Bill "Bass" Gordon & the) (aka Coins (1))		
Two Loves Have I/Bring My Baby Back	54	Gee 12

ARTIST/SONG	YEAR	LABEL
Colonials (2)		
Where Is My Love/Why Didn't You Tell Me Girl	N/A	Senate 1003
Colos (David Dayton & the)		
The Search Is Over/I Gotta Have Love	55	Lomar 704
Colts		
Adorable/Lips Red As Wine	55	Vita 112/Mambo 112 (55)
Sweet Sixteen/Honey Bun	56	Vita 121
Never No More/Hey You, Shoobeoohbee	56	Vita 130
Never No More/Sheik Of Araby	59	Antler 4003
Guiding Angel/Sheik Of Araby	59	Antler 4007
I Never Knew/Oh, When You Touch Me (by the Red Coats)	59	Del-Co 4002
Sweet Sixteen/Hey, Hey, Pretty Baby	62	Plaza 505
Colts (Jackie Kelso & the)		
Kwela, Kwela/Rat-A-Tat	55	Vita 114
Columbo, Joe (& group)		
I Need You/I Wonder If I Care As Much	63	Taurus 359
Columbus Pharaohs (aka Four Pharaohs)		
Give Me Your Love/China Girl	58	Esta 290/Ransom 101 (58)/ Paradise 109 (59)/ Nanc 1120 (59)
Combinations		
Back Home Again/I'm A Travelin' Man	60	Combo 167
Just One More Chance/Voodoo	N/A	Carrie 010
Combo Kings		
All I Could Do Was Cry/Mish Mash	N/A	Flo-Jo 4095
Combo-Nettes (Clemons Penix & the)		
I've Been Searching/No Evil	56	Combo 117
Combo-Nettes (Jane Porter & the) (female)		
If I Had My Wish/Hi-Diddle-Diddle	55	Combo 74
I Ain't Got Time/What Kind Of Man Is This?	56	Combo 118
Got To Have You Baby	88	Relic LP 5076
Comets (1) (Herb Kenny & the)		
Only You/When The Lights Go On Again	52	Federal 12083
Comets (2) (Lynn Tiatt & the)		
Dad Is Home/Vilma's Jump-Up	N/A	Pussycat 1
Comic Books		
Manuel/Black Magic And Witchcraft	62	Citation 5001/New Phoenix 6199 (62)
What Do You Do When	62	Cuca 6494
Commodores (1)		
Riding On A Train/Uranium	55	Dot 15372
Close To My Heart/Cream Puff	55	Dot 15425
Speedoo/Whole Lotta Shakin' Goin' On	56	Dot 15439
Two Loves Have I/Who Said I Said That	56	Dot 15461
Not A Day Goes By/Sweet Angel	57	Challenge 1004
I'll Be There/Faith	57	Challenge 1007
Laughing With Tears In My Eyes/Who Dat	59	Brunswick 55126
Home	N/A	4-S
Commodores (2) (Darrell Glenn & the)		
Hello Baby/Zinga Zingo	57	RPM 488

ARTIST/SONG	YEAR	LABEL
Como, Nicky (bb the Del Satins)		
Your Guardian Angel/Just A Little While	N/A	Tang 1231
Companions (1)		
Falling/Oh, What A Feeling!	58	Dove 240
Why Oh Baby Why/I Didn't Know	59	Brook's 100/Federal 12397 (60)
No Fool Am I/How Could You	62	Amy 852
It's Too Late/These Foolish Things	63	Arlen 722/Gina 722 (63)
Companions (2)		
I'll Always Love You/A Little Bit Of Blue	62	Columbia 42279
Companions (3)		
Be Yourself/Help A Lonely Guy	62	General American 711
Compliments (1) (Michael Zara & the)		
Angels Of Mercy/Nobody Knows	63	Shell 313
Compliments (2)		
Borrow Til Morning/Beware Beware	68	Midas 304
Composers		
I Had A Dream/You And Yours	63	Era 3118
Woe Is Me/Elephant Drag	N/A	Ampen 221
Computones		
Flip Flip Zoo-Wah	N/A	N/A
Con Chords (Bob Brady & the)		
I Love You Baby/Illusion	66	Chariot 525
Con-Dons		
Dear Abby/Centennial March	62	Carlton 587
Concepts (1)		
Jungle/Whisper	61	Apache 1515/ Musictone 1109 (61)
Concepts (2)		
Sad Little Boy/Blue Sea	64	ABC 10526
Concepts (3)		
Yo Me Pregunto/The Vow (a capella)	66	Catamount 112
Concepts (4) (with the Emanons)		
Cry	N/A	J&J 3000
Concertones		
Just One More Time/All Is Well And Fine	61	Legrand 1011
Concords (1)		
Candlelight/Monticello	54	Harlem 2328
I'm Satisfied With Rock 'N' Roll/I'll Always Say Please	56	Ember 1007
Concords (1) (Pearl Reaves & the)		
You Can't Stay Here (Step It Up And Go)/ I'm Not Ashamed (Ugly Woman)	55	Harlem 2332
Concords (2) (aka Snowmen/aka Sherwoods (3))		
Cross My Heart/Our Last Goodbye	61	Gramercy 304
Again/The Boy Most Likely	61	RCA 7911
My Dreams/Scarlet Ribbons	62	Gramercy 305
Marlene/Our Love Wasn't Meant To Be	62	Herald 576
Cold And Frosty Morning/Don't Go Now	62	Herald 578 (first pressing, second is by the Snowmen)

ARTIST/SONG	YEAR	LABEL

One Step From Heaven/Away — 62 — Rust 5048
Should I Cry/It's Our Wedding Day — 64 — Epic 9697
Down The Aisle Of Love/I Feel A Love Comin' On — 66 — Boom 60021/Polydor 14036 (70)

Concords (2) (fb Neal Scott)
Bobby/I Haven't Found It With Another — 61 — Portrait 102
Run To Me/Tomboy — 62 — Comet 2151
One Piece Bathing Suit/Little Girl — 63 — Herald 581
I Don't Stand A Ghost Of A Chance/Let Me Think It Over — 67 — Cameo 476

Concords (3) (Tony Colton & the)
Goodbye Cindy Goodbye/Tell The World — 63 — Roulette 4475

Condors
Sweetest Angel/Little Curly Top — N/A — Hunter 2503/2504

Cones (Connie & the)
Let Us Pretend/I See The Image Of You — 59 — NRC 5006
Lonely Girl's Prayer/I Love My Teddy Bear — 60 — Roulette 4223
Take All The Kisses/No Time For Tears — 60 — Roulette 4313

Confessions
Be-Bop Baby/Before You Change Your Mind — 61 — Epic 9474

Confidentials (Billy Joe & the)
Feeling Blue/Got You On My Mind — 65 — BJ 64

Connotations
Two Hearts Fall In Love/Before I Go — 62 — Technichord 1000/1001

Conquerors
Billy Is My Boyfriend/Duchess Conquers Duke — 62 — Lu Pine 108

Conservatives
That's All — 68 — Tribe

Consoles (Bobby & the)
My Jelly Bean/Nita, I Need You So — 63 — Diamond 141
Karine/Maybe — 66 — Verve 10402

Consorts (1) (Les Ledo & the)
Nina/Got Me A Sweetheart — 59 — Nina 1601

Consorts (2) (aka 4 Clefs)
Please Be Mine/Time After Time — 61 — Cousins 1004/Apt 25066 (62)

Constellations
Come Sit By Me/God Loves You Child — 56 — Groove 0140

Consuls (1)
Runaway/I'm Happy — 59 — Abel 222

Consuls (2) (Little Caesar & the) (aka Little Caesar & the Romans)
My Girl Sloopy/Poison Ivy — 65 — Mala 512

Contels
Hey You/Lover's Dream — 59 — Warwick 103

Contenders
Mr. Dee Jay/Yes I Do — 59 — Blue Sky 105
The Clock/Peace Of Mind — 63 — Long Fiber 201
Whenever I Get Lonely/That's The Way — 63 — Saxony 1001
The Dune Buggy/Go Ahead — 64 — Chattahoochie 644
Johnny B. Goode/Rise And Shine — 64 — Chattahoochie 656
The Clock/Look At Me — 66 — Java 101

ARTIST/SONG	YEAR	LABEL
Lonely Lover/I Like It Like That	66	Java 103
Hetta Hetta/I Know Somewhere	66	Java 104
Gunga Din/Wake Up In The Morning	N/A	Whitney Sound 1929

Contessas (female)
Boy Of My Heart/Hard Guy To Please	63	Witch 113

Continental Five
Moe & Joe/Perdelia	59	Nu Kat 10132
My Lonely Friend/King Of Rock And Roll	59	Nu Kat 104/105

Continental Gems
My Love Will Follow You/Everywhere	63	Guyden 2091

Continentals (1) (aka Quinns)
Peace Of Mind	59	Relic LP 5036
Dear Lord/Fine Fine Frame	56	Whirlin' Disc 101/ Port 70018 (60)
Picture Of Love/Soft And Sweet	56	Whirlin' Disc 105/ Port 70024 (61)
You're The Reason	N/A	N/A

Continentals (2)
Don't Do It Baby/Tongue Twister	59	Davis 466

Continentals (3)
Take A Gamble On Me/Meanwhile Back At The Ranch	56	Key 517
You're An Angel/Giddy-Up And Ding-Dong	56	Rama 190

Continentals (4) (Bill Harris & the)
Danny Boy/I'm So Glad	58	Eagle 1002

Continentals (5)
Sad Love Affair/White Buck Shoes	59	Red Top 121

Continentals (6) (Teddy & the)
Tick Tick Tock/Everybody Pony	61	Richie 1001/Pik 235 (61)
Do You/Tighten Up	61	Richie 445
Crying Over You/Crossfire With Me Baby	61	Richie 453
Tick Tick Tock/Wild Christening Party (by the Teen Kings)	62	Rago 201

Continentals (7) (Billy John & the)
Ooh Pooh Pah Doo/Does Someone Care (For Me)	62	N-Joy 1012
Lover Boy Blue/Put The Hurt On You	62	N-Joy 1014

Continentals (8) (Lenny & the)
Little Joe And Linda Lee/The Shack (instrumental)	63	Tribute 119
Dance The Last Dance/Rosebud	63	Tribute 125

Continentals (9) (Joey & the)
She Rides With Me/Rudy Vadoo	65	Claridge 304
Sad Girl/Baby	65	Laurie 3294
Linda/Will Love Ever Come My Way	N/A	Komet 1001

Continentals (10) (Michael & the)
Little School Girl/Rain In My Eyes	65	Audio Fidelity 139

Continentals (11)
My Lonely Friend/Impossible (by the Velvatones)	74	Candlelite 412

Continentals (12)
It Doesn't Matter/Whisper It	N/A	Hunter 3503

Continentals (13)
No Money No Luck Blues	N/A	Vandan 8067

ARTIST/SONG	YEAR	LABEL

Continentals (14)
Man With A Broken Heart — N/A — M

Continentals (15) (Morris Rogers & the)
Wonders Of Love/The Leg — N/A — Delta 601

Continettes
Boys Who Don't Understand/Billy The Kidder — 63 — Ritchie 4300

Contours (Texas Red & the)
Comin' Home/Turn Around — 57 — Bullseye 1009
Funny/The Stretch — 61 — Motown 1012

Contours (Mike Hanks & the)
Christen/Can I Be Your Lover Boy — 60 — Brax 221

Contrails
Someone/Mummy Walk — 65 — Reuben 711/Diamond 213 (66)
Make Me Love You/Feel So Fine — 67 — Millage 104

Contrasts (Billy Vera & the)
My Heart Cries/All My Love — 62 — Rust 5051

Convincers
Rejected Love/Go Back Baby — 62 — Movin' 100

Cook, Johnny (& group)
My Dear My Darling/It's All In Your Mind — 57 — Lamp 2006

Cooke, Dale (aka Sam Cooke) (& group)
Loveable/Forever — 57 — Specialty 596

Cooke, L.C. (& group)
Please Think Of Me/I'm Falling — 59 — Checker 925

Cooke, Sam (& group)
Just For You/Made For Me — 61 — Sar 122

Cookies (1) (female)
Don't Let Go/All Night Mambo — 54 — Lamp 8008
Precious Love/Later, Later — 55 — Atlantic 1061
In Paradise/Passing Time — 56 — Atlantic 1084/Atlantic 2079 (60)
My Lover/Down By The River — 56 — Atlantic 1110
Hippy-Dippy-Daddy/King Of Hearts — 57 — Josie 822

Cookies (2) (fb Earl-Jean McCree) (female)
Chains/Stranger In My Arms — 62 — Dimension 1002
Don't Say Nothin' Bad (About My Baby)/Softly In The Night — 63 — Dimension 1008
Will Power/I Want A Boy For My Birthday — 63 — Dimension 1012
Girls Grow Up Faster Than Boys/Only To Other People — 63 — Dimension 1020
I Never Dreamed/The Old Crowd — 64 — Dimension 1032

Cool Cats (Robin & the)
Give Me Your Love — N/A — Pussy Cat 501

Cool Gents (Deroy Green & the)
Beggar To A Queen/At The Teen Center — 61 — Cee Jay 584

Cool Tones
Cry All Night — N/A — Dice 750

Cool-Tones
Ginchy/Movin' Out — 59 — Warwick 505
The Dixie Blues/Daylight In Dixie — 62 — Radiant 1510

ARTIST/SONG	YEAR	LABEL
Coolbreezers		
You Know I Go For You/My Brother	57	ABC 9865
The Greatest Love Of All/Eda Weda Bug	58	Bale 100/101
Let Christmas Ring/Hello, Mr. New Year	58	Bale 102/103
Cooper, Babs (& group)		
Just Couldn't Please You/Honest I Do	62	Indigo 144
Cooper, Dolly (& group)		
I'm Looking Through Your Window/Big Rock Inn	56	Dot 15495
Cooper, Wade (& group)		
Oh Me Oh My/I'm Gonna Love You So	60	Ember 1059
Copasetics		
Collegian/Believe In Me	56	Premium 409
Copycats (Suzy & the)		
No Other Love (Like Yours)/Come Back To Me	61	Brent 7020
Coquettes (Mike Burnette & the)		
Ricky/Parking Meter	59	Imperial 5610
Coralairs (T. Renaldi & the)		
Baby Blue Eyes/A Lover Is A Fool	58	Bee 1543
Coralites		
True Love/Unchained Melody	N/A	Carib 1008
Corals (female)		
Tell Me Yes/The Puppet	62	Cheer 1001
My Best Friend/Dancin' And Cryin'	62	Kram 1001/Rayna 5010 (62)
Cordell, Richie (& group)		
Tick Tock/Please Don't Tell Her	62	Rori 707
Cordells		
Please Don't Go/Believe In Me	58	Bullseye 1017
The Beat Of My Heart/Laid Off	61	Bargain 5004
Cordials (1)		
Dawn Is Almost Here/Keep An Eye	61	7 Arts 707
A Fool In Love/Eek	61	Stan 111
Once In A Lifetime/What Kind Of Fool Am I?	62	Felsted 8653
Eternal Love/The International Twist	62	Reveille 106
Listen To My Heart/My Heart's Desire	62	Whip 276
Oh How I Love Her/You Can't Believe In Love	65	Liberty 55784
Cordials (2)		
I'm Not Crying Anymore/What's The Matter With Me	62	Bethlehem 3019
Cordials (3)		
I'm Ashamed/Sentimental Journey	60	Cordial 1001
Cordovans		
Come On Baby/My Heart	60	Johnson 731
Corduroys		
Forever Yours/Ain't Gonna Let You Go	61	Hale 100
Corey, John (with the Four Seasons)		
Pollyanna/I'll Forget	61	Vee Jay 466
Corlettes		
I Love You/Crazy Baby	62	Kansoma 02

ARTIST/SONG	YEAR	LABEL
Tears On My Pillow/How Do You Feel	N/A	Pace/Nita 711

Corona, Larry (& group)

Revenge/Jane	56	Fortune 523

Coronados (1)

Let's Get Acquainted/I Came Back To Say I'm Sorry	56	Vik 0217
My Beautiful Dream/No No Blues	57	Vik 0265
Good Night Kiss/World Of Confusion	58	United Artists 135

Coronados (2)

The Nature Of My Love/I Believe	60	Columbia 41550

Coronados (3)

Saturday Hop/Why	61	Peerless 5134
My Elise/Lying	61	Ric 979

Coronas

I Need Your Lovin' Again/All Out Vota (instrumental)	65	Corona 520

Corondolays (Chico & the)

My Wishes/Little Green Man	N/A	Style 1927

Coronets (1)

Nadine/I'm All Alone	53	Chess 1549
It Would Be Heavenly/Baby's Coming Home	53	Chess 1553
I Love You More/Crime Doesn't Pay	55	Groove 0114
Hush/The Bible Tells Me So	55	Groove 0116

Coronets (2)

Don't Deprive Me/Little Boy	55	Sterling 903

Corridors

Dear One/I Want To Marry You	59	Zone 4323/Wildcat 0057 (59)

Corsairs (1)

Goodbye Darling/Rock Lilly Rock	57	Hy-Tone 110

Corsairs (2)

Time Waits/It Won't Be A Sin	61	Smash 1715
Smoky Places/Thinkin' (Maybe She's Changed Her Ways)	61	Tuff 1808/Chess 1808 (61)
I'll Take You Home/Sittin' On Your Doorstep	62	Tuff 1818/Chess 1818 (62)
Dancing Shadows/While	62	Tuff 1830/Chess 1830 (62)
At The Stroke Of Midnight/Listen To My Little Heart	62	Tuff 1840/Chess 1840 (62)
Stormy/(It's Almost) Sunday Morning	63	Tuff 1847/Chess 1847 (63)
Save A Little Monkey (flip is instrumental)	63	Tuff 375

Corsairs (2) (Landy McNeil & the)

The Change In You/On The Spanish Side	64	Tuff 402

Corsells

Nobody Heard About Me/Party Time	64	Hudson 8104

Corvairs (1)

Sing A Song Of Sixpence/Yeah Yeah	60	Cub 9065
Whatcha Gonna Do/Love Her So	61	Clock 1037
Something Wild/Darlin'	61	Crown 004
True True Love/Hey Sally Mae	62	Comet 2145

Corvairs (2)

Get A Job/Ain't No Soles In These Old Shoes	66	Columbia 43861

Corvairs (3)

The Girl With The Wind In Her Hair/ I Don't Wanna Be Without You Baby	63	Leopard 5005
Because I Love You	N/A	Relic LP 5028

ARTIST/SONG	YEAR	LABEL

Corvairs (4)
Gee Whiz/It's Aw'rite	62	Twin 1001
I'm Gonna Marry You/I Need You So	62	Twin 19671

Corvairs (5)
A Victim Of Her Charms/Love Is Such A Good Thing	N/A	Sylvia 5003

Corvairs (6) (Billy Martin & the)
I Found My Baby	N/A	Monitor 1402

Corvans
Sleepless Nights/Love Angel	59	Cabot 131

Corvells
We Made A Vow/Miss Jones	57	Lido 509/Tip Top 509 (57)
The Bells/Don't Forget	61	Blast 203
Daisy/Take My Love	62	ABC 10324
He's So Fine/Baby Sitting	62	Lu Pine 104/Lu Pine 1004 (62)
One (Is Such A Lonely Number)/The Joke's On Me	63	Cub 9122

Corvets (1)
Lenora/My Darling	58	Way-Out 101
Only Last Night (In A Garden)/Shark In The Park	60	20th Fox 223
So Long/Alligator In The Elevator	60	Laurel 1012
I'm Pleadin'/Let's Do The Pony	61	Sure 1003

Corvets (2) (Arthur & the)
I'm Going To Cry/You're Blue	59	Moon 100
Darling I Love You/Poor Girl	64	Na-R-Co 203
I Believe/Miracles	64	NRC 2781
Aritha/Flossie Mae	64	NRC 2871

Corvets (3)
You Don't Want Me/Want To Be Happy	65	Soma 1425

Corvettes (1)
String Band Hop/Don't Restrain Me Joe	58	ABC 9891

Corvettes (2)
Rockin' Around The Mountain/Shasta	59	Arco 104

Corvettes (3) (Irving Fuller & the)
And Mine/I Can't Stop	60	Emery 121

Corvettes (4)
In The Chapel/The Swinging Smitty	61	Sheraton 201

Corvettes (5) (Little Sonny & the)
She's Mine	86	Relic LP 8008

Corwins
Little Star/When	N/A	Gilmar 222

Cosmic Rays
Bye Bye/Somebody's In Love	60	Saturn 222
Daddy's Gonna Tell You No Lies/Dreaming	60	Saturn 401

Cosmo (& group)
Sweetheart Please Don't Go/Just Words	62	Tilt 789

Cosmos
You're Torturing My Heart/Angel, Angel	N/A	Big L 502

Cosytones (1)
Speak To Me Of Love/Ride Along	56	Melba

ARTIST/SONG	YEAR	LABEL
Cosytones (2) (aka Cozytones)		
I'm Alone/Little Flirt	57	Willow 1001
Cotillions (1)		
What Kind Of Day Has It Been/This Road	62	Ascot 2105
Cotillions (2)		
Surf Twist/Sahara	62	Alley 1003
Sometimes I Get Lonely/One Of These Days	63	ABC 10413
Count Downs (Chuck Hix & the)		
Sandy/Sixteen	59	Verve 10169
Ballad Of A Badman/Is You Is	59	Verve 10190
Loretta/Cookie Duster	61	Flair 101
Count Five		
Bells Of Love (a capella)	75	Relic LP 103
I Do Believe (a capella)	75	Relic LP 103
There Was A Time (a capella)	75	Relic LP 103
Sound Of Heartbreak (a capella)	75	Relic LP 105
Countdowns		
Satellite Dan/The Answer In Your Heart	62	Rori 706
Counts (1)		
Darling Dear/I Need You Always	54	Dot 1188/Dot 16105 (61)
Hot Tamales/Baby Don't You Know?	54	Dot 1199
My Dear, My Darling/She Won't Say Yes	54	Dot 1210
Baby I Want You/Waitin' Around For You	54	Dot 1226
Let Me Go Lover/Wailin' Little Mama	55	Dot 1235
From This Day On/Love And Understanding	55	Dot 1243
Sally Walker/I Need You Tonight	55	Dot 1265
Heartbreaker/To Our Love	55	Dot 1275
Sweet Names/I Guess I Brought It All On Myself	56	Note 20000
Counts (2) (Frankie Brent with the)		
Cold As Ice/Playing The Field	58	Vik 0322
Counts (2) (Frankie Brent & the)		
No Rock And Rollin' Here/Lover's Lane	60	Strand 25014
Counts (3)		
Teen-Age Guy And Gal/Shake The Town	58	Mercury 71318
Counts (4) (Bobby & the)		
Three Signs Of Love/Cellar Stomp	N/A	Count 6985
Counts (4) (Bobby Comstock & the)		
Sweet Talk/Tennessee Waltz	59	Blaze 349
Jealous Fool/Zig Zag	59	Triumph 602
Let's Talk It Over/Jambalaya	60	Atlantic 2051
Bony Maronie/Do That Little Thing	60	Jubilee 5392
Everyday Blues/Wayward Wind	60	Mohawk 124
The Garden Of Eden/Just A Piece Of Paper	61	Festival 25000
I Want To Do It/Let's Stomp	62	Lawn 202
Jezebel/Your Big Brown Eyes	63	Jubilee 5396
Susie Baby/Take A Walk	63	Lawn 210
Sunny/Chicken Back	63	Lawn 217
This Little Love Of Mine/Your Boyfriend's Back	63	Lawn 219
I Can't Help Myself/Run My Heart	63	Lawn 224
Since You Been Gone/The Beatle Bounce	64	Lawn 229
Ain't That Just Like Me/Can't It Be True	64	Lawn 232
Counts (4) (Freddy Davis & the)		
I Hope You're Happy/Faith Can Move Mountains	58	Count 405

ARTIST/SONG	YEAR	LABEL

Counts (5)
Touch Me — 61 — Sunset 502

Counts (6) (Tommy Burk & the)
You'll Feel It Too/Counted Out — 62 — Nat 100
Stormy Weather/True Love Gone — 62 — Nat 101/Smash 1821 (63)
Cute/Dinga-Ling — N/A — Rich Rose 1001
You Took My Heart/She Told A Lie — N/A — Rich Rose 1003

Counts (6)
Don't Hafta Shop Around/Just A Little Bit — 64 — Rich Rose 711

Counts (7) (Cosmo & the)
Things I'd Like To Do/Small Town Gossip — 63 — Sound Stage 7 2504

Couplings
Young Dove's Calling/I Can See — 58 — Josie 831

Court Jesters
The Trial Of My Love/Roaches — 63 — Blast 208

Courtiers
I've Been Mistreated — N/A — Case 107

Cousins (1)
Mademoiselle — 57 — Nar 224

Cousins (2)
Be Nice To Me/I'm In Love With You — 58 — Decca 30609
What'd I Say/Boston Hop (by the Playboys) — 61 — Chancellor 1074

Cousins (3)
Little Girl/Molly Bee — 60 — Swirl 102
Down That Lonely Road/Everlovin' (Baby Mine) — 60 — Versatile 105

Covacs
Say You'll Be Mine/Shouldn't I — N/A — Herald (unreleased)

Covay, Don (& group)
Please Don't Let Me Know/Take This Hurt Off Me — 64 — Rosemart 802

Covinas
Thanks For The Memories/Five Minutes More — N/A — Hilton 3751

Cox, Herbie (bb the Cleftones)
Vacation In The Mountains/Leave My Woman Alone — 57 — Rama 233

Coyne, Ricky (& group)
Angel From Heaven/I Want You To Know — 59 — Event 4294

Craftys (aka Halos)
L-O-V-E/Heart Breaking World — 61 — Lois 5000/Seven Arts 5708 (61)
Zoom Zoom Zoom/I Went To A Party — 62 — Elmor 310

Cravers
Windstorm/Flavor Craver — 58 — Chock Full Of Hits 109

Crayons
Crazy Dream/Teach Me Mama — 63 — Counsel 121
Love At First Sight/I Saw You — 63 — Counsel 122

Creations (1)
There Goes The Girl I Love/You Are My Darling — 56 — Lido 501/Tip Top 501 (56)
Every Night I Pray/Mommy And Daddy — 56 — Tip Top 400
The Bells/Shang Shang — 61 — Jamie 1197

ARTIST/SONG	YEAR	LABEL
Woke Up In The Morning/Strolling Through The Park	61	Pine Crest 101
This Is Our Night/You Are My Inspiration	62	Mel-o-Dy 101
I've Got A Feeling/The Wedding	62	Meridian 7550
Don't Listen To What Others Say, Pt. 1/	64	Radiant 103
Don't Listen To What Others Say, Pt. 2		

Creations (1) (Johnny Angel & the)
We're Old Enough/Where's My Love	59	Jamie 1134

Creations (2)
Lady Luck/We're In Love	62	Penny 9022/Take Ten 1501 (63)
Oh Baby/Plenty Of Love	67	Globe 1000
Just Remember Me/Times Are Changing	67	Globe 102
I've Got To Find Her/Times Are Changing	67	Globe 103

Creations (3) (Bobby Richardson & the)
This Is My Love/Nobody Loves Me	61	Ember 1076

Creations (4)
Seventeen/You'll Always Be Mine	62	Patti-Jo 1703

Creations (5)
My Best Friend's Girl (a capella)	75	Relic LP 109
Through Eternity (a capella)	75	Relic LP 109

Creators
I've Had You/Drafted, Volunteered And Enlisted	61	Dooto 463
Do You Remember?/There's Going To Be An Angel	61	Time 1038
Too Far To Turn Around/Hello There Mister Grave Digger	62	Dore 635
I'll Never, Never Do It Again/Boy, He's Got It!	62	T-Kay 110
Cross Fire/Crazy Love	63	Epic 9605
Boy, He's Got It!/Yeah, He's Got It	63	Philips 40058
I Stayed Home (New Year's Eve)/Shoom Ba Boom	63	Philips 40060
Too Far To Turn Around	N/A	Lummtone

Creators (with the Alamos)
Wear My Ring/Booga Bear	57	Hi-Q 5021

Creels
See Me Once Again/Do You Wanna Jump	59	Judd 1005

Crenshaws (ref Sharps/ref Rivingtons)
Moonlight In Vermont/He's Got The Whole World In His Hands	61	Warner Bros. 5254
Wishing Star/Off Shore	65	Warner Bros. 5505
Manana	61	Warner Bros EP 5505

Crescendos (1)
Sweet Dreams/Finders Keepers	56	Atlantic 1109
I'll Be Seeing You/Sweet Dreams	59	Atlantic 2014

Crescendos (2)
My Heart's Desire/Take My Heart	57	Music City 831/Gone 5100 (61)
Oh Julie/My Little Girl	57	Tap 7027/Nasco 6005 (57)
Crazy Hop/School Girl	58	Nasco 6009
School Girl/Crazy Hop	58	Nasco 6009
Young And In Love/Rainy Sunday	58	Nasco 6021
Let's Take A Walk/Strange Love	60	Scarlet 4007
Angel Face/I'm So Ashamed	61	Scarlet 4009

Crescendos (3) (Johnny Woodson & the)
All That's Good/Dreamer From My Heart	58	Spry 108

ARTIST/SONG	YEAR	LABEL
Crescendos (4)		
A Fellow Needs A Girl/Black Cat	63	Domain 1025
Crescents (1)		
Roseann/You Have No Secrets	57	N/A
Everybody Knew But Me/You Have No Heart	57	Joyce 102
Crescents (1) (Pat Cordel & the)		
Darling Come Back/My Tears	56	Club 1011/Michele M 503 (59)/ Victory 1001 (63)
Crescents (2) (Billy Wells & the)		
Julie/I Love Only You	56	Reserve 105
Crescents (3) (Dick Watson & the)		
Be On The Lookout For The Woman/Groover	62	Gone 5144
Crescents (4)		
Smoke Gets In Your Eyes/Johnny Won't Run Around	63	Arlen 743
When You Wish Upon A Star/Hey There	63	Hamilton 50033
Crescents (5)		
Here You Come Again/That's All She Left Me	65	Watch 1902
Crescents (6)		
Be Mine	85	Relic LP 5053
Bewitched	85	Relic LP 5053
Please Don't Tease	85	Relic LP 5053
Sympathy	85	Relic LP 5053
You Are	85	Relic LP 5053
You're A Sweetheart	85	Relic LP 5053
Zoom	85	Relic LP 5053
Crescents (7)		
I'll Make A Vow/Come Back Baby	65	Seven B 7013
Creschendals		
Oh My Love/Oh My Love (instrumental)	63	Fortune 566
Creschendos (aka Crescendos (2))		
My Heart's Desire/Take My Heart	60	Music City 831/Gone 5100 (61)
Teenage Prayer/I Don't Mind	60	Music City 839
Creslyns		
Boom Chip-A-Boom	63	Beltone 2036
Crestones		
She's A Bad Motorcycle/The Grasshopper Dance	64	Markie 117
The Chopper	64	Markie 127
Crestones (Jimmy & the)		
Angel Maureen/New Girl On My Block	64	Maria 101
Crests		
My Juanita/Sweetest One	57	Joyce 103/Musictone 1106 (62)
Let Me Be The One	58	Coed (unreleased)
Strange Love	58	Coed (unreleased)
Pretty Little Angel/I Thank The Moon	58	Coed 501
Sixteen Candles/Beside You	58	Coed 506
Journey Of Love	59	Coed (unreleased)
Young Love	59	Coed (unreleased)
Six Nights A Week/I Do	59	Coed 509
Flower Of Love/Molly Mae	59	Coed 511
The Angels Listened In/I Thank The Moon	59	Coed 515
A Year Ago Tonight/Paper Crown	59	Coed 521

ARTIST/SONG	YEAR	LABEL
Keep Away From Carol	60	Coed (unreleased)
Learning About Love	60	Coed (unreleased)
Let True Love Begin	60	Coed (unreleased)
You Took The Joy Out Of Spring	60	Coed (unreleased)
Step By Step/Gee (But I'd Give The World)	60	Coed 525
Trouble In Paradise/Always You	60	Coed 531
Journey Of Love/If My Heart Could Write A Letter	60	Coed 535
Isn't It Amazing/Molly Mae	60	Coed 537
A Rose And A Baby Ruth	60	Coed LP 901
Butterfly	60	Coed LP 901
My Special Angel	60	Coed LP 901
Party Doll	60	Coed LP 901
Silhouettes	60	Coed LP 901
Dream Maker	61	Coed (unreleased)
Out In The Cold Again	61	Coed (unreleased)
I Remember (In The Still Of The Night)/Good Golly Miss Molly	61	Coed 543
Little Miracles/Baby I Gotta Know	61	Coed 561
Guilty/Number One With Me	62	Selma 311
The Actor/Three Tears In A Bucket	62	Trans Atlas 696
Fifty Million Heartbeats/Before I Loved her	62	United Artists 474
I'll Be True/Over The Weekend	63	Cameo 256
Tears Will Fall/Did I Remember	63	Selma 4000
Baby/I Love You So (a capella)	63	Times Square 6/ Times Square 97 (64)
Lean On Me/Make Up My Mind	64	Cameo 305
You Blew Out The Candles/A Love To Last A Lifetime	64	Coral 62403
Phone Booth On The Highway/She's All Mine Alone	65	Apt 25075
I'm Stepping Out Of The Picture/Afraid Of Love	65	Scepter 12112
Try Me/Heartburn	66	Parkway 987
I Care About You/Come See Me	66	Parkway 999
My Time/Is It You?	67	Parkway 118
Earth Angel/Tweedle Dee	N/A	King Tut 172

Crests (with Johnny Maestro)
No One To Love/Wish She Was Mine	57	Joyce 105/Times Square 2 (62)

Crestwoods
Angel Of Love/Lucky Star	61	Impact 6

Crew (Frank Motley & the)
A Prayer Of Love	60	DC 0436

Crew (Ron & Joe & the)
Riot In Cell Block #9/Ain't Love Grand	59	Strand 25001

Crewe, Bob (& group)
Oh How I Miss You Tonight/Ev'ry Time	60	Warwick 601

Crewnecks
I'll Never Forget You/Crewnecks And Khakis	59	Rhapsody 71960
Rockin' Zombie/When I First Fall In Love	59	Rhapsody 71961

Crickets (Dean Barlow & the)
Be Faithful/Sleepy Little Cowboy (by the Deep River Boys)	53	Beacon 104
When I Met You/Dreams And Wishes	53	Jay-Dee 777
I'm Not The Same One You Love/Fine As Wine	53	Jay-Dee 781
You're Mine/Milk And Gin	53	MGM 11428
I'll Cry No More/For You I Have Eyes	53	MGM 11507
Changing Partners/Your Love	54	Jay-Dee 785
Just You/My Little Baby's Shoes	54	Jay-Dee 786
Never Give Up Hope/Are You Looking For A Sweetheart	54	Jay-Dee 789
I'm Going To Live My Life Alone/The Man From The Moon	54	Jay-Dee 795/Davis 459 (58)
Be Faithful/I'm Not The Same One You Love	63	Beacon 555

ARTIST/SONG	YEAR	LABEL
Crisis (Lonnie & the)		
Bells In The Chapel/Santa Town, U.S.A.	61	Universal 103/Times Square 25 (63)/Relic 532 (65)
Criterions (1)		
Don't Say Goodbye/Crying The Blues Over You	59	Cecelia 1010
I Remain Truly Yours/You Just You	59	Cecelia 1208/Laurie 3305 (65)
Criterions (2) (Tygh & the)		
To Be Mine/Do What You Wanna	63	Flite 101
Cronies (Herb & the)		
In The Middle Of Love	N/A	Personality 700
Croom Brothers (fb Dillard Croom Jr.)		
It's You I Love/Rock And Roll Boogie	58	Vee Jay 283
Crosstones (bb the Chriss Chross Orchestra)		
Congratulations/Lies	55	Jaguar 3014
Crowns (1) (Arthur Lee Maye & the)		
Set My Heart Free/I Wanna Love	54	Modern 944
Please Say You Love Me/Cool Lovin'	55	RPM 420
Truly/Oochie Pachie	55	RPM 424
Love Me Always/Loop De Loop De Loop	55	RPM 429
Please Don't Leave Me/Do The Bop	55	RPM 438
Earth Angel/Honey Love	56	Dig 100 (unreleased)
This Is The Nite For Love/Honey, Honey	56	Dig 124
Gloria/Oh-Rooba-Lee	56	Specialty 573
A Fool's Prayer/Whispering Winds	57	Dig 133
Cause You're Mine Alone/Hey Pretty Girl	57	Flip 330
Honey, Honey/Will You Be Mine	58	Cash 1063/Imperial 5790 (61)
All I Want Is Someone To Love/Pounding	58	Cash 1065
Breaks Of Life/Only A Dream	64	Jamie 1284
That's What I'm Gonna Do	85	Relic LP 5052
Don't You Know (I Love You So)	85	Relic LP 5054
Gee/Only You	N/A	Dig 146 (unreleased)
Sh-Boom/Sincerely	N/A	Dig 149 (unreleased)
Crowns (2) (aka Five Crowns/ref Drifters)		
Kiss And Make Up/I'll Forget About You	58	R&B 6901
Crowns (3) (Henry Strogin & the)		
Why Do You Go Away/I'll Tag Along	60	Dynamic 1002/Ball 1015 (63)
I'll Tag Along/I Love L.A.	62	Amazon 1001
I Wanna Love	N/A	Ball 1012
Crowns (4)		
Heart Breaking Train/Lonely For You	59	Wheel 1001
Lonely For You	87	Relic LP 8011
Crowns (5) (Stark Whiteman & the)		
Graduation Day/Noise	60	Sho-Biz 1004
Crowns (6)		
Party Time/Amazon Basin Pop	62	Chordette 1001
Possibility/Watch Out (with Larry Chance)	63	Old Town 1171
Crowns (7) (fb Philip Harris)		
I Wonder Why (You Make Me Blue)/Better Luck Next Time	63	Vee Jay 546
Crowns (8) (Danny & the)		
Night Moon/The Story Of Jack And Jill	63	Mercury 72096

ARTIST/SONG	YEAR	LABEL

Crowns (9)
| Gonna Get Right Tonight/It's Still Love | 64 | Limelight 3031 |

Crows (aka Jewels (1))
Seven Lonely Days/No Help Wanted	53	Rama 3
Gee/I Love You So	53	Rama 5
Heartbreaker/Call A Doctor (by the Jewels)	54	Rama 10
Untrue/Baby	54	Rama 29
Miss You/I Really Really Love You	54	Rama 30
Baby Doll/Sweet Sue (It's You)	55	Rama 50
Mambo Shevitz/Mambo #5 (by Melino & Orchestra) (instrumental)	55	Tico 1082

Cruisers (1)
Baby, What A Fool I've Been/The Moon Is Yours	57	Finch 353
A Ring Around A Chain/Buoys And Gulls	58	Era 1052
Foolish Me/There's A Girl	58	Zebra 119
I Want Your Love/I Said Hear	59	Arch 1611
Betty Ann/You Made A Fool Out Of Me	59	Coda 3005
My Mary Lou/Cruisin'	59	Winston 1033
Another Lonely Night/Please Let Me Be	61	Pharaoh 128

Cruisers (2)
| Miss Fine/If I Knew | 60 | V-Tone 207 |
| Don't Tease Me/Crying Over You | 60 | V-Tone 213/Guyden 2069 (62) |

Cruisers (3)
| Cruisin' Baby | N/A | N/A |

Crusaders
| I Found Someone/Swinging Week-End | 63 | Dooto 472 |

Crystal Tones
| Debra-Lee/A Girl I Love | 59 | MZ 007/008/Zebra |

Crystal, Lou (& group)
| Dreaming Of An Angel/Sheila Baby | 6262 | SFAZ 1001 |

Crystalaires
| Pinocchio | N/A | N/A |
| Nobody Knows/Henry Said Goodbye | N/A | Sound Souvenir 1 |

Crystalairs
| Mona | N/A | Adam & Eve LP 504 |

Crystalettes (female)
Shy Guy/Please Stay Away	62	Crystalette 752
Just Think Of Me/Billy, My Billy	63	Crystalette 753
I've Got Everything/We're In Love	63	Crystalette 755

Crystaliers (1) (Cleo & the)
| Please Be My Guy/Don't Cry | 57 | Cindy 3003/Johnson 103 (57) |

Crystaliers (2)
| Teenage Ding Dong Bells | N/A | N/A |

Crystals (1) (aka Opals (1))
Four Women/My Dear	53	DeLuxe 6013
My Girl/Don't You Go	53	Rockin' 518
Have Faith In Me/My Love	54	DeLuxe 6037
Come To Me, Darling/Squeeze Me, Baby	54	Luna 100/101/Luna 5001 (54)
God Only Knows/My Girl	55	DeLuxe 6077

Crystals (2) (female)
| I Love My Baby/I Do Believe | 57 | Aladdin 3355 |

ARTIST/SONG	YEAR	LABEL
Crystals (3) (Sam Hawkins & the)		
King Of Fools/The Whatchamacallit	59	Gone 5042
Crystals (4)		
Blind Date/Mary Ellen	59	Felsted 8566
Crystals (5)		
Love You So/In The Deep	59	Specialty 657
Crystals (6)		
That's Where I Belong/Better Come Back To Me	59	Metro 20026
Malaguena/Gypsy Ribbon	60	Brent 7011
Watching You/Oh My, You	60	Cub 9064
Crystals (7) (female)		
Dreams And Wishes/Mr. Brush	61	Indigo 114
There's No Other (Like My Baby)/Oh Yeah Maybe Baby	61	Philles 100
Pony In Dixie/Espresso	61	Regalia 17
Uptown/What A Nice Way To Turn Seventeen	62	Philles 102
He Hit Me (And It Felt Like A Kiss)/No One Ever Tells You	62	Philles 105
He's A Rebel/I Love You Eddie	62	Philles 106
He's Sure The Boy I Love/Walkin' Along (instrumental)	62	Philles 109
Let's Dance The Screw Pt. 1/Let's Dance The Screw Pt. 11	63	Philles 111
Da Doo Ron Ron (When He Walked Me Home)/Git It (instrumental)	63	Philles 112
Then He Kissed Me/Brother Julius (instrumental)	63	Philles 115
Little Boy/Harry (from W. Va.) And Milt (instrumental)	64	Philles 119/Philles 119X (63)
All Grown Up/Irving (Jaggered Sixteenths) (instrumental)	64	Philles 122
My Place/You Can't Tie A Good Girl Down	65	United Artists 927
I Got A Man/Are You Trying To Get Rid Of Me Baby	66	United Artists 994
Ring-A-Ting-A-Ling/Should I Keep On Waiting	67	Michelle 4113
Crystals (8) (Claudia & the)		
This Is Your Life/Little Love Of Mine	61	Dore 601
Crystals (9) (Howie & the)		
Golly Gee	N/A	Fleetwood 4521
Crystals (10) (Jesse & the)		
Tell Me	N/A	Geno 12348
Crystals (11)		
Laughing On The Outside	N/A	Iona 1009
Cubans (1) (Joe Alexander & the)		
Oh Maria	55	Ballad 1008
Cubans (2)		
Don't Go Baby/Oh Miss Dolly	58	Flash
Cubans (2) (fb Davie "Little Caesar" Johnson)		
Tell Me (Will You Ever Be Mine)/You've Been Gone So Long	58	Flash 133
Cubs		
I Hear Wedding Bells/Why Do You Make Me Cry	56	Savoy 1502
Cues		
Forty 'Leven Dozen Ways/Scoochie Scoochie	54	Lamp 8007
Oh My Darlin'/Burn That Candle	55	Capitol 3245
Only You/I Fell For Your Loving	55	Jubilee 5201
Charlie Brown/You're On My Mind	56	Capitol 3310
Don't Make Believe/	56	Capitol 3400
Destination Twenty-One Hundred And Sixty-Five		
The Girl I Love/Crackerjack	56	Capitol 3483
Why/Prince Or Pauper	56	Capitol 3582
Crazy Crazy Party/I Pretend	57	Prep 104

ARTIST/SONG	YEAR	LABEL
Cuff Links (aka Cuff Linx)		
How You Lied/The Winner	57	Dooto 413
Off-Day Blues/Twinkle	57	Dooto 414
It's Too Late Now/Saxophone Rag	57	Dooto 422
Guided Missles/My Heart	57	Dootone 409
Cuff Linx (aka Cuff Links)		
So Tough/My Love Is With You	58	Dooto 433
A Fool's Fortune/Trick Knees	58	Dooto 434
Lawful Wedding/Zoom	58	Dooto 438
Changing My Love/I Don't Want Nobody	63	Dooto 474
My Heart Longs For You	N/A	N/A
Cufflinks		
Only One Love/Next To You	62	Gait 543
Culmer, Little Iris (bb the Majestics)		
Frankie, My Eyes Are On You/Show Me The Way To Your Heart	56	Marlin 803
Cunningham, Dale (& female group)		
Trust Me/Too Young	58	Cash 1067
Cupcakes (1) (Cookie & the) (aka Twilights) (fb Terry "Cookie" Clinton)		
Matilda/Married Life	58	Judd 1002
Until Then/Close Up The Back Door	59	Judd 1015/Lyric 1012 (63)
Part Of Everything/Matilda Has Finally Come Back	61	Mercury 71748
I've Been So Lonely/Got You On My Mind	63	Chess 1848
Matilda/I'm Twisted	63	Lyric 1003/Paula 221 (65)
Until Then/Close Up The Back Door	63	Lyric 1004
I Heard That Story Before/All My Lovin' Baby	63	Lyric 1008
Breaking Up Is Hard To Do/I Cried	63	Lyric 1009/Paula 312 (68)
Hey, Little Schoolgirl/Charged With Cheating	64	Lyric 1015
Even Though/Walking Down The Aisle (by Little Alfred)	64	Lyric 1016/Jewel 744 (65)
Long Time Ago/Kissin' Someone Else	64	Lyric 1017
Belinda/Trouble In My Life	64	Lyric 1020/Paula 230 (65)
Cupcakes (1) (L. Alfred with the)		
Even Though/Walking Down The Aisle	65	Jewel 744
Cupcakes (1) (Shelton Dunaway & the)		
I Had The Blues/Who Would Have Thought	59	Khoury's 715
Since Your Love Has Grown Cold/Frankochinese Cha Cha Cha	61	Khoury's 727
Cupcakes (2)		
It's Willy/Deutsche Rock And Roll	59	Time 1011
Winter Blue/Pied Piper	65	Diamond 177
Cupids (1)		
I Don't Know/Troubles Not At End	56	Chan 107
Cupids (2) (female)		
My Dog Likes Your Dog/The Answer To Your Prayer	57	Decca 30279
Cupids (3)		
Now You Tell Me/Lillie Mae	58	Aladdin 3404
Cupids (4) (Carlo & the)		
Teenage Blues/Crazy Rock	59	Parker 501/Judd 1007 (59)
Cupids (5) (Darwin & the)		
How Long/Chloe (instrumental)	60	Jerden 1
Goodnight My Love/Won't You Give Me A Chance	60	Jerden 9
Cupids (6) (aka Camelots (2)/aka Harps (2))		
True Love, True Love/Let's Twist	62	UWR 4241/4242
Brenda/For You	63	AAnko 1002/KC 115 (63)

The Cupids/Camelots

Cupids (7) (Sandy & the)
Rebel/I Didn't Know Him   63   Charter 2

Cupids (8)
Lorraine/Little Girl Of Mine   63   Musicnote 119

Cupids (9)
Pretty Baby/Let's Rock   64   Times Square 1

Cupons (Materlyn & the)
I'll Be Your Love Tonight/Turn Her Down   64   Impact 28

Curios (1) (Bucky Brown & the)
Dream Date/Everybody Had A Dream   60   XYZ 610

Curios (2) (Bobby Brown & the)
I Got The Blues/Down At Mary's House   59   Vaden 100

Curls
Imaginez Vous/Why Didn't I Go   59   Everest 19319
Like A Waterfall/He's My Hero   60   Everest 19350

Curry, James (bb the Jayhawks)
Please Baby/My Promise   56   Flash 110

Curtis, Eddie (& group)
Don't Cry/You're Just Too Pretty For Me   56   Dot 15505

Curtis, Tex (& group)
Prayer To The Moon/Shake, Pretty Baby, Shake   54   Gee 9

Curtiss, Jimmy (& group)
Without You/Simple Things   60   United Artists 215

ARTIST/SONG	YEAR	LABEL
Customs		
Because Of Love/Earthquake	63	Arlen 511
Cute-Teens		
When My Teen-Age Days Are Over/From This Day Forward	59	Aladdin 3458
Cutouts (Brian Brent & the)		
For Eternity/Vacation Time	63	Penny 2201
Cutups		
She Has Gone/Double Date	62	Jim 852
Cutups/Romeo	62	Music Makers 301
Cyclones (1)		
My Dear/Do You Love Me	57	Flip 324
Good Goodnight/Big Mary	59	Forward 313
Give Me Love/Say What	61	Festival 25003
Cyclones (1) (Wayne Brooks & the)		
Secret Love/Runaways	61	Warwick 629
Cyclones (2)		
Angel/I Need Love	N/A	Cyclone 500
Cymbals (1)		
One Step Too Far/Shout Mama Linda	62	Amazon 709
The Voice Of A Fool/Way In The Night	63	Dot 16472
Cymbals (2) (Lee Williams & the)		
What Am I Guilty Of	N/A	Rapda
Say It Isn't So	68	N/A
Cymbols (Little Sonny Knight & the)		
My Darling/Tears On My Pillow	N/A	New Teenage 5001
Cytations (Chris & the)		
The Glory Of Love/Unbelievable	63	Catamount 100
Cytones (Johnny Duraine & the)		
My Last Love/Shang-Dang-Do	61	Dore 624
Czars Of Rhythm		
You Show Me The Way/Please Don't Leave Me	65	De-Voice 2501
D'Accords		
Runnin' Around/Who's Been Loving You?	61	Don-El 110
Da-Prees		
Sometimes/Pay Day	63	Twist 70913
Daarts		
Beloved Stranger/Cut Me Up	61	Dyna 109
Dabettes (Karen Caple & the) (female)		
One Dab Man/Why Do You Care	62	Advance 3933
Daddy-O's		
Freddie	N/A	Shell
Daddy-O's (Joey Castle & the)		
Rock And Roll Daddy/Wild Love	59	Headline 1008
Daffodils		
Wine/These Kissable Lips	55	CJ 100
Walk	55	CJ 101

ARTIST/SONG	YEAR	LABEL
Dahills		
Michelle/Why Do We Have To Say Goodnight	64	Musicor 1041
Do You Want To Go Steady/Please Be My Girlfriend	76	Clifton 13/14
She's An Angel/I Who Love You	78	Crystal Ball 107
Dahlias		
Storm Tossed Sea Of Love/Go 'Way And Leave Me	57	Big 612
Daidems		
What More Is There To Say?/Ala Vevo	61	Lavere 187
Daisies		
I Wanna Swim With Him/You Just Said You Love Me	64	Roulette 4571
Dale, Alan (& group)		
Monday To Sunday/That's A Teenage Girl	61	Sinclair 1003
Dale, Bobby (& group)		
You Love Me Only In Your Dreams/Love Me More	N/A	De Rose 8469
Dales (1)		
If You Are Meant To Be/Lonely Women, Lonely Men	57	Onyx 509
Dales (2)		
Rockin' Nellie/Sweet Annie	60	Crest 1069
Dalton, Danny (& group)		
Who's Gonna Hold Your Hand/Walkin'	59	Teen 505
Dame, Freddy (& group)		
Love Is A Game	N/A	Nic Nac 331
Damons (Carl Lawrence & the)		
High School Dreams	58	Jean 0001
Danderliers (aka Dandoliers)		
Chop Chop Boom/My Autumn Love	55	States 147/B&F 1344 (61)
Shu-Wop/My Loving Partner	55	States 150/B&F 150
May God Be With You/Little Man	55	States 152
All The Way/Walk On With Your Nose Up	67	Midas 9004
Dandevilles		
Heavenly Angel/Psychology	59	Forte 314
Nasty Breaks/There's A Reason	59	Guyden 2014
Dandies		
Have I Lost Your Love/Red Light	59	Peach 726
Dandleers (aka Danleers)		
One Summer Night/Wheelin' And Dealin'	58	Amp-3 2115 (first pressing, second is by the Danleers)
Dandoliers (aka Danderliers)		
My Love/She's Mine	56	States 160/B&F 160

ARTIST/SONG	YEAR	LABEL

The Danleers

Danes

Most Of All/Come On Baby	61	Le Cam 718

Daniels (aka Elgins (1))

Big City/Finally	N/A	Lantam 01

Daniels, Dotty (& group)

Play A Sad Song/I Wrote You A Letter	63	Amy 885

Danleers (aka Dandleers)

One Summer Night/Wheelin' And Dealin'	58	Amp-3 2115 (second pressing, first is by the Dandleers)/Merc
I Really Love You/My Flaming Heart	58	Mercury 71356
A Picture Of You/Prelude To Love	59	Mercury 71401
I Can't Sleep/Your Love	59	Mercury 71441
If You Don't Care/(I Live) Half A Block From An Angel	60	Epic 9367
I'll Always Be In Love With You/Little Lover	60	Epic 9421
Foolish/I'm Lookin' Around	61	Everest 19412
The Truth Hurts/Baby You've Got It	64	Lemans 004
I'm Sorry/This Thing Called Love	64	Lemans 008
If/Were You There?	64	Smash 1872
Where Is Love?/The Angels Sent You	64	Smash 1895

Dante's Infernos

My First True Love (There She Goes)/Teenage Blues	57	Lido 507

Dantes (1)

Zebra Shoot/Dragon Walk	64	Courtney 713
Top Down Time/How Many Times	65	Rotate 5008

Dantes (2)

Can't Get Enough Of Your Love/80-96	66	Jamie 1314

Dapper Dans

Bird Brain/Lonely One	60	Ember 1065

Dappers (1)

Come Back To Me/Mambo Oongh	55	Peacock 1651
Bop Bop Bu/How I Need You, Baby!	56	Rainbow 373
My Love Is Real/Baby You Know You're Wrong	60	Epic 9423

Dappers (2)

Unwanted Love/That's All, That's All, That's All	56	Groove 0156

ARTIST/SONG	YEAR	LABEL
Dappers (3)		
We're In Love/Spellbound	58	Star-X 505
Dappers (4)		
Chicken Twist/Lonely Street	61	Foxie 7005
Dappers Quintet		
Look What I've Found	55	Flayr 500
Dapps (Johnnie Mae Matthews & the)		
Dreamer/Indian Joe	60	Northern 3727
Some Day/Mr. Fine	60	Northern 3729
Daps		
When You're Alone/Down And Out	56	Marterry 5249
Dar-Letts (female)		
He's Gonna Get It/Til I Fell In Love	64	Shell 101
Darchaes		
Pain In My Heart/Danny Boy	83	Nobell 7001
Darchaes (Ben White & the)		
Jocko Sent Me/Nationwide Stamps	62	Aljon 1247/1248/Coney Island
Darchaes (Nicky Addeo & the) (aka Uniques)		
Gloria/Bring Back Your Heart	63	Savoy 200/Earls 1533
Where There Is Love/You Can Depend On Me	64	Melody 1417
Over The Rainbow/Fool #2	64	Selsom 104
Darchaes (Ray & the)		
Carol/Little Girl So Fine	62	Aljon 1249/1250
Darling Forever/There Will Always Be	62	Buzzy 202
Dardenelles		
Now You're Gone/Feel Allright	53	Entre 102
A Thing Worth Remembering	60	Pennington 108
My Baby/Soft Is The Breeze	N/A	Playgirl 501
Dares (Joey Daye & the)		
True True Love/Talking About My Love	61	Fortune 868
Dariens		
Tell Me Love/Kid Me Not Baby	N/A	Carlson International
Darin, Bobby (& group)		
Judy, Don't Be Moody/Splish Splash (no group)	58	Atco 6117
Lost Love/Queen Of The Hop (no group)	58	Atco 6127
Dream Lover (with Neil Sedaka on piano)/Bullmoose (no group)	59	Atco 6140
Somebody To Love/Artificial Flowers (no group)	60	Atco 6179
Darlenes		
(I'm Afraid) You Hurt Me/I Still Like Rock And Roll	63	Stacy 965
Darlettes (Diane & the) (female)		
Just You/Here She Comes	62	Dunes 2016
Just You/The Wobble	62	Dunes 2016
Darlettes (female)		
Lost/Sweet Kind Of Loneliness	65	Mira 203
Love Will Make You Cry/To Reconcile	N/A	Taffi 100
Darlin, Chris (& group)		
A Casual Look/Please Write Me A Letter	60	Dore 578

ARTIST/SONG	YEAR	LABEL
Darling, Johnny (& group)		
Baseball Baby/I Don't Want To Wind Up In Love	58	DeLuxe 6167
Darlings (1)		
In The Evening/Let's Go Fishing	59	Penguin 0698
Darlings (2)		
To Know Him Is To Love Him/Train Of Of Memphis	63	Dore 663
He Played 1, 2, 3, 4/My Pillow	63	Dore 677
Please Let Me Know/Two Time Loser	63	Mercury 72185
Darnell, Larry (& group)		
That's All I Want From You/Who Showed My Baby How To Love	55	Savoy 1151
If You Go/Fing Fang Foy	57	DeLuxe 6136
Darnells (aka Marvelettes)		
Come On Home/Too Hurt To Cry, Too Much In Love To Say Goodbye	63	Gordy 7024
Darnels (1) (Gus Gordon & the)		
In The Valley Of The Roses/My Little Homin' Pigeon	57	Bana 525
Darnels (2) (Debbie & the) (female) (aka Teen Dreams)		
The Time/Why, Why	61	Vernon 100
Daddy/Mr. Johnny Jones	62	Columbia 42530
The Time/Santa, Teach Me To Dance	62	Vernon 101
Darrells		
So Tenderly/Without Warning	61	Lyco 1003
Darrow, Jay (& group)		
Girl Of My Dreams/I Love That Girl	61	Keen 82124
Darts		
On My Mind/Well Baby	58	Apt 25023
Sweet Little Baby/Gee-Ver-Men-Nee-Vers	58	Dot 15752
Darts (Herb Price & the)		
Gone Too Long/Shimmy Shimmy Cha Cha	59	Tempus 1506
Darts (Sherman & the)		
Remember/Rockin' At Midnight	57	Fury 1014
Darvel, Barry (& group)		
Lost Love/Silver Dollar	61	Atlantic 2128
Fountain Of Love/Little Angel Lost	61	Cub 9088
Adam And Eve/A King For Tonight	62	Atlantic 2138
Darvels (1)		
I Lost My Baby/Gone	63	Eddies 69
Darvels (2) (Frankie & the)		
Mr. Fortune Teller	N/A	N/A
Darwin, Ricky (& group)		
The Great Thinker/Deep In Love	59	Buzz 103
Dates (Lincoln Fig & the)		
Kiss Me Tenderly/Way Up	58	Worthy 1006
Dave & Larry (& group)		
Only A Dream/My Confession To You	65	B'n Kc 102
Davi (bb the Spidels)		
Reason For Love/Go, Charley, Go	62	Stark 110

ARTIST/SONG	YEAR	LABEL
Davies (Johnny Greco & the)		
High School Dance/Hogwalk	59	Sonic 813
Rocket Ride/Why Don't You Love Me	63	Pageant 602
Davis Brothers		
Why Can't They Understand/The Best You Can	65	Guyden 2120
Davis, Billy (& group)		
Anne Marie/Small Fry	60	R-Dell 118
Davis, Eunice (& group)		
24 Hours A Day/Get Your Enjoys	54	DeLuxe 6068
Davis, George (& group)		
Out Of A Million Girls/Soft Touch	62	Philips 40082
Davis, Hal "Sonny" (& female group)		
The Way You Look Tonight/Way To My Heart	59	Kelley 105
Davis, Hal "Sonny" (& group)		
Sweet And Lovely/My Young Heart	59	Alden 1301
King Of Lovers/Sweet And Lovely	59	Alden 1303
You're Playing With Me/Read The Book Of Love	60	Del-Fi 4146
What Do You Mean To Me/Merchant Of Love	61	Wizard 101/Vee Jay 387 (61)
One More Chance/Show Me	62	Gardena 125
I Don't Know/Lover's Plan	63	G.S.P. 2
Davis, Jan (& group)		
You're Not Welcome (Anymore)/Don't Walk Away	63	Rendezvous 214
Dawn (aka Five Discs)		
I'm Afraid They're All Talking About Me/Lovers' Melody	67	Laurie 3388
Sandy/For The Love Of Money	67	Laurie 3417
Bring It On Home/Baby I Love You	68	Rust 5128
Dawn Quartet (Billy Dawn Quartet) (aka Four Dukes/aka Donny Miles & the Dukes)		
This Is The Real Thing Now/Crying For My Baby	52	Decatur 3001
Miracle Of Love/Proud Of You	73	Vintage 1010
Dawns		
Love You So Tonight/Travelin'	59	Catalina 1000
How Deep Is The Ocean/Why Did You Let Me Love You	59	Climax 104
It Seems Like Yesterday/From You, Only You	64	Atco 6296
Dawns (Billy Horton & the)		
Like To See You In That Mood/Shadow	64	Lawn 241
I Wanna Know/No One Can Take Your Place	70	KayDen 403
Dawson, Ronnie (& group)		
Decided By The Angels/Summer's Comin'	60	Swan 4054
Day Brothers		
A Thousand Miles Away/Somebody Else	60	Chancellor 1059
Day Dreams (Tony & the)		
I'll Never Tell/Why Don't You Be Nice	58	Planet 1008/1009
Christmas Lullabye/Hand In Hand	58	Planet 1054
Hand In Hand/I'll Never Tell	61	Planet 1055
Day, Darlene (bb the Imaginations)		
Will/I Love You So	61	Music Makers 106
Day, Dawn & Dusk		
Let The Tears Fall/Miss Petunia	55	Apollo 476
Let The Tears Fall/A Cheat's A Cheat	55	Dent 519

ARTIST/SONG	YEAR	LABEL
Anytime, Anyplace, Anywhere/Who Are You Kissing	56	Josie 794

Day, Tracey (& group)

Jerry (I'm Your Sherry)/Once In A Blue Moon	61	Vee Jay 467

Daybreakers

I Wonder Why?/Up, Up And Away	58	Lamp 2016/Aladdin 3434 (58)

Daychords (Roxy & the)

I'm So In Love/Mary Lou	62	Don-El 116/Candlelite 430 (74)
Too Bad/One More Time	62	Don-El 120

Daylighters

Mad House Jump/You're Breaking My Heart	59	Bea & Baby 103
I'll Never Let You Go/Something Is Wrong	59	Domino 904
Come On Home/Reap What You Sow	59	Key Hole 107
Tough Love/Sweet Rocking Mama	60	C.J. 614
Oh What A Way To Be Loved/Why Do You Do Me Wrong	61	Nike 10011/Dot 16326 (62)/ Tip Top 2001 (62)
This Heart Of Mine/Bear Mash Stomp	61	Nike 1011/Astra 1001 (65)
Cool Breeze/Baby I Love You	62	Tip Top 2002
No One's Gonna Help You/War Hoss Mash	63	Checker 1051
Whisper Of The Wind/I Can't Stop Crying	63	Tip Top 2007
Hard Headed Girl/Oh Mom	64	Tip Top 2008
I Can't Stop Crying/Magic Touch	64	Tip Top 2009
For My Baby/Sweeter	64	Tip Top 2010
Whisper Of The Wind/Here Alone	64	Tollie 9028
Tell Me/What About Me	66	Smash 2040

Daylighters (Betty Everett & the)

Please Come Back/Why Did You Have To Go	60	C.J. 611

Daylighters (Chuck & the)

I Can't Stop Crying/Bottomless Pit	63	Tip Top 2006

Daylights

Billy Is The Boy/A Tear Fell From My Eyes	63	Propulsion 601

Daytones

Bless My Love/Krambuli	63	Jubilee 5452

Daytons

King Of Broken Hearts/Friday Better Come	59	Norgolde 101

Dazzlers

Gee Whiz/Somethin' Baby	58	Lee 100

Dazzlers (Teddy Randazzo & the)

Dance To The Locomotion/Cotton Fields	62	ABC 10350

De Bonairs

Lanky Linda/Mother's Son	56	Ping 1000
Say A Prayer For Me/Cracker-Jack Daddy	56	Ping 1001

De Havilons (Eddie & the)

Baby Dumplin'/Xmas Party	62	Peacock 1920

De Marco, Lou (& group)

Careless Love/My Lady Fair	56	Ferris 903

De Vaurs (female)

Baby Doll/Teenager	56	D-Tone A-3
Where Are You/Boy In Mexico	59	Moon 105/Red Fox 104

ARTIST/SONG	YEAR	LABEL
De Ville Sisters (Rueben Grundy & the)		
Every Word/Sail Away	58	Spry 110
De Villes		
Do Wop/Kiss Me Again And Again	58	Aladdin 3423
Without Warning/Troubled Heart	60	Dixie 1108
De-Icers		
Callin' My Love/After Five	57	De-Icer 100
De-Lights		
I'm Comin' Home/One, Two, Button My Shoe	62	Ad Lib 0207/Pop Line
Dealers (Floyd White & the)		
Cinderella/Cha Cha Rock (instrumental)	58	Criterion 1
Dean & Jean (bb the Del Satins)		
Please Don't Tell Me Now/Hey Jean, Hey Dean	64	Rust 5075
Dean, Terry (& group)		
Dream Boy (Oh, Oh, Oh)/It's Just Your Kiss	57	Poplar 102
Deane, Janet (bb the Skyliners)		
Another Night Alone/I'm Glad I Waited	58	Gateway 719
Deans (1) (Barry & the)		
Rock With Me Baby/I'll Love You	60	Zirkon 1001
Deans (2)		
My Heart Is Low/I'll Love You Forever	60	Mohawk 114
Humpty Dumpty/Le Chaim (Good Luck)	60	Mohawk 119
Little White Gardenia/I Don't Want To Wait	61	Laurie 3114
It's You/I Don't Want To Wait	61	Mohawk 126
Deans (3)		
Oh Little Star/You Got Me Baby	61	Star Maker 1928
Chills, Chills, Chills/(Lady Of The) Caravan	62	Star Maker 1931
Deans (4) (Dolly & the)		
The Happiest Years	N/A	Thornett 1008
Deb-Teens (female)		
Miss Lonely Hearts/Cuddly Baby	58	RCA 7242
Give It Up/Rock-A-Bye	58	RCA 7384
Darling/Drip Drop	59	Boss 403
Knock, Knock, Who's There/I'm In Love Again	59	RCA 7539
Debelaires (female)		
The Wa-Wabble/So Long, My Sailor	62	Lectra 502
Deberons		
It Only Takes One	N/A	Bond 1408
Debonaires (1)		
Won't You Tell Me/I'm Gone	56	Gee 1008
Darling/Whispering Blues	57	Herald 509
So Blue	58	Debonair
Every Once In A While/Mama Don't Care	59	Dore 526
Every Other Day/Jivin' Guy	59	Maske 804
We'll Wait/Make Believe Lover	60	Gee 1054
Every Once In A While/Gert's Skirts	61	Dore 592/Dore 702 (63)
Hold Back The Dawn/Mama Don't Care	62	Dore 654
Everybody's Movin'/Mama Don't Care	64	Dore 712
I Want To Talk About It (World) Pt. 1/ I Want To Talk About It (World) Pt. 2	67	Galaxy 787

ARTIST/SONG	YEAR	LABEL
Cause Of A Bad Romance	87	Relic LP 5069
Best Love/I'd Climb The Highest Mountain	N/A	Gee

Debonaires (2)

| This Must Be Paradise/I Need You Darling | 58 | Elmont 1004 |

Debonaires (3) (Dickie & the)

| Please Mr. Disc Jockey/Yo Yo Girl | 65 | Valli 302 |

Debonairs (1)

| As Other Lovers Do/The Bill Collector | 57 | Combo 129 |
| Casue Of A Bad Romance/For The Woman I Love | 58 | Combo 149 |

Debonairs (2)

| Crazy Kind Of Love/To Be Without You | 60 | Winter 502 |

Debonairs (3)

| Fools Love/Ah-La-La | 61 | B&F 1353 |

Debs (1) (female)

| Shoo Doo De Doo/Whadaya Want? | 55 | Bruce 129 |
| If You Were Here Tonight/Look What You're Doin' To Me | 55 | Crown 153 |

Debs (2) (female)

| Johnnie, Darling/Doom-A-Rocka | 57 | Keen 34003 |

Debs (3) (female) (with the Escorts)

| (We Like) Crew Cuts/Swingin' Sam (by the Pastels) | 58 | Josie 833 |

Debs (4) (female)

| If Wishes Were Kisses/Mucha Cha | 61 | Echo 1008 |
| Just Another Fool/Danger Ahead | 63 | Double L 727 |

Debutantes (1)

| Just Leave It To Me/It It Too Soon? | 56 | Savoy 1191 |

Debutantes (2)

| Going Steady/Memories | 58 | Kayo 928 |

Decades (Brother Zee & the)

| Sha-Boom Bang/Smokey The Bear | 62 | Ramco 3725 |

Deccors (Marie & the)

| Queen Of Fools/I'm The One | 62 | Cub 9115 |

Deckers (1) (Lynn Christie & the)

| Oh Where Did You Go/What Did I Do | 57 | Nar 225 |

Deckers (2)

| Sincerely With All My Heart/Come Back Baby | 58 | Yeadon 101 |
| Sincerely With All My Heart/The Thing | 58 | Yeadon 1041 |

Deckers (3) (Jigger & the)

| Falling Teardrops | N/A | GWS 3105 |

Decoys (1) (aka Belairs (3))

I Only Want You/For You	63	Aanko 1005
It's Gonna Be Allright/Oh Baby (by the Bel-Airs)	63	Times Square 8
Tomorrow/I Only Want You	64	Times Square 9/ Times Square 96 (64)

Decoys (2)

| Memories/Happy Honeymoon (by the Four Fellows (2)) | 63 | Aljon 1261 |

ARTIST/SONG	YEAR	LABEL
Decoys (3)		
Listen To Me/Always Be Good	64	Velvet 1001
Dedications (1)		
Shining Star/Mary Lou	63	C&A 506
Someone To Love/Mr. Taxicab Driver	64	Ramarca 602
Why Don't You Write Me/Boppin' Around	62	Card 335/336
Dedications (2) (Denny & the)		
Lost Love/I'll Show You How To Love	65	Susan 1111
Dee Cals		
Stars In The Blue What Should I Do/A Wonderful Day	59	Co-Ed 1960/Mayhams 1960 (61)
Dee Jays (1)		
I'm Really In Love	54	After Hours 102
Dee Jays (2)		
You Took Your Love From Me/Canadian Sunset	62	Sonata 1100
Dee, Fern (& group)		
Dream Man/You'll Never Know	58	Ember 1035
Dee, Joey (& group)		
Lorraine/The Girl I Walk To School	58	Little 813/814/Bonus 7009
Dee, Larry (& group)		
Am I Just Your Clown/Turtle Dove	61	Lagree 703
Dee, Ronnie (& group)		
Little Boy Blue/Never Leave The One You Love	61	Wye 1008
Dee, Sonny (& group)		
Here I Stand/I'm Not The One For You	61	Kapp 421
Dee-Vines		
I Believe/World's Greatest Lover	60	Lano 2001/Relic 514 (64)
Dee-Vines (fb Neil Stevens)		
More And More/What Could Be Better	58	Brunswick 55095
Deejays		
Love Me Baby/Don't Leave Me Here To Cry	N/A	SRC 101
Deep River Boys		
Truthfully/Doesn't Make Sense To Me	51	Beacon 9143
Deeps		
Calypso Rock 'N' Roll/The Night Is Young	57	Que 1000
Deeptones		
My Prayer	54	Music City 736/Musicon 736
Defenders		
Island Of Love/I Laughed So Hard	64	Parkway 926
Del Amos		
She's So Wonderful/I'm So Weak	59	Nikko 703
Del Cades		
World's Fair U.S.A./Two To Fall In Love	64	United Sound Associates 175
Del Capris		
Speak To Me Of Love/Theresa	63	Almont 304
Forever My Love/Hey Little Girl	67	Ronjerdon 39/ Kama Sutra 235 (67)

ARTIST/SONG	YEAR	LABEL
Del Chords		
September Song/In Togetherness	62	Midas 09
Del Counts (Ronald Bobo & the)		
Mother Nature/Lone Stranger	N/A	Rose 23
Del Knights		
Wrapped Too Tight/Wherever You Are	61	Chancellor 1075
Del Mates (John Steele & the)		
You're Gonna Miss Me/Fat Man	65	Wand 194
Del Pris		
Womp/The Time	61	Varbee 2003
I Don't Want To Cry/It Must Have Been Love	N/A	unreleased
Del Rays (1)		
My Darling/The One I Adore	58	Warner Bros. 5022
Around The Corner/Have A Heart	59	Moon 110
Del Rays (2)		
Lily Maebelle/When We're Alone	58	Future 2203
Del Rays (3)		
Our Love Is True/One Kiss, One Smile And A Dream	58	Cord 101
Del Rays (4)		
Fortune Teller	N/A	R&H 1005
Del Reys		
Let's Stay Together/Young And Innocent	60	Columbia 41784
Del Rios (1)		
The Vines Of Love/The Session	58	Big 613
Valerie/Mystery	63	Rust 5066
Del Rios (2)		
Alone On A Rainy Nite/Lizzie	56	Meteor 5038
I'm Crying/Wait, Wait, Wait	59	Neptune 108
There's A Love/Just Across The Street	62	Stax 125
Del Rios (3) (Jimmy Hurt & the)		
You Know Darling/Oh, What A Feeling	61	Do-Ra-Mi 1401
Del Rios (4) (Linda & the)		
Come On, Let Me Try/I Don't Want To Be Loved	62	Crackerjack 4005
Del Rios (5)		
Heavenly Angel/Dangerous Lover	62	Bet-T 7001
Del Royals		
You Can't Run Away/Trust In Love	60	Destiny 101
Who Will Be The One?/She's Gone	60	Minit 610
Barbara/I'd Wait Forever	60	Warwick 111
Got You On My Mind/Close To You	61	Minit 620
I Fell In Love With You/Always Naggin'	61	Minit 637
Del Roys		
Love Me Tenderly/Pleasing You	61	Carol 4113
Del Roys (aka Delroys)		
Strange Land/Wise Old Owl	59	Sparkell 102
Love Me Tenderly/Pleasing You	61	Carol 4113
Alimony	64	Moon LP AB1
Happy Life	N/A	Carol unreleased
Mexico	N/A	Carol unreleased

ARTIST/SONG	YEAR	LABEL

Del Satins

Counting My Teardrops/Remember	58	Win 702
I'll Pray For You/I Remember The Night	61	End 1096
Teardrops Follow Me/Best Wishes, Good Luck, Goodbye	62	Laurie 3132
Ballad Of A D. J./Does My Heart Stand A Chance	62	Laurie 3149
Feelin' No Pain/Who Cares	63	Columbia 42802
Two Broken Hearts/Believe In Me	64	Mala 475
Hang Around/My Candy Apple Vet	65	B.T. Puppy 506
Sweets For My Sweet/A Girl Named Arlene	65	B.T. Puppy 509
Relief/Throwaway Song	65	B.T. Puppy 514
A Little Rain Must Fall (with Carl Parker)/Love, Hate And Revenge	67	Diamond 216
A Girl Named Arlene/I'll Do My Crying Tomorrow	69	B.T. Puppy 563

The Del Satins

Del Tones

Please Talk To Me/And The Angels Sang	61	USA 711

Del Victors

Baby Sitter I Love You/Oh Lover	63	Hi-Q 5028

Del-Airs (1) (aka Del-Aires/aka Ronnie & the Delaires)

While Walking/Lost My Job	60	MBS 001
It Took A Long Time/Ma Ma Marie	61	Delsey 302
Elaine/Just Wigglin' 'N Wobblin'	63	Coral 62370
My Funny Valentine/Drag (Ronnie & the Delaires)	64	Coral 62404
Arlene/I'm Your Baby	64	Coral 62419

Del-Airs (2) (female)

Why Did He Leave/I'm Lonely	62	Arrawak 1003

Del-Capris

Up On The Roof/If I Should Lose You (a capella)	66	Amber 854
Teardrops Follow Me/Man In The Moon	66	Catamount 115

Del-Capris (Beverly & the)

Mildred/Mama I Think I'm In Love	64	Columbia 43107

Del-Chords (1)

Help Me/Say That You Love Me	60	Jin 126

Del-Chords (2) (Donnie & the)

When You're Alone/So Lonely	61	Taurus 352/Epic 9495 (62)
I Don't Care/I'll Be With You In Apple Blossom Time	63	Taurus 357
That Old Feeling/Transylvania Mist	63	Taurus 361

ARTIST/SONG	YEAR	LABEL
I Found Heaven/Be With You	63	Taurus 363
I'm In The Mood For Love/I've Got A Woman	63	Taurus 364

Del-Chords (3)

Marsha-Mellow/At The Hop	60	Cool 5816

Del-Cords

Everybody's Gotta Lose Someday/Your Mommy Lied To Your Daddy	60	Impala 215/Genius 401 (63)

Del-Hearts (Dale & the)

I've Waited So Long/Always And Ever	61	Herald 564
High Blood Pressure/Please	61	Herald 565

Del-Knights

Everything/Compensation	59	Unart 2008
I'm Comin' Home	N/A	Sheryl

Del-Larks

Remember The Night/Lady Love	58	East West 116

Del-Larks (Sammy & the)

I Never Will Forget/Baby Come On	61	Ea-Jay 100
Little Darling/Sleep Walk	61	Stop 101

Del-Lourds

Alone/All Alone (a capella)	63	Solar 1001
Gloria/All Alone (a capella)	63	Solar 1003

Del-Mars

That's My Desire/You Know	63	ABC 10426
Snacky Poo, Part. 1/Snacky Poo, Pt. 2	64	Mercury 72244

Del-Mingos

Young Queen Chunka Bo Bo/Goodnight My Love	63	Lomar 702

Del-Phis (female) (aka Martha & the Vandellas)

It Takes Two/I'll Let You Know	61	Checkmate 1005

Del-Prados

Oh, Baby/The Skip	62	Lucky Four 1021

Del-Rays (1) (Detroit Jr. & the)

Zig Zag/I'm Gonna Find Me Another Girl	64	CJ 636
Can't Take It/Mother-In-Law	64	CJ 637

Del-Rays (2)

I Want To Do It/Don't Let Her Be Your Baby	68	Stax 162

Del-Rays (3) (Dave T. & the)

Girl In My Heart/Scooter Town	64	Carousel 213

Del-Rays (3) (fb Dave T.)

Lorraine/The Bounce	61	Planet 52

Del-Reys

Should I Ever Love Again/Fannie Mae	60	Delreco 500

Del-Rhythmetts

I Need Your Love/Chic-A-Boomer	58	J-V-B 5000

Del-Sharps (Sonny Ace & the)

If My Teardrops Could Talk/Swingin' Stroll	58	TNT 153

Del-Tinos

Pa Pa Ooh Mau Mau/Nightlite	64	Conic 1451

ARTIST/SONG	YEAR	LABEL
Del-Tones		
Best Wishes/Walking Out The Back Door	59	Ro-Ann 1001
Del-Vons (aka Chanters (2))		
All I Did Was Cry/Gone Forever	63	Wells 1001
Delacardos		
A Letter To A School Girl/I'll Never Let You Down	59	Elgey 1001
I Got It/Thing-A-Ma-Jig	60	United Artists 276
Dream Girl/I Just Want To Know	61	Shell 308
Hold Back The Tears/Mr. Dillon	61	United Artists 310
Love Is The Greatest Thing/Girl Girl	62	Shell 311
Delairs (fb Ray Adams)		
I'm Gone/Rattle My Bones	56	Rainbow 348
Delatones		
Ik-Heb-Je-Lief/Teenager's Love	60	TNT 9028
Genie	68	N/A
Delchords (David Campanella & the)		
Somewhere Over The Rainbow/Everythng's That Way	59	Kane 25593
Delconte, David (& group)		
Face In The Crowd/I Lie	N/A	Delcon 1
Delcos		
Those Three Little Words/Arabia	62	Ebony 01/02/Showcase 2501 (63)/Sound Stage 7 2501 (63)
Still Miss You So/Just Ask	63	Sound Stage 7 2515
When You Dance/Why Do You Have To Go	N/A	Monument
Delegates (1) (aka Kool Gents)		
The Convention/Jay's Rock (Big Jay McNeely)	56	Vee Jay 212
Mother's Son/I'm Gonna Be Glad	57	Vee Jay 243
Delegates (2)		
The Peeper/Pygmy	65	Aura 88120
Delfonics (gm Carlton Lee)		
There They Go/You Can Tell	62	Fling 727
Deli-Cados		
Now I've Confessed/Granny Baby	N/A	PMP
Delicates		
Black And White Thunderbird/Ronnie Is My Lover	59	Unart 2017
Meusurry/Ringa Ding	59	Unart 2024
Flip, Flip/Your Happiest Years	60	United Artists 210
Too Young To Date/The Kiss	60	United Artists 228
My Pillow/I Played 1, 2, 3, 4	61	Celeste 676/Dee Dee 677 (61)
Not Tomorrow/Little Ship	61	Roulette 4321
Little Boy Of Mine/Dickie Went And Did It	61	Roulette 4360
Strange Love/I Don't Know Why	61	Roulette 4387
C'Mon Everybody/I've Been Hurt	64	Challenge 59232
I Want To Get Married/I've Been Hurt	65	Challenge 59267
Comin' Down With Love/Stop Shovin' Me Around	65	Challenge 59304
Delighters (Donald & the) (aka Fortunes)		
Adios My Secret Love/Somebody Help Me	63	Cortland 112
Delighters (Donald Jenkins & the) (aka Fortunes)		
(Native Girl) Elephant Walk/Wang Dang Dula	63	Cortland 109

ARTIST/SONG	YEAR	LABEL

Delights

My One Desire/Please Take My Love	61	Nite 1034
I Cry/Breaking Hearts To Him Is Just A Game	64	Arlen 753

Del Vikings (aka Dell Vikings/aka Del-Vikings)

Come Go With Me/How Can I Find True Love	56	Fee Bee 205/Dot 15538 (57)/ Dot 16092 (60)
Down In Bermuda/Maggie	56	Fee Bee 206
True Love/Uh Uh Baby	56	Fee Bee 210
What Made Maggie Run?/Uh, Uh, Baby	56	Fee Bee 210
What Made Maggie Run?/Down By The Stream	56	Fee Bee 210/Dot 15571 (56)
True Love/Baby, Let Me Be	56	Fee Bee 902
What Made Maggie Run?/Little Billy Boy	57	Dot 15571
I'm Spinning/When I Come Home	57	Dot 15636/Mercury 71198 (57)
Whispering Bells/Don't Be A Fool	57	Fee Bee 214/Dot 15592 (57)
I'm Spinning/You Say You Love Me	57	Fee Bee 218/Dot 15636 (57)
Willette/I Want To Marry You	57	Fee Bee 221
Willette/Woke Up This Morning	57	Fee Bee 221/Dot 15673 (58)
Tell Me I'm The One For You/Finger Poppin' Woman	57	Fee Bee 227
Somewhere Over The Rainbow/Hey, Senorita	57	Luniverse 106
A Sunday Kind Of Love/Come Along With Me	57	Mercury 30112
Cool Shake/Jitterbug Mary	57	Mercury 71132
Come Along With Me/What'Cha Gotta Lose	57	Mercury 71180
Your Book Of Love/Snowbound	57	Mercury 71241
Heart And Soul	57	Mercury EP 3362
I'm Sittin' On Top Of The World	57	Mercury EP 3362
My Foolish Heart	57	Mercury EP 3362
Is It Any Wonder	57	Mercury LP 20314/ Mercury EP 3363 (57)
Summertime	57	Mercury LP 20314/ Mercury EP 3363 (57)
Yours	57	Mercury LP 20314/ Mercury EP 3363 (57)
Yours/Heaven And Paradise	58	Luniverse 110
In The Still Of The Night/The White Cliffs Of Dover	58	Luniverse 113
There I Go/Girl Girl	58	Luniverse 114
The Voodoo Man/Can't Wait	58	Mercury 71266
You Cheated/Pretty Little Things Called Girls	58	Mercury 71345
Flat Tire/How Could You	58	Mercury 71390
Pistol Packin' Mama/The Sun	60	Alpine 66
I'll Never Stop Crying/Bring Back Your Heart	61	ABC 10208
I Hear Bells (Wedding Bells)/Don't Get Slick On Me	61	ABC 10248
Kiss Me/Face The Music	61	ABC 10278
One More River To Cross/The Big Silence	62	ABC 10304
Confession Of Love/Kilimanjaro	62	ABC 10341
An Angel Up In Heaven/The Fishing Chant	63	ABC 10385
Too Many Miles/Sorcerer's Apprentice	63	ABC 10425
Be Mine	63	Crown LP 5368
This Heart Of Mine	63	Crown LP 5368
We Three/I've Got To Know	64	Gateway 743
Cold Feet/I Want To Marry You	72	Bim Bam Boom 111
Come Go With Me/When You're Asleep	72	Scepter 12367
Watching The Moon/You Say You Love Me	73	Bim Bam Boom 113
Girl Girl/I'm Spinning	73	Bim Bam Boom 115
Hey Senorita/Over The Rainbow	73	Blue Sky 104
How Do You Like It (a capella)	75	Relic LP 109
Milk Shake Mama (a capella)	75	Relic LP 109
Come Go With Me/How Can I Find True Love	80	Collectables 1251
Whispering Bells/Don't Be A Fool	80	Collectables 1252
Can't You See/Oh I	N/A	D.R.C. 101
Hollywood And Vine	N/A	Fee Bee 173
Come Go With Me/Whispering Bells	N/A	Lightning 9013

Del Vikings (Buddy Carle & the) (aka Dell Vikings/aka Del-Vikings)

Understand/It's Too Late	N/A	Eedee 3501/Star 223

ARTIST/SONG	YEAR	LABEL
Del Vikings (with Charles Jackson)		
Cold Feet/Watching The Moon	59	Petite 503
Dell Mates		
Angela/Cross My Heart And Hope To Die	64	Fontana 1934/Smash 1934 (64)
Dell Tones		
Yours Alone/My Heart's On Fire	53	Brunswick 84015
Dell Woods		
Don't Put Onions On Your Hamburger/Her Moustache	63	Big Top 3137
Dell, Joey (& group)		
Let's Find Out Tonight/Only Last Night	62	Roulette 4422
Dell, Tony (& group)		
My Girl/Magic Wand	63	King 5766
Dell-Coeds		
Love In Return/Hey Mr. Banjo	62	Enith 712/Dot 16314 (62)
Dell-Fi's (Leon Peterson & the)		
Together Just We Two/My Love Came Tumbling Down	N/A	Kable 437
Dell-Os (John Shaw & the) (aka Sensational Dell-Os)		
Why Did You Leave Me/Why Does It Have To Be Her	58	U-C 5002/U-C 1031
Dell-Rays		
Darling I Pray/Pauline	58	Boptown 102
Dellrays		
The Way You Look Tonight/Hum Gully Gully	N/A	Lavette 1007

The Dells

Dells (aka El Rays)

Tell The World/Blues At Three (by Count Morris)	55	Vee Jay 134
Dreams Of Contentment/Zing Zing Zing	55	Vee Jay 166
Oh What A Night/Jo Jo	56	Vee Jay 204
Movin' On/I Wanna Go Home	56	Vee Jay 230
Why Do You Have To Go?/Dance, Dance, Dance	57	Vee Jay 236
A Distant Love/O-Bop, She-Bop	57	Vee Jay 251
Time Makes You Change/Pain In My Heart	57	Vee Jay 258
What You Say Baby/The Springer	57	Vee Jay 274
Jeepers Creepers/I'm Calling	58	Vee Jay 292

ARTIST/SONG	YEAR	LABEL
Wedding Day/My Best Girl	58	Vee Jay 300
Dry Your Eyes/Baby Open Up Your Heart	59	Vee Jay 324
Oh What A Night/I Wanna Go Home	59	Vee Jay 338
Swingin' Teens/Hold On To What You've Got	61	Vee Jay 376
God Bless The Child/I'm Going Home	62	Argo 5415
The (Bossa Nova) Bird/Eternally	62	Argo 5428
If It Ain't One Thing It's Another/Hi Diddley Dee Dum Dum	63	Argo 5442
After You/Goodbye Mary Ann	63	Argo 5456
Shy Girl/What Do We Prove?	64	Vee Jay 595
Oh What A Good Night/Wait 'Til Tomorrow	64	Vee Jay 615
Stay In My Corner/It's Not Unusual	65	Vee Jay 674
Hey Sugar (Don't Get Serious)/Poor Little Boy	65	Vee Jay 712
At The Bandstand (The Springer)	83	Charly LP 1056
Baby Do	83	Charly LP 1056
Cherry Bee	83	Charly LP 1056
Come On Baby	83	Charly LP 1056
I Can't Dream	83	Charly LP 1056
Restless Days, Sleepless Nights	83	Charly LP 1056
She's Just An Angel	84	Solid Smoke LP 8029
Someone To Call Me Darling	84	Solid Smoke LP 8029
Don't Tell Nobody	84	Solid Smoke LP 8029/ Charly LP 1055 (85)
Let's Do It Over	84	Solid Smoke LP 8029/ Charly LP 1055 (85)
Now I Pray	84	Solid Smoke LP 8029/ Charly LP 1055 (85)
Rain	84	Solid Smoke LP 8029/ Charly LP 1055 (85)
You're Still In My Heart	84	Solid Smoke LP 8029/ Charly LP 1055 (85)
I Can't Help Myself	84	Solid Smoke LP 8029/ Charly LP 1056 (85)
It Looks Like It's Over	85	Charly LP 1055

Delltones (1)

Baby Say You Love Me/Don't Be Long	55	Baton 212
My Special Love/Believe It	56	Baton 223

Delltones (1) (& the Kelly Owens Orchestra)

I'm Not In Love With You/Little Short Daddy	54	Rainbow 244

Delltones (2)

No Darlin' No/Lookin' For A Gal	N/A	Maestro 1919

Delltones (3) (J. Jay & the)

Too Late To Forgive/Just A Matter Of Time	N/A	Cobra 5555

Delmar, Eddie (bb the Bob Knight Four)

Garden In The Rain/My Heart Beckons You	65	Vegas 628

Delmar, Eddie (with the Bob Knight Four)

Blanche/Love Bells	61	Madison 168

Delmiras

Dry Your Eyes/The Big Sound	61	Dade 1821

Delmonicos

There They Go/You Can Call	63	Aku 6318
Until You/World's Biggest Fool	64	Musictone 6122

Delmonicos (fb Denise Germaine)

Teenage Idol/I'm Fed Up	63	Aku 6139

Delongs

I Want Your Love/You're Never Too Young	N/A	Art Flow 3906

ARTIST/SONG	YEAR	LABEL

Delphis (Tony & the)

Please Don't Say Goodbye — N/A — New Group 6001

Delrays

Our Love Is True/One Kiss, One Smile And A Dream — 58 — Cord 1001

Delrons (1) (Reperata & the) (female)

Your Big Mistake/Leave Us Alone	64	Laurie 3252
Whenever A Teenager Cries/He's My Guy	64	World Artists 1036
I Can Tell/Take A Look Around You	65	RCA 8721
I'm Nobody's Baby Now/Loneliest Girl In Town	65	RCA 8820
Tommy/Mama Don't Allow	65	World Artists 1051
The Boy I Love/I Found My Place	65	World Artists 1062
He's The Greatest/Summer Thoughts	65	World Artists 1075
Mama's Little Girl/He Don't Want You	66	RCA 8921
I Believe/It's Waiting There For You	67	Mala 573
The Kind Of Trouble I Love/Boys And Girls	67	RCA 9123
I Can Hear The Rain/Always Waitin'	67	RCA 9185
Captain Of Your Ship/Toom Toom (Is A Little Boy)	68	Mala 589
We're Gonna Hold The Night/San Juan	69	Kapp 2010
(That's What Sends Men To The) Bowery/	69	Kapp 989
I've Got An Awful Lot Of Losing To Do		
Walking In The Rain/I've Got An Awful Lot Of Losing To Do	70	Kapp 2050
Octopus' Garden/Your Life Is Gone	71	Laurie 3589

Delrons (2)

This Love Of Ours/Over The Rainbow — 61 — Forum 700

Delroys (aka Del Roys)

Bermuda Shorts/Time (Milton Sparks bb Delroys) — 57 — Apollo 514

The Delroys

The Deltairs

Delshays

I'll Love You Forever/Fake It — 64 — Charger 102

ARTIST/SONG	YEAR	LABEL
Delstars		
Zoop Bop (a capella)/For Your Love (a capella)	64	Mellomood 1001
Why Do You Have To Go (a capella)/	64	Mellomood 1004/Relic 1014 (65)
Who Said You Wasn't Mine (a capella)		
Your Way (a capella)	75	Relic LP 102
Deltairs (female)		
Lullaby Of The Bells/It's Only You Dear	57	Ivy 101
You Won't Be Satisfied/Who Would Have Thought It	58	Felsted 8525
I Might Like It/Standing At The Altar	58	Ivy 105
Deltars (Pearl & the) (fb Pearl McKinnon)		
Teenager's Dream/Dance, Dance, Dance	61	Fury 1048
Where Are You?/Back To School Again	N/A	unreleased
Deltas (1)		
Lamplight/Let Me Share Your Dreams	57	Gone 5010
Deltas (2) (Jim Waller & the)		
I've Been Blue/What I Want	61	Trac 502
Surfin' Wild/Church Key	62	Arvee 5072
Goodnight My Love/Give My Love A Chance	64	Cambridge 124/125
Deltas (3)		
My Own True Love/Hold Me, Thrill Me, Kiss Me	62	Philips 40023
My Own True Love/The Work Song	62	Philips 40023
Deltas (4) (Jay & the)		
Bells Are Ringing/Super Hawk	64	Warner Bros. 5404
Deltears (female)		
There He Goes/Whoever You Are	N/A	Ray-Born 132/133
Delteens		
A Lover's Prayer/First Man To The Moon	58	Vee Jay 303
Delteens (with the Orbits)		
Listen To The Rain/(Why Don't You) Love Me	61	Fortune 541
Deltones (1)		
I'm Coming Home/Early Morning Rock	58	Vee Jay 288
Deltones (2)		
Bow Legged Annie/La La La	59	Jubilee 5374
I Never Knew/Framed	60	20th Century Fox 175
Since I Met You/Hey, Little Girl	61	Dayhill 1002
Deltones (3) (Ronnie Baker & the)		
My Story/I Want To Be Loved	62	Laurie 3128
Delusions (W. Kelley & the)		
Do What You Did	N/A	Kelway 115
Delvets		
I Want A Boy For Christmas/Repeat After Me	61	End 1106
Will You Love Me In Heaven/Repeat After Me	61	End 1107
Delvons		
Stay Clear Of Love/Please Stay	67	JDF 760
DeMarco, Ralph (with the Paramounts)		
More Than Riches/Old Shep	59	Guaranteed 202
Dematrons		
The Boy Who's Sixteen	N/A	Southern Sound 202

ARTIST/SONG	YEAR	LABEL
Demens (aka Emersons)		
Take Me As I Am/You Broke My Heart	57	Teenage 1006
I'm Not In Love With You/Short Daddy	57	Teenage 1007
The Greatest Of Them All/Hey, Young Girl	57	Teenage 1008
Demensions		
Over The Rainbow/Nursery Rhyme Rock	60	Mohawk 116
Don't Take Your Love From Me/	60	Mohawk 120
Zing! Went The Strings Of My Heart		
Ave Maria (Schubert)/God's Christmas	60	Mohawk 121
A Tear Fell/Theresa	60	Mohawk 123
Count Your Blessings Instead Of Sheep/Again	61	Coral 62277
As Time Goes By/Seven Days A Week	61	Coral 62293/Coral 65611 (67)
Young At Heart/Your Cheatin' Heart	62	Coral 62323
My Foolish Heart/Just One More Chance	63	Coral 62344
Fly Me To The Moon/You'll Never Know	63	Coral 62359
Just A Shoulder To Cry On/Don't Worry About Bobby	63	Coral 62382
Don't Cry Pretty Baby/A Little White Gardenia	63	Coral 62392
This Time Next Year/My Old Girl Friend	64	Coral 62432
Over The Rainbow/Zing Went The Strings Of My Heart	66	Coral 65559
As Time Goes By/My Foolish Heart	66	Coral 65611
Demensions (Lenny Dell & the)		
Ting Aling Ting Toy/Once A Day	64	Coral 62444
Demilles (gm Carlo Mastrangelo)		
Donna Lee/Um-Ba-Pa	64	Laurie 3230
Cry And Be On Your Way/Lazy Love	64	Laurie 3247
Demires		
Wheels Of Love/The Spiders	59	Lunar 519
Demolyrs		
Rain/Hey Little Rosie	64	UWR 900/Jason 45-7
Demons (1) (Bobby & the)		
Oh, Dale/The Woo	60	MCI 1028
Demons (2) (Eddie Jones & the)		
The Greatest Of Them All/Long Tall Texan (with Jim Mann)	N/A	Kairay 1003
Demures		
Raining Teardrops/He's Got Your Number	63	Brunswick 55284
Denhams		
I'm So Lonely/Cry Baby Cry	57	Note 10009
Denims		
Sad Girl/Everybody Let's Dance	65	Columbia 43367
Dennis, Bradford (& group)		
The Wings Of An Angel/Hey Girl	N/A	Canadian 1600
Denny & Lenny (bb the Hollywood Ghouls)		
Monster's Love/Ghoul Love	63	Chance (N.Y.) 569
Denotations		
Nena/Lone Stranger	65	Lawn 253
Denton, Mickey (& group)		
Mi Amore/Ain't Love Grand	65	Impact 1002
Depippo Sisters		
This Time Last Year/He Said	64	Magnifico 104

ARTIST/SONG	YEAR	LABEL
Deputees (Peter Marshall & the)		
My Lovely One/Nice And Cozy	56	Melba 103
Derbys		
I Ain't Gonna Love You	53	Central 1001
Night After Night/Just Leave Me Alone	59	Mercury 71437
Lead Me On/Traveling Man	62	Savoy 1609
Any Old Way/The Huckster Man	63	KC 111
Derringers		
True Love, True Love (If You Cry)/Sheree	61	Capitol 4532
Maybe Baby/Don't Deceive Me	61	Capitol 4572
Desideros		
I Pledge My Love/Flat Foot Charlie	63	Renee 1040
Desires (1) (aka Jivetones)		
Bobby You/Cold Lonely Heart	58	Herald 532
Let It Please Be You/Hey, Lena	59	Hull 730
I Wanna Rendezvous With You/Set Me Free (My Darling)	60	Hull 733
A Talk To Mother	N/A	Hull (unreleased)
Coast Of Red	N/A	Hull (unreleased)
I Love Paris	N/A	Hull (unreleased)
Me And You	N/A	Hull (unreleased)
Sidewalks Of New York	N/A	Hull (unreleased)
So Close To An Angel	N/A	Hull (unreleased)
Desires (2)		
I Don't Know Why/Longing	60	20th Fox 195
Need Someone/Ha-Ha-Ha-Ha, Ha	62	Dee Impulse/ Moneytown 602 (62)
There I Go Again/I Never Loved Like This	62	Smash 1763
Desires (3) (aka Regents (3))		
Story Of Love/I Ask You	62	Seville 118
Desires (4)		
Phyllis Beloved/The Girl For Me	62	Dasa 102
Desires (5) (Rosko & the)		
Pledging My Love/The EMT	63	Domain 1021
Desires (6) (Julie & the)		
Kiss And Tell/Sand Dune	64	Laurie 3266
Destinaires		
Rag Doll/Teardrops (a capella)	65	Old Timer 609
Chapel Bells/It's Better This Way (a capella)	65	Old Timer 610
Diamonds And Pearls/More	65	Old Timer 613
You're Cheating On Me/The Spy	65	Old Timer 614
Destinations		
Valley Of Tears/Come On And Let Me Love You	61	Fortune 864
Tell Her/I'd Rather Be Hurt All At Once	66	Cameo 422
I Can't Leave You	N/A	Ando 114
Destineers		
So Young/Take A Look	62	RCA 8049
Determinations		
Only Love, Sweet Love/Memories Can't Be Broken	59	Space 304
Detroit Harmonettes		
I Gave Up Everything/I Need Thee	54	DeLuxe 6039

ARTIST/SONG	YEAR	LABEL
Detroit Jr. (& group)		
This Time For Christmas/Christmas Day	61	Foxy 002
Deuces Wild		
Meaning Of Love/I'm In A Whirl	58	Specialty 654
By Golly Gee/Just The Boy Next Door	60	Sheen 108
Devilles		
Joan Of Love/Tell Me So	59	Orbit 540
Mary Lou/Searching For Love	60	Jerden 107
Just Keep Me In Mind/Goddess Of Angels	60	Talent 103
Give Your Love To Me/Down On The Farm	61	Acclaim 1002
I Do Believe/No Money	62	Arrawak 1001
Devlin, Johnny (& group)		
Angel Of Love/Stayin' Up Late	62	Coral 62335
Devons		
Wise Up And Be Smart/Groovin' With My Thing	69	Mr. G 825
Devotions (1)		
Silly Milly/Worried About You Baby	58	Cub 9020
Devotions (2)		
Rip Van Winkle/I Love You For Sentimental Reasons	61	Delta 1001/Roulette 4406 (61)/ Roulette 4541 (64)
A Sunday Kind Of Love/Tears From A Broken Heart	64	Roulette 4556
Zindy Lou/Snow White	64	Roulette 4580
How Do You Speak To An Angel?/Teardrops Follow Me	N/A	Kape 701
Devotions (3) (Little Marcus & the)		
The Lone Stranger Went Mad/I'll Always Remember	64	Gordie 1001
Dew Drops (1) (Henry Clement & the)		
I'm So In Love With You/Please, Please Darling	61	Zynn 503
Dew Drops (1) (Little Clem & the) (aka Gaynotes)		
Plea Of Love/Waiting In The Chapel	58	Zynn 504
Dew Drops (2) (female)		
No Other Guy/Johnny Run Run	63	Jeff 1963
Dewdrops (Honey & the) (female)		
Come My Little Baby/Confucius Say	59	MMC 005
Dewtones		
Rockalick Baby	54	States (unreleased)
When My Baby Was Born	54	States (unreleased)
Diablos (aka Velvet Angels)		
Harriet/Come Home, Little Girl	58	Fortune 841
Playboy (Don't You Play In School)/I Won't Be Your Fool	63	Fortune 551
Fools Rush In	84	Fortune LP 8016
Old McDonald	84	Fortune LP 8016
Tender Passion	84	Fortune LP 8016
That's What You're Doing To Me	84	Fortune LP 8016
Wild Side Of My Baby	84	Fortune LP 8016
(So Long) Gee, I Hate To See You Go	84	Fortune LP 8020
Come Home With Me	84	Fortune LP 8020
Daddy Nolan Strong	84	Fortune LP 8020
I Want To Know	84	Fortune LP 8020
My Kind Of Lovin'	84	Fortune LP 8020
Remember Me (I'm The One Who Loves You)	84	Fortune LP 8020
Since I Fell For You & Rockin' Robin	84	Fortune LP 8020
Someday You'll Want Me To Want You	N/A	Fortune LP 8010

ARTIST/SONG	YEAR	LABEL
White Christmas	N/A	Fortune LP 8010

Diablos (Andre Williams & Gino Parks with the)

(Georgia May Is) Movin' (Andre Williams & Gino Parks)/ (H-mmm, Andre Williams Is) Movin'	60	Fortune 851

Diablos (featuring Nolan Strong) (aka Velvet Angels)

Adios My Desert Love/(I Want) An Old Fashioned Girl (as the Diablos)	54	Fortune 509/510
The Wind/Baby Be Mine	54	Fortune 511
Hold Me Until Eternity/Route 16	55	Fortune 514
Daddy Rockin' Strong/Do You Remember What You Did?	55	Fortune 516
The Way You Dog Me Around/Jump, Shake And Move	55	Fortune 518

Diablos (Nolan Strong & the) (aka Velvet Angels)

You Are/You're The Only Girl, Dolores	55	Fortune 519
A Teardrop From Heaven/Try Me One More Time	56	Fortune 522
Can't We Talk This Over?/The Mambo Of Love	57	Fortune 525
For Old Time's Sake/My Heart Will Always Belong To You	59	Fortune 529
I Am With You/Goodbye Matilda	59	Fortune 531
If I Could Be With You Tonight/I Wanna Know	59	Fortune 532
Since You're Gone/Are You Gonna Do	60	Fortune 536
Blue Moon/I Don't Care	62	Fortune 544
Mind Over Matter (I'm Gonna Make You Mine)/Beside You	62	Fortune 546
If I, Oh I/I Wanna Know	63	Fortune 532
I Really Love You/You're My Love	63	Fortune 553
You're Every Beat Of My Heart/(Yeah, Baby) It's Because Of You	63	Fortune 556
Are You Making A Fool Out Of Me/I Want To Be Your Happiness (N. S. with the Diablos & Tony Valla & the Alamos)	63	Fortune 564
(What Did That Genie Mean When He Said) Ali Coochie/ (You're Not Good Looking- But) You're Presentable	63	Fortune 569
Village Of Love/(I'm In Love) Real True Love	64	Fortune 563
The Way You Dog Me Around/Jump With Me (N.S. with the Diablos/a capella)	80	Fortune 574

Diadems

Goodnight Irene/I'll Do Anything	61	Goldie 715
Why Don't You Believe Me/Yes I Love You Baby	63	Star 514

Dials (1)

· Wondering About Your Love/Sorrento	60	Hilltop 2009
School Bells Are Ringing/Ring Ting-A-Ling	60	Hilltop 2010
Ring Ting-A-Ling/All Kinds Of Twistin'	60	Norgolde 105
No Hard Feelings/Win Yourself A Lover	61	Hilltop 219

Dials (2) (fb Sal Corrente/aka Sal Anthony)

These Foolish Things/At The Start Of A New Romance	62	Philips 40040

Dialtones (1)

Cherry Pie/Again	59	Dandy Dan 1
So Young/Chicago Bird	63	Lawn 203

Dialtones (2) (Johnny & the)

I Ran Around/My Dream Love	60	Jin 134

Dialtones (2) (Johnny Bersin & the)

The Only Girl/Don't Feel That Way	59	Jin 117

Dialtones (3) (aka Randy & the Rainbows)

Till I Heard It From You/Johnny	60	Goldisc 3005/Goldisc 3020 (61)

Diamond, Ronnie (& group)

Close To My Heart/Zig Zag	58	Imperial 5554

ARTIST/SONG	YEAR	LABEL
Diamonds (1)		
A Beggar For Your Kisses/Call Baby Call	52	Atlantic 981
Two Loves Have I/I'll Live Again	53	Atlantic 1003
Romance In The Dark/Cherry	53	Atlantic 1017
Diamonds (2)		
Black Denim Trousers And Motorcycle Boots/Nip Sip	55	Coral 61502
Be My Lovin' Baby/Smooch Me	55	Coral 61577
Why Do Fools Fall In Love/You Baby You	56	Mercury 70790
Church Bells May Ring/Little Girl Of Mine	56	Mercury 70835
Love, Love, Love/Ev'ry Night About This Time	56	Mercury 70889
Ka-Ding-Dong/Soft Summer Breeze	56	Mercury 70934
My Judge And Jury/Put Your House In Order	56	Mercury 70983
A Thousand Miles Away/Ev'ry Minute Of The Day	56	Mercury 71021
Little Darlin'/Faithful And True	57	Mercury 71060
Words Of Love/Don't Say Goodbye	57	Mercury 71128
Zip Zip/Oh, How I Wish	57	Mercury 71165
Silhouettes/Daddy Cool	57	Mercury 71197
The Stroll/Land Of Beauty	57	Mercury 71242
High Sign/Chick-Lets (Don't Let Me Down)	58	Mercury 71291
Kathy-O/Happy Years	58	Mercury 71330
Walking Along/Eternal Lovers	58	Mercury 71366
Young In Years/Twenty Second Day	59	Mercury 10017/ Mercury 71505 (59)
She Say (Oom Dooby Doom)/From The Bottom Of My Heart	59	Mercury 71404
Mother's Love/Gretchen	59	Mercury 71449
Holding Your Hand/Sneaky Alligator	59	Mercury 71468
Walkin' The Stroll/Batman, Wolfman, Frankenstein Or Dracula	59	Mercury 71534
Tell The Truth/Real True Love	60	Mercury 71586
Slave Girl/Pencil Song	60	Mercury 71633
You'd Be Mine/The Crumble	60	Mercury 71734
I Sho Lawd Will/You Short Changed Me	61	Mercury 71782
Munch/Woomai	61	Mercury 71818
One Summer Night/It's A Doggone Shame	61	Mercury 71831
The Horizontal Lieutenant/Vanishing American	62	Mercury 71956
Diante, Denny (& group)		
Little Lover/Faraway Places	64	Holiday 1210
What Makes Little Girls Cry	N/A	Holiday 1121
Diatones		
Oh, Baby, Come Dance With Me/Ruby Has Gone	60	Bandera 2509
Diaz, Vickie (& group)		
For Eternity/Your Mama Said No	60	Del-Fi 4149
Dickson, Richie (& group)		
You Broke My Heart/Moonlight And Roses	62	Class 308
Dikes		
Light Me Up/Don't Leave Me Poor	55	Federal 12249
Dillard, Varetta (bb the Four Students)		
Got You On My Mind/Skinny Jimmy	56	Groove 0159
Dimensionals		
Sleepy Time Girl/Drinkin' Pop Sodee Odee	53	Rainbow 219
Dimensions		
She's Boss/Penny	66	Panorama 25/HBR 1477 (66)/ Hanna Barbera 477 (66)
Baby What Do You Say/Knock You Flat	67	Panorama 41
Dimples (1) (Eddie Cooley & the)		
Priscilla/Got A Little Woman	56	Royal Roost 621

ARTIST/SONG	YEAR	LABEL
A Spark Met A Flame/Driftwood	57	Royal Roost 626
Hey You/Pull, Mon, Pull	57	Royal Roost 628
Leona/Be My Steady	59	Triumph 609
Priscilla/A Spark Met A Flame	60	Roulette 4272

Dimples (2)

Toy Telephone/Gimme Jimmy	58	Era 1079/Era 3079 (62)
Invitation To A Party/My Sister's Beau	59	Dore 517
Dreaming Of You/Please Don't Be Angry With Me	64	Cameo 325

DiMucci, Dion (& group)

Lonely Teenager/Little Miss Blue	60	Laurie 3070
Havin' Fun/Northeast End Of The Corner	61	Laurie 3081
Kissin' Game/Heaven Help Me	61	Laurie 3090
Somebody Nobody Wants/Could Somebody Take My Place Tonight?	61	Laurie 3101
Runaround Sue/Runaway Girl	61	Laurie 3110
The Wanderer/The Majestic	61	Laurie 3115
Runaround Sue/Ya Ya Twist (by Joey Dee & the Starliters)	61	Monument (No #)
Lovers Who Wander/(I Was) Born To Cry	62	Laurie 3123
Little Diane/Lost For Sure	62	Laurie 3134
Love Came To Me/Little Girl	62	Laurie 3145
Ruby Baby/He'll Only Hurt You	63	Columbia 42662
This Little Girl/The Loneliest Man In The World	63	Columbia 42776
Be Careful Of Stones That You Throw/ I Can't Believe (That You Don't Love Me Anymore)	63	Columbia 42810
Donna The Prima Donna/You're Mine	63	Columbia 42852
Drip Drop/No One's Waiting For Me	63	Columbia 42917
Sandy/Faith	63	Laurie 3153
Come Go With Me/King Without A Queen	63	Laurie 3171
Lonely World/Tag Along	63	Laurie 3187
Then I'll Be Tired Of You/After The Dance	63	Laurie 3225
I'm Your Hoochie Coochie Man/The Road I'm On	64	Columbia 42977
Johnny B. Goode/Chicago Blues	64	Columbia 43096
Shout/Little Girl	64	Laurie 3240
Unloved, Unwanted Me/Sweet Sweet Baby	65	Columbia 43213
Spoonful/Kickin' Child	65	Columbia 43293
I Got The Blues/(I Was) Born To Cry	65	Laurie 3303
Southern Train/I Can't Help But Wonder Where I'm Bound	69	Columbia 44719
I'm Your Hoochie Coochie Man/Gloria	69	Warner Bros.

DiMucci, Dion (bb the Wanderers)

Tomorrow Won't Bring The Rain/You Move Me, Babe	65	Columbia 43423

Ding Dongs (1) (aka Rinky-Dinks) (Featuring Bobby Darin)

Early In The Morning/Now We're One	58	Brunswick 55073

Ding Dongs (2)

Ding Dong/Sweet Thing	60	Eldo 109
Late Last Night/Lassie Come Home	60	Todd 1043

Ding-A-Lings

Oink Jones/C. Percy Mercy (Of Scotland)	60	Capitol 4467

Dingoes

What Would You Do/Dallas	57	Dallas 2001

Dinks

Ugly Girl/Rocka-Mow-Mow	66	Sully 925

ARTIST/SONG	YEAR	LABEL
Dinos		
Lover's Holiday	58	Fox 105
Darling Oh Darling/Twistin' Irene	62	Fox 0101
This Is My Story	N/A	Van 03265
Diplomats (1) (Debbie & the)		
Burnin' The Torch/Unchangeable Heart	58	Stepheny 1826
Diplomats (2) (Dino & the)		
My Dream/I Can't Believe	61	Laurie 3103
Hushabye My Love/Homework	61	Vida 0100/0101
Soft Wind/Such A Fool For You	61	Vida 0102/0103
Diplomats (3)		
Janie Girl/Let's Be In Love	61	May 105
Dippers (Georgie Torrence & the)		
So Good To Me (You've Been)/Go Away (Far Away)	60	King 5376
Such A Fool Was I/Way Over Yonder	61	Epic 9453
Together At Last/Fine Foxy Frame	65	Duo-Disc 117
Dischords		
Wipe Out/Mary's Little Lamb	63	Bonneville
Disciples		
I Found Out/Disciples	64	Fortune 573
Discorders		
Nothing Else Matters/My Hula Hula Lulu	57	Stepheny 1806
Discords (Eddie Quarter & the)		
The World Of Make Believe/Bad Habit	N/A	Smoke 101
Discounts (Bobby & the)		
Doreen	N/A	Generation 100
Distants		
Always/Come On	60	Northern 3732/ Warwick 546 (60)
Open Your Heart/Always	60	Warwick 577
Distants (Richard Street & the) (gm Eddie Kendricks)		
Answer Me/Save Me From This Misery	62	Harmon 1002
Dittos		
Come On Strong/Mustard	61	Warner Bros. 5247
Divots		
Diddy-Wah-Diddy/Missing You	61	Savoy 1596
Dry Cereal	N/A	Mark 3516
Dixon, Willie (& group)		
Twenty-Nine Ways/The Pain In My Heart	56	Checker 851
Do-Reys		
I Live For Your Love	N/A	Joy 2401
Do-Wells (Tony Morra & the)		
Looking For My Baby/I Can't Believe	60	Du-Well 1005
Dockett, Jimmy (& group)		
How Hurt I Am	N/A	Camille 3002
Dodd, Cally (& group)		
Too Young/Empty Halls	59	Calico 110

ARTIST/SONG	YEAR	LABEL
Dodgers (1)		
Let's Make A Whole Lot Of Love/You Make Me Happy	55	Aladdin 3259
Drip Drop/Cat Hop	55	Aladdin 3271
Dodgers (2)		
Pretty Baby/Boogie Man	57	Skyway 117
Oh Little One/Where Did The Bums Go	58	Skyway 118
Poor Little Fool/Big Mo	58	Skyway 119
Dollars (Little Eddie & the)		
Yellow Moon/My Momma Said	59	Fortune 845
Dollettes (Jimmy Carter & the)		
I'll Never Let You Go	N/A	Cayce 2002
Dolls (female)		
Tell Me Now/Suspicious Of You, Baby	58	Kangaroo 101
Just Before You Leave/I Love	58	Teenage 1010
In Love/Please Come Home	59	Okeh 7122
This Is Our Day/What's Next	65	Maltese 100
Dolphins (1) (Dougie & the)		
Yesterday's Dreams/Double Date	59	Angle Tone 542
Dolphins (2)		
Tell-Tale Kisses/I Found True Love	60	Shad 5020
Rainbow's End/One More For The Road	61	Empress 102
Hang On/Swingin' Soiree	63	Laurie 3202
Hey-Da-Da-Dow/I Don't Want To Go On Without You	64	Fraternity 937
Little Donna/Beautiful Woman	65	Fraternity 940
Surfin' East Coast/I Should Have Stayed	66	Yorkshire 125
Dolphins (3) (Davey Jones & the)		
Love Is Strange/Velvet Waters	61	Audicon 116
Bull Fight/Strictly Polynesian	61	Audicon 117
Dance Dance, Little Girl Dance/Annabelle-Lee	61	Sinclair 1005
Hell Cats/The Only Way To Fly	68	Tower 4527
Dolphins (4)		
Dance/Pony Race	62	Tip Top 2003/Gemini 501 (62)
It Might Break Your Heart/Why Will You Break My Heart	62	Tip Top 2005
Domains (Jerry Wright & the)		
Do You Remember/At The Party	60	Lanjo 2394
Domineers		
Nothing Can Go Wrong/Richie, Come On Down	60	Roulette 4245
Dominions		
Spanish Harlem/I Need Her	N/A	Graves 1091
Domino, Bobby (& group)		
Marilyn/Your Love For Me	61	Donna 1339
Dominoes (1) (Billy Ward & the) (fb Jackie Wilson)		
These Foolish Things Remind Me Of You/Don't Leave Me This Way	53	Federal 12129
Rags To Riches/Don't Thank Me	53	King 1280
Over The Rainbow/Give Me You	55	King 1502
Dominoes (1) (fb Clyde McPhatter)		
Harbor Lights/No! Says My Heart	51	Federal 12010
Sixty Minute Man/I Can't Escape From You	51	Federal 12022
I Am With You/Weeping Willow Blues	51	Federal 12039
That's What You're Doing To Me/ When The Swallows Come Back To Capistrano	52	Federal 12059
That's What You're Doing To Me/Love, Love, Love	52	Federal 12072

ARTIST/SONG	YEAR	LABEL
Dominoes (2) (Joe Taylor & the)		
Never Let Me Go/You Don't Love Me	N/A	HMF 2002
Dominos (Don & the)		
Weary Blues/Whole Lotta Love	62	Cuca 1109
Don Clairs (Harold Perkins & the)		
I Lost My Job/Santa Fe	58	Amp-3 1001/1002
Don Juans (1)		
I'm On My Merry Way	56	Fortune 831
Baby I Don't Care/Yum Yum	56	Jaguar 3020
Don Juans (1) (Andre Williams & the)		
Going Down To Tia Juana/Pulling Time	56	Fortune 824
It's All Over/Bobby Jean	56	Fortune 828
Just Because Of A Kiss/Bacon Fat	56	Fortune 831/Epic 9196 (56)
You Are My Sunshine (with Gino Purifoy)/Mean Jean	56	Fortune 834
My Tears (with Gino Purifoy)/Jail Bait (no group)	56	Fortune 837
Come On Baby/The Greasy Chicken (no group)	56	Fortune 839
My Last Dance With You/Hey! Country Girl	58	Fortune 842
Don Juans (1) (Don Lake & the)		
Ooh, Ooh, Those Eyes/Cha Cha Of Love	56	Fortune 520
Don Juans (1) (Joe Weaver & the)		
Baby I Love You So/It Must Be Love	56	Fortune 825
Baby Child/Looka Here, Pretty Baby	56	Fortune 832
Don Juans (1) (Little Eddie & the)		
This Is A Miracle/Calypso Beat	55	Fortune 836
Don Juans (1) (Marsha Renay & the)		
It's Nice/Our Cha-Lypso Of Love	60	Hi-Q 5017
Don Juans (2)		
The Girl Of My Dreams/Dolores	59	Onezy 101
Don-Tels		
I Found A Love/People Gonna Talk	63	Witch 119
Lonely Boy/The Old Man	63	Witch 121
Donato, Mike (& group)		
Dora/Summertime Love	N/A	PM 0101
Donays (female)		
Bad Boy/The Devil In His Heart	62	Brent 7033
Donettes (Don Eddy & the)		
Carrot Top/Sugar Coated Candy Kisses	60	Rona 1002
Donna Lou (& group)		
Only Heaven Knows	63	Lomar 703
Donnells (Jo Baby & the)		
I'm Gonna Move To The Outskirts/Little Sally Walker	65	Ty-Tex 114
Donnels (female)		
Johnny Oh/Here Comes The Bride	N/A	Alpha 001
Donnybrooks		
Every Time We Kiss/Break The Glass	59	Calico 108
Coming Home From School/Mandolins Of Love	59	Calico 112

ARTIST/SONG	YEAR	LABEL
Dons (1) (Gene Kennedy & the)		
If You Give Me A Chance/I'll Still Be Loving You	59	Paradise 112
Dons (2)		
Dream Girl/Marcheta	N/A	Heartbeat 1
Dontells		
Lover's Reunion/Make A Chance	63	Beltone 2040
In Your Heart/Nothing But Nothing	65	Vee Jay 666
I Can't Wait/Gimmie Some	N/A	Ambassador 3346
Doo Drops (Misty & the)		
Answer Me My Love/Come Shake Hands With A Fool	63	Imperial 5975
Doo Rays (Davey & the)		
It's The Beat/Do Dee Do Dee Do Wah	58	Guyden 2002
Doodlers		
Two Hearts/Don't Shake The Tree	55	RCA 6074
Dootones		
Teller Of Fortune/Ay, Si, Si	55	Dootone 366
Strange Love Affair/The Day You Said Goodbye	62	Dooto 470
Sailor Boy/Down The Road	62	Dooto 471
Dorells		
Maybe Baby/The Beating Of My Heart	63	Gei 4401/Atlantic 2244 (64)
Dories (female)		
I Loved Him So/Tragedy Of Love	59	Dore 528
Don't Jump/They Go Ape	60	Dore 556
Stompin' Sh-Boom/Breakup	62	Dore 629
Dorn, Jerry (bb the Hurricanes)		
Wishing Well/Sentimental Heaven	56	King 4932
The Key/Quicksand	57	King 5029
Dorsets		
Pork Chops/Cool It	61	Asnes 101
Dots (1) (fb Jeanette Baker) (female)		
I Confess/I Wish I Could Meet You	56	Caddy 101
I Lost You/Johnny	57	Caddy 107
Good Luck To You/Heartsick And Lonely	57	Caddy 111
Dots (2) (Lenny Capello & the)		
Cotton Candy/Tootles	60	Ric 960
Genevieve/90 Pound Weakling	62	Ric 991
Dots (3) (Tiny Dee & the)		
My Honey/Telegraph	63	Success 104
Double Daters		
Blondie Baby/Senior Stroll	58	Carlton 457
Beach Umbrella/Summer In The Mountains	58	Dot 15780
Double Dates		
I Love You Girl/Tatoo	59	Luck 103
Doug & Freddy (with the Pyramids)		
A Lover's Plea/I Believe In Love	598	Rendezvous 111
Doug & Freddy (bb the Pyramids)		
Need Your Love	598	K&G 100

ARTIST/SONG	YEAR	LABEL
Douglas, Ronnie (& group)		
You Say/Run, Run, Run	61	Everest 19413
Candy And Gum/You'll Come Back	61	Everest 19425
Say Didd-I-Lee Hey (Gonna See My Baby)/Worth Waiting For	65	Epic 9843
Dove, Diane (& group)		
Why/To Prove My Love	59	NRC 018
Dovells (fb Len Barry)		
No No No/Letters Of Love	61	Parkway 819
Bristol Stomp/Out In The Cold Again	61	Parkway 827 (first pressing)
Bristol Stomp/Letters Of Love	61	Parkway 827 (second pressing)
Do The New Continental/Mope-itty Mope Stomp	62	Parkway 833
Bristol Twistin' Annie/The Actor	62	Parkway 838
Hully Gully Baby/Your Last Chance	62	Parkway 845
The Jitterbug/Kissin' In The Kitchen	62	Parkway 855
You Can't Run Away From Yourself/Help Me Baby	63	Parkway 861
You Can't Sit Down/Stompin' Everywhere	63	Parkway 867
You Can't Sit Down/Wildwood Days	63	Parkway 867
Betty In Bermudas/Dance The Froog	63	Parkway 882
Stop Monkeyin' Aroun'/No No No	63	Parkway 889
Be My Girl/Dragster On The Prowl	63	Parkway 901
Happy Birthday Just The Same/One Potato, Two Potato	64	Parkway 911
Watusi With Lucy/What In The World's Come Over You?	64	Parkway 925
(Hey Hey Hey) Alright/Happy	65	Swan 4231
Happy Summer Days/Long After	66	Diamond 198
There's A Girl/Love Is Everywhere	66	MGM 13628
Here Comes The Judge/Girl (by the Magistrates)	68	MGM 13946
One Winter Love/Blue	69	Jamie 1369
Kiss The Hurt Away/He Cries Like A Baby	70	Decca 32919
Roll Over Beethoven/Something About You Boy	70	Event 3310
Mary's Magic Show/Don't Vote For Luke McCabe	72	MGM 14568
Sometimes/Far Away	72	Verve 10701
Dancing In The Street/Back On The Road Again	74	Event 216
Baby Work Out/Hully Gully Baby	83	Abkco 4029
L-O-V-E, Love/We're All In This Together	N/A	Paramount 0134
Dovers (1)		
Sweet As A Flower/Boy In My Life	59	Davis 465
The Sentence/Devil You May Be	61	New Horizon 501
Only Heaven Knows (a capella)	88	Relic LP 5075
Your Love (a capella)	88	Relic LP 5075
Dovers (1) (Miriam Grate & the)		
My Angel/Please Squeeze	55	Apollo 472
My Love	88	Relic LP 5075/Relic LP 5078 (89)
Dovers (2)		
Alice My Love/A Lonely Heart	62	Valentine 1000
Doves		
Don't Turn Away From Me/Let's Make Up	60	Big Top 3046
Down Beats		
Amor/Drifting Easy (instrumental)	60	Conn 201
Again/I'm Gonna Put You Down	61	Entente 001
Soul Fool/I Can't Hear You No More	65	Down Beat
Dedicated To The One I Love/Over My Room	65	Down Beat 1029
You're No Good/Bony Maronie	65	Down Beat 1030
Why Do You Love Another/You're The One	N/A	Dawn 1031
Say The Word/Together	N/A	Dawn 4531
Hard Rockin' Daddy/Down Beat (instrumental)	N/A	Dee-Cee 714
Downbeats (1)		
Come On Over/Lady Of The Sea	56	Sarg 162

ARTIST/SONG	YEAR	LABEL
Come On Over (Baby)/Darling Of Mine	56	Sarg 168
Run To Me, Baby/I Need Your Love	56	Sarg 173
I Couldn't See/Oh, Please	56	Sarg 186
Playing Possum/One At A Time	60	Wilco 16

Downbeats (1) (Beth Murphy with Gene Terry & the)
Where Were You/Walking On Air	59	Goldband 1083

Downbeats (1) (Gene Terry & the)
This Should Go On Forever	59	Goldband
No Mail Today/Never Let Her Go	59	Goldband 1081
Cinderella, Cinderella/Guy With A Million Dollars	59	Goldband 1088
Fine, Fine (with Ronnie Dee)/This Should Go On Forever	59	Savoy 1559

Downbeats (1) (O. S. Grant & the)
Falling Stars/I Just Can't Understand	56	Sarg 197
You Did Me Wrong/Tanya	56	Sarg 200

Downbeats (2)
My Girl/China Doll	56	Gee 1019
Let's Go Steady/So Many Tears	58	Peacock 1679
Someday She'll Come Along/You're So Fine	59	Peacock 1689
You Gotta Tell Me/It Won't Be Easy	62	Dynamite 243/Diamond 243

Downbeats (3)
Here	58	Safari 1010

Downbeats (4)
Request Of A Fool/Your Baby's Back	62	Tamla 54056

Downbeats (5)
Growing Love/Sweet Little Jane	N/A	Hampshire 1002

Downbeats (6)
1-2-3	N/A	Kanwic 137

Downes, Vinnie (& group)
Foolish Pride/An Angel Never Cries	59	Transcontinental 1011

Doyle, Dicky (& group)
Dreamland Last Night/My Little Darlin'	61	Wye 1009

Dragons (St. George & the)
Donna Alone	N/A	Dragon

Drakes (1)
Let Them Talk	55	States (unreleased)
Take A Giant Step	55	States (unreleased)

Drakes (2)
Oo Wee So Good/Kitty	58	Conquest 1001

Drakes (3)
I Made A Wish/Ole King Cole	65	Olimpic 252

Drapers (1)
Merry Go Round/The Love I Wish I Had	60	Unical 3001
Best Love/One More Time	60	Vest 831

Drapers (2) (ref Drifters)
You Got To Look Up/Your Love Has Gone Away	62	Gee 1081

Dream Girls (Bobbie Smith & the) (female)
Don't Break My Heart/Oh, This Is Why	59	Cameo 165
Crying In The Night/I'm In Love With You	59	Metro 20029

ARTIST/SONG	YEAR	LABEL
I Could Write A Book/Don't Break My Heart	60	Big Top 3059
Love Him/Heartaches	60	Metro 20034
Mr. Fine/Wanted	61	Big Top 3085
Dutchess Of Earl/Mine All Mine	62	Big Top 3100
Here Comes Baby/I Get A Feeling, My Love	62	Big Top 3111
Your Lovey Dovey Ways/Now He's Gone	62	Big Top 3129

Dream Kings

More Than Yesterday, Less Than Tomorrow/Oh, What A Baby	57	Checker 858

Dream-Timers (bb the Flippin' Teens Orchestra)

An Invitation/The Dancin' Lady	61	Flippin' 107

Dreamers (1)

No Man Is An Island/Melba	54	Rollin' 5/Rollin' 1001 (55)
Tears In My Eyes/535	55	Grand 131

Dreamers (2) (Eloise Brooks & the)

My Plea/Charles My Darling	55	Aladdin 3303

Dreamers (2) (fb Richard Berry)

Do Not Forget/Since You've Been Gone	56	Flip 319

Dreamers (2) (Jennell Hawkins & the)

Since You've Been Gone/Do Not Forget	61	Flip 354

Dreamers (2) (Richard Berry & the)

At Last/Bye, Bye	54	Flair 1052
Daddy, Daddy/Baby Darling	55	Flair 1058
Jelly Roll/Together	55	Flair 1075
Baby Baby	63	Crown LP 5371
Good Love	63	Crown LP 5371
I Am Bewildered	63	Crown LP 5371
Next Time	63	Crown LP 5371
Please Tell Me	63	Crown LP 5371
Pretty Brown Eyes	63	Crown LP 5371
The Big Break	63	Crown LP 5371
Wait For Me	63	Crown LP 5371

Dreamers (2) (Sidney Ester & the)

After You've Gone/Let Me Walk With You	59	Goldband 1087

Dreamers (3)

Right Time For Love/Girl Down The Street	56	ABC 9746

Dreamers (4) (female)

No Obligation/Lips Were Meant For Kissing	56	Manhattan 503

Dreamers (5)

Oh Yeah/Only Your Love	58	Bullseye 1013

Dreamers (6) (Joy Anthony & the)

Earth Angel/Eternally Yours	58	Sinclair 1001

Dreamers (7)

Don't Cry/It's Gonna Be Alright	59	Nugget 1000

Dreamers (8)

I Sing This Song (That's Why)/Mary's Little Lamb	60	Apt 25053
Natalie/Teenage Vows Of Love	60	Goldisc 3015
Mary Mary/Canadian Sunset	60	Guaranteed 219
Because Of You/Little Girl	61	Cousins 1005/May 133 (61)

Dreamers (9) (Donnie & the) (aka Kenny & the Whalers)

Carole/Ruby My Love	61	Decca 31312

ARTIST/SONG	YEAR	LABEL
Count Every Star/Dorothy	61	Whale 500
My Memories Of You/Teenage Love	61	Whale 505

Dreamers (10) (Leon & the)
If It Hadn't Been For You/Haircut	62	Parkway 843

Dreamers (11) (Hal Hedges & the)
On My Knees/Pennies From Heaven	63	ABC 10406

Dreamers (12)
Daydreamin' Of You/The Promise	63	Fairmount 612

Dreamers (13) (Denny & the)
Stars In The Sky	N/A	N/A

Dreamers (14)
Seconds/Mama Lucie	58	Dream 101

Dreamers (14) (Danny & the)
Forgive Me/Venus	60	Dream 7

Dreamers (15)
I Really Love You/You Made Me Darling	60	Blue Star 8001

Dreamliners
Just Me And You/Daiquiri (instrumental)	63	Cobra 013

Dreamlovers
Take It From A Fool/For The First Time	60	Len 1006
Annabelle Lee/Home Is Where The Heart Is	60	V-Tone 211
When We Get Married/Just Because	61	Heritage 102
Welcome Home/Let Them Love	61	Heritage 104
Zoom Zoom Zoom/While We Were Dancing	61	Heritage 107
Time/May I Kiss The Bride	61	V-Tone 229
If I Should Lose You/I Miss You	62	Down/End 1114 (62)
Sad Sad Boy/If I Were A Magician	63	Columbia 42698
Sad Sad Boy/Black Bottom	63	Columbia 42752
Pretty Little Girl/I'm Thru With You	63	Columbia 42842
Together/Amazons And Coyotes	63	Swan 4167/Casino 1308 (63)/ Swan 5619
These Will Be The Good Old Days/Oh Baby Mine	64	Cameo 326
You Gave Me Somebody To Love/Doin' Things Together With You	65	Warner Bros. 5619
Bad Times Make The Good Times/Bless Your Soul	66	Mercury 72595
Callin' Joann/You Gave Me Somebody To Love	66	Mercury 72630
Let Them Talk	82	Collectables LP 5004
Let's Twist Again	82	Collectables LP 5004
Mother	82	Collectables LP 5004
For The First Time	82	Collectables LP 5005/ Relic LP 5066

Dreams (1)
Darlene/A Letter To My Girl	54	Savoy 1130
I'm Losing My Mind/Under The Willow	54	Savoy 1140
I'll Be Faithful/My Little Honeybun	55	Savoy 1157

Dreams (2) (Frank Rossi & the)
Dream Boy/Around The Corner	57	Mark 7001

Dreams (3) (Johnny & the)
You're Too Young For Me/Are You With That	61	Richie 457

Dreams (4)
Too Late/Inexperience	62	Smash 1748
I Love You/Popeye	63	Talent 1004
Do What You Wanna/Do What You Wanna (instrumental)	69	DC 181

ARTIST/SONG	YEAR	LABEL
Dreams (5) (Darnell & the)		
The Day Before Yesterday/I Had A Love	64	West Side 1020/Cousins
Dreams (6)		
They Call Me Jesse James	68	DC
Dreams (6) (Frankie Carle & the)		
Don't Be Afraid/I'm So Glad	68	DC 180
Dreamtones		
Was I Dreaming/Say Hey Baby	57	Mercury 71222
Stand Behind Me/Love Me In The Afternoon	58	Klik 8505/Sold 501
A Lover's Answer/Mean Man	59	Astra 551
Praying For A Miracle/Jelly Bean	59	Express 501
Drew-Vels (Patti Drew & the)		
He's The One	N/A	N/A
Drifters		
Money Honey/The Way I Feel	53	Atlantic 1006
Summertime/Besame Mucho	53	Rama 22
Such A Night/Lucille	54	Atlantic 1019
Honey Love/Warm Your Heart	54	Atlantic 1029
Bip Bam/Someday You'll Want Me To Want You	54	Atlantic 1043
White Christmas/The Bells Of St. Mary's	54	Atlantic 1048
The World Is Changing/Sacroiliac Swing	54	Crown 108
Gone/What'cha Gonna Do	55	Atlantic 1055
Everyone's Laughing/Hot Ziggety	55	Atlantic 1070
Adorable/Steamboat	55	Atlantic 1078
Ruby Baby/Your Promise To Be Mine	56	Atlantic 1089
Soldier Of Fortune/I Gotta Get Myself A Woman	56	Atlantic 1101
Fools Fall In Love/It Was A Tear	57	Atlantic 1123
Hypnotized/Driftin' Away From You	57	Atlantic 1141
I Know/Yodee Yakee	57	Atlantic 1161
Drip Drop/Moonlight Bay	58	Atlantic 1187
There Goes My Baby/Oh My Love	59	Atlantic 2025
Dance With Me/(If You Cry) True Love, True Love	59	Atlantic 2040
This Magic Moment/Baltimore	60	Atlantic 2050
Let The Boogie Woogie Roll/Deep Sea Ball	60	Atlantic 2060
Lonely Winds/Hey Senorita	60	Atlantic 2062
Save The Last Dance For Me/Nobody But Me	60	Atlantic 2071
I Count The Tears/Suddenly There's A Valley	60	Atlantic 2087
Honky Tonk	60	Atlantic LP 8041
Sadie My Lady	60	Atlantic LP 8041
Souvenirs	60	Atlantic LP 8041
Some Kind Of Wonderful/Honey Bee	61	Atlantic 2096
Please Stay/No Sweet Lovin'	61	Atlantic 2105
Sweets For My Sweet/Loneliness Or Happiness	61	Atlantic 2117
Room Full Of Tears/Somebody New Dancin' With You	61	Atlantic 2127
When My Little Girl Is Smiling/Mexican Divorce	62	Atlantic 2134
Stranger On The Shore/What To Do	62	Atlantic 2143
Sometimes I Wonder/Jackpot	62	Atlantic 2151
Up On The Roof/Another Night With The boys	62	Atlantic 2162
On Broadway/Let The Music Play	63	Atlantic 2182
Rat Race/If You Don't Come Back	63	Atlantic 2191
I'll Take You Home/I Feel Good All Over	63	Atlantic 2201
Vaya Con Dios/In The Land Of Make Believe	64	Atlantic 2216
One Way Love/Didn't It	64	Atlantic 2225
Under The Boardwalk/I Don't Want To Go On Without You	64	Atlantic 2237
I've Got Sand In My Shoes/He's Just A Playboy	64	Atlantic 2253
Saturday Night At The Movies/Spanish Lace	64	Atlantic 2260
The Christmas Song/I Remember Christmas	64	Atlantic 2261
At The Club/Answer the Phone	65	Atlantic 2268
Chains Of Love/Come On Over To My Place	65	Atlantic 2285
Follow Me/The Outside World	65	Atlantic 2292

ARTIST/SONG	YEAR	LABEL
I'll Take You Where The Music's Playing/ Far From The Maddening Crowd	65	Atlantic 2298
We Gotta Sing/Nylon Stockings	65	Atlantic 2310
As Long As She Needs Me	65	Atlantic LP 8113
Desifinado	65	Atlantic LP 8113
I Wish Your Love	65	Atlantic LP 8113
More	65	Atlantic LP 8113
On The Street Where You Live	65	Atlantic LP 8113
Quando, Quando, Quando	65	Atlantic LP 8113
Temptation	65	Atlantic LP 8113
The Good Life	65	Atlantic LP 8113
Tonight	65	Atlantic LP 8113
What Kind Of Fool	65	Atlantic LP 8113
Who Can I Turn To	65	Atlantic LP 8113
Memories Are Made Of This/My Islands In The Sun	66	Atlantic 2325
Up In The Streets Of Harlem/You Can't Love Them All	66	Atlantic 2336
Baby What I Mean/Aretha	66	Atlantic 2366
Aint It The Truth/Up Jumped The Devil	67	Atlantic 2426
Still Burning In My Heart/I Need You Now	68	Atlantic 2471
Steal Away/Your Best Friend	69	Atlantic 2624
Black Silk/You Got To Pay Your Dues	70	Atlantic 2746
Be My Lady/A Rose By Any Other Name	71	Atlantic 2786
Kissin' In The Back Row of the Movies/I'm Feelin' Sad	74	Bell 45,600
Don't Cry On The Weekend	N/A	N/A
I Should Have Done Right	71	Atco LP 375
Three Thirty Three	71	Atco LP 375

Drifters (Charlie Thomas & the)

A Midsummer Night In Harlem/Lonely Drifter Don't Cry	N/A	N/A

Drifters (Charlie Thomas Group)

Peace Of Mind/The Struggler	73	Steeltown 671

Drifters (Johnny Moore Group)

Every Night/Something Tells Me	72	Bell 1269
You've Got Your Troubles/I'm Feeling Sad (And Oh So Lonely)	73	Bell 45,320
Like Sister And Brother/The Songs We Used To Sing	73	Bell 45,387
Say Goodbye To Angelina/I'm Free (For The Rest Of Your Life)	74	Bell 1339

Drivers (1)

A Man's Glory/Teeter Totter	54	Lin 1002

Drivers (2)

Smooth, Slow And Easy/Women	56	DeLuxe 6094
My Lonely Prayer/Midnight Hours	57	DeLuxe 6104
Oh, Miss Nellie/Dangerous Lips	57	DeLuxe 6117
Blue Moon/I Get Weak	57	RCA 7023

Drivers (3) (& the Spacemen)

Doe Doe/Ho Ho	59	Alton 252

Drivers (4)

Mr. Astronaut/Dry Bones Twist	62	King 5645

Du Droppers

Can't Do Sixty No More/Chain Me, Baby (Blues Of Desire)	52	Red Robin 108
I Wanna Know/Laughing Blues	53	RCA 5229
I Found Out (What You Do When You Go Around There)/ Little Girl, Little Girl (You'd Better Stop Talkin' In Your Sleep)	53	RCA 5321
Whatever You're Doin'/Somebody Work On My Baby's Mind	53	RCA 5425
Don't Pass Me By/Get Lost	53	RCA 5504
Come On And Love Me Baby/Go Back	53	Red Robin 116
Dead Broke/Speed King	54	Groove 0001
Just Whisper/How Much Longer?	54	Groove 0013
Let Nature Take It's Course/Boot 'Em Up	54	Groove 0036

ARTIST/SONG	YEAR	LABEL
Talk That Talk/Give Me Some Consideration	55	Groove 0104
You're Mine Already/I Wanna Love You	55	Groove 0120
Honeybunch	55	Groove EP only
I Only Had A Little	55	Groove EP only
Rollin' Stone	55	Groove EP only
Smack Dab In The Middle	55	Groove EP only
Story Untold	55	Groove EP only
That's All I Need	55	Groove EP only
You're Wrong	N/A	Groove unreleased
Baby Don't Leave Me In This Mood	N/A	unreleased
Balabam	N/A	unreleased
Drink Up	N/A	unreleased
Had To Play My Number	N/A	unreleased
If You Just Don't Leave	N/A	unreleased
My Thrill Girl	N/A	unreleased
Ten Past Midnight	N/A	unreleased
Train Keep Rolling On	N/A	unreleased
You've Been Good To Everybody	N/A	unreleased

Du Droppers (Sunny Gale & the)

Mama's Gone, Good Bye/The Note In The Bottle	53	RCA 5543

Du Droppers (Sunny Gale with the)

Goodnight, Sweetheart, Goodnight/Call Off The Wedding	54	RCA 5746

Du Mauriers

All Night Long/Baby, I Love You	57	Fury 1011

Dual Tones

Bubble Gum Bop/I'll Belong To You	60	Sabre 204

Duals (1)

Wait Up Baby/For Ever And Ever	57	Fury 1013

Duals (2)

Nearest To My Heart/Bye Bye	59	Arc 4446

Dubs

Angel Mine	55	unreleased
Hurry Up Honey	55	unreleased
Workin' For My Baby	56	unreleased
Could This Be Magic/Such Lovin'	57	Gone 5011/Musictone 1141 (61)
Don't Ask Me To Be Lonely/Darling	57	Johnson 102/Gone 5002 (57)/ Musictone 1142 (61)
Beside My Love/Gonna Make A Change	58	Gone 5020
Be Sure My Love/Song In My Heart	58	Gone 5034/Mark-X 8008 (60)
Chapel Of Dreams/Is There A Love for Me	58	Gone 5046/Gone 5069 (59)
Early In The Morning/No One	59	ABC 10056
Don't Laugh At Me/You'll Never Belong To Me	60	ABC 10100
For The First Time/Ain't That So	60	ABC 10150
If I Only Had Magic/Joogie Boogie	61	ABC 10198
Down, Down, Down I Go/Lullaby	61	ABC 10269
Now That We Broke Up/This To Me Is Love	61	End 1108
Two Hearts Are Better Than One	61	unreleased
You've Discovered Love	61	unreleased
You're Free To Go/Is There A Love For Me	62	Gone 5138
This I Swear/Wisdom Of A Fool	63	Josie 911
Your Very First Love/Just You	63	Wilshire 201
Could This Be Magic (version 2)/Blue Velvet	64	Lana 115
Your Very First Love/Don't Ask Me To Be Lonely (version 2)	64	Lana 116
We Three/We Build A Nest (by the Actuals)	73	Candlelite 438
Where Do We Go From Here/I Only Have Eyes For You	73	Clifton 2
Connie/Home Under My Hat	73	Johnson 097 (recorded in 1957)
Somebody Goofed/I Won't Have You Breaking My Heart	73	Johnson 098 (recorded in 1957)
You're Welcome/This To Me Is Love	75	Clifton 5

ARTIST/SONG	YEAR	LABEL

Dubs (Richard Blandon & the)

| I'm Downtown/Lost In The Wilderness | 71 | Vicki 229 |

Ducanes

| I'm So Happy (Tra La La)/Little Did I Know | 61 | Goldisc 3024 |

Duchesses (female) (aka Four Duchesses)

| Why/You Told Everyone But Me | 60 | Chief 7019 |
| Every Boy In Town/Will I Ever Make It | 60 | Chief 7023 |

Dudads

| I Heard You Call Me Dear/My Baby Misses Me Too | 55 | DeLuxe 6083 |

Dude (Dougie & the)

| Lifetime/Cowboy Joe | 63 | Amy 869 |

Dudes (gm Freddy Douglas)

| Who Would Have Thought/You Ought To Be Ashamed | 61 | Keith 6501 |

Duets (Leo & the)

| Down The Aisle/Goodnight Sweetheart | N/A | Co-Op 514 |

Dukays

The Girl's A Devil/The Big Lie	61	Nat 4001
Nite Owl/Festival Of Love	62	Nat 4002/Vee Jay 430 (62)
Please Help/I'm Gonna Love You So	62	Vee Jay 442
I Feel Good All Over/I Never Knew	62	Vee Jay 460
Combination/Every Step	63	Vee Jay 491
The Jerk/Mo' Jerk	64	Jerry-O 105
Mellow-Feznecky/Sho Nuf M.F.	64	Jerry-O 106

Duke Of Earl (& group) (aka Gene Chandler bb the Dukays)

| Daddy's Home/The Big Lie | 62 | Vee Jay 450 |

Dukes (1)

I'll Find Her/So Long Love	54	Specialty
Ooh Bop She Bop/Oh-Kay	54	Specialty 543
I'll Find A Love/Come On And Rock	55	Imperial 5344 (unreleased)
Someday Somewhere/Tell Me Why	56	Imperial 5385 (unreleased)
My Love Is Blue/I Was A Fool	56	Imperial 5399 (unreleased)
Teardrop Eyes/Shimmies And The Shakes	56	Imperial 5401
Lovin' You/Three Time Loser	56	Imperial 5408
Wini Brown/Cotton Pickin' Hands	56	Imperial 5415
Looking For You/Groceries, Sir	59	Flip 343
I Love You/Leap Year Cha Cha	59	Flip 345
Bad Luck Blues	N/A	Imperial unreleased
Lost Dreams	N/A	Imperial unreleased
The Last Ride	N/A	Imperial unreleased

Dukes (1) (Lloyd Price & the)

| Oo-Ee-Baby/Chee Koo Baby | 54 | Specialty 535 |

Dukes (2) (Billy Duke & the)

I Cried/The High And The Mighty	54	Coral 61203
Flip, Flop And Fly/Fun Lovin' Mama	55	Casino 138
This Is What I Ask/By Now	56	Sound 130
I Know I Was Wrong/Paradise Princess	56	Teen 110
Daddy Rock And Roll/Rocky Piano	56	Teen 112
Chalypso	57	Peak

Dukes (3) (Don Barber & the)

| What's Your Name/The Waddle | 60 | Thunderbird 105 |

Dukes (4) (Keith Alexander & the)

| Poor Orphan Boy/Cheater Sam | 62 | Gemini 901 |

ARTIST/SONG	YEAR	LABEL
Dukes (5) (Skip Arne & the)		
Sunshine And Rain/Angel	64	Little Fort 8688/Dot 16627 (64)
Dumonts		
But Only With You/Hoopla	61	King 5552
Dundees (Carlyle Dundee & the)		
Evil One/Never	54	Space 201
Dunes		
Lonely Sands/Sloppy Jalopy	61	Madison 156
Dungaree Darlings (female)		
Little Wallflower/Boy Of My Dreams	56	Rego 1003/Karen 1005 (59)
Dunham, Jackie (& group)		
Slow Down Your Life/I Think Of You	61	Imperial 5768
Dunhills		
Sound Of The Wind/Ricochet	N/A	Royal 110
Dunn, Leona (& group)		
Our Songs Of Love/Baby Don't Play Around	N/A	Hallmark 500
Duotones		
I Just Got Kissed/Tumblin' Down	N/A	Harlequin 611026
Duponts (1) (fb Little Anthony Gourdine)		
You/Must Be Falling In Love	55	Winley 212/Savoy 1552 (58)
Prove It Tonight/Somebody	57	Royal Roost 627
Duponts (2)		
Screamin' At Dracula's Ball/Half Past Nothing	58	Roulette 4060
Dupree, Lebron (& group)		
Wanda/Yea, Yea, Yea	59	Spann 411
Duprees		
You Belong To Me/Take Me As I Am	62	Coed 569
My Own True Love/Ginny	62	Coed 571
I'd Rather Be Here In Your Arms/I Wish I Could Believe You	63	Coed 574
Gone With The Wind/Let's Make Love Again	63	Coed 576
I Gotta Tell Her Now/Take Me As I Am	63	Coed 580
Why Don't You Believe Me/My Dearest One	63	Coed 584
Why Don't You Believe Me/The Things I Love	63	Coed 584
Have You Heard?/Love Eyes	63	Coed 585/Heritage 826 (69)
It's No Sin/The Sand And The Sea	64	Coed 587
Where Are You/Please Let Her Know	64	Coed 591
So Many Have Told You/Unbelievable	64	Coed 593
It Isn't Fair/So Little Time	64	Coed 595
I'm Yours/Wishing Ring	64	Coed 596
Around The Corner/They Said It Couldn't Be Done	65	Columbia 43336
She Waits For Him/Norma Jean	65	Columbia 43464
Let Them Talk/Exodus Song	66	Columbia 43577
It's Not Time Now/Don't Want To Have To Do It	66	Columbia 43802
Be My Love/I Understand	67	Columbia 44078
My Special Angel/Ring Of Love	68	Heritage 804
Goodnight My Love/Ring Of Love	68	Heritage 805
My Love, My Love/The Sky's The Limit	69	Heritage 808
Two Different Worlds/Hope	69	Heritage 811
The Sky's The Limit/Delicious	75	RCA 10407
Summertime	N/A	Regatta 2000
Dupries		
Baby Doll/Kissy Face	60	Thunderbird 106

ARTIST/SONG	YEAR	LABEL
Durhams		
Sincerely/Seconds Of Soul	65	Relic 1018
Don't Say We're Through (a capella)	75	Relic LP 103
Maureen (a capella)	75	Relic LP 103
This Is My Love (a capella)	75	Relic LP 103
I Remember (a capella)	75	Relic LP 104
Dusters		
Give Me Time/Sallie Mae	56	Arc 3000
Don't Leave Me Today/Why Do I Love You	56	Hudson 4
Pretty Girl/Coolation	57	ABC 9886
Darling Love/Teenage Jamboree	58	Glory 287
The Great Pretender	N/A	4 Hits EP only
Duvals (1)		
Guide Me/Happiness	56	Gee 1003
Duvals (2) (ref Five Crowns (1)/ref Drifters)		
You Came To Me/Ooh Wee Baby	56	Rainbow 335/Riviera 990 (56)
Duvals (3) (Phil Johnson & the) (aka Royal Notes)		
Kisses Left Unkissed/Three Speed Girl (by the Royal Notes)	58	Kelit 7032
I Lied To My Heart	58	Kelit 7033
Wee Small Hours/You Are My Love (by the Royal Notes)	58	Kelit 7034
Duvals (4)		
I Wanna Be Free/Yes I Do	61	La Salle 502
Duvals (5)		
What Am I/Cotton	63	Boss 2117/Red Rocket 471 (63)
Duvals (6)		
The Last Supper/Ferny Roast	63	Prelude 110
Duvells		
Danny Boy/How Come	62	Rust 5045
Dwellers		
Lonely Guy/Come Home Right Away	60	Conrose 101
Tell Me Why/Annie	58	Howard 503
Oh, Sweetie/What's That Thing Called Love	59	Oasis 101
Dymnestics (Evonne Robinson & the)		
Darling Hear My Plea	N/A	Spacey
Dyna-Sores		
Alley-Oop/Jungle Walk	60	Rendezvous 120
Dynamics (1)		
When The Saints Come Marching In/Gone Is My Love	57	Cindy 3005
Dynamics (2)		
A Hundred Million Lies/Ka Joom	57	Warner 1016
Enchanted Love/Happiness And Love	59	Arc 4450
No One But You/Always, I Have Loved You	59	Capri 104
Blue Moon/Pigeon	59	Delta 1002
Don't Leave Me/Wasted	59	Dynamic 1001
The Girl I Met Last Night/Nobody's Going Out With Me	59	Dynamic Sound 504
Aces Up/Baby	59	Guaranteed 201
Someone/Moonlight	59	Seeco 6008/Impala 501
Seems Like Only Yesterday/How Should I Feel	60	Decca 31046/Decca 31450 (62)
At The End Of Each Day/The Girl By The Gate	60	Decca 31129
If She Should Call/Dream Girl	61	Dynamic 1008
Wrap Your Troubles In Dreams/ I Can't Give You Anything But Love	61	Lavere 186

ARTIST/SONG	YEAR	LABEL
Christmas Plea/Dream Girl	62	Dynamic Sound 578/9
If I Give My Heart To You/Blind Date	62	Liban 1006
Misery/I'm The Man	63	Big Top 3161
Delsinia/So Fine	63	Dynamic Sound 1002/ Reprise 20183 (63)
Chapel On A Hill/Conquistador	63	Liberty 55628
I Wanna Know/And That's A Natural Fact	64	Big Top 516
Take The Freeway	N/A	Corsican 651

Dynamics (2) (fb Skip Milo)
Jo Baby/What's Wrong With Me	59	Arc 4453

Dynamics (3) (Johnny Christmas & the)
Soft Lips/Dum Dum	59	P.D.Q. 5002

Dynamics (4) (Ray Murray & the)
Baby What You Want Me To Do/With All My Love	60	Arbo 222

Dynamics (5) (Tony Maresco & the) (aka Anthony & the Sophomores)
Betty My Own/Forever Love	61	Herald 569

Dynamics (6) (Mickey Farrell & the)
Baby Mine/I'm Calling On You	63	Bethlehem 3080

Dynamics (7) (Susan & the)
Letter To An Angel/Happy Birthday To Julie	63	Dot 16476

Dynamics (8)
I Guess You Don't Love Me (No More)/Oh Night Of Nights	63	Do-Kay-Lo 101

Dynamics (9)
I Love To Be Loved/You Don't Seem To Realize	61	Douglas 200

Dynamics (10)
That's Bad/Nothing Can Change My Love For You (by the Bandits)	63	Emjay 1928/1935
This Love Of Ours/Nothing Can Change My Love For You (by the Bandits)	63	Emjay 1935

Dynamics (11)
Yes I Love You Baby/Soul Sloopy	N/A	Top Ten 100
Whenever I'm Without You/Love To A Guy	N/A	Top Ten 927

Dynamo, Skinny (& group)
So Long So Long/Jingle Bell	56	Excello 2097

Dynamos (1)
Woh Woh Yea Yea/Manhunt	61	Cub 9096
Teen Blues/Harem	61	Press 101

Dynamos (2)
Darling/No One But You	64	Azuza 1002

Dynatones
The Girl I'm Searching For/Pushin' And A-Slidin' (instrumental)	59	Bomarc 303

Dynels
Boy Friend/Let's Do It Again	62	Dot 16382
C'Mon Little Darlin'/Just A Face In The Crowd	64	Natural 7001

Eager, Johnny (& group)
So Glad/Stay By Me	59	End 1054
I Understand/Blessing Of Love	59	End 1061

Eagleaires
Cloudy Weather/Number One Baby	54	J.O.B. 1104

ARTIST/SONG	YEAR	LABEL
Eagles		
Please, Please/Tryin' To Get To You	54	Mercury 70391
(Will You, Won't You, Can't You)	54	Mercury 70464
Don't You Wanna Be Mine?/Such A Fool		
What A Crazy Feeling/I Told Myself	55	Mercury 70524
Kiss Them For Me/Ladies In The Sky	57	Prep 118
Earlington, Lyn (& group)		
Love Drops/My Last Phone Call	N/A	Lemonade 1501
Earls (1)		
Believe Me, My Love/Spinnin'	54	Gem 221/Crystal 100
My Marie/Out Of This World	54	Gem 227
Earls (1) (Paul Crawford & the)		
Let Me Back In There Again	56	DC 0400
Earls (2) (aka Five Thrills)		
Darlene	90	Relic LP 5087
Laverne	90	Relic LP 5087
Earls (3)		
My Hearts Desire/I'll Never Cry	61	Gone 5117
Life Is But A Dream/It's You	61	Rome 101
Life Is But A Dream/Without You	61	Rome 101
Lookin' For My Baby/Cross My Heart	61	Rome 102/Clifton 39 (74)
Remember Then/Let's Waddle	62	Old Town 1130
Never/Keep A-Tellin' You	63	Old Town 1133
Eyes/Lookin' My Way	63	Old Town 1141
Cry Cry Cry/Kissin'	63	Old Town 1145
I Believe/Don't Forget	64	Old Town 1149/Barry 1021
Ask Anybody/Oh What A Time	64	Old Town 1169
Remember Me Baby/Amor	65	Old Town 1181/1182
If I Could Do It Over Again/Papa	66	Mr. G. 801
My Lonely Lonely Room/It's Been A Long Time Coming	69	ABC 11109
Dreams Come True/My Heart's Desire	74	Clifton 47
Goin' Uptown/Mrs. Women	76	Columbia 10225
Stormy Weather/Could This Be Magic (by the Pretenders)	76	Rome 111/ Power-Martin 1005 (76)
Little Boy And Girl/Lost Love	76	Rome 112
Whoever You Are/Lost Love	76	Rome 113
All Through Our Teens/Whoever You Are	76	Rome 114
Get On Up And Dance The Continental/Love Epidemic	76	Woodbury 1000
Tonight (Could Be The Night)/Meditation	77	Woodbury 101
A Sunday Kind Of Love/Dream Come True	N/A	Harvey 100
Old Man River	N/A	Woodbury LP 104
Our Day Will Come	N/A	Woodbury LP 104
Out In The Cold Again	N/A	Woodbury LP 104
Earthboys		
Barbara Ann/Space Girl	58	Capitol 4067
Earthquakes		
Darling, Be Mine/Bashful Guy	59	Fortune 534
Earthquakes & Rhythm Kings		
This Is Really Real/Crazy Bop	60	Fortune 538
Earthquakes (Armando King with the)		
Look What You've Done/Baby, Only You	62	Fortune 549
Earthquakes (Tino Cairo with the)		
Love In Portofino/Wow Baby Sitter	57	Hi-Q 5020

ARTIST/SONG	YEAR	LABEL
East-Men (Hal Jaxon & Watsie Lumbard & the) (aka Eastmen)		
Hum-Dibby-Do-Wah/Passion	N/A	Glow 100
Eastmen (ref Del Vikings)		
Lover, Come Home/Bye, Bye, My Baby	59	Mercury 71434
Ebb Tides		
Only Be Mine/What's Your Name Dear	57	Teen 121
Ebb Tides (Nino & the)		
Franny Franny/Darling I'll Love Only You	57	Acme 720
Puppy Love/You Make Me Want To Rock And Roll	58	Recorte 405
Purple Shadows/The Real Meaning Of Christmas	58	Recorte 408
I'm Confessin'/Tell The World I Do	59	Recorte 409
I Love Girls/Don't Look Around	59	Recorte 413
Tonight/Nursery Rhymes	61	Madison 151
Those Oldies But Goodies (Remind Me Of You)/Don't Run Away	61	Madison 162
Juke Box Saturday Night/(Someday) I'll Fall In Love	61	Madison 166
Little Miss Blue/Someday	61	Marco 105
A Happy Guy/Wished I Was Home	61	Mr. Peacock 102
Stamps Baby Stamps/Lovin' Time	62	Mr. Peacock 117
Low Tide/A Ballad Of Jed Clampett	62	R&R 303
A Week From Sunday/Say No More	63	Mr. Peeke 123
(by Miss Frankie Nolan with the Ebbtides)		
Automatic Reaction/Linda Lou Garrett (Likes 24 Karat)	64	Mala 480
Mr. Moto/Surfin' '69	69	R&R
Ebb Tones		
Boogie Woogie/Rebel Beat	61	Bee 301
Ebb Tones (Don Grissom & the)		
Recess In Heaven/Just Fall In Love	56	Million $ 2011
Baby Stop	56	Million $ 2012
Ebb-Tones		
I Want You Only/That's All	56	Crest 1016
Baby/What Makes A Man Fool Around?	56	Crest 1024
Dust Off The Bible/Hum	57	Crest 1032
Ebbonaires (Jackson Trio & the) (aka Ebonaires)		
Let's Kiss Hello Again/Jivarama Hop	56	Hollywood 1062
Ebbs (aka Ebb Tides)		
Cartoons/Vickie Sue	59	Dore 521
Ebbtides (1) (David Ford & the)		
My Confession/The Sound Of Your Voice	56	Specialty 588
Ebbtides (2)		
Come On And Cry/Straightaway	62	Monument 520
Ebbtides (3) (ref Rivingtons)		
Lonesome/Love Doctor	59	Jan-Lar 101
Ebbtides (4)		
Star Of Love/First Love	64	Duane 1022
Ebbtones		
I've Got A Feeling/Danny's Blues	57	Ebb 100
Ebon-Knights		
Poor Butterfly/The Way The Ball Bounces	58	Stepheny 1817
First Date/Only Only You	58	Stepheny 1822

ARTIST/SONG	YEAR	LABEL
Ebonaires		
Love For Christmas/Jingle Bell Hop	55	Hollywood 1046
The Very Best Luck In The World/Hey, Baby, Stop	56	Money 220
We're In Love/Thinkin' And Thinkin'	59	Colonial 117
Love Call/Somewhere In My Heart	59	Lena 101
Love Call/Don't Leave Me Baby (a capella) (by the Camelots)	64	Cameo 334
Bring Me A Bluebird	88	Relic LP 5076
Doodle Doo Doo	88	Relic LP 5076
Rosetta	88	Relic LP 5076
Sioux City Sioux	88	Relic LP 5076
Sposin'	88	Relic LP 5076
You	88	Relic LP 5076
Ebonaires (bb the Maxwell Davis Orch.)		
Three O'Clock In The Morning/Baby, You're The One	53	Aladdin 3211
You're Nobody Till Somebody Loves You/Lawd, Lawd, Lawd	53	Aladdin 3212
Ebonettes (female)		
All Alone/Wild Man Walk	58	Ebb 147
Eboniers		
Hand In Hand/Shut Your Mouth	59	Port 70013
Ebony Moods		
I've Got News For You/Grand, Nice, Swell	55	Theron 108
Eccentrics		
Share Me/Stars	64	Applause 1008
Echelons		
A Christmas Long Ago	N/A	N/A
Echoes (1)		
All That Wine Is Gone/Please Say You're Mine	53	Rockin' 523
My Little Honey/Aye Senorita	56	Combo 128
Have A Heart	87	Relic LP 5069
Take My Hand	88	Relic LP 5076
Echoes (1) (Allan Roberts & the)		
School Days/Walk In With Love	N/A	Spotlight 101
Echoes (2) (Benny Barnes & the)		
Lonely Street/Moon Over My Shoulder	58	Mercury 71284
Echoes (3) (Frankie & the)		
Come Back Baby/Until We Meet Again	58	Savoy 1544
Echoes (4)		
Ding Dong/My Heart Beats For You	57	Gee 1028
Over The Rainbow/Someone	57	Specialty 601
Bye-Bye My Baby/Do I Love You	60	Columbia 41549
Loving And Losing/Ecstasy	60	Columbia 41709
Born To Be With You/My Guiding Light	60	Dolton 18
Angel Of Love/Twistin' Town	61	Hi Tide 106/Felsted 8614 (61)
Angel Of My Heart/Gee Oh Gee	61	Seg-Way 1002
Sad Eyes/It's Rainin'	61	Seg-Way 106
Baby Blue/Boomerang	61	SRG 101/Seg-Way 103 (61)
Love Candy/Paper Roses	65	Ascot 2188
Soldier Boy	N/A	4 Hits EP 11
Echoes (4) (Sonny Roberts & the)		
Honey Chile/I'll Never Let You Go	58	Impala 1001
Scratch My Back/The Little Green Man	58	Swan 4013
Echoes (5)		
Time/Dee-Dee-Di-Oh	59	Andex 22102

ARTIST/SONG	YEAR	LABEL
Echoes (6) (Jerry Starr & the)		
Teenage Tangle/Do Be True	59	Ron 321
Echoes (7)		
Bluebirds Over The Mountain/A Chicken Ain't Nothin' But A Bird	62	Smash 1766
Keep An Eye On Her/A Million Miles From Nowhere	63	Smash 1807
Annabelle Lee/If Love Is	63	Smash 1850
Echoes (8) (Billy & the)		
Come Softly/Bodacious Twist	62	Gala 121
Echoes (9) (Mitch & the)		
One Chance/I Could Try	63	Bethlehem 3077
Echoes (10) (Tommy Vann & the)		
Too Young/Give A Little Bit	66	Academy 118
Is This Love/What Can You Do With A Broken Heart	66	Academy 123
I'm Hopin' You'll Be Mine	N/A	Hollywood 101
Echoes (11)		
Without You/Heartbeat	60	Edco 100
Echolettes		
My Beau Joe/My Baby Loves Me	63	Imperial 5934
Echomores		
Cute Chick/Little Chick	N/A	Rocket 1042
Echotones		
So In Love/My Baby Doll	59	Dart 1009
Echotones (Skip & the)		
Born To Love/Ooh-La-La	59	DR 1001/Warwick 634 (60)
Ecstasies		
That Lucky Old Sun/A Time For Love	62	Amy 853
Ecuadors		
Say You'll Be Mine/Let Me Sleep Woman	59	Argo 5353
You're My Desire/Someone To Call My Own	61	Miracle 7
Edsels		
Lama Rama Ding Dong/Bells	58	Dub 2843
Do You Love Me?/Rink-A-Din-Ki-Do	59	Roulette 4151
What Brought Us Together?/Don't Know What To Do	60	Tammy 1010
My Jealous One/Bone Shaker Joe	61	Capitol 4588
Shake Shake Sherry/If Your Pillow Could Talk	61	Capitol 4675
Rama Lama Ding Dong/Bells	61	Dub 2843/Twin 600/Winley 700/Musictone1144 (61)
Three Precious Words/Let's Go	61	Tammy 1014/Ember 1078 (61)
The Girl I Love/Got To Find Out About Love	61	Tammy 1023
Count The Tears/Twenty Four Hours	61	Tammy 1027
Shaddy Daddy Dip Dip/Don't You Feel	62	Capitol 4836
Could It Be/My Whispering Heart	62	Dot 16311
Edwards, Jack (& group)		
All Night Long/When We Get The Word	63	Michelle 508
Edwards, Joey (& group)		
This Little Girl/Shirley Shirley	60	Lilly 501
Edwards, Sonny (& group)		
This Time I'm Gonna Cry	63	Cavetone 508
I Love You Tenderly	63	Cavetone 516

ARTIST/SONG	YEAR	LABEL

Efics (with Harvey Connell)
| Autumn Heart/Sentimental Journey | 61 | Fraternity 891 |

Egyptian Kings (aka Four Pharaohs)
| Give Me Your Love/Baby I Need Love | 63 | Nanc 1120 |
| School Days/The Move Around | N/A | unreleased |

Egyptians
| That's Alright/Flippin' Their Top | N/A | Danae 1002 |

Egyptians (King Pharaoh & the) (aka Four Pharaohs)
| By The Candlelite/Shimmy Sham | 61 | Federal 12413 |

Ekhoes (Con Pierson & the)
| I Heard Those Bells/Six Pretty Girls | 64 | LeMans 007 |

El Caminos (Mr. Lee & the)
| My Woman/I'm A Hog For You Baby | 64 | Camelot 107/Nolta |

El Capris
(Shimmy, Shimmy) Ko Ko Wop/Oh, But She Did	56	Bullseye 102/Argyle 10 (61)
Your Star/To Live Again	57	Fee Bee 216
They're Always Laughing At Me/Ivy League Clean	58	Paris 525
Safari/Quit Pulling My Woman	65	Ring-O 308

El Capris (fb Sam Crunby)
| Girl Of Mine/These Lonely Nights | 58 | Hi-Q 5006 |

El Deens
| Why Can't I Find You/My Love For You | 59 | Federal 12347 |
| Where Are You/Club For Broken Hearts | 59 | Federal 12356 |

El Domingoes
| Evening Bells/I'm Not Kidding You | 58 | Kappa Rex 206/ Candlelite 418 (74) |

El Domingos
| Lucky Me, I'm In Love/Made In Heaven | 62 | Chelsea 1009/ Candlelite 418 (74) |
| Are You Ready To Say I Do/I Want To Know | 64 | Karmin 1001 |

El Dorados (1)
Baby I Need You/My Lovin' Baby	54	Vee Jay 115
One More Chance/Little Miss Love	55	Vee Jay 127
At My Front Door/What's Buggin' You, Baby?	55	Vee Jay 147
I'll Be Forever Loving You/I Began To Realize	55	Vee Jay 165
Now That You've Gone/Rock 'n' Roll's For Me	56	Vee Jay 180
A Fallen Tear/Chop Ling Soon	56	Vee Jay 197
Bim Bam Boom/There In The Night	56	Vee Jay 211
Tears On My Pillow/A Rose For My Darling	57	Vee Jay 250
Three Reasons Why/Boom Diddle Boom	57	Vee Jay 263
Lights Are Low/Oh What A Girl	58	Vee Jay 302
In Over My Head/You Make My Heart Sing	70	Torrid 100
She Don't Run Around	81	Charly LP 1022
Trouble Trouble	81	Charly LP 1022
Love Of My Own	84	Solid Smoke LP 8025
It's No Wonder	N/A	Oldies 45

El Dorados (1) (with Hazel McCollum)
| Annie's Answer/Living With Vivian (Al Smith's Combo) | 54 | Vee Jay 118 |

El Dorados (2) (aka Kool Gents)
| Since You Came Into My Life/Looking In From The Outside | 71 | Paula 347 |
| Loose Bootie/Loose Bootie (instrumental) | 72 | Paula 369 |

El Jays (Leo Wright & the)
| It Is I/I Wonder | N/A | CB 5008/Pam |

ARTIST/SONG	YEAR	LABEL
El Pollos		
School Girl/Why Treat Me This Way?	57	Neptune 1001
High School Dance/These Four Letters	58	Studio 999
Three Little Letters	N/A	N/A
El Rays (1) (aka Dells)		
Darling I Know/Christine	54	Checker 794
El Rays (2) (female)		
Till The End Of Time/My Baby From Me	63	M.M. 104/Wolf 104
El Reyes (aka El Reys)		
Mr. Moonglow/Need Your Love	58	Jade 501
El Reys (aka El Reyes)		
Diamonds And Pearls/Rocket Of Love	65	Ideal 94706
Beverly/Angalie	65	Ideal 95388
El Sierros (aka Tommy & the Tears/aka Tear Stains)		
Sunday Kind Of Love/Daddy's Comin' Home	63	Yussels 7702
Life Is But A Dream/Pretty Little Girl	64	Times Square 101
Love You So/Valerie	64	Times Square 29/Relic 534 (65)
Picture Of Love/Sweeter Than (by the Young Ones)	64	Times Square 36/Relic 527 (65)
El Tempos		
My Love Grows Deep/My Dream Island	63	Vee Jay 561 (first pressing)
My Dream Island/My Love Goes Deep Within	63	Vee Jay 580 (second pressing)
El Tempos (Big Mike Gordon & the)		
Rain Or Shine/Down In New Orleans	55	Savoy 1152
El Tempos (Mike Gordon & the)		
You Got To Give/Why Don't You Do Right?	54	Cat 101
El Tones		
Like Mattie/Lovin' With A Beat	58	Cub 9011
El Torros (1)		
Dance With Me/Yellow Hand	57	Duke 175
You Look Good To Me	58	Duke 194
What's The Matter/Dance With Me	60	Duke 321
You May Say Yes/Two Lips	61	Duke 333
Mama's Cookin'/Doop Doop A Walla Walla	62	Duke 353
El Torros (2)		
All The Tears Is Gone/Love Is Love	58	Fraternity 811
El Venos (aka El Vinos)		
Now We're Together/Geraldine	56	Groove 0170
My Heart Beats Faster/You Must Be True	57	Vik 0305
My Heart Beats Faster/You WON'T Be True	64	RCA 8303
El Vireos		
First Kiss/Silly Willy	59	Revello 1002
El-Derocks		
Back Room	58	Sapphire 1004
El-Rich Trio		
This I Swear/House Of Blue Lights	N/A	Elco SK-1
Elads (aka Little Joey & the Flips)		
African Twist/Ring Dong	N/A	unreleased

ARTIST/SONG	YEAR	LABEL

Elbert, Donnie (& group)
My Confession Of Love/Peek-A-Boo	58	DeLuxe 6161

Elchords (Butchie Saunders & the)
Peppermint Stick/Gee, I'm In Love	57	Good 544/Musictone 1107 (59)

Eldaros
Rock-A-Bock/Please Surrender	58	Vesta 101/102

Eldees
Don't Be Afraid To Love/You Broke My Happy Heart	N/A	Dynamics 1013

Elder, Nelvin (& group)
I Dream/Find Me A Dream	61	Brent 7027

Eldorays
Nights Of Ecstacy/Everything's Gonna Be Alright	61	Bud 114

Electras
You Lied/Ten Steps To Love	61	Infinity 012/Constellation
Boo Babe/The Stomp	62	Infinity 016
You Know/Boo Baby	62	Lola 100
You Know/Don't Tell Me (by the Surgeons)	63	Cee Jam 100
Boo Baby/Can't You See It In My Eyes	63	Challenge 59245
Little Girl Of Mine/Mary, Mary	66	Ruby-Doo 2

Electronaires (Chuck Ranado & the)
My Baby's Gone/Why Did I Cry	56	Count 507

Electrons
For Sale/They Talk Too Much	64	Laguna 103

Elegant IV
Time To Say Goodbye/I'm Tired	61	Cousins 1005/ Mercury 72516 (65)

Elegants
Little Star/Getting Dizzy	58	Apt 25005
Please Believe Me/Goodnight	58	Apt 25017
True Love Affair/Payday	59	Apt 25029
Little Boy Blue (Is Blue No More)/Get Well Soon	59	Hull 732
Let My Prayers Be With You/Speak Low	60	United Artists 230
I've Seen Everything/Tiny Cloud	61	ABC 10219
Happiness/Spiral	61	United Artists 295
Promises/The Young Years	63	Limelight 3013
A Dream Can Come True/Dressin' Up	63	Photo 2662
Barbara, Beware/A Letter From Vietnam	65	Laurie 3283
Bring Back Wendy/Wake Up	65	Laurie 3298
Lonesome Weekend/It's Just A Matter Of Time	74	Bim Bam Boom 121
I Tried/Love Me And Don't Fool Around	N/A	Elegants 101
Still Waiting	N/A	Hull LP 1002
Rain Rain Go Away	N/A	United Artists (unreleased)

Elegants (Vito Piccone with the)
Path In The Wilderness/Get On The Right Track	63	IPG 1016

Elegants (Vito & the)
Belinda/Lazy Love	65	Laurie 3324

Elektras
Poor Amigos Rock/Little Lamb	60	End 1082
All I Want To Do Is Run/It Ain't As Easy As That	63	United Artists 594

Elements
Lonely Hearts Club/Bad Man	60	Titan 1708

ARTIST/SONG	YEAR	LABEL
Elgins (1)		
Mademoiselle/A Picture Of You	58	MGM 12670
Uncle Sam's Man/Casey Cop	61	Flip 353
Extra, Extra/My Illness	61	Titan 1724 (first pressing)
Heartache Heartbreak/My Illness	61	Titan 1724 (second pressing)
Cheryl/Tell Gina	63	Dot 16563
Johnny I'm Sorry/A Winner Never Quits	63	Lummtone 109
Johnny I'm Sorry/You Got Your Magnet On Me Baby	63	Lummtone 110
Finally/I Lost My Love In The Big City	63	Lummtone 112
Once Upon A Time/The Huddle	64	Joed 716
Your Lovely Ways/Finding A Sweetheart	64	Lummtone 113
Elgins (2) (Little Tommy & the)		
Never Love Again/I Walk On	62	Elmar 1084/ABC 10358 (62)
Elgins (3)		
The Times We've Wasted/Ritha Mae	64	Congress 214
Here In Your Arms/We're Gonna Have A Good Time	64	Congress 225
Street Scene/You Found Yourself Another Fool	65	Valiant 712
Elgins (4) (De Jan & the)		
That's My Girl/Heartbeat (by the Whirlwinds (1))	67	Times Square 112
Elgins (5)		
Pretending/Lonesome	N/A	A-B-S 113
Elites (1)		
You Mean So Much To Me/Tell Him Again	54	Hi-Lite 106
Tree Of Love/You'll Break Two Hearts	63	ABC 10460
Elites (2)		
In The Little Chapel/Northern Star	59	Abel 225
Elites (3) (female)		
Dapper Dan/Darling What About You	60	Chief 7028
Jack The Ripper/Mama Look At Me	60	Chief 7032
Come On And Dance/The Blues	61	Chief 7040
Eljays (Leo Wright & the)		
It Is I/I Wonder	62	CB 5008/Red Fox 103 (65)
Ellingtons		
Hurry Home	64	G-Clef 708
Elliots (Andre & the)		
Willie Jones Got Married/Willie Jones	62	Barry 106
Ellis Brothers		
Wow Baby/Sneaky Alligator	58	ABC 9954
Ellis, Lorraine (bb the Crows)		
Piano Player Play A Tune/Perfidia	54	Gee 1/Bullseye 100 (55)
Elrods (Ronnie Speeks & the)		
What Is Your Technique/Please Wait For Me	61	King 5548
Eltones (Joanne Boswell & the)		
You Were Meant For Me/I Won't Be Your Fool	60	Chief 800
Emanon Four		
Oh! That Girl/Blues For Monday	56	Flash 106
Emanons (1)		
Change Of Time/Hindu Baby	56	Gee 1005
Blue Moon/Wish I Had My Baby	56	Josie 801

ARTIST/SONG	YEAR	LABEL

Emanons (2)
We Teenagers (Know What We Want)/Dear One	58	Winley 226/ABC 9913 (58)
Connie/Buzz Buzz	N/A	Connie (unreleased)
You Know I Miss You	N/A	GGS 443

Emanons (3)
Ol' Man River/Emanons Rock	60	Delbert 5290

Emberglows
Sack And Chemise Gang Fight/Have You Found Someone New	61	Dore 591
Sentimental Reasons/Make Up Your Mind	62	Amazon 1005

Embers (1)
Paradise Hill/Sound Of Love	53	Ember 101/Herald 410 (53)
Sweet Lips/There'll Be No One Else But You	54	Columbia 40287

Embers (2)
Wait For Me/Couldn't Wait Any Longer	60	Dot 16101
My Dearest Darling/Please, Mr. Sun	60	Dot 16162

Embers (2) (Willis Sanders & the)
Your Souvenirs/Taking A Chance On You	57	Juno 213/Jvpiter 213 (57)
Honey-Bun/Lovable	58	Millionaire 775/Unart 2004 (58)
Time Out For Tears/Hungry For Your Love	59	Coral 62146

Embers (3) (Frankie Joe & the)
Down Be The Stream/Margaritte	57	Fee Bee 224

Embers (4) (Jeff Milner & the)
No Greater Love/Let Me Know, Let Me Know, Let Me Know	59	Dale 113
My Vow To You/Then (I'll Stop Loving You)	59	Dale 114

Embers (5) (Billy Scandlin & the)
You'll Always Have Someone/I Keep On Walking	59	Viking 1002

Embers (6) (Jerry Bright & the)
Be Mine/I'll Always Be	59	Yucca 143

Embers (7) (Joe D'Ambra & the)
Please Come Home/Don't Forget To Write	60	Mercury 71725

Embers (8)
Solitaire/I'm Feeling Alright Again	61	Empress 101
I Won't Cry Any More/I Was Too Careful	61	Empress 104
Abigail/I Was Too Careful	61	Empress 107
What A Surprise/I Was Too Careful	61	Empress 108
I Wish I Didn't Love You So	N/A	Valmor

Embers (9) (Ray Allen & the)
Ham The Space Monkey/The Wibble	61	Sinclair 1002

Embers (10) (Pete Bennett & the)
Fever/Soft	61	Sunset 1002

Embers (11)
In My Lonely Room/Good Good Lovin'	64	JCP 1008

Embers (12) (Gene Pitney & the)
Darkness	90	Relic LP 5085
Runaway Lover	90	Relic LP 5085
So Tired	90	Relic LP 5085
Victory	90	Relic LP 5085

ARTIST/SONG	YEAR	LABEL
Embers (12) (Larry Lee & the)		
That Little Girl Was Mine	90	Relic LP 5085
Tremble	90	Relic LP 5085
Winter's Romance	90	Relic LP 5085
Embers (13)		
I Wonder Why/Little Girl Next Door	65	Ara 210
Embertones		
I Remember/Falling For You	62	Bay 203
Emblems (1)		
Please Forgive Me	59	Topic 8570
Poor Humpty Dumpty/Would You Still Be Mine	62	Bay Front 107
Too Young/Bang Bang, Shoot 'Em Up Daddy	62	Bay Front 108
Emblems (2) (Eddie Carl & the)		
Little Willie Wampum/Every Little Dream Comes True	62	Oh My 1000
The Thrust, Pt. 1/The Thrust, Pt. 2	62	Oh My 1001
Emblems (3) (Patty & the)		
Mixed Up, Shook Up Girl/Ordinary Guy	64	Herald 590
The Sound Of Music Makes Me Want To Dance/ You Took Advantage Of A Good Thing	64	Herald 593
You Can't Get Away From Me/And We Danced	64	Herald 595
Easy Come, Easy Go/It's The Little Things	66	Congress 263
Let Him Go Little Heart/Try It, You Won't Forget It	66	Kapp 791
All My Troubles Are Gone/Please Don't Ever Leave Me Baby	67	Kapp 850
I'll Cry Later/One Man Woman	67	Kapp 870
I'm Gonna Love You A Long Long Time/My Heart Is So Full Of You	67	Kapp 897
Embraceables		
From Somebody Who Loves You/Gotta Pretty Little Baby	59	Sandy 1025
Don't Call For Me/My Foolish Pride	62	Cy 1004
(There's A) Wall Between Us/Sam	62	Dover 4100
Come Back/Destiny	62	Dover 4101
Emeralds (1) (Luther Bond & the)		
What If You/See What You Done?	54	Savoy 1124
You Were My Love/Starlight, Starbright	54	Savoy 1131
I Won't Believe You Anymore/It's Written In The Stars	55	Savoy 1159
He Loves You, Baby/I Cry	56	Federal 12279
Old Mother Nature/Six Foot Hole	59	Federal 12368
Gold Will Never Do/Jitterbug Jamboree	59	Showboat 1501/Briar 114
Someone To Love Me/Should I Love You So Much?	60	Showboat 1505
Emeralds (2)		
Sally Lou/Why Must I Wonder?	54	Kicks 3/Allied 10002/10003 (54)
The One I Adore/You Belong To My Heart	57	ABC 9889
Confess/I'm Dreaming	58	ABC 9948
That's The Way It's Got To Be/Maria's Cha Cha	59	Bobbin 107
All The Time/Gotta Be On Time	59	Rex 1004
Lover's Cry/Rumblin' Tumblin' Baby	60	Bobbin 121
I Kneel At Your Throne/Custer's Last Stand	60	Rex 1013
The Web/Trapped	60	Yale 232
Silver/Roadrunner	61	Toy 7734
Emeralds (2) (with Little Milton)		
Cross My Heart/I'm In Love	60	Bobbin 128
Emeralds (3) (Bobby Woods & the)		
Falling Rain/Friendly Mr. Hendley	60	Dot 16053
I Need Your Love	N/A	Rumble 348

ARTIST/SONG	YEAR	LABEL
Emeralds (4) (female)		
Dancing Alone/Wanna Make Him Mine	64	Jubilee 5474
Did You Ever Love A Guy/I'm Gonna Ask That Boy To Dance	64	Jubilee 5489
Emeralds (5)		
Please Don't Crush My Dreams/(Soda Pop) Juke Box Rock	67	Times Square 111
Emeralds (6)		
You're A Fallen Angel/You Hold The Strings To My Heart	62	Pel 3836
Emeralds (7)		
Mademoiselle/The Lover	59	Venus 1002
Marsha/You're Driving Me Crazy	59	Venus 1003
Emerals		
Please Don't Crush My Dreams/Jukebox Rock	60	Triple X 100/101
Emerson, Billy "The Kid" (& female group)		
Somebody Show Me/The Pleasure Is All Mine	57	Vee Jay 247
Emersons (aka Demens)		
Joannie Joannie/Hungry	58	Newport 7004
Hokey Pokey/Dr. Jekyll And Mr. Hyde	59	Cub 9027
Down In The Valley/Loneliness	61	United Artists 379
Emjays (fb Jimmy Curtis)		
This Is My Love/Waitin' (The Pitty Pat Song)	59	Greenwich 411
Cross My Heart/All My Love, All My Life	59	Greenwich 412
Over The Rainbow/Cookie Jar	59	Paris 538
Emmets (fb Chip Fisher)		
No One/Poor Me	59	Addison 15002
Emmy Lou (& group)		
Love Ya, Need Ya/I Wanna Know	61	Lute 6018
Emotions (1)		
The Nearest Thing To Heaven/Lover's Lane	59	Pio 107
Mr. Night/Make Me A Love	61	Laurie 3112
Echo/Come Dance Baby	62	Kapp 490
A Story Untold/One Life, One Love, One You	63	20th Fox 430
Rainbow/Little Miss Blue	63	20th Fox 452
L-O-V-E/A Million Reasons	63	Kapp 513
Starlit Night/Fool's Paradise	63	Laurie 3167
Boomerang/I Love You Madly	64	20th Fox 478
I Wonder/Hey Baby	64	Karate 506
She's My Baby/Baby I Need Your Loving	65	Calla 122
Heart Strings/Every Time	66	20th Fox 623
You're A Better Man Than I/Are You Real?	N/A	Johnson 746
Color My World/You're A Better Man Than I	N/A	South Park 1000
Emotions (2)		
It's Love/Candlelight	58	Fury 1010
I Ran To You/Been Lookin' Your Way	61	Flip 356
Been Lookin' Your Way/I Can Tell	61	Flip 358
(By The Light Of The) Silvery Moon/Do You Love Me	62	Card 600
Love Of A Girl/Do This For Me	65	Vardan 201
Emotions (2) (Lena Calhoun & the)		
I Ran To You/First Love Baby	61	Flip 357
Emperors (1)		
I May Be Wrong/Come Back, Come Back	54	Haven 511

ARTIST/SONG	YEAR	LABEL
Emperors (2) (Ernie & the)		
Meet Me At The Corner/Got A Lot I Want To Say	65	Reprise 0414
Emperors (3)		
No Regrets/Nursery Rhyme	58	3-J 121
Emperors (4)		
If You Don't Want Me	N/A	Graham
Emperors (5)		
Darlin' In The Moonlight/Steve Allen	64	Olimpic 245
Emperors (6)		
I Want My Woman	N/A	Sabra 5555
Empires (1)		
Corn Whiskey/My Baby, My Baby	54	Harlem 2325
Make Me Or Break Me (vocal by Johnny Ace Jr.)/Magic Mirror	55	Harlem 2333
I Want To Know/Shirley	55	Wing 90023
Tell Me, Pretty Baby/By The Riverside	55	Wing 90050
Linda/Whispering Heart	56	Whirlin' Disc 104
My First Discovery/Don't Touch My Gal	56	Wing 90080
If I'm A Fool/Zippety Zip	57	Amp-3 132
Empires (1) (Lightning Junior & the)		
Ragged And Hungry/Somebody Changed The Lock	55	Harlem 2334
Empires (2)		
Only In My Dreams/Definition Of Love	61	Calico 121
Over The Summer Vacation/You're So Popular	61	Lake 711
Love You So Bad/Come Home Girl	62	Chavis 1026/Candi 1026 (62)
Everybody Knew But Me/Three Little Fishes	62	Colpix 680
You're On Top, Girl	63	Candi 1033
Love Is Strange/Have Mercy	64	DCP 1116
Empires (2) (Eddie Friend & the)		
Tears In My Eyes/Single And Free	59	Colpix 112
Empires (3) (fb Jay Black)		
A Time And A Place/Punch Your Nose	62	Epic 9527
En-Solids (Drake & the)		
Please Leave Me/I'll Always Be There	N/A	Alteen 8652
Encenadas		
Love I Beg Of You	64	N/A
Enchanted Five		
Try A Little Love/Have You Ever	61	CVS 1002
Enchanters (1) (aka Sugar Tones (1))		
I've Lost/Housewife Blues	52	Jubilee 5080
Today Is Your Birthday/How Could You (Break My Heart)	52	Onyx 2007/Jubilee 5072 (52)
Enchanters (2)		
True Love Gone (Come On Home)/Wait A Minute, Baby	56	Mercer 992/Coral 61756 (57)
There Goes (A Pretty Girl)/Fan Me, Baby	57	Coral 61832
Bottle Up And Go/Mambo Santa Mambo	57	Coral 61916
True Love Gone/The Day	63	Coral 62373
True Love Gone/There Goes A Pretty Girl	63	Coral 65610
One Hand, One Heart	N/A	Coral
Enchanters (3) (aka Enchantments)		
Spellbound By The Moon/Know It All	56	Stardust 102
Come On Baby, Let's Do The Stroll/Rock Around	58	Bald Eagle 3001

ARTIST/SONG	YEAR	LABEL
Touch Of Love/Cafe Bohemian	59	Orbit 532/Bamboo 513 (61)
We Make Mistakes/The Decision	60	Sharp 105
I Lied To My Heart/Talk While You Walk	61	Musitron 1072
I Need Your Love/Goddess Of Love	62	Epsom 103
Oh Rosemarie/Bewildered	62	JJ&M 1562
On A Little Island	63	Tee Pee 65
I Should Be Loving You	N/A	Delta Ltd. 156

Enchanters (4)

You Worry Me/So Much	64	Vargo 10

Enchantments (aka Enchanters (3))

(I Love You) Sherry/Come On Home	62	Gone 5130
Popeye/Lonely Heart	62	Romac 1001
Oh Rosemarie/Bewildered	63	JJ&M 1562
I Love My Baby/Pains In My Heart	63	Ritz 17003
I'm In Love With Your Daughter, Pt. 1/	64	Faro 620
I'm In Love With Your Daughter, Pt. 2		
Down On My Knees (a capella)	75	Relic LP 103
Rock 'N' Roll Cha Cha (a capella)	75	Relic LP 103
Good Old Acappella/I Could Never Love Another	N/A	Rogue (no #)

Enchantones

My Picture Of You/We Fell In Love	62	Poplar 116

Enchords

Zoom Zoom Zoom/I Need You, Baby	61	Laurie 3089

Encores

When I Look At You/Young Girls, Young Girls	53	Checker 760
Ha-Chi-Bi-Ri-Bi-Ri/Time Is Moving On	54	Look 105/Ronnex 1003 (54)/
		Hollywood 1034 (55)
Barbara/Thank You	57	Bow 302

Encounters

Don't Stop/A Place In Your Heart	64	Swan 4205

Endells

Vicky/The Monkey Dance	63	Heigh Ho 605

Endorsers

Crying/Hold My Hand	59	Moon 109

Ends

It Ain't No Use/Row Row Your Boat	60	Vin 1029

English, Anna (& group)

Baby Come Home/My Favorite Record	58	Felsted 8524

English, Scott (bb the Accents (4))

White Cliffs Of Dover/4000 Miles Away	60	Dot 16099
When/Ugly Pills (You're Takin')	62	Joker 777
High On A Hill/When (by the Dedications)	63	Sultan 4003/Spokane 4003 (63)
Rags To Riches/Where Can I Go	63	Sultan 5500
Here Comes The Pain/All I Want Is You	64	Spokane 4007
Brandy/Lead Me Back	71	Janus 171
Woman In My Life/Ballad Of The Unloved	72	Janus 192

Ensenators

Just Like Before/I Had A Little Too Much	62	Tarx 1001
On And On/Love I Beg Of You	63	Tarx 1005

Entertainers (1)

Danny Boy/How Much Do You Love Me	63	Demand 2932

ARTIST/SONG	YEAR	LABEL
Entertainers (2) (Cortez & the)		
Life	N/A	Your Town
Entrees (Chuck Corley & the)		
Honey Let Me Stay/I Need Your Love	57	Fee Bee 219
City Of Strangers/Bring My Daddy Home	N/A	Sonic 118
Entros (Gloria Fowler & the)		
Will You Be My Guy/Train Of Love	65	CJ 654
Envoys (Bill Tally & the)		
Summer Sun/Stop On Red, Go On Green	59	Canadian American 104
I've Waited/Goodbye, Goodbye	59	Canadian American 105
Epics (1)		
Let's Dance/Lonely	58	Lifetime 1004
So Many Times/I Want To Be Your Girl	60	Dante 3004
Rowdy Mae/Summer's Coming In	61	Bandera 2512
Ho-Hum-Deedle-Dum/Girl By The Wayside	61	Lynn 510
Magic Kiss/Last Night I Dreamed	61	Lynn 516
Epics (2) (Linda & the)		
Memories Of Love/Gonna Be Loved	59	Blue Moon 415
Epics (3)		
The Bells Are Ringing/White Cliffs Of Dover	64	Mercury 72283
Epics (4)		
Wishing You Were Mine/Grounded	62	Eric 7001
Epiks		
When We're Apart	65	Process 146
Episodes		
Where Is My Love/The Christmas Tree	65	Four Seasons (no number)
Epitomes (Buford Busbee & the)		
Nobody But Me/This Is All I Ask	59	Dee Dee 101
Epps, Arthur (& group)		
Mona/There Was A Party	61	Spark 900
Epsilons		
I'm So Devoted/Mad At The World	N/A	Shrine 106
The Echo/Really Rockin'	69	Stax 0021
Equadors		
A Vision	58	RCA EP 4286
I'll Be The One	58	RCA EP 4286
Sputnik Dance	58	RCA EP 4286
Stay A Little Longer	58	RCA EP 4286
Equallos		
Beneath The Sun/In Between Tears	55	M&M/Romantic Rhythm (55)
Equalos (aka Plaids (3) (Willie Logan & the)		
Yodelin' Mad/Patty Patty	59	Mad 1296
Ermines (gm Cornel Gunter) (aka Flairs)		
True Love/Peek, Peek-A-Boo	55	Loma 701
You Broke My Heart/I'm So Used To You Now	56	Loma 703
Keep Me Alive/Muchacha, Muchacha	56	Loma 704
I'm Sad/One Thing For Me	56	Loma 705

ARTIST/SONG	YEAR	LABEL
Errico, Ray (bb the Honeytones)		
Humpty Dumpty Rock	56	Masquerade 56003
Ervin, Frankie (& female group)		
Believe Me/Why Don't You Go	59	Guyden 2010
Ervin, Frankie (& group)		
Annie Laurie/Wilhemina	59	Contender 1316
The Story/Blessing In Disguise	59	Rendezvous 112
You Hurt Me/If We Should Meet Again	60	Rendezvous 126
Such A Fool/Detour	62	Indigo 138
Ervin, Frankie (bb the Shields)		
Some Other Guy/Be My Girl	60	Hart 1691
Escapades (1) (Georgie Salo & the)		
End Of Time/I'll Love You Forever	60	Hi-Q 5014
Escapades (2)		
Nobody Knows/Peaches	N/A	Glow 87896
Escorts (1)		
Oh Honey/You Won't Be Satisfied	54	Essex 372
Paradise Hill/Bluebird Of Happiness	54	Essex 383
I've Been Thinking	55	Essex 389
Bad Boy/Tore Up Over You	57	RCA 6834
Lonely Man/So Hard To Laugh, So Easy To Cry	57	RCA 6963
You Can't Even Be My Friend	63	RCA 8228
Escorts (2)		
Sorry/It's Love To Me	56	Premium 407
Escorts (3)		
Misty Eyes/Arrow Two Hearts	57	O.J. 1010
Escorts (3) (Bobby Chandler & the)		
Winter Time/Junior Prom	58	O.J. 1012
Escorts (4) (Debs & the)		
Crew Cuts (We Like)/Swingin' Sam (instrumental by the Pastels)	58	Josie 833
Escorts (5) (Don Crawford & the)		
Why Why Why/Ugly Duckling	59	Scepter 1201
Escorts (6)		
One More Kiss Goodnight	59	Wells 102
Escorts (7)		
My First Year/Clap Happy	59	Judd 1014
I Will Be Home Again/Leaky Heart And His Red Go-Kart	60	Scarlet 4005
Judy Or Jo Ann/Main Drag	61	Soma 1144
Escorts (8) (Del & the) (ref Earls (2))		
You Don't Love Me/Skokian	60	Symbol 913
Baby Doll/Someone To Watch Over Me	61	Rome 103
Happy/You're For Me (And I'm For You)	61	Taurus 350/351
Escorts (9) (Felix & the) (gm Felix Cavaliere)		
The Syracuse/Save	62	Jag 685
Escorts (10)		
Gloria/Seven Wonders Of The World	62	Coral 62302
As I Love You/Gaudamaus	62	Coral 62317
Back Home Again/Something Has Changed Him	63	Coral 62372
My Heart Cries For You/Give Me Tomorrow	63	Coral 62385

ARTIST/SONG	YEAR	LABEL
Escorts (10) (Goldie & the)		
Somewhere/Submarine Race Watching	62	Coral 62336
One Hand, One Heart/I Can't Be Free	63	Coral 62349
Escos		
Chick-A-Dee/I'm Lonesome For You	59	Esta 100
Diamonds And Pearls/We Dance	60	Federal 12380
Golden Rule Of Love/Watcha Bet	61	Federal 12430
Yes I Need Someone/Thank You Mister Ballard	61	Federal 12445
(For Creating The Twist)		
Shame Shame Shame/That's Life	63	Federal 12493
Esquires (1) (aka Five Tinos)		
If You Only Knew What A Three Cent Stamp Could Do/	54	Epic 9024
Now, Now, Now		
Only The Angels Know/One Word For This	55	Hi-Po 1003
Yackety Yak/A Girl Named Joe	56	Meteor 5022
Esquires (2) (Lord Luther & the)		
Tremble/Tell Ya What (by the Five Hearts)	60	Music City 833
Esquires (3)		
Mission Bells/When I Fall In Love	62	Meridian 6283
Essentials (1) (Billy & the)		
Maybe You'll Be There/Over The Weekend	62	Jamie 1239
Lonely Weekend/Young At Heart	63	Mercury 72127
Last Dance/Yes Sir, That's My Baby	63	Mercury 72210
Remember Me, Baby/The Actor	65	Cameo 344
Babalu's Wedding Day/My Way Of Saying	66	Smash 2045
Don't Cry (Sing Along With The Music)/Baby, Go Away	66	Smash 2071
I Wrote A Song/Oh What A Feeling	67	SSS International 706
Essentials (1) (Little Billy & the)		
Steady Girl/The Dance Is Over	62	Landa 691/Jamie 1229 (62)
Essentials (2) (Johnny Lloyd & the)		
On Our Wedding Day	N/A	Reading 16000
Essents		
Barbara/I Just Can't Understand	66	Laurie 3335
Essex (1)		
Easier Said Than Done/Are You Going My Way	63	Roulette 4494
A Walkin' Miracle/What I Don't Know Won't Hurt Me	63	Roulette 4515
She's Got Everything/Out Of Sight, Out Of Mind	63	Roulette 4530
The Eagle/Moonlight, Music And You	66	Bang 537
Essex (1) (Anita Humes & the)		
Curfew Lover/What Did I Do?	64	Roulette 4542
Are You Going My Way/Everybody's Got You	67	Roulette 4750
Essex (2)		
Barbara Ann	N/A	N/A
Eternals		
Rockin' In The Jungle/Rock 'n' Roll Cha Cha	59	Hollywood 68/ Musictone 1111 (61)
Babalu's Wedding Day/My Girl	59	Hollywood 70/71/ Musictone 1110 (59)
Blind Date/Today	61	Warwick 611
Come Go With Me/Love Me With All Your Heart	68	Quality 1884
Etiquettes (Little Nat & the)		
You're So Close/Blah Blah Blah	61	Clock 2001

ARTIST/SONG	YEAR	LABEL
Euniques		
Pretty Baby/Cry Cry Cry	61	620 1003
Cry Cry Cry/Chicken (Yeah)	61	620 1006
Evans, Donna (& group)		
Sorry/Foolish Me	62	Cheer 1003
Evans, Jerry (bb the Off Keys)		
Out Of My Mind	62	Bubble 1333
Evans, Kay (& group)		
Lover	61	Whip 274
Evels (female)		
The Magic Of Love/Wonderful Guy	N/A	Tra-X 14-152
Eventuals		
Just The Things That You Do/Charlie Chan	61	Okeh 7142
Everglades		
While Waiting In The Chapel/Do You Miss Me	63	BPV 112577
Everglades (Jerry Hayward & the)		
You Stole My Heart Away/Shimmy, Shimmy, Shimmy, Shimmy	63	Symbol 916
Evergreens (1)		
Very Truly Yours/Guitar Player	55	Chart 605
Evergreens (2) (Dante & the)		
Alley-Oop/The Right Time	60	Madison 130
Time Machine/Dream Land	60	Madison 135
What Are You Doing New Year's Eve/Yeah Baby	60	Madison 143
Think Sweet Thoughts/Da Doo	61	Madison 154
Evergreens (3) (Eddie & the) (ref Sha Na Na)		
In The Still Of The Night/In The Still Of The Night	72	Kama Sutra 578
Excellents (aka Excellons)		
Coney Island Baby/You Baby You	62	Blast 205
I Hear A Rhapsody/Why Did You Laugh	63	Blast 207
Love No One But You/Red Red Robin	63	Mermaid 106
Excellons (aka Excellents)		
Sunday Kind Of Love/Helene (Your Wish Came True)	64	Bobby 601/Old Timer 601 (64)
Excels (1)		
You're Mine Forever/Baby Doll	57	Central 2601
Baby Doll/My Greatest Thrill	65	Relic 1007
Excels (2)		
On Bended Knee/I Miss You So	55	X 0108
My Foolish Heart/Just You And I Together	60	Gone 5094
Til You Were Gone/Can't Help Lovin' That Girl Of Mine	61	R.S.V.P. 111
Excels (2) (Bill Daniels & the)		
Rock And Roll Baby	N/A	X
Exceptions		
Down By The Ocean/Pancho's Villa	63	Pro 1/Cameo 378 (65)
Excitements (Elroy & the)		
My Love Will Never Die/No One Knows	61	Alanna 188/Alanna 565 (63)
Exciting Invictas		
I Don't Care/Not Again	60	Kingston 427

ARTIST/SONG	YEAR	LABEL
Exclusives		
My Girl Friend/It's Over	58	K&C 102/103
Execs		
Walkin' In The Rain/Palladium	58	Fargo 1055
Executive Four		
You Are/I Got A Good Thing Going	N/A	Lumar 202
Executives (1) (Margie Mills & the)		
Knock On Any Door/All Of Me	63	Vee Jay 549
Executives (2) (aka Challengers)		
River Of Tears/Come On Now	63	Explosive 3821/Mink 5004
Why/Come On Baby	63	Revenge 5003/
		Explosive 3621 (63)
Exodus (aka Four Epics)		
M And M/Silhouettes-You Cheated	72	Wand 11248
Exotics		
That's My Desire/Darling I Want To Get Married	61	Coral 62268
The Gang That Sang "Heart Of My Heart"/Hotcha Mighty Knows	61	Coral 62289
Manpower/Fortune Hunter	62	Coral 62310
My Life's Desire, Pt. 1/My Life's Desire, Pt. 2	62	Coral 62343
Lorraine/Gee	63	Springboard 101
Sad Sad Song/Let's Get Together	64	Coral 62399
Like You Hurt Me/Big Time Charlie	64	Coral 62439
Exploits (Bobby Maxwell & the)		
You're Laughing At Me/Stay With Me	59	Fargo 1009
Explorers		
In The Wee Small Hours Of The Morning/Don't Be A Fool	60	Coral 62175
Vision Of Love/Don't Be A Fool	63	Coral 65575
Explorers (Dennis & the)		
Vision Of Love/On A Clear Night	60	Coral 62147
Remember/Every Road	61	Coral 62295
Expressions (1)		
Now That You're Gone/Crazy	56	Teen 101
My Love, My Love/The Sign Of Happiness	61	Arliss 1012
Come Back Karen/Thrill	63	Smash 1848
You Better Know It/Out Of My Life	64	Federal 12533
Be Bop A Lula/Skinny Minnie	65	Guyden 2122
One Plus One/Playboy	65	Reprise 0360
Expressions (2) (aka Imaginations)		
To Cry/On The Corner	63	Parkway 892
Expressions (3) (Billy Harner & the)		
Anymore/Watcha Gonna Do	64	Lawn 239
Expressions (4) (Johnny & the)		
Where Is The Party/Something I Want To Tell You	65	Josie 946
Shy Girl/Now That You're Mine	66	Josie 955
Give Me One More Chance/Boys And Girls Together	66	Josie 959
Extensions (female)		
I Want To Know/My Need	63	Success 109
Extremes (aka Bobby & the Velvets)		
Come Next Spring/Let's Elope	58	Everlast 5013
The Bells/That's All I Want (with Bobby Sanders)	62	Paro 733

ARTIST/SONG	YEAR	LABEL
Exzels		
Canadian Sunset/Hit Talk	N/A	Crossfire 1914
Fabians (female)		
Confidential	N/A	Blue Rocket 315
Fables		
Angel/Cleopatra 30 B.C.	62	Elgo 3001
Fabulaires		
While Walking/No, No	57	Main Line 103/ East West 103 (57)
Wedding Song/Lonely Days, Lonely Nights	63	Chelsea 103
Fabuleers		
If I Had Another Chance/I Had A Feeling This Morning	60	Kenco 5002
Fabulons (1)		
Smoke From Your Cigarette/Give Me Back My Ring	60	Ember 1069
Connie/This Is The End	63	Benson Ritco 100/Benson 100
Fabulons (2) (with the Tikis)		
Since You've Been Gone/Don't Ask Me	66	Tower 259
Fabulons (3) (female)		
Lonely Boy/Trying	63	Jo-Dee 1001
Fabulons (4) (Bobby Winslow & the)		
House Of Tears	N/A	Fabulous 1001
Fabulous Blends (Big John & the)		
Hey Little Fool/Baby You're Wrong	64	Casa Grande 5001
Fabulous Chimes		
Faithful To Me	N/A	Invincible Arts 1177
Fabulous Clovers (aka Clovers)		
They're Rockin' Down The Street/Be My Baby	61	Winley 265
Fabulous Denos		
Bad Girl/Once I Had A Love	64	King 5908
Hard To Hold Back Tears/I've Enjoyed Being Loved By You	65	King 5971
Fabulous Dials		
Forget Me Not/Bossa Nova Stomp	63	Joy 276/DnB 1000
Fabulous Dinos		
That Same Old Song/Where Have You Been	62	Musicor 1025
Instant Love/Retreat	64	Saber 1009
Fabulous Earthquakes		
Please Be My Girl/In The Chapel In The Moonlight	60	Meridian 1518
Fabulous Echoes		
I Never Knew/Keep Your Love Strong	64	Liberty 55769
Sunshine	65	Diamond 187
Fabulous Egyptians		
End Of Time/The Cowboy	N/A	Cindy 96750
Fabulous El Dorados (ref El Dorados)		
Ease The Pain/Remember Sherrie	87	Delano 1099
Fabulous Embers (Willis Sanders & the) (aka Embers)		
Lovable You/Honey Bun	58	Millionaire 775

ARTIST/SONG	YEAR	LABEL
Fabulous Enchanters		
Why Are You Crying/Something Blue	61	Finer Arts 1007
Fabulous Fabuliers		
She Is The Girl For Me/I Found My Baby	59	Angle Tone 539
Fabulous Falcons		
Dolly/I Wanna Be With You	66	White Cliffs 249
Fabulous Fanatics		
Givin' Up On Love/Sweeter Than Wine	61	T-Bird 201
Fabulous Fidels		
Westside Boy, Eastside Girl	N/A	Jaa Dee 106
Fabulous Five		
Gettin' Old/Janie Made A Monster	59	King 5220
Fabulous Five Flames		
Lonely Lover/No More Tears	60	Time 1023
Fabulous Flames		
My Joan/Josephine	58	Rex 3000
Do You Remember?/Get To Stepping	61	Bay-Tone 102
Lover/I'm So All Alone	61	Bay-Tone 105
Fabulous Fortunes (Norm N. Nite & the)		
Let's Try It Again/Good Old Rock & Roll Music	71	Globe 107
Fabulous Four (aka Four Js)		
In The Chapel In The Moonlight/Mr. Twist	60	Chancellor 1062
Let's Try Again/Precious Moments	61	Chancellor 1068
Why Do Fools Fall In Love/The Sound Of Summer	61	Chancellor 1078
Betty Ann/Prisoner Of Love	61	Chancellor 1085
I'm Comin' Home/Everybody Knows	61	Chancellor 1090
Mr. Twist/Everybody Knows	61	Chancellor 1098
Forever/It's No Sin	62	Chancellor 1102
Oop-Shoobie-Doop Bam-A-Lam/Welcome Me Home	62	Melic 4114
Got To Get Her Back/Now You Cry	64	Brass 311/Coral 62479 (64)
Happy/Who Could It Be	64	Brass 314
Yound Blood/I'm Always Doing Something Wrong	64	Brass 316
Fabulous Four (with Fabian)		
The Love That I'm Giving To You/You're Only Young Once	61	Chancellor 1079
Fabulous Futuras		
La Do Da Da/When You Ask About Love	N/A	Okon (no #)
Fabulous Gardenias (aka Gardenias)		
What's The Matter With Me?/It's You, You, You	61	Liz 1004/Fairlane 21019 (62)
Fabulous Idols		
Baby/Nellie	61	Kenco 5011
Fabulous Koolcats (Ruben Siggers & the)		
Those Love Me Blues/Please Pretty Baby	57	Spinks 600
Fabulous Marcels (aka Marcels)		
That Lucky Old Sun/Peace Of Mind	75	St. Clair 13711
Fabulous Pearl Devines		
So Lonely/You've Been Gone	63	Alco 101
Fabulous Pearls		
My Heart's Desire/Jungle Bunny	59	Dooto 448

ARTIST/SONG	YEAR	LABEL

Fabulous Persians
Save The Last Dance For Me/Ling Ting Tong	N/A	Bobby-O 3123

Fabulous Playboys (aka Falcons (5))
I Fooled You/Sweet Peas And Bronc Busters	59	Contour 004
Honkey Tonk Woman/Tears, Tears, Tears	61	Apollo 760
Nervous/Forget The Past	61	Daco 1001/Apollo 758 (61)

Fabulous Royals
I Only Have Eyes For You/Land Of 1000 Dances	N/A	Aegis 1006

Fabulous Silver Tones
Dimples	N/A	West Coast 452

Fabulous Splendors
Canadian Sunset/Your Change Of Heart	60	O-Gee 105

Fabulous Tears (Little Dooley & the)
I Love You/She's So Fine	65	Baylor 101

Fabulous Twilights (Nathaniel Mayer & the)
My Last Dance With You/My Little Darling	61	Fortune 542
Village Of Love/I Want A Woman	62	Fortune 545/United Artists 449 (62)/Fortune 563 (63)
Hurtin' Love/Leave Me Alone	62	Fortune 547
Well, I've Got News/Work It Out	62	Fortune 550
Well, I've Got News/Mr. Santa Claus	62	Fortune 550X
I Had A Dream/I'm Not Gonna Cry	63	Fortune 554
Going Back To The Village Of Love/My Last Dance With You	63	Fortune 557
Place I Know/Don't Come Back	63	Fortune 562
From Now On/I Want Love And Affection	63	Fortune 567

Fabulous Uptones
New Love I Have Found/Turtle	62	Tulip 100

Fabulous Valients
Your Golden Teardrops/Carmelita	62	Holiday 61005

Fabulous Winds (Joe Boot & the)
That's Tough/Rock And Roll Radio	58	Celestial 111

Faces
Christmas/New Year's Resolution	65	Iguana 601
What Is This Dream (I Have)/Skier Jones	65	Regina 1326
I'll Walk Alone/I Didn't Want Her	65	Regina 1328

Fads (Buddy & the)
Won't You Love Me/Is It Just A Game	58	Morocco 1001

Fairfield Four
Memories (Of My Mother)/Don't Let Nobody	60	Old Town 1081

Fairlanes (1)
Seventeen Steps/Johnny Rhythm	59	Lucky Seven 102
If The World Don't End Tomorrow	60	Argo
Little Girl, Little Girl/Comin' After You	60	Argo 5357
I'm Not The Kind Of Guy/The Dagwood	62	Minaret 103
Surf Train/Lonely Weekends	63	Reprise 20213
Baby Baby/Tell Me	64	Radiant 101
The New York Sound, Pt. 1/The New York Sound, Pt. 2	64	Radiant 104
Memories Of The Past	89	Relic LP 5079

Fairlanes (2)
Just For Me/Bullseye	59	Dart 109

ARTIST/SONG	YEAR	LABEL
Fairlanes (3)		
Writing This Letter/Playboy	61	Continental 1001
Fairlanes (4) (Charles Perrywell & the)		
Come Along With Me/You're Lonesome Now	N/A	Tic Toc 104
Fairmounts		
Times And Places/Lucky Guy	62	Planet 53
Faithfuls (Philip & the)		
Love Me/Rhythm Marie	64	Goldwax 109
Falcons (1)		
I Can't Tell You Now/How Blind Can You Be	52	Regent 1041
You're The Beating Of My Heart/It's You I Miss	53	Savoy 893
Stepping Stone/Jigsaw Puzzle	57	RCA 7076
Falcons (2)		
Stay Mine/Du-Bi-A-Do	54	Flip 301
Tell Me Why/I Miss You, Darling	55	Cash 1002
Falcons (2) (Candy Rivers & the)		
Baby Tonight/You Are The Only One	54	Flip 302
Falcons (3) (aka Lyrics)		
My Only Love/Now That It's Over	57	Quality 1721/Falcon 1006 (57)/ Abner 1006 (57)
Falcons (4)		
Baby That's It (lead by Eddie Floyd)/This Day	56	Mercury 70940
Can This Be Christmas? (lead by Eddie Floyd)/Sent Up	57	Silhouette 521
This Heart Of Mine (lead by Eddie Floyd)/Romanita	58	Kudo 661
Just For Your Love/This Heart Of Mine (lead by Eddie Floyd)	59	Chess 1743/Anna 1110 (60)
You're So Fine/Goddess Of Angels (lead by Eddie Floyd)	59	Flick 001/Unart 2013 (59)/ United Artists 2013X (59)
You're Mine/Country Shack	59	Unart 2022
That's What I Aim To Do/You Must Know I Love You	60	Flick 008
Waiting For You (lead by Eddie Floyd)/The Teacher	60	United Artists 229
I + Love + You/Wonderful Love (lead by Eddie Floyd)	60	United Artists 255
Workin' Man's Song/Pow! You're In Love (lead by Wilson Pickett)	61	United Artists 289
Lah-Tee-Lah-Tah/Darling	62	Atlantic 2153
I Found A Love (lead by Wilson Pickett)/Swim	62	Lu Pine 103/Lu Pine 1003
Take This Love I've Got (lead by Wilson Pickett)/ Let's Kiss And Make Up (lead by Wilson Pickett)	63	Atlantic 2179
Oh Baby/Fine Fine Girl	63	Atlantic 2207
Lonely Nights/Has It Happened To You	64	Lu Pine 124/Lu Pine 1020 (64)
You're On My Mind (lead by Wilson Pickett)/Anna (lead by Wilson Pickett)	65	Lu Pine 003
Anytime, Anyplace, Anywhere	85	Relic LP 8005
Girl Of My Dreams	85	Relic LP 8005
I Wonder	85	Relic LP 8005
I'll Never Find Another Girl Like You	85	Relic LP 8005
Juke Hop	85	Relic LP 8005
Let It Be Me	85	Relic LP 8005
No Time For Fun	85	Relic LP 8005
Please Don't Leave Me Dear	85	Relic LP 8005
Whose Little Girl Are You	85	Relic LP 8005
Billy The Kid	86	Relic LP 8006
Feels Good	86	Relic LP 8006
Part Time Love	86	Relic LP 8006
She's My Heart's Desire	86	Relic LP 8006
What To Do	86	Relic LP 8006

ARTIST/SONG	YEAR	LABEL

Falcons (5) (aka Fabulous Playboys)

I Can't Help It/Standing On Guard	66	Big Wheel 1967
(I'm A Fool) I Must Love You/Love, Love, Love	66	Big Wheel 321/322
Love Look In Her Eyes/In Time For The Blues	67	Big Wheel 1971
Good Good Feeling/Love You Like You've Never Been Loved	67	Big Wheel 1972

Falcons (6) (Jack Richards & the)

| Pretty Baby/We Dream | 58 | Dawn 233 |

Fallen Angels

So Young, So Fine/Up On The Mountain	65	Tollie 9049
A Little Love From You Will Do	66	Laurie
Bad Woman/Pimples And Braces	N/A	Eceip 1004

Famous Flames

| So Long My Darling/I'm Going To Live My Life Alone | 60 | Harlem 114 |

Famous Flames (with Johnny Spain)

| I'm In Love/Family Rules | 58 | Back Beat 516 |

Famous Hearts (aka Lee Andrews & the Hearts)

| Aisle Of Love/Momma | 62 | Guyden 2073 |

Fanados

| The One I Love/She Must Be From A Different Planet | 57 | Carter 2050 |

Fanatics

| Is There Still A Chance/Oogly Googly Eyes | 61 | Skyway 127 |

Fantastic Five Keys (aka Five Keys)

| From The Bottom Of My Heart/Out Of Sight, Out Of Mind | 62 | Capitol 4828 |

Fantastic Vontastics

| Oh Happy Day (Tra-La-La)/Gee What A Boy | 65 | Tuff 406 |

Fantastics (1)

There Goes My Love/I Wanna Be A Millionaire Hobo	59	RCA 7572
This Is My Wedding Day/I Got A Zero	60	RCA 7664
Dancing Doll/I Told You Once	61	United Artists 309

Fantastics (2)

| I Don't Know | N/A | DMD 103 |

Fantastics (3)

| In Times Like These/Where There's A Will | 61 | Impresario 124 |

Fantasys

| No One But You/Why, Oh Why | 60 | Guyden 2029 |

Farrer, Tony (& group)

| A Blast From The Past/Following You | 61 | Trans Atlas 001 |

Fascinations (1)

| It's Midnight/Boom Bada Boom | 60 | Sure 106 |
| If I Had Your Love/Why | 61 | Paxley 750/Dore 593 (61) |

Fascinations (2) (Jordan & the)

Give Me Your Love/Once Upon A Time	61	Carol 4116
My Imagination/I'll Be Forever Loving You	61	Dapt 203
Love Will Make Your Mind Go Wild/My Baby Doesn't Smile Anymore	61	Dapt 207
I'm Goin' Home/If You Love Me Really Love Me	62	Josie 895
Delores	N/A	N/A

Fascinations (3) (female)

| Mama Didn't Lie/Someone Like You | 63 | ABC 10387 |
| Tears In My Eyes/You're Gonna Be Sorry | 63 | ABC 10443 |

ARTIST/SONG	YEAR	LABEL

Fascinations (4)

I'm Gonna Cry/Since You Went Away (recorded in 1962)	72	A&G 101

Fascinators

Dear Lord	N/A	Relic LP

Fascinators (1)

The Bells Of My Heart/Sweet Baby	52	Your Copy 1135
My Beauty, My Own/Don't Give It Away	52	Your Copy 1136
Can't Stop/Don't Give My Love Away	55	Blue Lake 112

Fascinators (2)

Teardrop Eyes/Shivers And Shakes	58	Dooto 441
Cuddle Up With Carolyn/Tee Vee	58	King 5119

Fascinators (3)

Chapel Bells/I Wonder Who	58	Capitol 4053/Capitol 4544 (60)
Who Do You Think You Are/Come To Paradise	59	Capitol 4137
Oh Rose Marie/Fried Chicken And Macaroni	59	Capitol 4247
I'll Be Gone/Can't You See I'm Lonely	65	Burn 845
Oh Rose Marie/Forgive Me My Darling	72	Bim Bam Boom 110
Recess/Teenage Wedding	N/A	Capitol (unreleased)

Fascinators (4)

You're To Blame	62	Trans Atlas 688

Fashionettes

Daydreamin' Of You/Only Love	64	GNP Crescendo 322

Fashions (1)

I'm Dreaming Of You/I Love You So	59	V-Tone 202
I'm Dreaming Of You/Lonesome Road	59	V-Tone 202
I Just Got A Letter/Try My Love	61	Ember 1084
Dearest One/All I Want	61	Warwick 646

Fashions (2)

Fairy Tales/Please Let It Be Me	62	Elmor 301
When Love Slips Away	68	20th Fox

Fashions (3)

Why Don't You Stay A Little Longer/I Set A Trap For You	63	Amy 884
Surfer's Memories/Surfin' Back To School	63	Felsted 8689

Fashions (4) (Dolly & the)

Just Another Fool	65	Ivanhoe 5019

Fat Boys (Freddie & the)

Why Do Fools Fall In Love/Ballad Of Freddie And Rich	N/A	Fat Man 101

Faulkner, Freddy (& group)

Cigarettes And Matches/Little Drifter Amy	63	Swan 4134

Fawns

Until I Die/Come On	58	Apt 15035/Apt 25015 (58)
Wish You Were Here With Me/Nothing But Love Can Save Me	67	Capacity 105
Girl In Trouble	N/A	Tec 3015

Fay, Flo (& group)

I'm The Richest One Of All/I Promise	63	Lawn 206

Fayettes (Hattie Littles & the)

Here You Come/Your Love Is Wonderful	62	Gordy 7007

ARTIST/SONG	YEAR	LABEL

Feathers

Johnny Darling/Shake 'Em Up	54	Aladdin 3267/
		Showtime 1104 (54)
Nona/Johnny, Darling	54	Show Time 1104
Why Don't You Write Me?/Busy As A Bumble Bee	54	Show Time 1105
(by Johnny & Louis Stanton)		
Love Only You/Crashing The Party	54	Show Time 1106
I Need A Girl/Standin' Right There	55	Aladdin 3277
Dear One/Lonesome Tonight	55	Hollywood 1051
Walkin' And Talkin'	55	Show Time

Feathers (June Moy & the)

Desert Winds/Castle Of Dreams	55	Show Time 1103

Federals

Come Go With Me/Cold Cash	57	DeLuxe 6112
While Our Hearts Are Young/You're The One I Love	57	Fury 1005
Dear Lorraine/She's My Girl	57	Fury 1009

Fellows (Eugene Church & the)

Pretty Girls Everywhere/For The Rest Of My Life	58	Class 235

Fender, Freddy (& group)

Holy One/Mean Woman	59	Duncan 1000/Imperial 5659 (60)
In The Still Of The Nite/You Don't Have To Go	64	Norco 108

Fentones (Shane Fenton & the)

Don't Do That/I'll Know	63	Laurie 3287/20th Fox 439 (63)

Fenways

Number One Song In The Country/Nothing To Offer You	64	Ricky L 106

Ferns (Baby Ray & the) (gm Frank Zappa)

How's Your Bird/World's Greatest Sinner	63	Donna 1378

Ferros

Come Home My Love/Tough Cat	58	Hi-Q 5008

Fi Dells

Time And Time Again	N/A	India 5822

Fi Dels

You Never Do Right (My Baby)/Try A Little Harder	N/A	Keymen 106

Fi-Dells (1) (female)

No Other Love/Come Back To Me	57	Warner 1014

Fi-Dells (2)

What Is Love/Don't Let Me Love You	61	Imperial 5780

Fi-Dells (3) (D. Purkiss & the)

Alone Without Love	64	United Sounds 110

Fi-Tones (aka Fi-Tones Quintette/aka Caverliers Quartet)

Foolish Dreams/Let's Fall In Love	55	Atlas 1050
My Faith/My Heart	57	Old Town 1042
You'll Be The Last/Wake Up	58	Angle Tone 525
What Am I Goin' To Do?/It Wasn't A Lie	58	Angle Tone 530
I Found My Baby/She Is The Girl For Me	59	Angle Tone 53
Deep In My Heart/Minnie	59	Angle Tone 536
Delores	73	Relic LP 5010
Peddler Of Dreams	73	Relic LP 5010

Fi-Tones (Carl Thomas & the)

I Love You Judy/Sweet Lovin' Maryann	59	Stroll 101/O Gee 1004

ARTIST/SONG	YEAR	LABEL

The Fi-Tones Quintette

Fi-Tones Quintette (aka Fi-Tones/aka Caverliers Quartet)

It Wasn't A Lie/Lots And Lots Of Love	55	Atlas 1051
I Call To You/(Don't You Know) Love You, Baby	56	Atlas 1052
I Belong To You/Silly And Sappy	56	Atlas 1055
Waiting For Your Call/My Tired Feet	56	Atlas 1056

Fiats

Speak Words Of Love/Before I Walk Out The Door	64	Universal 5003

Fidelitones

Pretty Girl/Game Of Love	58	Aladdin 3442
Say Hey Pretty Baby/Playboy	61	Marlo 1518
It It Too Late	N/A	Aladdin (unreleased)

Fidelitys

The Things I Love/Hold On To What Cha Got (And Get One More)	58	Baton 252
Can't You Come Out/Memories Of You	58	Baton 256
Captain Of My Ship/My Greatest Thrill	59	Baton 261
Marie/The Invitation	59	Sir 271
Walk With The Wind/Only To You	59	Sir 274
Wishing Star/Broken Love	59	Sir 277
Where In The World/This Girl Of Mine	60	Sir 276

Fidels

Love Me Tender/After The Lights Go Down	57	Music City 806

Fideltones

Whispering Words Of Love/For Your Love	60	Poop Deck 101

Fiestas

So Fine/Last Night I Dreamed	58	Old Town 1062
I'm Your Slave/Grandma Gave A Party	59	Old Town 1067
Our Anniversary/I'm Your Slave	59	Old Town 1069
That Was Me/Good News	59	Old Town 1074

ARTIST/SONG	YEAR	LABEL
It Don't Make Sense/Dollar Bill	60	Old Town 1080
You Could Be My Girl Friend/So Nice	60	Old Town 1090
Look At That Girl/Mr. Dillon, Mr. Dillon	61	Old Town 1104
She's Mine/The Hobo's Prayer	61	Old Town 1111
Julie/Come On Everybody	61	Strand 25046
Broken Heart/The Railroad Song	62	Old Town 1122
I Feel Good All Over/Look At That Girl	62	Old Town 1127
The Gypsy Said/Mama Put The Law Down	63	Old Town 1134
The Party's Over/Try It One More Time	63	Old Town 1140
Rock-A-Bye Baby/Foolish Dreamer	63	Old Town 1148
Rock-A-Bye Baby/All That's Good	64	Old Town 1166
Anna/Think Smart	64	Old Town 1178
Love Is Strange/Love Is Good To Me	65	Old Town 118
Ain't She Sweet/I Gotta Have Your Lovin'	65	Old Town 1189
So Fine/Darling You've Changed	74	Vigor 712

Fifes (Edward Hamilton & the)

Call Me	N/A	Jameco 1630

Fingerpoppers (Ronny Williams & the)

Strange Are The Ways Of Love/Feeling Is Real	60	Ultra Sonic 111

Fire Balls (Billy Eldridge & His)

Let's Go Baby/My Blue Tears	59	Unart 2011/Vulco 1501 (59)

Fireballs (Chuck Tharp & the)

Let There Be Love/Long, Long Ponytail	60	Jaro 77029/Lucky 0012

Fireflies (fb Richie Adams)

The Crawl/Where The Candlelight Glows	58	Roulette 4098
You Were Mine/Stella's Got A Fella	59	Ribbon 6901
I Can't Say Goodbye/What Did I Do Wrong	59	Ribbon 6904
Marianne/Give All Your Love To Me	60	Canadian American 117
My Girl/Because Of My Pride	60	Ribbon 6906
You Were Mine For Awhile/One O'Clock Twist	62	Taurus 355
Blacksmith Blues/Tuff-A-Nuff	63	Hamilton 50036
My Prayer For You/Good Friends	64	Taurus 366
Runaround/Could You Mean More	66	Taurus 376
Tonight/A Time For Us	67	Taurus 380

Fireside Singers

Pretty Girl/Darlin' Come Home	63	Herald 582

Firesiders

One And All/No One Cares For Me	61	Swan 4074

First Platoon

Ten Ways/Physical Fitness	63	SPQR 3303

5 Bell Aires (Henry Hall & the)

Come On To My Love House	90	Relic LP 5085
House Of Love	90	Relic LP 5085
I'm So Happy	90	Relic LP 5085
My Friends	90	Relic LP 5085

5 Bell Aires (John Hall & the)

Come On Home	90	Relic LP 5085
Wedding Bells	90	Relic LP 5085

5 Gents

I Never Told You/Rock With Me Marie	58	Crest 516
Sandy/Baby Doll	N/A	Viking 101

5 Kids

Carolyn/Oh Baby	55	Maxwell 101

ARTIST/SONG	YEAR	LABEL
Five Arcades		
Ruby Lee/Heaven's Own Desire	N/A	Sacto
Five Arrows (Gloria Valdez, the Paul Bascomb orch. & the)		
Pretty Little Thing/You've Got Me Losing My Mind	55	Parrot 816
Five Barons		
Fine As Wine (single sided)	52	Beacon 9144/Krazy Kat LP 797
Five Bars		
Somebody Else's Fool/Stormy Weather	57	Money 224
Deep In My Heart	63	Bubble 1010
Five Bells		
My Pledge To You/It's You	60	Clock 1017
My Cutie Pie/Please Remember	N/A	Stolper 100
Five Bills		
Can't Wait For Tomorrow/Till I	53	Brunswick 84002
Till Dawn And Tomorrow/Waiting, Wanting	53	Brunswick 84004
Five Birds (Willie Headen & the)		
Back Home Again/I Wanna Know	56	Authentic 703
Let Me Cry/The Skinny Woman Story	57	Authentic 410/Dootone 410
Five Blacks		
Forever In Love/Come One	N/A	B&C 100
Five Blue Flames (Chris Powell & the)		
My Love Has Gone/In The Cool Of The Evening	51	Columbia 39407
Five Blue Notes		
My Gal Is Gone/Ooh Baby	54	Sabre 103
You Gotta Go Baby/The Beat Of Our Hearts	54	Sabre 108
Thunderbird/My Special Prayer (by the Jammers)	59	Onda 108
My Special Prayer/Something Awful	64	Onda 888
Five Bobolinks		
Trying/Mailman Blues	52	Okeh
Five Bops		
Unforgotten Love/Jitterbuggin'	59	Hamilton 50023
Five Budds		
I Was Such A Fool (To Fall In Love With You)/Midnight	53	Rama 1
I Want Her Back/I Guess It's All Over Now	53	Rama 2
Five C's		
Tell Me/Whoo-Wee, Baby	54	United 172
My Heart's Got The Blues/Goody, Goody	55	United 180
Going My Way	81	P-Vine Special LP 9036
I Long For You	81	P-Vine Special LP 9036
Only By You (I Want To Be Loved)	81	P-Vine Special LP 9036
There's No Tomorrow	81	P-Vine Special LP 9036
Five Campbells		
Hey, Baby/Morrine	56	Music City 794
Five Cashmeres		
Walkin' Through The Jungle	61	Golden Leaf 108
Five Cats		
He Follows She/Santa Lucie	54	RCA 5885
Rockin' Chair/Mine Mine Mine	55	RCA 6012
I Was So Wrong/Someone's Gonna Cry	55	RCA 6181

ARTIST/SONG	YEAR	LABEL

Five Chancellors (aka Chancellors (1))
There Goes My Girl/Tell Me You Love Me	57	Port 5000

Five Chancells
Love No One But You/Please Let Me Love You (a capella)	65	Fellatio 103/Dawn 302

Five Chances
I May Be Small/Nagasaki	54	Chance 1157
All I Want/Shake-A-Link	55	Blue Lake 115
Bashful Boy	56	States (unreleased)
Gloria/Sugar Lips	56	States 156
My Days Are Blue/Tell Me Why	57	Federal 12303
Need Your Love/Land Of Love (despite label, not by Five Chances)	60	Corina 2002
Need Your Love/Is This Love	60	P.S. 1510
Make Love To Me/California	N/A	Atomic 2494

Five Chanels (aka Chanels) (female)
The Reason/Skiddily Doo	58	Deb 500

Five Chestnuts (Hayes Baskerville & the)
My One And Only Love/Billy	58	Drum 003/004

Five Chimes
Rosemarie/Never Love Another	55	Betta 2011
A Fool Was I/Dearest Darling	55	Betta 2017/Royal Roost 577 (55)

Five Chords
Jeannie/Red Wine	61	Cuca 1031

Five Chords (Johnny Jones & the)
Love Is Like Music/Don't Just Stand There	58	Jamie 1110

Five Chums
High School Affair/Give Me The Power	58	Excello 2123

Five Classics
My Imagination/Come On Baby	60	Arc 4454/A 317 (61)
Love Me/Mississippi Mud	61	Pova 6142
Old Cape Cod/Magic Star	62	Medieval 204

Five Cookies
Cook, Cook, Cookie/Keep Twisting	62	Everest 19429

Five Crowns (1) (aka Crowns (2)/ref Drifters)
Good Luck Darlin'/Again	52	Old Town 777 (unreleased)/ Relic LP 5030
The End Of The Fair/The Man From The Moon	52	Old Town 778 (unreleased)/ Relic LP 5030
You Could Be My Love/Good Luck Darlin'	52	Old Town 790
Lullaby Of The Bells/Later Later Baby	52	Old Town 792
A Star/You're My Inspiration	52	Rainbow 179
Who Can Be True/$19.50 Bus	52	Rainbow 184
Keep It A Secret/Why Don't You Believe Me	53	Rainbow 202
Alone Again/Don't Have To Hunt No More	53	Rainbow 206
I Was Wrong/Hug Me Baby	54	Rainbow 251
You Ran Away With My Heart	54	Rainbow 281
I Can't Pretend/Popcorn Willie	55	Caravan 15609/ Trans-World 717 (56)
You Came To Me/Ooh Wee Baby	55	Riviera 990/Rainbow 335 (56)
God Bless You/Do You Remember	56	Gee 1001
Kiss And Make Up/I'll Forget About You	58	R&B 6901
Memories Of Yesterday/A Surprise From Outer Space	59	De Besth 1122
I Want You/Hillum Boy	59	De Besth 1123
Just A Part Of Life/Just A Part Of Life	N/A	Five-O 503

ARTIST/SONG	YEAR	LABEL
Five Crowns (2) (with Jan Andre)		
It's Funny To Everyone But Me/Speak With Your Eyes	55	Emerald 2007
Five Crowns (3) (Chuck Edwards & the)		
If I Were King/Lucy And Jimmy Got Married	59	Alanna 557
Five Crystals		
Path Of Broken Hearts/Heaven's Own Choir	58	Music City 821/Delcro 827
Hey, Landlord/Good Looking Out	59	Kane 25592/Relic 1003 (65)
Five Daps		
Do Whop-A-Do/You're So Unfaithful	58	Brax 207/208
Five Debonaires		
Darlin'/Whispering Blues	57	Herald 509
Five Delights		
There'll Be No Goodbye/Okey Dokey, Mama	58	Newport 7002/Unart 2003 (58)
The Thought Of Losing You/That Love Affair	59	Abel 228
Five Diamonds		
Ten Commandments Of Love/I Cried And Cried	55	Treat 501
Five Dips		
Teach Me Tonight/That's What I Like (by the Allen Trio)	56	Original 1005
Five Discs (aka Boyfriends/aka Dawn/aka Impalas (4))		
Adios/My Baby Loves Me	58	Calo 202
I Remember/The World Is A Beautiful Place	58	Emge 1004/Vik 0327 (58)/ Rust 5027 (60)
My Chinese Girl/Roses	59	Dwain 6072/Dwain 803 (59)/ Mello Mood 1002 (64)
When Love Comes Knocking/Go-Go	61	Yale 240
Come On Baby/I Don't Know What I'll Do	61	Yale 243/244
Never Let You Go/That Was The Time	62	Cheer 1000
Rock 'N' Roll Revival/Gypsy Women	72	Laurie 3601
Five Dollars		
Doctor Baby/Harmony Of Love	55	Fortune 821/Fraternity 821 (58)
That's The Way It Goes/My Baby-O	55	Fortune 854
So Strange/You Know I Can't Refuse	56	Fortune 826
Hard-Working Mama/I Will Wait	56	Fortune 830
You Fool/How To Do The Bacon Fat	57	Fortune 833
You Fool/I'm Wanderin' (by the Five Jets)	57	Fortune 833
The Bells	84	Fortune LP 8016
Weekend Man	84	Fortune LP 8016
Five Dollars (Andre Williams & the)		
(H-mmm, Andre Williams Is) Movin'/(Georgia May Is) Movin' (Andre Williams & Gino Parks)	60	Fortune 851
Five Dollars (Jim Sands with the)		
We're Gonna Rock/You Don't Know My Mind	58	Hi-Q 5010
Five Dots		
The Other Night/Each Night	54	Dot 1204
I Just Love The Things She Do/Well, Little Baby	55	Note 10003
Five Dreamers (1) (Eddie Banks & the)		
Sugar Diabetes/Rock A Bye Blues	56	Josie 804
Five Dreamers (2) (aka 5 Dreamers)		
You Don't Know/Beverly	57	Port 5001

ARTIST/SONG	YEAR	LABEL

Five Dreams
You Are My Only/Up All Night — 57 — Mercury 71150

Five Dukes (Bennie Woods & the)
Wheel Baby Wheel/I Cross My Fingers — 55 — Atlas 1040

Five Dukes Of Rhythm
Soft, Sweet And Really Fine/Everybody's Singing The Blues — 54 — Rendezvous 812/Fortune 812 (54)

Five Echoes (aka Five Echos)
Baby, Come Back To Me/Lonely Mood — 53 — Sabre 102
So Lonesome/Broke — 54 — Sabre 105
That's My Baby/Why Oh Why — 54 — Sabre 111
Soldier Boy/Down The Road I Go — 56 — Vee Jay 190

Five Echos (aka Five Echoes)
Tell Me, Baby/I Really Do — 55 — Vee Jay 129
Fool's Prayer/Tastee Freeze — 55 — Vee Jay 156

Five Embers
Please Come Home/Love Birds — 54 — Gem 224
Love Tears — 55 — Gem 227 (unreleased)
I'm Free/My Fragile Heart — 60 — Royce 0006

Five Emeralds
I'll Beg/Let Me Take You Out Tonight — 56 — S-R-C 106
Darling/Pleasure Me — 56 — S-R-C 107

Five Encores
Double Date/Whistlin' Willie — 55 — Rama 180
Readin' Ritin' Rithmetic' & Rock 'n' Roll/Ben Ben Quaker Ben — 55 — Rama 185
Dance With The Rock/One Scotch, One Bourbon, One Beer — 55 — Rama 187

Five Fabulous Demons
You'd Better Come Home/Yeah Since You Went Away — 63 — King 5761

Five Fashions
Over The Rainbow/Solitaire — 65 — Catamount 103

Five Flames
I Want You So Bad/There Must Be A Reason — 59 — Federal 12348

Five Fleets
I Been Crying/Oh, What A Feeling — 58 — Felsted 8513
Slight Case Of Love/Yo' Good Lovin' — 58 — Felsted 8522
Cheer Up/Pitter Patter — 61 — Seville 112

Five Fortunes
You Are My Only Love — 58 — Ransom 103

Five G's
Forget Her/I Think I Know — 59 — Washingtonian (no number)

Five Glow Tones
At A Dance/Quiet Village — 59 — Jax 101

Five Grands
Kiss Me/Two For The Blues — 58 — Brunswick 55059

Five Harmonaires (Elaine Gay & the) (aka Harmonaires)
Rock Love/Ebony Eyes — 55 — DeLuxe 2029

Five Hearts (1) (aka Flairs/aka Five Hollywood Blue Jays)
Please, Please, Baby/The Fine One — 54 — Flair 1026

ARTIST/SONG	YEAR	LABEL
Five Hearts (2)		
Tell Ya What/Tremble (by Lord Luther & the Esquires)	60	Music City 833
Five Hearts (3) (ref Lee Andrews & the Hearts)		
Unbelievable/Aunt Jenny	59	Arcade 107
Five Hearts (4)		
My Prayer Tonight	N/A	Ransom
Five Hi Lighters (aka Highlighters (2))		
Sweet Little Baby Of Mine/Mi Amor	59	Cannon 580488
Five Hollywood Blue Jays (aka Flairs) (aka Flairs/aka Five Hearts (1))		
Put A Nickel In The Jukebox/Safronia Ida B. Brown	52	Recorded In Hollywood 162
I Had A Love/Tell Me You're Mine	52	Recorded In Hollywood 396
Cloudy And Raining/So Worried	51	Recorded In Hollywood 185
Five Hungry Men		
We Belong Together	64	Melmar 122
Five Ivories (aka Ivorys)		
Why Don't You Write Me/Deep Freeze	62	Sparta 001
Five J's		
My Darling/Calypso Jump	58	Fulton 2454
Five Jades (1)		
Without Your Love/Rock And Roll Molly	58	Duke 188
Five Jades (2) (aka Five Shadows)		
Rosemarie (a capella)/My Reverie (a capella)	65	Your Choice 1011
My Girl Friend (a capella)/How Much I Love You (a capella)	65	Your Choice 1012
Are You Sorry (a capella)	75	Relic LP 107
Begin The Beguine (a capella)	75	Relic LP 107
Ebb Tide (a capella)	75	Relic LP 107
Endless Night (a capella)	75	Relic LP 107
I Was Such A Fool (a capella)	75	Relic LP 107
I Wish You Love (a capella)	75	Relic LP 107
If I Were To Lose You (a capella)	75	Relic LP 107
If Someone Would Care (a capella)	75	Relic LP 107
In The Still Of The Nite (a capella)	75	Relic LP 107
Tell Her That I Love Her (a capella)	75	Relic LP 107
That's My Desire (a capella)	75	Relic LP 107
That's The Way It Goes (a capella)	75	Relic LP 107
Unchained Melody (a capella)	75	Relic LP 107
When I Fall In Love (a capella)	75	Relic LP 107
Shout (a capella)	75	Relic LP 108
When You Dance (a capella)	75	Relic LP 109
Five Jets (1)		
Not A Hand To Shake/I Am In Love	53	DeLuxe 6018
I'm Stuck/I Want A Woman	54	DeLuxe 6053
Tell Me You're Mine/Give In	54	DeLuxe 6058
Crazy Chicken/Everybody Do The Chicken	54	DeLuxe 6064
Please Love Me Baby/Down Slow	54	DeLuxe 6071
I'm Wanderin'/You Fool (by the Five Dollars)	57	Fortune 833
Five Jets (2)		
Sugaree/The Shake	64	Jewel 739
Five Johnson Brothers		
Sleep With A Dream/Happy Rock & Roll	58	Fulton 2455
Five Joys (Juanita Rogers & the)		
Teenager's Letter Of Promises/I'm So Glad You Love Me	58	Pink Clouds 333

ARTIST/SONG	YEAR	LABEL
Five Keys		
Ling Ting Tong/I'm Alone	54	Capitol 2945
I Took Your Love For A Toy/Ziggus	59	King 5251
Dream On/Dancing Senorita	59	King 5273
How Can I Forget You?/I Burned Your Letter	60	King 5302
Gonna Be Too Late/Rosetta	60	King 5330
I Didn't Know/No Says My Heart	60	King 5358
Valley Of Love/Bimbo	60	King 5398
Girl You Better Stop It	60	King LP 692
Now I Know I Love You	60	King LP 692
Will You	60	King LP 692
Wrapped Up In A Dream	60	King LP 692
You Broke The Only Heart/That's What You're Doing To Me	61	King 5446
Stop Your Crying/Do Something For Me	61	King 5496
I'll Never Stop Loving You/I Can't Escape From You	64	King 5877
Hey Girl/No Matter	65	Inferno 4500
Goddess Of Love/Stop	73	Landmark 101
Teeth & Tongue Will Get You Hung	N/A	Detour LP 33-010
When Will My Troubles End	N/A	Detour LP 33-010
Five Keys (featuring Rudy West)		
Happy Am I	51	Aladdin (unreleased)
Just Like Two Drops Of Water	51	Aladdin (unreleased)
Your Teardrops	51	Aladdin (unreleased)
With A Broken Heart/Too Late	51	Aladdin 3085
The Glory Of Love/Hucklebuck With Jimmy	51	Aladdin 3099
Hucklebuck With Jimmy/Ghost Of A Chance	51	Aladdin 3099A (unreleased)
It's Christmas Time/Old McDonald (Had A Farm)	51	Aladdin 3113
Do I Need You/Can't Keep From Crying	51	Aladdin 3113A (unreleased)
I'll Follow You/Lawdy Miss Mary	51	Groove 0031
Yes Sir, That's My Baby/Old McDonald Had A Farm	52	Aladdin 3118
Darling/Goin' Downtown	52	Aladdin 3119
Red Sails In The Sunset/Be Anything But Be Mine	52	Aladdin 3127
Mistakes/How Long	52	Aladdin 3131
I Hadn't Anyone Till You/Hold Me	52	Aladdin 3136
Serve Another Round/I Cried For You	52	Aladdin 3158
Can't Keep From Crying/Come Go My Bail, Louise	53	Aladdin 3167
Serve Another Round/If You Only Knew	53	Aladdin 3167A (unreleased)
There Ought To Be A Law (Against Breaking A Heart)/ Mama (Your Daughter Told A Lie On Me)	53	Aladdin 3175
When You're Gone/White Cliffs Of Dover	53	Aladdin 3175A (unreleased)
I'll Always Be In Love With You/Rocking And Crying Blues	53	Aladdin 3182
Will My Heart Stand A Chance/Yearning	53	Aladdin 3182A (unreleased)
These Foolish Things/Lonesome Old Story	53	Aladdin 3190
Teardrops In My Eyes/I'm So High	53	Aladdin 3204
My Saddest Hour/Oh! Babe!	53	Aladdin 3214
How Could You Do This To Me	53	Audio-Video (unreleased)
Someday Sweetheart/Love My Loving	54	Aladdin 3228
Deep In My Heart/How Do You Expect Me To Get It	54	Aladdin 3245
My Love/Why Oh Why	54	Aladdin 3263
I'm Just A Fool	54	Capitol (unreleased)
So Glad	54	Capitol (unreleased)
Trapped, Lost, Gone	54	Capitol (unreleased)
Story Of Love/Serve Another Round	55	Aladdin 3312
Shook My Head	55	Capitol (unreleased)
Close Your Eyes/Doggone It, You Did It	55	Capitol 3032
The Verdict/Me Make Um Pow Wow	55	Capitol 3127
Don't You Know I Love You/I Wish I'd Never Learned To Read	55	Capitol 3185
Gee Whittakers/Cause You're My Lover	55	Capitol 3267
Just Sittin'	56	Capitol (unreleased)
What Goes On/You Broke The Rules Of Love	56	Capitol 3318
She's The Most/I Dreamed I Dwelt In Heaven	56	Capitol 3392
Peace And Love/My Pigeon's Gone	56	Capitol 3455
Out Of Sight, Out Of Mind/That's Right	56	Capitol 3502
Wisdom Of A Fool/Now Don't That Prove I Love You	56	Capitol 3597

ARTIST/SONG	YEAR	LABEL
From The Bottom Of My Heart	56	Capitol LP 828/ Capitol EP 1-828 (57)
Dog Gone Baby	57	Capitol (unreleased)
Open Sesame	57	Capitol (unreleased)
Let There Be You/Tiger Lily	57	Capitol 3660
Four Walls/It's A Groove	57	Capitol 3710
This I Promise/The Blues Don't Care	57	Capitol 3738
The Face Of An Angel/Boom Boom	57	Capitol 3786
Do Anything/It's A Crying Shame	57	Capitol 3830
From Me To You/Whippety Whirl	57	Capitol 3861
To Each His Own	57	Capitol LP 828/ Capitol EP 1-828 (57)
Who Do You Know In Heaven	57	Capitol LP 828/ Capitol EP 1-828 (57)
All I Need Is You	57	Capitol LP 828/ Capitol EP 2-828 (57)
C'Est La Vie	57	Capitol LP 828/ Capitol EP 2-828 (57)
Dream	57	Capitol LP 828/ Capitol EP 2-828 (57)
Maybe You'll Be There	57	Capitol LP 828/ Capitol EP 2-828 (57)
The Gypsy/Just For A Thrill	57	Capitol T-828 (D.J. copy)
With All My Love/You're For Me	58	Capitol 3948
Emily Please/Handy Andy	58	Capitol 4009
One Great Love/Really-O Truly-O	58	Capitol 4092
Just To Be With You/You Were Mine	59	King 5276
My Mother's Prayers/As Sure As I Live	59	King 5285
The Measure Of My Love/This Is Something Else	59	King 5305
I've Always Been A Dreamer	60	King LP 688
When Paw Was Courtin' Maw	60	King LP 688
Your Teeth And Your Tongue	60	King LP 688
Out Of Sight, Out Of Mind (a capella)/Close Your Eyes (a capella)	73	Bim Bam Boom 116
Lawdy Miss Mary	89	Detour LP 33-010
Every Heart Is Home At Christmas	90	Capitol CDP 7-94701-2
If You Only Knew	91	EMI CDP7-92709

Five Keys (Rudy West & the)

Out Of Sight, Out Of Mind/You're The One	61	Seg-Way 1008

Five Kings

Light Bulb/Don't Send Me Away	64	Columbia 43060
Here Comes My Baby/Tina	66	Yvette 101

Five Knights

Miracle/Yo Te Amo	59	Specialty 675
She's Allright/Take Me In Your Arms	59	Tau 104
Let Me In/Times Are Getting Harder	61	Minit 626
Dark Was The Night/She's My Baby	63	Bumps 1504

Five Knights (Tommy Taylor & the)

I Want Somebody/Polly Want A Cracker	61	Minit 636

Five Larks (aka Larks (1))

Coffee, Cigarettes And Tears/My Heart Cries For You	51	Apollo 1177

Five Letters

Hold My Baby/Your First Love	58	Ivy 102

Five Lords

Oo-La-La/Falling Tears	60	D.S. 2078

Five Lyrics

I'm Traveling Light/My Honey, Sweet Pea	56	Music City 799

ARTIST/SONG	YEAR	LABEL

Five Masks
| Polly Molly/Forever And A Day | 58 | Jan 101 |

Five Masqueraders (Seaphus Scott & the) (aka Masquerades)
| Nature's Beauty/Summer Sunrise | 58 | Joyce 303 |

Five Masters
| We Are Like One/Cheap Skate | 59 | Bumble Bee 502 |
| Cheap Skate | 86 | Relic LP 8008 |

Five Moneys
| Believe | N/A | Charlie |

Five Notes (1) (Henry Pierce & the)
| Thrill Me Baby/Hey Fine Mama | 52 | Specialty 461 |

Five Notes (2) (aka Notes)
| Park Your Love/Show Me The Way | 55 | Chess 1614 |
| You Are So Beautiful/Broken Hearted Baby | 55 | Jen D 4185/Josie 784 (55) |

Five Notes (3) (Sammy & the)
| North By Northeast/African Cha Cha | 60 | Lucky Four 1010 |
| The Lion Is Awake (answer song)/Doodle Bug Twist | 62 | Lucky Four 1019 |

Five Owls
| Pleading To You/I Like Moonshine | 55 | Vulcan 1025 |

Five Palms (aka Palms)
| Little Girl Of Mine/Tear Drops | 57 | States 163 |

Five Pastels
| You're Just An Angel/Listen Baby | 62 | Dome 249 |

Five Pearls
| Please Let Me Know/Real Humdinger | 54 | Aladdin 3265 |

Five Pennies
Mr. Moon/Let It Rain	55	Savoy 1182
My Heart Trembles/Money	56	Savoy 1190
Wedding Bells/Put This Ring On Your Finger	N/A	Herald (unreleased)

Five Pennies (Big Miller & the)
| All Is Well/Try To Understand | 55 | Savoy 1181 |

Five Playboys
When We Were Young/Page Of My Scrapbook	57	Fee Bee 213/Dot 15605 (57)
Love Me Right/Pages Of My Heart	58	Fee Bee 213
Why Be A Fool/Time Will Allow	58	Mercury 71269
Angel Mine/She's My Baby	59	Fee Bee 232
She's My Baby/Mr. Echo	59	Petite 504

Five Quails (1)
| Jungle Baby/Hop Scotch Rock | 57 | Mercury 71154 |

Five Quails (2) (fb Harvey Fuqua)
| Been A Long Time/Get To School On Time | 62 | Harvey 114/Harvey 4818 |
| My Love/Never Felt Like This Before | 62 | Harvey 116 |

Five Ramblers
| I Want You To Know/Slide, Slide, Slide | 63 | Lummtone 111 |

ARTIST/SONG	YEAR	LABEL

Five Reasons
Go To School/Three O'Clock Rock	58	Cub 9006

Five Roses
Romance In The Spring/Don't Cry, Della	59	Nu Kat 100/101

Five Rovers
Down To The Sea/Change Your Mind	56	Music City 798

Five Satins (ref Scarlets)
Wonderful Girl/Weeping Willow	56	Ember 1008
All Mine/Rose Mary	56	Standord 100
I Remember (In The Still Of The Nite)/The Jones Girl	56	Standord 200/Ember 1005 (56)
Oh Happy Day/Our Love Is Forever	57	Ember 1014
To The Aisle/Wish I Had My Baby	57	Ember 1019
Our Anniversary/Pretty Baby	57	Ember 1025
A Million To One/Love With No Love In Return	57	Ember 1028
Again	57	Ember LP 100
Sugar	57	Ember LP 100/Ember EP 101
I'll Get Along	57	Ember LP 100/Ember EP 102
Moonlight and I	57	Ember LP 100/Ember EP 102
Pretty Baby	57	Ember LP 100/Ember EP 104
A Night To Remember/Senorita Lolita	58	Ember 1038
Shadows/Toni My Love	59	Ember 1056
When Your Love Comes Along/Skippity Doo	59	First 104
Your Memory/I Didn't Know	60	Cub 9071
These Foolish Things/A Beggar With A Dream	60	Cub 9077
I'll Be Seeing You/A Night Like This	60	Ember 1061
Candlelight/The Time	60	Ember 1066
Wishing Ring/Tell Me Dear	60	Ember 1070
I've Got Time	60	Ember LP 401
I've Lost	60	Ember LP 401
You Must Be An Angel	60	Ember LP 401
Can I Come Over Tonight?/Golden Earrings	61	Cub 9090
To The Aisle/Just To Be Near You	61	Musictone 1108
On A Lover's Island/Till The End	61	United Artists 368
The Masquerade Is Over/Raining In My Heart	62	Chancellor 1110
Downtown/Do You Remember	62	Chancellor 1121
Paradise On Earth/Monkey Business (by the Pharotones)	63	Times Square 21/ Times Square 94 (64)
Remember Me/Kangaroo	63	Warner Bros. 5367
You Can Count On Me/Ain't Gonna Cry	64	Roulette 4563
In The Still Of The Night "67"/Heck No (instrumental)	67	Mama Sadie 1001
Summer In New York/Dark At The Top Of My Heart	71	RCA 74-0478
Very Precious Oldies/You Are Love	73	Kirshner 4251
Story To You/I Love You So	73	Klik 1020
She's Gone With The Wind/(Somewhere) A Voice Is Calling	74	Candlelite 411
Two Different Worlds/Love Is Such A Beautiful Thing	74	Kirshner 4252
Annie's Back	N/A	Relic LP 5024
Church Bells Played The Blues	N/A	Relic LP 5024
Lonely Hearts	N/A	Relic LP 5024
Lover's Hill	N/A	Relic LP 5024
My Present Love	N/A	Relic LP 5024
Silver Waters	N/A	Relic LP 5024
Wonder Why	N/A	Relic LP 5024
Noone Knows/Musical Chairs	N/A	Sammy 103

Five Scalders
Girlfriend/Willow Blues	56	Drummond 3001
If Only You Were Mine/There Will Come A Time	56	Sugarhill 3000/ Drummond 3000 (56)

Five Scamps
With All My Heart/Red Hot	54	Okeh 7049

ARTIST/SONG	YEAR	LABEL

Five Scripts (aka Contenders/aka Kaptions/aka Lytations/aka Zippers)

Peace Of Mind/The Clock	63	Long Fiber 201
My Friends Call Me/You Left My Heart	65	Script 103

Five Secrets (aka Secrets (1)/aka Loungers)

Queen Bee/See You Next Year	57	Decca 30350 (first pressing, second is by the Secrets)

Five Sequins (Gary Haines & the)

Another Girl Like You/Tsetse Fly	61	Kapp 383

Five Shades

Mary Had A Little Lamb/Lonely Boy	61	Ember 1074
One Hot Dog/Sherlock Jones	61	MGM 13035
Vickie/I'll Give You Love	65	Veep 1208

Five Shadows (aka Five Jades (2))

Sunday Kind Of Love/Don't Say Goodnight	65	Mellomood 011/012

Five Sharks (aka Sharks)

Gloria (a capella)/Flames (a capella)	64	Old Timer 604/Siamese 404 (64)
Stand By Me (a capella)/I'll Never Let You Go (a capella)	64	Old Timer 605
Stormy Weather (Short & Long Versions)/If You Love Me	64	Times Square 35/Relic 525 (65)
The Lion Sleeps Tonight (a capella)/ Land Of A 1000 Dances (a capella)	66	Amber 852

Five Sharps

Stormy Weather/Sleepy Cowboy	52	Jubilee 5104
Stormy Weather/Mammy Jammy	64	Jubilee 5478

Five Shillings

Letter To An Angel/The Snake	58	Decca 30722

Five Sounds

The Greatest Gift Of All/Chalypso Baby	58	Deb 1006
Good Time Baby/That's When I Fell In Love	60	Baritone 940/941

Five Sounds (Russ Riley & the)

Tonight Must Live On/Crazy Feeling	57	Aljon 115

Five Sparks

Little Bo Peep/A Million Tears	59	Jimbo 1

Five Speeds

Tell Me/Goodbye	59	Wiggie 131

Five Spenders (aka Regents (2))

No Hard Feelings/That's What I Call A Good Time	60	Versatile 113

Five Splendors

Your Dog Hates Me/The Elephant Walk	60	Stroll 106

Five Stars (1)

Where Did Caledonia Go?/Walkin' An' Talkin'	54	Show Time 1102
Let's Fall In Love/We Danced In The Moonlight	55	Treat 505

Five Stars (2)

Take Five/Humpty Dumpty	56	Atco 6065
Dreaming/Pickin' On The Wrong Chicken	58	Note 10011/Hunt 318 (58)/ ABC 9911 (58)
Friction/My Paradise	58	Note 10016
Am I Wasting My Time/Gamblin' Man	59	Note 10031

Five Stars (3)

So Lonely, Baby/Hey, Juanita	57	Blue Boys Kingdom 106
Atom Bomb Baby/You Sweet Little Thing	57	Kernel 319574/Dot 15579 (57)

ARTIST/SONG	YEAR	LABEL
Ooh, Shucks/Dead Wrong	57	Mark-X 7006
Baby, Baby/Blabber Mouth	58	End 1028/Columbia 42056 (61)

Five Stars (4) (Gary Roberts & the)

You Made Me A Prisoner Of Love	N/A	Sterling 681

Five Superiors

Big Shot/There's A Fool Born Every Day	62	Garpax 44170

Five Swans

Li'l Girl Of My Dreams/Li'l Tipa-Tina	56	Music City 795

Five Techniques

Heaven Above/Don't Tell Me	61	Imperial 5742

Five Teenbeats

Autumn Mood/Time To Rock	60	Big Top 3062

Five Thrills (aka Earls (1))

My Baby's Gone/Feel So Good	53	Parrot 796
Wee, Wee Baby/Gloria	54	Parrot 800
All I Want	90	Relic LP 5087
Ride Jimmy Ride	90	Relic LP 5087
So Long Young Girl	90	Relic LP 5087
Rockin' At Midnight	90	Relic LP 8020

Five Tinos

Sitting By My Window/Don't Do That!	55	Sun 222

Five Trojans

Alone In This World/Don't Ask Me To Be Lonely	58	Tender 516
Little Doll/Lola Lee	59	Edison International 412

Five Trojans (Nicky St. Clair & the)

I Hear Those Bells/Creator Of Love	59	Edison International 410

Five Vets

You're In Love/Right Now	56	Allstar 713/Bruce

Five Whispers

Moon In The Afternoon/Midnight Sun	62	Dolton 61

Five Willows (aka Willows (1))

My Dear, Dearest Darling/Rock, Little Francis	53	Allen 1000
Dolores/All Night Long	53	Allen 1002
White Cliffs Of Dover/With These Hands	53	Allen 1003
Love Bells/Please, Baby	53	Pee Dee 290
Baby, Come A Little Closer/Lay Your Head On My Shoulder	54	Herald 433
Look Me In The Eyes/So Help Me	54	Herald 442

Five Wings (1)

Johnny Has Gone/Johnny's Still Singing	55	King 4778
Teardrops Are Falling/Rock-A-Locka	55	King 4781/King 5199

Five Wings (2) (Billy Nelson & the)

Walk Along/Shack, Pack And Stack Your Blues Away	56	Savoy 1183
My Gal/Hurry Up Honey	N/A	Savoy 999 (unreleased)

Flairs (1)

I Had A Love/She Wants To Rock	53	Flair 1012
You Should Care For Me/Tell Me You Love Me	53	Flair 1019
Gettin' High/Love Me Girl	54	Flair 1028
Baby Wants/You Were Untrue	54	Flair 1041
This Is The Night For Love/Let's Make With Some Love	54	Flair 1044
Hold Me, Thrill Me, Chill Me/I'll Never Let You Go	55	Flair 1056

ARTIST/SONG	YEAR	LABEL
My Darling, My Sweet/She Loves To Dance	55	Flair 1067
I'd Climb The Hills And Mountains/Swing Pretty Mama	59	Antler 4005
Cool, Baby, Cool	84	Cadet
I Love You	63	Crown LP 5356
I Want You To Be Mine	63	Crown LP 5356
Lonesome Desert	63	Crown LP 5356
My Heart's Crying For You	63	Crown LP 5356
Rock Bottom	63	Crown LP 5356
Tell Me You're Mine	63	Crown LP 5356

Flairs (1) (Cornel Gunter & the)

In Self Defense/She Loves To Rock	56	ABC 9698
Aladdin's Lamp/Steppin' Out	56	ABC 9740
Where You Live/You Got To Steal	N/A	Rap 007

Flairs (1) (Etta James & the)

Sunshine Of Our Love/Baby Baby Every Night	59	Kent 304

Flairs (1) (Fatso Theus & the)

Be Cool, My Heart/Rock 'N' Roll Drive-In	56	Aladdin 3324

Flairs (1) (James Stallcup & the)

Baby Let's Make Love/Sad Feeling	61	Le Cam 724

Flairs (1) (Richard Berry & the)

The Big Break/What Would You Do To Me	55	Flair 1055
(Oh Oh) Get Out Of The Car/Please Tell Me	55	Flair 1064
God Gave Me You/Don't Cha Go	55	Flair 1068

Flairs (1) (Shirley Gunter & the)

How Can I Tell You?/Ipsy Opsie Ooh	55	Flair 1076
Fortune In Love/I Just Got Rid Of A Heartache	56	Modern 1001
Headin' Home/I Want You	56	Modern 989

Flairs (2)

The Memory Lingers On/Shake Shake Sherry	61	Epic 9447
Roll Over Beethoven/Brazil	N/A	Palms 5961

Flame Tones (Richard Willans & the)

Oldies But Goodies/Little Sister Nell	72	Bell 192

Flames (1) (aka Hollywood Flames)

Young Girl/Please Tell Me Now	50	Selective 113
Strange Land Blues/Cryin' For My Baby	52	Spin 101
Keep On Smiling/Baby, Baby, Baby	53	7-11 2106
Baby, Pretty Baby/Together	53	7-11 2107
Let's Talk It Over/Tears Keep Tumbling Down	53	7-11 2108 (unreleased)
Volcano/Sorrowful Heart (lead by Patti Anne Mesner)	53	7-11 2109 (unreleased)
I'll Hide My Tears/Got A Little Shadow	53	7-11 2110 (unreleased)
So All Alone/Flame Mambo	56	Aladdin 3349

Flames (1) (Patti Anne Mesner & the)

Midnight/My Heart Is Free Again	52	Aladdin 3162
Sorrowful Heart/Beginning To Miss You (no group)	53	Aladdin 3198

Flames (2) (Tommy "Mary Jo" Braden & His)

Do The Do/Did You Ever See A Monkey	55	United 177

Flames (3)

I'll Never Let You Go/Crazy	59	Bertram 203

Flames (4) (Allan & the)

Till The End Of Time/Winter Wonderland (instrumental)	60	Colonial 7006/Campbell 225-1

ARTIST/SONG	YEAR	LABEL
Flames (5) (Farrell & the)		
Dreams And Memories/You'll Be Sorry	61	Fransil 14
Flames (6) (Carol Pegues & the)		
Darling Jane/Blues Around My Door	N/A	GM 101
Flames (7) (Alton & the)		
Nothing Sweeter	N/A	Duchess
Flamettes		
You You You/Hee Hee Ha Ha	61	Laurie 3109
Flaming Embers		
Gone Gone Gone/You Can Count On Me	61	Fortune 869
Flaming Hearts		
I Don't Mind/Baby	58	Vulco V1
Flamingo, Johnny (& female group)		
Will She Think Of Me/Paradise Hill	58	Specialty 640
Flamingo, Johnny (& group)		
I/It Were You	57	Canton 1785
United/I Just Cry	59	Malynn 101
Flamingos		
If I Can't Have You/Someday Someway	53	Chance 1133
That's My Desire/Hurry Home Baby	53	Chance 1140
Golden Teardrops/Carried Away	53	Chance 1145/Vee Jay 384 (61)
Plan For Love/You Ain't Ready	53	Chance 1149
Cross Over The Bridge/Listen To My Plea	54	Chance 1154
Blues In A Letter/Jump Children	54	Chance 1162
Dream Of A Lifetime/On My Merry Way	54	Parrot 808
When/(Chica Boom)That's My Baby	55	Checker 815
Please Come Back Home/I Want To Love You	55	Checker 821
I Really Don't Want To Know/Get With It	55	Parrot 811
I'm Yours/Ko Ko Mo	55	Parrot 812
Cry	56	Checker (unreleased)
I'll Be Home/Need Your Love	56	Checker 830
A Kiss From Your Lips/Get With It	56	Checker 837
The Vow/Shilly Dilly	56	Checker 846
Would I Be Crying/Just For Kicks	56	Checker 853
That Love Is You	57	Decca (unreleased)
The Ladder Of Love/Let's Make Up	57	Decca 30335
My Faith In You/Helpless	57	Decca 30454
Where Mary Go/Rock And Roll March	58	Decca 30687
Without A Song	58	End (unreleased)
Lovers Never Say Goodbye/That Love Is You	58	End 1035
Dream Of A Lifetime/Whispering Stars	59	Checker 915
Chickie Um Bah	59	Checker LP 3005/ Chess LP 1433 (59)
Nobody's Love	59	Checker LP 3005/ Chess LP 1433 (59)
Stolen Love	59	Checker LP 3005/ Chess LP 1433 (59)
Kiss-A-Me/Ever Since I Met Lucy	59	Decca 30880
Jerri Lee/Hey Now	59	Decca 30948
River Of Tears	59	End (unreleased)
We Were Made For Each Other	59	End (unreleased)
But Not For Me/I Shed A Tear At Your Wedding	59	End 1040
Love Walked In/At The Prom	59	End 1044
I Only Have Eyes For You/At The Prom	59	End 1046
I Only Have Eyes For You/Goodnight Sweetheart	59	End 1046
Love Walked In/Yours	59	End 1055
I Was Such A Fool/Heavenly Angel	59	End 1062

ARTIST/SONG	YEAR	LABEL
As Time Goes By	59	End LP 304
Begin The Beguine	59	End LP 304
The Breeze And I	59	End LP 304
Where Or When	59	End LP 304
I'm In The Mood For Love	59	End LP 304/End EP 205 (59)
Music Maestro Please	59	End LP 304/End EP 205 (59)
Mio Amore/You, Me And The Sea	60	End 1065
Nobody Loves Me Like You/Besame Mucho	60	End 1068
Besame Mucho/You, Me And The Sea	60	End 1070
Mio Amore/At Night	60	End 1073
When I Fall In Love/Beside You	60	End 1079
Your Other Love/Lovers Gotta Cry	60	End 1081
Kokomo/That's Why I Love You	60	End 1085
Bridge Of Tears	60	End LP 307
Crazy, Crazy, Crazy	60	End LP 307
Maria Elena	60	End LP 307
My Foolish Heart	60	End LP 307
Never In This World	60	End LP 307
Sweet And Lovely	60	End LP 307
Tell Me How Long	60	End LP 307
You Belong To My Heart	60	End LP 307
Every Time I Think Of You	60	End LP 308
Everybody's Got A Home	60	End LP 308
Happy Birthday Elise	60	End LP 308
In The Still Of The Night	60	End LP 308
Tenderly	60	End LP 308
You'll Never Walk Alone	60	End LP 308
Lover Come Back	61	End (unreleased)
Dream Girl/Time Was	61	End 1092
My Memories Of You/I Want To Love You	61	End 1099
I'm No Fool Anymore/It Must Be Love	62	End 1111
For All We Know/Near You	62	End 1116
I Know Better/Flame Of Love	62	End 1121
(Talk About) True Love/Come On To My Party	62	End 1124
(When You're Young And) Only Seventeen	62	End LP 316
Danny Boy	62	End LP 316
Moonlight In Vermont	62	End LP 316
Ol' Man River	62	End LP 316
The Sinner	62	End LP 316
Too Soon To Know	62	End LP 316
You're Mine	62	End LP 316
Shout It Out	63	End (unreleased)
I'm Coming Home	63	End LP 316
My Lovely One	63	End LP 316
Without His Love	63	End LP 316
Ol' Man River Pt. 1/Ol' Man River Pt. 2	63	Roulette 4524
Lover Come Back To Me/Your Little Guy	64	Checker 1084
Goodnight Sweetheart Goodnight/Does It Really Matter	64	Checker 1091
September Song	64	Constellation LP 3
Lovely Way To Spend An Evening/Walking My Baby Back Home	64	Times Square 102
I Found A New Baby	90	Relic LP 5088/ Chess LP 702 (76)
If I Could Love You	90	Relic LP 5088/ Chess LP 702 (76)

Flannels

Hey Rube/So Shy	56	Tampa 121

Flares (aka Cadets (1)/aka Jacks)

Loving You/Hotcha Cha-Cha Brown	60	Felsted 8604
Jump And Bump/What Do You Want If You Don't Want Love?	60	Felsted 8607
Foot Stomping Pt. 1/Foot Stomping Pt. 2 (instrumental)	61	Felsted 8624
Rock And Roll Heaven Pt. 1/Rock And Roll Heaven Pt. 2	61	Press 2800
Doing The Hully Gully/Truck And Trailer	61	Press 2802
Mad House/Make It Be Me	61	Press 2803

ARTIST/SONG	YEAR	LABEL
Do It With Me/Yon We Go	61	Press 2807
Hand Clappin'/Shimmy And Stomp	61	Press 2808
The Monkey Walk/Do It If You Wanna	61	Press 2810
Doing The Watusi	N/A	London (England) LP 8034
Fish And Twist	N/A	London (England) LP 8034
Huckle-Buck	N/A	London (England) LP 8034
Shake, Shimmy And Stroll	N/A	London (England) LP 8034
Sock Hop	N/A	London (England) LP 8034
The Pony	N/A	London (England) LP 8034
The Stroll	N/A	London (England) LP 8034
The Twist	N/A	London (England) LP 8034

Flares (Cookie Jackson & the) (ref Cadets (1)/ref Jacks)
I Didn't Lose A Doggone Thing/Write A Song About Me	61	Press 2814

Flares (Paul Ballenger & the) (ref Cadets (1)/ref Jacks)
I Still Love You/Seven Times Heaven	58	Reed 711

Flasher Brothers
Love Gave Me To You/To Live The Life Of A Lie	52	Aladdin 3156

Flashes (Jess Davis & the)
With All My Heart And Soul/Come What May	59	Bob-O-Link 100

Fleas
Tears/Scratchin'	61	Challenge 9115

Fleetones
Your Lover Man/Please Tell me	61	Bandera 2511

Fleetwoods
Come Softly To Me/I Care So Much	59	Dolton 1/Liberty 55188 (59)/ Liberty 77188 (59)
Graduation's Here/Oh Lord, Let It Be	59	Dolton 3/Dolton S-3 (59)
Mr. Blue/You Mean Everything To Me	59	Dolton 5
Outside My Window/Magic Star	60	Dolton 15
Runaround/Truly Do	60	Dolton 22
The Last One To Know/Dormilona	60	Dolton 27
Confidential/I Love You So	60	Dolton 30
Tragedy/Little Miss Sad One	61	Dolton 40
(He's The) The Great Impostor/Poor Little Girl	61	Dolton 45
Billy Old Buddy/Trouble	61	Dolton 49
Lovers By Night, Strangers By Day/They Tell Me It's Summer	62	Dolton 62
You Should've Been There/Sure Is Lonesome Downtown	63	Dolton 74
Goodnight My Love/Jimmy Beware	63	Dolton 75
What'll I Do/Baby Bye-O	63	Dolton 86
Before And After (Losing You)/Lonely Is As Lonely Does	64	Dolton 302
I'm Not Jimmy/Come Softly To Me	64	Dolton 307
Rainbow/Just As I Needed You	64	Dolton 310
For Lovin' Me/This Is Where I See Her	64	Dolton 315
Lonesome Town/Ruby Red, Baby Blue	64	Dolton 93
Ten Times Blue/Ska Light, Ska Bright	64	Dolton 97
Mr. Sandman/This Is My Prayer	64	Dolton 98

Flints
Over The Ocean/Chickie Chop Chop	58	Petite 101
People Say/Skippin' And Jumpin'	59	Okeh 7126
Why Do You Go/When Summer Gets Back	62	Heart 100

Flippers
You Yakity Yak Too Much/My Aching Heart	55	Flip 305

Flips (1)
Why Should I (flip has no group)	55	Sapphire 1052
Gone Away/It Will Never Be The Same	59	Mercury 71426

ARTIST/SONG	YEAR	LABEL
Flips (2) (Kip Tyler & the)		
Jungle Hop/Ooh Yeah Baby	58	Challenge 59008
Flips (3) (Mario & the)		
Once In A While/Nobody's Sweetheart	59	Cross Country 100
Twistin' Train/You Made Me Love You	61	Decca 31252
Flips (4) (Joey & the)		
The Beachcomber/Fool, Fool, Fool	64	Cameo 327
Flips (4) (Little Joey & the)		
Our Own Little World/My First Love Letter	60	Joy 243
Bongo Stomp/Lost Love	62	Joy 262
Bongo Gully/It Was Like Heaven	62	Joy 268
The Mystery Of The Night/Hot Rod	76	Monogram 111 (bootleg)
Flips (5)		
Rockin' With Rosie	N/A	Arctic 102
Flores, Bob (& group)		
Church Bells Twist	N/A	Arctic 102
Flores, Teddy (& group)		
Karen My Darling	N/A	Deflor 65729
Florescents		
What Are You Doing Tonight?/Being In Love	63	Bethlehem 3079
Floridians		
That Lucky Old Sun/I Love Marie	61	ABC 10185
Fluorescents		
The Facts Of Love/Shoopy Pop-A-Doo	59	Hanover 4520/ Candelite 420 (59)
Flyers		
On Bended Knee/My Only Desire	57	Atco 6088
Island Love	N/A	Fabbi
Foote, Chuck (& group)		
Come On Back/You're Running Out Of Kisses	61	Soncraft 401
Ford, Ann (& group)		
The Fool/Can't Tell You	59	Apollo 532
Foreign Intrigue (aka Ernie Maresca & the Del Satins)		
The Wanderer/Blind Date	N/A	E.M. 1001
Foretells		
Exodus (a capella)/Return To Me (a capella)	65	Catamount 109
Forevers		
Isn't That A Lovely Way To Say Goodnight	58	Apt
Baby/Slow Down	58	Apt 25022
Fortes		
Waiting For My Baby/Why Won't You Change Your Ways For Me	64	Current 103
Fortune Bravos (Spider Turner & the)		
Ride In My 225/One Stop	63	Fortune 570
Fortune Tellers		
Song Of The Nairobi Trio/Camel Train	61	Music Makers 105
School Prom/Just A Little Bit Of Your Love	61	Sheryl 340
Marry Her Joe/I Love You (Inka Doo)	63	Atlantic 2197

ARTIST/SONG	YEAR	LABEL
Fortune, Jimmy (& group)		
Moonlight Shadows/I Feel A Heartache Comin' On	61	Chancellor 1097
Fortune, Johnny (bb the Paramours)		
I'm Talking About You/My Wandering Love	63	Park Ave. 4905
Fortuneers		
Look-A-There/Oh, Woh, Baby	N/A	Skytone 1000
Fortunes (1) (aka Donald & the Delighters)		
Believe In Me/My Baby Is Fine	55	Checker 818
Bread	90	Relic LP 5088
Love	90	Relic LP 5088
Fortunes (2)		
Who Cares?/Tarnished Angel	58	Decca 30541
How Clever Of You/Trees	58	Decca 30688
Fortunes (3)		
Steady Vows/In The Night	59	Top Rank 2019
Congratulations/Look At Me, Look At You	60	Argo 5364
Nothing Matters Anymore/Ugly Duckling	61	Queen 24010
The Laugh Of The Town/This Is Love	64	Yucca 168/170
Fortunes (4)		
The Ghoul In School/You Don't Know (What I've Been Through)	63	Cub 9123
Fortunes (5)		
Running Away From Love/Tell Me	62	DRA 320
Foster Brothers		
Tell Me Who/I Said She Wouldn't Do	57	El-Bee 161
Never Again/I Could Cry	58	Hi Mi 3005
Show Me/If You Want My Heart	58	Mercury 71360
Trust In Me/Why-Yi-Yi	59	Profile 4004
Revenge/Pretty, Fickle Woman	60	B&F 1333
Foster Brothers (Lefty "Guitar" Bates & the)		
Land Of Love/Let's Jam	60	Dilly 101
Fountain, Morris (& group)		
Cryin' My Heart Out/Juicin' And Goofin'	54	Savoy 1139
4 Gents		
I Refuse To Pay/My Bernadette	63	Vida 0123
4 Thoughts		
When I'm With You/Kisses And Roses	N/A	Womar 103
4 Uniques		
Endlessly/Maybe Next Summer	64	USA 753
Four After Fives (aka Rivingtons)		
Hello, Schoolteacher!/I Gotta Have Somebody (Lonely Boy)	61	All Time 9076
Four Arcs (aka Imperials (1))		
Life Of Ease/It Won't Be Very Long	54	Boulevard 102
Four B's		
Love Eternal/I Played The Fool	58	D 1013
Four Barons (1) (aka Larks)		
Got To Go Back Again/Lemon Squeezer	50	Regent 1026

ARTIST/SONG	YEAR	LABEL

Four Barons (2)

| Old Enough To Know/Bambinella | 57 | Roman 400 |

Four Bars (1)

Hey Baby/Grief By Day, Grief By Night	54	Josie 762
If I Give My Heart To You/Stop It! Quit It!	54	Josie 768
Memories Of You/When Did You Leave Heaven?	54	Republic 7101
Why Do You Treat Me This Way/Let Me Live	55	Josie 783
Love Me Forever More/What's On Your Mind?	60	Cadillac 2006
Phony Baloney/Why Did You Do It	60	Time 4

Four Bars (2)

Try Me One More Time/Comin' On Home	62	Dayco 101/Shelley 180
Poor Little Me/Stay On My J.O.B.	62	Dayco 2500
Try Me One More Time/What's On Your Mind	63	Shelley 180/Dayco 101 (62)
I've Got To Move/Waitin' On The Right Guy	64	Falew 108
Lean On Me When Heartaches Get Rough/Why I've Got To Know	62	Dayco 4564

Four Bars (2) (Betty Wilson & the)

| I'm Yours/All Over Again | 62 | Dayco 1631 |

Four Bars (2) (Shane Hunter & the)

| I'm So Helpless/Follow Me | 59 | IPS 101 |

Four Bars (3)

| Just Bid Me Farewell/The Game Of Romance | 61 | Len 1014 |

Four Bars (4)

| We Are Together | N/A | Flying Hawk 1501 |

Four Beats (Donn Bruce & the)

| Love Leads A Fool/Let's Start All Over Again | 56 | Tuxedo 914 |

Four Beaus

| Tight Shoes/Partners Paradise | 59 | Todd 1028 |

Four Bel-Aires

| Tell Me Why/Where Are You | 58 | X-Tra 113 |

Four Bel-Aires (Larry Lee & the)

| Can I Be In Love/Stolen Love | 59 | M-Z 006 |

Four Bells

Please Tell It To Me/Long Way To Go	53	Gem 207/Crystal 102
Here/Dream, Dream, Dream	54	Bell 1039
Hey Nita/When I Needed You Most	54	Bell 5047
Only A Miracle/My Tree	54	Gem 220

Four Bits

| Hey Dreamboat/Glad Glad Glad | 58 | Coin 1501 |

Four Blades

I Want You To Be My Girl/Can You Find It In Your Heart	56	Gateway 1170
Church Bells May Ring/Stardust	56	Gateway 1174
You Didn't Sign Your Letter With Love/Bake That Chicken Pie	63	Alert 422

Four Bluebirds (gm Bobby Nunn)

| My Baby Done Told Me/Court Room Blues (Johnny Otis & Orchestra) | 49 | Excelsior 540 |

Four Blues

| Re Bop-De-Boom/The Vegetable Song | 50 | Apollo 1145 |
| Missing You/As Long As I Live | 50 | Apollo 1160 |

ARTIST/SONG	YEAR	LABEL
Four Brothers And A Cousin		
Trust In Me/Whistle Stop Blues	54	Jaguar 3003
Whispering Winds/Can It Be	54	Jaguar 3005
Four Buddies (1)		
I Will Wait/Just To See You Smile Again	51	Savoy 769
Don't Leave Me Now/Sweet Slumber	51	Savoy 779
My Summer's Gone/Why At A Time Like This	51	Savoy 789
I'm Yours/Moonlight In Your Eyes	51	Savoy 809 (unreleased)
Heart And Soul/Sin	51	Savoy 817
Simply Say Goodbye/Window's Eyes	51	Savoy 823
You're Part Of Me/Story Blues	52	Savoy 845
What's The Matter With Me/Sweet Tooth For My Baby	52	Savoy 866
My Mother's Eyes/Ooh-Ow	53	Savoy 888
I Love You Yes I Do/It Could Have Been Me	N/A	Savoy 951 (unreleased)
You Left Me Blue/Got Everything But You	N/A	Savoy 955 (unreleased)
Close To You/Stop Your Hittin' On Me	N/A	Savoy 959 (unreleased)
Four Buddies (1) (Dolly Cooper & the)		
I'd Climb The Highest Mountain/I Wanna Know (no group)	53	Savoy 891
Four Buddies (2)		
Delores/Look Out	56	Club 51 105
Four Buddies (2) (Bobbie James & the)		
I Need You So/Baby, I'm Tired (Bobbie James)	56	Club 51 104
Four Buddies (2) (Rudy Greene & the)		
You Mean Everything To Me/Highway No. 1	56	Club 51 103
Four Buddies (3)		
Hurt/Moonglow	61	Coral 62217
The Light/Cin Cin	62	Coral 62325
Slow Locomotion/Lonely Summer	63	Philips 40122
I Want To Be The Boy You Love/Just Enough Of Your Love	64	Imperial 66018
Four Buddies (4)		
Allright Already	59	Willett 100
Four Buds (aka Four Buddies (1)/aka Buddies (2)/aka Barons (1))		
Just To See You Smile Again/I Will Wait	50	Savoy 769
Four Cal-Quettes (aka Four Couquettes)		
Starbright/Billy, My Billy	61	Capitol 4574
Most Of All/I'm Gonna Love Him Anyway	61	Capitol 4657
I Cried/Movie Magazines	63	Liberty 55549
Four Casts		
Stormy Weather/Working At The Factory	64	Atlantic 2228
Four Chanels (Virgil & the) (aka 5 Chanels)		
Waiting/Don't Keep It To Yourself	59	Deb 508
Four Chaps		
Completely Yours/Foolish Little Butterfly	56	Rama 195
Roll Over Beethoven/Wrong Number	56	Rama 199
True Lovers/Will You Or Won't You	62	Co & Ce 231 (65)
Four Checkers		
Broken Heart/Sheila	59	Ace 129
Four Checks		
I'll Be Around/Big Feet Mary	61	Tri Disc 101

ARTIST/SONG	YEAR	LABEL
Four Cheers		
Fatal Charms Of Love/Perriwinkle Blue	58	End 1034
Four Chevelles		
This Is Our Wedding Day/Darling, Forever	57	Band Box 357
I Can't Believe/I Know	57	Band Box 358
Four Chickadees (female)		
Ding Dong/Teenage Blues	56	Checker 849
Four Chimes (aka Moroccos)		
Before I Met You	54	States (unreleased)
My Easy Baby	54	States (unreleased)
When My Baby Was Born	54	United (unreleased)
Four Chymes		
The Gypsy/Now Look At Who's Crying	63	Musicnote 121
Four Classmates (aka Classmates (2))		
A Kiss Is Not A Kiss/What Am I Gonna Do	55	King 1487
Four Clefs		
Time After Time (a capella)/Please Be Mine (a capella)	66	B-J 1000
Four Clippers		
You Can't Trust A Woman/Rain	57	Fox (no #)
Four Closures		
Maybe/Rock-A-My Soul	58	Specialty 643
Four Coachmen		
If You Believe/Nothing But Love, Love, Love	59	Castle 507
Shalom/Swamp Legend	60	Adonis 106/Dot 16297 (61)
Wintertime/That Thing Called A Girl	60	Adonis A-102
Four Counts (1)		
Young Hearts/I'm Gonna Love You	58	Dart 1014
Four Counts (2)		
I Love You With All My Heart/Rock & Roll's Good For The Soul	58	Cham 003
Yum-mee, Yum-mee/Cuckoo	58	Josie 840/Go 103
Four Counts (3)		
Heavenly/Blue Eyes	60	Ace 597
Four Counts (4)		
Graduation/Fanny Mae	62	Fine 2562
Four Couquettes (aka Four Cal-Quettes) (female)		
Sparkle And Shine/In This World	61	Capitol 4534
Again/I'll Never Come Back	62	Capitol 4725
Four Cousins (Bill Murray & the)		
Time And Time Again/Guaranteed	58	20th Century 75020
Four Crickets		
A Thousand Miles Away	N/A	Tops 702
Four Cruisers (Joseph Dobbin & the)		
On Account Of You/Beale St. Shuffle	53	Chess 1547
Four Dates		
I Say Babe/Hey Roly Poly	58	Chancellor 1019

ARTIST/SONG	YEAR	LABEL

Four Dates (fb Fabian Forte)
I'm Happy/Eloise	58	Chancellor 1014
Lilly Lou/Be My Steady Date	58	Chancellor 1024
Teenage Neighbor/I Feel Good	58	Chancellor 1027

Four Deals
It's Too Late Now/There Ain't No Bears In The Forest	50	Capitol 1313

Four Del-Aires (Lucy Ann Grassi & the)
Boy Crazy/Scuba Duba	64	Volcanic 1002

Four Deuces
W-P-L-J/Here Lies My Love (by Mr. Undertaker)	55	Music City 790
Down It Went/Goose Is Gone	56	Music City 796
Polly/Yella Shoes	59	Everest 19311

Four Directions
Tonight We Love/Arthur	65	Coral 68456

Four Dolls
Proud Of You/Three On A Date	57	Capitol 3766
Whoop-A-Lala/I'm Following You	58	Capitol 3895

Four Dots (1)
You Won't Let Me Go/My Dear	51	Dot 1043

Four Dots (2) (aka Heartbreakers)
Rita/He Man Looking For A She Girl	56	Bullseye 103
Peace Of Mind/Kiss Me, Sugar Plum	56	Bullseye 104

Four Dots (3) (Jerry Stone & the) (with Eddie Cochran & Jewel Akens)
It's Heaven/My Baby (She Loves Me)	58	Freedom 44002
Pleading For Your Love/Don't Wake Up The Kids	59	Freedom 44005

Four Dots (4) (Deke Watson & the)
Strange As It Seems/Saturday Night Function	N/A	Castle 2006

Four Duchesses (female) (aka Duchesses)
Cry For My Baby/Queen Without A King	60	Chief 7014
Why	N/A	unreleased

Four Dukes (1)
Crying In The Chapel/I Done Done It	53	Duke 116

Four Dukes (2)
Baby Won't You Please Come Home/John Henry	60	Imperial 5653

Four Ekkos
My Love I Give/Toodaloo Kangaroo	58	RIP 12558
Hand In Hand/Think Twice	59	Label 2022

Four Ekkos (Bernie Campbell & the)
Baby You Belong To Me/Will I Ever Find My Baby	N/A	Fine 26571

Four Ekkos (Jerry Engler & the)
Unfaithful One/Sputnik (Satellite Girl)	57	Brunswick 55037

Four Eldorados (aka El Dorados (1))
A Lonely Boy/Go! Little Susie	58	Academy 8138

Four Embers
But Beautiful/You've Been Away Too Long	63	Smash 1846

Four Epics (aka Exodus/aka Vespers)
I'm On My Way To Love/When The Music Ends	62	Heritage 109

ARTIST/SONG	YEAR	LABEL
Again/I Love You Diane	63	Laurie 3155
How I Wish I Was Single Again/Dance Joanne	63	Laurie 3183
Mr. Cupid/When I Walk With My Angel (by the Vespers)	63	Swan 4156
I Love You Alanne	N/A	N/A

Four Escorts (1)

Love Me/Loop De Loop Mambo	54	RCA 5886

Four Escorts (2)

My Special Girl/Don't You Remember	61	Skyla 1113

Four Escorts (3) (Dave Passecallo & the)

By The Fire/Baby, Where Are You?	N/A	N/A

Four Esquires

Follow Me/Summer Vacation	56	Pilgrim 717
Follow Me/Land Of You And Me	58	Paris 526
Can't Help Falling In Love/Merry-Go-Round Of Home	62	Terrace 7502

Four Exceptions

A Sad Goodbye	66	Parkway

Four Feathers (Gene Forrest & the)

Wiggle/Dubio	54	Aladdin 3224

Four Fellows (1)

I Tried/Bend Of The River	54	Derby 862
I Wish I Didn't Know You/I Know Love	55	Glory 231
Soldier Boy/Take Me Back, Baby	55	Glory 234
Angels Say/In The Rain	55	Glory 236
Fallen Angel/Hold 'Em, Joe	56	Glory 238
Petticoat Baby/I'm Past Sixteen (with Bette McLaurin)	56	Glory 241
Darling You/Please Don't Deprive Me Of Love	56	Glory 242
I Sit In My Window/Please Play My Song	56	Glory 244
You Don't Know Me/You Sweet Girl	56	Glory 248
Give Me Back My Broken Heart/Loving You, Darling	57	Glory 250

Four Fellows (1) (Bette McLaurin & the)

Grow Old Along With Me/So Will I	55	Glory 233
Just Come A Little Bit Closer/A Love That's True	55	Glory 237

Four Fellows (1) (Cathy Ryan & the)

24 Hours A Day/With You	55	King 1495

Four Fellows (1) (Miss Toni Banks & the)

Johnny The Dreamer/You're Still In My Heart	57	Glory 263

Four Fellows (2)

Break My Bones/Stop Crying	53	Tri-Boro 101
Remember/That Kiss You Gave Me	55	Nestor 27
That's Why I Pray/The City	62	Ad Lib 0208
Happy Honeymoon/Memories (by the Decoys (2))	63	Aljon 1261

Four Fifths

Come On Girl (Be Mine)/After Graduation	63	Hudson 8101
If You Still Want Me/Have You Ever Loved A Girl	66	Columbia 43913

Four Flames (aka Hollywood Flames)

Tabarin/W-I-N-E	51	Fidelity 3001
The Bounce Pt. 2/The Bounce Pt. 1	51	Fidelity 3002
(instrumental by Sherman Williams)		

Four Flames (aka Hollywood Flames) (Bobby Day & the)

Wheel Of Fortune/Later	52	Specialty 429

ARTIST/SONG	YEAR	LABEL
Four Flares		
Jump Back Honey Ride/Riders In The Sky	58	Edison International 402
Four Flickers		
Is There A Way/Yo Yo	59	Lee 1002
Long Tall Texan/Aimez-Moi	59	Lee 1003
Four Friends		
My Young And Foolish Heart/Save This Fallen Heart	57	Fee Bee 225
Four Gabriels		
Gloria/Recess In Heaven	48	World 2505
Four Gems		
Outside Of Paradise/Darling You Know	N/A	Broadcast 4
Four Gents		
On Bended Knee/Linda	57	Park 113
You're Just A Little Too Young/Please Don't Ask Me	61	Nite Owl 50
Four Graduates (aka Happenings)		
Lovely Way To Spend An Evening/Picture Of An Angel	63	Rust 5062
Candy Queen/A Boy In Love	64	Rust 5084
Four Guys (1)		
This May Be Your Life/By Bye For Just A While	55	Wing 90036
Drive-In Rock/Do Unto Others	56	Mercury 70908
Four Guys (2)		
You Took My Heart By Surprise/You Didn't Have To Tell Me	59	Kent 311
Four Guys (3)		
Teardrops From My Eyes/Hey Junior	N/A	Stride 5001
Four Haven Knights (aka Haven Knights)		
In My Lonely Room/I'm Just A Dreamer	56	Atlass 1066/Josie 824 (57)
Why Go On Pretending?/Just To Be In Love	57	Atlas 1092
Four Hits & A Miss		
She Wobbles (All Night Long)	62	Flamingo
Do It	62	Flamingo 540
Four Holidays		
Nobody Loves You Like-A Me/Who Can Say	59	United Artists 163 (unreleased)
I Don't Wanna Go To School/Love Ya	60	Verve 10204/Verve 740
Four Hollidays		
Step By Step/Grandma Bird	63	Markie 109
I Won't Need You	63	Markie 115
Four Horsemen		
A Dear John Letter/No Story Unturned	53	MGM 11566
My Heartbeat/A Long Long Time	58	United Artists 134
Four Hues		
Rock-A-Bye/Take Me Out Of Your Heart	56	Crown 159
Four Imperials		
My Girl/Teen Age Fool	58	Chant 10067
Look Up And Live/Give Me One More Chance	58	Fox 102
Lazy Bonnie/Let's Make A Scene	58	Lorelei 4444/Dot 15737 (58)
Valley Of Tears/Time Out	59	Dial 101
Santa's Got A Coupe De Ville/Seven Lonely Days	59	Twirl 2005

ARTIST/SONG	YEAR	LABEL
Four Interns		
I'm Troubled/It's All Right Now	55	Federal 12239
Four Intruders (aka Intruders)		
My Baby/This Is My Song	62	Gowen 1404
Four J's (i.e. James, Joseph, Jimmy & Joe) (aka Fabulous Four)		
Dreams Are A Dime A Dozen/Kissin' At The Drive-In	58	Herald 528
Rock And Roll Age/Be Nice, Don't Fight	58	United Artists 125
The Nursery/Will You Be My Love	63	4-J 506
Here I Am Broken Hearted/She Said That She Loved Me	64	Jamie 1267
By Love Possessed/My Love, My Love	64	Jamie 1274
Dreamin'/Love My Love	69	Congress 6003
Four Jacks		
You Met A Fool/Goodbye Baby	52	Federal 12075
I'll Be Home Again/The Last Of The Good Rockin' Men	52	Federal 12087
R-O-C-K/Gum Drop	56	Gateway 1136
Only You	56	Gateway 1147
My Prayer	56	Gateway 1183
Little Darlin'	56	Gateway 1211
I Can't Forget/Becky Ann	58	Rebel 1313
Whispering Bells	N/A	Big 4 Hits EP 213
Four Jacks (Ben Joe Zeppa & the)		
Why Do Fools Fall In Love/No Not Much	56	Gilmar 278
Four Jacks (Bill Erwin & the)		
Too Young To Be Blue/Too Young To Be Blue	60	Pel 501/Fairlane 21020 (62)
I've Waited Long Enough/Like Man It's Spring	60	Pel 601
Four Jacks (Janet Shay & the)		
Busy Bee/If And When	60	Alcar 1502
Four Jacks (Lil Greenwood & the)		
My Last Hour/Monday Morning Blues	52	Federal 12082
Never Again/Grandpa Can Boogie Too	52	Federal 12093
Four Jacks (Mac Burney & the)		
Tired Of Your Sexy Ways/This Is My Last Affair	55	Aladdin 3274
Let Me Get Next To You/Walking And Crying	56	Hollywood 1058
Four Jacks (Shirley Haven & the)		
Troubles Of My Own/Stop Foolin' Around	52	Federal 12092
Four Jacks (with Cora Williams & Shirley Haven)		
I Ain't Comin' Back Anymore/Sure Clue For The Blues	52	Federal 12079
Four Jays		
Class Ring/Weird	58	MGM 12687
Four Jewels (aka Impalas (3))		
Dapper Dan/Loaded With Goodies	63	Checker 1039
Johnny Jealousy/Someone Special	63	Start 638 (same # used twice)
Loaded With Goodies/Fire	63	Start 638 (same # used twice)
Time For Love/That's What They Put Erasers On Pencils For	64	Checker 1069
All That's Good/I Love Me And You	64	Start 641
Baby It's You/She's Wrong For You Baby	64	Tec 3007
Four Joes		
Lifetime Of Happiness/Uh-Huh	57	Darl 1005
Four Jokers (1)		
Caring/Tell Me Now	54	MGM 11815

ARTIST/SONG	YEAR	LABEL
Four Jokers (2)		
You Did/Transfusion	56	Diamond 3004
Four Jokers (3)		
Written In The Stars/The Run Around	58	Sue 703
Four Jokers (4)		
Uggaboo/She's A Flirt	62	Amy 832
Four Kays (Leroy Taylor & the)		
I'll Understand/Takin' My Time	N/A	Shrine 101
Four Kings (1)		
Hurry Back Home/She Don't Want Your Rocking (no group)	52	Fortune 807
My Head Goes Acting Up/You Don't Mean Me, Right?	54	Fortune 811
Doo-Li-Op/Rose Of Tangier	55	Fortune 517
Willingly/It's Not The End Of The World	56	Fraternity 752
Walking Along/Rag Mop	58	Stomper Time
Early In The Morning/I Want To Be There	63	M.O.C. 655
Hallelujah/The Graveyard Is Waiting	N/A	Gotham 763
Four Kings (1) (Ben & the)		
Forever Mine/Imprison Me Baby	N/A	Revival 635
Four Kings (1) (Willie Mitchell & the)		
Walking At Your Will/Tell It To Me Baby	58	Stomper Time 1160
Four Kings (2)		
You Never Knew/Do You Want To Rock?	54	Jax 323
Four Kings (3)		
I Don't Want Nobody But You/Guess Who	60	Cee Jay 580
Four Kings (4) (Ray Agee & the)		
Pray For Me/Swingin' Partner	60	Check 102/Plaid 105
Four Kings (5) (Sue Tornay & the)		
You Went Away/Tell Me	61	Dore 594
Four Kings (6)		
One Night/Lonely Lover	64	Canadian American 173
Four Kings And A Queen		
Grass In Your Own Backyard	52	United (unreleased)
Just A Fool	52	United (unreleased)
Lean Pretty Baby	52	United (unreleased)
Wheelin' And Dealin'	52	United (unreleased)
Four Kittens ("Fat Man" Matthews & the)		
When Boy Meets Girl/Later Baby	52	Imperial 5211
Four Knights		
La La/Tic-Toc	62	Triode 104
Four Labels		
Susie/Lookin'	58	Gralow 5524
Four Larks		
Go, Baby, Go/Night And Day	54	Guyden 707
It's Unbelievable/Keep Climbing Brothers	67	Uptown 761
Four Locks		
A Little Bit Of Soap	N/A	Uptown 761

ARTIST/SONG	YEAR	LABEL

Four Lovers (aka Four Seasons)

The Girl In My Dreams/You're The Apple Of My Eye	56	RCA 6518
Honey Love/Please Don't Leave Me	56	RCA 6519
Be Lovey Dovey/Jambalaya	56	RCA 6646
Happy Am I/Never Never	56	RCA 6768
Pucker Up/My Life For Your Love	57	Epic 9255
Shake A Hand/The Stranger	57	RCA 6812
The Stranger/Night Train	57	RCA 6819
It May Be Wrong/Please Take A Chance	59	Decca 30994

Four Mints

What'Cha Gonna Do/Night Air	56	Choctaw 8002/ Imperial 5432 (57)
Gold/Ruby Baby	57	Decca 30465
Hey, Little Neil/Teenage Wonderland	58	NRC 003
You Belong To My Heart/Wolf	58	NRC 011
Tomorrow Night/Pina Colada	59	NRC 037

Four Most (1) (aka 4 Most)

Ooh! Baby It Scares Me/Let A Smile Be Your Umbrella	56	Dawn 220

Four Most (2)

The Breeze And I/I Love You	59	Milo 107/Relic 501 (63)

Four Naturals (aka Naturals (1))

How Strange/Blue Moon	58	Red Top 113
I Hear A Rhapsody/When I'm In Your Arms	59	Red Top 119
The Thought Of You Darling/Long Long Ago	59	Red Top 125

Four Nuggets

No Time For Lovin'/Shortcut To A Heartache	63	Songbird 204

Four Of A Kind

Dedicated To You/Rock My Heart	56	Melba 110
Fools Fall In Love/Dreamy Eyes	57	Melba 117
You Were Made To Love/Love Every Moment	58	Cameo 154
It's Better That Way/I Care For You	58	Chancellor 1012/ Bomarc 302 (59)
Next Fall/U-Turn Baby	61	Rex 104

Four Of Us

Loving A Girl Like You/I'm Some Kind Of Wonderful	61	Adore 902/Bruce
I Don't Need No One/Iga Diga Doo	63	Brunswick 55288
Be Mine	N/A	Modern 222

Four Pages

Autograph Book/Much As I Do	62	Plateau 101

Four Palms

Consideration/Jeanie, Joanie, Shirley, Toni	58	Aladdin 3411

Four Pals (1)

If I Can't Have The One I Love/I Flipped	55	Royal Roost 610
No One Ever Loved Me/Can't Stand It Any Longer	56	Royal Roost 616

Four Pals (2) (Dean Beard & the)

On My Mind Again/Rakin' And Scrapin'	57	Atlantic 1137

Four Pals (3)

Long Black Stockings/Yours To Possess	59	Roulette 4127

Four Pearls

Look At Me/It's Almost Tomorrow	60	Dolton 26

ARTIST/SONG	YEAR	LABEL
Four Pennies (1) (aka Chiffons) (female)		
When The Boy's Happy/Hockaday Pt. 1	63	Rust 5070
My Block/Dry Your Eyes	63	Rust 5071
Four Pennies (2) (male)		
You Have No Time To Lose/You're A Gas	64	Brunswick 55304
Four Pharaohs		
Pray For Me/The Move Around	57	Ransom 100
Give Me Your Love/China Girl	57	Ransom 101/Paradise 109 (58)
Is It Too Late/It Was A Night Like This	58	Ransom 102
Four Pips (Pop & the)		
For You/Teenage Rock	N/A	Mercedes 5001
Four Plaid Throats		
My Inspiration/The Message	53	Mercury 70143
Four Rivers (Little Lynn & the)		
Send My Records C.O.D./I Walk In Circles	62	Music City 845
Four Saints		
Window Of Dreams/When I'm With You Again	70	Era 701
Four Seasons (Gigi Parker & the)		
Lonely Girl Blue/Someday, Someday	62	Coral 62314
Four Sensations		
Heaven Knows/Believing In You	51	Rainbow 157
Four Sevilles		
Heartbeat	N/A	Rainbow 157
Four Shades Of Rhythm		
My Blue Walk/Baby I'm Gone	49	Old Swingmaster 13
I Can Dream/Master Of Me	49	Old Swingmaster 23
Yesterdays/So There	52	Chance 1126
I Don't Stand A Ghost Of A Chance/Come Here	58	Mad 1206
Four Shots		
Love Hit Me And I Hollered/Get Off The Fence Hortence	55	Cadillac 154
Four Sierras (aka Sierras (1))		
Chance/Stormy Weather	63	Mail Call 2333/2334
Four Sounds		
Afraid/Tall Lanky Papa	57	Celeste 3010
You Stole My Heart/Noisy Clock	57	Celeste 3013
When I Find My Love/Someone To Show Me The Way	61	Federal 12421
The Ring/Peter's Gun	61	Tuff 1
It Won't Be A Sin/The Change In You	N/A	N/A
Four Sounds (Lois Blaine & the)		
I Need You So/Here Am I	N/A	Open-G 00
Four Sparks		
My Sweet Juanita/Out Of This World	58	ABC 9906
The Same Way/The Key To My Heart	N/A	Cliff
Four Speeds		
I Need You, Baby/The Girls Back Home	54	DeLuxe 6070
Four Sportsmen		
Surrender/Franklin Delano Brown	60	Sunnybrook 1
Lucille/Mother In Law	61	Sunnybrook 2

ARTIST/SONG	YEAR	LABEL
Pitter Patter/Git Up Paint	61	Sunnybrook 4
Sixty Minute Man/Jelly Roll Brown	62	Sunnybrook 5
If Your Heart Can Take It/Records, Records, Records	62	Sunnybrook 6

Four Stars

Win Or Lose/Honey, I Could Fall In Love	54	King 1382
My Sentimental Heart/The Chapel By The Sea	58	Kay-Y 66781

Four Steps (Bill Johnson & the)

Right To Love/You Better Dig It	59	Talos 402

Four Students

So Near And Yet So Far/Hot Rotten Soda Pop (Oh, My Toe)	55	Groove 0110

Four Students (Big John Greer & the)

A Man And A Woman/Blam (instrumental)	55	Groove 0131

Four Students (Charles Calhoun & the)

Jamboree/My Pigeon's Gone	56	Groove 0149

Four Students (Lil McKenzie & the)

Run Along/The Others Like I	55	Groove 0113

Four Students (Sue Allen & the)

Think Of Tomorrow/Set A Wedding Day	55	Groove 0130

Four Students (Tommy Brown & the)

The Thrill Is Gone/Gambler's Prayer	56	Groove 0143

Four Students (Varetta Dillard & the)

Mama Don't Want (What Poppa Don't Want)/Darling, Listen To The Words Of This Song	56	Groove 0139
Cherry Blossom/I'm Gonna Tell My Daddy	56	Groove 0152

Four Students (Zilla Mays & the)

Come Back To Me/Right Now	55	Groove 0127

Four Teens

Spark Plug/Go Little Go Cart	58	Challenge 59021

Four Tees

I Said, She Said/Like My Baby	64	Vee Jay 627

Four Temptations (aka Temptations (2))

Cathy/Rock And Roll Baby	58	ABC 9920

Four Tones (Dusty Brooks & the)

Heaven On Fire/Tears And Wind (by Juanita Brown)	53	Sun 182

Four Tops (1)

Could It Be You?/Kiss Me Baby	56	Chess 1623
Lonely Summer/Ain't That Love	60	Columbia 41755/Columbia 43356 (65)
Pennies From Heaven/Where You Are	62	Riverside 4534

Four Tops (2) (Carolyn Hayes & the)

Baby Say You Love Me	56	Chateau 2001

Four Tops (2) (Delores Carroll & the)

Everybody Knows/I Just Can't Keep The Tears From Tumblin' Down	56	Chateau 2002

Four Townsmen

It Wasn't So Long Before/Sometimes	60	Artflow 145
Graduation Is Here	N/A	N/A

ARTIST/SONG	YEAR	LABEL

Four Triumphs
I've Waited All My Life For You/Rivers In The Sky — 58   Mira 2050

Four Troys
In The Moonlight/Suddenly You Want To Dance — 59   Freedom 44013

Four Trumpets (Susie & the)
Starry Eyes/Blue Little Girl — 62   United Artists 471

Four Uniques
Looking For A Love/Too Young — 61   Adam 9002
Island Of Love/Good Luck Charm — 61   Deer 3002
She's The Only Girl/Twistin' Around — 62   Adam 9004

Four Vagabonds
P.S. I Love You/Lazy Country Side — 53   Lloyds 102

Four Vanns
So Young And So Pretty/Sha-Bee-Dah-Ah Ding — 56   Vik 0246

Four Vibes
You're All I Live For/You Got Soul — 62   Sway-Ray 1001

Four Wheels
Grateful/Adios, My Pretty Baby — 56   Spin-It 108

Four Wheels (fb Terri Dean)
I Blew Out The Flame/I'm Confessin' That I Love You — 59   Laurel 1003

Four Winds (1) (Sonny Woods & the)
I Promise/Do You Love Me? — 56   Middle-Tone 008
Living In A Dream/Do You Mean It — 56   Middle-Tone 013

Four Winds (2)
Find Someone New/Colorado Moon — 56   Vik 0221
Short Shorts/Five Minutes More — 57   Decor 175
Daddy's Home/Bull Moose Stomp — 61   Warwick 633
Playgirl/Jennifer — 64   Derby 10022/Felsted 8703 (64)
Come Softly To Me/Dear Judy — 78   Crystal Ball 102
Arlene/Goodbye, Maureen — 78   Crystal Ball 105
Doin' The Stroll — N/A   Explorer 713
Old Man River/Popcorn Party — N/A   Sherlock 1027

Four Winds (3) (aka Tokens (2))
Remember Last Summer/Strange Feelings — 64   Swing 100
Let It Ride/One Face In The Crowd — 68   B.T. Puppy 555

Four Winds (4)
To Love Or Not To Love/Down And Out — 64   Chattahoochie 655

Four Winds (5)
Mission By The Sea/These Hearts Were Mine — 58   Hide-A-Way 101

Four Xs (aka Four Zs)
I'll Remember/Why Can't You Love Me — 60   Lost 103

Four Young Men
You Been Torturing Me/See Them Laugh — 61   Crest 1076
Sweetheart Of Senior High/Just For Tonight — 61   Crest 1083
Garden In The Rain/That Man Paul — 61   Dore 621

Four Zs (aka Four Xs)
I'll Remember/Why Can't You Love Me — 60   Lost 20

ARTIST/SONG	YEAR	LABEL

Four-Evers (aka Four Evers)

You Belong To Me/Such A Good Night For Dreaming	62	Columbia 42303
I Confess/Sooner Or Later	62	Josie 901
One More Time/Everybody South Street	63	Jamie 1247
Lover Come Back To Me/It's Love	63	Smash 1853
Come Up In The World/Colors	64	Chattahoochie 630
Please Be Mine/If I Were A Magician	64	Smash 1887 (first pressing)
Be My Girl/If I Were A Magician	64	Smash 1887 (second pressing)
Doo Be Dum/Everlasting	64	Smash 1921
Stormy/I'm Walkin' (Into The Crowd)	65	Constellation 151
A Lovely Way To Spend An Evening/The Girl I Wanna Bring Home	66	Columbia 43886
What A Scene/You Never Had It So Good	66	Red Bird 10-078

Fourmost

Why Can't I Have You/Twist-A-Taste	62	Lu Pine 105
Hello Little Girl/Just In Case	63	Atco 6280
Respectable/I'm In Love	63	Atco 6285
If You Cry/Little Bit Of Loving	64	Atco 6307
How Can I Tell Her/You Got That Way	64	Atco 6317
Why Do Fools Fall In Love/Girls, Girls, Girls	66	Capitol 5591
Here There And Everywhere/You've Changed	66	Capitol 5738
It Was A Lie/Girl You Do Something	66	Red Bird 10-071/D.W. 105

Fourmost (Bobby Moore & the)

Dance Of The Land/You Got To Live For Yourself	64	Fantasy 585

Foxes

I Just Might Fall In Love/Tip Toe Through The Tulips With Me	63	ABC 10446

Foxes (Johnny Fox & the)

You Laff Too Much/Mountain Dew	62	Newtime 507

Foxettes (Lady Fox & the) (female)

I Think Of You/Our Love	62	Don-El 114
It Must Be Love/How Are You	62	Don-El 118

Francettes

He's So Sweet	63	Wolfie 104

Franciscans

Mother Please Answer Me/Walk To The Bottom Of The Sea	N/A	Jimbo 4001

Frank, Carol (& group)

Emmitt Lee/One Look At You	57	Excello 2118
Hold Me/One More Chance	59	Excello 2175

Fraternity Brothers

Big Town/Sad Little Boy	60	Date 1528
Dearest Darling/Moonlight And Roses	60	Verve 10195

Fraternity Men

Little Star/Lynne	64	Courier 114

Frazier, Ray (& group)

Days/Turn Me On	55	Excel 111
Walking With My Love	62	Excel 111

Frazier, Ray (bb the Moonrays)

All My Love/Fat Mouth	56	Excel 112

Freckles

Little Star/Freckle Face	61	Madison 158

Frederick, Tommy (& group)

Sundown/Where'd Ja Go	60	Coral 62170

ARTIST/SONG	YEAR	LABEL
Freedoms		
Ten Steps To Love/You Lied	64	Constellation 105
Freelancers (Dan Williams & the)		
High School Flame/Why	N/A	Beth 20/Freelance 20
Freeloaders (Bobby Sue & the)		
It Takes A Lot Of Love/Relief Check	55	Harlem 2335
Freeways		
My Baby Loves Me/I've Been A Fool	65	Hugo 11723
Fresandos		
Your Last Goodbye/I Mean Really (by Eddie Bartell)	58	Star-X 501
Fretts		
Full Moon Above/Rock'n Baby	59	Blue Moon 414
Friday Knights		
Don't Open That Door/Poor Mans Roses	60	Strand 25019
Friends (1) (Junior & his)		
ABC's Of Love/Who's Our Pet, Annette	60	ABC 10089
Friends (2) (Gary Cane & His)		
C'Mere Baby Doll/The Fight	60	Shell 717
The Yen Yet Song/I'll Walk The Earth	60	Shell 719
Friends (3) (Dante & His) (aka Dante & the Evergreens)		
Something Happens/Are You Just My Friend	61	Imperial 5798
Miss America/Now I've Got You	62	Imperial 5827
Friends (4) (Morningside Drive &)		
Na-Na-Na/Lazy Love (instrumental)	73	Laurie 3615
Frontera, Tommy (& group)		
After Tonight/How To Love Him	60	Rem 103
Frontiers (1)		
Ding Dong Doo/Why Pretend	61	King 5481
Nearest Thing To Heaven/Oh Nurse	61	King 5534
Each Night I Pray/You Shake Me Up	62	King 5609
Frontiers (2) (fb Roger Koob)		
I Only Have Eyes For You/Don't Come Crying	63	Philips 40113
I Just Want You/I'm Still Loving You	63	Philips 40148
You/When I See You	67	MGM 13722
Fugitives (fb Delna Lee)		
One Year Today/Big Man	57	Fabor 141
Fuller, Jerry (& group)		
Betty My Angel/Memories Of You	59	Challenge 59052
Fuller, Walter (& group)		
Closer To My Heart/Pecan Mambo	54	Kicks 4
Fullylove, Leroy (& group)		
I'm So Lonely/Jumpin' Over The Moon	61	Tandem 7002
Fulton, Sonny (& group)		
A Lovely Relationship	N/A	Lash 1127
Fulton, Sonny (& His Group)		
Honest I Do/Fire	59	Chelsea 533

ARTIST/SONG	YEAR	LABEL

Fun-Atics
Wise Guy/I Wanna Know How To Twist	62	Versailles 100
Just In The Nick Of Time/I Don't Wanna Make You Cry	67	Select 571

Funkytones (Vincent MacRee & the)
Oh Baby You	57	Gametime

Funny Bunnies
Midnight Sun/Sick Song	60	Dore 542

Furness Brothers
Paul Revere/I'm In The Mood For Love	52	MGM 11356
Please Don't Call Me Fool/King Of The Blues	57	Prep 107
You Name It/I Want A Date	60	Future 1002
One Little Moment With You/Duke's Place	60	Rae-Cox 104
Only Fate/Lookin' Out The Window	64	Melmar 114
Please Don't Call Me A Fool	64	Melmar 115
Say It Isn't So/King Of The Blues	64	Melmar 116

Furys
Zing! Went The Strings Of My Heart/Never More	63	Mach IV 112
I Really Feel Good	63	Mach IV 115
I Lost My Baby	63	Mach IV 118
Anything For You/Cat 'N' Mouse	63	World Pacific 386
Gone In The Night	N/A	Fleetwood 4569

Futures (1)
Breaking Up	N/A	Amjo 3033

Futures (2) (Vic Fontaine & the)
Rosina	N/A	Adam & Eve LP 504

Futuretones
Roll On/I Know	59	Tress 1/2

Futuretones (Jim Holiday & the)
All I Want Is You/Voice Of The Drums	58	4 Star 1720

Fydells
That Certain One/Pandora	59	Camelia 100

G-Clefs
Ka-Ding-Dong/Darla My Darlin'	56	Pilgrim 715
'Cause You're Mine/Please Write While I'm Away	56	Pilgrim 720
Symbol Of Love/Love Her In The Mornin' And Love Her In The Night Time	57	Paris 502
Is This The Way/Zing Zang Zoo	57	Paris 506
I Understand (Just How You Feel)/Little Girl, I Love You	61	Terrace 7500
I'll Remember All You Kisses/Ka-Ding-Dong	62	Ditto 503
A Girl Has To Know/Lad	62	Terrace 7503
Make Up Your Mind/They'll Call Me Away	62	Terrace 7507
Lover's Prayer (All Through The Night)/Sitting In The Moonlight	62	Terrace 7510
All My Trials/The Big Rain	63	Terrace 7514
I Believe In All I Feel/To The Winner Goes The Prize	64	Regina 1314
Angel, Listen To Me/Nobody But Betty	64	Regina 1319
On The Other Side Of Town/I Have	65	Veep 1218
Little Lonely Boy/Party '66	66	Loma 2034
I Can't Stand It/The Whirlwind	66	Loma 2048
This Time/On The Other Side Of Town	66	Veep 1226

G-Notes
I Would/Ronnie	58	Tender 510/Jackpot 48000 (59)
If They Only Knew/Say You're Mine	59	Form 102
Johnny, Johnny, Johnny/Broken Down Merry-Go-Round	59	Guyden 2012

ARTIST/SONG	YEAR	LABEL

Gadabouts
By The Waters Of Minnetonka/Giuseppe Mandolino	54	Mercury 70495
Go Boom Boom/Oochi Pachi	55	Mercury 70581
Two Things I Love/Glass Heart	55	Wing 90008
Teen Age Rock/If You Only Had A Heart	55	Wing 90043
Busy Body Rock/All My Love Belongs To You	56	Mercury 70823/Wing 90062 (56)
Stranded In The Jungle/Blues Train	56	Mercury 70898

Gailtones (female)
| Lover Boy/Please Don't Go | 58 | Decca 30726 |

Gainors
The Secret/Gonna Rock Tonite	58	Cameo 151
You Must Be An Angel/Follow Me	59	Cameo 156
Message With Flowers/She's My Lollipop	59	Mercury 71466
She's Gone/Please Consider	60	Mercury 71569
I'm In Love With You/Nothing Means More To Me	60	Mercury 71630/Mercury 71632
This Is A Perfect Moment/Where I Want To Be	61	Tally-Ho 102
Tell Him/Darlin'	61	Tally-Ho 105

Galaxies (1) (bb Eddie Cochran on guitar)
| My Tattle Tale/Love Has Its Ways | 60 | Guaranteed 216 |

Galaxies (2)
The Big Triangle/Until The Next Time	60	Capitol 4427
Tremble/My Blue Heaven	61	Dot 16212
Dear Someone/The Leopard	61	Richie 458

Galaxies (3)
| Just Another Date/Little Man | 76 | Ronnie 201 |

Galaxys
| A Lover's Prayer/Jelly Bean | 59 | Carthay 103 |

Gale, Sunny (& group)
| Church Bells May Ring/My Foolish Heart | 60 | Warwick 540 |

Galens
Baby I Do Love You/Love Bells	63	Challenge 59212
Stranger In Paradise/Chinese Lanterns	64	Challenge 59253
Young Dreams/I Love You More Than You Know	66	Challenge 59402

Gales
Guiding Angel/Boy Come Home	58	Mel-O 111
Josephine/If I Could Forget	58	Mel-O 113
Tommy/Around The Clock With You	63	Debra 1002

Gales (aka Marvels (2)/aka Senators)
Don't Let The Sun Catch You Crying/My Eyes Keep Me In Trouble	55	J.V.B. 34
Darling Patricia/All Is Well, All Is Well	55	J.V.B. 35/J.O.B. 3001
I Love You/Squeeze Me	60	Winn 916

Gallahads
Ooh Ah/Careless	55	Capitol 3060
Do You Believe Me/If It Wasn't For You	55	Capitol 3175
If I Give You My Word/Take My Love	56	Jubilee 5259
One Love Alone/Take Back My Ring	57	Vik 0291
Best Wishes/Steady Man	58	Vik 0316
Silently/Barracuda	58	Vik 0332
Keeper Of Dreams/Sad Girl	60	Beechwood 3000/Starla 15
Lonely Guy/Jo Jo The Big Wheel	60	Donna 1322/Del-Fi 4137 (59)
Gone/So Long	61	Nite Owl 20
Why Do Fools Fall In Love/Gone	61	Rendezvous 153
Have Love, Will Travel/My Offering	64	Sea Crest 6005

ARTIST/SONG	YEAR	LABEL
Gallahads (fb James Pipkin)		
The Fool/The Morning Mail	56	Jubilee 5252
Be Fair/I'm Without A Girl Friend	60	Del-Fi 4148
Gallahads (Jimmy Pipkin & the)		
This Letter To You/The Answer To Love	62	Donna 1361
Gallant Men		
Last Romance/Foreign Girl	62	Ford 117
Gallant, Billy (bb the Roulettes)		
Scribbling On The Wall/Thinking, Hoping And Wishing	61	Dee Dee 501
Thinking, Hoping And Wishing/If You'd Only Be My Love	62	Goldisc G6
Gallaway, Bill (& group)		
It's For Real	N/A	Clarke 1605
Galleons		
I Played The Fool/Pick Up	59	Vita 184
Gang (Teddy Field & the)		
When We Get Married	N/A	Vita 184
Gants		
My Unfaithful Love/Happening After School	57	Aladdin 3387
Gardenias (1)		
Flaming Love/My Baby's Tops	56	Federal 12284
I'm Laughing At You/Houdini	58	Hi-Q 5005
Gardenias (2)		
What's The Matter With Me/Darling It's You, You, You	62	Fairlane 21019
Gardner, Don (& group)		
A Dagger In My Chest/This Nearly Was Mine	57	DeLuxe 6133
I Don't Want To Go Home/There! I've Said It Again	57	DeLuxe 6155
Gari, Frank (& group)		
There's Lots More	61	Crusade 1024
Do-Be-Do	N/A	Ritco 555
Garnets (1) (Buel Moore & the)		
Really Really Baby/Sputnik 3	57	Vita 174
Garnets (2) (Lord Luther & the)		
Turn The Key/Teenage Creature (by the Kingsmen)	58	Frantic 107
Gassers		
Tell Me/Hum De Dum	56	Cash 1035
Dody Mighty/Doggonit	57	Encino 1011
Gates		
Letter To Dick Clark/Wrapped In Green Made For A Teen	59	Peach 628
Summer Night Love/Wedding Bells Gonna Ring	59	Peach 716
Gates, David (& group)		
What's This I Hear/You'll Be My Baby	60	Mala 413
Gatorvettes		
If It's Tonight/Midnight	58	Thunder 1001/ Bocaldun 1001 (59)
Gay Charmers (female)		
Groovey Shoes/Dance D-D-Dance	58	Savoy 1549
What Can I Do/Get In And Shut The Door	59	Grand 2001/Swan 4032 (59)
Walk Beside Him/Why Do You Hurt Me Darling	59	Savoy 1561

ARTIST/SONG	YEAR	LABEL
Gay Knights		
Angel/The Loudness Of My Heart	58	Pet 801
Gay Notes (1) (female) (aka Honey Bees)		
Hear My Plea/Crossroads	55	Post 2006
Gay Notes (2)		
For Only A Moment/Pu Pu Pa Doo	55	Drexel 905
Gay Notes (3)		
Something Special/Cherie	59	Vim 501
Gay Notes (3) (aka Little Clem & the Dew Drops)		
Waiting In The Chapel/Plea Of Love	58	Zynn 504
Gay Poppers		
You Better Believe/I Need Your Love	59	Savoy 1573
I've Got It/I Want To Know	60	Fire 1026
You Got Me Uptight/Please Mr. Cupid	61	Fire 1039
Gay Tunes (aka Gaytunes)		
Wh-y-y Leave Me This Way-ay-ay/Thrill Of Romance	53	Timely 1002
Got You On My Mind/Don't Go	58	Dome 502
I Want You To Love Me Too	87	Relic LP 5071
I'll Always Love You	87	Relic LP 5071
Gaylads		
Popeye The Sailor Man/Ah So	61	Audan 120
Gaylarks		
Tell Me, Darling/Whole Lot Of Love (by the Rovers (2))	55	Music City 792
Romantic Memories/Lil' Dream Girl	55	Music City 793
My Greatest Sin/Teenage Mambo	56	Music City 805
Mr. Rock 'n' Roll/Church On The Hill	57	Music City 809
Somewhere In This World/Just One More Chance (no group)	57	Music City 812
Ivy League Clothes/The Doodle-Doo	58	Music City 819
Gayles		
My Boy Flat Top/I Get So Happy	55	King 4846
I Had To Lose You/Too Late I Learned	55	King 4860
Yes Sir, That's My Baby/All I Want Is You	56	Media 1021
Gaylords (aka Imperials (1))		
Get Mad Baby/Go On Baby	52	Savoy 852
Gaynels		
Chubby/Uh-Huh	59	Okeh 7114
Gaynotes (female)		
Once He Loved Me/Strange As It May Seem	58	Aladdin 3424
Gays		
Alone At The Harbor/Command My Heart	59	Decca 30988
Gaytunes (aka Gay Tunes)		
I Love You/You Left Me	57	Joyce 101
Plea In The Moonlight/Pen Pal	58	Joyce 106
Gazelles		
Honest/Pretty Baby, Baby	56	Gotham 315
Gee, Billy (& group)		
King Of Hearts/If You Have Faith	59	Coronet 1303

ARTIST/SONG	YEAR	LABEL

Gee, Frankie (& group)
Date With The Rain/Ya Ya — 75 — Claridge 410

Gee-Chords
Dreams Come True/Mello-Jello Pt. 2 — N/A — Romantic Rhythm 101

Gee-Tones (aka Gregory Howard with the Cadillacs)
When In Love (Do As Lovers Do)/Sweet Pea — 56 — Gee 1013 (unreleased)

Gees (1) (Dickie & the)
Foolish Tears/Baby Bye Bye — 58 — Argo 5288

Gees (2)
It's All Over/Love Is A Beautiful Thing — 66 — Port 3011

Gems (1)
'Deed I Do/Talk About The Weather — 54 — Drexel 901
I Thought You'd Care/Kitty From New York City — 54 — Drexel 903
You're Tired Of Love/Ol' Man River — 54 — Drexel 904
One Woman Man/The Darkest Night — 56 — Drexel 909
Till The Day I Die/Monkey Face Baby — 57 — Drexel 915

Gems (2)
I Never Dreamed — 55 — 20th Century 5037

Gems (3)
Waiting/Please Change Your Mind — 58 — Recorte 407
Nursery Rhymes/The Night Is Over — 58 — Win 701
Crazy Chicken/Hippy Dippy — 61 — Mercury 71819
School Rock/There's No One Like My Love — 61 — Pat 101
Runch Happy — 61 — Vergelle 711

Gems (4) (Pearl Woods & the)
Think Of Poor Me/I'll Be A Cry Baby — 62 — Wall 551
One More Time/Sloppin' — 62 — Wall 552

Gemtones (Eddie Woods & the)
Heaven Was Mine/Prima Vera — 53 — Gem 204

Genells
Linda Please Wait/Rainy Night — 63 — Dewey 101

Generals
Never Too Late/I'm Searchin' — 60 — Tammy 1009

Genies (1) (gm Eugene Pitt)
No More Knockin'/On The Edge Of Town — 59 — Hollywood 69
Who's That Knockin'/First Time — 59 — Shad 5002
There Goes That Train/Crazy Love — 60 — Warwick 573
Just Like The Bluebird/Twistin' Pneumonia — 60 — Warwick 607
Crazy Feeling/Little Young Girl — 61 — Warwick 643

Genies (2) (Gene Wilson & the)
Come Here My Darling/Love, Love, Love D-R-E-A-M — 61 — King 5568

Genies (3) (female)
I'm Going Home/Shoo Fly Pie — 63 — Lennox 5562

Genos
Wishful Dreaming/Slim Little Annie — 59 — Sundance 202

Genotones
City Lights (Thank Her For Me)/Counting Stars — 61 — Casino 52261
Rita My Teenage Bride/Midnight Walk — N/A — WGW 3003

ARTIST/SONG	YEAR	LABEL
Gentlemen		
Something To Remember You By/Tired Of You	54	Apollo 464
Don't Leave Me Baby/Baby Don't Go	54	Apollo 470
Story Of A Love Gone Cold/You're Driving Me Crazy	55	Apollo
Gentrys		
There's A Love/You Make Me Feel So Good	67	MGM 13690
Gents (1)		
Why Do I Love Her/Jump In The Line	61	Liberty 55332
Gents (2)		
I'll Never Let You Go/Darling I Love You (by the Teen 5) (a capella)	64	Times Square 2/ Times Square 99 (64)
Island Of Love/Till The End Of Time (by the Teen 5) (a capella)	64	Times Square 4/ Times Square 98 (64)
Gents (3) (Little Freddie & the)		
Betty/Push, Kick And Shout	65	Showcase 402
Gents (4) (Larry & the)		
Little Queenie/Can't You Tell	64	Delaware 1700
You Mean Everything To Me/I'm Just A Loser In Love	65	Delaware 1711
Gents (5) (Vic & the)		
Lydia (a capella)/The Sign From Above (a capella)	64	Dorana 1170
Gents (6)		
Facing This World Without You	N/A	Midnight 102
Gents (7) (Gin & the)		
Boy And Girl	N/A	Eldorado 102
Gents (8)		
Golly Golly/It's Too Late To Cry	61	All Boy 8501
Geoles (Lil Millet & the)		
Rich Woman/Hopeless Love	55	Specialty 565
George, Othea (& group)		
Now That You're Gone	62	Chex 1008
Come To Me/Keep On Writin'	N/A	Volume 1100
George, Sunny (& group)		
Lip Lockin'/Tell Me Tell Me	58	MGM 12697
Georgettes (female)		
Oh Tonight/Love Like A Fool	57	Ebb 125
Dizzy Over You/Oh, Oh Yes	59	Jackpot 48001
Down By The River/Pair Of Eyes	60	Fleet 1111/ United Artists 237 (60)
Forget Me Not/How Do I Know	60	Goldisc 3006
The Story/Little Boy	63	Troy 1001
Giant, Jimmy (& group)		
Everything's Gonna Be Alright/Suddenly	60	Vee Jay 345
Giants (Little Guy & the)		
So Young/It's You	60	Lawn 103
Gibralters (Jimmy Barnes & the)		
No Regrets/Keep Your Love Handy	58	Gibraltar 101
Be Careful With My Love/I Need You So Much	59	Gibraltar 102
Love Made Me A Fool/Don't Let Nothing Stand In Your Way	59	Gibraltar 106
Our Wedding Day/Crying Cause I Lost	60	Savoy 1581

ARTIST/SONG	YEAR	LABEL
Gibralters (Nappy Brown & the)		
My Baby Knows/Down In The Alley	60	Savoy 1582
Gibson, Cindy (& group)		
(A Lovely) Summer Night	N/A	General 700
Gifts (Little Natalie & Henry & the)		
Teardrops Are Falling/It's Uncle Willie	63	Roulette 4540
Gifts (Young Henry Ford & the)		
Treat Her Nice/Two Hearts Make A Romance	64	Roulette 4552
Gigi (& group)		
This Time Next Summer/Little Bit Of Lovin'	61	Seg-Way 1010
Gillettes		
24 Hours A Day/The Same Identical Thing	64	J&S 1391
Gilman, Tony (& group)		
Who Put The Bomp	N/A	J&S 1391
Ginger (bb the Safaris)		
Spare Time/Dry Tears	61	Titan 1717
Gingersnaps		
Gingerbread/Lenny Lenny	58	Kapp 226
Gino (& group)		
Gotta Travel On	63	Golden Crest 588
Gino (bb the Dells)		
Altar Of Dreams/Baby Don't Go Now	61	Golden Crest 567
Ginos (Jeff & the)		
One Summer In A Million/Let Me Out	63	Mercury 72138
Girlfriends (1) (female)		
Four Shy Girls (In Their Itsy Bitsy Teenie Weenie Yellow Polka-Dot Bikinis) (answer song)/Jackie	60	Pioneer 71833
My One And Only, Jimmy Boy/For My Sake	63	Colpix 712
No More Tears/I Want To Be Happy	63	Melic 4125
Baby Don't Cry/I Don't Believe In You	64	Colpix 744
Girlfriends (2) (Erlene & the) (female)		
A Guy Is A Guy/My Dada Say	63	Old Town 1150
Because Of You/Casanova	63	Old Town 1152
Glad Rags		
My China Doll/Just One Love	57	Excello 2121
Gladiators (1)		
Girl Of My Heart/My Baby Doll	57	Dig 135
Gladiators (2) (Bruno & the)		
Istambul/Warm Is The Sun	62	Vault 901
Gladiators (3)		
I Need You/Turning To Stone	58	Donnie 701
Gladiolas (fb Maurice Williams)		
Little Darlin'/Sweetheart Please Don't Go	57	Excello 2101
Run, Run, Little Joe/Comin' Home To You	57	Excello 2110
Hey! Little Girl/I Wanna Know	57	Excello 2120
Say You'll Be Mine/Shoop Shoop	58	Excello 2136

ARTIST/SONG	YEAR	LABEL
Glasers (Tompall & the)		
Yakety Yak/Sweet Lies	58	Robbins 1006
Gleams (1)		
Give Me A Chance/Bad Boy	60	J-V 101
You Broke My Heart/I Don't Know Why You Sent For Me	62	Kip 236/237
Mr. Magic Moon/Pile Driver	63	Kapp 565
Gleams (2) (Berlin Perry & the)		
Tennessee Waltz/Put That Tear Back	59	Ribbon 6902
Gleems		
Sandra Baby/Are You The One	63	Parkway 893
Gleepers (Coke Willis & the)		
Ooh, But You're Nice To Hold/The Gleep	N/A	Daco 101
Glenns		
In The Chapel In The Moonlight/More And More	60	Rendezvous 118
Glens (1) (Billy & the)		
I Believe In You/Oh Boy	59	Jaro 77006
Glens (2)		
A Little Less Talk	N/A	Laitini 6666
Image Of Love/I Feel So Blue	N/A	Ro-Nan 1002
Glenwoods (aka Chateaus)		
Elaine/That's The Way It'll Be	60	Jubilee 5402
Gliders		
School Days/Baby Come On	62	Southern Sound 103
No Time	N/A	Alva 112
Gliders (Glen Pace & the)		
Tell Me/Next Year	60	ABC 10091
Glitters		
You Don't Know/Lighten-Up Slim	N/A	Rubaiyat 413
Little Star	N/A	Rubaiyat 413
Globeliters		
Gotta Find Me A Love/Turn It On	64	Guyden 2119
Globetrotters		
Rainy Day Bells	N/A	Collectables LP 7000
Glory Tones		
You Only Came Back To Hurt Me/Was That The Right Thing To Do	57	Epic 9243
Glowtones		
The Girl I Love/Ping Pong	57	East West 101/ Atlantic 1156 (57)
Goboys (Dudley Callicutt & the)		
Get Ready Baby/Heart Trouble	59	DC 0412
Gold Bugs		
Stop That Wedding/It's So Nice	65	Coral 62453
Gold Tones (Bill Bryan & the)		
Wasted Words/Rocking Chair	62	Pike 5913
Golden Bells		
Pretty Girl/Bells Are Ringing	59	Sure 1002

ARTIST/SONG	YEAR	LABEL

Golden Nuggets

| I Was A Fool/Teenage Josephine | 59 | Futura 2-1691 |

Golden Tones

| I'm Wrong/Crying The Blues | 55 | Samson 107/108 |

Golden Tones (fb Joe Simon and bb Johnny Guitar's Band)

| Little Island Girl/Doreetha | 59 | Hush 101 |

Golden Tones (fb Joe Simon)

| You Left Me Here To Cry Alone/Ocean Of Tears | 60 | Hush 102 |
| Blackboard Of My Heart/Mister Moon | 61 | Lodestar 22 |

Golden Tones (Marie Reynaud & the)

| My Man/This Little Man Of Mine | 58 | Goldband 1049 |

Golden Tones (Sticks Herman & the)

| The Natural Thing To Do/Wipe The Tears From Your Eyes | 58 | Goldband 1056 |

Goldenaires

| My Only Girl/All About You | 59 | Ron 325 |
| Love Letters/Dingbats | 60 | Ron 332 |

Goldenkeys

| Let's Vote For Tom Berkeley | 56 | Irma 100 |

Goldenrods

| Wish I Was Back In School/Color Cartoons | 59 | Vee Jay 307 |

Goldentones

| The Meaning Of Love/Run, Pretty Baby | 55 | Jay-Dee 806/Beacon 560 (55) |
| She's Funny That Way/Our Love Is Our Affair | 56 | Rainbow 351 |

Goldtones

| Wings Of An Angel/I'm So Lonely | 61 | YRS 1001 |
| Without You/Journey Bells | 62 | YRS 1002 |

Gomez, Yvonne (& group)

| Ease The Pain/My Man A-Go-Go | 67 | Hawaii 128 |

Gondoliers (Johnny Adams & the)

| Knocked Out/You Call Everybody Darling | 59 | Ric 957 |
| Nowhere To Go/Come Home | 60 | Ric 963 |

Good Guys (1)

| Dom-De-Dom/I Love My Baby | 64 | San-Dee 1007 |

Good Guys (2) (Doug Robertson & the)

Love You So/Desirie	64	Jerden 703/Uptown 703 (64)
Greenfields/Sweets For My Sweet	64	Jerden 729
Quiet Riot/Sweets For My Sweet	64	Jerden 729
Desirie/Driving Home	64	Jerden 739
Runaround Sue/Gloria	65	Jerden 767

Goode, Ray (& group)

| Stupid Heart/Fool's Paradise | 59 | Vel-Tone 25 |

Goodfellows

| Another Chance | 58 | Sun-Nel 0535 |

Goodies

| In Bermuda/The Deep Blue Sea | 59 | Chess 1731 |

Goofers

| Hearts Of Stone/You're The One | 54 | Coral 61305 |
| Flip Flop And Fly/My Babe | 55 | Coral 61383 |

ARTIST/SONG	YEAR	LABEL
Goofy Dry Bone/Nare	55	Coral 61431
Dee-Do Dee-Do/What Does That Dream Mean	55	Coral 61480
Sick Sick Sick/Twenty-One	55	Coral 61545
Crave Me/Oh How I Miss You Tonight	56	Coral 61593
Teardrop Motel/Tennessee Rock And Roll	56	Coral 61650
I'm Gonna Rock And Roll 'Til I Die/Our Miss Brooks	56	Coral 61664
'S O.K., 'S Alright/Little Bit Square, But Nice	59	Tiara 6123
Nameless/Perfidia	59	Tiara 6127

Googles (Barney & the)
Fall Is Here/Doin' The Shimmy	60	Shimmy 1055

Gordan, Joni (& group)
I'm Watching A Wedding	64	Musicnote 125

Gordon, Gary (& group)
No One/Let's Have A Ball	59	Fleetwood 1002

Gordon, Roscoe (& group)
What I Wouldn't Do/Let 'Em Try	61	Vee Jay 385

Gothics
Marilyn/Sunday Kind Of Love	59	Dynamic 101
My Dream/Love You Too Much	61	Carol 4115

Gothics (Stephanie & the)
Oh Happy Day/I'll String Along With You (no group)	61	Shelley 126

Graduates
What Good Is Graduation/Lonely	59	Corsican 0058
Ballad Of A Girl And Boy/Care	59	Shan-Todd 0055
Wendy, Wendy, Went Away	60	Malvern 500
Ballad Of A Boy And Girl/Goodbye My Love	63	Lawn 208

Grady, Paul (& group)
Darling I Understand/Baby Boy And Girl From Home	63	Glaze 109

Granahan, Gerry (& group)
Girl Of My Dreams/No Chemise Please	58	Sunbeam 102

Granahan, Gerry (bb the Wildwoods (ref Five Satins))
Dance Girl, Dance/Too Big For Her Bikini	61	Caprice 108

Grand Prees
Alone/I'm Gone	62	Haral 780
Sit And Cry/Jungle Fever	63	Candi 1020

Grand Prixs
Linda	62	Sara 6354
Last Summer Love	63	Pancho

Grant, Jason (& group)
It Doesn't Matter/House Of Cards	59	20th Fox 151

Grasshoppers
Hushabye	N/A	20th Fox 151

Gray, Carol (& group)
Cha-Cha Bop/Cha Cha Baby (no group)	58	Rhythm 126

Gray, Maureen (& group)
Crazy Over You/Today's The Day	61	Chancellor 1082
I Don't Want To Cry/Come On And Dance	61	Chancellor 1091
I'm So Young/There Is A Boy	61	Chancellor 1100
Dancin' The Strand/Oh My	62	Landa 689

ARTIST/SONG	YEAR	LABEL
Gray, Wilhemina (& group)		
Don't Wake Me Up/When The One You Love Loves You	57	MGM 12500
Graydon, Joe (& group)		
Again/It Happened To Me	59	Hamilton 50027
Green, Barbara (& group)		
Young Boy/I Should Have Treated You Right	64	Vivid 105/Hamilton 50027
Green, Birdie (& group)		
How Come/Tremblin'	62	End 1117
Green, Janice (& group)		
With All My Heart/Jackie	58	Nasco 6013
Greenwood, Paul (bb the Four Bel-Aires)		
You Won My Heart	58	Arc
Grier Quartet (The Frankie Grier Quartet)		
Oh Gloria/Lonesome For You	58	Swan 4019
Griffin Brothers		
My Baby's Done Me Wrong/Black Bread	54	Dot 1145
Griffin, Herman (& group)		
I Need You/I'm So Glad I Learned To Do The Cha Cha Cha	59	House Of Beauty 112
Griffin, Jimmy (& female group)		
A Love Like You/You Took My Loving	54	Dot 15223
Griffins (1) (aka Warblers)		
I Swear By All The Stars Above/Sing To Me	55	Mercury 70558
Bad Little Girl/Scheming	55	Mercury 70650
My Baby's Gone/Why Must You Go?	56	Mercury 70913
Forever More/Leave It To Me	56	Wing 90067
Griffins (2) (Jean Simms & the)		
Groovy/Goin' Steady	N/A	Dot
Grogan, Toby (& group)		
Angel/Just A Friend	63	Vee Jay 560
Groovers (Joe Dodo & the)		
Goin' Steady/Groovy	58	RCA 7207
Gross Sisters		
Oom Baby!/My Baby Ain't Nothing But Bad	59	Checker 932
Groves		
Out Of The Blue	N/A	Riff 104
Guides (aka Swallows (2))		
You Must Try/How Long Must A Fool Go On	59	Guyden 2023 (second pressing, first is by the Swallows)
Gum Drops		
Gum Drop/Don't Take It So Heard	55	King 1496
Don't Take It So Hard/I'll Wait For One More Train	55	King 8853/King 1499 (55)
I'll Follow You/I Wonder And Wonder	56	King 4913
Chapel Of Hearts/Natural Born Lover	56	King 4963
Pigeon/Ba-Bee Da Boat Is Leaving	57	King 5051
My Own True Love/On The Wings Of The Wind	58	Coral 62003
You're The One/Gum Drop Shoes And Bells In Her Hair	58	Decca 30584
I Spoke Too Soon/Sie Tu (It's You, It's You)	59	Coral 62102
It Happens Every Day/They Wake Me	59	Coral 62138

ARTIST/SONG	YEAR	LABEL

Gunter, Cornel (& group)
Wishful Thinking/Key To Your Heart — 64 — Challenge

Gunter, Cornel (bb the Ermines)
Call Me A Fool/You Send Me — 57 — Dot 15654
Baby Come Home/I Want You Madly — 57 — Eagle 301

Gunter, Cornell (& group)
Lift Me Up Angel/Rope Of Sand — 62 — Warner Bros. 5266

Guys (1)
Walkin' By The School/Funny Feelin' — 65 — Original Sound 56

Guys (2) (Little Sammy Rozzi & the) (aka Little Sammy & the Tones)
Over The Rainbow/Christine — N/A — Pelham 722/Jaclyn 1161

Guys (2) (Sammy & the)
Let It Please Be You — N/A — N/A

Guytones
You Won't Let Me Go/Ooh Bop Sha Boo (Give All Your Love To Me) — 57 — DeLuxe 6144
She's Mine/Not Wanted — 57 — DeLuxe 6152
This Is Love/Hunky Dory — 58 — DeLuxe 6159
Baby I Don't Care/Young Dreamer — 58 — DeLuxe 6163
Tell Me (How Was I To Know)/Your Heart's Bigger Than Mine — 58 — DeLuxe 6169

Gypsies (1)
One, Two, Three, Go/I'm Good To You Baby — 55 — Groove 0117
You've Been Away Too Long/Rock Around The Christmas Tree — 55 — Groove 0129
You've Been Away Too Long/Rockin' Pretty Baby — 56 — Groove 0137

Gypsies (2) (female)
Why?/Young Girl To Calypso — 57 — Atlas 1073

Haff-Tones
I Need You/Turnaround — 61 — Twilight 001

Hall Brothers
My White Convertible/Now You Say We Are Through — 58 — Arc 4444
I'm Still Lonely/Toy Boy — 62 — Four Star 1760

Hall, Betty (& group)
Paradise For Two/I'm On A Holiday — 62 — Ember 1096

Hall, Ronnie (& group)
Donna The Primadonna — N/A — Ember 1096

Hallmarks
Congratulations/My Little Sailor Boy — 62 — Dot 16418

Hallmarks (Rickie & the) (fb Ricki Lisi)
Wherever You Are/Joanie Don't You Cry — 63 — Amy 877

Halo, Johnny (with the Four Seasons)
Betty Jean/More Lovin' Less Talkin' — 62 — Topix 6004

Halos (1) (aka Craftys)
Nag/Copy Cat — 61 — 7 Arts 709
Come On/What'd I Say — 61 — 7 Arts 720
Village Of Love/Mean Old World — 62 — Trans Atlas 690

Halos (1) (Cammy Carol & the)
Until The Day I Die/Out Of Sight — 61 — Elmor 302

ARTIST/SONG	YEAR	LABEL
Halos (1) (Carl Spencer & the)		
Prayer	62	N/A
Halos (1) (Ernie & the) (fb Ernie K-Doe)		
Girl From Across The Sea (Angel Marie)/Darling Don't Make Me Cry	63	Guyden 2085
Halos (1) (Johnny Angel & the)		
Lady Of Spain/Without Her Heart	61	Felsted 8633
One More Tomorrow/Mashed Potato Stomp	62	Felsted 8646
Roller Motion/Looking For A Fool	62	Felsted 8659
Halos (2) (female)		
Do I/Just Keep On Loving Me	65	Congress 244
Since I Fell For You/You're Never Gonna Find	65	Congress 249
Baby What You Want Me To Do/Hey Hey Love Me	65	Congress 253
Hamilton Sisters		
Oop Shoop/Do You Wanna Ride	54	Columbia 40319
My Blue Heaven/Garden Of Eden	54	Columbia 40368
You Are The One	56	Columbia 40368
Hamilton, Bob (& group)		
Geraldine	N/A	Lu Pine
Hamilton, Gil (& group)		
When Are You Coming Home/Move And Groove	62	Vee Jay 479
Hamilton, Judd (& group)		
Dream/Your Only Boy	63	Dolton 80
Hamilton, Roy (bb the Cues)		
Don't Let Go/The Right To Love	57	Epic 9257
Hamilton, Willie (& group)		
I'm So Glad You're Mine/Hangin' Around	60	Contour 500
Hamiltons (Alexander & the)		
Over The Rainbow/I Don't Need You	66	Warner Bros. 5844
Hammel Jr., Karl (& group)		
Summer Souvenirs/The Magic Of Summer	61	Arliss 1007
Sittin' Alphabetically/A Smile On My Face, A Tear In Your Eye	61	Arliss 1011
Hamptons (gm Brother Kennedy)		
I Know Why Dreamers Cry/Once In A Lifetime	61	Legrand 1007
Happy Jesters		
Just Because/Heart Of My Heart	57	Dot 15566
Happy Teens		
One More Kiss/Cha Cha Boots	60	Paradise 114
Happytones		
Summertime Nights/Papa Shame	63	Colpix 693
Harbor Lights (aka Harbor Lites) (with Jay Black)		
Angel Of Love/Tick-A-Tick-A-Tock	60	Mala 422
Harbor Lites (aka Harbor Lights) (with Jay Black)		
What Would I Do Without You/Is That Too Much To Ask	60	Jaro 77020
Hargro, Charles (& group)		
Baby Oh Baby/Over And Over	59	DAB 101

ARTIST/SONG	YEAR	LABEL
Harlems (Little "D" & the)		
Who's Gonna Pick Up The Pieces/Deep In The Heart Of A Woman	63	Josie 914
Harlequins		
Confession Of Love/Haunting Memories	58	Juanita 102
Harmonaires		
Lorraine/Come Back	57	Holiday 2602
Harmonaires (Billy Ford & the)		
Put Yourself In My Place	61	Slate 3065
Harmonaires (Bonnie Lou & the)		
Drop Me A Line/Old, Faithful And True Love	55	King 1476
Miss The Love/Barnyard Hop	55	King 1506
Miss The Love/Daddy-O	55	King 4864
Harmonaires (Eddie Elders & the)		
With A Tear In My Heart/Gee! I Love You Baby	57	Vita 176
Harmonaires (Elaine Gay & the) (aka Five Harmonaires)		
Rock Love/Ebony Eyes	55	DeLuxe 2029
Harmonaires (Lula Reed & the)		
Heavenly Road/My Mother's Prayers	53	King 4590
Harmonizers (Premo & the)		
So Good	N/A	Doctor Bird
Harmony Grits (ref Original Drifters)		
Am I To Be The One/I Could Have Told You	59	End 1051
Gee/Santa Claus Is Coming To Town	59	End 1063
Harmony Kings		
Swinging Affair/It Makes No Difference	58	Cash 1064
Harper, Chuck (& group)		
Summer Is Through/Call On Me	62	Felsted 8658
Harper, Thelma (& group)		
At Last	62	Jell 191
Harps (1) (Little David (Baughan) & the)		
I Won't Cry/You'll Pay	55	Savoy 1178
Harps (2) (aka Camelots (2)/aka Cupids (6))		
Marie/Daddy's Going Away Again	64	Laurie 3239
Harptones		
A Sunday Kind Of Love/I'll Never Tell	53	Bruce 101/Relic 1022 (73)
My Memories Of You/It Was Just For Laughs	54	Bruce 102/Relic 1023 (73)
I Depended On You/Mambo Boogie	54	Bruce 104
Why Should I Love You/Forever Mine	54	Bruce 109
Since I Fell For You/Oobidee-Oobidee-Oo	54	Bruce 113
Loving A Girl Like You/High Flyin' Baby	54	Bruce 123
Life Is But A Dream/You Know You're Doing Me Wrong	54	Paradise 101
I Almost Lost My Mind/Oo-Wee, Baby	55	Bruce 128
My Success (It All Depends On You)/I've Got A Notion	55	Paradise 103
It All Depends On You/Guitar Shuffle	55	Paradise 105
What Is Your Decision/Gimme Some	56	Andrea 100
That's The Way It Goes/Marie	56	Rama
I Got A Fine Little Girl	56	Rama (unfinished)
Three Wishes/That's The Way It Goes	56	Rama 203
On Sunday Afternoon/The Masquerade Is Over	56	Rama 214
My Memories Of You/High Flyin' Baby	56	Tip Top 401

ARTIST/SONG	YEAR	LABEL
Cry Like I Cried/So Good, So Fine, You're Mine	57	Gee 1045
The Shrine Of St. Cecilia/Oo-Wee, Baby	57	Rama 221
Laughing On The Outside/I Remember	59	Warwick 500
Love Me Completely/Hep Teenager	59	Warwick 512
Rain Down Kisses/Answer Me, My Love	60	Coed 540
No Greater Miracle/What Kind Of Fool (Do You Think I Am)	60	Warwick 551
All In Your Mind/The Last Dance	61	Companion 102
What Will I Tell My Heart/Foolish Me	61	Companion 103
Devil In Velvet/Your Love Is A Good Love	61	Cub 9097
A Sunday Kind Of Love/Mambo Boogie	62	Raven 8001
Sunset/I Gotta Have Your Love	63	KT 201
Until The Real Thing Comes Along	72	Roulette LP 114/
		Murray Hill LP 001098 (88)
School Girl	85	Murray Hill LP 000083
You're Gonna Need My Help Someday	85	Murray Hill LP 000083
What Is Your Secret	88	Murray Hill LP 001098

Harptones (with Bunny Paul)

I'll Never Tell/Honey Love	54	Essex 364

Harris, Bill (& group)

I'm So Glad	N/A	Essex 364

Harris, Billy (& group)

The Wedding	59	Plaid 101

Harris, Dimples (& group)

This I Do Believe/If You'll Be True	56	Crest 1013

Harris, Thurston (bb the Sharps)

Little Bitty Pretty One/I Hope You Won't Hold It Against Me	57	Aladdin 3398
Do What You Did/I'm Asking Forgiveness	57	Aladdin 3399
Be Baba Leba/I'm Out To Getcha	58	Aladdin 3415
Only One Love Is Blessed/Smokey Joes	58	Aladdin 3428
Over And Over/You're Gonna Need Me	58	Aladdin 3430
Tears From My Heart/Over Someone Else's Shoulder	58	Aladdin 3435
From The Bottom Of My Heart/	59	Aladdin 3448
You Don't Know How Much I Love You (no group)		
My Love Will Last/Hey Little Girl	59	Aladdin 3450
Bless Your Heart/Runk Bunk	59	Aladdin 3452
Paradise Hill/Slip-Slop	59	Aladdin 3456

Harrison, Lee (& group)

Mine Alone/So Unimportant	58	Judd 1003

Hart, Rocky (bb the Passions)

Every Day/Come With Me	59	Cub 9052
Crying	61	Big Top 3069
I Play The Part Of A Fool/	61	Glo 216
Someone Stole My Baby While Doing The Twist		

Harvey (actually Harvey Fuqua with the Moonglows)

Ten Commandments Of Love/Mean Old Blues	58	Chess 1705
I Want Somebody/Da Da Goo Goo	58	Chess 1713
Don't Be Afraid To Love/Twelve Months Of The Year	59	Chess 1725
Unemployment/Mama Loocie	59	Chess 1738
Oooh Ouch Stop! (Teacher, You're Hurting Me)/Blue Skies	59	Chess 1749

Harvey Boys

Nothing Is Too Good For You/Marina Girl	56	Cadence 1306

Hatfield, Bobby (& group)

I Need A Girl/Hot Tamale	63	Moonglow 220

ARTIST/SONG	YEAR	LABEL
Havens		
Want You/Only You	63	Poplar 123
Hawketts		
Mardi Gras Mambo/Your Time's Up	55	Chess 1591
Hawkins, Sam (& group)		
When Nobody Loves You/She Didn't Notice Me	59	Gone 5054
Hawks (1)		
Joe The Grinder/Candy Girl	54	Imperial 5266
Good News/She's All Right	54	Imperial 5281
It Ain't That Way/I-Yi	54	Imperial 5292
Give It Up/Nobody But You	54	Imperial 5306
All Women Are The Same/That' What You Are	54	Imperial 5317
It's Too Late Now/Can't See For Lookin'	55	Imperial 5332
These Blues/Why Oh Why?	55	Post 2004
It's All Over/Ever Since You Been Gone	56	Modern 990
A Little More Wine, My Dear/Fussy	58	Del-Fi 4108
He's The Fatman	N/A	Imperial (unreleased)
I Want My Loving Now	N/A	Imperial (unreleased)
Schoolgirl	N/A	Imperial (unreleased)
Hawks (2) (Ronnie Hawkins & the)		
Need Your Lovin'/Mary Lou	59	Roulette 4177
Southern Love/Love Me Like You Can	59	Roulette 4209
Hawks (3) (Little Tony & the)		
Cry Cry Cry/Do What You Did	66	Original Sound 63
Hayden Sisters		
Silent Tears/Mr. Blues	61	Tilt 784
Hayden, Gil (& group)		
So Left Alone/Think Before You Say Goodbye	61	V-Tone 219
Hayes, Linda (& group)		
Our Love's Forever Blessed/You're The Only One For Me	55	Recorded In Hollywood 1032/ Decca 29644 (55)
Hayes, Linda (bb the Flairs)		
I Had A Dream/You Ain't Movin' Me	56	Antler 4000
Hayes, Linda (bb the Platters)		
Let's Babalu/My Name Ain't Annie	55	King 4752
Headhunters (Cannibal & the)		
Show You How To Make Love To Me/Land Of 1,000 Dances (not doo-wop)	65	Rampart 642
Headliners (1)		
Comin' On Down With Love/B.I. Moore	62	Beltone 2020
Headliners (2) (George Goodman & the)		
Let Me Love You/Let Me Love You (instrumental)	64	Val 1
Let Me Love You/I'm So Tired	65	Val 1000/Warner Bros. 5632 (65)/A&M 1011 (68)
I'll Cherish You Love/Secret Love	65	Val 5
Starlight And Moonbeams/I'm So Tired	65	Val 6
Headliners (3)		
Back To School Again/Traveler Traveler	N/A	Keno 1002
Healeys (Tom Austin & His)		
Summer's Over/Maybe You'll Be There	63	Old Town 1147

ARTIST/SONG	YEAR	LABEL

Heard, Lonnie (& group)
| A Sunday Kind Of Love/Romance In The Park | 61 | Arliss 1008 |

Heart-Attacks
| Babba Diddy Baby/I'm Angry Baby | N/A | Remus 5000 |

Heart-Throbs
| So Glad/All The Way Home | 57 | Aladdin 3394/Lamp 2010 (57) |

Heartaches (Jo Ann & the)
| I'm So Young (a capella)/A Lovers Call (a capella) | 66 | Catamount 114 |

Heartbeats (1) (aka Three Friends)
| Finally/Boil And Bubble | 55 | Jubilee 5202 |

Heartbeats (2)
Crazy For You/Rock 'n' Rollin' 'n' Rhythm 'n' Blues-n'	55	Hull 711
Be Mine, Be Mine	55	Rama (unreleased)
Darling How Long/Hurry Home Baby	56	Hull 713/Gee 1062 (61)
People Are Talking (Slow Version)/Your Way	56	Hull 716/Gee 1061 (61)
A Thousand Miles Away/Oh Baby Don't	56	Hull 720/Rama 216 (57)
Stars In The Sky	56	Rama (unreleased)
Tell Me	56	Rama (unreleased)
When I Found You/Hands Off Baby	57	Gee 1043
After New Year's Eve/Five Hundred Miles To Go	57	Gee 1047
Be Mine	57	Rama (unreleased)
Lovin' Sickness	57	Rama (unreleased)
Wedding Bells/I Won't Be The Fool Anymore	57	Rama 222
Everybody's Somebody's Fool/I Want To Know	57	Rama 231
Down On My Knees/I Found A Job	58	Roulette 4054
One Day Next Year/Sometimes I Wonder	58	Roulette 4091
One Million Years/Darling, I Want To Get Married	59	Guyden 2011
Down On My Knees/Crazy For You	59	Roulette 4194
Have Rock, Will Roll	60	Roulette LP 25107
It's Alright With Me	60	Roulette LP 25107
Lonely Lover	60	Roulette LP 25107
Easy To Remember	81	Collectables 1021

Heartbeats (2) (as the Heart Beats Quintet)
| Tormented/After Everybody's Gone | 55 | Network 71200 |

Heartbreakers (1) (fb Paul Himmelstein)
1, 2, I Love You/Without A Cause	57	Vik 0261
Love You Till/My Love	57	Vik 0299
Come Back My Love	59	Fordham 109/Vanguard 9093
Corrida Mash/I'm Leaving It All Up To You	62	Brent 7037
Since You've Been Gone/John Law	62	Markay 106
The Willow Wept/You Had Time	63	Atco 6258
Please Answer/She Is My Baby	64	Linda 114

Heartbreakers (2) (TV Slim & His)
| Darling Remember/Flatfoot Sam (no group) | 57 | Cliff 103/Checker 870 (57) |

Heartbreakers (3) (fb Frank Zappa)
| Everytime I See You/Cradle Rock | 63 | Donna 1381 |

Heartbreakers (4) (female)
| It's Hard Being A Girl/Special Occasions | 63 | MGM 13129 |

Hearties (Kip Hale & the)
| Don't You Care/Don't Say You Love Me | 54 | Jubilee 5166 |

Hearts (1) (Billy Austin & the)
| Angel Baby/Night Has Come | 52 | Apollo 444 |

ARTIST/SONG	YEAR	LABEL
Hearts (2)		
Lonely Nights/Oo Wee	55	Baton 208/Main Line 102 (57)
All My Love Belongs To You/Talk About Him, Girlie	55	Baton 211
Until The Real Thing Comes Along/Gone, Gone, Gone	55	Baton 215
Like, Later Baby/I Want Your Love Tonite	55	J&S 1626/1627
Goin' Home To Stay/Disappointed Bride	56	Baton 222
She Drives Me Crazy/I Had A Guy	56	Baton 228
You Weren't Home/I Couldn't Let You See Me Crying	56	J&S 1180
A Thousand Years From Today/I Feel So Good	56	J&S 995/Zells 3377 (70)
Dancing In A Dream World/You Wouldn't Tell	57	J&S 1657
So Long Baby/You Say You Love Me	57	J&S 1660
Dear Abby/Dear Abby (instrumental)	63	Tuff 370
If I Had Known/There Are So Many Ways	56	J&S 1002/1003
My Love Has Gone/You Or Me Have Got To Go	56	J&S 425/426
There Is No Love At All/Goodbye Baby	57	J&S 4571/4572
Do You Remember	N/A	Zells
Hearts (2) (with Clarence Ashe)		
Dancing In A Dreamworld/Trouble I've Had	64	J&S 1466
Hearts (3) (aka Lee Andrews & the Hearts)		
On My Honor/It's Unbelievable	60	Chancellor 1057
Hearts (3) (Lee Andrews & the)		
Maybe You'll Be There/Baby, Come Back	54	Rainbow 252/Riviera 965 (54)
The White Cliffs Of Dover/Much Too Much	54	Rainbow 256
The Bells Of St. Mary's/The Fairest	54	Rainbow 259
Bluebird Of Happiness/Show Me The Merengue	56	Gotham 318
Lonely Room/Leona	56	Gotham 320
Just Suppose/It's Me	56	Gotham 321
Teardrops/The Girl Around The Corner	57	Grand 156/Main Line 105 (57)/ Argo 1000 (57)/Chess 1675 (57)
Long, Lonely Nights/The Clock	57	Grand 157/Main Line 102 (57)/ Chess 1665 (57)
Try The Impossible/Nobody's Home	58	Casino 452/ United Artists 123 (58)
Why Do I/Glad To Be Here	58	United Artists 136
All I Ask Is Love/Maybe You'll Be There	58	United Artists 151
Lonely Room/Together Again	62	Gowen 1403
Much Too Much/The Fairest	65	Lost Nite 104
Quiet As It's Kept/You're Taking A Long Time Coming Back	66	RCA 8929
Island Of Love/Nevertheless	67	Crimson 1009
I've Had It/Little Bird	68	Crimson 1015
Cold Grey Dawn/All You Can Do	68	Lost Nite 1001
Oh My Love/Can't Do Without You	68	Lost Nite 1004
Quiet As It's Kept/Island Of Love	68	Lost Nite 1005
Sipping A Cup Of Coffee/Just Suppose	81	Gotham 323
Window Eyes/Long Lonely Nights (alternate)	81	Gotham 324
I Miss My Baby/Boom (alternate)	81	Gotham 325
Abide (By The Golden Rule)	N/A	Collectables LP 5003
Strollin' Baby	N/A	Collectables LP 5003
Hearts (3) (Lee Andrews & the) (as Lee Andrews)		
I Wonder/Baby Come Back	59	Casino 110
Just Suppose/Boom	59	United Artists 162
A Wise Man Said/If You Only Cared	60	Jordan 121
I've Got A Right To Cry/I Miss You So	61	Swan 4065
A Night Like Tonight/You Gave To Me	61	Swan 4076
P.S. I Love You/I Cried	61	Swan 4087
I'm Sorry Pillow/Gee But I'm Lonesome	62	Parkway 860/Parkway 5213/ 5214 (63)
Looking Back/Operator	63	Parkway 866
You You You/Hug-A-Bee	65	V.I.P. 1601

ARTIST/SONG	YEAR	LABEL
Hearts (4) (Eugene Ball with the)		
California Baby/Why Oh Why	57	Melatone 1001
Hearts (5) (Buddy & the)		
Thirty Days/Let It Rock	64	Landa 701
Heartspinners (1)		
I've Searched/Oh So Much	58	X-Tra 109
I've Searched/Mixture Of Love	63	Times Square 20
Heartspinners (2) (Dino & the)		
Cry Like I Cried/That's My Girl	72	Bim Bam Boom 108/ Barrier 103 (76)
I Love You So/Two Kinds Of People In The World	72	Bim Bam Boom 112
Hey Senorita/I'm Not A Know It All	73	Bim Bam Boom 119
Flames/Shirley	N/A	Pyramid 164
Zoom!/Let's Go Back To Yesterday	N/A	Robin Hood 141
Who Do You Think You Are?/A Thousand Miles Away	N/A	Robin Hood 142
The Lover's Plea/Mexico	N/A	Starlight 11
The Bells Of Love	N/A	Starlight 13
I Believe In You/Gee	N/A	Starlight 9
Heartstrings (Johnny Jason & the)		
Last Years Christmas Tree/Be There (by the Shadettes)	N/A	Romantic 101/102
Hemlocks (Little Bobby Rivera & the)		
Coralee/The Joys Of Love	57	Fury 1004
Hendricks, Bobby (bb the Coasters)		
Itchy Twitchy Feeling/A Thousand Dreams	58	Sue 706
Dreamy Eyes/Molly Be Good	58	Sue 708
It's Misery/Cast Your Vote	59	Sue 710
Henry, Earl (& group)		
My Suzanne/Believe A Traveler	58	Dot 15875
Henry, Stacy (bb the Dream-Timers)		
Sweetest Darlin'/I'm Not Ashamed	61	Flippin' 108
Hep Cats		
What In The World Can I Do/The Dilly Up	61	Del-Fi 4159
Hepcats (Daisy Mae & the)		
Woman Trouble/Lonesome Playgirl	56	Gotham 317
Hepsters		
I Had To Let You Go/Rockin' 'n' Rollin' With Santa Claus	55	Ronel 107
I Gotta Sing The Blues/This-A-Way	56	Ronel 110
Heptones		
I'm So In Love With You	56	Abco 105
Heralds		
Eternal Love/Gonna Love You Every Day	54	Herald 435
Freeze	N/A	Herald (unreleased)
Why Can't I Have You	N/A	Herald (unreleased)
Peggy/Wonder Boy	68	Tamborine 2
Hi Fi's		
Why Can't I Stop Loving You/I Keep Forgettin'	65	Cameo 349
Hi Larks		
Mine/Take A Hike	59	Beat 0050

ARTIST/SONG	YEAR	LABEL
Hi Lighters		
Feeling Alright	N/A	Charly LP 1115
Hi Liters (Buddy Roberts & the)		
Ding Dong/Black And Blue	60	Bonanza 689/690
Hi Lites		
Love You So Much	59	Key M82
Hi Tensions		
Got A Good Feeling/Ebbing Of The Tide	63	Milestone 2018
Come What May	N/A	Milestone
Old Times	N/A	Milestone
Traveling Lady	N/A	Milestone
Wedding Song (If You Say I Do)	N/A	Milestone
Hi Tensions (Leon Peels & the)		
So Far Away/The Clock	60	Audio 201/K&G 101
She'll Break Your Heart/Mary Had A Little Man	64	Whirlybird 2005
A Magic Island/Darlene	64	Whirlybird 2008
Hi Timers		
You're Everything/Why Should We Keep On Pretending	59	Sonic 1502
Hi Tones (Charles Andrea & the)		
Didn't We Have A Nice Time/Open Up Your Heart	61	Tori Ltd. T-2X
Hi Toppers (V. James & the)		
My Heart Is Not A Toy/By And By My Love	61	Kent 354
Hi-Fashions		
Yes, Oh Yes/Ooh, What A Guy	58	Paris 524
Hi-Fi Four		
Band Of Gold/Davy You Upset My Life	55	King 4856
Hi-Fi-Dels		
Did I Cry/Tricky Tricky	61	Atlantic 2121
Hi-Fidelities		
Street Of Loneliness/Help! Murder! Police!	57	Hi-Q 5000
Hi-Fidelities (Gino Parks & the)		
Last Night I Cried/Just Go (by Gino Parks)	58	Fortune 528
Hi-Fis		
I'm So Lonely/My Dear	59	Montel 1005
Each Passing Day/Sally	60	Mark 148/Devere 006
Hi-Fives (1)		
Hong Kong/Throwing Pebbles In The Pond	56	Flair-X 3000
Hi-Fives (2)		
My Friend/How Can I Win	58	Decca 30576
Dorothy/Just A Shoulder To Cry On	58	Decca 30657
What's New, What's New/Lonely	58	Decca 30744
Felicia/Windy City Special	60	Bingo 1006
Hi-Fives (3)		
Julie/Son Of Raunchy	64	Bell 634
Hi-Jacks		
Wonderful One/The Letter I Wrote Today	56	ABC 9742

ARTIST/SONG	YEAR	LABEL
Hi-Lighters		
Ain't Giving Up Nothing/Undecided Now	56	Celeste 3005
You Must Come In/Dance Everyone, Dance	58	Hanover 4506
Cha Cha Rock/Dance Me To Death	58	Mercury 71342
Hi-Lights		
Oh Lover Of Mine	63	JR 5003
Hi-Liters		
Route 66/Baby Don't Treat Me This Way	55	Wen-Dee 1927
Hi-Liters (with King Bassie & the Three Aces)		
In The Night/Let Me Be True To You	58	Hico 2432
Hi-Lites (1)		
I Found A Love/Zanzee	54	Okeh 7046
Hi-Lites (2)		
The Next Four Years/The Girl With The Bells	56	Mercury 70987
Friday Night Go Go/Chicka-Rocka-Chee-Che-Cho	58	Brunswick 55102
Beach Baby/One Love For Me	58	Wonder 102
The Pony Pt. 1/The Pony Pt. 2	61	Jet 501
4000 Miles Away/Woke Up This Morning	61	Jet 502
Walking My Baby Back Home/I'm Falling In Love	61	Record Fair 500
Gloria My Darling/For Your Precious Love	62	Julia 1105
For Sentimental Reasons/For Your Precious Love	62	Record Fair 501
Twistin' Time/Twistin' Pony	62	Twist Time 12
Death Of An Angel/Our Winter Love	63	King 5730
Groovy/Hey Baby	65	Wassel 701
Hi-Lites (3) (Ronnie & the)		
I Wish That We Were Married/Twistin' And Kissin'	62	Joy 260
Send My Love/Be Kind	62	Joy 265
Valerie/The Fact Of The Matter	62	Raven 8000
A Slow Dance/What The Next Day May Bring	63	Win 250/Reo
The Fact Of The Matter/You Keep Me Guessin'	63	Win 251
High School Romance/Uptown-Downtown	63	Win 252
Too Young/High School Romance	65	ABC 10685
For Lovers/What A Pretty You'd Be	N/A	N/A
Hi-Lites (4)		
Pretty Face	62	N/A
Hi-Lites (5) (Skippy & the)		
Waiting To Take You Home/Old Man River	N/A	Streamlite 1027/Elmor
Hi-Notes (Tommy Frederick & the)		
The Prince Of Players/I'm Not Pretending	58	Carlton 450
Hi-Tones (aka Hitones)		
That's All I Want To Do/You Didn't Have To Laugh	58	Skyline 701
The Special Day/I've Never Seen A Straight Banana	60	Candix 307
Fool, Fool, Fool/Let's Have A Good Time	60	King 5414
What Was The Cause Of It All/Don't Leave Me No Choice	61	Eon 101
Lover's Quarrel/Just For You	61	Fonsca 201
No More Pain/I Don't Know Why	61	Fonsca 202
Girls/Sure As The Flowers	61	Seg-Way 105
Hi-Tones (Bob Jaxon & the) (aka Hitones)		
Why Does A Woman Cry/Ali Baba	55	Cadence 1264
Hi-Tones (Johnny Wyatt & the)		
Wondering Why/We Met At A Dance	59	Big Time 1927

ARTIST/SONG	YEAR	LABEL
Hi-Tones (Willie & the) (aka Hitones)		
Don't Talk Back	N/A	Irma 13
Hide-A-Ways		
Cherie/Me Makem Powwow	55	MGM 55004
Hideaways		
Can't Help Loving That Girl Of Mine/I'm Coming Home	54	Ronni 1000
Lovin' Time/You're So Hard To Say Goodnight To	63	Duel 521
Higgins, Ben (& group)		
Really Paradise/A Whole Lot Of Lovin'	62	Jamie 1217
Higgins, Chuck (& group)		
Shot Gun Wedding/Groove	54	Kicks 6
I'll Be There/Broke	54	Specialty 532
Higgs & Wilson (& group)		
When You Tell Me Baby/Mannyon	60	Time 1028
High Liters		
Hello, Dear/Bobby Sox Baby	56	Vee Jay 184
High Seas		
Sunday Kind Of Love/We Go Together	60	D-M-G 1001/D-M-G 4000
High Tensions		
Looking For A Summertime Girl	64	Hitt 6601
High Type Five (Billy Carr & the)		
Champagne	59	C&P 105
High Type Five (Clarence Green with the)		
Mary My Darling/Old Grandpa	59	Chess 1732
Highbrows (Shadoe & the)		
Tomboy/Pony Express Riders	61	Gem 102
Highlanders (1)		
Sunday Kind Of Love/Beg And Steal	57	Ray's 36
Highlanders (2) (Sandra & the)		
Written In The Stars	61	Highland 1015
Highlands		
I Laughed	61	N/A
Highlighters (1)		
Christmas Is Coming At Last/White Christmas	50	Apollo 1141
Flang Dang Do/The Bull	58	New Song 116
Las Vegas Drive	59	New Song 133
Highlighters (2)		
Sweet Little Baby Of Mine/Mi Amor	59	Cannon 372
Highlighters (2) (Jimmy Hall & the)		
Jeannie/At The Hippety Hop	59	Cannon 369
Highlighters (3) (Walter Webb & the)		
Your Time Is Gonna Come/Lulu	70	Chess 2091
Highlights (1) (fb Frank Pizani)		
City Of Angels/Listen My Love	56	Bally 1016
To Be With You/Will I Ever Know	57	Bally 1027
Indiana Style/Turn Around Shoes	58	Bally 1044

ARTIST/SONG	YEAR	LABEL
Highlights (2) (Barry & the)		
Christmas Bell Rock/Chil-E Baby	60	Baye 511/Airmaster 700 (60)
Highlights (3)		
Ah So	N/A	Play
Highlites (Little Angie & the)		
Baby Doll	N/A	Essay
Highschool Chanters		
Hoodoo The Voodoo/Teenage Chant	59	Fashion 001
Hightones (Claude & the)		
Bucket Head/Doodle Bug	59	Baytone 113
Monkey Stuff/High Sailing	N/A	Pammar 614
Hightower, Donna (bb the Jacks)		
Dog Gone It/Love Me Again	55	RPM 432
Since You/Bob-O-Link (by the Jacks)	55	RPM 439
I Ain't Gonna Tell/He's My Baby	56	RPM 481
Hilites (Roy Smith & the)		
She's Fine/Love You So Much	61	Nu Tone 1182
Hill, Grant (& group)		
She's Going Away	N/A	Topaz 1300
Hillsiders (Bobby Angel & the)		
Baby-O/That's The Way I Want To Go	61	Rhum 101
Heartbreak Hotel/Submarine Races	62	Astra 300
Hinton, Joe (& group)		
I Know/Ladder Of Prayer	58	Back Beat 519
Pretty Little Mama/Will You	59	Back Beat 526
Hippies (aka Stereos (1)/aka Tams (1))		
Memory Lane/Teenage Kids	63	Parkway 863
Historians (Barbaroso & the) (fb Nicky Addeo)		
Zoom/When I Fall In Love	57	Jade 110
Hit-Makers		
Pretty Little Mama/Will You	59	Beat 526
Hitchhikers (Chuck Thomas & the)		
Let Our Hearts Be Our Guide/Why Baby	57	Band Box 360
Hitmakers (1)		
Chapel Of Love/Cool School	58	Original Sound 1
I Can't Take It Anymore/Too Cool	59	Angle Tone 1104
How To Make A Hit Record/Buttermilk	65	Dore 738
Hitmakers (2) (Linda Lou & the)		
The Torch Is Out/The Difference In Our Ages	65	Lama 7786
Hitones (Leonard Wayne & the) (aka Hi-Tones)		
That's All I Want To Do/You Don't Have To Laugh	64	Andre 701
Hits (Tiny Tim & the)		
Wedding Bells/Doll Baby	58	Roulette 4123
Hobson, Emmett (& group)		
Looka Here, Mattie Bee/Oo-Wee Mr. Jeff	53	Central 1001

ARTIST/SONG	YEAR	LABEL
Hodges, Charles (bb the Fi-Tones)		
There Is Love/Can I Run To You	65	Alto 2016
Hodges, Eddie (with Sue Wright & group)		
Bandit Of My Dreams/Mugmates	61	Cadence 1410
Holiday, Bobby (& group)		
My Letter/Come Home	61	Port 70027
Holiday, Jimmy (& group)		
Janet/How Can I Forget	63	Everest 2022
Holidays (1)		
Ima-Lika-You (Pizza Pie)/Rolling River	53	King 1217
(Shine 'Em! Shake 'Em! Roll 'Em!) Let The Dice Decide/	54	King 1246
Just Out of Reach		
You'll Never Get Away/List'nin' To The Green Grass Grow	56	King 1520
Holidays (2)		
Irene/Aw-Aw Baby	54	Specialty 533
Holidays (3)		
Desperately/The Robin	57	Melba 112
Sands Of Gold/French Riviera	58	Brunswick 55084
Never Go To Mexico (flip has no group)	58	Music City 818
Refreshing/Crazy Discharge	59	Pam 111
Very Merry Christmas/Merry Christmas Song	60	Monument 431
Pretend/Miss You	60	Robbee 103
Then I'll Be Tired Of You/Lonely Summer	60	Robbee 107
I Got News For You	N/A	Dixie 1145
Holidays (4) (Tony & the)		
There Goes My Heart Again/My Love Is Real	59	ABC 10029/ABC 10295 (61)
Holidays (5)		
Who Knows/My Heart Never Knows	59	Wonder 115
Stars Will Remember/Who Knows, Who Cares	60	Andie 5019
Come Back To Me/No Other Love	61	Brent 7018
One Little Kiss/My Girl	61	Nix 537
Patty Ann/Big Brown Eyes	62	Track 101
Send Back My Love/Deacon Brown	63	Galaxy 714
Got Your Letter/The New Trucking	N/A	Lyons 107
Holidays (6) (Dick Holler & the)		
King Kong/The Girl Next Door	61	Herald 566
Mooba-Grooba	62	Comet 2146
Holidays (7) (Buddy Sheppard & the) (aka Belmonts)		
Brahm's Lullabye/(Time To Dream) My Love Is Real	62	Sabina 506
Now It's All Over/That Back Sound	63	Sabina 510
Holidays (8)		
I Want You To Love Me/Love And Learn	64	Coral 62430
Holidays (9)		
This I Swear/Summertime	66	Relic 542
Adios (a capella)	75	Relic LP 102
Chant Of The Isles (a capella)	75	Relic LP 102
It Happened Today (a capella)	75	Relic LP 102
My Baby Loves Me (a capella)	75	Relic LP 102
Time After Time (a capella)	75	Relic LP 102
Holidays (10)		
Cathy Darling/Down By The Shore	N/A	Mark IV 725

ARTIST/SONG	YEAR	LABEL
Holidays (11)		
Love That's True/To Me	N/A	Willjer 6002
Holland, Bryant (& group)		
Where's The Joy In Nature Boy/Shock	58	Kudo 667
Holland, Eddie (bb the Rayber Voices)		
Merry-Go-Round/It Moves Me	59	United Artists 172
Hollidays		
The Wonder Of Love/I'm Not Ashamed	58	Prep 136
Holloway, Brenda (bb the Carrolls)		
Echo/Hey Fool	62	Donna 1358
Hollyhawks		
I Cry All The Time/When Came The Fall	63	Jubilee 5441
Hollyhocks		
Don't Say Tomorrow/You for Me	57	Nasco 6001
Hollywood Allstars		
Justine/Dance The Slossin	63	Admiral 501
Hollywood Argyles		
Alley Oop/Sho' Know A Lot About Love	60	Lute 5905
Gun Totin' Critter Named Jack/Bug Eye	60	Lute 5908
Hully Gully/So Fine	60	Lute 6002
See You In The Morning/Morning After	61	Finer Arts 1002
You've Been Torturing Me/The Grubble	61	Paxley 752
Bossy Nover/Find Another Way	63	Felsted 8674
Long Haired Unsquare Dude Named Jack/Ole	65	Chattahoochie 691
Hollywood Arist-O-Kats		
Amazon Beauty/I'll Be Home Again	53	Recorded In Hollywood 406
Hollywood Bluejays		
I Had A Love/Tell Me You Love Me	53	Recorded In Hollywood 396
Hollywood Flames (aka Satellites) (fb Bobby Day)		
Let's Talk It Over/I Know	53	Swing Time 345/Lucky 009 (55)/ Decca 48331 (55)
One Night With A Fool/Ride, Helen, Ride	54	Lucky 001
I Shall Return	54	Lucky 002
Peggy/Ooh-La-La	54	Lucky 006/Decca 29284 (55)/ Hollywood 104
Fare Thee Well/Clickety Clack, I'm Leaving	54	Money 202
Go And Get Some More/Another Soldier Gone (by the Question Marks (1))	54	Swing Time 346
Buzz-Buzz-Buzz/Crazy	57	Ebb 119/Mona Lee 135
Give Me Back My Heart/A Little Bird	58	Ebb 131
Strollin' On The Beach/Frankenstein's Den	58	Ebb 144
Chains Of Love/Let's Talk It Over	58	Ebb 146
I'll Get By/A Star Fell	58	Ebb 149
If I Thought You Needed Me/Every Day, Every Way	59	Atco 6155
I'll Be Seeing You/Just For You	59	Ebb 153
So Good/There Is Something On Your Mind	59	Ebb 158
Now That You're Gone/Hawaiian Dream	59	Ebb 162
In The Dark/Much Too Much	59	Ebb 163
Ball And Chain/I Found A Boy	60	Atco 6164
Devil Or Angel/Do You Ever Think Of Me	60	Atco 6171
Money Honey/My Heart's On Fire	60	Atco 6180
Yes They Do/Gee	61	Chess 1787
Believe In Me/I Can't Get A Hit Record	62	Coronet 7025
Drop Me A Line/Letter To My Love	63	Vee Jay 515

ARTIST/SONG	YEAR	LABEL
Dance Senorita/Annie Don't Love Me Anymore	65	Symbol 211
I'm Comin' Home/I'm Gonna Stand By You	65	Symbol 215
Ooh Baby Ooh	88	Specialty LP 2166
So Good	88	Specialty LP 2166
This Heart Of Mine	88	Specialty LP 2166
Two Little Bees	88	Specialty LP 2166

Hollywood Flames (Dave Ford & the) (aka Satellites)

Elizabeth/Believe In Me	62	Goldie 1101

Hollywood Four Flames

Dividend Blues/W-I-N-E	51	Unique 003
Tabarin/Cry For My Baby	51	Unique 005
Please Say I'm Wrong/The Masquerade Is Over	51	Unique 015
I'll Always Be A Fool/She's Got Something	52	Recorded In Hollywood 164
Young Girl/Baby Please	52	Recorded In Hollywood 165 (first pressing)
Young Girl/Glory Of Love	52	Recorded In Hollywood 165 (second pressing)

Hollywood Playboys

I'm Lonely/You Can't Fool Me Baby	61	Rita 118

Hollywood Playboys (fb Nick Massi)

Talk To Audrey/Ding Dong, School Is Out	60	Sure 105

Hollywood Producers

You're Not Welcome/White Silk Gloves	66	Parkway 993

Hollywood Saxons (aka Saxons (1))

Everyday's A Holiday/L. A. Lover	61	Hareco 102/Swingin' 631 (61)/Elf 101 (61)/20th Century 312
I'm Your Man/It's You	61	Swingin' 651/Elf 103 (61)
Loving You/Laughing Blues	62	Action-Pac 111
Is It True?/Rock & Roll Show	65	Relic 1011
Merry Go Round/Laughing Girl	68	Swingin' 654

Hollywood Saxons (Stan Beverly & the)

Spinning/Diamonds	58	Entra 711
The Tears Came Rolling Down/Diamonds	63	Entra 1214

Hollywood Teeners (Jimmy Norman & the)

A Boy And A Girl/Bride	60	Fun 101
My Thanks/Para Siempre	60	Fun 102

Holman, Eddie (& group)

This Can't Be True/A Free Country (no group)	65	Parkway 960
Never Let Me Go/Why Do Fools Fall In Love	66	Parkway 157

Holmes, Eddie (& group)

Together Again/At Night	58	Eagle 1000

Hometowners

Ding Dong/I Wanna Go Home	59	Fraternity 842

Hondas

Send It/Twelve Feet High	62	Eden 4

Honey Bears (male)

One Bad Stud/It's A Miracle	54	Spark 104
I Love Brooklyn/Cuca Monga	55	Cash 1004
I Shall Not Fail/Whoa!	55	Spark 111

Honey Bees (1)

Let's See What's Happening/Endless	56	Imperial 5400
What's To Become Of Me/Just To Live Again	56	Imperial 5416

ARTIST/SONG	YEAR	LABEL

Honey Bees (2)
Kiss Me My Love/Give Your Love To Me	64	Bee 1101
One Wonderful Night/She Don't Deserve You	64	Smash 1939
One Girl, One Girl/No Guy	64	Vee Jay 611
Some Of Your Lovin'/You Turn Me On Boy	65	Fontana 1505
Let's Get Back Together/Never In A Million Years	66	Wand 1141

Honey Boys
Never Lose Faith In Me/Vippity Vop	56	Modern 980

Honey Dreamers
Time Was/Copper Kettle	59	Dot 15925

Honey-Do's (male)
Honey-Dew/Someone	61	Sue 746

Honeybirds
Ain't That Just Like A Boy/Who You Gonna Run To	64	Coral 62414

Honeycones
Betty Morretti/Cool It Baby	58	Ember 1033
Op/Vision Of You	58	Ember 1036
Gee Whiz/Rockin' In The Knees	58	Ember 1042
Tell Me Baby/Your Face	59	Ember 1049

Honeydreamers (Kirk Stuart & the)
Gladly/The Swingin' Shepherd Blues	58	Josie 832

Honeymoons (Denny Dale & the)
Why Did You Leave Me/Mr. Moon	66	Soma 1447

Honeytones (1)
Somewhere, Sometime, Someday/Too Bad	55	Mercury 70557
False Alarm/Honeybun Cha Cha	55	Wing 90013

Honeytones (1) (Gene Worth & the)
When You Are Mine	N/A	Ace

Honeytones (2)
Don't Look Now, But/I Know I Know	58	Big Top 3002

Hong Kong White Sox
Cholley-Oop (parody)/He'd Better Go	60	Trans-World 6906

Honkers
Do You Promise/Honk	59	Okeh 7124

Honorables
Castle In The Sky/How About A Date	61	Honor Records 100

Hood, Darla (bb the Rocketeers)
No Secret Now/Witches Brew	57	Encino 1007/Acama 122 (60)

Hootenaires
Baby Baby (I Love You)/Bill Bailey	63	Enjoy 2003

Hoppers
Linda Loves Me	N/A	Valley's Mead 104

Horizons (1)
Hey Now Baby/Strange Oh Strange	64	Regina 1321

Horizons (1) (Sunny & the)
Nature's Creation/Because They Tell Me	62	Luxor 1015

ARTIST/SONG	YEAR	LABEL
Horizons (2)		
Why Did You Make Me Cry (a capella)	75	Relic LP 103
A Story Of Love (a capella)	75	Relic LP 104
Hornets (1) (aka Cleveland Quartet)		
I Can't Believe That You're In Love With Me/Lonesome Baby	53	States 127
Big City Bounce	81	P-Vine Special LP 9036
Ridin' And Rockin'	81	P-Vine Special LP 9036
You Played The Game	81	P-Vine Special LP 9036
Hornets (2)		
Crying Over You/Tango Moon	57	Flash 125
Strollin'/Slow Dance	58	Rev 3515
Hornets (3)		
She's My Baby/Give Me A Kiss	64	V.I.P. 25004
Hornets (4) (Don Ray & the)		
I Dreamed Of You/Silly Dilly	59	Hornet 501
Hosea, Don (& group)		
Since I Met You/Uh Huh Huh	61	Sun 368
Hot Rods (1) (Little Shy Guy & the)		
My Little Baby	56	Calvert 107
Hot Rods (2) (Doug Connell & the)		
On Our Way From School/You're My Girl	59	Alton 600
Hot Shots		
Blue Hours/Horse's Neck	54	Savoy 1128
Blue Nights/Blue Dreams	54	Savoy 1136
Hot Tamalas		
Mr. Starlight/Loves Intentions	64	Detroit 101
Hounddogs		
I'm Beginning To Understand Them/The Girl	64	Dee Dee 773
House, Herman (& group)		
Evie My Darling	N/A	Call 106
Houston, David (& group)		
Waited So Long/All I Do Is Dream Of You	58	NRC 005
Houston, Joe (& group)		
Shtiggy Boom/Joe's Gone	55	RPM 426
Howard, Gregory (bb the Cadillacs) (aka Gee-Tones)		
When In Love (Do As Lovers Do)/Sweet Pea	63	Kapp 536
Howard, Vince (& group)		
If You Believe, If You Believe/Moonlight Mountain	61	Era 3056
Howards		
Lola/Mi Mi Girl	58	ABC 9897
Hubbcaps (Frank Hubbell & the)		
Broken Date, Pt. 1/Broken Date, Pt. 2	63	Topix 6005
Hubcaps (Holt Davey & the)		
Pittery Pat/You Move Me	58	United Artists 110X
Hudson, Eddie (& group)		
She's Sugar Sweet/That Long Lost Baby	58	Excello 2135

ARTIST/SONG	YEAR	LABEL
Hudson, Glinda (& group)		
I'll Wait	N/A	Smalltown 300
Hueys		
Coo Coo Over You/You Ain't No Hippie	68	Instant 3289
Huff, Chauncey (& group)		
Does She Love Me/Swimmin' U.S.A.	64	Fantasy 587
Hull, Terry (bb the Starfires)		
Those Pretty Brown Eyes/Meant To Be	N/A	Staff 103
Humdingers		
Necklace Of Tear Drops/The Clock In Lovers Lane	57	Dale 106
Hummingbirds		
You And Me/My Ship	62	Cannon 4600
Humphries, Fatman (bb the Four Notes (aka Crows))		
I Can't Get Started With You/Lulubell Blues	52	Jubilee 5085
Humphries, Teddy (& group)		
This Love Is True Love/Without A Song	58	King 5151
Hunter, Herbert (& group)		
I'm So Satisfied/Don't Pity Me	61	Poncello 711
Hunters (1) (aka Flairs)		
Rabbit On A Log/Down At Hayden's	53	Flair 1017
Hunters (2) (Little Moose & the)		
Lovely One/Granny Rock	59	SMC 1373
Hurley, John (& group)		
Lonely Boy/Cry Baby	58	AKA 103
Hurricanes (1)		
I Keep Crying/Teardrops	54	Audivox 109
Hurricanes (2)		
Poor Little Dancing Girl/Pistol Packin' Mama	55	King 4817
Maybe It's All For The Best/Yours	56	King 4867
Raining In My Heart/Tell Me, Baby	56	King 4898
Little Girl Of Mine/Your Promise To Me	56	King 4926
Sentimental Heaven/Wishing Well	56	King 4932
Dear Mother/You May Not Know	56	King 4947
Fallen Angel/I'll Always Be In Love With You	57	King 5018
Priceless/Now That I Need You	57	King 5042
I'll Be Glad	N/A	UGHA LP 001
Hushabyes (Hale & the)		
Yes Sir, That's My Baby/900 Quetzals	64	Apogee 104/Reprise 0299
Huskies		
Go Out And Buy Yourself A Hat/Alaska, U.S.A.	58	Imperial 5544
Huskies (Kenny Kole & the)		
Sorry/Who	58	Klik 8205
Hustlers		
Goodbye/That's What Makes Her Boss	65	Fascination 6570
Hustlers (Carl Burnett & the)		
Sweet Memories/Jerk Baby Jerk	65	Carmax 102

ARTIST/SONG	YEAR	LABEL
Hy-Tones		
I'm A Fool/Chinese Boogie	58	Hy-Tone 120
I've Got My Baby/Bigger And Better	66	A-Bet 9415
Hy-Tones (Georgia Harris & the)		
Let Me Hold Your Hand/I Want To Kiss You	58	Hy-Tone 121
Hypnotics		
Eloise/Your'er The Best For Me	59	Warkee 905
I. V. Leaguers		
Ring Chimes/The Story	57	Porter 1003/1004/Dot 15677 (58)
Told By The Stars/Jim Jam	59	Nau-Voo 803
Ideals (1)		
Do I Have The Right/You Won't Like It	58	Cool 108
Ideals (2)		
My Girl/Annie Was A Stroller	58	Decca 30720
Ivy League Lover/Don't Be A Baby, Baby	59	Decca 30800
Please Jan/Always Yours	59	Stars Of Hollywood 1001
Together/What's The Matter With You, Sam	61	Paso 6401/Dusty Disc
Ideals (2) (Johnny Brantley & the)		
Mary's Lamb/Knee Socks	59	Checker 920/Checker 979 (61)
Ideals (3)		
Teens/Magic	61	Paso 6402/Dusty Disc
Trans Zistor/The Duchess	62	Fargo 1024
Identicals		
Jamie/Dreaming Of You	63	Firebird 101
Identities		
When You Find Love Slipping Away	N/A	Together 1410
Idets		
Look My Way	N/A	Shiptown 007
Idols (1)		
Just A Little Bit More/Why Must I Cry (by the Swans)	61	Reveille 1002/Dot 16210 (61)
Idols (2)		
The Prowler/Thirty Days	58	RCA 7339
Jeannine/Can't Tag Along	61	E-Z 1214
Idols (3)		
The Stars Will Remember/Tell Me	61	Galaxie 77
Idols (4)		
You're Good For Me/That's The Game To Play	N/A	Redd-E 1017
Idols (5)		
I Love You	N/A	Collectables LP 5039
Idylls		
Annette/Love Me Again	60	Spinning 6012
Illusions (1)		
The Letter/Henry And Henrietta	60	Coral 62173
Can't We Fall In Love/How High Is The Mountain	61	Ember 1071
The Closer You Are/For Sentimental Reasons	62	Kape 1001
Hey Boy/Lonely Soldier	62	Mali 104/Sheraton 104 (62) Northeast 801 (62)/ Relic 512 (64)
In The Beginning/Maybe	64	Laurie 3245
I Know/Take My Heart	66	Columbia 43700

ARTIST/SONG	YEAR	LABEL
Illusions (2)		
Story Of My Life/Walking Boy	64	Little Debbie 105
Imaginations (1)		
I Want A Girl/I Love You More (Than Anyone)	61	Bacon Fat 101
Imaginations (2)		
Hey You/Guardian Angel	61	Duel 507/Bo Marc 301 (61)/ Music Makers 108 (61)
Goodnight Baby/The Search Is Over	61	Music Makers 103
Mama's Little Baby/Wait A Little Longer Son	62	Ballad 500
Autumn Leaves	85	Relic LP 5058
Chapel Bells	85	Relic LP 5058
Fannie Brown	85	Relic LP 5058
Harry Goody	85	Relic LP 5058
My Little Girl	85	Relic LP 5058
Mystery Of You	85	Relic LP 5058
Never Let You Go	85	Relic LP 5058
I'll Never Let You Go/The Mystery Of Love	N/A	Harvey 101
Imaginations (2) (Darlene Day & the)		
I Love You So/Will	61	Music Makers 106
Impacs		
Forever And A Day/Hold-Out	63	Arlen 741
I'm Gonna Make You Cry/Tears In My Heart	63	Parkway 865
Jo-Ann/Two Strangers	64	King 5851
Shimmy, Shimmy/Zot (instrumental)	64	King 5863
Kool It/She Didn't Even Say Hello	64	King 5891
Ain't That The Way Life Is/Don't Cry Baby	64	King 5910
Impacts (1)		
Croc-O-Doll/Bobby Sox Squaw	59	RCA 7583
Now Is The Time/Soup	59	Watts 5599
Canadian Sunset/They Say	59	Watts 5600/RCA 7609 (59)
Help Me Somebody/Darling, Now You're Mine	61	Carlton 548
Summer/Linda	64	Anderson 104
Impacts (2)		
Where Are You/I'm So Glad	66	Brunswick 55393
Impaks		
Make Up Your Mind/Climb Upon Your Rockin' Chair	62	Express 716
Impalas (1)		
All But The Memory	58	Cub EP CX5000
Chum	58	Cub EP CX5000
Sorry (I Ran All The Way Home)/Fool Fool Fool	59	Cub 9022
Oh What A Fool/Sandy Went Away	59	Cub 9033
Peggy Darling/Bye Everybody	59	Cub 9053
First Date/I Was A Fool	59	Hamilton 50026
Impalas (1) (Speedo & the)		
When My Heart Does All The Talking/All Alone	60	Cub 9066
Impalas (2)		
The Lonely One/Lost Boogie	59	Sundown 115
Last Night I Saw A Girl/There Is Nothin' Like A Dame	63	20th Fox 428
Impalas (2) (Bobby Byrd & the)		
Why?/Gotta Girl	58	Corvet 1017
Impalas (3) (female) (aka Four Jewels)		
I Need You So Much/For The Love Of Mike	61	Checker 999

ARTIST/SONG	YEAR	LABEL

Impalas (4) (aka Five Discs)

When You Dance/I Can't See Me Without You	66	Red Boy 113/Steady 044
I Can't See Me Without You/Old Man Mose	N/A	Rite-On 101

Impalos

You're To Blame/Wrong About You	61	United Artists 327

Impax

Baby, You're My Love/Cool Breeze	60	Warner Bros. 5153

Imperial Gents

Little Darlin'/The Imperial Gents Stomp	70	Laurie 3540

Imperial Wonders

When I Fall In Love/Trying To Get To You	N/A	Black Prince 317

Imperialites

Have Love Will Travel/Let's Get One	64	Imperial 66015

Imperials (1) (aka Four Arcs/aka Gaylords)

You'll Never Walk Alone/Ain't Gonna Tell It Right	53	Gem 212/Great Lakes 1212 (54)
My Darling/You Should Have Told Me	53	Savoy 1104/Buzzy 1 (62)
Why Did You Leave Me?/Hard Workin' Woman	54	Derby 858
Life Of Ease/It Won't Be Very Long	54	Great Lakes 1201

Imperials (2)

Tears On My Pillow/Two People In The World	58	End 1027 (first pressing, second is by Little Anthony & the)
A Short Prayer/Where Will You Be	60	Newtime 503
The Letter/Go And Get Your Broken Heart	60	Newtime 505
Faithfully Yours/Vut Vut	61	Carlton 566
I'm Still Dancing/Bermuda Wonderful	62	Capitol 4924

Imperials (2) (Little Anthony & the)

I Cover The Waterfront	58	End (unreleased)
Little Girl	58	End (unreleased)
Tears On My Pillow/Two People In The World	58	End 1027 (second pressing, first is by the Imperials)
So Much/Oh Yeah	58	End 1036
The Diary/Cha Cha Henry	58	End 1038
The Glory Of Love/Come On Tiger	58	Liberty 55119
Must Be Falling In Love/You	58	Savoy 1552
Dry Your Eyes	59	End (unreleased)
When You Wish Upon A Star/Wishful Thinking	59	End 1039
A Prayer And A Juke Box/River Path	59	End 1047
So Near And Yet So Far/I'm Alright	59	End 1053
Shimmy, Shimmy, Ko-Ko-Bop/I'm Still In Love With You	59	End 1060
Love Is A Many Splendored Thing	59	End LP 303/End EP 204 (59)
Over The Rainbow	59	End LP 303/End EP 204 (59)
What Did I Do	59	End LP 303/End EP 204 (59)
My Empty Room/Bayou Bayou Baby	60	End 1067
I'm Taking A Vacation From Love/Only Sympathy	60	End 1074
Limbo Pt. 1/Limbo Pt. 2	60	End 1080
Formula Of Love /Dream (or Two People In The World)	60	End 1083
Please Say You Want Me/So Near And Yet So Far	60	End 1086
The Fires Burn No More/I Know (Lift Up Your Head)	61	Apollo 755
Traveling Stranger/Say Yeah	61	End 1091
A Lovely Way To Spend An Evening/Dream	61	End 1104
All Or Nothing At All	61	End LP 311
Don't Get Around Much Anymore	61	End LP 311
I Couldn't Sleep A Wink Last Night	61	End LP 311
I'll Never Smile Again	61	End LP 311
I've Got A Crush On You	61	End LP 311
If You Are But A Dream	61	End LP 311
Ooh Looka There, Ain't She Pretty	61	End LP 311

ARTIST/SONG	YEAR	LABEL
They Say It's Wonderful	61	End LP 311
This Love Of Mine	61	End LP 311
Undecided	61	End LP 311
That Lil' Ole Lovemaker Me/It Just Ain't Fair	63	Roulette 4379
Lonesome Romeo/I've Got A Lot To Offer Darling	63	Roulette 4477
I'm On The Outside (Looking In)/Please Go	64	DCP 1104/Veep 1240 (66)
Goin' Out Of My Head/Make It Easy On Yourself	64	DCP 1119/Veep 1241 (66)
Hurt So Bad/Reputation	65	DCP 1128/Veep 1242 (66)
Take Me Back/Our Song	65	DCP 1136/Veep 1243 (66)
I Miss You So/Get Out Of My Life	65	DCP 1149/Veep 1244 (66)
Hurt/Never Again	66	DCP 1154/Veep 1245 (66)
It's Not For Me	N/A	Rhino LP 70919

Implaceables

| My Foolish Pride/Don't Call For Me | N/A | Kain 1004 |

Impollos (fb Bobby Russell)

| The Raven/She's Gonna Be Right | 58 | Felsted 8520 |

Impollos (Johnny Inman & the)

| You Never Realized/I'm So Sorry | 58 | Aladdin 3426 |

Impossibles

Chapel Bells/Little By Little	63	Blanche 029
Mr. Maestro/Well It's Alright	64	RMP 1030
Well It's Alright/Everywhere I Go	66	RMP 501

Impossibles (Linda Carr & the)

| Shy One/Garbage Man | 61 | Ray Star 779 |
| I'll Never Get Married/Happy Teenager | 61 | Skyla 1111 |

Impressions

Listen/Shorty's Got To Go	54	Great Lakes 1212/Bandera 2504 (59)/Port 70031 (62)
Lonely One/Senorita I Love You	59	Abner 1025
Meanwhile, Back In My Heart/All Through The Night	60	20th Fox 172
That You Love Me/New Love	60	Abner 1034
I Need Your Love/Don't Leave Me	62	Swirl 107
Say That You Love Me/Senorita I Love You	62	Vee Jay 424/Vee Jay 621 (64)

Impressions (Jerry Butler & the)

Come Back My Love/Love Me	58	Abner 1017
For Your Precious Love/Sweet Was The Wine	58	Vee Jay 280/Falcon 1013 (58)/Abner 1013 (58)/Vee Jay 396 (61)
The Gift Of Love/At The Country Fair	59	Abner 1023/Vee Jay 574 (64)

Impressors

| Is It Too Late/No No No | 57 | Onyx 514 |
| Do You Love Her/Loneliness | 58 | Cub 9010 |

Imps

| Uh-Oh/That'll Get It | 61 | Do-Ra-Mi 1414 |

Inadequates

| Pretty Face/Audie | 59 | Capitol 4232 |

Incidentals

Barbara/Where's My True Love	61	Gar-Lo 1000
All Night/Driving Guitars	64	Ford 134
Lucille/Fireside	64	Ford 138

Incognitos

| Dee Jay's Dilemma/Forget It | 61 | Zee 001 |

ARTIST/SONG	YEAR	LABEL
Inconquerables		
Wait For Me/For Your Love	N/A	Flodavieur 803
Incredables		
If You Give A Party/Little Bitty Bandit	N/A	Kelrich 850/851
Indelgents		
Give Up	N/A	Jenges
Indexes (John Golden & the)		
Take A Chance/You Changed My Mind (with Blanton McFarlin)	61	Douglas 101
Indigos		
Woo Woo Pretty Girl/Servant Of Love	58	Cornel 3001
Everything Plus/High School Social	58	Cornel 515
Girl By The Wayside/Ho-Hum Deedle-Dum	61	Image 5001
He's Coming Home/What Good Am I Without You	65	Cor 6581/Verve Folkways 5002
My Dream Girl/Beyond Your Wildest Dreams	N/A	Cadette 8003
Individuals (1)		
Met Her At A Dance/Jungle Superman	59	Show Time 595
Dear One/Jungle Superman	59	Show Time 598/Red Fox 105
Without Success/I've Been Hurt	59	Sparrow 101
Individuals (2) (Andy Taylor & the)		
Beverly My Darling	60	Music City 838
Individuals (3) (Chuck Rio & the)		
Cell Block #9/If You Were The Only Girl In The World	61	Tequila 103
Individuals (4) (with the Merceedees)		
Please Baby Be Mine/Not Me	62	Gold Seal 1000
Individuals (5)		
Wedding Bells/Pillow Wet With Tears	64	Chase
Individuals (6)		
Here I Am	59	Delwood
Ineligibles		
Just The Things That You Do/Do The Groove	60	Capella 501
Infascinations		
One Chance/I'm So In Love	61	Clauwell 003/004
Infatuators		
I Found My Love/Where Are You?	61	Destiny 504/Vee Jay 395 (61)
Informers (1)		
Don't Cry, Sure It Hurts/Dora, He Told Me To Tell You It Hurts	60	Dore 562
Informers (2)		
If You Love Me/Hard Way To Go	65	J-Rude 1400
Initials		
You Didn't Answer My Letter/Someday Someway	73	Vintage 1006
Initials (Angelo & the)		
Bells Of Joy/You	59	Dee 1001/Sherry 667
School Day/This Song Is Number One	64	Congress 207
Seventeen Guys On A Blanket At The Beach/Dancing On The Sand	64	Congress 219
Someday She'll Love Me/I Should Have Listened	64	Congress 229
Innocents		
Time/Dee Dee Di Oh	59	Andex 22012/Indigo 141 (62)
Honest I Do/My Baby Hully Gully's	60	Indigo 105

ARTIST/SONG	YEAR	LABEL
Tick Tock/The Rat (instrumental)	60	Trans World 7001
Gee Whiz/Please Mr. Sun	61	Indigo 111
Kathy/In The Beginning	61	Indigo 116
Beware/Because I Love You	61	Indigo 124
Donna/You Got Me Goin'	61	Indigo 128
Pains In My Heart/When I Become A Man	61	Indigo 132
Oh How I Miss My Baby/Be Mine	62	Reprise 20112
Come On Lover/Don't Cry	63	Decca 31519
Oh How I Miss My Baby/You're Never Satisfied	63	Reprise 20125
My Heart Stood Still/Don't Call Me Lonely Any More	64	Warner Bros. 5450

Innocents (Kathy Young & the)

A Thousand Stars/Eddie My Darling	60	Indigo 108/Port 3025 (60)
Happy Birthday Blues/Someone To Love	61	Indigo 115
Our Parents Talked It Over/Just As Though You Were Here	61	Indigo 121
Magic Is The Night/Du Du'nt Du	61	Indigo 125
Baby Oh Baby/The Great Pretender	61	Indigo 137
Lonely Blue Nights/I'll Hang My Letters Out To Dry	62	Indigo 146
Dream Awhile/Send Her Away	62	Indigo 147
Dream Boy/I'll Love That Man	62	Monogram 506
All You Had To Do (Was Tell Me)/Love Me (with Chris Montez)	62	Monogram 517
Sparkle And Shine	N/A	Indigo EP 1001

Inspirations (1)

Raindrops/Maggie	56	Apollo 494
Don't Cry/Indian Jane	58	Lamp 2019
Pretty Mama	89	Relic LP 5080
Oh What A Feeling	N/A	Old Town LP
Starlight Tonight	N/A	Old Town LP

Inspirations (2)

Dry Your Eyes/Goodbye	56	Jamie 1034/Jamie 1212 (62)
The Genie/Feeling Of Her Kiss	59	Sultan 1
Angel In Disguise/Stool Pigeon	60	Al-Brite 1650/1651/Sparkle 102 (60)/Gone 5097 (60)
The Girl By My Side/Neckin'	63	Beltone 2037

Inspirations (3) (Ronnie Vare & the)

Let's Rock Little Girl/Love Is Just For Two	59	Dell 5202/5203

Inspirations (4) (Benny Bunn & the)

If I Were King/In Desperation	59	Eastmen 790

Inspirations (5) (Andre "Bacon Fat" Williams & the)

I Still Love You/Jailhouse Blues	60	Fortune 856

Inspirations (6)

Ay Yai Yai/My Inspiration	72	Bim Bam Boom 109

Inspirations (7) (Maurice Williams & the)

The Day Has Come/Never Leave You Again	63	Candi 1031

Inspirations (8)

Ring Those Bells/The Cumberland And The Merrimac	61	Rondak 9787

Inspirators

If Loving You Is Wrong/Three Sixty	55	Treat 502
Starlight Tonight/Oh, What A Feeling!	58	Old Town 1053

Instants

Always Be True/Gravy Train	62	Rendezvous 193

Intentions

Summertime Angel/Mr. Misery	63	Jamie 1253
I'm In Love With A Go-Go Girl/Wonderful Girl	64	Melron 5014

ARTIST/SONG	YEAR	LABEL
Time/Cool Summer Night	65	Uptown 710
My Love She's Gone/Dancing Fast, Dancing Slow	67	Kent 455
Don't Forget That I Love You/Night Rider	67	Philips 40428
What Am I Gonna Do With You/Hey Baby	N/A	Black Pearl 100

Interiors

Darling Little Angel/Voodoo Doll	61	Worthy 1008
Echoes/Love You Some More	61	Worthy 1009

Interludes (1)

I Shed A Million Tears/Oo-Wee	58	RCA 7281

Interludes (2)

I Want You To Know/Split A Kiss	59	Star-Hi 103
Heartbreaker/Scandalous	59	Valley 1005
No One For Me/Fort Lauderdale	60	Valley 106
White Sailor Hat/Evil	60	Valley 107

Interludes (3)

Number One In The Nation/Beautiful, Wonderful, Heavenly You	61	ABC 10213
Darling I'll Be True/Wilted Rose Bud	62	King 5633

Internationals

Goin' To A Party/I Love You So	58	ABC 9964

Interpreters

Pretty Little Thing/Be Kind To Love	67	A-Bet 9425

Intervals

Side Street/I Still Love That Man	58	Ad 104/Apt 25019 (58)
Love So Sweet/Try To Realize	58	Irma 820
Please Come Back To Me/Don't Leave Me	59	Ad 103
You Are My Only Love/Funny How Time Goes By	62	Class
Here's That Rainy Day/Wish I Could Change My Mind	62	Class 304

Intimates

Got You Where I Want/Only Girl For Me	64	Amcan 402
Smart Too Late/I've Got A Tiger In My Tank	64	Epic 9743

Invaders

Paradise/Sloop It Out	59	El Toro 503
I Won't Be Lonely	64	Calendar 223

Inventions (aka Catalinas (3))

Hey, Peanuts/Row Boat	60	Up 111

Invictas

Lest You Forget/Over The Wall	58	Pix 1101
Gone So Long/Nellie	59	Jack Bee 1003
I Met Him At A Dance/Oh Mama	63	Mavis 221

Invictors

I'll Always Care For You/I Don't Wanna Go	59	Bee 1117
This Thing Called Love/The Wiggle	62	TPE 8217
Don't Take My Love/Babalonian	63	TPE 8219
Where All Lovers Meet/That's All Right	63	TPE 8221
I Took A Chance/Put Her Down	63	TPE 8223

Invincibles

Mr. Moonglow/Swayback	59	Chess 1727

Iridescents (female)

Three Coins In The Fountain/Strong Love	63	Hudson 8102

ARTIST/SONG	YEAR	LABEL
Irridescents		
The Angels Sang/I Know	60	Ultrasonic 104
Islanders (1)		
Hey, Hey Baby (a capella)	75	Relic LP 103
My True Story (a capella)	75	Relic LP 103
Walking In The Rain (a capella)	75	Relic LP 104
You Never Loved Me (a capella)	75	Relic LP 105
When We Get Married (a capella)	75	Relic LP 108
Islanders (2) (Rick & the)		
Just For You (Dance Dance)/Everybody	N/A	H&G 185
Isley Brothers		
Angels Cried/The Cow Jumped Over The Moon	56	Teenage 1004
This Is The End/Don't Be Jealous	58	Cindy 3009
I Wanna Know/Everybody's Gonna Rock & Roll	58	Gone 5022
My Love/The Drag	59	Gone 5048
The Drag/Rockin' MacDonald	59	Mark-X 8000
Turn To Me/I'm Gonna Knock On Your Door	59	RCA 7537
Italian Asphalt And Pavement Company (aka Duprees)		
Check Yourself/The Sky's The Limit	70	Colossus 110
Itels		
Star Of Paradise/Chubby Isn't Chubby Anymore	61	Magnifico 101
Ithacas		
If You Want My Love/Gonna Fix You Good	57	Fee Bee 220
Ives, Jimmy (& group)		
My Fumbling Heart/Settle Down	61	Comet 2141
Ivies		
Sunshine/Come On	58	Ivy 110/Brunswick 55112 (58)
I Really Want To Know/Voodoo	59	Roulette 4183
Ivies (Ezra & the)		
Comic Book Crazy/Rockin' Shoes	59	United Artists 165
Ivoleers		
Lover's Quarrel/Come With Me	59	Buzz 101
Ivories (1)		
Alone/Baby, Send A Letter	56	Jaguar 3019/Jaguar 3023 (57)
Ivories (2) (female)		
Me And You/I'm In Love	57	Mercury 71239
Ivorys (aka Five Ivories)		
Wishing Well/Deep Freeze	62	Darla (no number)
Why Don't You Write Me/Deep Freeze	62	Sparta 001
Ivorytones		
Little Fool/The Things We Did Last Summer	60	Norwood 101
Wo! Wo! Wo!/Move It Over	60	Unidap 448
Ivy Jives		
Million Dollar Girl/Knockout	60	Jaro 77036
Ivy League		
What More Do You Want/Wait A Minute	65	Cameo 343
Lonely Room/Funny How Love Can Be	65	Cameo 356
That's Why I'm Crying/A Girl Like You	65	Cameo 365
Graduation Day/Tossing And Turning	65	Cameo 377

ARTIST/SONG	YEAR	LABEL
Ivy Leaguers		
Beware Of Love/Deposit Your Love In The Bank Of My Heart	57	Flip 325
Ivy Three		
Yogi/Was Judy There	60	Shell 720
Hush Little Baby/Alone In The Chapel	60	Shell 723
Nine Out Of Ten/I've Cried Enough For Two	61	Shell 302
Bagoo/Suicide	61	Shell 306
Ivy, Sheron (& group)		
I Need You/Believe Me	61	Heritage 106/Coed 572 (62)
Ivy-Tones		
Oo-Wee Baby/Each Time	58	Red Top 105
Ivyliers		
Echo From The Blue/When The Reign Of Love Begins	57	Donna A-3
Ivys		
All I Want/Lost Without You	59	Coed 518
J's (1) (Jimmy J. & the)		
Girlfriend (Please Be My)/I've Lost	61	Salco 647
J's (2) (with Jamie)		
Little Me/Come On Strong	62	Columbia 42635
Jac-O-Lacs (fb Cornel Gunter)		
Cindy Lou/Sha-Ba-Da-Ba-Doo	55	Tampa 103
Jack, Johnny (& group)		
The Beggar That Became King/Touch Me	62	Gone 5132
Let's Have A Party/True Love At First Sight	64	Lawn 226
Forever (And A Day)/Love Must Be	64	Lawn 230
Jackaels (J. J. Jackson & the) (aka Jackals (2))		
A Lifetime From Today/That Look In Your Eye	59	Storm 501
Oo-Ma-Liddi/Let The Show Begin	59	Storm 502/Prelude 502 (59)
Jackals (1) (Frank Sandy & the)		
Let's Go Rock 'N Roll/Midnight Stomp	58	MGM 12678
Jackals (2) (J. J. Jackson & the) (aka Jackaels)		
Ring Telephone/False Face	63	Everest 2012
Jacks & Jills		
I Hear A Melody/Roses Never Fade	56	Empire 101
I Can't Forget/Red Dog	58	MGM 12671
Jacks (aka Cadets (1))		
Why Don't You Write Me/Smack Dab In The Middle	55	RPM 428 (first pressing)
Why Don't You Write Me/My Darling	55	RPM 428 (second pressing)
I'm Confessin'/Ever Since My Baby's Been Gone	55	RPM 433
Bob-O-Link/Since You (Donna Hightower)	55	RPM 439
This Empty Heart (My Love Has Gone)/My Clumsy Heart	55	RPM 444
So Wrong/How Soon?	56	RPM 454
Why Did I Fall In Love/Sugar Baby	56	RPM 458
Dream A Little Longer/Let's Make Up	56	RPM 467
I Confess/Blau-Wile Devest Fontaine (P. Anka)	56	RPM 472
Oo Wee Baby	57	RPM LP 3006
Wiggie Waggie Woo	57	RPM LP 3006/ Crown LP 5021 (57)
You Belong To Me	57	RPM LP 3006/ Crown LP 5021 (57)

ARTIST/SONG	YEAR	LABEL
Do You Wanna Rock (aka Hey Little Girl)	57	RPM LP 3006/ Crown LP 5372 (58)
Why Don't You Write Me/This Empty Heart	60	Kent 344
Lovey Dovey	63	Crown LP 5372
You Are The First One	63	Crown LP 5372
Why Don't You Write Me/So Wrong	75	Relic 1031
Away	N/A	Relic LP 5023
Why Don't You Write Me/Sugar Baby	N/A	Victory

Jackson Brothers

The Wrong Door	52	Arrow 1003
Love Me/Tell Him No	54	Atlantic 1034
Troubles/Baby Baby	59	Candy 002

Jackson Trio

Love For Christmas/JingleBell Hop	55	Hollywood 1046

Jackson, Chuck (& group)

Baby I Want To Marry You/Never Let Me Go	61	Atco 6197

Jackson, Lee (& group)

The Christmas Song/Santa Came Home Drunk (by Clyde Lasley)	57	Bea & Baby 121

Jades (1)

Beverly/Leave Her To Me	58	Dot 15822
Leave Her For Me/So Blue	58	Time 1002
Big Beach Party/Oh Why	59	Christy 110
Applesauce/Tell Me Pretty Baby	59	Christy 111
Don't Be A Fool/Friday Night With My Baby	59	Christy 113
Blue Memories	59	Christy 114
Hey Little Girl/Walking All Alone	59	Nau-Voo 807
Hold Back The Dawn/When They Ask About You	63	Dore 687

Jades (1) (Bobby Klint & the)

Moana/Rock Me The Blues	59	Christy 109
Lovely Lady Please Be Mine/Pretend	59	Christy 117

Jades (2) (Emmett & the)

No One/Blowin' The Rock	61	Rustone 1405

Jades (3) (Freddy Koenig & the)

One Last Teardrop/Hey, Clarice	63	Valerie 225

Jades (4)

He's My Guy/There Will Come A Day	64	Port 70042

Jades (5)

Hey Senorita	N/A	Adona 1445
Walking Along	N/A	Prism 1924

Jades (6)

My Loss, Your Gain	N/A	Poncello 7703

Jags (Steve Carl with the)

Curfew/Eighteen Year Old Blues	58	Meteor 5046

Jaguars (1)

Rock It, Davy, Rock It/The Big Bear (with Patti Ross)	55	Aardell 107
I Wanted You/Rock It, Davy, Rock It	56	Aardell 0003
Be My Sweetie/Why Don't You Believe Me?	56	Aardell 0006
The Way You Look Tonight/Moonlight And You	56	Aardell 0011
The Way You Look Tonight/Baby Baby Baby	56	R-Dell 11/Baronet 1 (62)
I Love You Baby/(City Zoo) Baby Baby Baby	57	R-Dell 16
Hold Me Tight/Picadilly	58	Ebb 129
I Wanted You/Rock It, Davy, Rock It	58	R-Dell 45

ARTIST/SONG	YEAR	LABEL
Roundabout/Jaguar	59	Epic 9308
Exit 6/Drive In	59	Epic 9325
Big Noise/I Could If I Would	59	Janet 201
Thinking Of You/Look Into My Eyes	59	Original Sound 06/
		Original Sound 20 (62)
Girl Of My Dreams/Don't Go Home	60	R-Dell 117
Fine, Fine, Fine/It Finally Happened	61	Rendezvous 159/
		Rendezvous 216 (63)
The Way You Look Tonight/Baby, Baby, Baby, Baby	66	Original Sound 59

Jaguars (2) (Nick & the)

Cool And Crazy/Ichi Bon, Volume I	60	Tamla 5501

Jaguars (3)

Where Lovers Go/Discover A Lover	64	Faro 618

Jamecos (Diana Tyler & Nat Brown with the)

Most Of All/Second Hand Love	65	Jameco 2004

James Boys

Ah Ha Crazy	60	Edsel 780

James, Artamer (& group)

Congratulations/Ditty Bop Walk	58	Code 711

James, Jesse (bb the Royal Aces)

Somebody Really Mine/Dreams Never Hurt Nobody	61	Musicor 1008

James, Tammy (& group)

Congratulations/Caesar Haircut	63	Janlene 776

Jamies

Summertime, Summertime/Searching For You	58	Epic 9281
Snow Train/When The Sun Goes Down	58	Epic 9299/Epic 9565 (63)
Don't Darken My Door/The Evening Star	59	United Artists 193

Jammers

My Special Prayer/Thunderbird (by the Five Blue Notes)	59	Onda 108

Jammers (Johnny & the) (fb Johnny Winter)

School Day Blues/You Know I Love You	60	Dart 131

Janettes

He's Crying Inside/We Belong To Each Other	62	Goldie 1102

Janssen, Danny (& group)

Mirror On The Wall/Blue Moon	60	Stepheny 1841

Januarys (Little June & His) (fb June Coleman)

Hello/Burgers, Fries And Shakes	57	Salem 188
Oh, What A Feeling/Oh, My Love	59	Profile 4009

Jarmels

Little Lonely One/She Loves To Dance	61	Laurie 3085
A Little Bit Of Soap/The Way You Look Tonight	61	Laurie 3098
I'll Follow You/Gee Oh Gosh	61	Laurie 3116
Red Sails In The Sunset/Loneliness	62	Laurie 3124
One By One/Little Bug	62	Laurie 3141
Come On Girl/Keep Your Mind On Me	63	Laurie 3174
Why Am I A Fool For You	N/A	Collectables LP 5044
You Don't Believe A Word I Say	N/A	Collectables LP 5044

Javalons

Took A Chance (I Took A Chance)/That Is Why (I Love You)	61	Eko 6901/6902

ARTIST/SONG	YEAR	LABEL
Jay Birds (1) (Vinnie Monte & the)		
Your Cute Little Ways/Without Your Love	56	Josie 793
Always/A Love Of My Own	58	Decanter 101
Jay Birds (2) (Lenny Young & the)		
Joyce/Lovable	58	Jay Scott 1001/
		Jackpot 48006 (58)
Jay Cees		
Just Say The Word/The Waddle	62	Enjoy 1004
Jay, Lori (& group)		
Thrills And Heartaches	56	Rim 2016
Jaybirds (Bobby Darin & the)		
Silly Willie/Blue-Eyed Mermaid	56	Decca 29922
Jaycees (Chuck Jackson & the)		
Forever Is A Long Long Time	64	Gateway 738
Jaye Sisters		
Going To The River/Pitter Patter Boom Boom	58	Atlantic 1171
Real Love/School's Out	58	Atlantic 1190
Little Daddy/Stop, You're Knocking Me Out	58	Atlantic 2000
Jaye, Jerry (& group)		
I'm Goin' Home/Let's Make Love	63	Carlton 598
Jayes		
You're Gonna Grieve When I Leave/Panic Stricken	58	Arc 4443
Jayhawks (aka Vibrations/aka Marathons)		
Counting My Teardrops/The Devil's Cousin	56	Flash 104/105
Stranded In The Jungle/My Only Darling	56	Flash 109
Love Train/Don't Mind Dyin'	56	Flash 111
The Creature/Everyone Should Know	57	Aladdin 3393
Start The Fire/I Wish The World Owed Me A Living	57	Eastman 792
New Love/Betty Brown	58	Eastman 798
Lonely Highway/La Macerena	61	Argyle 1005
Jayhawks (Earl Palmer & the)		
Johnny's House Party, Pt. 1 (instru.)/	57	Aladdin 3379
Johnny's House Party, Pt. 2 (instru.)		
Jaynells		
I'll Stay Home New Year's Eve/Down Home	63	Cameo 286/Diamond 153
Hollywood Actor	N/A	N/A
Out Of A Million Girls	N/A	N/A
Portrait Of Love	N/A	N/A
So Close	N/A	N/A
Jaynes (Lonnie Jay & the)		
Somewhere/Around And Around We Go	63	Arlen 724
Jayos (Johnny Otis & the)		
Tough Enough/The Blooper (no group)	57	Dig 131
Jayos (Mel Williams & the)		
Don't Cry Baby/My Love	56	Dig 123
Jays (1) (Armonda & the)		
Present Of Love/Pony Tails	59	Apollo 540
Jays (2) (Mike & the)		
Dingle Dangle Doll/My Only Girl	60	Doyl 1001

ARTIST/SONG	YEAR	LABEL

Jays (3)
Turn To Me/Stanwyck Theme — 61 — Barry 103

Jays (4) (Jimmy & the)
Lugene — N/A — Fairbanks 2001

Jaytones (aka Revlons (3)/aka Centuries (3))
The Clock/Gasoline — 58 — Brunswick 55087
Oh Darling/The Bells — 58 — Timely 1003/1004
My Only Love/Absolutely Right — 60 — Cub 9057
Oh Darling/Crying For You (by the Centuries) — 63 — Times Square 5

Jaywalkers
Oh Babe/My Bonnie (Lies Over The Ocean) — 62 — Pam 210

Jeanettes (Gene & the)
You're A Star/A Lover — 63 — Fortune 565

Jeeters (Ron Willis & the)
Don't Come Too Late/Someday You'll Want Me To Want You — 60 — Ace 588

Jeffries, Bob (bb the Mondellos)
Never Let Me Go/Irina Special (instrumental) — 57 — Rhythm 110

Jelly Beans
I Wanna Love Him So Bad/So Long — 64 — Red Bird 10-003
The Kind Of Boy You Can't Forget/Baby Be Mine — 64 — Red Bird 10-011
I'm Hip To You/You Don't Mean No Good To Me — 65 — Eskee 001

Jerome, Patti (& group)
Johnny Has Gone/After The Lights Go Down Low — 55 — Josie 774

Jeromes
Rockin' Chair Song/Getting Even — 61 — Dar 300

Jesters (1)
So Strange/Love No One But You — 57 — Winley 218
Please Let Me Love You/I'm Falling In Love — 57 — Winley 221
I Laughed/Now That You're Gone — 58 — Cyclone 5011
The Plea/Oh Baby — 58 — Winley 225
The Wind/Sally Green — 60 — Winley 242
That's How It Goes/Tutti Fruitti — 61 — Winley 248
Come Let Me Show You/Uncle Henry's Basement — 61 — Winley 252
The Buffalo/Alexander Graham Bull — 62 — Amy 859

Jesters (1) (Lendon Smith with the)
Women/Lost Love — 56 — Meteor 5030

Jesters (2)
Since You're Gone/Messy Bessy — 60 — Shimmy 1054

Jesters (3) (Richie Thompson & the)
Ring A Ling A Ding/Too Late To Worry — 61 — Diamond 103

Jesters (4)
My Babe/Cadillac Man — 66 — Sun 400

Jesters (5)
To Be Or Not To Be — N/A — Spry 118

Jet Streams
Who Me/Hey Phoebe, Get Off The Phone — 58 — Decca 30743

Jets (1)
The Lovers/Drag It Home, Baby — 53 — Rainbow 201

RTIST/SONG	YEAR	LABEL
ets (2)		
Volcano/Gomen Nasai	53	7-11 2101/2102
Got A Little Shadow/I'll Hide My Tears	54	Aladdin 3247
ets (2) (Ronnie Grett & the)		
Sweet Baby/Run Manny Run	55	Capitol 3174
ets (3)		
Heaven Above Me/Millie Brown	56	Gee 1020
ets (4) (Roy Jordan & the)		
Keep Cool/Jeebla Jabla Jingo	56	Orpheus 1102
ets (5) (Buck Rogers & the)		
Rose Marie/Crazy Baby	59	Montel 2002
ets (6) (ref Marcels)		
You Still Got Time/Soul Dinner	63	Arrow 100
ewels (1) (aka Crows)		
Call A Doctor/Heartbreaker (by the Crows)	53	Rama 10
ewels (2)		
Hearts Of Stone/Runnin'	54	R&B 1301
A Fool In Paradise/Oh Yes I Know	54	R&B 1303
Try And Get Me	54	R&B 1313/Ram 1102
Hearts Can Be Broken/Angel In My Life	55	Imperial 5351
Please Return/Natural, Natural Ditty	55	Imperial 5362
How/Rickety Rock	56	Imperial 5377
My Baby/Goin', Goin', Gone	56	Imperial 5387
She's A Flirt/B-Bomb Baby	56	RPM 474
The Wind/Pearlie Mae	59	Antler 1102
I Worry 'Bout You/Are You Comin' To The Party	59	Shasta 115
Hearts Of Stone/Oh Yes I Know	64	Original Sound 38
One Night	N/A	Imperial (unreleased)
Skid Row	N/A	Imperial (unreleased)
Keep Your Feet On The Floor	N/A	Imperial LP only
No Shoulder To Cry On	N/A	Imperial LP only
ewels (2) (Johnny Torrance with the)		
Rosalie/Living From Day To Day	54	R&B 1306
ewels (3)		
My Song/This Is My Story	63	Federal 12541
ewels (4) (Billy Abbott & the)		
Groovy Baby/Come On And Dance With Me	63	Parkway 874
ewels (5) (female) (aka Four Jewels)		
Opportunity/Gotta Find A Way	64	Dimension 1034
Smokey Joe/But I Do	64	Dimension 1048
Jimmy Lee/The Hash	64	Olimpic 244
Smokie Joe's/Lookie Cookie	66	King 6068
llettes (female)		
Daddy Do/Please Say You'll Love Me	62	Amazon 711
Why Did I Cry/Can't Play A Playgirl	63	Philips 40140
lls (Jacqueline & the)		
He Loves Me He Loves Me Not/Gee But It's Great To Be In Love	61	Goldisc 3023
v-A-Tones		
Flirty Gertie/Fire Engine Baby	58	Felsted 8506

ARTIST/SONG	YEAR	LABEL

Jive Bombers

It's Spring Again/Pork Chop Boogie	52	Citation 1160
Brown Boy/Peewee's Boogie	52	Citation 1161
Bad Boy/When Your Hair Has Turned To Silver	57	Savoy 1508
The Blues Don't Mean A Thing/If I Had A Talking Picture	57	Savoy 1513
Cherry/You Took My Love	57	Savoy 1515
Is This The End/Just Around The Corner	58	Savoy 1535
You Give Your Love To Me/Stardust	59	Savoy 1560
Anytime/The Days Of Wine And Roses	64	Middle-Tone 020

Jive Five

My True Story/When I Was Single	61	Beltone 1006/Relic 1026 (75)
Never, Never/People From Another World	61	Beltone 1014/Relic 1030 (78)
No Not Again/Hully Gully Callin' Time	62	Beltone 2019/Relic 1027 (75)
What Time Is It/Beggin' You Please	62	Beltone 2024/Relic 1028 (76)
These Golden Rings/Do You Hear Wedding Bells	62	Beltone 2029/Relic 1029 (77)
You Know What I Would Do/Hurry Back	62	Beltone 3001
The Girl With The Wind In Her Hair/	62	Beltone 3002
I Don't Want To Be Without You Baby		
Johnny Never Knew/Lili Marlane	63	Beltone 2030
Rain/She's My Girl	63	Beltone 2034

Jiveleers

Boom Chic-A-Boom/Cheryl (by the Camerons (1))	60	Cousins 1/2

Jivers (1)

Cherie/Little Mama	56	Aladdin 3329
Ray Pearl/Dear Little One	56	Aladdin 3347

Jivers (2)

I Wonder If You Know/What Do You Know About Heartaches	59	RCA 7478

Jives (Bobby Taylor with Charlie & the)

Seven Steps To An Angel/Ubangi Stomp	61	Hour 102

Jives (Charlie & the)

Coffee Grind, Pt. 1/Coffee Grind, Pt. 2	62	Hour 104

Jivetones

Ding Ding Dong/Geraldine	58	Apt 25020
When	N/A	Apt (unreleased)
Zip Zip	N/A	Apt (unreleased)

Jiving Juniors

Moonlight Lover/Sweet As An Angel	61	Asnes 103
I Wanna Love/Duke's Cookies	61	Blue Beat 24
Dearest Darling/Lollipop Girl	61	Blue Beat 4

Jo-Vals

Ballerina/I Want You To Be My Girl	64	Alwil 101
Sometimes I'm Happy/You You My Love	64	Laurie 3229
Well It's Alright/Well It's Alright (instrumental)	N/A	Grove 105

Joey (& group)

I Got Feelings/A Place In Your Heart	62	Taurus 353

Joey, Guy (& group)

Philly Stomp/Anna	61	Coed 563

Jogettes

Your Love/Johnnie's Coming Home	62	Mar 102

Johnny & Dell (& group)

There Is Love/The Bounce	59	Luck 101

ARTIST/SONG	YEAR	LABEL

Johnson 3 Plus 1
High School Queen/Treatment For The Cure — 69 — Tangerine 1013

Johnson Quartet, Bill (The Bill Johnson Quartet)
Maria Mia/We're Gonna Love — 55 — Jubilee 5211

Johnson, Bill (the Bill Johnson Quintet)
So Sweet Of You/Traveling Stranger — 57 — Baton 239

Johnson, Bubber (bb the Wheels)
Drop Me A Line/Ding Dang Doo — 55 — King 4793

Johnson, Dave (& group)
Angel Of Mine/Teenage Jamboree — 60 — Apt 25054

Johnson, Delores (& female group)
Give Me Your Love/Gotta Find My Baby — 61 — Bobbin 132

Johnson, Ernie (& group)
Tell Her For Me/You Need Love — 61 — Asnes 104

Johnson, Herb (bb the Cruisers)
Guilty/Have You Heard — 60 — Len 1007

Johnson, Jesse (& group)
So Loved Am I/Cute Little Girl — 58 — Symbol 901

Johnson, Kripp (& group)
A Door That Is Open/Still I Forgive You — 59 — Mercury 71486

Johnson, Marv (& group) (bb the Rayber Voices)
Once Upon A Time/Baby You (Baby-O) — 58 — Kudo 663

Johnson, Stella (& male group)
The Ways Of Love/What Do They Know — 60 — Vin 1022

Jokers (1) (Jivin' Gene & the)
Up, Up And Away/Going Out With The Tide — 59 — Jin 109/Jin 7331
My Need For Love/Breaking Up Is Hard To Do — 59 — Jin 116
Breakin' Up Is Hard To Do/My Need For Love — 59 — Mercury 71485
You're Jealous/Go On, Go On — 60 — Mercury 71561
Poor Me/That's What It's Like — 61 — Mercury 71751

Jokers (2) (Johnny & the)
Do-Re-Mi Rock/Why Must It Be — 59 — Harvard 804
I Know/Where Did My Baby Go — 62 — Beltone 2028

Jokers (3)
I Do/Pretty Little Hula Girl — 60 — Danco 117

Jokers (3) (Darlene & the)
Love Me, Love Me/Frankie — 60 — Danco 115

Jokers (3) (Ty Stewart & the)
Young Girl/Here Am I — 61 — Amy 828

Jokers (4)
Little Mama/Say You're Mine — 61 — Grace 510

Jokers (5) (fb Kenny Tibbs)
I'm Still Alone/The Worm — 62 — Viking 1009

Jokers (5) (Willie & the)
She Won't Hang Up/I Promise — 62 — Viking 1007

ARTIST/SONG	YEAR	LABEL
Jokers (6) (Johnny Williams & the)		
Dearest Darling/Long Black Veil	61	Pic 1 105
Jokers (7) (J.W. & the)		
Only A Tear/Sidewalk Rock & Roll	59	Simpson 1130
Jokers (8)		
Don't Want No Woman	N/A	Teen 1006
Jolly Jacks		
There's Something On Your Mind/Rock The House	63	Landa 707
Jones Boys (1)		
The Song Is Ended/	54	S&G 5007
You Make Me Feel Like A Penny Waitin' For Change		
Jones Boys (2) (Jimmy Jones & the)		
Heaven In Your Eyes/The Whistlin' Man	57	Arrow 717
Jones Boys (3)		
Alone In The Night/Honey, Honey (by the Capitols)	73	Baron 103
Jones, Billy (bb the Squires)		
Listen To Your Heart/Every Word Of The Song	58	Deck 478
Jones, Davey (& group)		
Love Your Way/Come On And Love Me	58	Apt 25013
No More Tears/Tootsie Wootsie	59	Glades 601
Our Love/Change Your Mind	59	Marlin 6062
I'm In Pain/Let's Do It	61	Apt 25064
Jones, Hilliard (& group)		
Prison Of Love/What Have You Got	62	Cortland 101
Jones, Jimmy (bb the Cues)		
Handy Man/The Search Is Over	59	Cub 9049
Jones, Jimmy (bb the Pretenders)		
Close Your Eyes/Part Time Sweetheart	61	Port 70040
Jones, Toni (& group)		
Dear (Here Comes My Baby)/Love Is Strange	63	Smash 1814
Jordan, Lou (bb the Chaperones (1))		
Paradise For Two/Close Your Eyes	62	Josie 888
Joseph, Dave (& group)		
Another Mile To Go/Oo La La	58	Vanguard 35004
Joseph, Mike (& group)		
Sandy/King Of Wealth	62	Lucky Four 1017
Josie, Lou (& group)		
Lonely Years/I'm Gonna Getcha	59	Baton 269
Talk To The Angels/Jeannie	61	Rendezvous 143
Jovations		
Take You Back Agian/My Dreams	63	Taurus 362
Joy, Arlene (& group)		
Too Young/Twistin' Susie Q	62	Rendezvous 185
Joy-Tones		
This Love/I Wanna Party Some More	64	Coed 600

RTIST/SONG	YEAR	LABEL

oyettes (female)

Story Of Love/Boy Next Door	56	Onyx 502

oyjumpers (fb Jimmy Anderson)

Angel Please/I Wanna Boogie	62	Zynn 1014

oylarks

In The Rain/Betty, My Love	59	Snag 107

oylets (female)

Say Yeah/Stewed Tomatoes	63	ABC 10403

oys

I Still Love Him/(Sing Along) I Still Love Him	64	Valiant 6042

oytones (female)

All My Love Belongs To You/You Just Won't Treat Me Right	56	Rama 191
Gee! What A Boy/Is This Really The End?	56	Rama 202
My Foolish Heart/Jimbo Jango	56	Rama 215

uliana (& group)

You Can Have Any Boy/You're Saying Goodnight	61	RCA 7906

umpers (Jay Nelson & the)

Sleepytime Rock/A Fool That Was Blind	59	Excello 2149
Wild Love/To You, My Darling	59	Excello 2165

umpin' Jacks (1)

Do Let That Dream Come True/Why, Oh, Why?	53	Lloyds 101
Julocka Jolly	89	Relic LP 5077
Long Head Leggy Rascal	89	Relic LP 5077

umpin' Jacks (1) (Danny Lamego & the)

Embraceable You/Pa-Pa-Ya, Baby	54	Bruce 115
Hickory Dickory Rock/Chicken Feed	56	Andrea 101

umpin' Jacks (1) (Danny Peppermint & the)

The Peppermint Twist/Somebody Else Is Taking My Place	61	Carlton 565

umpin' Jacks (2)

Mop-Top/Let There Be Rockin'	54	One-O-One 100

umpin' Jaguars

Shut The Door, Baby/Knock-Kneed Nellie From Knox	56	Decca 29938

umpin' Tones

I Had A Dream/I Wonder	64	Raven 8004
Grandma's Hearing Aid/That Angel Is You	64	Raven 8005

umping Jacks (1)

About A Quarter To Nine/Lady, Play Your Mandolin	56	Capitol 3415
Valencia/Toki-Roll, Toki-Rock	56	Capitol 3496

umping Jacks (2)

Tried And Tasted/My Girl, My Girl	57	ABC 9859

unior Five

On My Birthday/I Can't Wait Till Tomorrow	63	Laurie 3213

uniors (1) (Jimmy Castor & the)

I Promise/I Know The Meaning Of Love	56	Wing 90078
This Girl Of Mine/Somebody Mentioned Your Name	57	Atomic 100

uniors (2) (Danny & the)

At The Hop/ Sometimes When I'm All Alone	57	ABC 9871/Singular 711 (57)

ARTIST/SONG	YEAR	LABEL
Rock And Roll Is Here To Stay/School Boy Romance	57	ABC 9888
Dottie/In The Meantime	58	ABC 9926
A Thief/Crazy Cave	58	ABC 9953
Sassy Fran/I Feel So Lonely	58	ABC 9978
Do You Love Me/Somehow I Can't Forget	59	ABC 10004
Playing Hard To Get/Of Love	59	ABC 10052
Twistin' U.S.A./A Thousand Miles Away	60	Swan 4060
O Holy Night/Candy Cane Sugary Plum	60	Swan 4064
Pony Express/Daydreamer	61	Swan 4068
Cha Cha Go Go (Chicago Cha Cha)/Mr. Whisper	61	Swan 4072
Back To The Hop/Charleston Fish	61	Swan 4082
Just Because/Your Hair's Too Long/ Some Kind Of Nut	61	Swan 4084
(3 songs on record)		
Oo-La-La-Limbo/Now And Then	62	Guyden 2076
Twistin' All Night Long (with Freddy Cannon)/Some Kind Of Nut	62	Swan 4092
Doin' The Continental Walk/(Do The) Mashed Potato	62	Swan 4100
We Got Soul/Funny	62	Swan 4113
Twistin' All Night Long/Twistin' England	62	Top Rank 604
Let's Go Skiing/Sad Girl	64	Mercury 72240
Rock And Roll Is Here To Stay/Sometimes	68	Lub 252
I Can't See Nobody/Mo'Reen	68	Ronn 24
Let The Good Times Roll/At The Hop	73	Crunch 18001
Tallahassee Lassie	N/A	Singular LP 569
When The Saints Go Twistin' In	N/A	Singular LP 569

Jupitors

I Want/It Takes Two	58	Planet X 9621

Justifiers

Lonely Boy/My Love Has Gone	58	Kim 101

Juveniles

Beat In My Heart/I've Lied	58	Mode 1

K-Doe, Ernie (& group)

Hello My Lover/Taint It The Truth	60	Minit 614

Kac-Ties (aka Kact-Ties)

Walking In The Rain/Smile	62	Trans Atlas 695/Kape 502 (63)
Happy Birthday/Girl In My Heart	65	Kape 501
Over The Rainbow (a capella)	75	Relic LP 108
The Rest Of My Life (a capella)	75	Relic LP 108
What Did I Do Wrong (a capella)	75	Relic LP 108

Kact-Ties (aka Kac-Ties)

Let Your Love Light Shine/Were-Wolf	63	Shelley 163/Kape 503 (63)
Oh What A Night/Let Me In Your Life	63	Shelley 165/Atco 6299 (64)

Kapers (Paul London & the)

Sugar Baby/Never Like This	62	Check Mate 1006
Rosie Lee	N/A	Fascination 1007

Kappaliers (gm Noel Sookey)

Down In Mexico/Goodbye Baby	N/A	Shadow 1229

Kappas

Sweet Juanita/Your Love	59	Wonder 112

Kaptions (aka Lytations)

Dreaming Of You/I Know Somewhere	N/A	Ham-Mil 1520

Kartunes (fb Teddy Randazzo)

Raindrops/Will You Marry Me	58	MGM 12598
Dedicated To Love/Willie The Weeper	58	MGM 12680

ARTIST/SONG	YEAR	LABEL
Kashmirs		
Heaven Only Knows/Tippi-Tippi-Wang-Wang	58	Wonder 104
Katz, Ronnie (& group)		
Long Time	61	N/A
Keens (Rick & the)		
Peanuts/I'll Be Home	61	Austin 313/Le Cam 721 (61)/ Smash 1705 (61)
Maybe/Popcorn	61	Smash 1722
Your Turn To Cry/Tender Years	62	Jamie 1219
Darla/Someone New	64	Le Cam 113/Tollie 9016 (64)
Keith, Ann (& group)		
Lonely Girl/Lover's Prayer	59	Memo 96
Keller, Jerry (& group)		
Never Wake Up/Be Careful How You Drive Young Joey	61	Capitol 4630
Kelley, Charles (bb the 3 Of Us Trio)		
Telegram/Sugar Jump (instrumental)	58	York 3332
Kelloggs (fb Vito Balsamo)		
Snap, Crackle, Pop/Like A Mad Fool	69	Laurie 3476
Kelly, Karol (& group)		
Slow Dance/I Wanna Talk To You	62	Joy 272
Kendall Sisters		
Three Wishes/Make It Soon	57	Checker 884
Kenjolairs		
Little White Lies/Story Of An Evergreen Tree	62	A&M 704
Kennedy, Ace (& group)		
I Made A Mistake/Buck Dancin'	61	Swan 4080
Kent, Al (& group)		
Hold Me/You Know Me	59	Wizzard 100
Kentones		
Marie/Please Make Up Your Mind	58	Siroc 202
Kents (1)		
I Found My Girl/With All My Heart And Soul	58	Argo 5299
I Love You So/Happy Beat	58	Dome 501
Kents (2)		
Don't Say Goodbye/My Juanita	65	Relic 1013
Kestrels		
In The Chapel In The Moonlight/There Comes A Time	60	Laurie 3053
Key, Troyce (& group)		
Drown In My Tears/Baby Please Don't go	58	Warner Bros. 5007
Ain't I Cried Enough/Watch Your Mouth	59	Warner Bros. 5035
Most Of All/She's Sumpin' Else	59	Warner Bros. 5070
Key-Noters		
The Vision/Starlight And You (instrumental)	59	Swan 4048
Keyavas (Harry & the)		
If This Is Goodbye/Tears	63	IPG 1011

ARTIST/SONG	YEAR	LABEL
Keymasters		
Been So Long (flip instrumental)	N/A	Quality Sound 001
Keynoters (fb Norma Brock)		
I'm Gonna Build A Mountain/Evergood	59	Pepper 896
Keynotes (1)		
Who/They Say	54	Dot 15225
Suddenly/Zenda	55	Apollo 478
I Don't Know (Why I Love You Like I Do)/A Star	55	Apollo 484
Oh Yeah Hm-m-m/A Star	56	Apollo 485
Really Wish You Were Here/Bye, Bye, Baby	56	Apollo 493
Zup Zup (Ooh You Dance So Nice)/Now I Know	56	Apollo 498
In The Evening/Oh, Yeah, Hm-m-m	56	Apollo 503
One Little Kiss/Now I Know	57	Apollo 513
Chapel Bells Are Ringing	89	Relic LP 5080
Early One Morning	89	Relic LP 5080
Tell Me You Love Me	89	Relic LP 5080
Girl In The Chapel	N/A	Apollo LP 1000/ Relic LP 5072 (87)
Surely	N/A	Apollo LP 1000/ Relic LP 5072 (87)
Zoop Zoop (Darling I Love You)	N/A	Apollo LP 1000/ Relic LP 5072 (87)
Keynotes (2) (B. Allen & the)		
Butterfly/Oo-Wee-Baby	57	Eldorado 505
Keynotes (3)		
A Sunday School Romance/Only In A Dream	59	Bell-O-Tonic 001
With These Rings/We're Not Getting Along (Like We Used To)	59	Top Rank 2005
Keynotes (4)		
Dum Doodee Dum Dum	N/A	Index
Keynotes (5)		
Congratulations Baby/Carelessly	57	Pop 111
Keynotes (6) (Gene Anderson & the)		
Susie/I've Got It Bad	N/A	Top Ten 252
Keys (1)		
Am I In Love/Barefoot Days	52	MGM 11168
Keys (2) (Ricky & the)		
Can't You See/Come On Liza	58	Savoy 1529
Keys (3)		
My Love Has Gone	N/A	Lee 0759
Keystoners		
Magic Kiss/I'd Write About The Blues	56	G&M 102
The Magic Kiss/After I Propose	56	G&M 102/Epic 9187 (56)/ Okeh 7210 (64)
Sleep And Dream/T. V. Gal	61	Riff 202
Keystones		
It's Too Soon To Know	N/A	N/A
Keytones (1)		
Wonder Of The World/A Fool In Love	57	Old Town 1041 (first pressing)
Seven Wonders Of The World/A Fool In Love	57	Old Town 1041 (second pressing)
Keytones (2)		
Don't Tell William/Parking Field 4	61	Chelsea 1002

ARTIST/SONG	YEAR	LABEL
I Don't Care/La-Do-Da-Da	62	Chelsea 101
One, Two, Three/Sweet Chariot	63	Chelsea 1013
Keytones (3)		
Time After Time/Lover Of Mine	62	Chess 1821
Kid, The (& group)		
Sleep Tight/True Love	N/A	Rumble 1347
Kiddieos (Jay Bryant & the)		
Don't Stop Now/Want You To Know	N/A	Alfa 201
Kidds		
Drunk, Drunk, Drunk/Are You Forgetting Me	55	Imperial 5335
You Broke My Heart/I Won't Be Back	55	Post 2003
Miss Lucy	N/A	Imperial (unreleased)
Down In Mexico	N/A	Post (unreleased)
Kidds (Morry Williams & the)		
Are You My Girlfriend/Oh Louise	58	Tee Vee 301/Carlton 477 (58)
Time Runs Out/Grasshopper (instrumental)	60	Luck 102
Kids (1) (Herman & the)		
Daddy Daddy/March On	59	Columbia 41411
Kids (2) (Billy & the)		
Take A Chance On Love/The Way It Used To Be	61	Lute 6016/Lute 312
Say You Love Me	N/A	Julian 104
Kids (3)		
Good Loving	N/A	Gaylord 2203
Kids (4)		
Dear Mom And Dad	N/A	Hurd 80
Kids From Texas		
Long Legged Linda/I'm So Lonely	58	Hanover 4500
Killers (Hank Blackman & the)		
Everyone Has Someone/Itchy Koo	62	Brent 7030
Kilts (1) (Herman Jones & the) (gm Tony LeMar)		
I'll Be True/Mashed Potatoes	58	Gaynote 105
Kilts (2) (Charlie Jester & the)		
Sylvia/If Only I Had Known	61	Le Cam 722
King Bees		
Puppy Love/Give Me Your Number	57	Flip 323
Can't You Understand?/Lovely Love	57	KRC 302
Buzzin'/Good Rockin' Tonight	58	Checker 909
What Could Have Been Can't Be/Tender Love	59	Noble 715
King Cobras		
To Hold Your Love/Blue Diamond	59	Irvanne 117
King Crooners (aka King Krooners)		
Now That She's Gone/Won't You Let Me Know	59	Excello 2168
Lonely Nights/She's Mine All Mine	59	Hart 1002
King Krooners (fb Little Rico) (aka King Crooners)		
Memoirs/School Daze	60	Excello 2187
King Toppers		
Walkin' And Talkin' The Blues/You Were Waiting For Me	57	Josie 811

ARTIST/SONG	YEAR	LABEL
King, Clydie (& group)		
Our Romance/Written On The Wall	57	Specialty 605
King, Mabel (bb the Harptones)		
Love/When We Get The Word	63	Amy 874
King, Sleepy (& group)		
Begging/My Time Ain't Long	59	Symbol 904
Kinglets		
You Gotta Go/Six Days A Week	56	Calvert 101
My Baby Don't Need Chargin'/Pretty Please	59	Bobbin 104
Kings & Queens		
Voices Of Love/I'm So Lonely	57	Everlast 5003
Kings (1)		
Fire In My Heart/You Never Knew	54	Harlem 2322
What Can I Do?/Til I Say Well Done	54	Specialty 497
God Made You Mine/The Good Book	56	Gotham 316
Don't Go/Love Is Something From Within	57	Gone 5013
Angel/Come On, Little Baby	58	Jalo 203
Till You/Elephant Walk	58	RCA 7419
Surrender/Hold Me	59	Jay-Wing 5805
Your Sweet Love/Troubles Don't Last	59	RCA 7544
I Want To Know/Bump-I-Dy Bump	60	Lookie 18/Epic 9370 (60)
Creation	N/A	Collectables LP 5037/ Collectables LP 7003
Kings (1) (Bobby Hall & the)		
Why? Oh, Why?/I Love You, Baby	53	Jax 314
Baby, Be There/You Made Me Cry	53	Jax 316
Sunday Kind Of Love/Love No One	53	Jax 320
Kings (1) (Little Hooks & the)		
Count Your Blessings/How To Start A Romance	63	Century 1300/Little Rick 909 (63)/Chess 1867 (63)
Kings (2) (fb Joe Van Loan)		
Long Lonely Nights/Let Me Know	57	Baton 245
Kings (3) (Vicki France & the)		
Cry On My Shoulder/My France	59	Sparkette 1002
Kings (4) (Chet Reni & the)		
A Love Of My Own/What's Wrong With Me?	N/A	Georgie 101
Kings (5)		
Your Gonna Miss Me	N/A	Vim 10990
Kings Five		
The Voodoo Man/I Hear The Rain	59	Trophy 1/2
Kings Men		
Don't Say You're Sorry/Kicking With My Stallion	57	Club 51 108
Kingsmen (1)		
One Foolish Mistake/Stranded Love	56	Neil 102
Guardian Angel/I'm Your Lover Man	57	Allstar 500/East West 115 (58)/ East West 120 (58)
Kingsmen (2)		
Teenage Creature/Turn The Key (by Lord Luther & the Garnets (2))	59	Frantic 107

RTIST/SONG	YEAR	LABEL
ingsmen (3) (Johnny Knight & the)		
Secret Heart/Push A Little Button	63	Chance (N.Y.) 568
ingsmen (4)		
Goodnight Sweetheart/Humpty Dumpty	N/A	Arnold 2106
ingtones		
Twins/Have Good Faith	64	Derry 101
The Girl I Love/A Love I Had	67	Drummond 105
To Have A Little Girl/A Love I Had	N/A	Kitoco (no number)
inney, Mary (& group)		
Bobby My Love/I'm Anxious	59	Andex 4031
it Kats		
You're An Angel/Cold Walls	65	Lawn 249
ittens (female)		
Letter To Donna/It's All Over Now	59	Unart 2010
Something Tells Me I'm In Love/Aching For You	60	Alpine 61
Itsy Bitsy, Teenie Weenie, Yellow Polka Dot Bikini/ Dark, Dark Sunglasses	60	Alpine 64
Letter On His Sweater/Broken Dreams	60	Alpine 67
Count Every Star/I'm Worried	63	Chestnut 203
Walter/Lite Bulb	63	Don-El 122
I Need Your Love Tonight/Johnny's Place	63	Don-El 205
He's My Guy	85	Relic LP 8004
I Love You So	85	Relic LP 8004
ittens (Terri & the) (female)		
Wedding Bells (Just For You And Me)/You Cheated	61	Imperial 5728
ittens Five (female)		
Don't Let It Happen Again/Nothin'	64	Herald 588
ixs		
It's All Over/This Is The End Of Love	58	Music City 817
Elaine/This Is The End Of Love	58	Music City 823
nick-Knacks		
Baby Sittin' With You/Loneliness	59	Cub 9030
Tracks Of My Tears (a capella)	75	Relic LP 108
nickerbockers (1)		
You Must Know/Somewhere, Somehow, Sweetheart	53	It's A Natural 3000
nickerbockers (2)		
Please Don't Love Him/Can You Help Me	66	Challenge 59348
nickerbockers (2) (Buddy Randell & the)		
All I Need Is You/Bite Bite Barracuda	65	Challenge 59268
Lies/The Coming Generation	65	Challenge 59321
night Lites (Gary & the)		
Will You Go Steady/I Can't Love You Anymore	64	Prima 1016
night, Alan (& group)		
Until I Know/Chills	60	Tide 007
night, Bob (The Bob Knight Four)		
Good Goodbye/How Old Must I Be	61	Laurel 1020
For Sale/You Gotta Know	61	Laurel 1023

ARTIST/SONG	YEAR	LABEL
Well, I'm Glad	61	Laurel 1025
So So Long (Good Goodbye)/You Tease Me	61	Taurus 100
Memories/Somewhere	62	Josie 899
I'm Selling My Heart/The Lazy Piano	62	Taurus 356
(instrumental by the Lazy Four)		
Two Friends/Crazy Love	63	Jubilee 5451
Tomorrow We'll Be Married/Willingly	64	Goal 4/Jubilee

Knight, Gloria (& group)

Lonely Girl	N/A	Emerson 2101

Knight, Marie (& group)

Look At Me/Grasshopper Baby	56	Mercury 70969
Tell Me Why/As Long As I Love	56	Wing 90069
Am I Reaching For The Moon/I'm The Little Fooler	57	Mercury 71055

Knight, Sonny (& group)

End Of A Dream/Worthless And Lowdown	57	Dot 15542
Barbara/I'm Lost Without You	59	Eastman 791
Those Oldies But Goodies Are Dedicated To You/She Had Me Reelin'	62	Original Sound 18

Knightbeats

Hey Girl	62	Planet 55

Knightcaps

Honey Bee	58	Punch 6000

Knights (1) (Frankie Daye & the)

Dance Party Rock/Drag It	59	Studio 9904

Knights (2)

Forgive Me/I've Got The Feeling	65	USA 800

Knights (3) (Mary Wheeler & the)

A Falling Tear/I Feel In My Heart	N/A	Atom 701

Knightsmen

Darlin' Why/Pistol Packin' Mama	61	Bocaldun 1006

Knockout Mays

You Are Laughing/Sweet Talk	60	Cos-De 1003

The Knockouts

RTIST/SONG	YEAR	LABEL
nockouts		
Darling Lorraine/Riot In Room 3C	59	Shad 5013
Rich Boy Poor Boy/Please Be Mine	60	Shad 5018
You Can Take My Girl/Fever	61	MGM 13010
Mo Jo, Pt. 1/Mo Jo, Pt. 2	64	Tribute 199
What's On Your Mind/Tweet-Tweet	64	Tribute 201
Don't Say Goodbye/Ecuador	65	Tribute 1039
o Kos (female)		
The First Day Of School/You've Been Cheating	57	Combo 141
Teardrops	N/A	Gilt-Edge
odaks (aka Kodoks)		
Little Boy and Girl/Teenager's Dream	57	Fury 1007
Oh Gee Oh Gosh/Make Believe World	57	Fury 1015
My Baby And Me/Kingless Castle	58	Fury 1019
Runaround Baby/Guardian Angel	60	Fury 1020
Don't Want No Teasing!/Look Up To The Sky	60	J&S 1683/1684
Dance Dance Dance	90	Relic LP 5083
odoks (aka Kodaks)		
Let's Rock/Twista Twistin'	61	Wink 1004
Love Wouldn't Mean A Thing/Mister Magoo	61	Wink 1006
okomos (with the Four Seasons)		
Yours Truly/Mamma's Boy	62	Gone 5134
Open House Party/No Lies	62	Josie 906
okonuts (fb Mel Cavin)		
I Love You/My Mummy	62	Bertram International 215
ool Gents (aka Delegates) (gm Dee Clark)		
This Is The Night/Do Ya Do?	56	Vee Jay 173
You Know/I Just Can't Help Myself	56	Vee Jay 207
Picture On The Wall/Come To Me	63	Bethlehem 3061
Crazy Over You	N/A	Charly LP 1115/ Solid Smoke LP 8026
Just Like A Fool	N/A	Vee Jay KP 1019/Charly LP 1113/Solid Smoke LP 8026
ooltones		
Traveling Stranger (a capella)	75	Relic LP 101
ooltoppers		
Is That Exactly What You Wanna Do/Cause I Love You So	55	Beverly 702
ounts (Lee Harrison & the)		
Mine Alone/So Unimportant	58	Pearl 717
raftones		
Memories/Everybody's Got A Home But Me	62	Medieval 206
ruisers		
Karen/C'Mon Sweet Baby	65	Kiski 2068
uf-Linx		
So Tough/What'Cha Gonna Do	58	Challenge 1013/ Challenge 59002 (58)
Eyeballin'/Service With A Smile	58	Challenge 59004
Climb Love's Mountain/All That Good	58	Challenge 59015
'Cap-Tans (aka L'Captans)		
The Bells Ring Out/Call The Doctor	58	Hollywood 1092

ARTIST/SONG	YEAR	LABEL
L'Captans (aka L'Cap-Tans)		
Say Yes/Home Work	59	Savoy 1567/D.C. 0416 (59)
La Chords		
To Be/Flame Out	N/A	Gay 629
La Dolls		
I'll Be Back	85	Relic LP 8004
Sick Spell	85	Relic LP 8004
La Donna, Marie (& group)		
How Can I Let You Know/Georgie Porgie	63	Gateway 730
La Fets & Kitty (aka La Fits & Kitty)		
Christmas Letters/Can Can Rock & Roll	57	Apollo 520
La Mar, Tony (& group)		
Come Out Tonight/Promises	N/A	Duco 5001
La Rells		
Everybody Knew/Please Be Fair	61	Robbee 109
Public Transportation/I Just Can't Understand	61	Robbee 114
I Guess I'll Never Stop Loving You/Sneaky Alligator	62	Liberty 55430
La Roc, Dal (& group)		
Stop What You're Doing/What A Fool	61	Arteen 1010
La Salles		
Chopsticks/Yum Yum	58	Back Beat 515
Labradors		
Queen Of Swing/When Someone Loves You	58	Chief 7009
Ladders		
Counting The Stars/I Want To Know	57	Holiday 2611
My Love Is Gone/Hey, Pretty Baby	59	Vest 826
Laddins		
Did It/Now You're Gone	57	Central 2602/ Times Square 3 (61)
My Baby's Left Me	58	Central unreleased
I'm Falling In Love	58	Central unreleased/ Isle unreleased (60)
Yes, Oh Baby Yes/Light A Candle	59	Grey Cliff 721
Eternally	59	Grey Cliff unreleased
So Long Darling	59	Grey Cliff unreleased
She's The One/Come On	60	Isle 801
A Certain Kind Of Love	60	Isle unreleased
Oh How I Hate To Go Home/There Once Was A Time	61	Theatre 111
I'll Kiss Your Teardrops Away/If You Need Me, I'll Be There	62	Angie 1790
Try, Try Again/That's What You Do To Me	62	Groove 4-5
Push, Shake, Kick And Shout/Push, Shake, Kick And Shout (instrumental)	63	Angie 1003/Bardell 776 (63)
Dream Baby/Dizzy Jones Birdland	63	Butane 779
A Hundred Pounds Of Clay	74	Relic LP 5018
Diamonds And Pearls	74	Relic LP 5018
Every Beat Of My Heart	74	Relic LP 5018
Mother-In-Law	74	Relic LP 5018
That's What You Do To Me	74	Relic LP 5018
Tossin' And Turnin'	74	Relic LP 5018
You Talk Too Much	74	Relic LP 5018
Ladds (George Dee & the)		
I Can't Go On Like This/More	N/A	Kon-Ti-Ki 230

ARTIST/SONG	YEAR	LABEL
Ladelles (female)		
Borrowed Time/No	N/A	Debonair 1218
Lady Bugs (female)		
Who Sent This Love Note/Fraternity, U.S.A.	62	Legrand 1033
Ladybirds		
Yes I Know/Yes I Know	64	Lawn 231
Lafayettes		
Nobody But You/Life's Too Short	62	RCA 8044
I Still Do/Caravan Of Lonely Men	62	RCA 8082
Laine, Linda (& group)		
After Today/Low Grades And High Fever	64	Tower 108
Lake, Tony (& group)		
I Declared My Love/Glamor Girl	59	Herald 543
Lakettes (female)		
Here Comes The Fool/Do You Know	60	Thunderbird 102
Lalarettes (La La & the)		
This Day Is Ours	63	Elpeco 2922
Lam, Tommy (& group)		
Teenagers Dream/Weeping Willow	62	R 303
Lamar, Chris (& group)		
Love So True/Treat Me So Good	63	Don-El 121
Lamarr, Gene (bb the Blue Flames (3))		
That Crazy Little House/You Don't Love Me Anymore	58	Spry 113
Close To Me/Moon Eyes	58	Spry 115
Lambert, Rudy (bb the Lyrics)		
That Old Feeling/Sunday Kind Of Love	58	Rhythm 128
Lamp Lighters		
Big Joke/After All	55	Decca 29669
Your Way/Beep Beep	N/A	N/A
Lampkin, Tommy (bb the Kidds)		
Lover's Plea/Eternal Love	55	Imperial 5361
Lamplighters (gm Thurston Harris)		
Turn Me Loose/Part Of Me	53	Federal 12149
Be Bop Wino/Give Me	53	Federal 12152
Smootchie/I Can't Stand It	53	Federal 12166
I Used To Cry Mercy, Mercy/Tell Me You Care	53	Federal 12176
Salty Dog/Ride, Jockey, Ride	54	Federal 12182
Five Minutes Longer/You Hear	54	Federal 12192
Yum Yum/Goody Good Things	54	Federal 12197
I Wanna Know/Believe In Me	54	Federal 12206
Roll On/Love, Rock And Thrill	55	Federal 12212
Hug A Little, Kiss A Little/Don't Make It So Good	55	Federal 12242
You Were Sent Down From Heaven/Bo Peep	56	Federal 12255
It Ain't Right/Everything's All Right	56	Federal 12261
Lamplighters (Jimmy Witherspoon & the)		
Sad Life/Move Me Baby	53	Federal 12156
Lance, Herb (bb the Classics)		
You Can't Be Sure Of Anything/By The Candle Glow	57	DeLuxe 6150

ARTIST/SONG	YEAR	LABEL
Lancers (1)		
Were You Ever Mine To Lose	53	Trend 63
It's You I Love	54	Trend 73
Live And Let Live	54	Trend 82
Lancers (2)		
Oh Little Girl/You're The Right One	63	Lawn 205
The Warmth Of The Sun/Hushabye	65	Vee Jay 654
Landers, Bob (& group)		
Cherokee Dance/Guitar Rock (by Willie Joe)	56	Specialty 576
Landis, Jerry (& group) (aka Paul Simon & group)		
Lone Teen Ranger/Lisa	62	Amy 875
Lands, Liz (bb the Temptations)		
Keep Me/Midnight Journey	63	Gordy 7030
Lanes		
Open Up Your Heart/You Alone	56	Gee 1023
Lanham, Richard (bb the Tempo-Tones)		
On Your Radio/Dance Of Love	55	Acme 712
Wishing All The Time/The Day I Met You	56	Acme 722
Don't Believe Him/Have A Little Faith	65	Josie 985
Lanterns		
Gloria (a capella)/I Miss You So Much	73	Baron 110
Lapels		
Sneakin' Around/Sneaky Blues	60	Melker 103/Dot 16129 (60)
Big Bad Mollie/I Want A True Friend	60	Melker 104
Bad Luck/Dusty Roads	61	Fortune 862
Larados		
Now The Parting Begins/Bad Bad Guitar Man	57	Fox 963
Will You Love Me Tomorrow?/You Didn't Care	80	Madog 801
Larados (Danny Zella & the)		
You Made Me Blue/Sapphire	57	Dial 100
Larand, Johnny (& group)		
Heaven To Me	N/A	Octavia 0005
Largos		
I Wonder Why?/Saddle Up	61	Starmaker/Dot 16292 (62)
Just A Picture	N/A	Starmaker 1002
Larks (1)		
My Heart Cries For You/Coffee, Cigarettes And Tears	51	Apollo 1177
Hopefully Yours/When I Leave These Prison Walls	51	Apollo 1180
My Reverie/Let's Say A Prayer	51	Apollo 1184
Eyesight To The Blind/I Ain't Fattenin' Frogs For Snakes	51	Apollo 427
Little Side Car/Hey! Little Girl	51	Apollo 429
Oh It Feels So Good/I Don't Believe In Tomorrow	51	Apollo 430
Shadrack/Honey In The Rock	52	Apollo 1189
In My Lonely Room/Stolen Love	52	Apollo 1190
Hold Me/I Live True To You	52	Apollo 1194
My Lost Love/How Long Must I Wait For You?	52	Apollo 435
Darlin'/Lucy Brown	52	Apollo 437
Margie/Rockin' In The Rocket Room	54	Lloyds 108
If It's A Crime/Tippin' In	54	Lloyds 110
When You're Near/Who Walks In When I Walk Out	54	Lloyds 111
No Other Girl/The World Is Waiting For The Sunrise	54	Lloyds 112
Forget It/Os-Ca-Lu-Ski-O	54	Lloyds 114

ARTIST/SONG	YEAR	LABEL
Johnny Darlin'/You're Gonna Lose Your Gal	54	Lloyds 115
Honey From The Bee/No, Mama, No	55	Apollo 475
Christmas To New Year's	88	Relic LP 8013
If You Were The Only Girl In The World	88	Relic LP 8013
It's Breaking My Heart	88	Relic LP 8013
Jam Session	88	Relic LP 8013
All I Want For Christmas	88	Relic LP 8014
For The Love Of You	88	Relic LP 8014
What's The Matter	88	Relic LP 8014
Danny Boy/Without A Song	N/A	Dreamtone 201 (unreleased)

Larks (2) (Don Julian & the)

Shorty The Pimp, Pt. 1/Shorty The Pimp, Pt. 2	65	Jerk 202

Larks (2) (gm Don Julian)

Fabulous Cars And Diamond Rings/Life Is Sweeter Now	61	Cross Fire 74-49/74-50/ Guyden 2103 (61)
It's Unbelievable/I Can't Believe It	61	Sheryl 334/Uptown (65)
There Is A Girl/Let's Drink A Toast	61	Sheryl 338
I Want Her To Love Me/I Want Her To Love Me (instrumental)	61	Violet 1051/Guyden 2098 (61)
For The Love Of Money/Another Sleepless Night	64	Arock 1010
The Jerk/Forget Me	64	Money 106
Mickey's East Coast Jerk/Soul Jerk	64	Money 110
Heavenly Father/The Roman	64	Money 112
Love You So/Love Me True	65	Jett 3001
Sad Sad Boy/Can You Do The Duck	65	Money 115
The Answer Came Too Late/Lost My Love Yesterday	65	Money 119
Philly Dog/Heaven Only Knows	65	Money 122
Come Back Baby/The Skate	65	Money 127
I Want You Back/I Love You	71	Money 601

Larks (3) (Irma & the)

Don't Cry/Without You Baby	N/A	Priority 322

Larktones

The Letter/Rockin', Swingin' Man	58	ABC 9909
Nosy Neighbor/Why Are You Tearing Us Apart	60	Riki 140

Lasabers (Lafayette & the)

Cure For Love/Free Way	60	Port 70036

Lassiter, Art (& group)

Just Another Day In The Life Of A Fool/Bermuda	56	Ballad 1020
Too Late For Tears/Just Another Day In The Life Of A Fool	56	Ballad 1024

Latin Lads (Julito & the)

Nunca (Never)/Poesia En Movim Iento	63	Rico-Vox 27

Latons

So In Love/Love Me	62	Port 70030

Laurels (1)

Truly, Truly/'Tis Night	55	X 0143

Laurels (1) (Bobby Relf & the)

Yours Alone/Farewell	55	Flair 1063

Laurels (2) (Jake Porter & the)

Fine Fine Baby/T. J.	55	Combo 66

Laurels (3) (Kenny Loran & the)

Lonely Boy/Change Of Love	58	Challenge 59010

Laurels (4)

Picture Of Love/Hand In Hand	59	ABC 10048
Baby Talk/You Left Me	60	Spring 1112

ARTIST/SONG	YEAR	LABEL
Laurie, Linda (& group)		
Prince Charming/Soupin' Up Your Motor	60	Rust 5022
Lavenders (1) (Robin Lee & the)		
Pretty Patti	60	Circle Dot 103
Lavenders (2)		
Angel/The Slide	61	C.R. 103
The Bells/I Said Look	61	Lake 706
One More Time/One More Once	63	Mercury 72126
This I Feel/Daddy, Daddy	64	Dot 16584
Lavette, Betty (& group)		
You Killed The Love/Witchcraft In The Air	64	LuPine 123
Lawrence, Bernie (& group)		
Collecting Girls/That Was Yesterday	61	United Artists 388
Lawrence, Bob (& group)		
Come My Little Baby/Honey Dew	57	Mark-X 7005
Lawson Boys (Teddy Lawson & the)		
There's No Return From Love/I Knew It Was You	57	Mansfield 611
Leaders		
Stormy Weather/A Lover Of The Time	55	Glory 235
Dearest, Beloved Darling/Nobody Loves Me	56	Glory 239
Can't Help Lovin' That Girl Of Mine/Lovers	56	Glory 243
Leaping Flames		
It's Been So Long/Hurts Me To Work	63	MRC 1201
Ledo, Les (& group)		
Scarlet Angel/Don't Fight	60	Shell 721
Lee (bb the Regents)		
Goddess Of Love/Lonely Summer	61	Scepter 1222
Lee, Addie (& group)		
C'Mon Home/Please Buy My Record	58	End 1018
Lee, Curtis (bb the Halos)		
Special Love/D-In Love	60	Dunes 2001
California GL-903/Then I'll Know	60	Dunes 801
I Never Knew What Love Could Do/Gotta Have You	60	Hot 7
I'm Asking Forgiveness/Let's Take A Ride	60	Sabra 517
With All My Heart/Pure Love	60	Warrior 1555
Pledge Of Love/Then I'll Know	61	Dunes 2003
Pretty Little Angel Eyes/Gee How I Wish	61	Dunes 2007
Under The Moon Of Love/Beverly Jean	61	Dunes 2008
Just Another Fool/A Night At Daddy Gee's	62	Dunes 2012
The Wobble/Does He Mean That Much To You	62	Dunes 2015
Lee, James Washington (& group)		
I Need Somebody/Don't Ask Me	62	L&M 1003
Lee, Jerry (& group)		
Unwritten Law/Count Ten	61	Rendezvous 147
Lee, Jimmy (& group)		
My Dear Little Doll/I Wonder (Can It Be True)	61	Canadian American 122
Lee, Jimmy (& Wayne Walker & group)		
Love Me	55	Chess 4863

ARTIST/SONG	YEAR	LABEL
Lee, Jimmy (bb the Earls)		
Daddy's Home/If I Could Do It Once Again	N/A	Bo-P-C 100
Lee, Mabel (& group)		
Dearest Dream/He's My Guy	56	Hull 712
Lee, Shirley (& group)		
Behind The Make Up/Keep The Magic Working	61	Seven Arts 711
Lee, Warren (& group)		
Geraldine/London Bridge	63	Jin 173
Leeds		
Heaven Only Knows/Mr. Cool	59	Wand 102
Leeds, Randy (& group)		
My Oh My/Insurance	59	Roulette 4153
Leen Teens		
So Shy/Dream Around You	59	Imperial 5593
Leerics		
Island Of Love/Hey Patty	N/A	Un-Released Gold 799
Lefemmes (Cole & the)		
Love Is No Stranger	N/A	Varbee 5001
Legacy (aka Bel-Aires)		
Loretta/Dreams Of Heaven	87	Crystal Ball 151
Down The Road/A Little Bit Of Soap	88	Crystal Ball 153
Legends (1)		
I'll Never Fall In Love Again/The Eyes Of An Angel	57	Melba 109
The Legend Of Love/Now I'm Telling You	58	Hull 727
Legends (2) (Billy Davis & the)		
Goodbye Jesse/Spunky Onions	60	Peacock 1694
Legends (3)		
Get Out Of The House/You Little Nothin'	61	Magenta 02
Jungle Lullabye/Go Away With Me	62	Caldwell 410
My Love For You/Say Mama	62	Ermine 39
Bop-A-Lena/I Wish I Knew	62	Ermine 43
Tell The Truth/You'll Never See The Forest	62	Jamie 1228
Run To The Movies/Summertime Blues	63	Capitol 5014
Well Darling/Over Yonder	63	Falco 305
Legends (4) (Rick & the)		
I Wonder Why/Love Me Like I Know You Can	63	JD 162/ United Artists 50093 (66)
Legends (5) (Larry & the) (with the Four Seasons)		
Don't Pick On Me Baby/The Creep	64	Atlantic 2220
Legends (6) (Lonnie & the)		
I Cried/Baby Without You	66	Impression 109
Leggeriors		
Flame Of Love/Justine	63	Goliath 1351
Leigh, Linda (& group)		
Move Out/It's Real	59	Rendezvous 103
Leisure Lads		
Baby, I'm All Alone/A Teenage Memory	59	Delco 801

ARTIST/SONG	YEAR	LABEL
Lemon Drops		
Cute Little Wiggle/Lo-o-ve	59	Coral 62145
Marcheta/Mexicali Moon	60	Aladdin 3465
Lendells (aka Lydells)		
(Don't Be A) Litterbug/Maryann	66	Reach 2
Leopards (1) (Lee & the)		
What About Me/Don't Press Your Luck	62	Fortune 867
Come Into My Palace/Trying To Make It	62	Gordy 7002/Laurie 3197 (63)
Leopards (2)		
Mah Mah (Chicken Pot Pie)/Valerie	63	Leopard 5006
Lester, Bobby (actually the Moonglows)		
Lonely Hearts/Am I The Man?	59	Checker 921
Levees		
Out Love Is A Vow/Walkie Talkie Baby	59	Karen 1004/Relic 515 (64)
Leverett, Chico (bb the Satintones)		
Work Work/Baby Don't Leave	63	Bethlehem 3062
Levons (female)		
Come To Me/Everytime	62	Columbia 42506
We're Just Friends Now/Love Is Better Than Ever	63	Columbia 42798
Lewis, Billy (& group)		
Stool Pigeon Baby/I Won't Tell A Soul	56	Flo-Lou 101
Lewis, Bobby (& female group)		
Tossin' And Turnin'/Oh Yes, I Love You	61	Beltone 1002
Lewis, James (& group)		
I Cried Last Night/Tell Me That You Love Me	58	Arrow 730
Lexing, Bobby (& group)		
Flame In My Heart	61	Good Sound 107
Lexingtons (1)		
When My Baby Went Away/I Found My Baby	60	Everest 19369
Lexingtons (2) (Joey & the)		
Heaven/The Girl I Love	62	Comet 2154
Bobbie/Tears From My Eyes	63	Dunes 2029
Lexingtons (3)		
My Honey Loves Another Girl/Ba Ba Doo	63	International 500
Lexons		
Angels Like You/Rock 'N Roll 'N Rock 'N Roll	58	Lexington 100
Lidos		
Trudy/Since I Last Saw You	57	Band Box 359
Lifesavers (Lucien Farrar & the)		
Didn't You Know/Tomorrow Night	57	Jupiter 45
Lile, Bobby (& group)		
Story-Book Love	63	Marsh 204
Limelighters		
Cabin Hideaway/My Sweet Norma Lee	56	Josie 795
This Lonely Boy/Sister Sookey Comes Home	57	Gilco 213

ARTIST/SONG	YEAR	LABEL

Limelites (Shep & the)

Freckle Face	59	Apt (unreleased)
Little Star	59	Apt (unreleased)
Too Young To Wed/Two Loving Hearts (Shane Sheppard)	60	Apt 25039
I'm So Lonely (What Can I Do?)/One Week From Today	60	Apt 25046
Daddy's Home/This I Know	61	Hull 740
Ready For Your Love/You'll Be Sorry	61	Hull 742/Hull 1009
Three Steps From The Altar/Oh What A Feeling	61	Hull 747
Three Steps To The Altar/Ready For Your Love	61	Roulette 102
Our Anniversary/Who Told The Sandman	62	Hull 748
What Did Daddy Do/Teach Me How To Twist	62	Hull 751
Everything Is Gonna Be Alright/Gee Baby What About You	63	Hull 753
Remember Baby/The Monkey	63	Hull 756
Stick By Me (And I'll Stick By You)/It's All Over Now	63	Hull 757
Steal Away (With Your Baby)/For You My Love	63	Hull 759
Why, Why Won't You Believe Me/Easy To Remember (When You Want To Forget)	63	Hull 761
Why Did You Fall For Me/I'm All Alone	64	Hull 767
Party For Two/You Better Believe	65	Hull 770
I'm A Hurtin' Inside/In Case I Forget	65	Hull 772

Lincoln's Quintett

Dream Of Romance/Tell Me What Is Wrong	58	Angle Tone 522

Lincolns (1)

I Cried/Madly In Love	57	Aljon 113/114
Don't Let Me Shed Any More Tears/Pleasin' You Pleases Me	57	Atlas 1100
Baby, Please Let Me Love You/Can't You Go For Me?	59	Mercury 71553

Lincolns (2)

Sometime, Somewhere/Sukiyaki Rocki	61	Bud 113

Links

Scrunchy/Pyramid	58	Brunswick 55081
Baby/She's The One	58	Teenage 1009

Linnettes

Someday/Big Eyed Baby	60	Palette 5112

Lions (1)

No One (No One But You)/Giggles	60	Everest 19388/Mark IV 1
Hickory Dickory/The Yokel (He Went To Town)	60	Imperial 5678
Two Timing Love/Feast Of The Beast	60	Rendezvous 116

Lions (2) (Lugee & the) (fb Lou Christie)

The Jury/Little Did I Know	61	Robbee 112

Lisi, Ricky (bb the Concords)

The River/Don't Go Now	63	Roulette 4511

Litations

Let Me Tell You	63	N/A

Litterbugs

Valerie/Calypso	63	Okeh 7164

Little Angel

Come On And Rock/Help Me Baby	59	Award 126

Little Angels

I'll Be A Little Angel/Santa Claus Parade	61	Warwick 672

Little Beats

Someone For Me/Love Is True	57	Mercury 71155

ARTIST/SONG	YEAR	LABEL
Little Beavers (Johnny Briscoe & the)		
Why Do Fools Fall In Love/Sugar Love	71	Atlantic 2822
Little Boys Blue (Bonnie & the)		
You'd Better Run/Bells	60	Nikko 611
Little Buck (& group)		
I'll Follow You/Let It Be Now	60	Duke 324
Little Caesar (& group)		
I'm Reachin'/Who Slammed The Door	58	RCA 7270
Little Cheryl (& group)		
Heaven Only Knows/Can't We Just Be Friends	63	Cameo 270
Come On Home/I Love You Conrad	64	Cameo 292
Little Coolbreezers		
Won't You Come In/Pack Your Bags And Go	56	Ebony 1015
Little David (& group)		
Love Me	N/A	521 1001
Little Dippers		
Forever/Two By Four	59	University 210
Be Sincere/Tonight	60	University 6053/6054
Lonely/I Wonder, I Wonder, I Wonder	60	University 608
Sails/For Just A Little While Tonight	64	Dot 16602
Little Dixie (& group)		
Be Fair/I'm Growing Up	59	Las Vegas 101/Strip 101
Little Ellen (& group)		
Answer Me My Love/That Other Guy	61	Smash 1724
Little Ernie (& group)		
You Lied And I Cried/Queen Of The Hop	63	Summit 0008
Little Esther (bb the Robins)		
Saturday Night Daddy/Mainliner (by Bobby Nunn with the Robins)	52	Federal 12100
Little Eva (& group)		
The Locomotion/He Is The Boy	62	Dimension 1000
Little Four Quartet		
Tee-U-Eee/Don't Forget To Be True	N/A	Southern 122
Little Herman (& group)		
Gotta Keep On Walking/I'm Gonna Put The Hurt On You	64	Arlen 751
Little Jerry (& group) (Jerry Williams)		
(I'll Always Remember) The Chapel On The Hill/I'm So Mad	60	Aldo 502
Little Kings (Phil Orsi & the)		
Oh My Darling/Come On Everybody	63	Lucky 1009
Little Nat (bb the Shells)		
Tally Wally/Do This Do That	61	Pik 242
Little People (Mike Lynam & the)		
Message To Pretty/I Need You	N/A	Emanon 101
Little Richard (& group)		
True, Fine Mama/Ooh My Soul (no group)	58	Specialty 633

ARTIST/SONG	YEAR	LABEL
Little Sammy (& group)		
Can You Love Me/Papa Did The Chicken	56	Shade 1002
Little Stevie (& group)		
I See A Star/The Letter	61	Guyden 2060
Little, Horace (& group)		
Five Hundred Years/Texas Stomp	62	Ascot 2102
Little, Lee Roy (& group)		
Hurry Back, Please Come Home/Let Me Go Home Whiskey	60	Cee Jay 579
Littlefield, Little Willie (& female group)		
Theresa/The Day The Rains Came	58	Rhythm 124
Littlefield, Little Willie (bb the Mondellos)		
Ruby, Ruby/Easy Go	57	Rhythm 108/Bullseye 1005 (57)/ Argyle
Live Wires (Andy & the)		
Maggie/You've Done It Again	60	Applause 1249
Lloyd, Jackie (bb the Harbor Lights)		
Come And Get Me/Warm Love	60	Heros 342
Lockets		
Don't Cha Know/Little Boy	63	Argo 5455
Lockettes (female)		
Puddin' Pie/You Don't Want Me	58	Flip 334
Lockettes (Richard Berry & the)		
Heaven On Wheels/The Mess Around	58	Flip 336
Locomotions		
Little Eva/Adios My Love	62	Gone 5142
Locos		
Professor Loco/Oh Yes, Indeed I Do	58	20th Fox 102
Logan, Dorothy (bb the Gems)		
Since I Fell For You (flip has no group)	54	Drexel 902
Logics		
One Love/Everybody's Doing The Pony	60	Everlast 5015
Lollipops (1) (Little Bob & the)		
Twisting Home/You Don't Have To Cry	62	Decca 31412
Lollipops (2) (Becky & the)		
I Don't Care/Come On Home	64	Troy 6493/Epic 9736 (64)
Lollypoppers		
A Bottle Of Pop And A Lollypop/Miss Selma's Boogie	55	Aladdin 3291
Miss Selma's Boogie/A Bottle Of Pop And A Lollypop	55	Harlem 104/Aladdin 3291 (55)
Lollypops		
Believe In Me/My Love Is Real	58	Universal International 7420/ Holland 7420 (58)
Dream Street/Norman	60	Kandee 6001
London, Lloyd (bb the Yachtsmen)		
Will There Ever Be A Girl/Cry Baby	59	Destiny 530

ARTIST/SONG	YEAR	LABEL
London, Ralph (& group)		
Someday You'll Be My Girl/Lovely Lovely Girl	64	Coed 588
Lonely Boys		
A Spoken Letter/My Girl	59	NuWay 555
Lonely Guys		
The Way You Look Tonight/Moon Flight	57	Caddy 117
Lonely Ones		
I Want My Girl/My Wish	59	Baton 270/Sir 270 (59)
Debbie/Swanee River Fling	60	Rendezvous 125
Long, Bobby (& His Cherrios)		
Patty/By My Side	58	Arrow 727
Hold Me/Ooh La La	59	Glow-Hill 504
Calling/Did You Ever Dream Lucky	59	Unart 2023
Lopez, Trini (& group)		
Since I Don't Have You/Rock On	59	King 5187
Love Me Tonight/Here Comes Sally	59	King 5198
Loran, Kenny (& group)		
Magic Star/Mama's Little Baby	59	Capitol 4276
Lord, Emmett (& group)		
Turn Him Down/Women	62	Liberty 55491
Been So Long/Beggar Of Love	N/A	Antel 520
Lords (Yvette & the)		
We Must Carry On/How Can I Tell Him	64	Yvette 103
Loreleis		
Have Fun Baby/Now I'm Broken Hearted	55	Dot 15268
You're So Nice To Be Near/Wildsville	55	Spotlight 390
Lornettes		
His Way With The Girls/Down The Block And Up To Heaven	65	Gallico 110
Loungers		
Remember The Nite/Dizzy Spell	58	Herald 534
Lourdes		
My Favorite Dream/Yours	60	Mercury 71655
Love Bugs (fb Preston Love)		
Boom Diddy Wawa Baby/A Man Goin' Crazy	55	Federal 12216
Love Bugs (Preston Love & the)		
If You Ever Get Lonesome	N/A	Ultra
Love Letters		
Walking The Streets Alone/Owee-Nellie	57	Acme 714
Love Notes (1)		
Crawling	53	Family Library Of Music EP 1040
You're Mine	53	Family Library Of Music EP 1040
Love Notes (2)		
Surrender Your Heart/Get On My Train	53	Imperial 5254
I'm Sorry/Sweet Lulu	54	Riviera 970/Rainbow 266 (54)
Since I Fell For You/Don't Be No Fool	54	Riviera 975

ARTIST/SONG	YEAR	LABEL

Love Notes (3)
United/Tonight	57	Holiday 2605
If I Could Make You Mine/Don't Go	57	Holiday 2607

Love Notes (4)
Gloria/Mathematics Of Love	62	Wilshire 203
Our Songs Of Love/Nancy	63	Wilshire 200

Love Notes (5) (Honey Love & the)
We Belong Together/Mary Ann	65	Cameo 380

Love, Darlene (& group)
(Today I Met) The Boy I'm Gonna Marry/ My Heart Beat A Little Faster	63	Philles 111
(Today I Met) The Boy I'm Gonna Marry/Playing For Keeps	63	Philles 111
Wait 'Til My Bobby Gets Home/Take It From Me (instrumental)	63	Philles 114
A Fine Fine Boy/Nino And Sonny (instrumental)	63	Philles 117
Christmas (Baby, Please Come Home)/Harry And Milt Meet Hal B. (instrumental)	63	Philles 119
(He's A) Quiet Guy/Stumble And Fall	64	Philles 123
Christmas (Baby, Please Come Home)/Winter Wonderland	64	Philles 125/Philles 125X (65)
White Christmas	64	Philles EP X-EP
Too Late To Say You're Sorry/If	66	Reprise 534
Christmas (Baby, Please Come Home)/ Wait Till My Bobby Gets Home	74	Warner-Spector 0401
Lord, If You're A Woman/Stumble And Fall	76	Warner-Spector 0410

Love, Jimmy (& group)
Let Me Down Easy/Way Down Yonder In New Orleans	63	Violet 1052

Love, Ronnie (& group)
Judy/Detroit, Michigan	65	D-Town 1047

Love-Lords
Burning Love/Simmerfast (instrumental)	62	Al-King 11021

Love-Tones (Gino Parks & the)
Fire/For This I Thank You	62	Tamla 54066

Lovejoys (female)
It's Mighty Nice/Payin' (For The Wrong I've Done)	64	Tiger 105/Red Bird 003 (64)

Lovejoys (Leola & the) (female)
He Ain't No Angel/Wait 'Round The Corner	64	Tiger 101

Lovelarks (1)
More And More/Diddle-Le-Bom	61	Masons 3-070

Lovelarks (2) (Steve Kass & the)
Darling My Love/You Made A Boo Boo	N/A	Class 10

Lovelites
I Found Me A Lover/You Better Stop It	67	Bandera 2515

Lovenotes (1) (aka True Loves)
A Love Like Ours/Never Look Behind	57	Premium 411

Lovenotes (2) (Sybil Love & the)
I Love You Darling/No More Tears	59	Valex 505

ARTIST/SONG	YEAR	LABEL

Lovers (1)

Don't Touch Me/Let Me Be The First To Know	56	Decca 29862
Darling It's Wonderful/Gotta Whole Lot Of Lovin' To Do	57	Lamp 2005
I Wanna Be Loved/Let's Elope	57	Lamp 2013
Tell Me/Love Bug Bit Me	58	Aladdin 3419/Lamp 2018 (58)
Strange As It Seems/Party Line	61	Keller 101
Darling It's Wonderful/I Want To Be Loved	62	Imperial 5845/Post 10007 (63)
You Are Welcome To My Heart/With All My Heart	62	MC B-003
Let's Elope/Tell Me	63	Imperial 5960
Someone/Do This For Me	66	Gate 501/Philips 40353 (66)

Lovers (1) (Billy Love & the)

| Legend Of Love/Hold Me Close | 64 | Dragon 4403 |

Lovers (2)

| Let's/Big Axe | 58 | Casino 103 |

Lovers (3) (Ray Frazier & the)

| King Of Lovers/Darling | 59 | Combo 161 |

Lovers (4) (Valentino & the)

| I'm Gonna Love/One Teardrop Too Late | 61 | Donna 1345 |

Lovers (5) (Little Louie & the)

| Someday You'll Pay/Nothing But The Two-Step | 62 | Viscount 102 |

Lovers (6)

| Caravan Of Lonely Men/In My Tenement | 65 | Agon 1011 |

Lovers (7) (Cliff Butler & the)

| I Can't Believe | N/A | Frantic 801 |

Lovers (8) (Pete Peter & the)

| A Lonely Island/Pistol Packing Mama | 60 | Derby 1030 |

Lovetones (1)

| Talk To An Angel/Take It Easy, Baby | 56 | Plus 108 |
| When I Asked My Love/You Can Tell That This Is Christmas | 62 | Love-Tone 101 |

Lovetones (2)

| It's Mighty Easy/I Want You Now | 61 | Marlo 1515 |

Lovetones (3) (Raymond Pope & the)

| I Love Nadine/Star | 62 | Squalor 1313 |

Lovettes

| Puzzling Love/Lost Weekend | 59 | Knight 2010 |
| Written In The Stars/Puzzling Love | 59 | Knight 2010 |

Low Notes

| Baby Oh Baby | N/A | N/A |

Loye Jr., Bobby (& group)

| Loving Tree/Another Mr. Blue | 63 | Wilshire 202 |

LP's (Denny & the)

| Why Not Give Me Your Heart?/Slide-Cha-Lypso | 58 | Rock-It 001 |

Lullabies (1) (Lisa & the) (ref Concords)

| Why Do I Cry/He's So Good | 64 | Coed 589 |

Lullabies (2) (Tommy Tucker & the)

| That Lucky Old Sun | N/A | N/A |

ARTIST/SONG	YEAR	LABEL
Lullabyes (1)		
My Heart Cries For You/You Touch Me	64	Dimension 1039
Lullabyes (2)		
You Belong To Me/Do What You Did	61	Embassy 204
Lumpkin, Henry (& group)		
We Really Love Each Other/I've Got A Notion	61	Motown 1005
Luvs		
We Kiss In The Shadows/You Used To Be	63	Stallion 1002
Ly-Dells		
Genie Of The Lamp/Teenage Tears	61	Master 111
Wizard Of Love/Let This Night Last	61	Master 251
Book Of Songs/Hear That Train	62	SCA 18001
Karen/Doing The Wiggle Wobble	63	Roulette 4493
Three Little Monkeys/Playing Hide And Seek	65	Southern Sound 122
Lydells		
There Goes The Boy/Talking To Myself	59	Pam 103/Parkway 897 (64)
Lyndon, Frank (bb the Regents)		
Tonight We Wail/Cry Cry Cry	N/A	Jab 1004
Lynn, Bill (& group)		
Only One For Me/Little Pony Tail	61	Amy 820
Lynn, Bobby (& group)		
Tonight My Love	N/A	CR 102
Lynn, Gloria (bb the Wheels)		
Run For Your Love/I Can't Waste My Tears	57	Premium 412
Lynn, Sandy (bb the Corvets)		
Hurry, Hurry Home/Little Johnny	61	Laurel 1024
Lyres (aka Nutmegs)		
Ship Of Love/Play Boy	53	J&G 101
Lyrics (1)		
I'm In Love/You	58	Hy-Tone 111
Let's Exchange Hearts For Christmas	N/A	N/A
Lyrics (2)		
Did She Leave You/Lovely Charms	58	Marvels 1005
Every Night/Come Back Baby	58	Rhythm 127
Come On Home/Why Don't You Stop?	58	Vee Jay 285
Oh, Please Love Me/The Girl I Love	59	Harlem 101/Wildcat 0028 (59)/ Coral 62322 (62)
I Want To Know/The Beating Of My Heart	59	Harlem 104
Crying Over You/Down In The Alley	59	Mid South 1500
Let's Be Sweethearts Again/You And Your Fellow	61	Fernwood 129/ Fleetwood 233 (61)
Cryin' The Blues	N/A	N/A
Lyrics (2) (Leo Valentine & the)		
Please Don't Leave Me This Way/Baby Doll	62	Skylight 201
Got To Get Along/Come Back	62	Skylight 202
Lyrics (2) (William Wigfall & the)		
Darling/How A Woman Does Her Man	63	(Russel's) Gold Wax 101/ Goldwax 910 (63)
So Hard To Get Along/The Side Wind	63	Goldwax 105/ABC 10560 (64)

ARTIST/SONG	YEAR	LABEL
Lyrics (3) (Kenneth Churchill & the)		
Fate Of Rock And Roll/Would You Rather	58	Joyce 304
Lyrics (4) (Ike Perry & the)		
Stairsteps To Heaven/The Love Bug's Got Me	58	Bridge 110
I've Got You Covered/You Can Be My Honey	60	Cowtown 801
At The Party	63	Courier 828
In My Letter To You/My Honey Sweet Pea	63	Mama 1/2/Mama 1074 (63)
Don't Let It Get You Down/Come Back To Me Darling	63	Mama 3614/Courier 828 (63)
Don't Let It Get You Down/At The Party	65	Naurline 100
Lovin' Papa/She's Got His Nose Wide Open	N/A	Bee 1875
Lyrics (5)		
Broken Love/I Can't Get Along Without You	62	Dan-Tone 1002
Lytations (aka Kaptions)		
Over The Rainbow/Look Into The Sky	64	Times Square 107
Mac, Bobby (& group)		
How Was Your Weekend/Shy Guy	N/A	Vended 104
Mac, Lou (bb the Palms)		
Slow Down/Baby (no group)	55	Blue Lake 114
Mack, Dell (bb the Golden Gate Quartet)		
The Way Love Goes/You Can't Judge A Book By The Cover	58	Goldband 1064
Mackinteers (Teddy Mack & the)		
Is There Any Doubt/Hey Hey Gypsy Woman	N/A	Monroe 1
Macree, Vincent (& group)		
Teenage Talk	57	Gametime 103
Macs (Terry & the)		
Baby-O-Mine/Love Is A Beautiful Thing	56	ABC 9668
You Don't Have To Explain/Spinning, Spinning, Spinning	56	ABC 9721
Mad Lads		
Why/Hey, Man	62	Mark Fi 1934
Mad Lads (Frank Deaton & the)		
My Love For You/Just A Little Bit More	57	Bally 1042
Mad Lads (Little Becky Cook & the)		
Let's Dance/Saving My Love For You	61	CBM 504
Madara, Johnny (& group)		
Lovesick/Be My Girl	57	Prep 110
A Story Untold/Vacation Time	61	Bamboo 511
Madhattans		
Wowie/A Basketful Of Blueberries	57	Atlantic 1142
Madison Brothers		
Trusting In You/What's The Matter, Baby	60	Cedargrove 314/Apt 25050 (60)
Give Me Your Heart/Baby Don't	61	Sure 1002
Madison Brothers (Farris Hill & the)		
Did We Go Steady Too Soon/The Twirl	62	V-Tone 231
Madison, Glen (& group)		
Why Do You Have To Go/When You Dance	62	Ebony 105/Monument
Madisons (fb Larry Santos)		
Can You Imagine/The Wind And The Rain	64	Lawn 240

ARTIST/SONG	YEAR	LABEL
Only A Fool/Stagger	65	Jomada 601/Jumaca 601
Cheryl Anne/Looking For True Love	65	MGM 13312
Valarie/I'll Be Around (by the Monterays)	65	Twin Hit 2865

Maestro, Johnny (bb the Del Satins)
Model Girl/Got To Tell Them	61	Coed 545
What A Surprise/The Warning Voice	61	Coed 549
Test Of Love/Mr. Happiness	61	Coed 552
I.O.U./The Way You Look Tonight	61	Coed 557
Besame Baby/It Must Be Love	61	Coed 562

Magic Notes
Never Again/The Wrong Door	57	Era 1035

Magic Tones
When I Kneel Down To Pray/Good Googa Mooga	53	King 4665
How Can You Treat Me This Way?/Cool, Cool Baby	54	King 4681
Tears In My Eyes/Spanish Love Song	57	Howfum 101

Magic Touch (aka Vito & the Salutations)
Baby, You Belong To Me/Lost And Lonely Boy	73	Roulette 7143

Magicians (female)
Rain Don't Fall/An Invitation To Cry	65	Columbia 43435
Why Do I Do These Foolish Things/Is It All Gone?	66	Villa 704
Why Must You Cry/Keep Your Hands Off	66	Villa 706

Magics
Chapel Bells/She Can't Stop Dancing	63	Debra 1003
If I Didn't Have You/Let's Boogaloo	N/A	RFA 100

Magnatones
I Need You/McDonald's Rock	60	Cedargrove 313/Time 108 (60)
Adios My Desert Love/I Love You With Tender Passion	63	Fortune 555

Magnetics (1)
Where Are You/The Train	62	Allrite 620

Magnetics (2)
Oh Love/Wasting Time	N/A	JV 2501

Magnets
You Just Say The Word/Surprise	55	Groove 0058
When The School Bells Ring/Don't Tarry Little Mary	58	RCA 7391

Magnificent 6
Forever More	N/A	L-Brown 01659

Magnificent Four
The Closer You Are/Uncle Sam	61	Whale 506/Blast 210 (63)

Magnificents
Up On The Mountain/Why Did She Go?	56	Vee Jay 183/Vee Jay 367 (60)
Caddy Bo/Hiccup	56	Vee Jay 208
Off The Mountain/Lost Lover	57	Vee Jay 235
Don't Leave Me/Ozeta	58	Vee Jay 281
Let's Do The Cha Cha/Up On The Mountain	60	Vee Jay 367
Do You Mind?/The Dribble Twist	62	Kansoma 03/Checker 1016 (62)
This Ole Love Of Mine	84	Solid Smoke LP 8030
Yes, She's My Baby	84	Solid Smoke LP 8030
It's No Wonder	N/A	Oldies 45

Magnificents (released as by the El Dorados)
My Heart Is Calling/On Main Street	66	Dee Gee 3008

ARTIST/SONG	YEAR	LABEL

Maharajahs

I Do Believe/Why Don't You Answer?	58	Flip 332
Sweet Loretta/Oh, Shirley	58	Flip 335

Maidens (Sir Joe & the)

Jivin' Jean/Pen Pal	62	Lenox 5563

Majestics (1)

Divided Heart/Please Don't Say No	58	NRC 502
TV Cowboys/So You Want To Rock	59	Faro 592
Sweet One (with the Nightwinds)/The Lone Stranger	59	Sioux 91459/20th Century 171 (59)/Foxie 7004 (59)
Teen Age Gossip/Hard Times	60	Contour 501

Majestics (2)

Nitey Nite/Cave Man Rock	56	Marlin 802
The Love Stranger/Sweet One	59	20th Fox 171
Searching For A New Love/Angel Of Love	61	Pixie 6901/Jordan 123 (61)/Nu-Tone 123 (61)
Oasis/Oasis, Pt. 2	62	Chess 1802
Shoppin' And Hoppin'/Give Me A Cigarette	62	Chex 1000
So I Can Forget/Give Me A Cigarette	62	Chex 1000
Treat Me Like You Want To Be Treated/Unhappy And Blue	62	Chex 1004
Lonely Heart/Gwendolyn	62	Chex 1006
Teach Me How To Limbo/Baby	62	Chex 1009
Strange World/Everything Is Gonna Be All Right	63	Linda 111
Girl Of My Dreams/It Hurts Me	65	Linda 121
Bobbi Ann	N/A	Fox 5014
Pennies For A Beggar	N/A	Knight 105

Majestics (2) (Kirk Taylor & the)

From Out Of This World/You Didn't Learn That In School	59	Bandera 2507

Majestics (3)

Smile Through My Tears/Love Has Forgotten Me	66	MGM 13488

Majestics (4)

Ave Maria (a capella)	75	Relic LP 104
Twilight (a capella)	75	Relic LP 105

Majestics (4) (Little Joe & the)

Every Day Of The Week (a capella)	75	Relic LP 104
I'm So Young (a capella)	75	Relic LP 104
This Magic Moment (a capella)	75	Relic LP 105

Majorettes (female)

White Levis/Please Come Back	63	Troy 1000
Let's Do The Kangaroo/Dance With Me	63	Troy 1004

Majors (1)

Laughing On The Outside, Crying On The Inside/Come On To My Room	51	Derby 763
You Ran Away With My Heart/At Last	51	Derby 779

Majors (2)

Big Eyes/Go Way	54	Original 1003

Majors (2) (Jesse Powell & the)

Oh Baby/String-A-Long	58	Josie 845

Majors (3) (Otis Blackwell & the)

It's Love And It's Real/Don't Take My Word	57	Gale 102

Majors (4)

Rockin' The Boogie/Blue Sunset	57	Felsted 8501
Come Go With Me/Les Qua	59	Felsted 8576
Go With Me/I Found My Love	65	Felsted 8707

ARTIST/SONG	YEAR	LABEL
Majors (5) (aka Versatiles/aka Performers)		
Lundee Dundee/I'll Whisper In Your Ear (as the Versatiles)	60	Rocal 1002
A Wonderful Dream/Time Will Tell	62	Imperial 5855
A Little Bit Now/She's A Troublemaker	62	Imperial 5879
Anything You Can Do/What In The World	63	Imperial 5914
Tra-La-La/What Have You Been Doin'?	63	Imperial 5936
Get Up Now/One Happy Ending	63	Imperial 5968
Your Life Begins (At Sweet Sixteen)/Which Way Did She Go	63	Imperial 5991
I'll Be There/Ooh Wee Baby	63	Imperial 66009
Maldoneers (with the Deltairs)		
Maria My Love/What A Pity	73	Vintage 1015
Malibus		
Cry/Leave Me Alone	63	Planet 58
Mandells		
Darling, I'm Home/Who, Me?	61	Smart 323/Chess 1794 (61)
I Don't Have You/Because I Love You	61	Smart 325
It's No Good/Don't Know What You've Got	63	York 202
True Love Is Hard To Find/Doin' The Look	66	Jubilee 5519
Mandels		
The Scotch/My Kissin' Cousin	61	Lilly 502
Manderins		
Going Away/Let The Bells Ring	60	Band Box 236
Manhattans (1)		
How Do I Say I'm Sorry/Love Is Where You Find It	58	Warner 1015
Manhattans (2) (Eli Price & the)		
My Big Dream/That'll Make It Nice	59	Dooto 445
Manhattans (3)		
La-La-La/Sing All The Day	62	Capitol 4730
Manhattans (4) (Ronnie & the)		
Come On Back/Long Time No See	63	Enjoy 2008
Manhattans (5)		
Why Should I Cry/The Feeling Is Mutual	N/A	Big Mack 3911
Manis, Georgie (& group)		
Teen Angel/Hep, 2, 3, 4	58	Eclaire 105
Mann, Barry (bb the Edsels)		
Who Put The Bomp (In The Bomp, Bomp, Bomp)/Love, True Love	61	ABC 10237
Mann, Billy (& group)		
Lost Angel/Find Yourself Another Guy	56	Dig 111
A Million Heartaches Ago/Just Like Before	56	Dig 120
Mann, Gloria (& group)		
I Played The Fool/Pretty Eyes	55	Sound 114
Manselles		
Love Him/Paradise Is Where He Is	65	Diamond 172
Maples		
I Must Forget You/99 Guys	54	Blue Lake 111
Mar, Jerry (& group)		
Sittin' On Top Of The World/Brokenest Heart In Town	57	Amp-3 131

ARTIST/SONG	YEAR	LABEL
Mar-Vells (aka Mar-Vels)		
Go On And Have Yourself A Ball/How Do I Keep The Girls Away	63	Butane 778
Tonight	N/A	Harlem 1002
Mar-Vels (aka Mar-Vells)		
Cherry Lips/Could Be You	58	Love 5011/5012
Somewhere In Life/Voo Doo Hurt	61	Tammy 1016
My Guardian Angel/Marvel Stomp	61	Tammy 1019
Endless Nights/Surfing At Makaha	64	IN 102
Mar-Villes		
The Drag/Nights Are So Lonely	62	Infinity 027
Marathons (1)		
Don't Know Why/The Stranger	59	JC 101/Sabrina 334 (59)
Marathons (2) (aka Jayhawks/aka Vibrations)		
Peanut Butter/Talkin' Trash	61	Arvee 5027
Peanut Butter/Down In New Orleans	61	Chess 1790/Argo 5389 (61)
Little Pancho/Mashed Potatoes One More Time	62	Plaza 507
Gee	N/A	Collectables LP 5081
High Blood Pressure	N/A	Collectables LP 5081
Oink Jones	N/A	Collectables LP 5081
Marathons (3)		
C. Percy Mercy Of Scotland Yard/Tight Sweater	61	Arvee 5038
Chicken Spaceman/You Bug Me Baby	62	Arvee 5048
Marauders (Hayward Lee & the)		
Mother Dear	N/A	Jet
Marbles (aka Jewels)		
Golden Girl/Big Wig Walk	54	Lucky 002
Marcel, Vic (& group)		
Come Back To These Arms/That's My Girl	63	Don-But 17349
Marcels		
Blue Moon/ Goodbye To Love	61	Colpix 186
Summertime/Teeter Totter Love	61	Colpix 196
You Are My Sunshine/Find Another Fool	61	Colpix 606
Heartaches/My Love For You	61	Colpix 612
Merry Twist-Mas/Don't Cry For Me This Christmas	61	Colpix 617
My Melancholy Baby/Really Need Your Love	61	Colpix 624
Sunday Kind Of Love	61	Colpix LP 416
Baby Where Y'Been	62	Colpix (unreleased)
Tell Them About It	62	Colpix (unreleased)
Footprints In The Sand/Twistin' Fever	62	Colpix 629
Hold On/Flowerpot	62	Colpix 640
Friendly Loans/Loved Her The Whole Week Through	62	Colpix 651
All-Right-OK You Win/Lollipop Baby	62	Colpix 665
That Old Black Magic/Don't Turn Your Back On Me	63	Colpix 683
I Wanna Be The Leader/Give Me Back Your Love	63	Colpix 687
One Last Kiss/Teeter Totter Love	63	Colpix 694
One Last Kiss/You Got To Be Sincere	63	Colpix 694
Honestly Sincere	63	Colpix LP 454
Comes Love/Your Red Wagon	64	Kyra
Betty Lou/Take Me Back	73	Baron 109
In The Still Of The Night/High On a Hill	73	Queen Bee 47001
Peace Of Mind/That Lucky Old Sun	75	St. Clair 13711
Blue Heartaches	86	Murray Hill LP 000229
Lonely Boy/How Deep Is The Ocean	N/A	888 101
Crazy Bells In My Heart/Sunday Kind Of Love	N/A	Cycle 2001 (unreleased)
Take Me Back/Betty Lou	N/A	Jody 123
I'll Be Forever Loving You/A Fallen Tear	N/A	Monogram 112

ARTIST/SONG	YEAR	LABEL
Over The Rainbow/Sweet Was The Wine	N/A	Monogram 113
Two People In The World/Most Of All	N/A	Monogram 115

Marcels (as the Fabulous Marcels)

Peace Of Mind/Crazy Bells	N/A	Owl 324

Marchan, Bobby (bb the Clowns)

Quit My Job/Hush Your Mouth	60	Ace 595

Marchand, Donny (& group)

Round In Circles/Along Came Susie	60	Craft 3000

Marco (& group)

Let's Leave It That Way/I'm So Alone	63	Mohawk 135

Mareno, Lee (bb the Regents)

Goddess Of Love/He's Gone	61	New Art 103/Scepter 1222 (61)

Maresca, Ernie (bb the Del Satins)

Shout! Shout! (Knock Yourself Out)/Crying Like A Baby Over You	62	Seville 117
Mary Jane/Down On The Beach	62	Seville 119
Lorelei/The Love Express	63	Seville 125
Please Be Fair/Rovin' Kind	63	Seville 129

Margilators

Wait For Me/Arlinda	59	Blue Moon 409

Margilators (Toby & Ray & the)

Bom Do Wa/Just Waiting For You	59	Blue Moon 411

Marglows (Andy & the)

Just One Look/Symphony	63	Liberty 55570
I'll Get By/Superman Lover	63	Liberty 55627

Marie Ann (& group)

Dream Boy/High Heel Shoes	60	Warwick 605

Marie, Elena (& group)

Soldier Boy/Blue Mood	N/A	Gee Bee 01

Marigolds

Rollin' Stone/Why Don't You?	55	Excello 2057
Two Strangers/Love You, Love You, Love You	55	Excello 2061

Marigolds (Johnny Bragg & the)

Foolish Me/Beyond The Clouds	56	Excello 2078
It's You, Darling, It's You/Juke Box Rock 'n' Roll	56	Excello 2091

Mariners

Zindy Lou/Everybody's Doin' It Now	55	Cadence 1278

Mark III

Valerie/The Man	61	ABC 10280/BRB 100

Mark IV

(Make With) The Shake/45 R.P.M.	58	Cosmic 704
I Got A Wife/Ah-OOO-Ga	59	Mercury 71403
Dante's Inferno/Move Over Rover	59	Mercury 71445

Mark IVs

The Tide Has Turned/Whoa Baby, That's All	62	Barry 105

Mark V

Cry Baby/Bull Fight Cha Cha Cha	60	Milo 110

ARTIST/SONG	YEAR	LABEL
Mark, Ronald (& group)		
Moonlight Sky/And Now You're Gone	64	Gateway Custom 102
Markays (Doug Sahm & the)		
If You Ever Need Me/Why, Why, Why	61	Harlem 107/Swingin' 625 (61)
Markeets		
Teardrops/Baby Please	57	Melatone 1005
Markells		
The Letter Of Love/Darling I Really Love You	58	R&M 407/408
Markeys		
Eternal Love/You've Got Me On A String	56	20th Century 1210
Along Came Love/Special Delivery	58	Gone 5028
Yakity Yak/Hot Rod	58	RCA 7256
A Time To Love/Make A Record Man	58	RCA 7412
Marksmen		
Don't Gamble With My Heart	57	Mercury
Don't Gamble With My Heart/You Hurt Me So	57	Starday 320
Marktones		
Hold Me Close/Talk It Over	57	Ember 1022
Yes, Siree/Hey, Girlee	58	Ember 1030
Marland, Cletus (& group)		
I'll Take Care Of You/Like I Never Felt Before	61	Roulette 4388
Maroons		
Don't Leave Me Baby, Don't/Someday I'll Be The One	62	Queen 24012
Marquees (1)		
The Bells/The Rain	56	Grand 141
Marquees (2) (Billy Stewart & the)		
Baby, You're My Only Love/Billy's Heartache	57	Okeh 7095
Marquees (2) (gm Marvin Gaye)		
Hey Little School Girl/Wyatt Earp	57	Okeh 7096
Marquees (3)		
Say Hey/I'm In Misery	58	Len 100
Marquees (4)		
Love Machine/Who Will Be The First One	59	Warner Bros. 5072
Christmas In The Congo/Santa Done Got Hip	59	Warner Bros. 5127
Don't Be Mean, Geraldine/Until The Day I Die	60	Warner Bros. 5139
Marquees (4) (Terry Brown & the)		
That's The Way I Feel/Stay With Me	60	Jo-Ann 128
I Need A Helping Hand/Don't You Do Me Like That	61	Jo-Ann 130
Marquees (5)		
Ecstasy	59	Day-Sel 1001
Marquees (6)		
In The Halo Of Your Love/Can It Be Wrong	60	Do-Ra-Mi 1407
Marquis (1)		
I Don't Want Your Love/Popcorn Willie	56	Rainbow 358
Marquis (2)		
Bohemian Daddy/Hope He's True	56	Onyx 505/Relic 505 (64)

ARTIST/SONG	YEAR	LABEL
Marquis (3)		
Strange Is Love/Six Gun	59	Class 251
Marsh, Billy (& group)		
Run And Tell/Don't Tell Me	56	Arrow 716
Marshall Brothers		
Who'll Be The Fool From Now On/Mr. Santas Boogie	51	Savoy 825
Why Make A Fool Out Of Me/Just A Poor Boy In Love	52	Savoy 833
Marshalls (Bill Cook & the)		
A Soldier's Prayer/Just Because (by Bill Cook)	51	Savoy 828
Marshans		
I Remember/It's Almost Tomorrow	64	Etiquette
Marsmen (Marvin & Johnny & the)		
Jo Jo/How Long Has She Been Gone	54	Specialty 488
Martells (1) (aka Martels)		
Forgotten Spring/Va Va Voom	61	Cessna 477/Bella 45 (61)/Relic 517 (64)
Martells (2)		
Since I've Been Away/What Can I Do	65	Atco 6336
Martels (aka Martells (1))		
Where Did My Woman Go/Teacher Don't Keep Me In	59	Nasco 6026
Martels (Eulis Mason & the) (aka Martells (1))		
Rockin' Santa Claus/Carol Lee	59	Bella 20
Martin, Benny (& group)		
Darling Goodbye/This Is Why I Love You	60	Astro 109
Martin, Jerry (& group)		
Lovers Promise/Young Boy's Love	62	R 507
Martin, Kenny (& group)		
I'm Sorry/Yum Yum	58	Federal 12330
Now I Know/Tell Me Not To Go	59	Federal 12350
Ask Me/It's All Over	59	Federal 12354
Martin, Sonny (& group)		
When True Love Is Gone/How To Win Your Love	59	Rocko 518
Martin, Steve (& group)		
Lonely Little Girl/My Little Angel	63	Magnasound 700
Martin, Trade (& group)		
Joanne/Liverpool Baby	64	Coed 594
Martinels		
Baby, Think It Over/I Don't Care	63	Success 110
Martineques		
Tonight Is Another Night/Unknown Love	62	Danceland 777/Roulette 4423 (62)
Broken Hearted Me/Everything Will Be Alright	62	Danceland 779
If You Want To Call Me	65	Me O 1002
Martino, Lou (& group)		
Someone To Watch Over Me/Please (Give Me A Little Love)	64	Columbia 43126

ARTIST/SONG	YEAR	LABEL
Marvel, Tina (& male group)		
I Can't Love No One But You/Beautiful Love	63	Lu Pine 121
Marveleers		
For The Longest Time/One-Sided Love Affair	53	Derby 829
All My Heart/I've Only Myself To Blame	53	Derby 842
Love Me, Want Me/I Miss You Most Of All	53	Derby 844
These Are The Things We'll Share/Marlina, Marlina	55	Dot 15320
Marvelettes		
Forever/Locking Up My Heart	63	Tamla 54077
Marveliers		
When We Dance/Down	60	Cougar 1868
Little Girl/The Spider	N/A	Joanie 4439
Marvellos (1)		
Red Hot Momma/I Need A Girl	55	Marvello 5005
You're The Dream/Calypso Mama	55	Theron 117
Come Back My Love/Boyee Yoing	58	Stepheny 1818/Cha Cha 756
Marvellos (2)		
She Told Me Lies/Salty Sam	62	Exodus 6214/Reprise 20008 (62)
I Ask Of You/Hip Enough	62	Exodus 6216
Marvells (aka Marvels (2))		
Did She Leave You/Lovely Charms	59	Magnet 1005
Miracle Of Life/What About The Mountain	61	Finer Arts 2019
For Sentimental Reasons/Come Back	61	Winn 1916
How Could You Hurt Me So/Cause I'm Loving You	62	Finer Arts 2024
Tomorrow/I'm A Fool For Losing You	62	Finer Arts 2026
This Can't Go On	N/A	Yorsey
Marvels (1) (aka Dubs)		
I Won't Have You Breaking My Heart/Jump, Rock And Roll	56	ABC 9771
Marvels (1) (Harry M & the)		
What's The Use/The "U-T	61	ABC 10243
Marvels (2) (aka Marvells/aka Gales/aka Senators (2))		
So Young, So Sweet/I Shed So Many Tears	58	Laurie 3016
Marvels (3)		
Just Another Fool/You Crack Me Up	59	Mun Rab 1008
Marvels (4)		
Somewhere In Love (You'll Find Your Love)	60	Bishop 1002
Marvels (5)		
Guiding Angel/Hallelulu-la	62	Pyramid 6211/Jason Scott 42021
Marvels (5) (Neil Sedaka & the)		
Oh Delilah/Neil's Twist	62	Pyramid 623
Marveltones		
So (It's Over)/My Heart Is Yours	52	Regent 194
Three Sundays/Care	52	Regent 196
Marx		
One Minute More/You Are My Love	N/A	Chante 1002
One More Time/You Are My Love	N/A	Dahlia 1002
Mascots (1)		
The Story Of My Heart/Do The Wiggle	60	King 5377
Lonely Rain/That's The Way I Feel	60	King 5435

ARTIST/SONG	YEAR	LABEL
Mascots (2)		
Once Upon A Love/Hey Little Angel	62	Blast 206
Bluebirds Over The Mountain/Timberlands	62	Mermaid 107
Mason, Barbara (bb the Larks)		
Dedicated To You	64	Crusader/Arctic (65)
Mason, Little Billy (bb the Rhythm Jesters)		
Make Me Your Own/I Love My Baby	56	Rama 212
School Kid/Young, Broke And In Love	57	Gee 1042
Thinking Of You/You Are My Sunshine	57	Rama 223
Mason, Peter (& group)		
Lonely Drummer Boy/Thank Heaven For Little Girls	60	Lawn 105
Masquerades (aka Seaphus Scott & the Five Masqueraders)		
These Red Roses/Mister Man The Guitar Man	60	Formal 1011/
		Formal 1012 (remastered)
Fanessa/The Whip	61	Boyd 1027
Good Golly Miss Molly	N/A	unreleased
Portia	N/A	unreleased
That's When Your Heartaches Begin	N/A	unreleased
These Foolish Things	N/A	unreleased
Masquins (Tony & the)		
My Angel Eyes/Fugi Womma	61	Ruthie 1000
Massey, Barbara (& group)		
You Call Me Angel/I'll Tell You In The Morning	61	Imperial 5786
Massi, Nick (& group)		
Little Pony	N/A	One Way 244
Master Four		
It's Not The End/Love From The Far East	N/A	Tay-Ster 6012
Masterettes (female)		
Never Never/Follow The Leader	58	Le Sage 716
Masters (1) (Scotty Mann & the)		
Just A Little Bit Of Loving/The Mystery Man	56	Peacock 1665
Masters (2) (Thurston Harris & the)		
I Hear A Rhapsody/Purple Stew	58	Aladdin 3440
Masters (3)		
Johnny Clean-Up/'Til I Return	58	Len 103
Masters (4)		
I'm Searching/Crying My Heart Out	58	Le Sage 713/714
A Lovely Way To Spend An Evening/Dore's Blues	60	Bingo 1008
A Man Is Not Supposed To Cry/Look Out	61	End 1100
Masters (5) (Rick & the)		
Bewitched Bothered And Bewildered/A Kissin' Friend	62	Haral 778
Flame Of Love/Here Comes Nancy	62	Taba 101/Cameo 226 (62)
Let It Please Be You/I Don't Want Your Love	63	Cameo 247
Masters, Johnny (bb the Crests)		
Say It Isn't So/The Great Physician	60	Coed 527
Mastertones (1)		
Tell Me/What'll You Do?	54	Bruce 111/Tip Top
Are You Lonely/I Made A Boo Boo	N/A	Future 1001

ARTIST/SONG	YEAR	LABEL
Mastertones (2)		
Fannie Mae	59	Band Box 226
Mastertones (2) (Elaine Taylor & the)		
Yes Sir, That's My Baby/Baby Won't You Please Come Home	60	Band Box 233
Mastertones (2) (Scotty & Bobo & the)		
For The Rest Of My Life/Mamacita Mia	60	Band Box 238
Mastertones (3) (fb Ray Williams)		
Baby (You Got To Change)/I Want To Know	61	Le Cam 717
Matadors (1)		
Vengeance (Will Be Mine)/Pennies From Heaven	58	Sue 700
Be Good To Me/Have Mercy Baby	58	Sue 701
Matadors (2) (Hank Ayala & the)		
Betty Jo/Handsome	59	Back Beat 530
Matadors (3)		
Listen/So Near	62	Jamie 1226
If You Left Me Today/It Ain't Nothin' But Rock 'N' Roll	63	Keith 6502
You'd Be Crying Too/My Foolish Heart	63	Keith 6504
Matadors (4)		
Ace Of Hearts/Perfidia	63	Colpix 698
La Corrida/I've Gotta Drive (by Jan & Dean)	64	Colpix 718
C'mon, Let Yourself Go/C'mon, Let Yourself Go, Pt. 2	64	Colpix 741
Matadors (5) (Tommy Liss & the)		
Just In Make Believe/Time Is Tough	63	Saxony 1005
Matadors (6)		
If I Had Another Chance/Nonsense	61	Duchess 1005
Matadors (7)		
Let Me Dream/Wobble Wobble	66	Forbes 230/Chartmaker 404
Matadors (8)		
Please Say You Want Me/Should I Ever Love Again	63	Lee 5466
Matches		
She Laughed At Me/Gonna Build Myself A Castle	N/A	Jaguar 712
Mates (Marci & the)		
Shall I Tell Him You're Not Here/Let Us Part For A Year	62	Big Top 3116
Suddenly We're Strangers/Oops, There Goes Another Year	63	Big Top 3136
Mathews Brothers		
Stupid/Mora Dora	63	ABC 10473
Matthews, Dino (& group)		
The Girl That I Love/Lenore	62	Dot 16365
Maye, Hartsy (& group)		
As The Years Go By	N/A	Zell 4397
Mayfield, Percy (& group)		
Please Believe Me/Diggin' The Moonglow	57	Specialty 607
One Love/My Reward (no group)	59	Imperial 5577
Maytones (Percy Mayfield & the)		
The Voice Within/Baby, You're Rich	54	Specialty 544

ARTIST/SONG	YEAR	LABEL
McCain, Jerry (& group)		
Love Me Right/Ting Tang Tagalu	65	Continental 777
McCall, Little J. (& group)		
My Love I Can't Hide/Half Ton Tillie	61	Wow 1000/Donna 1334 (61)
McCallister, Lon (& group)		
One Desire/Empty Heart	61	Apt 25061
McCleese, James (& group)		
I Love You So/A Million Tears	61	Marco 106
McCline, Charles (& group)		
You Conquered Me/Say That You Care	64	Larry-O 101
McCoy, Van (& group)		
Mr. D.J./Never Trust A Friend	61	Rock'N 101
McDonald, Ken (& group)		
One Love Alone/The Picture	58	Prep 128
McDowall, Chester (& group)		
I Wonder Why/Baby Don't Leave me	59	Duke 302
McElroy, Sollie (& female group)		
Angel Girl/Party Time	N/A	Ja-Wes 101
McFadden, Ruth (bb the Harptones)		
School Boy/United We Stand (no group)	56	Old Town 1030
McGee, Al (& group)		
Lucky Joe/You Can Count On Me	61	Aries 7-10-2
Tender Beloved/Oldies But Goodies Show	61	Donna 1348
McHugh, Jimmy (& group)		
I Don't Want Everything/Do The Kangaroo	63	Success 106
McHugh, Richie (& group)		
Jo Ann	63	Raewood 587
McKnight, June (& group)		
Why Don't You Come Home	62	Jeanne 1225
McNeil, Angele (& group)		
Can You Tell Me Why/Please Daddy	57	Felsted 8503
McPhatter, Clyde (& female group)		
I'm Lonely Tonight/Thirty Days	56	Atlantic 1106
McPhatter, Clyde (& female group))		
I'm Not Worthy Of You/Seven Days	55	Atlantic 1081
McPhatter, Clyde (& group)		
Let The Boogie Woogie Roll (with the Drifters)/Deep Sea Ball (with the Cookies & the Cues)	60	Atlantic 2060
I Just Want To Love You/You're For Me	60	Mercury 71692
McPhatter, Clyde (bb the Cookies & the Cues)		
Just To Hold My Hand (Cues only)/No Matter What	57	Atlantic 1133
Heartaches/Long Lonely Nights (Cues only)	57	Atlantic 1149
You'll Be There/Rock And Cry	57	Atlantic 1158
No Love Like Her Love/That's Enough For Me	58	Atlantic 1170
A Lover's Question (Cues only)/I Can't Stand Up Alone	58	Atlantic 1199
Since You've Been Gone/Try Try Baby	59	Atlantic 2028
You Went Back On Your Word/There You Go (with the Drifters)	59	Atlantic 2038
Go! Yes Go!/If I Didn't Love You Like I Do (with the Drifters)	60	Atlantic 2082

ARTIST/SONG	YEAR	LABEL

McPhatter, Clyde (bb the Cues)

| I Make Believe/Without Love (There Is Nothing) | 56 | Atlantic 1117 |

McPhatter, Clyde (bb the Drifters)

| Don't Dog Me/Just Give Me A Ring (with the Cookies & the Cues) | 60 | Atlantic 2049 |

Meadowbrooks

| Seems Like Only Yesterday/Time After Time | 65 | Catamount 106 |
| Lovers Quarrel (a capella)/Is Everybody Happy (a capella) | 65 | Catamount 108 |

Meadowlarks

Brother Bill/Raisin' A Ruckus	51	Imperial 5146
Real Pretty Mama/Love Only You	54	RPM 399
LSMFT Blues/Pass The Gin	54	RPM 406
Lie/The Booglay	64	Magnum 716

Meadowlarks (Don Julian & the)

Love Only You/Real Pretty Mama	54	RPM 399
Heaven And Paradise/Embarrassing Moments	55	Dootone 359
Always And Always/I Got Tore Up	55	Dootone 367
This Must Be Paradise/Mine All Mine	55	Dootone 372
Thrill Me Night And Day	55	Dootone EP 203
Please Love A Fool/Oop Boopy Oop	56	Dootone 394/
		Original Sound 004 (58)
I Am A Believer/Boogie Woogie Teenage	56	Dootone 405
Blue Moon/Big Momma Wants To Rock	57	Dooto 424
Untrue	57	Dooto LP 224
Please Say You Love Me/Doin' The Cha Cha Cha	58	Original Sound 03
Blue Mood/There's A Girl	59	Original Sound 12
Popeye/Heaven Only Knows	62	Dynamite 1112
Slauson Shuffle, Pt. 1/Slauson Shuffle, Pt. 2	62	Dynamite 1114
Philly Jerk/How Can You Be So Foul	65	Jerk 100
Everytime	N/A	Chance

Meadows, Larry (& group)

| Phyllis/We're Through | 59 | Strato-Lite 969 |

Med-Tones (Johnny Daril & the)

| Come Back/Weak In My Knees | 59 | Vita 188 |

Medalions (aka Medallions (3))

| Love Letters/Since You've Gone Away | 60 | Card 1 |

Medallionaires

| Magic Moonlight/Teen-Age Caravan | 58 | Mercury 71309 |

Medallions (1)

How/Meet Me Tonight	54	Dootone 344 (unreleased)
The Letter/Buick '59	54	Dootone 347
The Telegram/Coupe De Ville Baby	55	Dootone 357
Edna/Speedin'	55	Dootone 364
Dear Darling/Don't Shoot Baby	55	Dootone 379
I Want A Love/Dance And Swing	56	Dootone 393
Give Me The Right/She's The One (by the Penguins)	60	Dooto 456 EP

Medallions (1) (Johnny Twovoice & the)

| My Pretty Baby/I'll Never Love Again | 55 | Dootone 373 |

Medallions (1) (Vernon Green & the)

Shedding Tears For You/Pushbutton Automobile	56	Dootone 400
Did You Have Fun?/My Mary Lou	56	Dootone 407
For Better Or For Worse/I Wonder, I Wonder, I Wonder	57	Dooto 419
A Lover's Prayer/Unseen	57	Dooto 425
Magic Mountain/'59 Volvo	59	Dooto 446
Behind The Door/Rocket Ship	59	Dooto 454

ARTIST/SONG	YEAR	LABEL
Deep, So Deep/Dear Ann	62	Pan World 10000
Dear Ann/Shimmy Shimmy Shake	62	Pan World 71
Look At Me, Look At Me/Am I Ever Gonna See My Baby Again	64	Minit 30234
Can You Talk/You Don't Know	73	Dootone 479

Medallions (2)

I Know/Laki-Lani	55	Essex 901

Medallions (3) (aka Medalions)

A Broken Heart/Lolo Baby	57	Singular 1002
Love That Girl/Carachi	59	Sultan 1004

Medallions (4)

I Love You True/My Baby's Gone	61	Sarg 191
Lovin' Time/Home Town	61	Sarg 194
You Are Irresistible/Why Do You Look At Me	62	Reo 8693/Lenox 5556 (62)

Medwick, Joe (& group)

Searchin' In Vain/Johnny Brown	59	Duke 311

Mel-O-Aires (Rudy Jackson & the)

I'm Crying/Enfold Me	55	R&B 1310

Mel-O-Dots

One More Time/Just How Long	52	Apollo 1192
Baby Won't You Please Come Home	89	Relic LP 5077
Rock My Baby	89	Relic LP 5077

Mellards

That's Life/Love Me Crazy	56	Ballad 1016

Mellards (Fred Green & the)

My Sweetheart/You Can't Keep Love	55	Ballad 1012

Mello Kings

The Kiss/Shirley	50	Imperial 5105

Mello-Chords

Golden Vanity/Desperado	61	Lyco 1001

Mello-Dees (Herman Griffin & the)

Hurry Up And Marry Me/Do You Want To See My Baby	60	Anna 1115/Stepp 237

Mello-Fellows

Iddy Biddy Baby/My Friend Charlie	54	Lamp 8006

Mello-Harps

I Love Only You/Ain't Got The Money	55	Tin Pan Alley 145/146
Love Is A Vow/Valerie	56	Do-Re-Mi 203
What Good Are My Dreams?/Gone	56	Tin Pan Alley 157/158
I Couldn't Believe My Bleeding Heart	56	Tin Pan Alley 159
Gumma Gumma/No Good	59	Casino 104

Mello-Kings (aka Mellokings/aka Mellotones (1))

Tonight, Tonight/Do Baby Do	57	Herald 502 (second pressing, first is by Mellotones)
Chapel On The Hill/Sassafras	57	Herald 507
Baby Tell Me (Why, Why, Why)/The Only Girl (I'll Ever Love)	58	Herald 511
Valerie/She's Real Cool	58	Herald 518
Running To You/Chip Chip	59	Herald 536
Our Love Is Beautiful/Dear Mr. Jock	60	Herald 548
Kid Stuff/I Promise	60	Herald 554
Til There Were None/Penny	61	Herald 561
Love At First Sight/She's Real Cool	61	Herald 567
Walk Softly/But You Lied	62	Lescay 3009
Thrill Me	N/A	Relic LP 5035

ARTIST/SONG	YEAR	LABEL
Mello-Larks (Vince Massey & the)		
Smile/Did I Remember	53	Herald 414
Mello-Maids (female)		
Oh-h-h/Will You Ever Say You're Mine	56	Baton 231
I Remember, Dear/A Million Years Ago	57	Baton 238
Mello-Men		
My Love, The Blues, And Me/I'd Give A Million Yesterdays	53	MGM 11607
Mello-Moods		
I Couldn't Sleep A Wink Last Night/ And You Just Can't Go Through Life Alone	52	Red Robin 104
How Could You/Where Are You? (Now That I Need You)	52	Red Robin 105
I'm Lost/When I Woke Up This Morning	53	Prestige 856/Hamilton 143 (53)
How Could You (different version from Red Robin 105)	64	Oldies 45 167
Mello-Moods (bb Teacho Wiltshire Band)		
Call On Me/I Tried And Tried And Tried	52	Prestige 799
Mello-Queens (John Lester & the)		
Getting Nearer/At Last	59	C&M 500
Mello-Tone 3 (Little E & the)		
Bye Bye Pretty Baby/Candy Apple Red Impala	61	Falco 302
Mello-Tones (1)		
I'm Just Another One In Love With You/I'm Gonna Get	54	Decca 48319
Little Bit More/When Love Is Young	58	Key 5804
Mello-Tones (1) (Marga Benitez & the)		
Man Love Woman/Winos On Parade	54	Decca 48318
Mello-Tones (2)		
Rosie Lee/I'll Never Fall In Love Again	57	Fascination 1001/Gee 1037 (57)
Ca-Sandra/Rattlesnake Roll	57	Gee 1040
Mello-Tones (2) (Nat Williams & the)		
You Excite Me/A Friend	59	Aries 1014
Mellomen (Kitty White & the)		
If You Only Take The Time/Someone Like Joe	55	Century 711
Mellomen (Scatman Crothers & the)		
Dearest One/Keep That Coffee Hot	55	Century 710
Mellomoods		
Song Of Love/That Dubonnet Wine	54	Recorded In Hollywood 399
Mellomoods (Chuck Higgins & the)		
Beautiful Love/Rock & Roll (instrumental)	56	Money 214
Mellos (Terri Corin & the)		
Truly, I Love You Truly/Why Did You Do It	N/A	Rider 108
Mellos (Terry & the)		
Love Express/The Bell's Of St. Mary's	60	Amy 812
Mellotones (1) (aka Mello Kings)		
Tonight, Tonight/Do Baby Do	57	Herald 502 (first pressing, second is by Mello-Kings)
Mellotones (2) (Doug Williams & the)		
Sorrow Valley/The Battle Of Jericho	58	Hy-Tone 103/Hy-Tone 122 (59)
Send Me/Trust In God	59	Hy-Tone 125

ARTIST/SONG	YEAR	LABEL

Mellow Drops

When I Grow Too Old To Dream/The Crazy Song	54	Imperial 5324
I Want Your Love	N/A	Imperial (unreleased)
She'll Stand Up For You	N/A	Imperial (unreleased)

Mellow Jacks

Gina Baby/Mellow You Down	62	Marquee/Ascot 2115 (62)

Mellow Keys

Listen, Baby/I'm Not A Deceiver	56	Gee 1014

Mellow Larks

Farewell To You My Love/Sing A Silly Sing Song	57	Argo 5285

Mellows

How Sentimental Can I Be?/Nothin' To Do	54	Jay-Dee 793
Be Mine	89	Relic LP 5080

Mellows (Carl Spencer & the)

Farewell, Farewell/No More Loneliness	56	Candlelight 1012

Mellows (Lillian Leach & the)

Smoke From Your Cigarette/Pretty Baby, What's Your Name?	55	Jay-Dee 797
I Was A Fool To Let You Go/I Still Care	55	Jay-Dee 801
Yesterday's Memories/Lovable Lily	55	Jay-Dee 807
My Darling/Lucky Guy	56	Celeste 3002
Sweet Lorraine/I'm Yours	56	Celeste 3004
I Call To You	74	Relic LP 5014
So Strange	89	Relic LP 5080
Ain't She Got Nerve (acappella)/You're Gone	57	Celeste 3008
When The Lights Go On Again/	57	Celeste 3009
I'm Gonna Pick Your Teeth With An Ice Pick (a capella)		

Mellows (Lillian Lee & the)

Moon Of Silver/You've Gone	56	Candlelight 1011

Mellows (Mack Starr & the)

Drifting Apart/Oh, My Love	62	Cub 9117

Melo Gents

Baby Be Mine/Get Off My Back	59	Warner Bros. 5056

Melo-Aires

You Know Baby/Indebted To You	58	Nasco 6019

Melo-Aires (Rudy Jackson & the)

Teasing Me/Give Me Your Hand	57	Imperial 5425

Melodears

Summer Romance/Charock	58	Gone 5033
It's Love Because/They Don't Say	59	Gone 5040

Melodeers

Rudolph The Red-Nosed Reindeer/Wishing Is For Fools	60	Studio 9908
The Letter/Nairna Nairna	61	Shelley 127
Happy Teen-Age Times/Goo Goo (Sounds)	61	Studio 9909
Born To Be Mine/Three Deuces And Twin Pipes	62	Shelley 161

Melodeers (Tony Thomas & the)

Say You Care/Sometimes I'm Happy	55	Capri 777

Melodees

Daddy Daddy	60	Nu Kat 124

ARTIST/SONG	YEAR	LABEL
Melodettes (Norman Dunlap with the)		
A Dream And A Prayer/It's Easy To Remember	53	Aladdin 3213
Melody Masters		
I'll Never Be The Same/Problem Child	59	Renown 107
Melodymacks (George Mack & the)		
I Want To Be With You Baby	N/A	Mac
Melodymakers		
Let's Make Love Worthwhile/Carolina Moon	57	Hollis 1001
Melotones		
Father Time/Prayer Of Love	52	Lee Tone 700
Melson, Joe (& group)		
Love Is A Dangerous Thing/Dance	62	Hickory 1175
Melvettes		
Take One Step/Quiet Now	N/A	Tela-Star 110
Melvetts (Joyce Spivey & the)		
Dreaming/Angel	65	Olimpic 254
Memories (1)		
Love Bells/I Promise	62	Way-Lin 101
Memories (2) (Danny & the)		
Don't Go/Can't Help Lovin' That Girl Of Mine	64	Valiant 6049
Memories (3)		
Darling You're My Angel/Will I	64	Times Square 11/ Times Square 95 (64)
Love Me Once Again	N/A	Klik
Memos		
My Type Of Girl/The Biddy Leg	59	Memo 34891
I'm Going Home/My Most Precious Possession	59	Memo 5000/5001
Mendell, Johnny (& group)		
Pretty Little Rita/Please Be My Love	62	Jamie 1214
Merceedees (with the Individuals (4))		
Please Baby, Be Mine/Not Me	62	Gold Seal 1000
Mercurys		
Someone Touched Me/The B. B. Bug	59	Madison 119
Meridians		
Blue Victory/Have You Forgotten	N/A	Parnaso 107
Blame My Heart/He Can't Dance	N/A	Parnaso 120
Merri Men (Robin Hood & His) (aka Robin Hood & His Merry Men)		
Maryann/We Had A Quarrel	61	Delsey 303
Merry Men (1) (Robin Hood & His) (aka Robin Hood & His Merri Men)		
Mister Santa, Bring Me A Doll/Ellen	62	Mohawk 130
Merry Men (2) (Steve Douglas & His)		
Yes Sir, That's My Baby/Lt. Colonel Bogey's Parade	62	Philles 104
Metallics		
Drop By/Get Lost	62	Baronet 14
Let Me Love You/In The Middle Of The Night	62	Baronet 16
It Hurts Me/I'll Conquer The World	62	Baronet 18
Need Your Love/Itchy Twitchy Too	62	Baronet 2

ARTIST/SONG	YEAR	LABEL
Metaphors		
You Have Everything/Come On Back	N/A	Rad (no #)
Meteors (1) (Junior Thompson with the)		
Mama's Little Baby/Raw Deal	56	Meteor 5029
Meteors (2)		
Let's Start Anew/Trying To Get Back Home	63	Beltone 2041
Meteors (3) (Jimmy Dee & the)		
Don't Hurt Me No More/Wanda	61	Pixie 7411
Meter-Tones		
Believe In Me/Talk To Me	59	Jax 1002
Metrics		
I Found You/Wishes	64	Chadwick 101
Metro-Chords		
It's A Shame/Slide My Baby Slide	61	Admiral 300
Metro-Liners		
I Don't Stand A Ghost Of A Chance/	76	Catamount 132
Your Troubles Will Be My Troubles		
Metronomes (1)		
Ride/I Want You	53	Specialty 462 (unreleased)
Metronomes (1) (Gene Moore & the)		
She's Gone/That's Bad	53	Specialty 472
Metronomes (2)		
I Love My Girl/I'm Gonna Get Me A Girl Somehow	57	Cadence 1310
Dear Don/How Much I Love You	57	Cadence 1339
Heaven Help Me	N/A	Cadence (unreleased)
Lonely Woman	N/A	Cadence (unreleased)
Embraceable You	60	Wynne EP
Pennies From Heaven	60	Wynne EP
Metronomes (3)		
Tears Tears Tears/Hot Time	62	Challenge 9157
My Dearest Darling/The Chickie-Goo	62	Maureen 1000
Back Door Blues/This Could Be The Start Of Something Big	62	Riverside 4523
Metronomes (4) (Leon & the)		
Buy This Record For Me/I'll Catch You On The Rebound	65	Carnival 515
Metronomes (5)		
If You Care/Fountain Of Love	N/A	Milestone
Metropolitans		
So Much In Love/My Heart Is True	58	Junior 395
Metros (1) (Eddie Joy & the)		
Young Love Is An Old Story	59	Dart 1008
Metros (2)		
Lookin'/All My Life	67	Just 1502
Metros (3)		
Someone	N/A	Ra-Sel
Metrotones (1)		
A-Ting-A-Ling/Tonight	55	Columbia 40420
Write Me Baby/Even Then	55	Columbia 40486

ARTIST/SONG	YEAR	LABEL
Metrotones (2)		
More And More	57	Reserve 114
Metrotones (2) (bb the Little Walkin' Willie Quartet)		
Please Come Back/Skitter, Skatter	57	Reserve 116
Miamians		
Call Me A Coward/When My Teenage Days Are Through	58	Amp-3 1006
Michels, Ginny (& group)		
True Confession/Everyone Was There	62	Mala 446
Mid Knights		
Charlena	N/A	Arc 1028
Mid-Knighters		
Flower Of Love/Charlena	N/A	Paragon 814
Middleton, Tony (& group)		
Count Your Blessings/I Just Want Somebody	59	Triumph 600
Middletones		
Ain't Gonna Waste No Tears On You	55	Cadillac 156
Midnight Lighters (Hank Ballard & the) (aka Midnighters)		
Finger Poppin' Time/From The Love Side	72	Polydor 14128
Midnight Riders (Kasandrea & the)		
Turtle Dovin'/I Couldn't Let You Down	59	Imperial 5638
Midnighters (aka Royals (1))		
Work With Me Annie/Sinner's Prayer	53	Federal 12169
Work With Me Annie/Until I Die	53	Federal 12169
Give It Up/That Woman	53	Federal 12177
Sexy Ways/Don't Say Your Last Goodbye	54	Federal 12185
Annie Had A Baby/She's The One	54	Federal 12195
Annie's Aunt Fanny/Crazy Loving (Stay With Me)	54	Federal 12200
Stingy Little Thing/Tell Them	54	Federal 12202
Moonrise/She's The One	54	Federal 12205
Ring-A-Ling-A-Ling/Ashamed Of Myself	55	Federal 12210
Switchie Witchie Titchie/Why Are We Apart	55	Federal 12220
Henry's Got Flat Feet (Can't Dance No More)/Whatsoever We Do	55	Federal 12224
It's Love Baby/Looka Here	55	Federal 12227
Give It Up/That Woman	55	Federal 12230
That House On The Hill/Rock And Roll Wedding	55	Federal 12240
Don't Change Your Pretty Ways/We'll Never Meet Again	55	Federal 12243
Sweet Mama Do Right/Partners For Life	56	Federal 12251
Open Up The Back Door/Rock Granny Roll	56	Federal 12260
Tore Up Over You/Early One Morning	56	Federal 12270
I'll Be Home Some Day/Come On A Get It	56	Federal 12285
Let Me Hold Your Hand/Ooh Bah Baby	57	Federal 12288
In The Doorway Crying/E Basta Cosi	57	Federal 12293
Oh So Happy/Is Your Love For Real	57	Federal 12299
Let 'Em Roll/What Made You Change Your Mind	57	Federal 12305
Daddy's Little Baby/Stay By My Side	58	Federal 12317
Baby Please/Ow Wow Oo Wee	58	Federal 12339
Don't Go I Love You	60	King LP 700
Young Lady	60	King LP 700
Midnighters (fb Henry Moore)		
Doin' Everything/Big Frog	61	King 5513

ARTIST/SONG   YEAR LABEL

The Midnighters

Midnighters (Hank Ballard & the) (aka Royals (1))

The Twist/Teardrops On Your Letter	59	King 5171/Federal 12345 (59)
Kansas City/I'll Keep You Happy	59	King 5195
Sugaree/Rain Down Tears	59	King 5215
House With No Windows/Cute Little Ways	59	King 5245
Never Knew/I Could Love You	59	King 5275
Look At Little Sister/I Said I Wouldn't Beg You	59	King 5289
The Coffee Grind/Waiting	60	King 5312
Finger Poppin' Time/I Love You, I Love You So-o-o	60	King 5341
Let's Go, Let's Go, Let's Go/If You'd Forgive Me	60	King 5400
The Hoochi Coochi Coo/I'm Thinking Of You	60	King 5430
Rock Junction/Spongie	61	King 5449
Let's Go Again/Deep Blue Sea	61	King 5459
The Continental Walk/What's This I See?	61	King 5491
The Switch-A-Roo/The Float	61	King 5510
Nothing But Good/Keep On Dancing	61	King 5535
Can't You See, I Need A Friend/Big Red Sunset	61	King 5550
I'm Gonna Miss You/Do You Remember?	61	King 5578
Do You Know How To Twist/Broadway	62	King 5593
It's Twistin' Time/Autumn Breeze	62	King 5601
Good Twistin' Tonight/I'm Young	62	King 5635
I Want To Thank You/Excuse Me	62	King 5655
When I Need You/Dreamworld	62	King 5677
I Love And Care For You/Shakey Mae	62	King 5693
She's The One/Bring Me Your Love	62	King 5703
The Rising Tide/All The Things I Love	62	King 5713
That Low Down Move/House On The Hill	63	King 5719
Christmas Time For Everyone But Me/Santa Claus Is Coming	63	King 5729
Walkin' And Talkin'/How Could You Leave	63	King 5746
Those Lonely, Lonely Feelings/It's Love	63	King 5798
Buttin' In/I'm Learning	63	King 5821
Don't Let Temptation/Have Mercy	64	King 5835
Don't Fall In Love With Me/I'm So Mad	64	King 5860
These Young Girls/I Don't Know But One	64	King 5884

ARTIST/SONG	YEAR	LABEL
Stay Away From My Baby/She's Got Soul	64	King 5901
What's Your Name/Daddy Rolling Stone	64	King 5931
A Winner Never Quits/Let's Get Show	64	King 5954
One Monkey Don't Stop The Show/Watch What.....	64	King 5963
Poppin' The Whip/You Just You	65	King 5996
Sloop And Slide/My Sun Is Going Down	65	King 6018
I'm Ready/Togetherness	65	King 6031
He Came Along/Annie Had A Baby	66	King 6055
You're In Real Good Hands/Unwind Yourself	67	King 6119
Funky Soul Train/Which Way Should I Turn	67	King 6131
You Can't Keep A Good Man Down	69	King LP 1052
Hey There Sexy Lady/Hey There Sexy Lady (instrumental)	74	Stang 5058

Midnighters (Henry Booth & the)

Every Beat Of My Heart/Starting From Tonight	60	DeLuxe 6190

Midnighters (Lil' Ray & the)

Loretta/My Girl	64	Impact 30

Midnights

Annie Pulled A Hum-Bug/Hear My Plea	54	Music City 746
She Left Me/Cheating On Me	54	Music City 762

Midnite Raiders (Mills Allen & the)

Dorothy Jane	N/A	Black Gold 304

Midniters (Al Chase & the)

Oh Yes My Darling/Lubby Lou	60	Jin 118

Miflin Triplets

I Do/Someone Should Have Told Me	58	Ember 1045

Mighty Dukes

Not Other Love/Why Can't I Have You	52	Duke 104

Mighty Jupiters

Your Love/Hy Wocky Toomba	58	Warner 1020

Mighty Mellotones

Beams Of Heaven	N/A	Honey-B 1017

Milestones

Roasted Peanuts/One Week Romance (by the Calendars)	61	Swingin' 649

Milky Ways

Teenage Island/My Love	60	Liberty 55255

Miller Brothers

Try/If I Had A Car	58	Mercury 71293
Let Me Know/Lawrence Was His Name	63	Coed 577

Miller Sisters (female)

Until You're Mine/Hippity Ha	55	Herald 455/Herald 527 (58)
There Is No Right Way To Do Me Wrong/You Can Tell Me	55	Sun 230
Guess Who/How Am I To Know	56	Ember 1004
Someday You Will Pay/You Didn't Think I Would	56	Flip 504
Please Don't Leave/Do You Wanna Go	56	Hull 718
Finders Keepers/Ten Cats Down	56	Sun 255
The Flip Skip/Let's Start Anew	57	Acme 111/Acme 721 (58)
You Made A Promise/Crazy Billboard Song	57	Acme 717
My Own/Sugar Candy	57	Onyx 507
Just Wait And See/Black Pepper (instrumental by Leo Price)	60	Hull 736
Oh Lover/Remember That	60	Miller 1140
Pony Dance/Give Me Some Old Fashioned Love	60	Miller 1141
Please Mr. D.J.	60	Miller 1143

RTIST/SONG	YEAR	LABEL
Pop Your Finger/You Got To Reap What You Sow	61	Glodis 1003
I Cried All Night/Holly Golly Reel	62	Hull 752
I Miss You So/Dance Little Sister	62	Rayna 5001
Oh Why/Walk On	62	Rayna 5004
Tell Him/Dance Close	63	Riverside 4535
Baby Your Baby/Silly Girl	63	Roulette 4491
Cooncha/Feel Good	64	Stardust 3001
Looking Over My Life/Si Senor	65	Yorktown 75
I'm Telling It Like It Is/Until You Come Home I'll Walk Alone	67	GMC 10006
Hey You	N/A	Capri

iller Sisters (Jeannie & the) (female)

Don't You Forget/Roll Back The Rug (And Twist)	62	Hull 750

illionaires (1) (aka Blenders (1))

Somebody's Lyin'/Kansas Kapers	55	Davis 441

illionaires (2)

Cherry Baby/I Thought About You	65	Bunny 506

illionaires (3) (Rocky & the)

Remember Me/Frisco Sands	63	Orchestra 102

illionaires (4) (Benny Curtis & the)

I Wonder/Troubles	61	Bridges 1102

illionaires (5) (fb Ben E. King) (ref Drifters)

Once A Heart	N/A	N/A

ilner, Jimmy (& group)

A Place In My Heart/Is It Fair	59	Ember 1052

inor Chords

Many A Day/Let Her Go Man	62	Lu Pine 112
So What	86	Relic LP 8008

inor Chords (Charles Henderson & the)

Bad Bulldog/Fire	59	Flick 005

inor Chords (Sunnie Elmo & the)

Don't Let Me Down/I'm Falling In Love With You	60	Flick 006
Indian Love Call/Let Me	60	Flick 009

inor Tones (Robbie Meldano & the)

Forever Darling/I Need You Baby	58	Music City 816

inorbops

Need You Tonight/I Want You For My Own	57	Lamp 2012

inors

Jerry/Where Are You?	57	Celeste 3007/Mello 554

int Juleps

Bells Of Love/Vip-A-Dip	56	Herald 481
Queen Of Love	N/A	Herald (unreleased)

int, Little Eddie (& group)

Bring Yourself Back Here/Two More Days	59	Memo 17921

ints

Busy Body Rock/Don't Leave Me Alone	56	Lin 5001
Night Air/Pledge Of Love (by Ken Copeland)	56	Lin 5007/Imperial 5432 (57)
Magic Of Love/Swimming Around The World	58	Airport 103

ARTIST/SONG	YEAR	LABEL
Minute Men		
My Love Is Gone/Please Keep The Beatles In England	64	Argo 5469
Miracles (1)		
A Lovers' Chant/Come Home With Me	55	Baton 210
Miracles (2)		
You're An Angel/A Gal Named Jo	55	Cash 1008
Miracles (3) (Carl Hogan & the)		
I Love You So/Your Love (Is All I Need)	57	Fury 1001
Miracles (4) (fb Smokey Robinson)		
Got A Job/My Mama Done Told Me	58	End 1016
Money/I Cry	58	End 1029/End 1084 (60)
Bad Girl/I Love You Baby	59	Motown G1/G2/Chess 1734 (59)
All I Want Is You/I Need A Change	60	Chess 1768
Miracletones		
Tell Me My Darling	58	Jam 5803
Miranda, Billy (& group)		
Go Ahead/Run Rose	60	Checker 957
Misfits		
Midnight Star/I Don't Know	61	Aries 7-10-3
Give Me Your Heart/My Mother-In-Law	61	Hush 105
Missiles		
We Belong Together/Space Ship	60	Novel 200
Mission Bells		
Sincerely/When A Girl Really Loves You	65	London 9760
Mistakes		
Chapel Bells/I Got Fired	59	Lo-Fi 2311/2312/Tip Top
Misters (1)		
Too Many Girls/Why Don't We Do This More Often	59	Chante 1002/Decca 31026 (59)
Misters (2) (Mike Malone & the)		
It Must Be Raining	64	Token 1002
Mistics		
Memories/Without Love	63	Capri 631
You'll Be There/What Happened To Saturday	64	Kirk 636
Mitchell, Tony (& group)		
Candle In The Wind/Million Drums	63	Canadian American 157
Mitchum, Jim (& group)		
Lonely Birthday/Oh, What A Wonderful Feeling	60	20th Century 277
Mitlo Sisters		
Let Me Tell You/Lonely Sea	58	Klik 8405
Mixers		
You Said You're Leaving Me/Johnny's Got A Girl Friend	58	Bold 101
Love And Kisses/Casanova	59	Bold 102
Mixmasters (Sonny Fulton & the)		
Fingerprints/No Not Now	59	Sunbeam 125
Mobley, John (& group)		
Tunnel Of Love (Pt. 1)/Tunnel Of Love (Pt. 2)	N/A	Town & Country 6601

RTIST/SONG	YEAR	LABEL

Modern Red Caps
They Can Dream/Don't You Hear Them Laughing	63	Rowax 801
Our Love Will Never Be The Same/Empty World	65	Lawn 254
Lovers Never Say Goodbye/We Walked In The Moonlight	65	Penntown
Golden Teardrops/Never Too Young	66	Swan 4243

Modern Red Caps (George Tindley & the)
Done Being Lonely/I Couldn't Care Less	62	Smash 1768
Free/Never Kiss A Good Man Goodbye	65	Penntowne 101

Modernistics
Who Can I Turn To	61	Pioneer 7315

Modernistics (Al Lewis & the)
What Will The Outcome Be/Just One More Chance	59	Music City 829

Modifiers (Mike & the)
I Found Myself A Brand New Baby/It's Too Bad	62	Gordy 7006

Mohawks (1)
Bewitched (Bothered And Bewildered)/I Got A Girl	60	Val-Ue 211

Mohawks (2) (fb Richard "Popcorn" Wylie)
I'll Be Around/Money	61	Motown 1009

Mohawks (2) (Popcorn & the)
Shimmy Gully/Custer's Last Man	60	Motown 1002
Have I The Right/Real Good Lovin'	62	Motown 1019

Mohawks (3)
Shoplifting Molly	64	Mutual 504

Mon-Clairs
Please Come Back/Baby Sue	62	Joey 6101

Mon-Vails
Carol Ann/White Bucks	58	Pen Joy 501

Monarchs (1)
Angels In The Sky/Wanna Go Home	55	Wing 90040

Monarchs (2)
Pretty Little Girl/In My Younger Days	56	Neil 101/Melba 101 (56)
Always Be Faithful/How Are You?	56	Neil 103/Melba 103 (56)
Love You That's Why/Coming Home	61	Liban 1002

Monarchs (3) (Chuck Mills & the)
She's Mine/Who Was The Fool	59	Band Box 221
Who Was The Fool/Ding Dong	59	Band Box 227

Monarchs (4)
This Old Heart/'Til I Hear From You	62	Jam 104

Monarchs (5) (Porgy & the)
Stay/Somebody Said (I'd Cry Someday)	63	Mala 462

Monarchs (6)
Look Homeward Angel/What Made You Change Your Mind	64	Sound Stage 7 2516

Monarchs (7)
Over The Rainbow/Guess Who	N/A	Reegal 512

Monday, Julie (& group)
Baby, Let Me Be Your Girl/Come Share The Good Times With Me	66	Rainbow 500/501

ARTIST/SONG	YEAR	LABEL
Mondellos		
That's What I Call Love/Daylight Saving Time	57	Rhythm 106
Hard To Please/Happiness Street	57	Rhythm 109
Mondellos (Alice Jean & the)		
100 Years From Today/Come Back Home	57	Rhythm 102
Mondellos (Rudy Lambert & the)		
My Heart/That's What I Call Love	58	Rhythm 114
Mondellos (Yul McClay & the)		
Never Leave Me Alone/Over The Rainbow	57	Rhythm 105
While I'm Happy	N/A	N/A
Mondo, Joe (& group)		
Last Summer Love	63	Epi 1003
Moniques		
Hey Girl/Goin' Down To Birdland	62	Benn-X 55
Halo/Don't Throw Stones	63	Centaur 104
I'm With You All The Way/Rock Pretty Baby	63	Centaur 105
Love So Wonderful/Teach Me How To Dance	62	Benn-X 15
Monitors (1)		
Candy Coated Kisses/Tonight's The Night	55	Aladdin 3309
Our School Days/I've Got A Dream	57	Specialty 595
Closer To Heaven/Rock 'N' Roll Forever	57	Specialty 622
Hop Scotch/Mamma Linda	58	Specialty 636
Monitors (2)		
A Boyfriend's Prayer/Nita	58	Circus 219
Monograms		
My Baby Dearest Darling/Please Baby Please	57	Saga 1000
Tears And Dreams/That's What He Said	60	Safire 102
Baby Blue Eyes/Little Suzie	61	Rust 5036
Monorails		
Come To Me Darling/Will Ya William	61	Lute 6017
Monorays		
It's Love Baby/What's Your Name	58	Nasco 6020
You're No Good/Love	65	20th Fox 594
Monorays (with Tony March)		
My Guardian Angel/Five Minutes To Love You	59	Tammy Records 1005 (first pressing)/Tammy 1005 (59) (second pressing)
Monotones (1) (ref Terracetones)		
Tom Foolery/Zombi	58	Argo 5301
Book Of Love/You Never Loved Me	58	Mascot 124/Argo 5290 (58)
The Legend Of Sleepy Hollow/Soft Shadows	59	Argo 5321
Fools Will Be Fools/Tell It To The Judge	59	Argo 5339
Reading The Book Of Love/Dream	60	Hull 735
Daddy's Home But Mama's Gone/Tattletale	61	Hull 741
Book Of Dance	62	Hull LP 1002
Toast To Lovers	62	Hull LP 1002
Forever Yours	86	Murray Hill LP 000180
What Would You Do If There Wasn't Any Rock 'N' Roll	86	Murray Hill LP 000180
Monotones (2)		
What Would I Do/Is It Right	64	Hickory 1250

ARTIST/SONG	YEAR	LABEL

ontalvo, Lenny (bb the Crystal Chords)

Be Mine Again/When In The World	58	3-D 373

ontclairs (1)

Give Me A Chance/My Every Dream	56	Premium 404
All I Want Is Love/I've Heard About You	56	Sonic 104
Golden Angel/Don Juan	57	Hi-Q 5001

ontclairs (1) (Floyd Smith with the)

Grandpa's Gully Rock/This Is A Miracle	61	Fortune 540

ontclairs (1) (Mel Williams & the) (aka Capris (5))

O-O-Wah/Lessons In Love	54	Decca 29370
Ooh Wah/Fools Fall In Love	55	Rage 101

ontclairs (2)

Goodnight, Well It's Time To Go/A Broken Promise	60	Audicon 111
I Believe (In Your Love)/No Baby	63	ABC 10463

ontclairs (3)

Wait For Me/Happy Feet Time	65	Sunburst 106
Sore Feet/Poopsie	65	Sunburst 115

ontclairs (4)

Lisa/Tap Tap Daisy	67	United International 1007

ontclairs (5) (Eddie Carol & the)

Where Are You/Wow-Wow Baby	58	Rulu 6098

onte, Vince (& group)

Mashed Potato Girl/You Can't Compare With My Baby	62	Jubilee 5428

ontells

Ranga Lang Lang/Soldier Boy, I'm Sorry	63	Golden Crest 582
Gee Baby/My Prince Will Come	63	Golden Crest 585

ontels (1)

Union Hall/That's Alright With Me	56	Universal 101
Union Hall/Forever And Ever (by Frankie & the C-Notes)	63	Times Square 10

ontels (2)

Rondevous	N/A	Kink 9365

onterays (1)

Deep Within My Heart/Push-Em Up	64	Dominion 1019/Ultima 704

onterays (2)

I'll Be Around/Valerie (by the Madisons)	65	Twin Hit 2865

onterays (3)

You Never Cared/Blast Off	57	Planet 57

ontereys (1)

Someone Like You/Train Whistle Blues	56	Nestor 15/Teenage 1001 (56)

ontereys (1) (Dean Barlow & the)

Dearest One/Through The Years	57	Onyx 513/Relic 511 (64)
Angel/Tell Me Why	57	Onyx 517

ontereys (2)

My Girl/With You	56	Saturn 1002
I'll Love You Again/The American Teens	58	East West 124
You're The Girl For Me/Ape Shape	58	Rose 109
Goodbye My Love/It Hurts Me So	59	Arwin 130
Without A Girl/So Deep	59	Impala 213

ARTIST/SONG	YEAR	LABEL
Rita/Billy Budd	60	Prince 5060
Face In The Crowd/Step Right Up	63	Astra 1018/Blast 219 (63)
First Kiss/Just One More Kiss	64	Dominion 1019
I Still Love You/For Sentimental Reasons	64	GNP Crescendo 314
One More Fool Than I	N/A	Saturn

Montereys (2) (Sandra Patrick & the)

I Want Your Love/Broken Heart Prayer	64	Dominion 1008

Montereys (3)

A Crowded Room/You Said That You Loved Me	59	Major 1009

Montereys (4)

Darlin' Send Me A Letter/Late Darlin'	N/A	Trans American 1000/1001

Montereys Quartet

Ballad Of Take Me Back To Baltimore (Pt. 1)/ Ballad Of Take Me Back To Baltimore (Pt. 2)	64	JC Records 9317

Montgomerys

Promise Of Love/Gotta Make A Hit Record	63	Amy 883

Mood Makers

Dolores/Dream A Dream	61	Bambi 800

Moods

Little Alice/Lady Of The Sea	59	Sarg 162
Let Me Have Your Love/Broke Up	59	Sarg 179
Teenagers Past/Rockin' Santa Claus	59	Sarg 184

Moon Beams

Don't Go Away/A Lover's Plea	59	Grate 100

Moonbeams (aka Moonbeems)

Crying The Blues//Mardi Gras Mambo (by the Hawketts)	58	Sapphire 2250

Moonbeems (aka Moonbeams)

Teen Age Baby/Cryin' The Blues	55	Sapphire 1052/Sapphire 1003 (58)/Checker 912 (59)
Maria	N/A	Sapphire (unreleased)
The Way You'll Always Be	N/A	Sapphire (unreleased)

Moonglows

I Just Can't Tell No Lie/I've Been Your Dog (Ever Since I've Been Your Man)	52	Champagne 7500
Whistle, My Love/Baby, Please	53	Chance 1147
Just A Lonely Christmas/Hey! Santa Claus	53	Chance 1150
Secret Love/Real Gone Mama	54	Chance 1152/Vee Jay 423 (62)
I Was Wrong/Ooh Rocking Daddy	54	Chance 1156
219 Train/My Gal	54	Chance 1161
Fine Fine Girl/My Love	54	Chance 1166 (unreleased)
So All Alone/Shoo Doo Be Doo (My Lovin' Baby)	54	Checker 806
Sincerely/Tempting	54	Chess 1581
Most Of All/She's Gone	55	Chess 1589
Foolish Me/Slow Down	55	Chess 1598
Starlight/In Love	55	Chess 1605
In My Diary/Lover, Love Me	55	Chess 1611
We Go Together/Chickie Um Bah	56	Chess 1619
See Saw/When I'm With You	56	Chess 1629
Over And Over Again (fast version)/I Knew From The Start	56	Chess 1646
Over And Over Again (slow version)/I Knew From The Start	56	Chess 1646
I'm Afraid The Masquerade Is Over/Don't Say Goodbye	56	Chess 1651
Please Send Me Someone To Love/Mr. Engineer (Bring Her Back To Me)	57	Chess 1661
The Beating Of My Heart/Confess It To Your Heart	57	Chess 1669

ARTIST/SONG	YEAR	LABEL
Too Late/Here I Am	57	Chess 1681
In The Middle Of The Night/Soda Pop	58	Chess 1689
This Love/Sweeter Than Words	58	Chess 1701
Rock Rock Rock	58	Chess LP 1425
I'll Never Stop Wanting You/Love Is A River	59	Chess 1717
Cold Feet	59	Chess LP 1430
Kiss Me Baby	59	Chess LP 1430/
		Chess LP 701 (76)
Junior/Beatnik	60	Chess 1770
The First Time/Mama	61	Chess 1781
My Inspiration/Gee	61	Crimson 1003
Sincerely/Time After Time	64	Lana 130
What A Difference A Day Makes/Most Of All	64	Lana 131
Blue Velvet/In My Diary	64	Lana 132
See Saw/Love Is A River	64	Lana 133
We Go Together/Shoo Doo Be Doo	64	Lana 134
Half A Heart/Ten Commandments Of Love	64	Lana 135
I've Got The Right/Baby Please	64	Times Square 30
Sincerely "72"/You've Chosen Me	71	Big P 101
We Go Together/Please Send Me Someone	72	All Platinum 109
Sincerely '72/I Was Wrong	72	RCA 74-0759
When I'm With You/You've Chosen Me	72	RCA 74-0839
In The Still Of The Night/I Pray For Love	73	Relic 1024
Let's Go	76	Chess LP 701
Thrill Me	76	Chess LP 701

Moonglows (Bobby Lester & the)

Blue Velvet/Penny Arcade	62	Chess 1811

Moonglows (Harvey & the)

The Ten Commandments Of Love/Mean Old Blues	58	Chess 1705
Mama Loocie/Unemployment	59	Chess 1738

Moonlighters (1) (Bobby Lester & the) (aka Moonglows)

So All Alone/Shoo Doo Be Doo (My Lovin' Baby)	54	Checker 806
New Gal/A Hug and A Kiss	55	Checker 813

Moonlighters (2)

Broken Heart/Glow Of Love	58	Tara 100/Josie 843 (58)
Never, Never, Never/Rock-A-Bayou-Baby	58	Tara 102

Moonlighters (3) (Billy & the)

You Made Me Cry/Little Indian Girl	78	Crystal Ball 101

Moonrays (1) (Ray Frazier & the)

Days/Turn On Me	56	Excel 111
My Dream Love/Heaven's Not So Far	62	Dynamite 1009

Moonrays (2) (Lee Williams & the)

I'm So In Love/(No) I Won't Cry Any More	60	King 5409

Moontars (Don Deal & the)

Sweet Love/The First Teenager	58	Era 1070

Moontunes (Smiley Moon & the)

You Don't Understand/Whip It On	67	Star 601

Moore, Rudy May (bb the Raytones)

Easy Easy Baby/Miss Wonderful	60	World Pacific 821

Moore, Sonny (& group)

My True Love And I/Prisoner To You	58	Old Town 1063

Moovers

I Love You Baby/One Little Dance	67	Brent 7065

ARTIST/SONG	YEAR	LABEL

Moreland, Prentice (& group)
Oh Pretty Baby/Please, Please, Please	59	Edsel 778
You Are My Sunshine/Chubby Ain't Chubby No More	62	Challenge 9154

Morning Echoes
Dear Mother	51	Premium 877

Moroccans (aka Moroccos)
Believe In Tomorrow/You Fascinate Me (by the Phillipairs)	57	Salem 1014

Moroccans (Sammy Fitzhugh & the)
Sadie Mae/Linda Baby	58	Poplar 115

Moroccos
Morocco Chant	55	United (unreleased)
Pardon My Tears/Chicken	55	United 188
Somewhere Over The Rainbow/Red Hots And Chili Mac	55	United 193/B&F 193 (60)
My Love	56	United (unreleased)
What Is A Teen-Ager's Prayer?/Bang Goes My Heart!	56	United 204/B&F 1347
Sad, Sad Hours/The Hex	57	United 207

Moroccos (Lillian Brooks & the)
For Only You/She Boodle Dee, Boodle Dee	56	King 4934
Sweet Sweet William/No Parking	56	King 4956

Morris, Pete (& group)
When You're Hurt/Walkin' Together	57	End 1006

Morris, Roger (& group)
It's No Secret	62	Puff 1002

Morrocos (Little Joe & the)
Trouble In The Candy Shop/Bubble Gum	59	Bumble Bee 500

Morse, Ella Mae (& group)
Goodnight Sweetheart Goodnight/Happy Habit	54	Capitol 2800
Lovey Dovey/Bring Back My Baby To Me	54	Capitol 2992

Mosquitos
Wait A Minute/Blind Date	64	Herald 587

Motifs
She's My Girl/My Babe	N/A	Baton 23112

Motions (aka Emotions (1))
Mr. Night/Make Me A Love	61	Laurie 3112

Motions (Ron & the)
Last Nights Dream	N/A	Red Bug

Motivations
I'm Loving You, You're Leaving Me/I Love You	73	Eastbound 604

Motor Scooter (Beverly & the)
I Had To Walk Home Myself/He's My Boy	64	Epic 9654

Moy, June (bb the Feathers)
Desert Winds/Castle Of Dreams	54	Show Time 1103

Mr. Bassman (aka Devotions)
Rip Van Winkle/You're The One (by Marty & the Symbols)	63	Graphic Arts 1000

Mr. Lee (1) (bb the Cherokees)
The Decision/What's Your Name	60	Winter 501

Mr. Lee (2) (bb the Frank Andrade 5)
Let The Four Winds Blow/Hey Mrs. Jones	64	Skylark 503

ARTIST/SONG	YEAR	LABEL
Mudlarks		
Love Game/My Grandfather's Clock	59	Roulette 4143
Muffins		
Walk Alone/Just One More Time	63	Planet 59
Mulrays		
Lily Marlane/I Got The Blues	57	Trans World 719
Murals		
See You In September/Ambush	59	Climax 110
Murphy, Bob (& group)		
Hey You/Hootin' In The Kitchen (by Billy Boyle)	63	Lawn 221
Murraymen		
Oasis/It Won't Always Be Raining	55	Arcade 131
Muskateers (aka Royal Jokers)		
Goodbye My Love/Love You 'Til My Dying Day	53	Roxy 801
Deep In My Heart/Love You 'Til My Dying Day	53	Swingtime 331
Mustangs		
Over The Rainbow/Look	65	Vest 8005
Myron, Mitch (& group)		
Runnin' Around Town/True Love Is Hard To Find	60	Bay-Tone 109
Mystery Men		
Feel Like A Million	N/A	Pow 1001
Mystics (1)		
Hushabye/Adam And Eve	59	Laurie 3028
Don't Take The Stars/So Tenderly	59	Laurie 3038
All Through The Night/(I Begin) To Think Again Of You	60	Laurie 3047
White Cliffs Of Dover/Blue Star	60	Laurie 3058
Star Crossed Lovers/Goodbye Mr. Blues	61	Laurie 3086
A Sunday Kind Of Love/Darling I Know Now	61	Laurie 3104
Again	87	Collectables LP 5043
It's Only A Paper Moon	87	Collectables LP 5043
Let Me Steal Your Heart Away	87	Collectables LP 5043
Over The Rainbow	87	Collectables LP 5043
Mystics (1) (fb Don Press)		
More Than Ever/Ask The Robin	59	Laurie 3036
Mystics (1) (fb Rusty Lane)		
Karen/Comes The Day	59	Laurie 3031
Mystics (1) (fb Scott Garrett)		
Love Story/Graduation Souvenirs	59	Laurie 3029
Mystics (2)		
Life To Go/Ballad Of Barbara Allen	59	Lee 1004
Mash Potatoes With Me/The Hoppy Hop	62	King 5678
Just For Your Love/The Jumpin' Bean	63	King 5735
Fox/Dan	63	Nolta 353
Just A Loser/She Got Everything	64	Constellation 138/Safice 333
Didn't We Have A Good Time/Now And For Always	65	Dot 16862
Ooh Poo Pah Doo	66	Black Cat 501
Teenage Sweetheart/Rockin' Yodel	N/A	Chatam 350/351
Get A Job/That's All	N/A	Jenny Lynn 101
Steppin' Stones	N/A	Olympia 2131
Ride My Pony/This Is What I Was Made For	N/A	Ren-Vell 320

ARTIST/SONG	YEAR	LABEL
Mystics (2) (Gene Fisher & the)		
Remember (You're My Girl)/Listen To Me	62	Plateau 101
Mystics (3) (Ed Gates & the)		
In The Jungle/Chewing Gum	62	Robins Nest 2
Mystics (4)		
That's The Kind Of Love/I Really Love You	64	Teako 370
Nacks (Nicky & the)		
The Night/That Old Black Magic	62	Barry 108
A Lovely Way To Spend An Evening (a capella)	75	Relic LP 103
Love Is A Many Splendored Thing (a capella)	75	Relic LP 103
White Cliffs Of Dover (a capella)	75	Relic LP 104
Good Good-Bye (a capella)	75	Relic LP 105
Nash, Marvin (& group)		
Say A Prayer For Me	N/A	Pharoah 1001
Darling	N/A	Pharoah 115
Native Boys		
Native Girl/It Won't Take Long	54	Modern 939
Strange Love/Cherrlyn	56	Combo 113
Tears/When I Met You	56	Combo 115
Laughing Love/Valley Of Lovers	56	Combo 119
Oh, Let Me Dream/I've Got A Feeling	56	Combo 120
Naturals (1)		
You Give Me So Much/What A Shape I'm In	58	Beacon 462
Don't Send Me Away/The Mummy	59	Era 1089
Naturals (1) (aka Four Naturals)		
Blue Moon/How Strange	58	Red Top 113/Hunt 325 (58)
Naturals (2) (Jack Bailey & the)		
Your Magic Touch/Tiger Lil	59	Ford 113
Naturals (3) (Yolanda & the)		
My Memories Of You/Jawbone	62	Kimley 923
Naturals (4)		
Why Don't They Understand/Just In Case You Change Your Mind	64	Chattahoochie 633
Neanderthals (Dave Meadows & the)		
Angel/I Don't See Stars In Your Eyes	60	Magnum 41160
Neat-Teens		
Jeanie	N/A	N/A
Neevets		
The Hum/You're Gonna Pay	64	Reon 1303
Nelson, Vikki (bb the Wheels)		
By My Side/Bright And Early	56	Premium 402

RTIST/SONG	YEAR	LABEL

The Neons

Neons (1)

Angel Face/Kiss Me Quickly	56	Tetra 4444
Road Of Romance/My Chickadee	57	Tetra 4449
Golden Dreams/Angel Face	60	Gone 5090
Honey Bun/Golden Dreams	74	Vintage 1016

Neons (2)

My Lover/Tucson	61	Waldon 1001
Fat Girls/Magic Moment	62	Challenge 9147

Neptunes

Fraidy Cat/As Long As	57	Glory 269
If You Care/She Went That-A-Way	58	Payson 101/102
So Little Time/She'll Understand	60	Checker 967
This My Love/Curiosity Killed The Cat	61	RCA 7931
Make A Memory/House Of Heartache	63	Instant 3255
A King Without A Crown/I Met You	64	Marlo 1534
I'm Coming Home/I Don't Cry Anymore	64	Victoria 102

Neville, Aaron (& group)

Show Me The Way/Get Out Of My Life (no group)	60	Minit 618

Neville, Art (& group)

My Dear Dearest Darling/My Baby	65	Cinderella 1400
Little Liza Jane/My Dear Dearest Darling	65	Cinderella 1401

New Group (Otis Williams & His) (ref Charms)

Miss The Love (I've Been Dreaming Of)/Tell Me Now	55	DeLuxe 6088
Gumdrop/Save Me, Save Me	56	DeLuxe 6090
Too Late I Learned/That's Your Mistake (by O.W. & the Charms)	56	DeLuxe 6091

New Hollywood Argyles (aka Hollywood Argyles)

Alley Oop '66/Do The Funky Foot	66	Kammy 105

ARTIST/SONG	YEAR	LABEL
New Invictas		
Deeply In Love With You/She Wouldn't Quit	62	Hale 500
New Silhouettes (aka Silhouettes)		
Climb Every Mountain/We Belong Together	67	Jamie 1333
Not Me Baby/Gaucho Serenade	68	Goodway 101
New Yorkers (1) (fb Fred Parris)		
Miss Fine/Dream A Little Dream	61	Wall 547
Tears In My Eyes/A Little Bit	61	Wall 548
New Yorkers (2)		
You Should Have Told Me/Don't Want To Be Your Fool	64	Tac-Ful 101
New Yorkers (3)		
I Know Why/Little Girl 5'3"	63	Park Ave 100
New Yorkers 5		
Gloria, My Darling/Cha Cha Baby	55	Danice 801
Newcomers (Wade Flemons & the)		
Here I Stand/My Baby Likes To Rock	58	Vee Jay 295
Newlyweds		
Love Walked Out/The Quarrel	N/A	Homogenized Soul 601
Newmarks		
Why/Goody Goody Gum Drop	63	Chattahoochie 627
Newports (1) (aka Falcons (4))		
Chicky Chop Chop/Hurry, Arthur Murray (lead by Eddie Floyd)	59	Contour 301
Newports (2) (Cal Linley & the)		
Mess Around/Can't Find A Girl	60	DC 0431
Newports (3)		
If I Could Tonight/A Fellow Needs A Girl	61	Kane 007/Guyden 2067 (62)
Dixie Women/The Wonder Of Love	61	Kent 380
Tears/Disillusioned Love	64	Guyden 2116
Newports (4) (Tyrone & the) (aka Nu Ports)		
I Feel Like A Million/On A Saturday Night	63	Darrow 5-20
Newports (5)		
I Want You/The Trouble Is You	66	Laurie 3327
Newtones (1)		
Going Steady/Remember The Night	59	Baton 260
Newtones (2) (aka Nutones (2))		
Can't You See/I Remember The Night	65	Relic 1009
Come On/We're Going Steady	65	Relic 1010
Nic Nacks		
Jolene/Since You Came	63	Ovation 6201
Nichol, Joey (& group)		
Ashamed/Steady Love	58	ABC 9951
Nicholls, Dave (bb the Coins)		
Bells Will Ring/Time For Dreams	N/A	Sparton 1062
Nickels		
I Love Only You	N/A	Nu Sound 180

ARTIST/SONG	YEAR	LABEL
ight Owls		
Loop The Hoop/You Shouldn't Oughta Done It	57	NRC 015
Bells Ring/Let's Go Again	64	Bethlehem 3087
ight Owls (Tony Allen & the)		
I Found An Angel/I'm Dreamin'	56	Dig 109
Be My Love	60	Crown LP 5231
Cute Thing	60	Crown LP 5231
Dreamin'	60	Crown LP 5231
Give Me A Chance	60	Crown LP 5231
Have Faith In Me	60	Crown LP 5231
Home Wrecker	60	Crown LP 5231
If I Had Aladdin's Lamp	60	Crown LP 5231
If Love Was Money	60	Crown LP 5231
Lover's Mountain	60	Crown LP 5231
Why In The World	60	Crown LP 5231
ight Riders		
Lookin' For My Baby/St. Lou	59	Sue 719
Talk To Me Baby/Night Ridin'	60	Sue 731
ight Riders (Doc Starkes & the)		
Women & Cadillacs/Say Hey	54	Apollo 460
Rags/Doctor Velvet	54	Apollo 466
ight Riders (Johnny Fairchild & the)		
I Was A Fool/Please, Please, Please	59	Ace 565
ight Riders (Mel Smith & the)		
Pretty Plaid Skirt/I'll Never Change	59	Sue 713
ight Rockers (Freddie Hall & the)		
Love And Affection/She Was My First Love	59	CJ 610
ight-Riders (aka Night Riders)		
Big Game Hunter/Doin' The Cha Cha In Havana	61	Dore 613
ightbeats (Elray & the)		
My Secret	N/A	Revive 103
ightcaps		
Darlin'/Mystery Train	61	Vandan 7066
ighthawks (1)		
All'A Your Love/When Sin Stops	58	Hamilton 50006
ighthawks (2) (B. Guitar & the)		
Here Comes Night/You Should Have Loved Her More	58	Decca 30634
ighthawks (3) (Johnny Gosey & the)		
Fools Will Take Chances/I Lost My Baby	N/A	MOA 1001
ightingales		
Love In Return/Private Party	61	Ray Star 784
ightriders (aka Nite Riders)		
Never/Tell The Truth	56	Sound 128
ightwinds (Frank & Jack & the)		
Oh My Darling/Pretty Betty Jean	58	Felsted 8539
iptones (Nippy Hawkins & the)		
Angie/It's Gonna Be Too Late	65	Lorraine 1001

ARTIST/SONG	YEAR	LABEL

Nite Riders
When A Man Cries/Waiting In The Schoolroom	58	Teen 120

Nite Riders (aka Nightriders)
Starlight And You/I Know You're In There	58	Teen 116
Got Me A Six Button Benny/Don't Hang Up The Phone	58	Teen 118

Nite Riders (Doc Starkes & the)
Apple Cider/Six Button Benny	58	Swan 4003
Apple Cider/Way In The Middle Of A Dream	58	Teen 114
Keep It A Secret	89	Relic LP 5078

Nite Riders (Melvin Smith & the)
Ugly George/Nobodys Fault	62	Chime 101

Nite Sounds
Cheese Cake/I Love You With Tender Passion	62	Fortune 548
Harem Girl/The Roll	62	Fortune 552
Get Clean/On Broadway	62	Seafair 112

Nite Sounds (Melvin Davis with the Diablos & the)
Playboy (Don't You Play In School) (with the Diablos)/ I Won't Be Your Fool	62	Fortune 551

Nite-Liters
Fat Sally/Parents Keep-A Preachin'	60	Sudden 101

Nite-Lites
I Get Blue/Lover's Twist	N/A	Sequoia 502

Nitebeaters
Dream Lover	N/A	Carib 1010

Nitecaps
A Kiss And A Vow/Be My Girl	55	Groove 0134
Tough Mama/Sweet Thing	56	Groove 0147
Bamboo Rock & Roll/You May Not Know	56	Groove 0158
In Each Corner Of My Heart/Let Me Know Tonight	56	Groove 0176
Wine Wine Wine/Nightcap Rock	60	Vandan 7491
24 Hours/No Parking	61	Vandan 3587
Next Time You See Me	66	Vandan 4280
Wine Wine Wine/Walking The Dog	66	Vandan 4733
Oh, You Sweet Girl	N/A	Detour LP 33-010
Snap Crackle & Pop	N/A	Detour LP 33-010
You're Gonna Be Sorry	N/A	Detour LP 33-010

Nitecaps (Clyde Stacy & the)
Hoy Hoy/So Young	57	Candlelight 1015
I Sure Do Love You Baby/Honky Tonk Hardwood Floor	58	Bullseye 1008

Nitelites (Nickie & the) (fb Nick Massi)
I'm Lonely/Tell Me You Care	59	Brunswick 55155

No Names
Love/Jam (instrumental)	64	Guyden 2114

Nobells
Searchin' For My Love/Crying Over You	62	Mar 101

Noble, Beverly (& group)
You Cheated/Why Must I Cry	59	Sparrow 100

Noblemen (1)
Sleep Beauty Sleep/He Won't Tell	63	USA 1215

ARTIST/SONG	YEAR	LABEL
Noblemen (2) (aka Noblemen 4)		
Everytime/All The Love I Got	N/A	Clarity 103
On The Other Side Of The World/I Just Want To Know	N/A	Clarity 106
Noblemen 4 (aka Noblemen (2))		
What's Your Name/Get Out Of My Life Woman	N/A	Recap 291
I Can Hear Raindrops/Hang It In Your Ear	N/A	Recap 292
Nobles (1)		
Do You Love Me/Who's Been Riding My Mule	58	Sapphire 1051
Nobles (1) (Nicky & the)		
Oh Baby	57	Klik
Schoolhouse Rock/A Way To Tell Her	58	End 1021
School Bells/School Day Crush	58	Gone 5039/End 1098 (61)/Times Square 37 (64)/Relic 544 (66)
Poor Rock 'N' Roll/Ting-A-Ling	58	Klik 305/Times Square 1 (63)/ Lost Nite 153
Crime Don't Pay/Darkness	62	Times Square 12
Why Be A Fool/The Search	63	Times Square 33
Nobles (2) (aka Timbers (2))		
Till The End Of Time/Standing Alone	58	ABC 9984
Oops Oh Lawdy/Stop Crying	58	Tee Gee 101
Just For Me/To Me	59	ABC 10012
Nobles (3) (fb Sollie McElroy)		
Serenade/You Ain't Right	62	Stacy 926
Nobles (4) (Aki Aleong & the)		
Without Your Love/Tradewinds Tradewinds	61	Reprise 20021
Body Surf/Mary Ann	63	Vee Jay 520
Nobletones		
Who Cares About Love/Cha-Lyp-So Baby	58	C&M 182/Times Square 18 (63)
I'm Really Too Young/I Love You	58	C&M 183/Times Square 17 (63)/ Relic 529 (65)
I'm Really Crying/Mambo Boogie	58	C&M 188/189/C&M 438
I Still Love You/Rock And Roll Nursery Rhymes	73	Vintage 1014
Nolan, Miss Frankie (& group)		
I Still Care/(I Wish It Were) Summer All Year Round	61	ABC 10231
Nolan, Miss Frankie (bb Nino & the Ebbtides)		
A Week From Sunday/Say No More	61	Madison 151
Nomads (1)		
The Perfect Crime/Paris After Dark	58	Balboa 006/Josie 851 (58)
Tell It Like It Is/Rainbow's End	63	Josie 905
Nomads (2)		
You're The Only One/Heart Attack	59	Northern 503
Norman, Zack (& group)		
Hey Doll/Givin' Up Love	57	Poplar 111
Normanaires		
My Greatest Sin/Wrap It Up	53	MGM 11622
Nornetts		
Happy Boy/Pappa Knew	64	Wand 153
Nortones		
Susie Jones/That's The Way The Cookie Crumbles	59	Warner Bros. 5065
Smile, Just Smile/Boy	59	Warner Bros. 5115
Cookie Man/I'm Gonna Find You	60	Stack 502

ARTIST/SONG	YEAR	LABEL
Norvells		
Greasy Kid Stuff/As I Walk Alone	63	Checker 1037
Without You	N/A	Janis 6366
Notables		
Moonlight And Roses/Under The Bridges Of Paris	58	Big Top 3001
Surfside/Lisa Maree	63	Big Top 3141
Notations (1)		
What a Night For Love/Chapel Doors	58	Wonder 100
Notations (2) (Augie Rios & the)		
I've Got A Girl/There's A Girl Down The Way	63	Shelley 181
Notations (3)		
Danny Boy/You Can Run	65	Relic 1019
For Your Precious Love (a capella)	75	Relic LP 104
Kentucky Babe (a capella)	75	Relic LP 104
Lost Love (a capella)	75	Relic LP 104
Hang On Sloopy (a capella)	75	Relic LP 105
When I Fell In Love (a capella)	75	Relic LP 105
My Foolish Heart (a capella)	75	Relic LP 108
Peace Of Mind (a capella)	75	Relic LP 109
Note Makers		
It Hurts To Wonder/Do I Have A Chance	58	Sotoplay 007
Note-Torials		
My Valerie/Loved And Lost	59	Sunbeam 119
Notes (1) (aka Five Notes (2))		
Don't Leave Me Now/Cha Jezebel	56	Capitol 3332
Trust In Me/Round And Round	56	MGM 12338
Notes (2) (Reed Harper & the)		
I Miss You So/Sweetheart Of The Prom	58	Vik 0328
Three Charms/It's Worth Remembering	60	Luck 105
Notes (3)		
Little Girl/G.I. Blues	59	Sarg 177
Notes (4)		
I Miss You So	58	Smart 1001
Novars (Carl Bell & the)		
Birth Of The Beat/Open House In Your Heart	58	Laurie 3014
Novas (Little Ted & the)		
All Your Lovin'/Baby Baby Baby	N/A	Kay-Gee 440/Kay-Gee 1068
Nu Luvs		
Baby You Belong To Me/Hello Lover	61	Clock 2003
Nu Ports (Tyrone & the) (aka Newports)		
Feel Like A Million/On A Saturday Night	63	Darrow 5-20
Nu-Tones (1)		
Sharon Lee/Feel In Love For The Very First Time	61	Cha Cha 716
Nu-Tones (2)		
Teen-Age Heart/Guitar Shuffle	N/A	Spin Time 1001
Nu-Trons		
Searchin'	N/A	Eldee 85

ARTIST/SONG	YEAR	LABEL
Nuggets		
Curl Up In My Arms/So Help Me I Love You	54	Capitol 2989
Shtiggy Boom/Anxious Love	55	Capitol 3052
Before We Say Goodnight/Angel On The Dance Floor	61	RCA 7930
Just A Friend/Cat Snapper	62	RCA 8031
Whisper/Wish She Were Mine	73	Vintage 1003
Numbers		
Big Red/My Pillow	62	Bonneville 101/Dore 641 (62)
Nunn, Bobby (bb the Robins)		
Mainliner/Saturday Night Daddy (by Little Esther)	52	Federal 12100
Nunn, Bobby (with the Robins & Little Esther)		
You Took My Love Too Fast/Street Lights	53	Federal 12122
Nutmegs (aka Rajahs/aka Lyres)		
Story Untold/Make Me Lose My Mind	55	Herald 452
Ship Of Love/Rock Me, Squeeze Me	55	Herald 459
Whispering Sorrows/Betty Lou	55	Herald 466
Key To The Kingdom (Of Your Heart)/Gift O' Gabbin' Women	56	Herald 475
A Love So True/Comin' Home	56	Herald 492
My Story/My Sweet Dream	59	Herald 538
A Dream Of Love/Someone, Somewhere (Help Me)	60	Tel 1014
Crazy About You/Rip Van Winkle	62	Herald 574
The Way Love Should Be/Wide Hoop Skirts	63	Times Square 14/Relic 533 (65)
Down To Earth/Coo Coo Cuddle Coo (Admirations)	63	Times Square 19
Why Must We Go To School?/Ink Dries Quicker Than Tears (by the Volumes)	63	Times Square 22/Relic 535 (65)
Down In Mexico/My Sweet Dreams	63	Times Square 27/Relic 528 (65)
Let Me Tell You/Hello	63	Times Square 6/Relic 531 (65)
You're Crying/Wa-Do-Wa	64	Times Square 103
Shifting Sands/Out Of My Heart	65	Relic 1006
Help Me	71	Relic LP 5002
I Like To Cha Cha	71	Relic LP 5002
Story Untold '72/Tell Me	72	Baby Grand 800
The Joker	N/A	Herald (unreleased)
Nutones (1)		
Goddess Of Love/Niki Niki Mambo	55	Hollywood Star 797
Believe/Annie Kicked The Bucket	55	Hollywood Star 798
Believe/You're No Barking Dog	55	Hollywood Star 798
At Midnight/Beans 'N' Greens	56	Combo 127
Nutones (2) (aka Newtones (2))		
I Remember The Nite/Can't You See	65	Relic 1009
We're Going Steady/Come On	65	Relic 1010
Nutones (3)		
Love Me All The Time/Time And Again	63	Dart 135
Nutrends		
Together/Spooksville	63	Lawn 216
Oberle, Scott (& group)		
Cupid's Poison Dart/You're My Dream Girl	64	Lawn 216
Objectives		
Oh My Love/Love Went Away	65	Jewel 751
Obsessions		
Love Always/A Fool	64	Accent 1182
Ocapellos		
The Stars/Anytime	65	General 107/Checker 1144 (66)

ARTIST/SONG	YEAR	LABEL
Octaves		
Mambo Carolyn/You're Too Young	58	Val 1001
Octobers		
Stop It Little Girl/I Should'A Listened To Mama	63	Chairman 4402
Off Beats		
Doodlum/Have Love Will Travel	64	Guyden 2101
Off Keys		
Our Wedding Day/Singing Bells	62	Rowe 003/Technicord 1001 (62)
Off Keys (Jerry Evans & the)		
Oh Little Girl/You Are	62	Rowe 002
Offbeats (Harold L & the)		
Connie/Three Years	61	Happy Hearts 124
Offbeats (Jimmy Dee & the)		
You're Late Miss Kate/Here I Come	58	Dot 15721
I Feel Like Rockin'/Rock Tick Tock	59	TNT 161
You Say You Beat Me To The Punch (answer record)/ I've Got A Secret	63	Cutie 1400
Offbeats with the Montclairs (Jimmy Dee & the)		
Don't Cry No More/Henrietta (no group)	57	TNT 148/Dot 15664 (57)
Offitt, Lillian (& group)		
Can't Go On/Darling Please Don't Change	58	Excello 2139
Ohio Untouchables (bb Falcons (4))		
She's My Heart's Desire/What To Do	62	Lu Pine 1009/Lu Pine 109 (62)
I'm Tired/Up Town (instrumental)	62	Lu Pine 1011/Lu Pine 116/117 (64)
Love Is Amazing/Forgive Me Darling	62	Lu Pine 110/Lu Pine 1010 (62)
Oliver, Big Danny (& group)		
Sapphire/I Wanna Go Steady	58	Trend 012X
Oliver, Johnny (& group)		
I Must Have Love/Lemonade Baby	54	MGM 55001
Darling, Is It True?/My Love Lady	55	MGM 55012
I Need You So/The Things I Might Have Been	56	MGM 12319
Olympics		
Western Movies/Well	58	Demon 1508
Dance With The Teacher/Ev'rybody Needs Love	58	Demon 1512
(Baby) Hully Gully/Private Eye	59	Arvee 562
Chicken/Your Love	59	Demon 1514
I Wish I Could Shimmy Like My Sister Kate/Workin' Hard	60	Arvee 5006
Dance By The Light Of The Moon/Dodge City	60	Arvee 5020
Big Boy Pete/The Slop	60	Arvee 595
Boo-Dee Green	60	Arvee LP A-423
Stay Away From Joe	60	Arvee LP A-423
Little Pedro/Bull Fight (instrumental)	61	Arvee 5023
Dooley/Stay Where You Are	61	Arvee 5031
The Stomp/Mash Them 'Taters	61	Arvee 5044
Big Boy Pete '65/Stay Where You Are	61	Arvee 6501/Everest
Just Like That	61	Arvee LP A-424
Chicken/Cool Short	61	Titan 1718
Twist/Everybody Likes To Cha Cha Cha	62	Arvee 5051
The Scotch/Baby It's Hot	62	Arvee 5056
What'd I Say Pt. 1/What'd I Say Pt. 2	62	Arvee 5073
The Boogler Pt. 1/The Boogler Pt. 2	62	Duo Disc 104
Return Of Big Boy Pete/Return Of The Watusi	62	Duo Disc 105

The Olympics

The Bounce/Fireworks	63	Tri Disc 106
Dancin' Holiday/Do The Slauson Shuffle	63	Tri Disc 107
Bounce Again/A New Dancin' Partner	63	Tri Disc 110
The Broken Hip/So Goodbye	63	Tri Disc 112
I'm Comin' Home/Rainin' In My Heart	64	Loma 2010
Good Lovin'/Olympic Shuffle (instrumental)	65	Loma 2013
Baby I'm Yours/No More Will I Cry	65	Loma 2017
We Go Together (Pretty Baby)/Secret Agents	65	Mirwood 5504
Mine Exclusively/Secret Agents	66	Mirwood 5513
Baby Do The Philly Dog/Western Movies	66	Mirwood 5523
The Duck/The Bounce	66	Mirwood 5525
Mine Exclusively	66	Mirwood LP 7003
Pretty Baby	66	Mirwood LP 7003
We Go Together	66	Mirwood LP 7003
I'll Do A Little Bit More/The Same Old Thing	67	Mirwood 5529
Hully Gully/Big Boy Pete	67	Mirwood 5533
Lookin' For A Love/Good Things	68	Parkway 6003
The Cartoon Song/Things That Made Me Laugh	69	Jubilee 5674
Please Please Please/Girl, You're My Kind Of People	69	Warner Bros. 7369

Omegas

Crazy Bones/Razzamatazz	59	Chord 1305
When You Touch Me/Froze	59	Decca 31008
Study Hall/(So How Come) No One Loves You	60	Decca 31094
No One Will Ever Know/Falling In Love	60	Decca 31138
Midnight Run/I Wanna Go Home	61	Groove G-4

One, Bobby (& group)

Undecided/Hummingbird	59	NRC 021

One-O-Two's (102's) (Skip & the)

Gotta Pay The Price	62	KayBee 106

Onions (Tommy Sena & the)

Onions (Remind Me Of You)/The Wobble	N/A	Valmont 905

Ontarios

Memories Of You/Lovers' Mambo	65	Big Town 121
It's Wrong/Is This The Real Thing (by the Warblers)	73	Baron 101
I Really Had A Ball/Sorry (by the Clefs)	73	Baron 104
Love Me Baby/Scheming (by the Warblers)	73	Baron 106

Opals (1) (aka Crystals (1))

My Heart's Desire/Oh, But She Did	54	Apollo 462

ARTIST/SONG	YEAR	LABEL
Come To Me, Darling/Squeeze Me, Baby	54	Luna 100/101

Opals (2) (female)
Love/Hop, Skip And Jump	62	Beltone 2025

Opals (3)
No, No, Never Again/Just Like A Little Bitty Baby	65	Laurie 3288

Opposites
Karen/Ding Dong	62	Columbia 42641

Orbits (1)
Message Of Love/I Really Do	56	Flair-X 5000
Who Are You?/Mr. Hard Luck	57	Argo 5286
Knock Her Down/My Love	59	Nu Kat 116/117
Tell Me Baby/Two Crazy Scientists	N/A	Dooto 601

Orbits (2) (Bobby & the)
Felicia/Bandstand Dance	59	Seeco 6005/Seeco 6067 (61)
Teenage Love/What Do I Say (When I'm Close To You)	59	Seeco 6030
Your Cheatin' Heart/I Don't Stand A Chance	62	Gone 5126

Orbits (2) (Bobby Grayson & His)
I'll Follow You/Look Over Here Girl	63	Jamco 105

Orbits (2) (fb Lani Zee)
Funny, Funny, Funny/Sea Tides	61	Seeco 6074

Orbits (3) (J. Lyndon & the)
My One Desire	N/A	Whiteley 4282

Orbits (4)
I Need You/I'm Home	N/A	Don-J 48798

Orchids (1)
Oh Why?/All Night Long	53	King 4661
I've Been A Fool From The Start/Beginning To Miss You	53	King 4663

Orchids (2)
You're Everything To Me/Newly Wed	55	Parrot 815
I Can't Refuse/You Said You Loved Me	55	Parrot 819

Orchids (3)
My Story/Is It True	N/A	Savoy 964 (unreleased)

Orchids (4)
Soft Shadows/Good Gully	61	Wall 549

Orchids (5) (female)
I Don't Think You Missed Me	62	Harlow 101

Orchids (6) (Dick Bardi & the)
Stormy Weather/The Hard Way	N/A	Maestro 409/410

Orientals
Get Yourself To School/Please Come Back Home	58	Kayo 927
Misty Summer Night/Soul Ain't You Thrilled	N/A	New Dawn 413

Orients
Queen Of Angels/Shouldn't I?	64	Laurie 3232

Original Cadillacs (aka Cadillacs)
Lucy/Hurry Home	57	Josie 821
I'll Never Let You Go/The Wayward Wanderer	64	Josie 915

ARTIST/SONG	YEAR	LABEL
Original Cadillacs (Earl Carroll & the) (aka Cadillacs)		
Buzz-Buzz-Buzz/Yea, Yea, Baby	58	Josie 829
Original Casuals (aka Casuals (1))		
So Tough/I Love My Darling	58	Back Beat 503 (second pressing, first is by Casuals)
Ju-Judy/Don't Pass Me By	58	Back Beat 510
Three Kisses Past Midnight/It's Been A Long Time	58	Back Beat 514
Original Charmers		
For Sentimental Reasons/Bashful Boy	60	Angle Tone 550
Fools Rush In/Someday You'll Want Me	72	Blue Sky 102
Original Checkers		
Love Wasn't There/Over The Rainbow	62	King 5592
Original Drifters (Bill Pinkney & the) (ref Drifters)		
Don't Call Me/Do The Jerk	64	Fontana 1956
Original Drifters (ref Drifters)		
The Masquerade Is Over/I Found Some Lovin'	67	Veep 1264
Old Man River/Millionaire	71	Game 394
Original Emotions (aka Emotions (1))		
You're A Better Man Than I/Are You Real	N/A	Johnson 746
Original Four Aces (aka Four Aces)		
I Can See An Angel/You Were My First Affair	55	Big Town 118
Original Jaguars		
Our Young Love/Making Love Girl	N/A	Val-Vo 110
Original Mustangs (Dolores Curry & the)		
Oh Baby/Jump Lula	59	Hi-Q 5040
Original Pyramids (aka Pyramids (3))		
Ankle Bracelet/Hot Dog Dooly Wah	61	Shell 304
Original Rhythm Rockers		
Madness/Oh! Oh! Honey	59	Gone 5073
Original Three Friends (Joey & the)		
Blanche/The Oriental	N/A	Chevron 500
Originals (1)		
Anna/Sleepless Nights	59	Jackpot 48012
Originals (2) (Tony Allen & the)		
Let Me Hear You Say Yeah/Wishing Star	60	Original Sound 10
Little Lonely Girl/I Still Love You	60	Original Sound 13
Originals (3) (Rosie & the)		
A Kiss From Your Lips/Let Me Be Your Girl	60	Brunswick 55171
Angel Baby/Give Me Love	60	Highland 1011
Lonely Blue Nights/We'll Have A Chance	61	Brunswick 55205/ Highland 1031 (61)
My Darlin' Forever/The Time Is Near (Rosie)	61	Brunswick 55213
Angel From Above/Why Did You Leave Me?	61	Highland 1025
Originals (4)		
Lend Me Your Ear/Bandstand Sound	60	Poor Boy 110
Originals (5) (fb Lonnie Nye)		
Careless With Love/I Gotta Know	60	Lo-Lon 101

ARTIST/SONG	YEAR	LABEL
Originals (6)		
At Times Like This/Gimme A Little Kiss, Will Ya Huh	61	Diamond 102
You And I/Summer School	62	Diamond 116
Originals (7) (Bill Pinkney & the)		
The Masquerade Is Over/I Found Some Lovin'	67	Veep 1264
Originals (8)		
Old Enough To Break A Heart	N/A	Van 04166
Originals (9) (Rachael & the)		
I'll Always Remember/The Sound	62	Night Star 010
Originells 4		
I Can Make You Mine/Four Nights	65	Apt 25074
Orioles (Sonny Til & the)		
It's Too Soon To Know/Barbra Lee	48	It's A Natural 5000/ Jubilee 5000 (48)
Exactly Like You	48	Jubilee (unreleased)
I'm Losing Something I Never had	48	Jubilee (unreleased)
Lazy River Rolls By	48	Jubilee (unreleased)
Two Party Line	48	Jubilee (unreleased)
(It's Gonna Be A) Lonely Christmas/To Be With You	48	Jubilee 5001
To Be With You/Dare To Dream	48	Jubilee 5001
Please Give My Heart A Break/It Seems So Long Ago	49	Jubilee 5002
Tell Me So/Deacon Jones	49	Jubilee 5005
I Challenge Your Kiss/Donkey Serenade	49	Jubilee 5008
A Kiss And A Rose/It's A Cold Simmer	49	Jubilee 5009
Forgive And Forget/So Much	49	Jubilee 5016
What Are You Doing New Year's Eve/ (It's Gonna Be A) Lonely Christmas	49	Jubilee 5017
If It's To Be	50	Jubilee (unreleased)
Would You Still Be The One In My Heart/ Is My Heart Wasting Time	50	Jubilee 5018
At Night/Every Dog-Gone Time	50	Jubilee 5025
Moonlight/I Wonder When?	50	Jubilee 5026
You're Gone/Everything They Said Came True	50	Jubilee 5028
I'd Rather Have You Under The Moon/ We're Supposed To Be Through	50	Jubilee 5031
I Need You So/Goodnight Irene	50	Jubilee 5037
I Crossed My Fingers/Can't Seem To Laugh Anymore	50	Jubilee 5040
Oh Holy Night/The Lord's Prayer	50	Jubilee 5045
This I'll Do My Darling	51	Jubilee (unreleased)
I Miss You So/You Are My First Love	51	Jubilee 5051
Pal Of Mine/Happy Go Lucky Local Blues	51	Jubilee 5055
When You're A Long Long Way Away From Home/ Would I Love You (Love You, Love You)	51	Jubilee 5057
My Prayer/I Never Knew	51	Jubilee 5060
I'm Just A Fool In Love/Hold Me, Squeeze Me (Hold Me Tight)	51	Jubilee 5061
Baby, Please Don't Go/Don't Tell Her What's Happened To Me	51	Jubilee 5065
A Scandal	52	Jubilee (unreleased)
Baby, I Love You So	52	Jubilee (unreleased)
It Ain't Gonna Be Like That	52	Jubilee (unreleased)
Yes Indeed	52	Jubilee (unreleased)
How Blind Can You Be/When You're Not Around	52	Jubilee 5071
Trust In Me/Shrimp Boats	52	Jubilee 5074
Proud Of You/You Never Cared For Me	52	Jubilee 5076
Waiting/It's All Over Because We're Through	52	Jubilee 5082
Barfly/Getting Tired, Tired, Tired	52	Jubilee 5084
See See Rider/Don't Cry, Baby	52	Jubilee 5092
You Belong To Me/I Don't Want To Take A Chance	52	Jubilee 5102
Till Then/I Miss You So	53	Jubilee 5107
Teardrops On My Pillow/Hold Me, Thrill Me, Kiss Me	53	Jubilee 5108
Dem Days (Are Gone Forever)/Bad Little Girl	53	Jubilee 5115

ARTIST/SONG	YEAR	LABEL
I Cover The Waterfront/One More Time	53	Jubilee 5120
Crying In The Chapel/Don't You Think I Ought To Know	53	Jubilee 5122/Lana 109 (64)
Write And Tell Me Why/In The Mission Of St. Augustine	53	Jubilee 5127
Robe Of Calvary/There's No One But You	53	Jubilee 5134
Don't Go To Strangers/Secret Love	54	Jubilee 5137
Maybe You'll Be There/Drowning Every Hope I Ever Had	54	Jubilee 5143
In The Chapel In The Moonlight/Thank The Lord, Thank The Lord	54	Jubilee 5154
Longing/If You Believe	54	Jubilee 5161
Count Your Blessings (Instead Of Sheep)/Runaround	54	Jubilee 5172
Don't Cry	55	Jubilee (unreleased)
Sure Fire	55	Jubilee (unreleased)
I Love You Mostly/Fair Exchange	55	Jubilee 5177
I Need You Baby/That's When the Good Lord Will Smile	55	Jubilee 5189
Please Sing My Blues Tonight/Moody Over You	55	Jubilee 5221
Don't Go To Strangers/Angel	56	Jubilee 5231
Happy Till The Letter/I Just Got Lucky	56	Vee Jay 196
For All We Know/Never Leave Me Baby	56	Vee Jay 228
Sugar Baby/Didn't I Say	57	Abner 1016/Vee Jay 244 (57)
Tell Me So/At Night (with chorus)	59	Jubilee 5363
The First Of Summer/Come On Home (with the Helen Way Singers)	59	Jubilee 5384
Crying In The Chapel/Forgive And Forget (with chorus)	59	Jubilee 6001
Live It Up	60	Vee Jay LP 1021
Secret Love/Wobble	62	Charlie Parker 211
In The Chapel In The Moonlight/Hey! Little Woman	62	Charlie Parker 212
Back To The Chapel Again/Lonely Christmas	62	Charlie Parker 213
What Are You Doing New Year's Eve/ Don't Mess Around With My Love	62	Charlie Parker 214
It's Too Soon To Know/I Miss You So	62	Charlie Parker 215
I Miss You So/Hey! Little Woman	62	Charlie Parker 219
Write And Tell Me Why/Don't Tell Her What Happened To Me	63	Charlie Parker 216
What Are You Doing New Year's Eve/Crying In The Chapel	64	Lana 109
Along About Sundown	83	Murray Hill LP M61277
Blame It On Yourself	83	Murray Hill LP M61277
Bring The Money Home	83	Murray Hill LP M61277
Cigareetos	83	Murray Hill LP M61277
Don't Keep It To Yourself	83	Murray Hill LP M61277
Don't Stop	83	Murray Hill LP M61277
Feeling Low	83	Murray Hill LP M61277
Good Looking Baby	83	Murray Hill LP M61277
I Had To Leave Town	83	Murray Hill LP M61277
I May Be Wrong	83	Murray Hill LP M61277
I Promise You	83	Murray Hill LP M61277
I'm Beginning To Think You Care For Me	83	Murray Hill LP M61277
My Baby's Gonna Get It	83	Murray Hill LP M61277
My Loved One	83	Murray Hill LP M61277
Once Upon A Time	83	Murray Hill LP M61277
Pretty, Pretty Rain	83	Murray Hill LP M61277
Walking By The River	83	Murray Hill LP M61277
Wanted	83	Murray Hill LP M61277
Why Did You Go	83	Murray Hill LP M61277
What Happened To You	84	Collectables LP 5014

Orioles (Sonny Til & the) (bb the Sid Bass Orchestra)

If You Believe/Laughing	54	Jubilee 5161

Orlando, Tony (& group)

Ding Dong/You And Only You	59	Milo 101

Orlandos

Old MacDonald/Cloudburst	57	Cindy 3006

Orlons

I'll Be True/Heart Darling Angel	61	Cameo 198
Mr. Twenty One/Please Let It Be Me	62	Cameo 211

ARTIST/SONG	YEAR	LABEL
Oro, Emmy (& group)		
Is It A Sin/Some Of These Days	62	Chelsea 1005
Osburn, Bobby (& group)		
My Heart's Been Broken/Susie-Q	64	Arlen 747
Ospreys		
Do You Wanna Jump Children/It's Good To Me (You Don't Know And I Don't Know)	57	East West 110
Outcasts (Mac Boswell & the)		
Rang Dang Do Lally/I Thought You Knew	60	Wonder 117
Ovations		
Let's Make Love Tonight	N/A	N/A
Ovations (1)		
Whole Wide World/My Lullabye	60	Andie 5017
The Day We Fell In Love/My Lullabye	61	Barry 101
Oh What A Day (same song as Day We Fell In Love)/Real True Love	61	Epic 9470
Ovations (2)		
I Don't Wanna Cry/Loneliness Never Entered My Mind	63	Capitol 5082
Ovations (3)		
Remembering/Who Needs Love	64	Josie 916
Ovations (4)		
Runaround/I Still Love You	N/A	Hawk 153
Overtones		
I Can't Fall In Love	N/A	N/A
Please Let Me Know/I Been There Before	N/A	Ajax
You're The Only Girl	N/A	Ajax 173
Overtones (Penny & the)		
Walking My Baby Back Home	58	N/A
What Made You Forget	58	Rim 2021
Overtones (Tony Rice & the)		
My Darling Y-O-U/I Thank You, Baby	61	Action 100
Little School Girl/Bluebird Of Happiness	61	Rae-Cox 106
Owens, Freddy (& group)		
Heavenly One/Chapel	61	Wall 550
Owens, Garland (& group)		
Dancing With Tears In My Eyes	N/A	Lemonade 1502
Owls		
So Lost/Kasanutu	N/A	Arden 1000
Ox-Tones		
Fatty Patty	58	Phonograph 1024
Oxfords (Darrell & the) (aka Tokens (2))		
Picture In My Wallet/Roses Are Red	59	Roulette 4174
Can't You Tell?/But Your Mother She Said No	60	Roulette 4230
Ozells		
The Gossips/Please Don't Go	63	Cub 9126
Pacers (1)		
I Wanna Dance With You/I Found A Dream	58	Calico 101/102

ARTIST/SONG	YEAR	LABEL

Pacers (2)
How Sweet/No Wonder — 61 — Guyden 2064

Pacers (3)
You Got Me Bugged/Sassy Sue — 63 — Coral 62398

Pacesetters
That's All/Ronnie's Beat (instrumental) — 62 — Wink 1008

Pacettes
Don't Read The Letter/You Don't Know Baby — 63 — Regina 1306

Packards
Dream Of Love/Ding Dong — 56 — Paradise 105
Ladise/My Doctor Of Love — 56 — Pla-Bac 106

Pagans
Lover's Plea/Bad Man Brown — 60 — Music City 832

Pagans (Lynn Dee & the)
Fool That I Am/I've Got What You Want — 60 — Music City 835

Page Boys
Waiting/This I Give To You — 57 — Prep 117
Hey Now Baby/Out To Lunch — 59 — Tel 1007
If Tears Could Speak/Old Buttermilk Sky — 63 — Decca 3105
Our Love/Things Are Going To Break Up — N/A — Camelot 114

Page, Joey (& group)
Blue Velvet/Party Season — 61 — Roulette 4373

Page, Ricky (& female group)
I Understand/Everytime (You're Mine) — 61 — Coin 711/Dot 16261

Pageants (1)
Show Them You Can Dance/It's Been So Long — 55 — Beacon 559
We Belong Together/Theme From "Sleeping Moondog" — 61 — Paxley 753

Pageants (1) (fb Tony Dee)
Happy Together/Why Did You Go — 60 — Goldisc 3013
Saturday Romance/Make You My Queen — 62 — Du-Well 101/Arlen 731 (62)

Pageants (2)
She Is Your Girl/Make It Last — 65 — Groove 0056
I'm A Victim/Are You Ever Coming Home — 65 — RCA 8601

Pageants (3)
Tender Love — N/A — Club

Pageants (4)
Long Ago — N/A — Vira

Pageboys
When I Meet A Girl Like You/I Have Love — 63 — Seville 135

Pages (1) (Gene Morris & the)
I've Gotta A Love/Lovin' Honey — 57 — Vik 0287

Pages (2)
Donna Marie/Wind — 58 — Eagle 1005/Don Tan 0001

Pal, Ricki (& group)
Just Outside Of Love/No Need For Crying — 58 — Arwin 115

Palisades (1) (gm Carole King)
Close Your Eyes/I Can't Quit — 60 — Calico 113
Dear Joan/The Shrine — 60 — Leader 806

ARTIST/SONG	YEAR	LABEL
Oh My Love/Hometown Girl	61	Dore 609
This Is The Nite/Relic Rock	62	Medieval 205
Make The Night A Little Longer/It's Heaven Being With You	63	Chairman 4401

Palisades (2) (Frank Gonzales & the)

Let's Make Up/Sweet Little Surfing Girl	61	FG 1001

Palms

Dianne	56	States (unreleased)
Knew I Had A Chance	56	States (unreleased)
Love Is No Thing To Play With	57	States (unreleased)
One More Time	57	States (unreleased)
Edna/Teardrops	57	United 208

Palms (Artie Wilkins & the)

Darling Patricia/Please Come Back (no group)	56	States 157

Pals (1)

My Baby Likes To Rock/Summer Is Here	58	Turf 1000/1001/
		Guyden 2019 (59)

Pals (2) (Gerry Patt & His)

It's So Strange/Dancing By Myself	65	Ascot 2129

Panics

Heartaches/You're Driving Me Crazy	59	ABC 10072

Panthers (Charles Watson & the)

I Found My Love	N/A	Village 103

Paradons

Diamonds And Pearls/I Want Love	60	Milestone 2003
Bells Ring/Please Tell Me	60	Milestone 2005
Take All Of Me/So Fine, So Fine, So Fine	60	Warner Bros. 5186
I Had A Dream/Never, Never	62	Milestone 2015
Never Again/This Is Love	N/A	Tuffest 102

Paragons

Florence/Hey, Little School Girl	57	Winley 215
Let's Start All Over Again/Stick With Me Baby	57	Winley 220
Two Hearts Are Better Than One/Give Me Love	57	Winley 223
Twilight/The Vows Of Love	58	Winley 227
So You Will Know/Don't Cry, Baby	58	Winley 228/Times Square 9 (63)
Blue Velvet/Wedding Bells	60	Musicraft 1102/
		Musictone 1102 (62)
So You Will Know/Doll Baby	60	Winley 240
If/Hey Baby	61	Tap 500
In The Midst Of The Night/Begin The Beguine	61	Tap 503
These Are The Things I Love/If You Love Me	61	Tap 504
Time After Time/Baby, Take My Hand	63	Music Clef 3001/3002
Don't Ever Leave Me	N/A	Winley LP 6003

Paragons (Mack Starr & the)

Just A Memory/Kneel And Pray	61	Winley 250

Paragons (Tommy Collins & the)

Darling, I Love You/Doll Baby	59	Winley 236

Parakeets (1) (fb Frank Motley)

Give Me Time/I'm Losing My Mind Over You (by Frank Motley)	54	Gem 218
My Love Is True/Can't You See I Love You (by the Rainbows)	73	Baron 105

Parakeets (2) (Vic Donna & the)

Teenage Rose/Silly And Sappy	57	Atlas 1071
Love Was A Stranger To Me/Count The Tears	57	Atlas 1075

The Paradons

Parakeets (2) Quintet

I Have A Love/The Rain Starts To Fall	56	Atlas 1068

Parakeets (2) Quintet (Leroy Williams & the)

My Heart Tells Me/Yvonne	56	Atlas 1069

Parakeets (3)

Shangri-La/Come Back	61	Jubilee 5407
I Want You Right Now/I Love You Like I Do	62	Big Top 3130

Paramounts (1)

Take My Heart/Thunderbird Baby	59	Combo 156
Trying/Girl Friend	60	Carlton 524
Christopher Columbus/I Know You'll Be My Love	60	Fleetwood 1014
Congratulations/Why Do You Have To Go?	61	Dot 16175
When You Dance/You're Seventeen	61	Dot 16201
Where's Carolyn Tonight/When I Dream	63	Centaur 103
Shedding Teardrops/In A Dream	63	Ember 1099
Just to Be With You/One More For The Road	63	Laurie 3201
Time Will Bring A Change/Under Your Spell	64	Magnum 722
Rumba	87	Relic LP 5069

Paramounts (2) (Eddie Saxon &)

Blues No More/If It's Meant To Be	62	Empress 106

Paramours (Bill Medley & Bobby Hatfield)

That's The Way We Love/Prison Break	61	Smash 1701
Cutie Cutie/Miss Social Climber	61	Smash 1718
That's All I Want Tonight/There She Goes (She's Walking)	62	Moonglow 214

Paris, Bobby (& group)

Little Miss Dreamer/Who Needs You	63	Chattahoochie 631
Night Owl/Tears On My Pillow	66	Cameo 396

Parisians

Silhouettes/Planters Cafe	59	Bullseye 1028

ARTIST/SONG	YEAR	LABEL
Silhouettes/Esther	61	Argyle 1006
Fifi's Place/Ambush	61	Felsted 8627
Why/On The Sunny Side Of The Street	62	Pova 1003/1004

Park Avenue Jesters

Don't Turn Your Back On Me	N/A	N/A

Parkays

Late Date/Get It	61	ABC 10242

Parker, Bobby (& group)

Foolish Love/Stop By My House	60	Amanda 1001

Parker, Little Junior (& group)

Belinda Marie/Dangerous Woman (no group)	59	Duke 315

Parktowns

Stop, Look And Listen/You Hurt Me Inside	60	Impala 214/Thor 3258
That Day Will Never Come/You Hurt Me Inside	61	Crimson 1006

Parlay Brothers

My Girl/Do You Really Wanna Dance	65	Valjay 2725

Parlettes

Tonight I Met An Angel/Because We're Very Young	63	Jubilee 5467

Parliaments (1)

Don't Need You Anymore/Honey, Take Me Home With You	58	Len 101

Parliaments (2)

Party Boys/Poor Willie	59	Apt 25036
Lonely Island/You Make Me Wanna Cry	60	Flipp 100/101
To Be Alone/My Only Love	61	U.S.A. 719
You're Cute/I'll Get You Yet	63	Symbol 917

Parliaments (3) (Freddie & the)

Darlene/That Girl	59	Twirl 1003

Parliaments (4) (Sammy & the)

No Hard Feelings/Win Yourself A Lover	60	Arnold 1001

Parrish, Troy (& group)

Gloria/Laugh	62	Baronet 10

Parrots

Please Don't Leave Me/Weep, Weep, Weep	53	Parrot 758/Checker 772 (54)

Partylights (Shona & the)

Nice Guy/Miracle Maker	63	Chicory 1601

Passionettes

My Plea	N/A	Path 101

Passions (1)

Tango Of Love/Nervous About Love	58	Dore 505
Just To Be With You/Oh Melancholy Me	59	Audicon 102
I Only Want You/This Is My Love	60	Audicon 105
Gloria/Jungle Drums	60	Audicon 106
Beautiful Dreamer/One Look At You Is All It Took	60	Audicon 108
Made For Lovers/You Don't Love Me Anymore	60	Audicon 112
I Gotta Know/Aphrodite	61	Octavia 8005
Lonely Road/One Look Is All It Took	62	Jubilee 5406
The Bully/Empty Seat	63	ABC 10436
Sixteen Candles/The Third Floor (instrumental)	63	Diamond 146

ARTIST/SONG	YEAR	LABEL
Passions (2)		
Jackie Brown/My Aching Heart	58	Era 1063/Capitol 3963 (58)
Passions (3)		
Too Many Memories/The Reason (Why I Love You)	61	Unique 79X/79XX/Fantastic 79
Passions (4)		
Baby I Do/Man About Town	66	Back Beat 573
Passions (5)		
It Ain't Fair/I'm So Afraid	N/A	Topaz 1317
Pastel Keys (Ronnie Gill & the)		
Standing On The Mountain/Geraldine	58	Rip 108/Rio 129/Expiditus 500

The Pastels

ARTIST/SONG	YEAR	LABEL
Pastels (1)		
Bye Bye	55	States (unreleased)
Goodbye	55	States (unreleased)
Put Your Arms Around Me/Boom De De Boom	56	United 196
Pastels (2) (fb Big Dee Irwin)		
Been So Long/My One And Only Dream	57	Mascot 123/Argo 5287 (57)
Let's Go To The Rock & Roll Ball/You Don't Love Me Anymore	58	Argo 5297
So Far Away/Don't Knock	58	Argo 5314
Pastels (3)		
Swingin' Sam/(We Like) Crew Cuts (by the Debs & Escorts)	58	Josie 833
Pastels (4)		
King Of Fools/Mary	63	Limelight 3007
Pastels (5)		
Do You Ever Think Of Me/Sleep Tight	64	Pastel 506
Patios (Billy & the)		
Love Is A Story/You Name It	61	Lite 9002
Patti Anne (Patti Anne Mesner with the Flames)		
Shtiggy Boom/Baby, Baby I'm In Love With You (no group)	55	Aladdin 3280
Paul, Bunny (bb the Harptones)		
Such A Night/I'm Gonna Have Some Fun	54	Essex 352
Answer The Call/Lovey Dovey	54	Essex 359

ARTIST/SONG	YEAR	LABEL
Paul, Clarence (& group)		
I'll Be By Your Side/I Need Your Lovin'	59	Hanover 4519
Falling In Love Again/May Heaven Bless You	59	Roulette 4196
Pawns		
Summer	N/A	Baystate 1267
Payne, Chuck (& group)		
Baby/La De Da	57	Atlas 1072
Payne, Little Leon (& group)		
History Of Love	N/A	Daco 701
Peacheroos		
Be Bop Baby/Every Day My Love Is True	54	Excello 2044
Peachettes (Lynn Taylor & the) (female)		
Sweet Little Girl/The Bells Of St. Mary's	60	Clock 1033
Peacocks		
My New Hi-Fi/Teen Hoppers Ball	58	4 Star 1718
I Want You To Know/Tender Love	58	Noble 711
Peacocks (Junior Ryder & the)		
Sad Story/Better Stop (no group)	54	Duke 119
Peacocks (Nunnie Moore & the)		
Fontella/Bouquet Of Roses	57	L&M 1002/Firefly 322 (60)
Peanuts (M&M & the)		
Open Up Your Eyes/Lil Valley	64	Money 101
I Found My Love/The Phillie	64	Money 107
Pearlettes (female)		
He's Gone/Just In Case	61	Craig 501/502
Just In Case/Just In Case	61	Craig 562/Seg-Way 1003 (61)
Can I Get Him/Never Be Another Boy Like You	61	Vee Jay 422/Go 712
Can This Be Love/Cheated	62	Vault 100
Duchess Of Earl/Everybody	62	Vee Jay 435
Pearls (1)		
Shadows Of Love/Yum Yummy	56	Atco 6057
The Bells Of Love/Come On Home	56	Atco 6066
Let's You And I Go Steady/Zippety Zippety Zoom	56	Onyx 503/Relic 513 (64)
Tree In The Meadow/My, Oh My	56	Onyx 506/Relic 519 (64)
I Sure Need You/Your Cheatin' Heart	57	Onyx 510/Relic 520 (64)
Ice Cream Baby/Yuz-A-Ma-Tuz	57	Onyx 511/Relic 521 (64)
The Wheel Of Love/It's Love, Love, Love	57	Onyx 516/Relic 522 (64)
Band Of Angels/Ugly Face	59	On The Square 320
It Must Be Love/I Cried	61	Amber 2003
I Just Can't Stand It	N/A	Astor 1005
Pearls (2) (Speedo & the) (ref Cadillacs)		
Who Ya Gonna Kiss/Naggity Nag	59	Josie 865
Pearls (3)		
Jungle Bunny/My Heart's Desire (as the Fabulous Pearls)	59	Dooto 448
Look At Me/It's Almost Tomorrow	60	Dolton 26
Pearls (4) (female)		
If I Had A Choice/Happy Over You	62	Warner Bros. 5300
Pebbles		
Ooo Wee/Let Me Hear It Again	55	Middle-Tone 2002
Oh What A Beautiful Dream/That Was My Girl	N/A	Eiffel 2085

ARTIST/SONG   YEAR LABEL

The Pearls

Pedal Pushers (B. Dale & the)
Love You Lovely Stranger/Foolish Little Fool   N/A Ko Ko 8803

Pedestrians (Jaywalker & the) (featuring Pete Antell)
Hey Now/Never Happen   62   Amy 848

Pedrick, Bobby (& group)
Maybe/Karine   66   Verve 10402

Pee Wees
Tootsie Roll/Blue Jean Cinderella   58   Josie 838

Peek, Paul (& group)
I'm Not You Fool Anymore/Oldsmo William   58   NRC 008

Peels
Juanita Banana/Fun   66   Karate 522

Peels, Leon (bb the Blue Jays)
A Casual Kiss/Cottonhead Joe   64   Whirlybird 2002

Pelicans (1)
Chimes/Ain't Gonna Do It   54   Imperial 5307
Down In Mexico   N/A LP only
Miss Lucy   N/A LP only

Pelicans (1) (Earl Nelson & the)
I Bow To You/Oh Gee, Oh Golly   57   Class 209

Pelicans (2)
Aurelia/White Cliffs Of Dover   54   Parrot 793

Pemberton, Jimmy (bb the Chantels)
From Rags To Riches/That's What You Think   59   End 1059/Mark-X 8002 (59)

Pendulums
Time Marches On/Masquerader   62   May 109

Penguins
No There Ain't No News Today/When I'm Gone   54   Dootone 345
(by Willie Headen & D. Williams Orch.)
Earth Angel/Hey Senorita   54   Dootone 348/Power 7023 (54)
I Ain't Gonna Cry No More   55   Dooto EP 101 (55)/Dooto LP 224
                                                           (57)/Authentic LP 224 (57)
Love Will Make Your Mind Go Wild/Ookey-Ook   55   Dootone 353

ARTIST/SONG	YEAR	LABEL
Kiss A Fool Goodbye/Baby, Let's Make Some Love	55	Dootone 362
Be Mine Or Be A Fool/Don't Do It	55	Mercury 70610
Walkin' Down Broadway/It Only Happens To You	55	Mercury 70654
Devil That I See/Promises, Promises, Promises	55	Mercury 70703
A Christmas Prayer/Jingle Jangle	55	Mercury 70762
My Troubles Are Not At An End/She's Gone, Gone	56	Mercury 70799
Earth Angel/Ice	56	Mercury 70943
Dealer Of Dreams/Peace Of Mind	56	Wing 90076
Pledge Of Love/I Knew I'd Fall In Love	57	Atlantic 1132
That's How Much I Need You/Be My Lovin' Baby	57	Dooto 428
Will You Be Mine/Cool Cool Baby	57	Mercury 71033
Sweet Love/Let Me Make Up Your Mind	58	Dooto 432
Do Not Pretend/If You're Mine	58	Dooto 435
You're An Angel/Mr. Junkman	59	Dooto 456
Butterball	59	Dooto LP 242/Dooto EP 241
Cold Heart	59	Dooto LP 242/Dooto EP 241
Heart Of A Fool	59	Dooto LP 242/Dooto EP 241
Lover Or Fool	59	Dooto LP 242/Dooto EP 241
Money Talks	59	Dooto LP 242/Dooto EP 241
Want Me	59	Dooto LP 242/Dooto EP 241
Believe Me/The Pony Rock	62	Sun State 101
Memories Of El Monte/Be Mine	63	Original Sound 27
Heavenly Angel/Big Bobo's Party	64	Original Sound 54

Penguins (Cleve Duncan & the)

To Keep Our Love/Universal Twist	61	Eldo 119

Penn Boys

Have A Party	N/A	Bobby 502

Penn, Dan (& group)

Let Them Talk/Close To Me	64	Fame 6402

Penn, Tony (& group)

King Or A Fool/I Don't Like It	59	P.R.I. 101

Pennants

Don't Go/Workin' Man	61	World 102

Pentagons

Silly Dilly/It's Spring Again	58	Specialty 644
To Be Loved (Forever)/Down At The Beach	60	Fleet Int'l 100/Donna 1337 (61)
For A Love That Is Mine/I Like The Way You Look At Me	61	Donna 1344
I Wonder (If Your Love Will Ever Belong To Me)/She's Mine	61	Jamie 1201
Forever Yours/Gonna Wait For You	61	Sutter 100
Until Then/I'm In Love	62	Jamie 1210/Caldwell 411 (62)

Peppermints (1)

Teen Age Idol/Believe Me	59	House Of Beauty 1
Peppermint Jerk/We All Warned You	65	RSVP 1112

Peppermints (2)

Cheryl Ann/Now I Cry	65	Peppermint 1001

Peppers (1)

Rocking Chair Baby/Hold On	54	Chess 1577
Yoko Hoko Homa/Blossoms	58	Jane 105

Peppers (2)

One More Chance/A Place In My Heart	61	Ensign 1076
Little Piece Of Paper/It Wouldn't Be The Same	61	Press 2809

Percells (female)

Cheek To Cheek/What Are Boys Made Of	63	ABC 10401
Look At That Guy/Boy Friends	63	ABC 10449

ARTIST/SONG	YEAR	LABEL
My Guy/Hully Gully Guitar	63	ABC 10476
I Stand Alone/The Greatest	63	ABC 10516

Perenials
| I Need Your Lovin'/Please Please (by the Scholars) | N/A | Ruby-Ray 2 |

Perennials
| I'm Yours 'Til The End/My Big Mistake | 63 | Ball 1016 |

Perfections
| Hey Girl/My Baby | 59 | Lost Nite 111 |
| Am I Gonna Lose You/I Love You, My Love | N/A | SVR 1005 |

Performers (1)
| Give Me Your Heart/I'll Make You Understand | 56 | All Star 714/Tip Top 402 (57) |

Performers (2) (Bobby Sanders & the)
| Cleopatra/Dead Pigeon | 63 | Sound-O-Rama 117 |

Performers (3) (aka Majors/aka Versatiles)
| Just Dance/Love Is The Answer (by the Majors) | 66 | ABC 10777 |

Peridots
| Hully Gully All Nite Long/It's The Bomp | 61 | Deauville 100 |

Perkins, Roy (& group)
| You're Gone/Here Am I | 55 | Meladee 112 |

Perks (Bill Pinky & the) (gm Bill Pinckney)
| After The Hop/Sally's Got A Sister | 58 | Phillips International 3524 |

Permanents
| Oh Dear, What Can The Matter Be/Let Me Be Baby | 63 | Chairman 4405 |

Perri's
| Jerrilee/Ballad Of A Happy Heart | 58 | Madison 105 |

Perry, Charles (& group)
| Walk Through The Darkness/If There Wasn't Any You | 62 | Melic 4119 |

Perry, Tony (& group)
| Trust In Our Love/I'm Yours Forever | 57 | Ember 1015 |

Persianettes (Timmy Carr & the)
| Only Now And Then/I Could Never Stop Crying | 64 | Guyden 2104 |

Persianettes (Timmy & the)
| Timmy Boy/There Comes A Time | 63 | Olympia 100 |
| Summertime Is Near/Summertime Is Near | 63 | Olympia 101 |

Persians (1)
| Your Love/Keep On Moving | 55 | Capitol 3230 |

Persians (2)
Teardrops Are Falling/Vault Of Memories	61	Goldisc G1/Goldisc 1004 (63)
Gee What A Girl/Love Me Tonight	62	Gold Eagle 1813
Tears Of Love/Dance Now	62	RSVP 114
Sunday Kind Of Love/When We Get Married	62	RTO 100
(When You Said) Let's Get Married/(Let's Monkey) At The Party	63	Goldisc G17/Music World 102 (63)
Get A Hold Of Yourself/The Steady Kind	63	Pageant 601
That Girl Of Mine/Don't Let Me Down	63	Sir Rah 501

Persians (3) (Paris & the)
| Credit Man | 61 | AKU 921 |

Personalities
| Woe Woe Baby/Yours To Command | 57 | Safari 1002 |

ARTIST/SONG	YEAR	LABEL

Persuaders
| What Could It Be/Tears | 59 | Winley 235/Relic 1002 (65) |

Pery Mates
| It Was You/Great Red Rat | 61 | CaJo 210 |

Petite Teens
| My Singing Idol And Poor Little Fool/We're In Our Teens | 59 | Brunswick 55119 |

Petites
Marguerite/Blessed Are They	58	Spinning 6003
Sweetie Pie/Who Kicked The Light Plug Out Of The Socket	58	Spinning 6005
Get You Daddy's Car Tonight/Sun Showers	60	Columbia 41662
Making Miracle/Little Love	61	Columbia 42053
The Beating Of My Heart/Nobody But You	62	Elmor 304
I'm Gonna Love Him/Is Thirteen Too Young To Fall In Love	64	Ascot 2166

Pets
| Cha-Hua-Hua/Cha-Kow-Ski | 58 | Arwin 109 |

Pets (Jerry Warren & the)
| Street Of Love/Monkey Walk | 59 | Arwin 118 |

Petty, Eddie (& group)
| That's You, That's Me | 57 | Guest 1003 |

Phaetons (1)
| Fling/Homemade | 59 | Hi-Q 5012 |
| I Love My Baby/As You Know | 59 | Vin 1015 |

Phaetons (2) (gm Dean Torrence)
| I'm So Lonely/Road Of Blues | 63 | Sahara 102 |

Phantoms
| Lost And Found/Channel Fever | 57 | Baton 244 |

Phantoms (Lynn Roberts & the)
| Miss You Tonite/I'll Be Around | 56 | Oriole 101 |

Phantoms (Vernon Green & the)
| Sweet Breeze/The Old Willow Tree | 56 | Specialty 581 |
| Tell Me Why/How | 56 | Specialty unreleased |

Phantones
| This Is Love/Get Ready, Get Right | 58 | Code 707 |
| Is This The End/Waiting For Your Love | 59 | Bale 105 |

Pharaohs (1)
| Somewhere There's A Rainbow/I'll Never Ever Love Again | 60 | Flip 352 |
| My Little Girl | N/A | Specialty |

Pharaohs (1) (Richard Berry & the)
Take The Key (And Open Up My Heart)/No Kissin' And A Huggin'	56	Flip 318
Louie, Louie/You Are My Sunshine	57	Flip 321
Rock, Rock, Rock (This Dance Is Crazy)/Sweet Sugar You	57	Flip 327
You're The Girl/You Look So Good	58	Flip 331
Do I Do I/Besame Mucho	58	Flip 339
Have Love Will Travel/No Room	59	Flip 349
You Are My Sunshine/You Look So Good	62	Flip 360

Pharaohs (2) (Ricky & the)
| Teenager's Love Song/Watusi | 56 | Class 202 |

Pharaohs (3)
| My Dream Girl | 59 | Wildcat 0018 |

ARTIST/SONG	YEAR	LABEL

Pharaohs (4) (Artie & the)
I'll Take Care Of You/Foxy Devil — 64 — Cuca 1162

Pharaohs (5)
Come To Me/If I Had The Power — 61 — Pharaoh 1

Pharaohs (6)
Walking Sad/Come On Baby — 57 — Fascination 001/Skylor 101

Pharaos
Tender Touch/Heads Up, High Hopes Over You — 60 — Donna 1327

Pharoads
My Little Girl/All Alone — 52 — RPM 355 (unreleased)

Pharotones
Monkey Business/Paradise On Earth (by the Five Satins) — 63 — Times Square 21/ Times Square 94 (64)

Pheasants
Out Of The Mist/Hot Biscuits — 63 — Throne 802

Philadelphians
Church Bells/Coming Home To You — 61 — Campus 103
Dear/The Love That I Lost — 61 — Chesapeake/Campus 101 (61)
The Vow/I Missed Her — 62 — Cameo 216

Philadelphians (Big John & the)
My Love, My Love/Cleo's Theme (Vince Mon Tanta) — 63 — Guyden 2093

Philettes
Again Again And Again/Riddle Riddle Mar Randy O — 64 — Hudson 8105

Philharmonics
Why Don't You Write Me?/Teen Town Hop — 58 — Future 2200

Phillipairs
You Fascinate Me/Believe In Tomorrow (by the Moroccans) — 57 — Salem 1014

Phillips, Phil (bb the Twilights (aka Cookie & the Cupcakes))
Sea Of Love/Juella (with the Twilights) — 59 — Khoury's 711/ Mercury 71465 (59)

Picadilly Pipers
Where's My Baby/I Loved Only You — 56 — Chart 615

Picadillys
Lonely Lover's Prayer/Mr. Butterball — 56 — Chart 619

Pictures (C.L. & the) (fb Curtis Lee)
Let's Take A Ride/I'm Asking Forgiveness — 61 — Dunes 2010/Sabra 517 (60)
Afraid/Mary Go Round — 62 — Dunes 2017
Lonely Weekends/Better Him Than Me — 63 — Dunes 2020
Pickin' Up The Pieces Of My Heart/Mr. Mistaker — 63 — Dunes 2021
I'm Sorry/That's What's Happening — 63 — Dunes 2023
I'm Not A Know It All — 64 — Kirk 635
He'll Only Hurt You/Talking About My Baby — 64 — Kirk 639/Monument 854 (64)
Could This Be Magic/Yolanda — 65 — Monument 888
Baby Not Now/Jigsaw Puzzle — 66 — Monument 958
Love Will Find A Way/Then I'll Know — N/A — Cadette 8005

Pilgrims
Careless Love/Walkin' Down The Track — 56 — Baton 235

ARTIST/SONG	YEAR	LABEL
Pin-Ups		
Lookin' For Boys/Kenny	64	Stork 1
Ping Pongs (1)		
In The Chapel In The Moonlight/Big Ben (Hoffman-Siegel Orch.)	60	Cub 9062
Zyzzle/Summer Reverie	60	United Artists 236
Ping Pongs (2)		
You Belong To Me/Falabalon	62	Marco 107
Ping Pongs (3)		
You And Only You/I Don't Want To Wait	64	G-Note
Pioneers		
For You/48 Hours	61	Golden Crest 565
Pipes		
Be Fair/Let Me Give You Money	56	Dootone 388
I Love The Life I Live/You Are An Angel	56	Dootone 401
So Long/Baby Please Don't Go	58	Jacy 001
Teamwork/Soon I Will Be Done	62	Carlton 575
Pips (fb Gladys Knight)		
Ching Chong/Whistle, My Love	58	Brunswick 55048
Every Beat Of My Heart/Room In Your Heart	61	Huntom 2510/Vee Jay 386 (61)/ Fury 1050 (61)
Linda/Darling	62	Fury 1067
Happiness/I Had A Dream Last Night	63	Everlast 5025
Pirates (1) (Terry & the)		
What Did He Say/Talk About The Girl	58	Valli 100/Chess 1695 (58)
Pirates (2) (Black Beard & the)		
Lovers Never Say Goodbye/Show Me The Way To Go Home	58	Ad 101
Pirates (3) (Johnny Kidd & the)		
Yes Sir, That's My Baby/Shakin' All Over	60	Apt 25040
I'll Never Get Over You/Then I Got Everything	63	Capitol 5065
Pirates (4) (aka Motown Temptations)		
Mind Over Matter/I'll Love You 'Til The Day I Die	62	Mel-O-Dy 105
Pirouettes		
If You See My Baby/The Wrangler Stretch	64	Diamond 165
Pitch Pikes		
Zing Zong/Never Never Land	57	Mercury 71099
How Will I Know/Come Back To Me	57	Mercury 71147
Pitt, Eugene (& group)		
Why Why Why/Another Rainy Day	66	Veep 1229
Pitter Pats		
Baby You Hurt Me/Whatcha Bet	67	Instant 3284
Pixies		
Cry Like A Baby/Just Like A Tear	62	AMC 102/Don-Dee 102 (63)
Geisha Girl/He's Got You	65	Autumn 12
Pixies 3 (female)		
Birthday Party/Our Love	63	Mercury 72130
442 Glenwood Avenue/Cold, Cold Winter	63	Mercury 72208
Love Walked In/Orphan Boy	64	Mercury 72231
Gee/After The Party	64	Mercury 72250
The Hootch/It's Summer Time	64	Mercury 72288
Love Me, Love Me/Your Way	64	Mercury 72357

ARTIST/SONG	YEAR	LABEL
Pizani, Frank (bb the Highlights)		
Every Time/Angry	57	Bally 1040
It's No Fun/Wanna Dance	59	Afton 616
The Stars Will Remember	59	Afton 617
Plaids (1)		
Keeper Of My Heart/I Sing For You	56	Darl 1001
Al-Lee-O! Al-Lee-Ay!/Halfway To Heaven	56	Darl 1003
Plaids (2)		
Hungry For Your Love/Chit-Chat	58	Liberty 55167
My Pretty Baby/Till The End Of The Dance	58	Nasco 6011
Around The Corner (From My House)/He Stole Flo	59	Era 3002
Plaids (3) (Willie Logan & the) (aka Equals)		
You Conquered Me/Say That You Care	64	Jerry-O 103
Planets (1) (aka Rhythm Aces)		
Never Again/Stand There Mountain	57	Era 1038
Be Sure/Wild Leaves	57	Era 1049
Sharin' Lockers/I Need You So	59	Nu-Clear 7422
Be Sure/Once In A Lifetime	62	Aljon 1244
Planets (2)		
Mr. Moon/You Are My Sunshine	64	Roulette 4551
Planetts		
The Magic Age Of Sixteen/So Young, So Warm, So Wonderful	63	Goldisc G7
Plants		
Dear I Swear/It's You	57	J&S 1602
From Me/My Girl	58	J&S 1617/1618
I Searched The Seven Seas/I Took A Trip Way Over The Sea	58	J&S 248/249
Platinums		
One Summer Night	N/A	J&M 122648
Platters		
Give Thanks/Hey Now	53	Federal 12153
I Need You All The Time/I'll Cry When You're Gone	53	Federal 12164
Roses Of Picardy/Beer Barrel Boogie	54	Federal 12181
Tell The World/Love All Night	54	Federal 12188
Voo-Vee-Ah-Bee/Shake It Up Mambo	54	Federal 12198
Maggie Doesn't Work Here Anymore/Take Me Back, Take Me Back	54	Federal 12204
Only You (And You Alone)/You Made Me Cry	55	Federal 12244
I Need You All The Time/Tell The World	55	Federal 12250
Glory Of Love	55	Federal LP 395-549/King LP 549 (56)/Mercury LP 20146 (56)
Only You (And You Alone)/Bark, Battle And Ball	55	Mercury 70633
The Great Pretender/I'm Just A Dancing Partner	55	Mercury 70753
Only You (And You Alone)/Voo-Vee-Ah-Bee	55	Power 7012
Give Thanks/I Need You All The Time	56	Federal 12271
(You've Got) The Magic Touch/Winner Take All	56	Mercury 70819
My Prayer/Heaven On Earth	56	Mercury 70893
You'll Never Never Know/It Isn't Right	56	Mercury 70948
One In A Million/On My Word Of Honor	56	Mercury 71011
Heart Of Stone	56	Mercury LP 20216/ Mercury EP 3343
I'm Sorry/He's Mine	57	Mercury 71032
My Dream/I Wanna	57	Mercury 71093
Only Because/The Mystery Of You	57	Mercury 71184
For The First Time/Twilight Time	58	Mercury 30075
Helpless/Indiff'rent	58	Mercury 71246
Twilight Time/Out Of My Mind	58	Mercury 71289
My Old Flame/You're Making A Mistake	58	Mercury 71320

ARTIST/SONG	YEAR	LABEL
I Wish/It's Raining Outside	58	Mercury 71353
Smoke Gets In Your Eyes/No Matter What You Are	58	Mercury 71383/
		Mercury 10001 (58)
Enchanted/The Sound And The Fury	59	Mercury 71427
Remember When/Love Of a Lifetime	59	Mercury 71467
Wish It Were Me/Where	59	Mercury 71502/
		Mercury 10018 (59)
My Secret/What Does It Matter	59	Mercury 71538
Harbor Lights/Sleepy Lagoon	60	Mercury 71563
Ebb Tide/(I'll Be With You In) Apple Blossom Time	60	Mercury 71624
Red Sails In The Sunset/Sad River	60	Mercury 71656/
		Mercury 10038 (60)
To Each His Own/Down The River Of Dreams	60	Mercury 71697
By The River Sainte Marie	60	Mercury LP 20481/
		Mercury LP 60160 (60)
Lazy River	60	Mercury LP 20481/
		Mercury LP 60160 (60)
Moonlight On The Colorado	60	Mercury LP 20481/
		Mercury LP 60160 (60)
On A Slow Boat To China	60	Mercury LP 20481/
		Mercury LP 60160 (60)
Rainbow On The River	60	Mercury LP 20481/
		Mercury LP 60160 (60)
Reflections In The Water	60	Mercury LP 20481/
		Mercury LP 60160 (60)
Honeysuckle Rose	60	Mercury LP 20589/
		Mercury LP 60254 (60)
Jeanine	60	Mercury LP 20589/
		Mercury LP 60254 (60)
When You Wore A Tulip	60	Mercury LP 20589/
		Mercury LP 60254 (60)
Whispering Grass	60	Mercury LP 20589/
		Mercury LP 60254 (60)
If I Didn't Care/True Lover	61	Mercury 71749
Trees/Immortal Love	61	Mercury 71791
I'll Never Smile Again/You Don't Say	61	Mercury 71847
You'll Never Know/Song For The Lonely	62	Mercury 71904
It's Magic/Reaching For A Star	62	Mercury 71921
More Than You Know/Every Little Movement	62	Mercury 71986
Memories/Heartbreak	63	Mercury 72060
Once In A While/I'll See You In My Dreams	63	Mercury 72107
Here Comes Heaven Again/Strangers	63	Mercury 72129
Cuando Caliente El Sol/Viva Ju Juy	63	Mercury 72194
Full Moon And Empty Arms	63	Mercury LP 20759/
		Mercury LP 60759 (63)
In A Little Spanish Town	63	Mercury LP 20759/
		Mercury LP 60759 (63)
Moon Over Miami	63	Mercury LP 20759/
		Mercury LP 60759 (63)
Moonlight And Roses	63	Mercury LP 20759/
		Mercury LP 60759 (63)
Moonlight Memories	63	Mercury LP 20759/
		Mercury LP 60759 (63)
My Reverie	63	Mercury LP 20759/
		Mercury LP 60759 (63)
Oh How I Miss You Tonight	63	Mercury LP 20759/
		Mercury LP 60759 (63)
Sentimental Journey	63	Mercury LP 20759/
		Mercury LP 60759 (63)
Shine On Harvest Moon	63	Mercury LP 20759/
		Mercury LP 60759 (63)
Row The Boat Ashore/Java Jive	64	Mercury 72242
Sincerely/P. S., I Love You	64	Mercury 72305
Love Me Tender/Little Things Mean A Lot	64	Mercury 72359
Don't Blame Me	N/A	Mercury EP

ARTIST/SONG	YEAR	LABEL
I'd Climb The Highest Mountain	N/A	Mercury EP 3343
You've Changed	N/A	Mercury EP 3343
I'll Get By	N/A	Mercury EP 3344
I Don't Know Why	N/A	Mercury EP 3345
Take Me In Your Arms	N/A	Mercury EP 3345
Temptation	N/A	Mercury EP 3345
You Can Depend On Me	N/A	Mercury EP 3345
Darktown Strutter's Ball	N/A	Mercury EP 3353
No Power On Earth	N/A	Mercury EP 3353
Sweet Sixteen	N/A	Mercury EP 3353
You Are Too Beautiful	N/A	Mercury EP 3353
Don't Forget	N/A	Mercury EP 3355
Mean To Me	N/A	Mercury EP 3355
Oh Promise Me	N/A	Mercury EP 3355
Time And Tide	N/A	Mercury EP 3355

Platters '65 (featuring Linda Hayes)

Won't You Be My Friend/Run While It's Dark	65	Entree 107

Platters (Linda Hayes & the)

Please Have Mercy/Oochi Pachi	55	King 4773

Playboy Band (John Fred & His)

Mirror Mirror (On The Wall)/To Have And To Hold	62	Montel 2001

Playboys (1)

Tell Me (Are You Really Mine)/Rock, Moan And Cry	54	Cat 108

Playboys (1) (Charles White & the)

Good Golly, Miss Molly/Honey Bun	55	Cat 115

Playboys (2)

One Question/So Good	56	Tetra 4447

Playboys (3)

Don't Do Me Wrong/Why Do I Love You, Why Do I Care	57	Mercury 71228
Over The Weekend/Double Talk	58	Martinique 101/Cameo 142 (58)
Golly Gosh Oh Gee/Sugar Lump	58	United Artists 124
Memories/You're All I See	59	ABC 10070
Icy Fingers/Party Ice	59	Dolton 8
Crazy Daisy/Sweet Talk	59	Imperial 5586
Please Forgive Me/Sing Along	59	Martinique 400
Jungle Fever/Shotgun	59	Rik 572
Believe It Or Not/Hawaiian War Chant	59	Souvenir 1001
Boston Hop/What'd I Say? (by the Cousins)	61	Chancellor 1074
Duck Walk/If I Had My Way	62	Chancellor 1106
Careful With My Heart/Girl Of My Dreams	62	Cotton 1008
Mope De Mope/The Night Before Christmas	63	Legato 101
Shortnin' Bread/Cheater Stomp	N/A	Catalina 1069

Playboys (4)

Cross My Heart	61	Nite Owl 30

Playboys (5)

When I Meet A Girl Like You/I Have Love	63	Seville 135

Playboys (6) (Gene Vito & the)

Playboy/I Want You Back Again	64	Blast 214

Playboys (7) (Caleb & the)

I'm Yours/See About Me	63	Olimpic 4575

Playboys (8) (Gary Gillespie & the)

Honest I Do/Dancing Girl	62	Delta 520

ARTIST/SONG	YEAR	LABEL
Playboys (9) (John Fred & the)		
Shirley/High Heel Sneakers	62	Montel 998
Players (1) (Leroy Lovett & the)		
Unchained Melody/Midnight Sun	55	Atlantic 1058
Players (2)		
You Need A Love/What About Me	63	Tarx 1007
Playgirls (1) (aka Blossoms)		
Hey Sport/Young Love Swings The World	59	RCA 7546
Gee, But I'm Lonesome/Sugar Beat	60	RCA 7719
Playgirls (2)		
Bells/Donnie	62	Galaxy 713
Playmates (aka Three Playmates)		
It Must Be Love/Giddy-Up-A-Ding-Dong	57	Savoy 1523
Playthings		
Lipstick/Sittin'	58	Liberty 55147
Plazas (1) (Eric & the)		
I Wish/It's The Last Kiss	63	Production 612
Plazas (2) (Nicky Addeo & the)		
Danny Boy/Lovely Way To Spend An Evening	64	Revelation 7-101
Pleasers (1) (Little Wilbur & the)		
Heart To Heart/Alone In The Night	57	Aladdin 3402
Pleasers (1) (Wilbur Whitfield & the)		
P.B. Baby/The One I Love	57	Aladdin 3381
Plaything/I Don't Care	57	Aladdin 3396
Pleasers (2) (Bobbie Please & the)		
The Monster/The Switch	59	Jamie 1118
Your Drivers License, Please/Heartache Street	61	Era 3044
Pleasures		
Don't You Know (I Love You)/Plaything	64	RSVP 1102
Pledges (1) (aka Skip & Flip)		
Betty Jean/Her Bermuda Shorts	57	Revere 3517
Pledges (2)		
I'm Sorry/Won't You Give Your Love To Me	59	Hamilton 50028
Plurals		
Donna My Dear/Miss Annie	58	Wanger 186/187/ Bergen 186/187 (59)
Goodnight/I'm Sold	59	Wanger 188
Angel	N/A	N/A
Plush Pups (Terrie Parker & the)		
A Dream In The Night/'Cause I'm Your Friend	61	Queen 24011
Plushtones		
Raindrops/Penny Loafers	60	Plush 601
Poe Rats (Al Downing & the)		
Oh Babe/Down On The Farm	58	Challenge 59006
Poets (1)		
Vowels Of Love/Dead	58	Pull 129/Flash 129 (58)

ARTIST/SONG	YEAR	LABEL
Poets (2)		
I'm In Love/Honey Chile	60	Spot 107/Imperial 5664 (60)
Poka-Dotts (female)		
Ting-A-Ling/Stairway To Love	54	Modern 945
Poni-Tails		
It's Just My Luck To Be Fifteen/Wild Eyes And Tender Lips	57	ABC 9846
Can I Be Sure/Still In Your Teens	57	Marc 1001
Your Wild Heart/Que La Bozena	57	Point 8
Born Too Late/Come On, Joey, Dance With Me	58	ABC 9934
Seven Minutes In Heaven/Close Friends	58	ABC 9969
Moody/Oom-Pah Polka	59	ABC 10027
I'll Be Seeing You/I'll Keep Tryin'	59	ABC 10047
Before We Say Goodnight/Come Be My Love	59	ABC 10077
Father Time/Early To Bed	59	ABC 9995
Who, When And Why/Oh, My, You	60	ABC 10114
Poor Boys (King Richard & the)		
Didn't We Fool Them?/I'm Not Ashamed	61	Apollo 1201
Washboard/I'm Going To Spend My Money	61	Apollo 1203
Pop Overs		
Time's Run Out	N/A	Toppette 1020
Popcorns		
I Loved You/Pluto	63	Vee Jay 537
Popsicles		
Thumb Print/This Is The End	58	Knight 2002
Baby I Miss You/I Don't Want To Be Your Baby Anymore	65	GNP Crescendo 336
Populaires		
Island Of Paradise/I Lost My Heart	57	Marvello 5001
Popular Five		
Sh-Boom/Tomorrow Night	67	Rae-Cox 1001
I'm A Love Maker/Little Bitty Pretty One	68	Minit 32050
Baby I've Got It/Best Friend Worst Enemy	70	Mister Chand 8001
Pork Chops		
I Wanna See My Lovin' Baby/Everything's Cool	56	Herald 493
Porter, Jake (with the Buzzards)		
The Bop/Wine, Women And Gold	55	Combo 91
Porto, Billy (& group)		
Ruby Ruby/Foolish Dreams	57	Mercury 71205
Portraits		
Close To You/Easy Cash	59	Capitol 4181
Yo-Yo Girl/My Big Brother's Friend	61	RCA 7900
Three Blind Mice/We're Gonna Party	63	Tri-Disc 109
A Million To One/Let's Tell The World	67	Sidewalk 928
Over The Rainbow/Runaround Girl	68	Sidewalk 935
Posse (Marshall Laws & the)		
Mama's House/Little Baby	61	Forum 702
Possessions		
No More Love/You And Your Lies	64	Britton 1003/Parkway 930 (64)
Powell Quintet (The Austin Powell Quintet)		
Some Other Spring/All This Can't Be True	51	Decca 48206

ARTIST/SONG	YEAR	LABEL

Powell, Austin (bb the James Quintet)
Wrong Again/What More Can I Ask	52	Atlantic 968

Powell, Sandy (& group)
Bon Bon/Pistol Packin' Mama	61	Herald 557/Impala 211

Powell, Tiny (& group)
Take Me With You (flip has no group)	64	Wax 101/Wax 14

Powers, Roni (& group)
An Angel Up In Heaven/I Wish	61	LT Productions 1022

Powers, Wayne (& group)
My Love Song/Point Of View	58	Phillips International 3523

Prancers
Rudolph The Red-Nosed Reindeer/Short Short'nin'	59	Guaranteed 204

Precisions (1)
You Can't Play Games/Dream On	60	Strand 25038
Cleopatra/Someone To Watch Over Me	62	Golden Crest 571
Eight Reasons Why (I Love You)/Mama Told Me	62	Highland 300

Precisions (2) (Tommy Genova & the)
What Has Happened To You/The Lover	62	Bella 606

Precisions (3)
Sweet Dreams	63	Debra 1001

Precisions (4)
Brenda/White Christmas	N/A	Rayna 1001

Precisions (5)
The Love (I Found In You)/What Would You Do	N/A	Wild 903

Preeteens
What Makes Me Love You/Pass It On	59	J&S 1756

Prells
It's A Wig/Cash	64	Skyline 1004

Preludes (1)
Don't Fall In Love Too Soon/I Want Your Arms Around Me (All The Time)	56	Empire 103

Preludes (2)
Vanishing Angel/Kingdom Of Love	58	Acme 730/Cub 9005 (58)

Preludes (3)
Lorraine/Oh, Please, Genie	61	Arliss 1004
A Place For You (In My Heart)/That Would Be So Good	62	Octavia 8008

Preludes (4)
Flip Flop	N/A	Imperial

Preludes Five
Starlight/Don't You Know Love	61	Pik 231

Premeers
Diary Of Our Love/Gee Oh Gee	62	Herald 577

Premieres & the Invictas
Do It/Magic Of Love	59	F-M 677

ARTIST/SONG	YEAR	LABEL
Premiers (1)		
Baby/New Moon	56	Dig 106
Have A Heart/My Darling	56	Dig 113
Red Sails In The Sunset/Your Kiss	57	Dig 141 (unreleased)/ Relic LP 5052 (85)
When You Are In Love/The Trap Of Love	57	Fortune 527
Is It A Dream?/Valerie	57	Gone 5009
Hey Miss Fancy/Run Along Baby	57	RCA 6958
China Doll/Life Is Grand	58	Cindy 3008
Red Light Bandit (Caryl Chessman)/True Deep Love	60	Dore 547
Reverie/Double Date	61	Clock 1042
She Goes Oonka Chicka/What Makes Little Girls Cry	61	Dore 614
Frantic/The Beatle Walk (by the Phaetons)	64	Sahara 103
Lonely Weatherman	N/A	Mohican
Speaking Of You/Funky Monkey	N/A	Odex 1711
Premiers (1) (Artie & Linda & the)		
Laughing On The Outside/Blueberry Hill	64	Chancellor 1147
Premiers (1) (Julie Stevens & the)		
Blue Mood/Crazy Bells	56	Dig 115/Eldo 107 (60)/Dice 115
Take My Heart/I Don't Want To Know	57	Dig 129
Evening Star/Last Of The Real Smart Guys	61	Dore 603
Angel Love/False Love	62	Best 1004
Premiers (2) (John McKinney & the)		
Angels In The Sky/Gee, How I Love You	58	Mad 1009
Premiers (3)		
Hop And Skip/Uh-Huh	58	Bond 5803/5804
Firewater/Younger Than You	59	Nu-Phi 429/Nu-Phi 701
Premiers (4)		
I Think I Love You/Tonight	59	Mink 021/Parkway 807 (60)
Premiers (5) (fb Roger Koob) (aka Roger & the Travelers)		
Jolene/Oh Theresa	59	Alert 706
Pigtails Eyes Are Blue/I Pray	60	Fury 1029
Falling Star/She Gives Me Fever	61	Rust 5032
Run Along Baby	N/A	Coast 102
Premiers (6) (Ronnie & the)		
Sharon/Cha Cha Rock	61	Highland 1014
Premiers (7) (Herb Johnson & the)		
Help/Crying Blues	N/A	Palm
Premonitions		
My Girl Pearl	67	Jade
Presidents		
The Toast/Pots And Pans	62	Mercury 72016
Prestos		
Lookin' For Love/Till We Meet Again	55	Mercury 70747
Pretenders (1) (featuring Jimmy Jones) (aka Savoys (3))		
Close Your Eyes/Part Time Sweetheart	55	Whirlin' Disc 106/ Port 70040 (61)
Posessive Love/I've Got To Have You, Baby	56	Rama 198
Tonight/I Love You So	57	Holiday 2610
Blue And Lonely/Daddy Needs Baby	58	Central 2605/Apt 25026 (59)/ ABC 10094 (60)
Pennies From Heaven (a capella)	75	Relic LP 101

ARTIST/SONG   YEAR LABEL

The Pretenders

Pretenders (1) (Jimmy Jones & the) (aka Savoys (3))

Lover/Plain Old Love	56	Rama 207/Roulette 4322 (60)
The Day You Are Mine/Ding Dong Bells	62	Bethlehem 3050

Pretenders (2)

I'm So Happy/Smile	61	Power-Martin 1001/
		Relic 1004 (65)
Could This Be Magic/Stormy Weather (by the Earls on Rome 111)	76	Power-Martin 1005
Could This Be Magic/A Very Precious Love	76	Power-Martin 1006/1007

Pretenders (3) (Linda & the)

It's Not My Will/Believe Me	63	Assault 1880

Pretenders (4) (James Moore & the)

To Be Loved/A Man Should Never Cry	64	Tishman 905

Primettes (aka Supremes (3))

Tears Of Sorrow/Pretty Baby	61	Lu Pine 120

Primettes (aka Supremes (3)) (Al Garner & the)

All I Need Is You	86	Relic LP 8008

Prince, Rod (& group)

Rainbow Of Love/My Star All Alone	61	Comet 2140

Privateers (Joyce & the) (fb Joyce Heath)

Honor Role Of Love/The Bunny Tale	62	Agon 1003

Prizes

I Found Someone New/Summer's Here At Last	64	Parkway 917

Prodigals (1)

Judy/Marsha	58	Falcon 1011/Abner 1011 (58)/
		Tollie 9019 (64)
Won't You Believe/Vangie	58	Falcon 1015/Abner 1015 (58)

ARTIST/SONG	YEAR	LABEL
Prodigals (2)		
I Need You/You Better Move On	N/A	Acadian 1000
Professionals (Tommy Vann & the)		
I'm So Alone/Does Your Mama Know About Me	69	Congress 6001
Profiles (1)		
Take A Giant Step/Watusi Wobble	62	Goldie 1103
Profiles (2)		
Right By Her Side/Never	65	Gait 1444
Profits (aka Classics with Emil Stucchio)		
Wind/Vagabond	76	Sir 353
Prominents		
Just A Little/You're Gonna Lose Her	65	Lummtone 116
Prophets (1)		
Stormy/Baby Come Back	56	Atco 6078
Little Miss Dreamer/Sha-La-La	63	Jairick 201
Sugar Lump	N/A	Go-Lish
I Still Love You	N/A	Shell
Prophets (2) (Ronnie Dio & the)		
Love Pains/Ooh-Poo-Pah-Do	62	Atlantic 2145
Gonna Make It Alone/Swingin' Street	63	Lawn 218
10 Days With Brenda/Walking In Different Circles	67	Parkway 143
Pussycats		
Anniversary Of Love/Mickey Mouse March	63	Keyman 600
Puzzles		
I Need You/My Sweet Baby	68	Fatback 216
Pyramiders		
Don't Ever Leave Me/How It Feels	58	Scott 1505
Pyramids (1)		
Deep In My Heart For You/And I Need You	55	Federal 12233
Someday/Bow-Wow	55	Hollywood 1047/ "C" Note 1206 (56)
Pyramids (2)		
At Any Cost/Okay, Baby!	56	Davis 453
Why Did You Go?/Before It's Too Late	57	Davis 457
Pyramids (2) (Ruby Whitaker & the)		
I Don't Want To Set The World On Fire/I Get The Feeling	57	Mark-X 7007
Pyramids (3)		
Ankle Bracelet/Hot Dog Dooly Wah	58	Shell 711
Cryin'/I'm The Playboy	62	Cub 9112
Shakin' Fit/What Is Love	63	Vee Jay 489
Pyramids (4)		
Oh No You Won't/Long Long Time	59	RCA 7556
Here Comes Marsha/Penetration	63	Best 102/Best 13002 (64)
Pyramids (5) (Dave White & the)		
24 Hours/Write My Name	60	Pink 705
Pyramids (6) (Doug & Freddy & the) (aka Doug & Freddy with the Pyramids)		
Take A Chance On Love/I Know Your Lyin' (But Say It Again)	61	Finer Arts 1001

ARTIST/SONG	YEAR	LABEL
Q Tones (Don Q & the)		
Private Property/Baby I Don't Need You Now	N/A	Bullet 330
Q's (Bruce Clark & the)		
A Penny For Your Thoughts/Went To Chinatown	64	Hull 762
Quadrells		
Come To Me/What Can The Matter Be?	56	Whirlin' Disc 103
If I Give My Heart To You	N/A	Karen
Quadrells (Alan & the)		
The Woody Surfer/Loafin'	61	Goldisc G14
Quails (1)		
The Things She Used To Do/Pretty Huggin' Baby	55	DeLuxe 6085
The Cow/Take Me Back, Baby	63	American 1023
You're Mine	63	American 1024
Quails (1) (Bill Robinson & the)		
Lonely Star/Quit Pushin'	54	DeLuxe 6030
I Know She's Gone/Baby Don't Want Me No More	54	DeLuxe 6047
A Little Bit Of Love/Somewhere, Somebody Cares	54	DeLuxe 6057
Why Do I Wait?/Heaven Is The Place	54	DeLuxe 6059
Love Of My Life/Oh, Sugar	55	DeLuxe 6074
Quails (2) (fb Harvey Fuqua)		
It's Been A Long Time/Get To School On Time	61	Harvey 114
My Love/Never Felt Like This Before	62	Harvey 116
Over The Hump/I Thought	62	Harvey 120
Quailtones (Sax Kari & the)		
Tears Of Love/Roxanna	55	Josie 779
Quantrils		
If I Give My Heart To You/Thunderbird	N/A	Karem
Quardells (Billy Kope & the)		
It's All My Fault/Lulu	58	Kudo 662
Quarter Notes (1)		
Come De Nite/Loneliness	57	DeLuxe 6116
My Fantasy/Ten Minutes To Midnight	57	DeLuxe 6129
Quarter Notes (2)		
Like You Bug Me/Please Come Home	57	Dot 15685
Punkanilla/The Interview	58	RCA 7327
Record Hop Blues/Suki-Yaki-Rocki	59	Whizz 715
Frantic Flip/Canadian Sunset	60	Imperial 5647
Pretty Pretty Eyes/I Don't Want To Go Home	63	Guyden 2083
I've Been Loved/Hey Little Girl	66	Boom 60018
Quarter Notes (2) (Neil Darrow & the)		
Charlene/She's A Fine Chick	59	Whizz 717
Quarter Tones (Chip & the)		
Simple Simon/You Were My Baby	64	Carlton 604
Quarternotes		
Baby/Hold Me Darling	62	Little Star 112
Queens (Shirley Gunter & the)		
Oop Shoop/It's You	54	Flair 1050
You're Mine/Why?	55	Flair 1060
Baby, I Love You So/What Difference Does It Make?	55	Flair 1065
That's The Way I Like It/Gimme, Gimme, Gimme	55	Flair 1070

RTIST/SONG	YEAR	LABEL
uentins		
Mi Amore/You'll Never Know	60	Andie 5014
uestion Marks (1)		
Another Soldier Gone/Go And Get Some More	54	Swing Time 346
(by the Hollywood Flames)		
uestion Marks (2)		
Ballad Of A Girl And Boy/Concerto Rock	59	First 102
uin-Teens (female)		
I Hurt So/Dickie	63	Pike 5922
uin-Tones (female)		
Ding Dong/I Try So Hard	58	Chess 1685
Oh My Love	58	Red Top
Down The Aisle Of Love/Please Dear	58	Red Top 108/Hunt 321 (58)
What Am I To Do? (The Letter)/There'll Be No Sorrow	58	Red Top/Hunt 322 (58)
Oh, Heavenly Father/I Watch The Stars	59	Red Top 116
Choo Choo Boogie/Boogie Woogie Pony	N/A	Courtney 135
Fool That I Am/When My Sugar	N/A	Vo 5172
uinns (aka Continentals (1))		
Oh Starlite/Hong Kong	58	Cyclone 111
Unfaithful/Who Stole The Cookies	65	Relic 1012
uintones (1)		
I'm Willing/Strange As It Seems	56	Gee 1009
uintones (2)		
Power Of Love/Liverlips	61	Lee 1113
Times Sho' Gettin' Rough/Softie	62	Phillips International 3586
The Lonely Telephone/Just A Little Loving	N/A	Jordan 1601
uintones (2) (Jimmy Witherspoon & the)		
Still In Love/My Girl Ivy	56	Atco 6084
uintones (2) (Pat Foster & the)		
In The Doorway Crying/That's What They Say	60	Lee 1114
uintones (3)		
South Sea Island/More Than A Notion	57	Park 57-111/57-112
uotations		
Imagination/Ala-Men-Sa-Aye	61	Verve 10245
This Love Of Mine/We'll Reach Heaven Together	62	Verve 10252
See You In September/Summertime Goodbyes	62	Verve 10261
Listen My Children And You Shall Hear/	63	Liberty 55527
Speak Softly And Carry A Big Horn		
In The Night/Oh No, I Still Love Her	64	Admiral 753
It Can Happen To You/I Don't Have To Worry	68	DeVenus 107
Can I Have Someone/Havin' A Good Time (With My Baby)	68	Imperial 66368
Imagination (a capella)/Ala-Men-Sa-Aye (a capella)	73	Relic 1025
Night/Why Do You Do Me Like You Do	74	Downstairs 1003
I Wonder Why (a capella)	75	Relic LP 103
I've Seen Everything (a capella)	75	Relic LP 103
Maybe You'll Be There (a capella)	75	Relic LP 103
I'll Be Home (a capella)	75	Relic LP 104
Why Do You Do Me Like You Do (a capella)	75	Relic LP 104
I Don't Want To Cry (a capella)	75	Relic LP 105
To The Aisle (a capella)	75	Relic LP 105
My Blue Heaven (a capella)	75	Relic LP 108
Ala-Men-Sa-Aye (a capella)	75	Relic LP 109

ARTIST/SONG	YEAR	LABEL
R-Dells		
You Know Baby/You Say	60	Dade 1806
Candy Stick Twist/That's What I Want	62	Gone 5128
Radiants (1)		
I'll Never Be Mean/Ra Cha Cha	58	Wizz 713
Radiants (2) (Cleve Duncan & the)		
I'm Betting My Heart/To Keep Our Love (by the Penguins)	59	Dooto 451
Radiants (3) (Little Jan & the)		
Now Is The Hour/Is It True?	60	Clock 1028
Heart And Soul/If You Love Me	60	Vim 507
If You Love Me/Now Is The Hour	61	Goldisc G15
If You Love Me/Is It True	61	Queen 24007
Ragamuffins		
Don't Be Gone Long/The Fun We Had	64	Tollie 9027
Raging Storms		
Down At The Corner/So Hard To Take	62	Trans Atlas 691
Hound Dog/Dribble Twist	62	Warwick 677
Ragmops		
God Bless This Moment	N/A	CBM 314
Raiders (1) (Hal Goodson & the)		
Later Baby	57	Solo 108
Raiders (2)		
The Castle Of Love/Raiders From Outer Space	58	Atco 6125
My Steady Girl/Walking Through The Jungle	58	Brunswick 55090
Raiders (3)		
You Said/Blue Day	58	Mercury 71395
Raiders (4) (Tony Castle & the)		
Salty/Hi Lily, Hi Lo	61	Gone 5099
Sincerely/Tara's Theme	61	Gone 5105
Raiders (5) (Joey Vel & the)		
Acts Of Love/Goodbye	N/A	Promo Rel 102
Rainbeaus		
Maybe It's Wrong/That's All I'm Asking Of You	60	World Pacific 810
Rainbeaus (Vinnie Rome & the)		
Come Home/Crazy Maie	59	Apt 25035
Rainbows (1)		
My Heart Is Yours/Can't You See I Love You	54	Gem 214
Rainbows (2)		
Mary Lee/Evening	55	Red Robin 134/Pilgrim 703 (56)/Fire 1012 (60)
Shirley/Stay	56	Pilgrim 711/Argyle 1012 (62)
Stay/Shirley	56	Red Robin 141
They Say/Minnie	57	Rama 209
Baraboo	N/A	Red Robin (unreleased)
Honey Hush	N/A	Red Robin (unreleased)
Jelly Bean	N/A	Red Robin (unreleased)
The Bug	N/A	Red Robin (unreleased)
Rainbows (3) (Randy & the) (aka Dialtones)		
Denise/Come Back	63	Rust 5059
Why Do Kids Grow Up?/She's My Angel	63	Rust 5073
Dry Your Eyes/Happy Teenager	64	Rust 5080
Little Star/Sharin'	64	Rust 5091
Joyride/Little Hot Rod Susie	64	Rust 5101

The Rainbows

Song	Year	Label
Lovely Lies/I'll Forget Her Tomorrow	66	Mike 4001
Quarter To Three/He's A Fugitive	66	Mike 4004
Bonnie's Part Of Town/Can It Be?	66	Mike 4008
I'll Be Seeing You/Oh, To Get Away	67	B.T. Puppy 535
Angel Face/I Wonder Why	N/A	Crystal Ball 106

Rainbows (4)

Song	Year	Label
I Know/Only A Picture	63	Dave 908
It Wouldn't Be Right/Family Monkey	63	Dave 909
Till Tomorrow/Mama, Take Your Daughter Back	N/A	Gramo 5508

Rainbows (5)

Song	Year	Label
It's Terrific/Undertaker (by Sonny Walker)	73	Baron 100
Can't You See I Love You/My Love Is True (by the Parakeets)	73	Baron 105

Rainbows (6)

Song	Year	Label
Gonna Go Down	N/A	Mercury

Raindrops (1)

Song	Year	Label
(I Found) Heaven In Love/I Prayed For Gold	56	Spin-It 104
Little One/Rockin' On The Farm	58	Spin-It 106
Rock-A-Baby Rock/Rain	59	Capitol 4136
Without Love, Love, Love/Oh My	59	Hamilton 50021

Raindrops (2)

Song	Year	Label
Dim Those Lights/Oh, Oh, Baby	58	Vega 105

Raindrops (3)

Song	Year	Label
Love Is Like A Mountain/Maybe	60	Corsair 104/Dore 561 (60)

Raindrops (4)

Song	Year	Label
I Remember In The Still Of The Night/The Sweetheart Song	61	Imperial 5785

Raindrops (5) (Tony & the)

Song	Year	Label
While Walking/Our Love Is Over	61	Chesapeake 609
Tina/My Heart Cried	62	Crosley 340

Raindrops (6)

Song	Year	Label
What A Guy/It's So Wonderful	63	Jubilee 5444
The Kind Of Boy You Can't Forget/Even Though You Can't Dance	63	Jubilee 5455
That Boy John/Hanky Panky	63	Jubilee 5466
Book Of Love/I Won't Cry	64	Jubilee 5469
Let's Get Together/You Got What I Like	64	Jubilee 5475
One More Tear/Another Boy Like Mine	64	Jubilee 5487
Don't Let Go/My Mama Don't Like Him	64	Jubilee 5497

ARTIST/SONG	YEAR	LABEL
Raindrops (7)		
I Still Love You	64	Sotoplay 0028
Raindrops (8) (Jackie & the)		
My Heart Is Your Heart/Down Our Street	64	Colpix 738
Rainsford, Billy (& group)		
Starry Eyes/Magnolia	N/A	Hermitage 803
Rajahs (aka Nutmegs/aka Lyres)		
Shifting Sands/I Fell In Love	57	Klik 7805
Rose Ann/You're Crying	73	Klik 1019
Ramadas		
Teenage Dream/My Angel Eyes	63	Philips 40097
Summer Steady/Lonely Tears	63	Philips 40117
I'm Going To Be Blue/Walking Down The Hall	64	New World 2000
Ramblers (1)		
Search My Heart/50-50 Love	53	Jax 319
Vadunt-Un-Va-Da Song/Please Bring Yourself Back Home	54	MGM 11850
Bad Girl/Rickey-Do, Rickey-Do	55	MGM 55006
Ramblers (2)		
The Heaven And Earth/Don't You Know?	56	Federal 12286
Ramblers (3)		
Hurry Hurry Baby/Everything Is Wrong	56	Flash 101
Ramblers (4)		
Rambling/Devil Train	60	Addit 1257
Ramblers (5)		
Yaba Dab Ah Doo/Funny Papers	61	Impact 10
Ramblers (6)		
I Need You So	63	Larkwood 1104
Ramblers (7)		
Father Sebastian/Barbara (I Love You)	64	Almont 311
Birdland Baby/School Girl	64	Almont 313
Surfin' Santa/Silly Little Boy	64	Almont 315
Ramblers (8)		
Come On Back/So Sad	63	Trumpet 102
Ramblers (9)		
Bye Bye Bye/Lost Symphony	64	Cora 101
Rams		
Sweet Thing/Rock Bottom	55	Flair 1066
Ramsey, Gloria (& group)		
My Love/Good Poppin' Daddy	N/A	Hap 1894
Ran-Dells		
Sound Of The Sun/Come On And Love Me Too	63	Chairman 4407
The Martian Hop/Forgive Me Darling	64	Chairman 4403
Beyond The Stars/Wintertime	64	RSVP 1104
Rand, Johnny (& group)		
I'm Yours/Exodus	65	Keno 928
Rand, Rose Marie (& group)		
Lies, Lies, Lies/Gimmie	56	Vik 0206

ARTIST/SONG	YEAR	LABEL

Randell, Rick (& group)
Take My Name And Number/Stars — 62 — United Artists 448

Randells (Rick & the)
Let It Be You/Honey Doll — 59 — ABC 10055

Randle, Johnny (& female group)
My One And Only One — N/A — Jayree 2205

Randolph, Dean (& group)
False Love/Girl In The White Convertible — 63 — Chancellor 1138

Randolph, Leroy (& group)
I've Fallen Into The Tender Trap/Good To The Last Drop — 71 — Spring 121

Randolph, Lil (& group)
Satellite Love/Give Me A Girl — 58 — Chock Full Of Hits 103

Rannels
Blue Island/Boom, Baby — 63 — Boss 2122

Raphael, Johnny (& group)
We're Only Young Once/Lonely Road To Nowhere — 58 — Aladdin 3409

Rapid-Tones (Willie Winfield & the) (ref Harptones)
Sunday Kind Of Love/Memories Of You — 62 — Rapid 1002

Ravels (Sheriff & the)
Shombalor/Lonely One — 59 — Vee Jay 306

Ravenaires (aka Rivieras (2))
Together Forever/A Night To Remember — 58 — Algonquin 718 (second pressing, first is by the Rivieras)

Ravenetts
Too Young To Know/Misery — 59 — Moon 103

Ravens (1)
Count Every Star/I'm Gonna Paper My Walls With Your Love Letters — 50 — National 9111
A Simple Prayer/Water Boy — 56 — Argo 5261
Kneel And Pray/I Can't Believe — 56 — Argo 5255
Dear One/That'll Be The Day — 57 — Argo 5276/Checker 871
Here Is My Heart/Lazy Mule — 57 — Argo 5284

Ravens (2) (Mike & the)
I've Taken All I Can/Mr. Heartbreak — 62 — Empire 1

Ravens (3) (Rico & the)
In My Heart/Don't You Know — 65 — Rally 1601/Autumn 6 (65)

Ravens (4) (Billy & the)
Someone To Love — N/A — Sahara 108

Raves (1)
Don't Bug Me Baby/If I Knew The Way — 56 — Liberty 55013
Tell Me One More Time/Billy The Kid — 59 — Swade 104
I Must Be The One You Love — N/A — N/A

Raves (2) (Jimmy Ricks & the)
Homesick/Daddy Rollin' Stone — 62 — Atco 6220
Daddy Rollin' Stone/Umgowa — 62 — Festival 25004

Ravons (1)
Teenage Hop/Wrapped, Tangled And Tied — 58 — Arrow 734
Teen-Age Idol/I'm A Fugitive — 59 — Davis 464

ARTIST/SONG	YEAR	LABEL
Ravons (2)		
Why Did You Leave Me?/Everybody's Laughing At Me	62	Yucca 142
Ravons (3) (Bobby Roberts & the)		
I'm In Love Again/How Can I Make Her Mine	64	Cameo 339
Ray, Little Jimmy (& group)		
Make Her Mine/You Need To Fall In Love	59	Galliant 1001
Ray-Dots		
I Need Someone/Lu La	60	Vibro 1651
Ray-O-Vacs		
What Can I Say/Start Lovin' Me	52	Jubilee 5098
Darling (with Herb Milliner)/Riding High	54	Josie 763
Crying All Alone/Party Time	56	Kaiser 384
Wino O/Hong Kong	56	Kaiser 389
Party Time/Crying Alone	57	Atco 6085
Little Boy/I'll Always Be In Love With You	60	Sharp 103
Ray-O-Vacs ("Flap" McQueen & the)		
Daddy (vocal by Babe Hutton)/I Still Love You So (vocal by Herb Milliner)	55	Josie 781
Ray-Vons		
Judy/Regina	64	Laurie 3248
Rayber Voices (Marv Johnson & the)		
Come To Me/Whisper	59	United Artists 160/ Tamla 101 (59)
Raye, Cal (& group)		
We Belong Together/Lovely Lies	65	Providence 412
My Tears Start To Fall/You're My Lovin' Baby	66	Super 101
Raye, Jan (the Jan Raye Quartet)		
Sweet Sue/Whatever Happened To You (by W.L. Carroll)	55	Baton 213
Raye, Jean (& group)		
Open Your Eyes	62	Whip 275
Rays (1)		
Tippity Top/Moo Goo Gai Pan	55	Chess 1613
How Long Must I Wait?/Second Fiddle	57	Argo 1074/Chess 1678 (57)
My Steady Girl/Nobody Loves You Like I Do	57	XYZ 100
Silhouettes/Daddy Cool	57	XYZ 102/Cameo 117 (57)
Crazy Girl/Dressin' Up	58	Cameo 127
Triangle/Rendezvous	58	Cameo 128
Rags To Riches/The Man Above	58	Cameo 133
Elevator Operator/Souvenirs Of Summertime	58	XYZ 2001
Why Do You Look The Other Way/Zimba Lulu	59	XYZ 600
Mediterranean Moon/It's A Cryin' Shame	59	XYZ 605
Silver Starlight/Old Devil Moon	60	XYZ 608
Magic Moon (Claire De Lune)/Louie Hoo Hoo	61	XYZ 607
Sad Saturday/Love Another Girl	64	Amy 900
Rays (1) (Bob Crewe & the)		
Charm Bracelet/Do Be Do Be Do	57	Vik 0307
Rays (1) (Doug Warren & the)		
If The World Doesn't End Tomorrow (I'm Comin' After You)/ Around Midnight	60	Image 1011
Rays (1) (fb Frankie Valli)		
Are You Happy Now/Bright Brown Eyes	62	Perri 1004

ARTIST/SONG	YEAR	LABEL

Rays (1) (Hal Miller & the)
| An Angel Cried/Hope, Faith And Dreams | 61 | Topix 6003 |
| I Still Care/On My Own Two Feet | 64 | Amy 909 |

Rays (2) (Rich & the)
| My Heart/The Way You Look Tonight | 56 | Richloy 101 |

Raytones (1) (Laverne Ray & the)
| I've Got That Feeling/I'm In Love Again | 57 | Okeh 7091 |

Raytones (2)
| Until You're In My Arms/Ready, Willing And Able | 58 | Cash 1059 |
| My Baby Pt. 1/My Baby Pt. 2 | N/A | Ball 0503 |

Raytones (2) (Rudy Rae Moore & the)
| Dear Ruth/Skitter Skatter Pitter Patter | N/A | Ball 0500 |

Raytones (2) (Rudy Ray Moore & the)
| I'm Ready/So Good To Me | 58 | Cash 1060 |
| Your Tender Touch/My Country Gal | N/A | Ball 0504 |

Re'Vells
| Let It Please Be You/Love Walked In | 62 | Roman Press 201 |

Re-Vels (aka Re-Vels Quartette)
You Lied To Me/Later, Later, Baby	56	Sound 129
Dream, My Darling, Dream/Cha-Cha-Toni	56	Sound 135
So In Love/It Happened To Me	56	Teen 122
False Alarm/When You Come Back To Me	58	Chess 1708

Re-Vels Quartette (aka Re-Vels)
| My Lost Love/Love Me, Baby | 54 | Atlas 1035 |

Reactions
| Just A Little Love/Let Me Hang Around You | 64 | Cool Sound 701/ Cloud 10498 (64) |
| Our Wonderful Love/That Girl | 65 | Mutual 509 |

Reagan, Tommy (& group)
| The Santa Twist | N/A | N/A |

Real McCoys
| Gonna Take A Chance | N/A | Pico |

Realistics
| Please Baby Please/Too Shy | 70 | De-Lite 528 |

Reasons (Ria & the)
| Memories Linger On/Sorry I Lied | 64 | Amy 888 |

Rebelaires
| Once We Loved/Keep Singing And Look Ahead | 57 | B&K 103 |

Rebels (1) (Jimmy & the)
| Shiek Of Araby/You Are My Sunshine | 59 | Roulette 4201 |

Rebels (2)
| Just Give Me Your Heart/The Donkey Step | 61 | Peacock 1909 |

Rebels (3)
| In The Park/In My Heart | 59 | Kings-X 3362 |

Red Coats
| Oh, When You Touch Me/I Never Knew (by the Colts) | 59 | Del-Co 4002 |
| Teenage Broken Heart | N/A | Kikko 610 |

ARTIST/SONG	YEAR	LABEL
Red Hots (Johnny Hansley & the)		
Please Try To Love Me/Shaggin'	59	Kip 402
Redcoats (Steve Alaimo & the)		
Home By Eleven	59	Dade 1800
Love Letters/You Can Fall In Love	59	Dade 1805
I Want You To Love Me/Blue Fire	59	Marlin 6064/Imperial 5699 (60
She's My Baby/Should I Call	59	Marlin 6067
Blue Fire/My Heart Never Said Goodbye	60	Dickson 6445
Redjacks		
Big Brown Eyes/To Make You Mine	58	Apt 25006/Oklahoma 5005 (58
Redtoppers		
I Never Had A Girl Like You/All Night Jump	N/A	Dan 3214
Redtops (Eddie Dugosh & the)		
Release My Heart	58	Award 116
Redwoods (gm Jeff Barry)		
Never Take It Away/Unemployment Insurance	61	Epic 9473
Where You Used To Be/Please Mr. Scientist	62	Epic 9505
Shake Shake Sherry/The Memory Lingers On	66	Epic 9947
Reed, A. C. (& group)		
Talkin' 'Bout My Friends/Boogaloo Tramp (no group)	N/A	Nike 2002
Reed, John (& group)		
Darling Please/Yeah Little Girl	N/A	Fore 611
Reed, Johnny (& group)		
A Thousand Miles Away/Promises	58	Major 100
Reed, Lula (bb the Teeners)		
Just Whisper/If The Sun Isn't Shining	54	King 4714
Why Don't You Come On Home/I'm Giving All My Love	55	King 4811
Give Me The Right/Anything To Say You're Mine	58	Argo 5298
Reed, Michael (& group)		
Dream Lover	N/A	N/A
Reed, Ursula (bb the Solitaires)		
You're Laughing Cause I'm Crying/Ursula's Blues	54	Old Town 1001
Reeves, Harriet (& group)		
Come To Me	N/A	Eon 103
Reflections (1) (Howie Butler & the)		
Treasure Of Love/Have A Good Time	60	Gaity 6017
Reflections (2)		
I Really Must Know/Maybe Tomorrow	61	Crossroads 401
Rocket To The Moon/Because Of You	62	Crossroads 402
Tic Toc/In The Still Of The Night	62	Tigre 602
I Need Your Love/You Don't Love Me	N/A	Went 001
Reflections (3)		
Like Columbus Did/Lonely Girl	64	Golden World 12
Talkin' 'Bout My Girl/Oowee Wow	64	Golden World 15
Don't Do That To Me/A Henpecked Guy	64	Golden World 16
(Just Like) Romeo & Juliet/Can't You Tell By The Look In My Eyes	64	Golden World 8/9
You're My Baby/Shabby Little Hut	65	Golden World 19
Poor Man's Son/Comin' At You	65	Golden World 20
Deborah Ann/Wheelin' And Dealin'	65	Golden World 22
Out Of The Picture/June Bride	65	Golden World 24

RTIST/SONG	YEAR	LABEL
Girl In The Candy Store/Your Kind Of Love	65	Golden World 29
Like Adam And Eve/Vito's House	66	ABC 10794
Long Cigarette/You're Gonna Find Out	66	ABC 10822

Reflections (4)

No More Love For You/My Perfection	N/A	Pam-O 101

Regal, Mike (& group)

Too Young/Is It True What They Say About Barbara	63	Kapp 506

Regals

May God Bless And Keep You/Run Pretty Baby	54	Aladdin 3266
When You're Home/There'll Always Be A Christmas	54	MGM 11869
I'm So Lonely/Got The Water Boiling	55	Atlantic 1062
Yes My Love/See You In The Morning	60	Lavender 1452

Regan, Tommy (& female group)

I Adore You/Nine To Five	65	World Artists 1049

Regan, Tommy (bb the Marcels)

I'll Never Stop Loving You/This Time I'm Losing You	64	Colpix 725

Regents (1)

Bamboo Tree/Isle Of Trinidad	57	Argo 5268

Regents (2) (aka Five Spenders)

That's What I Call A Good Time/No Hard Feelings	60	Kayo 101
Summertime Blues	N/A	Peoria 0008

Regents (3) (aka Desires (3)/aka Runarounds (2))

Barbara-Ann/I'm So Lonely	61	Cousins 1002/Gee 1065 (61)
Runaround/Laura My Darling	61	Gee 1071
Liar/Don't Be A Fool	61	Gee 1073
Lonesome Boy/Oh Baby	61	Gee 1075
Let Them Talk	62	K-C
Unbelievable/Hooray For Love (by the Run-A-Rounds)	62	KC 116

Regents (4)

Me And You/Playmates	65	Blue Cat 110
Words/Worryin' Kind	66	Penthouse 502

Reid, Matthew (bb the Four Seasons)

Jane/Why Start	61	ABC 10259

Relations

Smile/Until We Two Are One	63	Kape 504
Too Proud To Let You Know/What Did I Do Wrong?	63	Kape 703
All Night Long	63	Michelle 506
Crowd With The Phony Tattoo/Say You Love Me	63	Zells 712
Burying Ground	N/A	Club
When We Get The Word	N/A	Club
Yes I Do	N/A	Club
Back To The Beach/Too Proud To Let You Know	67	Demand 501/Davy Jones 664

Relations (Gloria & the)

Date With My Man/ Hook, Line And Sinker	N/A	Bonnie 101/102

Relatives (1) (Ronnie & the) (aka Ronettes)

Sweet Sixteen/I Want A Boy	61	Colpix 481/Colpix 601 (61)
My Guiding Light/I'm Gonna Quit While I'm Ahead	61	May 111

Relatives (2)

Never Will I Love You Again	63	Almont 306

ARTIST/SONG	YEAR	LABEL
Relf, Bobby (bb the Laurels)		
Our Love/The Shuck (by Ernie Freeman)	56	Cash 1019
Little Fool/I'm Not Afraid	56	Dot 15510
Remainders		
Pen In Hand/Over The Rainbow	N/A	Vico 1
Remarkables (1) (Reggie & the)		
The Year That Gave Me You/Come On Baby	62	Musicor 1030
Remarkables (2)		
Write Me/Whirl-A-Round	64	Chase 1600
Reminiscents		
Cards Of Love/Flames	62	Marcel 1000
For Your Love/Please Lie To Me	63	Cleopatra 104
Zoom Zoom Zoom/Oh Let Me Dream	63	Day 1000
Hey You (a capella)	75	Relic LP 109
Oh Let Me Dream (a capella)	75	Relic LP 109
Renaults		
Stella/Melancholy	59	Warner Bros. 5094
Just Like Mine/Another Train Pulled Out	62	Wand 114
Only You/Hully Gully Lamb	62	Wand 120
Two Face/Ten Questions	63	Chicory 160
Renaults (Bobby Colquitt & the)		
Searching/Tell Daddy Baby	61	Colt 621/CJ 621
Rendezvous		
It Breaks My Heart/Take A Break	61	Rust 5041
Congratulations Baby/Faithfully	62	Reprise 20089
Ruby Baby/Ram-Bunk-Shus	N/A	Paradise 1017
Renditions (Billy De Marco & the)		
Out Of My Mind/Goodbye Mister Blues	60	Up 113
Renegades		
Stolen Angel/Keep Laughin'	61	Dorset 5007
I Love Him So	62	Counsel 119
Renegades (Patty McCoy & the)		
Goodbye/Stranger	62	Counsel 116
Reno, Al (& group)		
Cheryl/Congratulations	61	Kapp 432
Reno, Nicky (& group)		
I Had A Dream/My Darling	59	Ges 100
Renowns (1)		
My Mind's Made Up/Wild One	61	Everest 19396
Renowns (2) (Richie & the)		
Please Say You Want Me/That's What You're Doing To Me	63	Streke 247
Reptiles (Johnny Cole & the)		
Wrap My Heart In Velvet/Lizard Grizzard	61	Radiant 1503
Resolutions		
January 1st, 1962/Traveling Salesman	62	Valentine 1001
Resonics		
Split Personality/Pepe La Phew	63	Unity 101
I'm Really In Love/Think Right	64	Lucky Token 108
With Your Love To Guide Me/It Won't Be Long	N/A	Lil-Larry 1005

ARTIST/SONG	YEAR	LABEL

Restless Hearts (Fred Parris & the) (ref Five Satins)
Walk A Little Faster/No Use In Crying	65	Checker 1108
Land Of Broken Hearts/Bring It On Home To Daddy	66	Atco 6439
Blushing Bride/Giving My Love To You	66	Green Sea 106
I'll Be Hanging On/I Can Really Satisfy	66	Green Sea 107
In The Still Of The Night "67"/Heck No (instrumental)	67	Mama Sadie 1001

Rev-Lons (female)
| Give Me One More Chance/Boy Trouble | 62 | Garpax 44168 |
| Love Can't Be A One Way Deal/I Can't Forget About You | 63 | Reprise 20200/Starburst 123 |

Revalons
| Dreams Are For Fools/This Is The Moment | 58 | Pet 802 |

Revelaires
| It's A Miracle/Crazy Doctor | 54 | Burgundy 105 |
| You Must Be Blind/She Wears My Ring | 65 | Decca 31830 |

Revelations
| Spanish Harlem | N/A | N/A |

Revelletts (Jimmy Charles & the)
| A Million To One/Hop Scotch Hop | 60 | Promo 1002 |
| The Age For Love/Follow The Swallow | 60 | Promo 1003 |

Revellons (Ria & the)
| She Fell In Love/He's Not There | 64 | RSVP 1110 |

Revels
Dead Man's Stroll/Talking To My Heart	59	Norgolde 103 (first pressing)
Midnight Stroll/Talking To My Heart	59	Norgolde 103 (second pressing)
Foo Man Choo/Tweedley Dee	59	Norgolde 104
Good Grief/Six Pack	59	Swingin' 620
Please/Two Little Monkeys	60	Andie 5077
Oh How I Love You/I Met My Lost Love	61	Palette 5074
Lots Of Luck/Gotta Have Some Fun	63	Diamond 143

Reveres
| Leonore/Honeystrollin' (instrumental by the Honeystrollers) | 58 | Glory 272 |
| Beyond The Sea/The Show Must Go On | 63 | Jubilee 5463 |

Revieras
| Walk Away/I'll Wait | 64 | Victoria 103 |

Revivals
| No No No | N/A | N/A |
| Too Young | N/A | N/A |

Revlons (1)
This Restless Heart/I Promise Love	61	Rae-Cox 105
Dry Your Eyes/She'll Come To Me	62	Capitol 4739
It Could Happen To You/Ya Ya	66	Parkway 107

Revlons (2) (Tino & the)
Story Of Our Love/Black Bermudas And Knee Socks	60	Mark 154
Wedding Bells Will Ring/Heidi	63	Pip 4000
Little Girl, Little Girl/Rave On	65	Dearborn 525
Lazy Mary Memphis/I'm Coming Home	66	Dearborn 530

Revlons (3) (aka Centuries (3)/aka Jaytones)
| Ride Away/Betty (by the Centuries (3)) | 63 | Times Square 15 |
| My Love | N/A | Klik |

Revlons (4)
| What A Love This Is/Did I Make A Mistake | 62 | Toy 101 |

ARTIST/SONG	YEAR	LABEL
Revlons (5)		
Love's Burning Fire	N/A	VRC 112
Rey, Tony (& group)		
Something On Your Mind	N/A	KingBee 101
Rhythm Boys (Hank Farell & the)		
Bad Boy	60	Solar 1013
Rhythm Cadets		
Dearest Doryce/Rocking Jimmy	57	Vesta 501/502
Rhythm Casters		
Love, Love, Baby/Oh, My Darling	57	Excello 2115
Rhythm Five		
Baby Please Don't Go/I Tried	62	Tifco 829
Rhythm Four (Joe Therrien & the)		
Tell Me/Siam	61	Sentinel 8906
Rhythm Gents		
Linda	64	Merri 6008
Rhythm Heirs		
Strange World/Cradle Rock	59	Yucca 105
Rhythm Jesters		
Hole In The Bucket/Rock To The Music	56	Rama 213
Please Be Mine/Ooh Sha-La	62	Lectra 501
Rhythm Jesters (Bob Davis & the)		
Never Anymore/She'll Never Know	57	Rama 224
Rhythm Kings		
Night After Night/I Shouldn't Have Passed Your House	49	Ivory 751
Merry Christmas One And All/Christmas Is Coming At Last	51	Apollo 1171
Why My Darling Why/I Gotta Go Now	51	Apollo 1181
Rhythm Masters (aka Vel-Aires)		
Patricia/Baby We Two	56	Flip 314
Rhythm Rockers (1) (Jimmy Reagan & the)		
Lonely Lonely Heart/Can't You See It In My Eyes	59	G&G 128/129/Mona-Lee
Rhythm Rockers (2)		
Oh Oh Henry/Madness	N/A	Square 505
Rhythm Rockers (2) (fb Mike Patterson)		
We Belong Together/Oh Boy	60	Satin 921
Rhythm Stars		
Oh Moon/Lynn	59	Clock 1007
My Girl Babe/Bandstand March	59	Corsican 0057
Rhythm Steppers		
Hey Little Lola/My First Broken Heart	59	Spinning 6010
Rhythm Tones		
Please Come Back To Me/Something Wrong	59	Vest 828
Rhythmaires		
Just For You/If I Only Knew	58	Pet 806

RTIST/SONG	YEAR	LABEL
Rhythmeres		
Elaine/Bow Legged Baby	58	Brunswick 55083
Rhythmettes		
Mister Love/Mind Reader	57	Brunswick 55012
Till My Baby Comes Home/That's A Plenty	58	Brunswick 55050
High School Lovers/Snow Queen	60	Coral 62186
Rialtos (1) (Chano & the)		
Guardian Angel/Don't Forget To Write	60	Jin 154
Rialtos (2) (Bobby Hollister & the)		
Love's Gamble/Ring Around Your Neck	61	Pike 5910
Rialtos (3)		
Let Me In/It Hurts	62	CB 5009
Ricardos		
Mary's Little Lamb/I Mean Really	58	Star-X 512
Richards, Donald (bb the Volumes (3))		
I Cried For Your Love/Hello Operator	62	Chex 1003
Richards, Jay (& group)		
Echoes On My Mind/Little Sheryl	59	Hollywood 1100
Richards, Lee (& group)		
I'm Waitin'	59	Wanger 193
Richards, Norm (& group)		
Tease Me/Datin' With You	59	Imperial 5567
Richards, Ricky (& group)		
I Wish For Someone/Peek-A-Boo Mary Lou	61	Wye 1011
Richardson, Rudi (& group)		
Why Should I Cry/Fools Hall Of Fame	57	Sun 271
Richettes		
Love And Happiness/This Is Our First Date	62	Apt 25069
Richie (& group)		
Cherie/Dream Lover	61	Kip 240
Rickateers (Jimmy Ricks & the)		
She's Fine-She's Mine/The Unbeliever	56	Josie 796
Ricks, Jimmy (& female group)		
Romance In The Dark/Trouble In Mind	64	Atlantic 2246
Ricks, Jimmy (& group)		
Do You Promise/The Sugar Man Song	57	Paris 504
Goodnight My Love/At Sunrise	59	Signature 12013
Ricky (& group)		
Baby Please Come Home (flip has no group)	56	Empire 106
Ricquettes (Danny Skeene & the)		
Over The Rainbow/Seven Days	N/A	Valex 105/106
Ridgley, Tommy (& group)		
Double Eye Whammie/Should I Ever Love Again	61	Ric 978
Riffs (aka Chimes (5))		
Tell Her/I Been Thinkin'	64	Jamie 1296
Little Girl/Why Are The Nights So Cold	64	Sunny 22
Tell Tale Friends/Why Are The Nights So Cold	65	Old Town 1179

ARTIST/SONG	YEAR	LABEL
Rifftones (Riff Ruffin & the)		
I'm Confessin'/Solitude	N/A	Ball 0501
Riley, Pat (& group)		
Without You To Love/Get With It	57	Tin Pan Alley 175
Ring-A-Dings		
Snaky Poo, Pt. 1/Snaky Poo, Pt. 2	62	Infinity 014
Ringo, Eddie (& group)		
Teardrops On My Letter/Full Racing Cam	60	Twin Star 1016
Rinky-Dinks (aka Ding Dongs (1)) (featuring Bobby Darin)		
Early In The Morning/Now We're One	58	Atco 6121
Mighty Mighty Man/You're Mine	58	Atco 6128
Catch A Little Moonbeam/Choo Choo Cha Cha	59	Capitol 4146
Rip Chords (1)		
I Laughed So Hard/You And I	58	MMI 1236
Rip Chords (2)		
Ding Dong/Karen	62	Columbia 42641
Karen/Here I Stand	63	Columbia 42687
She Thinks I Still Care/Gone	63	Columbia 42812
Hey Little Cobra/The Queen	63	Columbia 42921
Three Window Coupe/Hot Rod USA	64	Columbia 43035
One Piece Topless Bathing Suit/Wah-Wahini	64	Columbia 43093
Don't Be Scared/Bunny Hill	65	Columbia 43221
Rip Tides (Johnny Hudson & the)		
Let's Run Away/Hanky Panky	59	Challenge 59062
Rip-Chords		
I Love You The Most/Let's Do The Razzle Dazzle	56	Abco 105
Ripples		
Battle Of Love/Let Me Love You	N/A	Bond 1479
Riptides		
April/Sally Ann	66	Sidewalk 904
Rituals		
Girl In Zanzibar/Guitarro	59	Arwin 120
This Is Paradise/Gone	59	Arwin 127
Rivals (1)		
Rival Blues/Don't Say You're Sorry	50	Apollo 1166
Rivals (2) (fb Letha Jones)		
I Need You/I Got That Feeling	60	Anna 1113
Rivals (3)		
I'll Never Walk Alone/Sally, Sally	63	Treyco 401
Rivals (4)		
Make Up Your Mind/She's Mine	62	Puff 3912
It's Gonna Work Out/Love Me	64	Puff 1001/Lu Pine 118 (64)
Rivals (5)		
Rigetty Tick/I Must See You Again	57	Darryl 722
Come To Me/I Must See You Again	63	Junior 990
River Rovers (Lydia Larsen & the)		
Bald Headed Daddy	89	Relic LP 5077
Just Love You So	89	Relic LP 5077

ARTIST/SONG	YEAR	LABEL
Rivera, Lucy (& group)		
Make Me Queen Again/I F I C	59	End 1041
Rivieras (1)		
Count Every Star/True Love Is Hard To Find	58	Coed 503
Moonlight Serenade/Neither Rain Nor Snow	58	Coed 508
Our Love/Midnight Flyer	59	Coed 513
Our Love/True Love Is Hard To Find	59	Coed 513
Since I Made You Cary/Eleventh Hour Melody	59	Coed 522
Moonlight Cocktails/Blessings Of Love	60	Coed 529
My Friend/Great Big Eyes	60	Coed 538
Stay In My Heart/Easy To Remember	60	Coed 542
El Dorado/Refrigerator	61	Coed 551
Moonlight Cocktails/Midnight Flyer	64	Coed 592
My Silent Love	N/A	Coed LP only
Scarlet Hour	N/A	Coed LP only
Serenade In Blue	N/A	Post LP 2000
Rivieras (2) (aka Ravenaires)		
Together Forever/A Night To Remember	58	Algonquin 718 (first pressing, second is by the Ravenaires)
Rivieras (3) (Bobby Meyer & the)		
You Got To Tell Me/Behold	64	Lawn 238
Rivileers		
Forever/Darling, Farewell	54	Baton 201
Eternal Love/Carolyn	54	Baton 205
For Sentimental Reasons/I Want To See My Baby	55	Baton 207
Don't Ever Leave Me/Little Girl	55	Baton 209
Rivileers (Gene Pearson & the)		
A Thousand Stars/Hey, Chiquita	54	Baton 200
A Thousand Stars/Who Is The Girl	57	Baton 241/Dark 241
Rivingtons (ref Sharps (1)/ref Crenshaws)		
Papa-Oom-Mow-Mow/Deep Water	62	Liberty 55427/Wand 11253 (63)
My Reward/Kickapoo Joy Juice	62	Liberty 55513
Mama-Oom-Mow-Mow/Waiting	63	Liberty 55528
The Bird's The Word/I'm Losing My Grip	63	Liberty 55553
The Shaky Bird Pt. 1/The Shaky Bird Pt. 2	63	Liberty 55585
Little Sally Walker/Cherry	63	Liberty 55610
Doin' The Bird	63	Liberty LP 3282/ Liberty LP 7282 (63)
Weejee Walk/Fairy Tales	64	Liberty 55671
I Tried/One Monkey	64	Reprise 0293
All That Glitters/You Move Me Baby	64	Vee Jay 634/ A.R.E. American 100 (64)
Years Of Tears/I Love You Always	64	Vee Jay 649
The Willy/Just Got To Be Mine	64	Vee Jay 677
Tend To Business/A Rose Growing In The Ruins	66	Columbia 43581
Yadi-Yadi-Yum-Dum/Yadi Yadi Revisited	66	Columbia 43772
Teach Me Tonight/Reach Our Goal	67	Baton Master 202
I Don't Want A New Baby/You're Gonna Pay	67	Quan 1379
I Lost The Love/Mind Your Man	68	AGC 5
Pop Your Corn Pt. 1/Pop Your Corn Pt. 2	69	RCA 74-0301
Papa-Oom-Mow-Mow/I Don't Want A New Baby	73	Wand 11253
Roaches		
Angel Of Angels/Beatlemania Blues	64	Crossway 447
Roamers		
I'll Never Get Over You/Deep Freeze	54	Savoy 1147
Never Let Me Go/Chop, Chop, Ching-A-Ling	55	Savoy 1156

ARTIST/SONG	YEAR	LABEL
Roamers (Varetta Dillard & the)		
You're The Answer To My Prayer/Promise, Mr. Thomas (no group)	55	Savoy 1160
Roamers (Wilbert Harrison & the)		
Da Dee Ya Da/Women And Whiskey	54	Savoy 1149
Rob Roys		
Conversation/Now, Only Me	60	Columbia 41650
Rob-Roys (Norman Fox & the)		
Tell Me Why/Audrey	57	Back Beat 501
Lover Doll/Little Star	57	Back Beat 499
Lover Doll/Do-Re-Mi	57	Back Beat 499M
Dance, Girl, Dance/My Dearest One	58	Back Beat 508
Dream Girl/Pizza Pie	58	Hammer 544/Capitol 4128 (59)
Rainy Day Bells/That's Love	75	Back Beat
Robbins (aka Robins)		
Rockin'/That's What The Good Book Says	51	Modern 807
I Made A Vow/Double Crossin' Baby	54	Crown 106
Key To My Heart/All I Do Is Rock	54	Crown 120/Cadet
Robbins, Eddie (& group)		
A Girl Like You/Dear Parents	58	Power 214/Dot 15702 (58)
Janice/It Was Fun	61	David 1001
Roberts, Allen (& group)		
Give Me Your Hand/Angel In My Life	59	Knight 2009
Roberts, Dave (& group)		
Wondrous/Fancy Talk	58	PL 14
Roberts, Lou (& group)		
My Promise To You/Rattle Snake Shake	66	Genie 102
Roberts, Penny (bb the Paramours)		
I'll Be Yours/The Only Way	62	Moonglow 201
Robins (1)		
If It's So Baby/If I Didn't Love You So	49	Savoy 726
Don't Like The Way You're Doin'/Come Back Baby	50	Aladdin 3031
School Girl Blues/Early Morning Blues	50	Recorded In Hollywood 150
I'm Not Falling In Love With You/Cry Baby	50	Regent 1016
(by Mel Walker & the Bluenotes)		
The Turkey Hop Pt. 1 (with Johnny Otis)/	50	Savoy 732
The Turkey Hop Pt. 2 (instrumental)		
Our Romance Is Gone/There Ain't No Use Beggin'	50	Savoy 738
I'm Living OK/There's Rain In My Eyes	50	Savoy 752
I'm Through/You're Fine But Not My Kind	50	Savoy 762
Around About Midnight/You Sure Look Good To Me	50	Score 4010
A Fool Such As I/My Heart's The Biggest Fool	52	RCA 5175
All Night Baby/Oh Why?	53	RCA 5271
How Would You Know/Let's Go To The Dance	53	RCA 5434
My Baby Done Told Me/I'll Do It	53	RCA 5486
Ten Days In Jail/Empty Bottles	53	RCA 5489
Don't Stop Now/Get It Off Your Mind	54	RCA 5564
Framed/Loop De Loop Mambo	55	Spark 107
If Teardrops Were Kisses/Whadaya Want	55	Spark 110
One Kiss/I Love Paris	55	Spark 113
I Must Be Dreamin'/The Hatchet Man	55	Spark 116
Smokey Joe's Cafe/Just Like A Fool	55	Spark 122/Atco 6059 (56)
Cherry Lips/Out Of The Picture	55	Whippet 200
Merry Go Rock/Hurt Me	56	Whippet 201X
Since I First Met You/That Old Black Magic	57	Whippet 203
A Fool In Love/All Of A Sudden My Heart Sings	57	Whippet 206

ARTIST/SONG	YEAR	LABEL
Every Night/Where's The Fire?	57	Whippet 208
Pretty Little Dolly/Quarter To Twelve	58	Knight 2001
A Little Bird Told Me/It's Never Too Late	58	Knight 2008
In My Dreams/Keep Your Mind On Me	58	Whippet 211
Snowball/You Wanted Fun	58	Whippet 212
Just Like That/Whole Lot Imagination	60	Arvee 5001
Live Wire Suzie/Oh No	60	Arvee 5013
Baby Love/We Loved	61	Gone 5101
White Cliffs Of Dover/How Many More Times?	61	Lavender 001
Magic Of A Dream/Mary Lou Loves To Hootchy Kootchy Koo	61	Lavender 002
I Found Out My Troubles	87	Savoy Jazz LP 1188
Trouble/Moving Out	N/A	Push 764
Have A Merry Christmas	N/A	Savoy (unreleased)
I Found Out	N/A	Savoy (unreleased)

Robins (1) (fb Richard Berry)

Riot In Cell Block #9/Wrap It Up	54	Spark 103

Robins (1) (Little Esther & the)

Double Crossin' Blues/Ain't Nothin' Shakin	50	Savoy 731
(with Little Esther & Johnny Otis)		
Double Crossin' Blues/Back Alley Blues (by the Beale Street Gang)	50	Savoy 731
Mistrustin' Blues/Misery	50	Savoy 735
Deceivin' Blues/Lost Dream Blues	50	Savoy 759

Robins (1) (Maggie Hathaway & the)

Race Of A Man/Bayou Baby Blues	50	Recorded In Hollywood 112
A Falling Star/When Gabriel Blows His Horn	51	Recorded In Hollywood 121
(vocals by Maggie Hathaway)		

Robins (2) (female)

Johnny/Doing The Popeye	62	Sweet Taffy 400/New Hit 3010

Robins (3) (aka Nobells)

Lucy Watusi/Cry Over You	64	Musicor 1050

Robinson, Mike (& group)

Lula/Red Light	61	Vibro 4000

Rocco, Lenny (& group)

Rochelle/Sugar Girl	61	Delsey 301

Rochells

Teardrops/Please Hear My Plea	N/A	Spacey 202

Rock-A-Bops (Jeannie Dell, Johnnie B & the)

Kiss You A Thousand Times/Rock-A-Bye Boogie	60	Josie 878

Rock-A-Bouts

She's A Fat Girl/Beatnik	59	Chancellor 1030

Rock-A-Byes (Baby Jane & the)

Hickory Dickory Dock/Half Deserted Street	62	Spokane 4001
My Boy John/How Much Is That Doggie In The Window	62	United Artists 560
Get Me To The Church On Time/Half Deserted Street	63	Spokane 4004

Rock-A-Fellas

Red Lips/Don't Torment Me	58	ABC 9923

Rock-A-Fellas (Eddie Bell & the)

High School Girl/Shindig	58	Coed 505
Countin' The Days/Night Party	59	Coed 512
Super Chick/To The School House	59	Coed 517

ARTIST/SONG	YEAR	LABEL
Rock-A-Tones		
Young Lady/Please Don't Talk About Me	N/A	Judytone 369
Rock-A-Ways (Ricky Vac & the)		
How Do You Think I Feel/Colleen	61	Hilltop 1871
Rock-Fellers		
Ours/Orange Peel	59	Valor 2004
Rock-Its		
It's Love/If You've Never Been In Love	58	Spangle 2010
Rockabeats (Jimmy Kelly & the)		
Little Chickie/Bonnie	58	Cobra 5028
Rockafellas (aka Rockafellers)		
Strike It Rich/My Baby, She's The Talk Of The Town	63	SCA 18003
Rockafellers (aka Rocka-Fellas)		
Dear Someone/Strike It Rich	63	Southern Sound 112
Rockaways (1) (Alicia & the)		
Why Can't I Be Loved?/Never Coming Back	56	Epic 9191
Rockaways (1) (Ken Darrell & the)		
I'm Not Going Steady/Faleroo	57	Epic 9226
Rockaways (2) (aka Tokens (2))		
Top Down Time/Don't Cry (Tomorrow's Tears Tonight)	64	Red Bird 10-005
Rockbusters		
Tough Chick/Chico	59	Cadence 1371
Rockers (1) (Paul Winley & the)		
My Confession/Angel Child	55	Premium 401
Rockers (2)		
Tell Me Why/Count Every Star	56	Carter 3029
What Am I To Do?/I'll Die In Love With You	56	Federal 12267
Down In The Bottom/Why Don't You Believe?	56	Federal 12273
Rockers (3) (Rick Randle & the)		
I'm Hurt/That Day	58	Arc 4445
Rockers (4) (Rockin' Bradley & the)		
She's Mine Not Yours/Loomy	58	Hull 729
Rocket-Tones		
Too Many Loves	63	3-Sons Records 928
Rocketeers (1)		
Foolish One/Gonna Feed My Baby Poison	53	Herald 415
Rocketeers (2) (aka Rhythm Aces)		
Hey Rube/Talk It Over	56	Modern 999
My Reckless Heart/They Turned The Party Out	58	M.J.C. 501
Down At Bessie's House		
Rocketones		
Mexico/Dee I	57	Melba 113
Rockets (1) (Herb Kenny & the)		
My Song/You Never Heard A Word I Said	52	MGM 11332
I Don't Care/Calling You	52	MGM 11360
Take A Little/I Miss You So	53	MGM 11397
But Always Your Friend/(I Dreamed Of A) Star Spangled Banner	53	MGM 11487

ARTIST/SONG	YEAR	LABEL
Don't Take My Word (Take My Heart)/	53	MGM 11648
Do I Have To Tell You I'm Sorry		

Rockets (2)

Open The Door/Big Leg Mama	53	Atlantic 988
My Love For You/Dance The Rhythm And Blues	56	Wrimus
(by Billy Matthews & the Balladiers)		

Rockets (3) (aka Rhythm Aces)

You Are The First One/Be Lovey Dovey	56	Modern 992
Johnny's House Party, Pt. 1/Johnny's House Party, Pt. 2	57	Modern 1021

Rockets (3) (Little Freddy & the)

All My Love/Too Fat	57	Chief 33

Rockets (4) (Bill Bodaford & the)

Little Girl/Teardrops	58	Back Beat 507

Rockets (5) (Dick Holler & His)

Uh-Uh-Baby/Livin' By The Gun	58	Ace 540

Rockets (6) (Randy & the)

Genevieve/If You Really Care	59	Viking 1000
Let's Do The Cajun Twist	62	Jin 161

Rockets (7) (Lois Lee & the)

Always Alone	N/A	Cool 712

Rockettes

Love Nobody/I Can't Forget	54	Parrot 789

Rockin R's

Walking You To School/Bewitched (Bothered And Bewildered)	60	Stepheny 1842

Rockin' Chairs

A Kiss Is A Kiss/Rockin' Chair Boogie	59	Recorte 402
Come On Baby/Please Mary Lou	59	Recorte 404

Rockin' Chairs (Lenny Dean & the)

Memories of Love/Girl Of Mine	59	Recorte 412

Rockin' Dukes (1)

Angel And A Rose/My Baby Left Me	57	O.J. 1007

Rockin' Dukes (2) (with Joe Hudson)

Baby, Give Me A Chance/Ooh-Wee, Pretty Baby	57	Excello 2112

Rockin' Kids

Yea Yea/Black Stockings	58	Dot 15749

Rockin' Kings (Ronnie & the)

You Know/Rock 'N Roll Sal	58	RCA 7248

Rockin' R's (Ron Volz & the)

I'm Still In Love With You/Mustang (instrumental)	59	Tempus 1515/Vee Jay 334 (59)

Rockin' Townies (Bennie Woods & the)

I Cross My Fingers/Wheel Baby Wheel	55	Atlas 1040

Rocking Rebels (Ray Fournia & the)

You Done Me Wrong/Settle Down	N/A	Diamond Disk 101

Rockmasters

My Lonely One/A Wonderful Thing	63	One-Derful 4820

ARTIST/SONG	YEAR	LABEL
Rocky Fellers (1) (Leroy & the)		
Unfinished Fifth/River Wide	61	Cameo 194
Rocky Fellers (2)		
Santa Santa/Great Big World	62	Scepter 1245
Killer Joe/Lonely Teardrops	63	Scepter 1246
Like The Big Guys Do/Great Big World	63	Scepter 1254
Ching-A-Ling Baby/Hey Little Donkey	63	Scepter 1258
She Makes Me Wanna Dance/Bye Bye Baby	63	Scepter 1263
The Beachcomber Song/Don't Sit Down	64	Donna 1383
Tiger (Everybody Wants To Be A)/Jeannie Memsah	64	Warner Bros. 5440
Nina/Better Let Her Go	64	Warner Bros. 5469
Don't Throw My Toys Away/The Man With The Blue Guitar	65	Warner Bros. 5497
Rented Tuxedo/Two Steps Downstairs In The Basement	65	Warner Bros. 5613
Rodans		
Time Is Passing/Queenie Bee	59	Vest 825
Rogers, Dan (& group)		
I'd Be Lost Without You/No Girl For Me	64	Era 3131
Rogers, Juanita (bb the Five Joys)		
Teenager's Love Letter/I'm So Glad You Love Me	61	Pink Clouds 333
Rogers, Kenneth (aka Kenny Rogers) (& group)		
That Crazy Feeling/We'll Always Have Each Other	58	Carlton 454
Rogers, Menard (& group)		
I Found Someone	N/A	Drum Boy 45104
Rogers, Pauline (& group)		
I've Been Pretending/Everything's All Right	56	Flair-X 5001
Rogues		
If You Love Me/World Of Love	56	Old Town 300
It's True/Puppy Love	56	Old Town 304
Dream/I've Been Dreaming	58	Old Town 1056
Bitter Tears	N/A	Beckingham 1083
Roleaks (female)		
As Long As You Love Me/Keep On Loving You	N/A	Hope 557
Rollers		
Bonneville/Got My Eye On You	61	Liberty 55303
The Continental Walk/I Want You So	61	Liberty 55320
Bounce/Teenager's Waltz	61	Liberty 55357
Rollettes (Googie Rene & the) (female)		
Sad Fool/Wham Bam (instrumental)	56	Class 201
Rollettes (female)		
More Than You Realize/Kiss Me, Benny	56	Class 203
An Understanding/I'm Trying (To Make You Love Me)	60	Melker 103
Rollins, Bird (& group)		
I'll Love You Forever/Bumble Bee	60	Harvard 805
Rollins, Debbie (& group)		
Meet Me Tonight/Don't Let It Get Your Girl	64	Ascot 2159
Roma, Teena (& group)		
Just For You/Love Is Like A Mountain	61	Arteen 1002
Romaines		
Your Kind Of Love/Till The Wee, Wee Morning	54	Groove 0035

ARTIST/SONG	YEAR	LABEL
Romaines (Romaine Brown & His)		
When Your Lover Has Gone/Satin Doll	57	Decca 30399
Roman, Nat (& group)		
Tears In My Eyes/This Is The Night	64	Sahara 103
Romanaires		
Is It Too Late/Lollypops And Shotguns	N/A	D&J 100
Romancers (1)		
I Still Remember/House Cat	56	Dootone 381
This Is Goodbye/Jump And Hop	56	Dootone 404
You Don't Understand/Baby, I Love You So	58	Bay-Tone 101
Romancers (2)		
Take Me To Paradise/We Met At The Altar	59	Marquee 701
Romancers (3) (Rocky Homan & the)		
My Precious Love/Love Me All The Way	61	Flip 355
Romancers (4)		
No Greater Love/You'll Never Know	61	Celebrity 701/Beacon 701
Romancers (5)		
Moody/Jumpin' Jungle	60	Palette 5067
Addio Maria/It Only Happens To You	61	Medieval 202/Palette 5075 (61)
That Lucky Old Sun/Hard Head	61	Palette 5085
What About Love/Marie That's You	62	Palette 5095
Don't Let Her Go/I Did The Wrong Thing	64	Linda 117
My Heart Cries/Tell Her I Love Her	65	Linda 119
Do You Cry/Love's The Thing	65	Linda 120
She Gives Me Love/Take My Heart	66	Linda 123
She Took My Oldsmobile/That's Why I Love You	66	Linda 124
Romancers (6)		
Eternal Love/You Win Again	73	Vintage 1013
Romans (1)		
Why Can't This Be So	56	Haven 111
Wild Ideas/Uh Uh	58	MMI 1238
Honey Love	N/A	Haven
Romans (2) (Frankie Valle & the) (ref Four Seasons)		
Real (This Is Real)/Come Si Bella	59	Cindy 3012
Romans (3) (Caesar & the)		
Baby Let's Wait	N/A	GJM 9000
Your True Love/Let The Four Winds Blow	N/A	Hi-Note 602
Romans (3) (Little Caesar & the)		
Those Oldies But Goodies (Remind Me Of You)/Fever	61	Del-Fi 4158
Those Oldies But Goodies (Remind Me Of You)/ She Don't Wanna (Dance No More)	61	Del-Fi 4158
Hully Gully Again/Frankie And Johnny	61	Del-Fi 4164
Memories Of Those Oldies But Goodies/Fever	61	Del-Fi 4166
The Ten Commandments Of Love/C. C. Rider	61	Del-Fi 4170
Popeye Once More/Yoyo Yo Yoyo	61	Del-Fi 4177
Annie Had A Baby	61	Del-Fi LP 1218
I Need You So	61	Del-Fi LP 1218
Little Star	61	Del-Fi LP 1218
Searchin'	61	Del-Fi LP 1218
Work With Me Annie	61	Del-Fi LP 1218
We Belong Together/Disco Hully Gully	77	Essar 7803

ARTIST/SONG	YEAR	LABEL
Romans (4)		
The Cat's Meow/You Are My Only Love	58	Juno 013/014
Rome, Billy (& group)		
Donna/You Runaround	61	Sultan 5501
Romeos (1) (aka Jumping Jacks (1))		
Love Me/I Beg You Please	54	Apollo 461
Rags/Doctor Velvet	54	Apollo 466
Oh Baby Oh	89	Relic LP 5078
Somebody's Been Plowing My Mule	89	Relic LP 5078
Romeos (2)		
Gone, Gone, Get Away/Let's Be Partners	57	Fox 749
Fine, Fine Baby/Moments To Remember You By	57	Fox 846/Atco 6107 (57)
Romeos (3)		
Two Innocent Loves/Love Mobile	58	Felsted 8528
Julie/I'm Gonna Rebuild This World	63	Felsted 8672
Romeos (4) (Kenny Gamble & the)		
Ain't It Baby, Pt. 1/Ain't It Baby, Pt. 2 (instrumental)	N/A	Arctic 114
Romeos (5) (Jimmy & the)		
Kathy	N/A	Southside 1003
Rommels		
Those Wedding Bells/Mister Sam	60	Trend 4104
Ron-Dells (aka Rondels)		
I'll Be Gone/Slow Down	63	Arlen 723
Ron-Dels (fb Delbert McClinton)		
If You Really Want Me To, I'll Go/Walk About	65	Brownfield 18/Smash 1986 (65)
Rondells (1)		
Dreamy/Good Good	58	Carlton 467
Rondells (2)		
My Prayer (a capella)	75	Relic LP 104
Rondels (aka Ron-Dells)		
Matilda/Tina	63	Shalimar 104/Dot 17323 (70)
Rookies (1) (Joe Perkins & the)		
Time Alone Will Tell/Ain't You Glad Nature Did It	57	King 5005
A New Feeling/How Much Love Can One Heart Hold	57	King 5030
Rookies (2)		
Blabbermouth/The Penalty	59	Donna 1313
Roomates (aka Roommates)		
I Want A Little Girl/Making Believe	60	Promo 2211
Glory Of Love/Never Knew	61	Valmor 008
Band Of Gold/Oh Baby Love	61	Valmor 010
My Foolish Heart/My Kisses For Your Thoughts	61	Valmor 013
Answer Me, My Love/Gee	63	Philips 40105
The Nearness Of You/Please Don't Cheat On Me	63	Philips 40153/Philips 40161 (63)
A Place Called Love/Knowing You	N/A	Ban 691
Song Of The Dreamer	N/A	Relic LP 5041
The Only Girl For Me	N/A	Relic LP 5041
To The Aisle	N/A	Relic LP 5041
Yes My Love	N/A	Relic LP 5041
Come Go With Me	N/A	Valmor
One Summer Night	N/A	Valmor

ARTIST/SONG	YEAR	LABEL
Roomates (Cathy Jean & the)		
Please Love Me Forever/Canadian Sunset (no group)	60	Valmor 007
Make Me Smile Again/Sugar Cake	61	Valmor 009
I Only Want You/One Love	61	Valmor 11
Believe Me/Double Trouble	62	Philips 40143
Please Tell Me/Sugar Cake	62	Valmor 16
You Don't Have To Say You Love Me/It's So Hard	91	Cure 91-02801
Roomates (fb Cathy Jean) (aka Roommates)		
My Heart Belongs To Only You/I Only Want You	63	Philips 40106
Roommates (aka Roomates)		
My Heart/Just For Tonight	60	Canadian American 166
Sunday Kind Of Love/A Lovely Way To Spend An Evening	62	Cameo 233
Roommates (Dick Dixon & the)		
Be Good, Be Good, Be Good/Caterpillar Crawl	59	Kapp 292
Roosters		
Fun House/Chicken Hop	59	Shar-Dee 704
Pretty Girl/Let's Try Again	62	Epic 9487/Felsted 8642 (62)
Rose, Andy (with the Thorns)		
Crazy For You/This Is The Nite	61	Coral 62271
Rosebuds (1) (female)		
Dearest Darling/Unconditional Surrender	57	Gee 1033
Joey/Kiss Me Goodnight	59	Lancer 102
Rosebuds (2) (Rosemary & the) (female)		
Dreamtime/What Do I Mean To You	63	Larkwood 1101
Roses		
Almost Paradise/I Kissed An Angel	58	Dot 15816
Roses (Don & His)		
Since You Went Away To School/Right Now	58	Dot 15755
Leave Those Cats Alone	58	Dot 15784
Rosettes		
You Broke My Heart/It Must Be Love	61	Herald 562
Roulettes (1)		
The Way You Carry On/You Don't Care Anymore	57	Ebb 124
I See A Star/Come On, Baby	58	Champ 102
Hasten Jason/Wouldn't Be Going Steady	59	Scepter 1204
Roulettes (2)		
Can You Go/Soon You'll Be Leaving Me	64	United Artists 718
Roulettes (2) (Adam Faith & the)		
I Just Don't Know/It's Alright (no group)	64	Amy 913
Round Robins		
Since I Don't Have You/Peter Gunn (instrumental by Joe Cenna)	53	Bell 108
Rovers (1) (Helen Foster & the)		
You Belong To Me/Oop Dee Doo	52	Republic 7013
Rovers (2)		
Why, Oh-H?/Ichi-Bon Tami Dachi	54	Music City 750/Capitol 3078 (55)
Salute To Johnny Ace/Jadda	55	Music City 780
Whole Lot Of Love/Tell Me, Darling (by the Gaylarks)	55	Music City 792

ARTIST/SONG	YEAR	LABEL
Rovers (3)		
Most Of All/Sweet Slumber	74	Vintage 1018
Royal Aces (Jesse James & the)		
I Will Go/Cha Cha Minnie	62	Shirley 103
Royal Boys		
Darling Angel/Lover's Bells	N/A	Tropelco 1007
Royal Counts		
That's How I Feel (a capella)/Way Over There	72	Catamount 1958
Royal Debs		
Jerry/I Do	62	Tifco 826
Royal Demons		
Baby Don't	58	Rhythm 5004
Kiss Kiss/Trembling Hand	61	Pek 8101
Royal Drifters		
Little Linda/S' Why Hard	59	Teen 506
To Each His Own/Da Kind	59	Teen 508
Royal Dukes (Don Ellis & the)		
Half Of Me/You Won't Remember Me	59	Bee 1114
Party Doll/A Woman's Love	60	Bee 201
Royal Five		
Ain't No Big Thing/Peace Of Mind	68	Arctic 160
Royal Halos		
Nobody But Me And My Girl/My Love Is True	59	Aladdin 3460
Royal Holidays		
I'm Sorry (I Did You Wrong)/Margaret	58	Penthouse 9357/ Carlton 472 (58)
Down In Cuba/Rockin' At The Bandstand	59	Herald 536
Royal Jacks		
I'm In Love Again/The Big Ring	58	20th Fox 100
Night After Night/Who, What, When, Where And Why?	59	Studio 9903
Tam-O-Shanter/Anticipation	62	Amy 865
Royal Jesters		
My Angel Of Love/Those Dreamy Eyes	60	Harlem 105
Love Me/Let's Kiss And Make Up	61	Cobra 2222
I Want To Be Loved/I Never Will Forget	61	Cobra 7777
Love Me	62	N/A
Ask Me To Move A Mountain/Is That Good Enough For You	62	Cobra 611025
Wisdom Of A Fool/What Love Has Joined Together	62	Jester 102
We Go Together	62	Jester 104
Let There Be You/I Really Don't Want To Know	62	Jester 106
Please Say You Want Me Too/What'Cha Gonna Do 'Bout It	65	Jox 029
Royal Jokers		
You Tickle Me, Baby/Stay Here	55	Atco 6052
Don't Leave Me, Fanny/Rocks In My Pillow	56	Atco 6062
Ride On, Little Girl/She's Mine, All Mine	56	Atco 6077
September In The Rain/Spring	57	Hi-Q 5004
Sweet Little Angel/I Don't Like You That Much	58	Fortune 840
Sam's Back/Grabitis	60	Metro 20032
Red Hot/Hard Times	61	Big Top 3064
You Tickle Me Baby/You Came Along	63	Fortune 560
Lovey Dovey/Nickel, Three Dimes and Five Quarters	60	Keldon 322

ARTIST/SONG	YEAR	LABEL
Royal Kings (1)		
Teachin' And Preachin'/Bouncin' The Boogie	52	Specialty 444
Royal Kings (2)		
Peter Peter/Keep It To Yourself	61	Forlin 502
Royal Knights		
You Should Have Told Me	N/A	Radio City
Have You Heard	N/A	Rendezvous 01
Royal Lancers (1) (Ronnie Premiere & the)		
So Loved Am I/You May Not Be An Angel	61	Sara 1020
Royal Lancers (2) (Paul Stefan & the)		
Say Mama	63	Citation 5003
Baby I Don't Care/Angel In My Eyes	63	Citation 5004
Good, Good Lovin'/This Time	63	Hi Mar HM-501
Royal Lancers (3)		
Hey Little One/Hey Everybody	63	Lawn 215
Together/Spooksville	63	Lawn 216
Royal Masters		
You're The One/Don't Leave Me This Way	62	Guyden 2078
Royal Notes		
Three-Speed Girl/Kisses Left Unkissed	58	Kelit 7032
(by Phil Johnson & the Duvals)		
You Are My Love/Wee Small Hours	58	Kelit 7034
Royal Playboys		
Walking On/Don't Be No Square	61	Imperial 5782
Royal Premiers		
Who Am I Without Your Love/I Wanna Love Love Love	62	Toy 103
Make Love To Me/I Can Make It If I Try	65	MBS 105
Royal Ravens		
Grand Spanish Lady/All Over You	N/A	Mah's 0015
Royal Reveres		
Such A Fool/If I Had My Life To Live Over	N/A	Jump Up 114
Royal Robins (1)		
The Country Fool/Turn Me Loose	63	ABC 10504
How High The Moon/Something You've Got Baby	64	ABC 10542
Royal Robins (2) (Patricia Conley & the)		
We're Gonna Get Married	62	Aldo 504
Royal Teens (gm Bob Gaudio & Joe Villa)		
Sittin' With My Baby/Mad Gas	57	Astra 1012/Power 113 (59)
Short Shorts/Planet Rock	57	Power 215/ABC 9882 (58)
Big Name Button/Sham Rock	58	ABC 9918
Harvey's Got A Girl Friend/Hangin' Around	58	ABC 9945
My Kind Of Dream/Open The Door (I Forgot My Key)	58	ABC 9955
Believe Me/Little Cricket	59	Capitol 4261
I'll Not Be The One (To Say Goodbye)/Royal Blue	59	Mighty 111
Royal Blue/Leotards	59	Mighty 111
Cave Man/Wounded Heart	59	Mighty 112
The Moon's Not Meant For Lovers (Anymore)/Was It a Dream?	60	Capitol 4335
It's The Talk Of The Town/With You	60	Capitol 4402
My Memories Of You/Little Trixie	61	Mighty 200
Short Short Twist/Royal Twist	62	Allnew 1415/Jubilee 5418 (62)

ARTIST/SONG	YEAR	LABEL
I'll Love You Till The End Of Time Pt. 1/ I'll Love You Till The End Of Time Pt. 2 (by the Blue Tones/instrumental)	65	Swan 4200/Blue Jay 101
Bad Girl/Do The Montoona	65	TCF 117
Smile A Little Smile For Me/Hey Jude	69	Musicor 139
Lazy Walker	N/A	Empire 1001

Royal Teentones (Bobby Sands & the)

Secret Lover/Teenage Joy	59	Nugget 1003

Royal Tones

Seesaw/Little Bo	59	Jubilee 5362

Royal, Billy Joe (& group)

We Haven't A Moment To Lose/Never In A Hundred Years	61	Fairlane 21009

Royal-Aires

Friendship Ring/Baby Baby	57	Gallo 108

Royale Cita Chorus

I Understand/Chang Chang A-Lang	56	Gee 1021

Royale Cita Chorus (fb Mabel King)

Second Hand Love/Symbol Of Love	56	Rama 204

Royalls (aka Five Royales)

Too Much Of A Little Bit/Give Me One More Chance	52	Apollo 434

Royals (1) (aka Midnighters)

Every Beat Of My Heart/All Night Long (with Wynonie Harris)	52	Federal 12064/ Federal 12064AA (52)
Starting From Tonight/I Know I Love You So	52	Federal 12077
Moonrise/Fifth St. Blues	52	Federal 12088
I'll Never Let Her Go/A Love In My Heart	52	Federal 12098
Are You Forgetting/What Did I Do	52	Federal 12113
The Shrine of St. Cecilia/I Feel So Blue	53	Federal 12121
Get It/No It Ain't	53	Federal 12133
I Feel That-A-Way/Hello Miss Fine	53	Federal 12150
Someone Like You/That's It	53	Federal 12160
Give It Up/That Woman	53	Federal 12177
Work With Me Annie/Until I Die	54	Federal 12169

Royals (1) (Chuck Willis & the)

I've Been Treated Wrong Too Long/Don't Deceive Me (no group)	53	Okeh 6985

Royals (1) (fb Chuck Willis)

If You Love Me/Dreams Of You	51	Okeh 6832

Royals (2) (aka Scooters)

Someday We'll Meet Again/I Want You To Be My Mambo Baby	54	Venus 103

Royals (3) (Fay Simmons & the)

Shake It Up/Forgive This Fool	60	Jordan 122

Royals (4) (Ronnie Bennett & the)

True Love, True Love/Have You Ever Watched A Teardrop	60	Jin 143

Royals (5) (Richie & the)

And When I'm Near You/Goody Goody	61	Rello 1
We're Strollin'	62	Golden Crest 573
Be My Girl/We're Strollin'	62	Rello 3

Royals (6)

I Lost My Love	N/A	Liban

ARTIST/SONG	YEAR	LABEL

Royals Five
Say It To My Face/Gonna Keep Lovin' You — N/A Tyler 200

Royaltones (1)
Crazy Love/Never Let Me Go — 56 Old Town 1018
Latin Love/Hey, Norman! — 56 Old Town 1028
Hong Kong Jelly Wong — N/A Murray Hill LP 000083
A Castle In The Sky — N/A Old Town (unreleased)
Do You Remember — N/A Old Town (unreleased)
I Give You My Word — N/A Old Town (unreleased)

Royaltones (1) (Ruth McFadden & the)
Two In Love (With Only One Heart)/You For Me (no group) — 56 Old Town 1020
Short Line/Big Wheel — 60 Goldisc 3004
The Flip/Secret Love — 60 Goldisc 3011
Butterscotch/Dixie Cup — 60 Goldisc 3016
Dixie Rock/Royal Whirl — 60 Goldisc 3017
Do The Early Bird/Scotch 'N' Soda — 61 Goldisc 3028

Royaltones (2) (El Pauling & the)
I'm A Cool Teenager/Solid Rock — 60 Federal 12383
Now Baby Don't Do It/Everybody Knows — 60 Federal 12396
You're Ruinin' My Gladness/The Way I See It — 60 Lute 5801

RPMs
Love Me/Street Scene — 63 Port 70032

Ru-Bee-Els
Evil/I'll Try — 62 Flip 359

Ru-Teens (aka Rue-Teens)
Happy Teenager (a capella)/Come A Little Bit Closer (a capella) — 65 Old Timer 612

Rubies (1)
Zing! Went The Strings Of My Heart/Wobble With Me Baby — 53 TNT 101/KT
Loaded With Goodies/Take It Easy Casanova — N/A District 301

Rubies (1) (female)
He Was An Angel/He Was Mine — 61 Empress 103
Spanish Boy/Deeper — 64 Vee Jay 596

Rubies (2)
Someday/Just You And I — 55 Verne 103

Rubies (3) (Jewell & the)
A Thrill/Kidnapper — 63 La Louisianna 8041/ ABC 10485 (63)

Rubies (4) (female)
Is A Man Really Worth It/Sugar Cane — 64 Enith International 720

Rue-Teens (aka Ru-Teens)
Lucky Boy/I Don't Cry Over Girls — 64 Louis 6805

Rumblers
Boss/I Don't Need You Anymore — 63 Downey 103/Dot 16421 (63)
Riot In Cell Block #9/The Hustler — 64 Downey 119

Run-A-Rounds (aka Runarounds (2)/aka Regents (3)/aka Desires (3))
Unbelievable/Hooray For Love (by the Run-A-Rounds) — 63 KC 116
Let Them Talk/Are You Looking For A Sweetheart — 63 Tarheel 065
(by the Run-A-Rounds)

ARTIST/SONG	YEAR	LABEL

Runarounds (1) (aka Emotions (1))

The Nearest Thing To Heaven/Lover's Lane	61	Pio 107

Runarounds (2) (aka Run-A-Rounds/aka Regents (3)/aka Desires (3))

Mashed Potato Mary/I'm All Alone	61	Cousins 1004
Carrie (You're An Angel)/Send Her Back	64	Felsted 8704
Perfect Woman/You're a Drag	66	Capitol 5644
You Lied/My Little Girl (with Tommy Cosgrove & the Elegant Four)	67	MGM 13763

Runaways

Pachuko Hop/The Stinger	62	Moonglow 202
18th Floor Girl/Your Foolish Ways	N/A	Alamo 105
What's Happening, Baby?	N/A	Hitt 2001
Kangaroo Hop/Teenage Style	N/A	Teensound 1924

Runners

Charlie Brown/She Say (by the Treetoppers)	53	Bell 107

Russ, Lonnie (& group)

Something Old Something New/My Wife Can't Cook	62	4-J 501

Russell, Bobby (& group)

You Were Mine/Once A Day	65	Monument 899

Ryan, Allen (& group)

My Reverie	57	Sonic 1600

Ryan, Cathy (bb the Admirals)

Come Home/The Cricket	55	King 4848
Only A Dream/High Falutin' Honey	56	King 4890

Rydell, Bobby (& group)

Please Don't Be Mad/Makin' Time	59	Cameo 160

Rydells (Bobby & the)

That's My Desire	N/A	N/A

Sa-Shays

Boo Hoo Hoo/You Got Love	61	Alfi 1/Zen 101

Saber, Johnny (& group)

The Note That I Wrote/Baby It's Gotta Be Love	N/A	Hitsville 1137

Saber, Johnny (bb the Passions)

Wish It Could Be Me/Dolly In A Toy Shop	60	Adonis 103

Sabers (1) (fb Billy Storm)

Cool, Cool Christmas/Always Forever	55	Cal-West 847

Sabers (2) (J. & the)

Twist Mary Sue/Little One	62	Vavrey 1003

Sabers (3)

It's Not Like You	N/A	Prism 1893

Sabians

Crazy Dream	61	Yale 241

Sabres

You Can Depend On Me/Calypso Baby	55	Bullseye 101
Your Face/Lulu	58	Liberty 55128
Most Of All	N/A	Jamieco

Sad Sacks

Sack Dresses/Guard Your Heart	58	Imperial 5517

RTIST/SONG	YEAR	LABEL

afaris (fb Jimmy Stephens) (aka Suddens)

	YEAR	LABEL
Image Of A Girl/Four Steps To Love	60	Eldo 101
Girl With The Story In Her Eyes/Summer Nights	60	Eldo 105
In the Still Of The Night/Shadows	60	Eldo 110
Soldier Of Fortune/Garden Of Love	61	Eldo 113
Legion Of The Lost	61	Image LP

aigons

You're Heavenly/Honey Gee	55	Dootone 375

aints (1)

With You	57	Cue 7934

aints (2) (Danny & the)

Peggy's Party/No One Has Eyes For Me	59	Warner Bros. 5134
Big Lulu/Long Long Ago	N/A	Fanelle 101

aints (3) (Dave & the)

Fever/Leavin' Surf City	63	Band Box 341

aints (3) (Orlie & the)

King Kong/Pittsburgh Twist And Freeze	61	Band Box 253

aints (3) (Tom Allen & the)

Lone Lonely One/Never	61	Band Box 249

aints (4) (Ricky & the)

When The Saints Twist/My Special Angel	62	7 Teen 101

aints (5)

Snap Dragon/Doin' The Stroll	58	Prescott 1570

aints (6) (Lola & the)

Crazy For You	N/A	N/A

alems

My Precious Love/I'll Still Go On Loving You	61	Mercury 71754

allycats (Sally & the)

Bread Fred/Depending On You	59	Rendezvous 105

alutations (Vito & the)

Walkin'/High Noon	62	Apt 25079
Hey, Hey Baby/Your Way	62	Kram 1202/Kram 5002
Gloria/Her Way	62	Rayna 5009
Gloria/Let's Untwist The Twist	62	Rayna 5009/Red Boy 5009
Unchained Melody/Hey, Hey Baby	63	Herald 583
Eenie Meenie/Extraordinary Girl	63	Herald 586
Girls I Know/Get a Job	64	Regina 1320
Can I Depend On You/Hello Dolly	64	Rust 5106
Can I Depend On You/Liverpool Bound	64	Wells 1008
Don't Count On Me/Day-O (Banana Boat Song)	64	Wells 1010
Bring Back Yesterday/I Want You To Be My Baby	66	Boom 60020
So Wonderful (My Love)/I'd Best Be Going	66	Red Boy 1001/Sandbag 103
Unchained Melody/So Much	78	Crystal Ball 104

Sams

Come On Back	N/A	N/A
Here's My Heart	N/A	N/A
My Guardian Angel	N/A	Ebony 008

Samuels, Clarence (& group)

Without You/We're Goin' To The Hop	59	Apt 25028

508 Sandelles

ARTIST/SONG	YEAR	LABEL
Sandelles		
Hit 'N Run Lover	64	Debonair 309
Sanders, Bobby (bb the Performers)		
It Was You/I'm On My Way	61	Kaybo 618
Sandetts (female)		
Without You/Cutting Silhouettes	60	Smokey 109
Sandmen (1)		
Somebody To Love/When I Grow Too Old To Dream	55	Okeh 7052
Sandmen (1) (Brook Benton & the)		
Ooh/The Kentuckian Song (Brook Benton)	55	Okeh 7058
Sandmen (1) (Chuck Willis & the)		
I Can Tell/One More Break (Chuck Willis)	55	Okeh 7055
Sandmen (1) (fb Brook Benton)		
Come On Be Nice/I Wanna Do Everything For You	57	Vik 0285
Sandmen (1) (Lincoln Chase & the)		
The Message/That's All I Need	55	Columbia 40475
Sandmen (2)		
Searching For A New Love	65	Blue Jay 5002
Sandpipers		
Ali Baba/Young Generation	66	Kismet 394
Sands Of Time (aka Tokens (2))		
Benji's Cincinnati/A Tribute To The Beach Boys '76	76	Kirshner 4263
Santells		
Why Are We Apart/There's A Time And Place For Everything	64	Courier 103
So Fine/These Are Love	64	Courier 115
Santos, Larry (bb the Four Seasons)		
Someday (When I'm Gone)/True	64	Atlantic 2250
Santos, Larry (bb the Tones (1))		
Three Little Lovers/We Belong Together	59	Baton 265
Sapphires (1)		
So Glad/Everyone Knows	58	RCA 7357
Sapphires (2) (Howie & the) (aka Pearls)		
More Than The Day Before/Rockin' Horse	59	Okeh 7112
Saratogas		
I'll Be Loving You/Get It In A Minute	61	Imperial 5738
Satelites (Baby Boy Jennings & the)		
Little Girl/Goin' Home	60	Savoy 1589
Satelites (Ronny & the)		
Blue Moon/Bunny Lee	N/A	Dolly 22254
Satellites (1) (Sonny King & the)		
You Shouldn't/So Doggone Lonely	55	Nocturne 1003/1004
Satellites (2) (Joe Potito & the)		
Say A Prayer/Can't Let Your Lovin' Go	57	Safari 1003

ARTIST/SONG	YEAR	LABEL
Satellites (3)		
Heavenly Angel/You Ain't Sayin' Nothin'	58	Class 234/Malynn 231 (58)
My Piggie's Gotta Dance/I Found A Girl	58	United Artists 141
Blast Off/Man In Orbit	61	Chess 1789
One More Time/Red And Yellow Polka Dots	N/A	Arc 149
Satellites (3) (Bobby Day & the)		
So Long Baby/Come Seven	57	Class 207
Little Bitty Pretty One/Heavenly Angel	57	Class 211
Little Bitty Pretty One/	57	Class 211
When The Swallows Come Back To Capistrano		
Beep Beep Beep/Darling If I Had You (no group)	57	Class 215
Sweet Little Thing/Honeysuckle Baby	58	Class 220
Little Turtle Dove/Saving My Love For You (no group)	58	Class 225
Rockin' Robin/Over And Over	58	Class 229/Trip 29
The Bluebird, The Buzzard And The Oriole/Alone Too Long	58	Class 241
That's All I Want/Say Yes	59	Class 245
Mr. & Mrs. Rock 'n' Roll/Gotta New Girl	59	Class 252
Love Is A One Time Affair/Ain't Gonna Cry No More	59	Class 255
Unchained Melody/Three Young Rebs From Georgia	59	Class 257
My Blue Heaven/I Don't Want To	59	Class 263
Undecided/Slow Pokey Joe	62	Rendezvous 175
Satellites (4)		
Linda Jean/Rockateen	59	ABC 10038
Each Night/Darktown Strutters Ball	60	D-M-G 4001
Buzz Buzz/We Like Birdland	60	Palace 102
Satellites (5) (Pat & the)		
Jupiter-C/Oh! Oh! Darlin'	59	Atco 6131
Satellites (6) (Dick & Slim & the)		
Chalypso Rock/My Truest Love	59	Cool 113
Satellites (7) (Collay & the)		
Last Chance/Little Girl Next Door	60	Sho-Biz 1002
Satellites (8) (Bobby Long & the)		
Red Roses Will Never Fade	64	Vegas 555-2
You've Got What It Takes	64	Vegas 700
Satellites (9) (Ronny & the)		
Dream Of You/Last Night I Dreamed	59	Rose 1001
Satin Angels (females)		
Pity Me	85	Relic 8004
Town Sensation	85	Relic 8004
Satins (Tommy Roe & the)		
I Got A Girl/Caveman	60	Judd 1018
Satins Four (with the Cinammon Angels)		
Oh Cathy/I Can't Find The Girl On My Mind	65	B.T. Puppy 515
Satintones		
My Beloved (versions with and without strings)/Sugar Daddy	60	Motown 1000
I'll Never Love Again	60	Tamla 54024
Motor City/Going To The Hop	60	Tamla 54026
Tomorrow And Always/A Love That Can Never Be	61	Motown 1006 (first pressing)
(versions with and without strings)		
Angel/A Love That Can Never Be	61	Motown 1006 (second pressing)
I Know How It Feels/My Kind Of Love	61	Motown 1010
Zing! Went The Strings Of My Heart/Faded Letter	61	Motown 1020

ARTIST/SONG	YEAR	LABEL
Satisfactions		
Oh Why/We Will Walk Together	62	Chesapeake 610
Satisfiers		
Lies/All Over Nothing	55	Jubilee 5205
Come Away, Love/Where'll I Be Tomorrow Night	56	Coral 61727
Solitude/Over The Rainbow	57	Coral 61788
Will-O-The-Wisp/Remember That Crazy Rock	58	Coral 61945
Ghost Of A Chance/Fair Exchange	60	Vegas 626
Saucers		
Why Do I Dream?/Oh Wailey Routa	59	Felco 104
Flossie Mae/Hi-Oom	64	Kick 100
Hello, Darling/Giggle Goo	64	Lynne 101
Saunders, Jay (& group)		
I'm Still In Love With You/Heaven Have Mercy	56	Club 1012
Savage, Al (& group)		
Trouble On My Mind/A Fool Was I	57	Herald 505
Savoys (1)		
Let's Ride, Ride, Ride/Oh, That'll Be Joyful (both by Jack McVea)	54	Combo 55
Darling Stay With Me/Yacka Hoom Boom	55	Combo 75
Evil Ways/Loving Man	55	Combo 81
Chop Chop Boom/Nobody In Mind (by Jack McVea)	55	Combo 90
Savoys (2) (Sonny Brooks & the)		
Here I Am/Rocka Rolla Rock	56	Tip Top 1007
Sweetheart Darling/I'm So Down Hearted	56	Tip Top 1008
Savoys (3) (aka Pretenders (1))		
You/Say You're Mine	56	Savoy 1188
Savoys (3) (Jimmy Jones & the) (aka Pretenders (1))		
With All My Heart/Please Say You're Mine	60	Savoy 1586
Savoys (4)		
I Love My Baby/You And I	59	Bella 18
Savoys (5) (Marva & the)		
Don't Let Him Go/Just In Your Imagination	63	Coed 582
Savoys (6)		
Oh What A Dream (a capella)/If You Were Gone From Me (a capella)	64	Catamount 101
Gloria (a capella)/The Closer You Are (a capella)	65	Catamount 105
Oh Gee Oh Gosh/Vision Of Love	N/A	Catamount 778
Saxons (1) (aka Hollywood Saxons)		
Please Be My Love Tonight/Home On The Range	57	Our
Is It True?/Rock And Roll Show	58	Contender 1313
My Love Is True/Trying	58	Tampa 139
Everyday Holiday/L.A. Lover	61	Hareco 102
Saxons (1) (Mary Edwards & the)		
Oh Oh Mama/Chilly Willy	56	Meteor 5031
Saxons (2)		
Camel Walk	60	Sho-Biz 1003
Saxons (3)		
The Power Of Love	N/A	Jim Dandy 1002
Scale-Tones		
Everlasting Love/Dreamin' And Dreamin'	56	Jay-Dee 810

RTIST/SONG	YEAR	LABEL

camps
Yes My Baby/Waterproof — 55 — Peacock 1655

carlets (Fred Parris & the) (ref Five Satins)
She's Gone (With The Wind)/The Voice (Fred Parris & the Scarlets) — 58 — Klik 7905/Candlelite 411 (74)

carlets (ref Five Satins)
Dear One/I've Lost — 54 — Red Robin 128/Event 4287 (55)
Love Doll/Darling I'm Yours — 55 — Red Robin 133
True Love/Cry Baby — 55 — Red Robin 135
Kiss Me/Indian Fever — 55 — Red Robin 138
Truly Yours/East Of The Sun — 60 — Fury 1036

cavengers
The Angels Listened In/My Lover Waits For Me — 63 — Mobile Fidelity 1005

chaefer, Freddy (& group)
Zoom Zoom Zoom/Why Is It — 62 — King 5621

charmeers
I've Waited So Long/Traveling Stranger (by the Jive Chords) — 74 — Vintage 1017

cholars
What Did I Do Wrong — 56 — Cue 7927
Rocky Road/Spin The Wheel — 56 — Dot 15498
If You Listen With Your Heart/Poor Little Doggie — 56 — Dot 15519
Beloved/I Didn't Want To Do It — 57 — Imperial 5449
Kan-Cu-Wa/I Didn't Want To Do It — 57 — Imperial 5459
Please Please/I Need Your Lovin' (by the Perenials) — N/A — Ruby-Ray 2

chool Belles
Waitin' For My Date/Billy Boy, Billy Boy — 58 — Dot 15746
Turtle Dovin'/Cool It Baby — 58 — Dot 15801
Swing Swang/Count Down — 59 — Hanover 4526
Whistling Bells/Whistling At The Boys — 61 — Buena Vista 378
Don't Believe Him/Valley High — 62 — Crest 1104

chool Boys
Dream Lover — 60 — Studio 1

chool Girls
The Reason Why I Love Him/Guess We're Not In Love — 62 — Express 712

choolboys (1)
Carol/Pearl — 56 — Okeh 7090
Shirley/Please Say You Want Me — 57 — Okeh 7076
Mary/I Am Old Enough — 57 — Okeh 7085
Angel Of Love/The Slide — 58 — Juanita 103

choolboys (2) (Bob Hamilton & the)
School's Beginning — 86 — Relic LP 8008

choolboys (2) (Professor Hamilton & the)
Back To School/Juanita Of Mexico — 61 — Contour 0001

choolgirls (Wendy & the) (female)
My Guy/Merry Go Round — 58 — Golden Crest 502

choolmates (1) (Colleen & the)
Mairzy Doats/My Heart Is On A Merry-Go-Round — 58 — Coral 62024

choolmates (2) (Ronnie & the)
Don't Don't Don't (Drop Out)/Just Born (To Be Your Baby) — 64 — Coed 605

ARTIST/SONG	YEAR	LABEL
Schooners (1)		
Viddley Biddley Baby/Schooner Blues	58	Ember 1041
Schooners (2) (Smokey Armen & the)		
Baby What Am I Gonna Do/Say You Love Me	58	Peek-A-Boo 102
Scooters (aka Royals)		
Someday We'll Meet Again/Really	57	Dawn 224
Everybody's Got A Girl/A Ring Around A Chain	58	Era 1065
Evertbody's Got A Girl/Big Lies	58	Era 1072
Scotchtones		
Do You Have The Right/Sake Wa Duke	60	Rustone 1402
Scott Brothers		
Do You Want My Love/Celebrity Party	59	Skyline 501
Part Of You/Kingdom Of Love	59	Skyline 502
Stolen Angel/Keep Laughing	60	Ribbon 6905
Lost Love/Only Then	60	Ribbon 6911
Love Me Tenderly/Welcome Me	63	Comet 2161
Scott, Jimmy (& group)		
What Sin/When Day Is Done	57	King 5086
Somewhere Down The Line/Home	58	King 5104
Scott, Neil (bb the Concords (2))		
Oh Genie/Go Bohemian	60	Clown 3011
Run To Me/Tomboy	62	Comet 2151
Scott, Ricky (& group)		
Darling Darlin'/I Didn't Mean It	60	X-Clusive/Cub 9079 (60)
Scotties		
Let Me Love You Tonight/Patiently	59	Scottie 1305
Searchers		
Wow Wow Baby/Ooo-Wee	58	Class 223
Yvonne/Little Wanda	61	Mac 351
Sebastian (& group)		
Too Young/Darlin' I Do	59	Mr. Maestro 801/ Take 2 2002 (59)
Secrets (1) (aka Five Secrets/aka Loungers)		
See You Next Year/Queen Bee	57	Decca 30350 (second pressing, first is by the Five Secrets)
Secrets (2)		
Quien Sabe (Who Knows, Who Knows)/Now Is The Hour	60	Columbia 41861
Secrets (3) (Carlo & the)		
Pony Party/100 Pounds Of Potatoes	62	Throne 801
Secrets (4) (Colleen Kaye & the)		
Joey's Diamond Ring/The One I Love	63	Big Top 3151
Secrets (5)		
Everyday/A Smile Upside Down	66	Red Bird 10-076
Sedates		
Please Love Me Forever/I Found	58	MRB 171/20th Century 1011 (59)/20th Century 1212 (61)/ Port 70004
Girl Of Mine/Bei Mir Bist Du Schon	62	Trans Atlas 692

ARTIST/SONG	YEAR	LABEL

Selections (featuring Al Reno)

Guardian Angel/Soft And Sweet	58	Antone 101/Mona Lee 129

Selectones (Jay Jay & the)

Humpty Dumpty/When I Look Around	62	Guest 6201/6202

Semesters

Laura My Darling (a capella)	75	Relic LP 104
Spiral (a capella)	75	Relic LP 104
Summer Nights (a capella)	75	Relic LP 104

Seminoles

True Love/Open Your Eyes	61	Go-Gee 287
I Can't Stand It/It Takes A Lot	62	Check Mate 1012
Forever/You Can Lump It	62	Mid Town 101

Semitones (Ron Ricky & the)

There's A Girl In My Heart	N/A	Semitone 1

Senators (aka Gales/aka Marvels (2))

Julie/It Doesn't Matter	59	Abner 1031
Scheming/Tafu	59	Bristol 1916
Loretta/Poor Little Puppet	59	Golden Crest 514
Wedding Bells/I Shouldn't Care	62	Winn 1917

Senders

Spinning/Pretty Little Pretty	58	Entra 711/Kent
The Ballad Of Stagger Lee/I Dream Of You	59	Kent 320
One More Kiss/Everybody Needs To Know	59	Kent 324

Seniors (1)

Evening Shadows Falling (I Think Of You)/I've Got Plenty Of Love	56	Tetra 4446
Why Did You Leave Me?/Sloo Foot Soo	58	Excello 2130

Seniors (2)

Who's Gonna Know/It's Been A Long Time	59	Tampa 163
I've Lived Before/When Will I Fall In Love	60	Decca 31112
Pitter Patter Heart/Hully Gully	60	Kent 342
When I Fall In Love/Baby, Say The Word	61	Decca 31244

Seniors (3)

Ah Sweet Mystery Of Love/Rock And Rolly	60	ESV 1016

Sensation-Ivies

Tell Me/God Bless The Child	61	Willow 23003

Sensational Dell-Os (aka John Shaw & the Dell-Os)

So Shy/That's Why I Dream	58	Mida 106
Lost Love/So Don't Go	58	Mida 109
Why Did You Leave Me/Why Does It Have To Be Her	58	U-C 5002/U-C 1031

Sensationals (1) (Jimmy Jones & the)

Come On And Go With Me/Walk In The Garden	59	Savoy 4116
Nobody But The Lord/Before This Time Another Year	59	Savoy 4126
I Can't Begin To Tell You/In The Storm	62	Savoy 4174
Lead Me On/So High	65	Savoy 4234

Sensationals (2)

Once In A While/Snow White Winter	60	Candix 306
Wouldn't Be The Same/The City Sleeps	61	Candix 319

Sensations (1)

I Can't Change	64	Junior 1071

ARTIST/SONG	YEAR	LABEL
Sensations (1) (fb Yvonne Baker/aka Yvonne Mills)		
Yes Sir, That's My Baby/Sympathy	56	Atco 6056
Please Mr. Disc Jockey/Ain't He Sweet	56	Atco 6067
My Heart Cries For You/Cry, Baby, Cry	56	Atco 6075
Little Wallflower/Such A Love	56	Atco 6083
My Debut To Love/You Made Me Love You	57	Atco 6090
Romance In The Dark/Kiddy Car Love	58	Atco 6115
Music, Music, Music/Part Of Me	61	Argo 5391
Let Me In/Oh Yes, I'll Be True	61	Argo 5405
We Were Meant To Be/It's Good Enough For Me	63	Junior 1002
That's What You Gotta Do/You Made A Fool Out Of Me	63	Junior 1005
Baby	63	Junior 1006
You Made A Fool Of Me/That's What You've Gotta Do	63	Junior 986/Tollie 9009 (64)
I Can't Change/Mend The Torn Pieces	64	Junior 1010
We Were Meant To Be/It's Good Enough For Me	64	Junior 1021
There's No You	N/A	N/A
Sensations (1) (Yvonne Baker & the)		
That's My Desire/Eyes	62	Argo 5412
No Changes/Party Across The Hall	62	Argo 5420
When My Lover Comes Home/Father Dear	63	Argo 5446
Sensations (2) (Sonya & the)		
Don't Feel Like The Lone Ranger	63	Gend
Sensations (3)		
The Price Of Love/Don't Take Your Love	62	River 228
Sentimentals (1)		
I Want To Love You/Teenie, Teenie, Teenager	57	Mint 801/Checker 875 (57)
Sunday Kind Of Love/Wedding Bells	57	Mint 802
I'm You Fool, Always/Rock Me, Mama	58	Mint 803
Found A New Baby/I'll Miss These Things	58	Mint 807
You're Mine/Danny Boy	59	Mint 805
This Time/I Want To Love You	62	Mint 808
Sentimentals (1) (Ann Nichols & the)		
Lover, I'm Waiting For You/I'm Sixteen Years	58	Tuxedo 926
Sentimentals (1) (James Carter & the)		
I Know/Hey, Baby, Hey	57	Tuxedo 922/Tuxedo 943
Sentimentals (2)		
We Three/Understanding Love	59	Coral 62100
Love Is A Gamble/If It Isn't For You	59	Vanity 589
Two Different Worlds/Deep Down In My Heart	60	Coral 62172
Señors		
May I Have This Dance/Searching For Olive Oil	62	Sue 756
Sequins & Rhythm Kings (Jimmy Burke with the)		
Ooh! Ooh! Those Eyes/Forbidden Love	60	Fortune 537
Sequins (1)		
Don't Fall In Love/Why Can't You Treat Me Right	56	Red Robin 140
Sequins (2)		
Wedding Bells/Look For A Job (by Little Joe Mosley)	58	Del-Fi 4107
Sequins (3) (Jessie & the)		
Hold My Hand/So Weak	59	Boxer 201/Profile 4008 (59)
Sequins (4) (female)		
To Be Young/The Mountains	59	Cameo 161
Love Me Forever/They're Dancing Now	62	Terrace 7511
You Can't Sit Still/Mr. Leader Of The Band	63	Ascot 2140
Hideaway/I Ain't Gonna Cry (No More)	63	Terrace 7515

ARTIST/SONG	YEAR	LABEL
Sequins (5) (Janice Rado & the) (female)		
I'm Coming Home/This Feeling	61	Edsel 782
Serenaders (1)		
It's Funny/Confession Is Good For The Soul	52	Coral 60720
Misery/But I Forgive You	52	Coral 65093
Tomorrow Night/Why Don't You Do Right?	52	J.V.B. 2001/2002
Please, Please Forgive Me/Baby	53	DeLuxe 6022
Will She Know/I Want To Love You, Baby	53	Red Robin 115
M-A-Y-B-E-L-L/Ain't Goin' To Cry No More	54	Swing Time 347
Serenaders (2)		
Never Let Me Go/I Wrote A Letter	57	Chock Full Of Hits 101/102/ MGM 12623 (58)
Dance, Darling, Dance/Give Me A Girl	58	MGM 12666
How Do You Mend A Broken Heart	59	Cross Country
My Girl Flip-Flop/Gotta Go To School	59	Rae-Cox 101
Adios, My Love/Two Lovers Make One Fool	63	Riverside 4549
I'll Cry Tomorrow/If Your Heart Says Yes	64	V.I.P. 25002
Serenaders (3)		
Summer Job/Honolulu	58	Hanover 4507
Alaska/Where Did You Go 'Out', What Did You Do 'Nothing'	58	Hanover 4514
Love Me Now/Gates Of Gold	58	Teen Life 9
My Last Affair/I Had My Moment	N/A	Colony 100
Serenaders (4) (Gene Mumford & the)		
Please Give Me One More Chance/When You're Smiling	56	Whiz 1500
Serenaders (5) (Larry Lee & the)		
All Alone	90	Relic LP 5085
Dreams Of Heaven	90	Relic LP 5085
Too Young	90	Relic LP 5085
Serenades		
A Sinner In Love/The Pajama Song	57	Chief 7002
Serenadetts		
Boyfriend/The Big Night	61	Enrica 1008
Servicemen		
My Turn/I Need A Helping Hand	67	Pathway 102
Sessions (1)		
Girls Go For Guys/Chico	64	Guyden 2105
Sessions (2)		
Look To The Rainbow (a capella)/For Her (a capella)	76	Arcade 100
Seventeens (1) (female)		
Steady Guy/Bug Out	58	Golden Crest 503
Seventeens (2) (Robby John & the)		
Teenage Bill Of Rights/Revolution	59	Del-Fi 4115
Sevilles (1) (Richard Barrett & the)		
Dream On/I Am Yours	60	Seville 104
Sevilles (2)		
Charlena/Loving You (Is My Desire)	61	JC 116/Galaxy 721 (64)
Louella/Salt Mine	61	JC 118
Fat Sally/Working Hard	61	JC 120
Don't You Know I Care, Pt. 1/Don't You Know I Care, Pt. 2	62	Cal Gold 172
Hey Hey Hey/Treat You Right	64	Galaxy 717
Baby/Creation	64	Galaxy 727

ARTIST/SONG	YEAR	LABEL
Sevilles (3) (Bobby Mathis & the)		
Girl In The Drugstore/Going To The City	60	Sioux 51860
Sh-Booms (aka Chords (1))		
Pretty Wild/Could It Be?	55	Cat 117
I Don't Want To Set The World On Fire/Lu Lu	57	Vik 0295
Blue Moon/Short Skirts	60	Atlantic 2074
Sh-Boom/Little Maiden	61	Atco 6213
Sha-Weez		
No One To Love Me/Early Sunday Morning	53	Aladdin 3170
Feeling Sad	N/A	Aladdin (unreleased)
Satisfied With My Love	N/A	Aladdin (unreleased)
Sha-Weez (Big Boy Myles & the)		
Who's Been Fooling You?/That's The Girl I Married	55	Specialty 564
Just To Hold My Hand/Hickory Dickory Dock	56	Specialty 590
Shades (1)		
Dear Lori/One Touch Of Heaven	55	Imperial 5358/Aladdin 3453 (59)
Strolling After Dark/Splashing	59	Scottie 1309
Shades (2)		
Sun Glasses/Undivided Attention	58	Big Top 3003
Wouldn't It Be Nice/The Combination	62	Joey 6206
The Chimes/Voodoo Man	63	Times Square 16/ Times Square 93 (64)
So Good	N/A	Klik
Time Stood Still	N/A	Klik
Shades (3) (Joey & the)		
My Love Is Gone/New York Honky Tonk	N/A	Wild 905
Shadows (1)		
Stay/No Use	53	Decca 28765
Tell Her/Don't Be Bashful	53	Decca 48307
Better Than Gold/Big Mouth Mama	54	Decca 48322
Shadows (2)		
Under The Stars Of Love/Jungle Fever	58	Del-Fi 4109
There Stands The Glass/Bop-Alena	58	Delta 1509
I Love You	59	El-Gee-Bee 101
I Wonder Why/Tell This Lonely Heart Goodbye	61	Dottie 1006
Shadows (3) (Dave & the)		
At The Fair/Dancing Cheek To Cheek	62	Checkmate 1016
Shadows (4)		
The Ten Commandments Of Love (a capella)	75	Relic LP 102
Shakers (Buddy Sharpe & the)		
Linda Lee/Bald Headed Baby	58	Fee Bee 230
Shakers (Pepper & the)		
Need Your Love/For My Baby	66	Chetwyd 45002
Shalimars		
I Didn't Mean To Hurt You/Baby That's What Love Is	N/A	Mr. Maestro 778
Shallows		
How Lucky I Am/Wrecking My Life	61	Rae-Cox 108
I Wonder/Do The Bug	62	Forlin 503
Shalons		
Angel/True Love Came My Way	76	Ronnie 203

ARTIST/SONG	YEAR	LABEL

Shamans

Valley Of Tears/Shubby Dubby Doo	59	Kayham 1/2
Southern California/I'll Wait Forever	59	Kayham 3/4

Shamrocks (Little Henry & the)

Baby Come To Me/The Ta Ta Song	61	Kent 398

Shannons

Born Too Late/Don't Ask Me	58	L&M 1003

Shanteers

You're Gone/Take Me Back	62	Rori 708

Shantones

Come To Me/Little Girl	56	Trilyte 5001

Shantons

Triangle Love/Lover's March	59	Jay-Mar
To Be In Love With You/Lucille	59	Jay-Mar 241

Shantons (Skip Brown & the)

Why Don't You Believe Me/Jenny Lee	59	Pam 112

Shantons (Skip Jackson & the)

Santa Claus Is Coming To Town/The Christmas Song	60	Jay-Mar/Dot-Mar (69)
I'm On To You Girl/Promise That You'll Wait	69	Dot-Mar 324

Sharell, Jerry (& group)

Everybody Knows/That's My Business	61	Alanna 560

Sharks (aka Five Sharks)

Blueberry Hill/I Love You For Sentimental Reasons	75	Clifton 10
Shirley/I'll Be Home	N/A	Broadcast 1128
You Belong To Me/The Glory Of Love	N/A	Broadcast 1132

Sharmeers

You're My Lover/A School Girl In Love	58	Red Top 109

Sharmettes (female)

Answer Me/My Dream	62	King 5648
Wonderful Love/I Gotta Tell It	62	King 5656
Tell Me/I Want To Be Loved	62	King 5686

Sharp, Bobby (& group)

Flowers Mr. Florist, Please	58	Wing

Sharpettes (King & the)

How Do I Stand Today/Did He Know	64	Aldo 503

Sharps (1) (ref Rivingtons)

Love Me My Darling/Heaven Only Knows (instrumental)	54	Two Mikes 101
What Will I Gain?/Shufflin'	57	Aladdin 3401
Come On/Sweet Sweetheart	57	Jamie 1040/Vik 0264 (57)/VDJ 6
Our Love Is Here To Stay/Lock My Heart	57	Lamp 2007
All My Love/Look What You've Done To Me	58	Combo 146/Dot 15806 (58)
Look At Me/Have Love Will Travel	58	Jamie 1108
Teenage Girl/We Three	58	Win 702
Here's My Heart/Gig-A-Lene	59	Jamie 1114
Double Clutch/If Love Is What You Want	60	Star-Hi 10406
Tapun Tapun	87	Relic LP 5069

Sharps (2)

6 Months, 3 Weeks, 2 Days, 1 Hour/Cha-Cho Hop (by Jack McVea)	57	Tag 2200/Chess 1690 (58)

ARTIST/SONG	YEAR	LABEL

Sharpsters

| My Baby Is Gone/Beneath The Moon | 59 | Bella 2208/2209 |

Sharptones (1)

| Since I Fell For You/Made To Love | 55 | Post 2009 |
| I'll Always Remember/Sock Hop | 59 | Ace 133 |

Sharptones (2) (Jesse Belvin & the)

| Sugar Doll/Let Me Dream | 58 | Aladdin 3431 |

Sharptones (3) (Billy Sharp & the)

| Hippity Hop/Stars In My Eyes | 58 | Kudo 668 |

Shaw, Joan (& group)

| Broken Heart/Hand Holdin' Baby | 56 | ABC 9724 |

Shaw, Ricky (& group)

| A Fools Memory/Young And In Love | 62 | President 822 |

Shaynes

| Valarie/Let's Go Steady | 61 | Pee Vee 5000 |

Sheiks (1) (fb Jesse Belvin)

Walk That Walk/The Kissing Song (Sweetie Lover)	55	Cat 116
Give Me Another Chance/Baby Don't You Cry	55	Ef-N-De 1000
So Fine/Sentimental Heart	55	Federal 12237/
		Federal 12355 (59)

Sheiks (2)

| Song Of Old/Candlestick Cafe | 59 | Jamie 1147 |

Sheiks (3)

| Come On Back To Me/Please Don't Take Away The Girl I Love | 60 | Amy 807 |

Sheiks (4)

| Why Should I Dance/What I'd Do For Your Love | 61 | Le Grand 1013 |
| Cocoanut Woman/Twist That Twist | 61 | Le Grand 1016 |

Sheiks (5) (Eddie Williams & the)

| I Just Can't Help Myself/You Left Your Happiness | N/A | Coronado 112 |

Shells (1)

Sippin' Soda/Pretty Little Girl	58	End 1022/Gone 5103 (61)
Pleading No More/Don't Say Goodbye	58	Johnson 106/Juanita 106 (58)
Explain It To Me/An Island Unknown	58	Johnson 107
In The Dim Light Of The Dark/O-Mi Yum-Mi Yum-Mi	58	Johnson 110
Sweetest One/Baby, Walk On In	58	Johnson 112
Deep In My Heart/(It's A) Happy Holiday	58	Johnson 119
Whispering Wings/Shooma Dom Dom	59	End 1050
She Wasn't Meant For Me/The Thief	59	Roulette 4156
Baby Oh Baby/Angel Eyes	60	Johnson 104
Baby Oh Baby/What's In An Angel's Eyes	60	Johnson 104
Better Forget Him/Can't Take It	61	Johnson 109
A Toast To Your Birthday/The Drive	63	Johnson 120
On My Honor/My Royal Love	63	Johnson 127
Our Wedding Day/Deep In My Heart	63	Josie 912
Dear One/Same Ol' Thing	65	Genie 100/101
Baby Oh Baby (a capella)	66	Candlelite LP 1000
Baby, Walk On In (a capella)	66	Candlelite LP 1000
Bad Girl (a capella)	66	Candlelite LP 1000
Be Sure My Love (a capella)	66	Candlelite LP 1000
Dream (When You're Feeling Blue) (a capella)	66	Candlelite LP 1000
Fine Little Girl (a capella)	66	Candlelite LP 1000
Happy Holiday (a capella)	66	Candlelite LP 1000
I'm A Happy Man (a capella)	66	Candlelite LP 1000

RTIST/SONG	YEAR	LABEL
If You Were Gone From Me (a capella)	66	Candlelite LP 1000
Life Is But A Dream (a capella)	66	Candlelite LP 1000
Misty (a capella)	66	Candlelite LP 1000
Oh, What A Dream (a capella)	66	Candlelite LP 1000
On The Outside Looking In (a capella)	66	Candlelite LP 1000
Ooh, Baby Baby (a capella)	66	Candlelite LP 1000
So Fine (a capella)	66	Candlelite LP 1000
The Closer You Are (a capella)	66	Candlelite LP 1000
The Way You Do The Things You Do (a capella)	66	Candlelite LP 1000
My Cherie/Explain It To Me	72	Johnson 099

hells (1) (gm Gene Holiday)

My Heart Runneth Over (with Love)/	63	Johnson 125
Scratch My Name Off The Mail Box		

hells (1) (Roy Jones & the)

Satisfied/Made For Lovers	60	Swirl 101

hells (2)

When I'm Blue/Whiplash	N/A	Conlo 879

hepherd Sisters (female)

Rock & Roll Cha Cha/Gone With The Wind	54	Capitol 2706/Melba 101 (56)
Alone/Congratulations To Someone	57	Lance 125
Remember That Crazy Rock 'N Roll Tune/I Walked Beside The Sea	57	Melba 108
Gettin' Ready For Freddy/The Best Thing There Is	57	Mercury 71244
(by the Sheppard Sisters)		
Heart And Soul/(It's No) Sin	59	MGM 12766
Here Comes Heaven Again/I Think It's Time	59	Warwick 511
Schoen-A, Schoen-A/Hapsburg Serenade	61	Big Top 3066
I'm Still Dancin'/Deeply	61	United Artists 350
Lolita/Ya Ya	62	United Artists 456
Don't Mention My Name/What Makes Little Girls Cry	63	Atlantic 2176
Talk Is Cheap/(Take A Look At My Guy) The Greatest Lover	63	Atlantic 2195
Alone (original version)/Alone (new version)	65	York 50002

hepherd, Johnnie (& group)

How Blue My Heart/Boom Boom Boomerang	61	Tilden 3001

heppard, Buddy (& group)

So Many Reasons Why/I'm Hypnotized	59	Play Me 3517

heppard, Shane (bb the Limelites) (aka Shep & the Limelites)

Too Young To Wed/Two Loving Hearts	59	Apt 25038

heppards (1)

Love/Cool Mambo	55	Theron 112
Sherry/Mozelle	56	United 198/B&F 198 (56)

heppards (2)

Island Of Love/Never Felt Like This Before	59	Apex 7750
Feel Like Lovin'/Just Like You	60	Apex 7752
It's Crazy/Meant To Be	60	Apex 7755
Society Girl/Just When I Needed You Most	60	Apex 7759
Feel Like Lovin'/Come Home, Come Home	60	Apex 7760
Just Like You/Tragic	61	Apex 7762
Never Let Me Go/Give A Hug To Me	61	Pam 1001
What's The Name Of The Game/Glitter In Your Eyes	61	Sharp 6039
Every Now And Then/Glitter In Your Eyes	61	Vee Jay 406
Elevator Operator/Loving You	62	Abner 7006
Tragic/Come To Me	62	Vee Jay 441
Pretend You're Still Mine/Walkin'	63	Okeh 7173
Give A Hug To Me/Island Of Love	64	Constellation 123
Forgotten	64	Constellation LP 4/
		Collectables LP 5078

ARTIST/SONG	YEAR	LABEL
I'm Not Wanted	64	Constellation LP 4/ Collectables LP 5078
Queen Of Hearts	64	Constellation LP 4/ Collectables LP 5078
Stubborn Heart/How Do You Like It	67	Mirwood 5534
A Hundred Years From Today	N/A	N/A
So In Need For Love	N/A	Collectables LP 5078

Sherry Sisters
The Prize	N/A	N/A

Sherwoods (1)
Uncle Sam/Three Love Letters Ago	60	V-Tone 506

Sherwoods (2)
The Gang's All Back/Little Big Horn (instrumental)	61	Johnson 111
Sneakin' Around/Shades Of Summer	61	Johnson 121

Sherwoods (2) (Tony Reno & the)
I'll Never Stand In Your Way/Maria Elena	63	Johnson 123

Sherwoods (3) (aka Concords (2)/aka Snowmen)
Cold And Frosty Morning/True Love Was Born (With Our Last Goodbye)	63	Dot 16540

Sherwoods (4)
Little Heart Take Care/Recipe For Going Steady	63	Mercury 72042

Sherwoods (5)
Happy Holiday/Molly	64	Magnifico 105

Sherwoods (6)
Love You Madly/Moffitt's Mess	67	Crimson 104/Ray Star

Sherwoods (7) (Johnny Schilling & the)
King Of The World/Marcelle	63	C&A 507

Shevelles
Like I Love You/Ooh Poo Pah Doo	64	World Artists 1023
I Could Conquer The World/How Would You Like Me To Love You	64	World Artists 1025

Shields
You Cheated/That's The Way It's Gonna Be	58	Tender 506/Tender 513 (58)/ Dot 15805 (58)
Nature Boy/I'm Sorry Now	58	Tender 518/Dot 15856 (58)
Play The Game Fair/Fare Thee Well My Love	58	Tender 521/Dot 15940 (58)
The Girl Around The Corner/You'll Be Coming Home Soon	60	Falcon 100/ Transcontinental 1013 (60)
You Told Another Lie/Barnyard Dance	61	Continental 4072

Shields, Johnny (& group)
Out Of Sight, Out Of Mind	N/A	Armour

Shirelles (female)
I Met Him On A Sunday/I Want You To Be My Boyfriend	58	Decca 25506/Decca 30588 (58)/ Tiara 6112 (59)
My Love Is A Charm/Slop Time	58	Decca 30669
I Got The Message/Stop Me	58	Decca 30761
Dedicated To The One I Love/Look A Here, Baby	59	Scepter 1203
A Teardrop And A Lollipop/Doin' The Ronde	59	Scepter 1205
Please Be My Boyfriend/I Saw A Tear	60	Scepter 1207
Tonight's The Night/The Dance Is Over	60	Scepter 1208
Tomorrow/Boys	60	Scepter 1211 (first pressing)
Will You Still Love Me Tomorrow/Boys	60	Scepter 1211 (second pressing)
Mama Said/Blue Holiday	61	Scepter 1217

RTIST/SONG	YEAR	LABEL
What A Sweet Thing That Was/A Thing Of The Past	61	Scepter 1220
Big John/21	61	Scepter 1223
Baby It's You/The Things I Want To Hear (Pretty Words)	61	Scepter 1227
Johnny On My Mind	61	Scepter LP 501
Lower The Flame	61	Scepter LP 501
Oh, What A Waste Of Love	61	Scepter LP 501
Tonight At The Prom	61	Scepter LP 501
Unlucky	61	Scepter LP 501
You Don't Want My Love	61	Scepter LP 501
Soldier Boy/Love Is A Swingin' Thing	62	Scepter 1228
Welcome Home Baby/Mama, Here Comes The Bride	62	Scepter 1234
It's Love That Really Counts/Stop The Music	62	Scepter 1237
Everybody Loves A Lover/I Don't Think So	62	Scepter 1243
I Don't Want To Cry	62	Scepter LP 502
I'll Do The Same Thing Too	62	Scepter LP 502
It's Mine	62	Scepter LP 502
My Willow Tree	62	Scepter LP 502
Rainbow Valley	62	Scepter LP 502
The First One	62	Scepter LP 502
What's Mine Is Yours	62	Scepter LP 502
Without A Word Of Complaint	62	Scepter LP 502
Foolish Little Girl/Not For All The Money In The World	63	Scepter 1248
Don't Say Goodnight And Mean Goodbye/I Didn't Mean To Hurt You	63	Scepter 1255
What Does A Girl Do/Don't Let It Happen To Us	63	Scepter 1259
It's A Mad, Mad, Mad, Mad World/31 Flavors	63	Scepter 1260
Tonight You're Gonna Fall In Love With Me/	64	Scepter 1264
Twentieth Century Rock And Roll		
Sha-La-La/His Lips Get In The Way	64	Scepter 1267
Thank You Baby/Doom's Day	64	Scepter 1278
Maybe Tonight/Lost Love	64	Scepter 1284
Are You Still My Baby/I Saw A Tear	64	Scepter 1292
Everybody's Goin' Mad/March (You'll Be Sorry)	65	Scepter 12101
My Heart Belongs To You/Love That Man	65	Scepter 12114
(Mama) My Soldier Boy Is Coming Home/Soldier Boy	65	Scepter 12123
I Met Him On A Sunday '66/Love That Man	65	Scepter 12132
Shhh, I'm Watching The Movies/Shhh, I'm Watching The Movies	65	Scepter 1296
Que Sera Sera/Till My Baby Comes Home	66	Scepter 12150
Shades Of Blue/After Midnight	66	Scepter 12162
Shades Of Blue/Looking Around	66	Scepter 12162
Shades Of Blue/When The Boys Talk About The Girls	66	Scepter 12162
Teasin' Me/Look Away	67	Scepter 12178
Don't Go Home (My Little Darlin')/Nobody's Baby After You	67	Scepter 12185
Too Much Of a Good Thing/Shiny Colors	67	Scepter 12192
Last Minute Miracle/No Doubt About It	67	Scepter 12198

Shirelles (Shirley & the)

A Most Unusual Boy/Look What You've Done To My Heart	69	Bell 760
Playthings/Looking Glass	69	Bell 787
Go Away And Find Yourself/Never Give Up	69	Bell 815

Shondelles

Don't Cry My Soldier Boy/My Love	62	King 5597
Special Delivery/Muscle Bound	62	King 5705
Ooo Sometimes/Watusi One More Time	63	King 5755

Shondelles (Rickey Leigh & the)

To Find An Angel Like You/Why Do Little Girls Hurt Little Boys	63	Savoy 1620

Shonnie (& group)

Sunset	54	TNT 113

Shortcuts

Don't Say He's Gone/I'll Hide My Love	59	Carlton 513

ARTIST/SONG	YEAR	LABEL
Show Stoppers		
When You See Me Hurt/Don't You Know What I Believe	61	Brent 7021
Cynthia	63	Amber 212
Showcases		
This Love Was Real/Anna, My Love	64	Galaxy 732
Showmen		
It Will Stand/Country Fool	61	Minit 632/Imperial 66033 (64)/
		Liberty 56166 (67)
Showmen (Carl Frost & the)		
I'm Still In Love With You/Mind Your Mama	63	Lawn 223
Showmen (Toni & the)		
Beware	N/A	Ten Star 103
Shufflers (1)		
Ain't Nothin' Wrong With That/Lovin' On My Mind	54	Okeh 7040
Shufflers (2) (Jay & the)		
Always Be Mine/When The Lights Are Low	62	Crackerjack 4010
Shuffles		
Do You Remember My Darling/Dancin' Little Girl	63	Rayco 508
Shy Guys		
A Love So True/Where You Belong	66	Palmer 5008
Shy-Tones (aka Hi-Tones/aka Trentons)		
A Lover's Quarrel/Just For You	60	1 Goodspin 401/Bruce
Annette/White Bucks	61	Spot 14
White Bucks/Bandstand Rock	61	Spot 14
Sierras (1) (aka Four Sierras)		
So Many Sleepless Nights/Nearer My Heart	62	Knox 102
Stormy Weather/Chance	63	Mail Call 2333/2334
Sierras (2) (female)		
I'll Believe It When I See It/I Should Have Loved You	62	Goldisc G4
A Plan For Love/Then I'll Still Love You	63	Cham 101/Dot 16569 (63)
Signatures		
Someone In Love/Julie Is Her Name	57	Whippet 210/
		Gen Norman 210X (57)
Silhouettes		
Wish I Could Be There/Which Way Did She Go	56	Grand 142
Get A Job/I Am Lonely	57	Junior 391/
		Junior 593 (57)/Ember 1029 (5
I Sold My Heart To The Junkman/What Would You Do	58	Ace 552/Junior 396 (58)
Heading For The Poor House/Miss Thing	58	Ember 1032
Bing Bong/Voodoo Eyes	58	Ember 1037
Never/Bull Frog	61	20th Fox 240
The Push/Which Way Did She Go	62	Imperial 5899
Your Love/Rent Man	62	Junior 993
Gaucho Serenade	N/A	N/A
Not Me Baby	N/A	Goodway
Silhouettes (Billy Horton & the)		
Evelyn/Never Will Part	59	Ace 563/Junior 400 (59)
Silks (Charles McCullough & the)		
My Girl/Zorro	61	Dooto 462
I Cried All Night/You're Not Too Young	62	Dooto 467

RTIST/SONG	YEAR	LABEL
ilva-Tones		
That's All I Want From You/Roses Are Blooming	57	Monarch 5281/Argo 5281 (57)
ilver Slippers (Barbara J & the)		
Laughing At Me/Love Is The Thing	61	Lescay 3001
ilvertones (1)		
Hey Good Looking/My Only Love	60	Elgin 005
You Gotta Change Your Ways/Sentimental Memory	60	Silver Slipper 1000
ilvertones (2)		
Thinking Of You/Canadian Sunset	62	Joey 302
ilvertones (3)		
Get It/Bathsheba	63	Goliath 1355/Valiant 6045 (64)
Seven Piece Bathing Suit/Wait For My Gal	64	Sweet 16
ilvertones (4) (Ronnie Rice & the)		
She's Not Yours/I Want You To Be My Girl	64	Limelight 3029
immons, Little Maxine (& group)		
Since I Lost You/In You Baby, In You Baby	N/A	Varbee 117
inceres (1)		
You're Too Young/Forbidden Love	60	Jordan 117
Darling/Do You Remember	60	Sigma 1003/1004
Please Don't Cheat On Me/If You Should Leave Me	61	Richie 545
Our Winter Love/Kookie Ookie	63	Epic 9583
Sincerely/Snap Your Fingers	64	Columbia 43110
The Magic Of Love/Tell Her	66	Taurus 377
inceres (2) (Johnny H & the)		
Why Don't You Write Me/Crazy Baby	63	El Zarape 122
inging Belles (female)		
The Empty Mailbox/Someone Loves You, Joe	60	Madison 126
High Noon/Oh Happy Day	60	Madison 132
inging Doves (Cliff Butler & the)		
When You Love/People Will Talk	53	States 123
inging Wanderers (aka Wanderers (1))		
Say Hey, Willie Mays/Don't Drop It	54	Decca 29230
The Wrong Party Again/Three Roses	54	Decca 29298
ingleton, Bebo (bb the Notes)		
Shrine Of The Echo/Feeny Jones	59	Stentor 101
inners		
Nightmare/Could This Be Love	62	Eden 1
intells		
Lundee Dundee (a capella)	75	Relic LP 105
Please Say It Isn't So (a capella)	75	Relic LP 105
My Imagination (a capella)	75	Relic LP 108
ir Nites (T.L. Clemons & the)		
I Love You So/Who's That Girl	60	Combo 168
irs		
Sixteen Candles/Wow (instrumental)	68	Charay 33
ix Teens (female)		
A Casual Look/Teenage Promise	56	Flip 315
Afar Into The Night/Send Me Flowers	56	Flip 317

ARTIST/SONG	YEAR	LABEL
Only Jim/My Special Guy	57	Flip 320
Arrow Of Love/Was It A Dream Of Mine?	57	Flip 322
Baby You're Dynamite/My Surprise	57	Flip 326
My Secret/Stop Playing Ping Pong (With My Heart)	57	Flip 329
Danny/Love's Funny That Way	58	Flip 333
Oh, It's Crazy/Baby-O	58	Flip 338
Heaven Knows I Love You/Why Do I Go To School?	59	Flip 346
So Happy/That Wonderful Secret Of Love	60	Flip 350
A Little Prayer/Suddenly In Love	60	Flip 351

Sixteens

Was It A Dream	64	Regency 626

Skarlettones (female)

Do You Remember/Will You Dream	59	Ember 1053

Skipper, Buddy (& group)

Back On The Beach Again/Make Believe Baby	61	Fury 1051

Sky Boys (Thurl Ravenscroft & the)

Mad, Baby, Mad/Never Doubt My Love	55	Fabor 4005

Skyhawks

Love Me Right	N/A	Collectables LP 5039

Skylarks (1) (aka Starlings)

The Glory Of Love/You And I	51	Decca 48241

Skylarks (2)

Home In Pasadena/I Had The Craziest Dream	53	RCA 5257
Ol' Man River/There's A Boat Leaving Soon For New York	57	Verve 10082

Skylarks (3) (Chet Barnes & the)

Is You Is/Everytime It Rains	61	Embassy 201

Skylarks (4)

Jeannie/Everybody's Got Somebody	62	Everlast 5022

Skylighters

How Foolish Am I/That My Man	N/A	Emjay 6152

Skyliners (1)

Since I Don't Have You/One Night, One Night	59	Calico 103/104/ Original Sound 35 (63)
This I Swear/Tomorrow	59	Calico 106
It Happened Today/Lonely Way	59	Calico 109
If I Loved You	59	Calico LP 3000
Tired Of Me	59	Calico LP 3000
Warm	59	Calico LP 3000
When I Fall In Love	59	Calico LP 3000
How Much/Lorraine From Spain	60	Calico 114
Pennies From Heaven/I'll Be Seeing You	60	Calico 117/ Original Sound 36 (63)
Believe Me/Happy Time	60	Calico 120
I'll Close My Eyes/The Door Is Still Open	61	Colpix 188
The End Of A Story/Baion Rhythms	61	Colpix 607
Close Your Eyes/Our Love Will Last	61	Colpix 613
Everyone But You/Three Coins In The Fountain	62	Cameo 215
Tell Me/Comes Love	62	Viscount 104
Since I Fell For You/I'd Die	63	Atco 6270/Motown 1046 (63)
This I Swear/It Happened Today	63	Original Sound 37
The Loser/Everything Is Fine	65	Jubilee 5506
Who Do You Love?/Get Yourself A Baby	66	Jubilee 5512
I Run To You/Don't Hurt Me, Baby	66	Jubilee 5520
Oh How Happy/We've Got Love On Our Side	78	Tortoise Int'l 11343

ARTIST/SONG	YEAR	LABEL
With All My Heart And Soul	85	Relic LP 5053
I Can't Sleep/Why Should You Taunt Me?	N/A	Doc 496

Skyliners (1) (Jimmy Beaumont & the)

Where Have They Gone/I Could Have Loved You So Well	74	Capitol 3979
The Day The Clown Cried/Our Day Is Here	76	Drive 6520

Skyliners (2)

Rock N' Roll Ruby/I Do All Right	N/A	Double AA 1045

Skylites

Oh Happy Day/My Only Girl	61	Ta-Rah 101

Skytones

Mr. Moon	N/A	Gaylo

Slades (aka Spades (1))

You Mean Everything To Me/Baby	57	Liberty 55118
You Cheated/The Waddle	58	Domino 500
No Time/You Gambled	58	Domino 800
Summertime/You Must Try	59	Domino 1000
Just You/It's Better To Love	61	Domino 901
Take My Heart/It's Your Turn	61	Domino 906

Slades (Joyce Harris & the)

I Cheated/Do You Know	61	Domino 903

Slicks (Jimmy Sommers & the)

I Love You, You Love Me	N/A	Space

Sliders

Love Is Like A Mountain/There Is A Great Big Moon	N/A	Chevron 012/Chevron 750

Sliders (Byron Gipson & the)

Honey Dew/The One I Love	55	Specialty 566

Sliders (Byron"Slick" Gipson & the)

I Want 'Cha Baby	56	Specialty

Sliders (Slick Gipson & the)

Footloose And Fancy-Free/Etta Mae	56	Specialty 587

Smart Tones

Ginny/Bob-O-Link	58	Herald 529

Smith Quartet, Ben

Big Fat Lips/The Cadillac Song	53	Rama 17

Smith, Arlene (& group)

Mon Cherie Au Revoir/To Live My Life Again	63	End 1120

Smith, Jimmie (& group)

I'll Cry And Cry Every Night/Night Time Is The Time	59	Flip 347

Smith, Kenny (& group)

Deep In My Heart/Money Talks	64	Fraternity 934

Smith, Melvin (with the Night Riders)

Zaki Sue/Open The Door, Richard	58	Cameo 135

Smith, Richard (& group)

Mama Cried/I Don't Wanna Cry	58	Hi-Q 5042

Smith, Roy (& group)

It's Love	N/A	Adaire 90

ARTIST/SONG	YEAR	LABEL
Smith, Savannah (& group)		
Anytime Anyplace Anywhere/Let It Be	60	End 1077
Smith, Wendell (& group)		
Tonight's My Night To Cry/Puddin' Pie	59	United Artists 166
Smooth Tones		
Dear Diary/Crazy Baby	56	Ember 1001
Smoothies		
Softly/Joanie	60	Decca 31105
Lonely Boy And Pretty Girl/Ride, Ride, Ride	60	Decca 31159
Smoothtones		
Bring Back Your Love (To Me)/No Doubt About It	55	Jem 412
Don't Keep Our Love Hidden In The Dark/Little Cupid	57	Okeh 7078
Snap Shots		
I Need You/That's What I Like	63	Federal 12496
Snappers		
If There Were/Big Bill	59	20th Century Fox 148
Snaps (Ginger Davis & the)		
I'm No Runaround (answer record to "Runaround Sue")/Laughin'	62	Swan 4090
Growing Up Is Hard To Do/Seven Days In September	65	MGM 13413
Sneakers		
You Belong To Me/Mary Lou	N/A	Delta 1868
Snowmen (aka Concords (2)/aka Sherwoods (3))		
Cold And Frosty Morning/You Started It	64	Herald 597 (second pressing, first is by the Concords)
So-And-Sos (Anita & the)		
Joey Baby/Rinky Tinky Rhythm	61	RCA 7974
Socialites (1) (Kenny & the)		
The King Tut Rock/I'll Have To Decide	58	Crosstown 001
Socialites (2) (female)		
Jimmy/The Click	63	Arrawak 1004
Society Girls (female)		
SPCLG (Society For The Prevention Of Cruelty To Little Girls)/You Better Stay Home	63	Vee Jay 524
Soft Tones (aka Softones)		
A Moth Around A Flame/My Mother's Eyes	55	Samson 103
Softones (aka Soft Tones)		
Oh Why	N/A	Cee Bee 1062
Softwinds		
Cross My Heart/Oh Baby	61	Hac 105
Soldier Boys		
I'm Your Soldier Boy/You Picked Me	62	Scepter 1230
Solitaires		
Wonder Why?/Blue Valentine	54	Old Town 1000
Please Remember My Heart/South Of The Border	54	Old Town 1006/1007
Chances I've Taken/Lonely	54	Old Town 1008
I Don't Stand A Ghost Of A Chance/Girl Of Mine	55	Old Town 1010
What Did She Say?/My Dear	55	Old Town 1012

TIST/SONG	YEAR	LABEL
The Wedding/Don't Fall In Love	55	Old Town 1014
Magic Rose/Later For You, Baby	55	Old Town 1015
The Honeymoon/Fine Little Girl	56	Old Town 1019
You've Sinned/You're Back With Me	56	Old Town 1026 (first pressing)
The Angels Sang/You've Sinned	56	Old Town 1026 (second pressing)
Give Me One More Chance/Nothing Like a Little Love	56	Old Town 1032
Walkin' Along/Please Kiss This Letter	57	Old Town 1034/Argo 5316 (58)
I Really Love You So (Honey Babe)/Thrill Of Love	57	Old Town 1044
Walkin' And Talkin'/No More Sorrows	57	Old Town 1049
Please Remember My Heart/Big Mary's House	58	Old Town 1059
Embraceable You/'Round Goes My Heart	59	Old Town 1066
Helpless/Light A Candle In The Chapel	59	Old Town 1071
Lonesome Lover/Pretty Thing	61	Old Town 1096
Honey Babe/The Time Is Here	63	Old Town 1139
Fool That I Am/Fair Weather Lover	64	MGM 13221

lotones

Pork And Beans/Front Page Blues	55	Excello 2060

ngettes (fb Kate Webster)

Sea Of Love/I Feel So Low	59	Decca 30945

ngspinners

Duffy	N/A	Leila 1601

nics

As I Live On/Bumble Bee	55	Groove 0112
Once In A Lifetime/It Ain't True	58	X-Tra 107
This Broken Heart/You Made Me Cry	59	Harvard 801/Harvard 922 (59)/ Checker 922 (59)
Evil Eye/Triangle Love	59	Nocturne 110/ RKO Unique 411 (59)
It's You/Preacher Man	62	Amco 001
Funny/I Get That Feeling	62	Armonia 102
Beautiful Brown Eyes/Sugaree	62	Jamie 1235
Say You'll Be Mine	87	Relic LP 8011
You Are My Sunshine	87	Relic LP 8011

nics (Vance Charles & the)

Closer To Me/Let's Fall In Love	63	Lori 9553

nnets

Why Should We Break Up/Please Won't You Call Me	56	Herald 477
Oh Judy/Angel Of My Dreams	58	Lane 501
Forever For You/I Can't Get Sentimental	64	Guyden 2112

nnettes (female)

I've Gotten Over You	63	Kayo 0001

notones

How Do You Speak To An Angel/Sonotone Bounce	54	Bruce 105

notones (fb Don Gardner)

I Hear A Rhapsody/It's A Sin To Tell A Lie	55	Bruce 127

notones (Harry Carlton & the)

Long Time Baby	N/A	Jarman

others (aka Harptones)

I Believe In You/The Little White Cloud That Cried	65	Port 70041

phisticates

I Need You/I Can't Stand It	N/A	Mutt 27318

ARTIST/SONG	YEAR	LABEL
Sophomores (1)		
Big Joke/After All	55	Decca 29669
Every Night About This Time/Cool, Cool Baby	56	Dawn 216
I Get A Thrill/Linda	56	Dawn 218
Charades/What Can I Do?	57	Chord 1302/Epic 9259 (57)
Ocean Blue/I Left My Sugar Standing In The Rain	57	Dawn 223
Is There A Someone For Me/Everybody Loves Me	57	Dawn 225
I Just Can't Keep The Tears From Tumblin' Down/	57	Dawn 228
If I Should Lose Your Love		
Checkers/Each Time I Hold You	57	Dawn 237
Sophomores (2) (Anthony & the) (aka Tony & the Twilighters (4))		
Gee (But I'd Give The World)/It Depends On You	59	ABC 10073
Embraceable You/Beautiful Dreamer	61	Grand 163
Play Those Oldies Mr. D.J./Clap Your Hands	63	Mercury 72103
Better Late Than Never/Swingin' At Chariot	63	Mercury 72168
It Depends On You/Gee	65	ABC 10737
Wild For Her/Get Back To You	66	ABC 10770
Heartbreak/I'll Go Through Life Loving You	66	ABC 10844
Workout/Serenade	66	Jamie 1330
One Summer Night/Workout (instrumental)	67	Jamie 1340
Sorrows (Nicky De Matteo & the)		
Suddenly/More Than Riches	60	Guyden 2024
I Wanna Be Lonely/Little Red Kitten	66	Cameo 407
Sound Masters		
I Want You To Be My Baby	N/A	Julet 102
Sounds (1) (aka Tangiers)		
Cold Chills/So Unnecessary	55	Modern 975
Sweet Sixteen/Anything For You	56	Modern 981
Sounds (2)		
Life/Charlie Chan	59	Sarg 172
My Pillow Of Dreams/Tell Me Baby	59	Sarg 181
Sounds (3) (Vikki Nelson & the)		
Like A Baby/I Was A Fool For Leaving	57	Vik 0273
Sounds (4) (Lee & the)		
What Is This Thing Called Love/Beautiful Romance	59	Lido 600
Sounds (5)		
Little Baby Be Mine/Judy, I Love You So	61	Queen 24008
Southwinds		
Build Me A Cabin/They Call Me Crazy	58	Fury 1017
Souvenirs (1)		
So Long, Daddy/Alene, Sweet Little Texas Queen	57	Dooto 412
Double Dealing Baby	57	Dooto LP 224
Souvenirs (2)		
I Could Have Danced All Night/It's Too Bad	67	Inferno 2001
Spaceriders (Mai Casselle & the)		
Don't Deceive Me/Do The Dipper	N/A	Half Peach 500
Spades (1) (aka Slades)		
Baby/You Mean Everything To Me	58	Liberty 55118
Spades (2)		
I'm On Fire/Close To You	59	Major 1007

ARTIST/SONG	YEAR	LABEL
Spades (3) (Dell Rays & the)		
Di Di/Full House (instrumental)	N/A	Dice 479
Spaniels		
Baby It's You/Bounce	53	Vee Jay 101/Chance 1141 (53)
The Bells Ring Out/House Cleaning	53	Vee Jay 103
Goodnight, Sweetheart, Goodnight/You Don't Move Me	54	Vee Jay 107
Play It Cool/Let's Make Up	54	Vee Jay 116
Do Wah/Don'Cha Go	55	Vee Jay 131
You Painted Pictures/Hey, Sister Lizzie	55	Vee Jay 154 (first pressing)
Painted Picture/Hey Sister Lizzie	55	Vee Jay 154 (second pressing)
False Love/Do You Really?	56	Vee Jay 178
Dear Heart/Why Don't You Dance	56	Vee Jay 189
Since I Fell For You/Baby Come Along With Me	56	Vee Jay 202
You Gave Me Peace Of Mind/Please Don't Tease	56	Vee Jay 229
Everyone's Laughing/I.O.U.	57	Vee Jay 246
I Need Your Kisses/You're Gonna Cry	57	Vee Jay 257
I Lost You/Crazee Baby	57	Vee Jay 264
Tina/Great Googley Moo	58	Vee Jay 278
Stormy Weather/Here Is Why I Love You	58	Vee Jay 290
Heart And Soul/Baby It's You	58	Vee Jay 301
This Is A Lovely Way To Spend An Evening	58	Vee Jay LP 1002
I Like It Like That/Trees	59	Vee Jay 310
100 Years From Today/These Three Words	59	Vee Jay 328
People Will Say We're In Love/The Bells Ring Out	59	Vee Jay 342
I Know/Bus Fare Home	60	Vee Jay 350
Little Joe	60	Vee Jay LP 1024
So Deep Within	60	Vee Jay LP 1024
The Posse	60	Vee Jay LP 1024
Baby Sweets	60	Vee Jay LP 1024/ Charly LP 1114 (86)
I Know, I Know/Jealous Heart (Pookie Hudson bb the Imperials)	63	Double L 711
For Sentimental Reasons/Miracles	64	Double L 720
Maybe/Goodnight Sweetheart	69	Buddah 153
Fairy Tales/Jealous Heart	70	North American 001/ Calla 172 (70)
Lonely Man/Stand In Line	70	North American 002
Come Back To These Arms/Money Blues	70	North American 3114
Peace Of Mind/She Sang To Me/Danny Boy	74	Canterbury EP101
Automobiles	81	Charly LP 1021
I'll Be Waiting	84	Solid Smoke LP/ Charly LP 1114 (86)
A Stranger In Love	86	Charly LP 1114
Lovey Dovey Baby	86	Charly LP 1114
Red Sails In The Sunset	86	Charly LP 1114
False Love	N/A	Vee Jay (unreleased)
Gerald's Blues	N/A	Vee Jay (unreleased)
I'm Gonna Thank Him	N/A	Vee Jay (unreleased)
Jessie Mae	N/A	Vee Jay (unreleased)
Lucinda	N/A	Vee Jay (unreleased)
Sloppy Drunk	N/A	Vee Jay (unreleased)
Spaniels (Pookie Hudson & the)		
(I Love You) For Sentimental Reasons/Meek Man	61	Neptune 124
John Brown/Turn Out The Lights	62	Parkway 839
Sparkels		
Try Love (One More Time)/That Boy Of Mine	64	Old Town 1160
Sparkles (1) (Lorelei Lynn & the)		
Bobby/Rock-A-Bop	59	Award 128
Sparkles (2)		
Where There's A Will/We Got It	63	Poplar 119

ARTIST/SONG	YEAR	LABEL
Sparkletones		
Dear Little Boy/Just One Chance	63	Pageant 604
Sparks (1) (Curtis Irvin & the)		
Make A Little Love/Cheatin' On Me	54	RPM 417
Sparks (2)		
Mary, Mary Lou/Ol' Man River (instrumental)	57	Decca 30378
A Cuddle And A Kiss/Roamin' Candle	57	Decca 30509
Danny Boy/Run, Run, Run	57	Hull 723
Adreann/The Finger	57	Hull 724
Robin Red Breast/Something Happened	58	Arwin 114
The Genie/Gee, That's Bad	59	Carlton 522
Why Did You Leave/La Macerena	59	Decca 30974
Sparks (3) (Nathan Ray & the)		
Teen Heart/Hold Me Close	58	Rocko 510
Sparks (4)		
Woe, Woe/Cool It	67	Cub 9151
Sparks Of Rhythm		
Cry On My Shoulder	89	Relic LP 5080
Somewhere	89	Relic LP 5080
Sparks Of Rhythm (fb Jimmy Jones) (aka Berliners)		
Don't Love You Anymore/Woman, Woman, Woman	55	Apollo 479
Stars Are In The Sky/Hurry Home	55	Apollo 481
Handy Man/Everybody Rock And Go	60	Apollo 541
Sparks, Milton (& group)		
The Voice Of Love/A Certain Smile	58	Vulcan/Hunt 320 (58)
Sparrows (1)		
Tell My Baby/Why Did You Leave Me?	53	Jay-Dee 783
I'll Be Lovin' You/Hey!	54	Jay-Dee 790
Love Me Tender/Come Back To Me	56	Davis 456/Jay Dee
I'm Gonna Do That Woman In/Don't Fuck Around With Love	71	Kelway 101 (unreleased)
(by the Blenders, recorded in 1953)		
I'm Gonna Hold My Baby Tight	85	Krazy Kat LP 797
Sparrows (2) (Little Jimmy & the)		
Two Hearts Together/Snorin'	58	Val-Ue 101
Sparrows (3)		
It's Written In The Stars	N/A	Broadcast 1000
Sparrows Quartet		
Please Come Back To Me	N/A	Del Tone 3001
Sparrows Quartette		
Love My Baby/Deep In My Heart	N/A	Jet 3000
Spartans (1)		
Faith, Hope And Charity/Lost	54	Capri 7201
Spartans (2) (Jimmy & the)		
You're My Girl/Why Doesn't She Notice Me	60	Satellite 106
Spartans (3)		
One More Chance/Love Is Strange	61	Audio International 102
Spears (Frankie Ervin & the)		
Why Did It End?/Try To Care	61	Don 202

ARTIST/SONG	YEAR	LABEL
Spears, Calvin (& group)		
Come On Home/Doing The Rock And Roll	60	Vin 1020
Specials		
I'm Leaving It All Up To You/Kissin' Like Lovers	63	Marc 103
Spectors Three (gm Phil Spector)		
I Really Do/I Know Why	60	Trey 3001
Mr. Robin/My Heart Stood Still	60	Trey 3005
Speidels		
Oh Baby/A Lovely One	60	Monte Carlo 101
Spellbounds (Johnny Adams & the)		
A Part Of Me/Some Day	63	Watch 6333
Spencer, Carl (& group)		
Prayer/Tired Of Work	62	Southside 1007
Spencer, Sonny (& group)		
Gilee/Oh Boy	59	Memo 17984
Spi-Dells		
Gee But I Wish/Never Ever	N/A	Little Town 575
Take Me As I Am/Over The Weekend	N/A	Tyme 200/Tyme 263
Spices (1)		
Tell Me Little Girl/Money, Fortune And Fame	58	Carlton 480
Spices (2) (Sugar & the)		
Bye Bye Baby/Do The Dog	63	Stacy 968
Spidels (aka Spiedels)		
Fat Lady/I'll Catch A Rainbow	63	Minaret 112
You Know I Need You/Like A Bee	N/A	Chavis 1035
Spiders		
You're The One/I Didn't Want To Do It	54	Imperial 5265/ Imperial 5618 (59)
Tears Began To Flow/I'll Stop Crying	54	Imperial 5280
I'm Slippin' In/I'm Searching	54	Imperial 5291
Mmm Mmm Baby/The Real Thing	54	Imperial 5305
21"/She Keeps Me Wondering	54	Imperial 5318
That's Enough/Lost And Bewildered	55	Imperial 5331
Am I The One/Sukey, Sukey, Sukey	55	Imperial 5344
For A Thrill/Bells In My Heart	55	Imperial 5354
Witchcraft/Is It True?	55	Imperial 5366
A-1 In My Heart/Dear Mary	56	Imperial 5393
That's The Way To Win My Heart/Goodbye	56	Imperial 5405
Honey Bee/That's My Desire	57	Imperial 5423
You're The One/Tennessee Slim	60	Imperial 5714
Witchcraft/You Don't Love Me (True)	61	Imperial 5739
Don't Knock	61	Imperial LP 9140
True You Don't Love Me	61	Imperial LP 9140
Walking Around In Circles	61	Imperial LP 9140
Love's All I'm Putting Down	N/A	Imperial (unreleased)
Mello Mama	N/A	Imperial (unreleased)
Why Do I Love You	N/A	Imperial (unreleased)
You Played The Part	N/A	Imperial (unreleased)
Spiders (Chuck Carbo & the)		
Don't Pity Me/How I Feel	56	Imperial 5376
Spiedells		
Dream Girl	66	Providence 418

ARTIST/SONG	YEAR	LABEL
Spiedels (aka Spidels)		
Dear Joan/No	58	Crosley 201
Spindles (Frankie & the)		
My Letter To You/Count To Ten	68	Roc-Ker 100
Handwriting On The Wall/Count To Ten	68	Roc-Ker 101
For Your Love	68	Roc-Ker 13314
Tomorrow/There Is A Beauty	68	Roc-Ker 575
Spindletoppers (Carl & the)		
It's Written In Your Eyes/Hey Moon	62	ABC 10346
Spindrifts		
Belinda/Cha Cha Doo	58	ABC 9904
Spinner, Alice (& group)		
Good For Me/Sweet Promises	N/A	Hugo 11722
Spinners (1)		
Goofin'/Love's Prayer	58	Capitol 3955
Marvella/My Love And Your Love	58	Rhythm 125
Bird Watchin'/Richard Pry, Private Eye	59	End 1045
Little Otis/Rag Mop	59	Warner Bros. 5084
Spinners (2) (Claudine Clark & the)		
Angel Of Happiness/Teenage Blues	58	Herald 521
Party Lights/Disappointed	62	Chancellor 1113
Walkin' Through A Cemetery/Telephone Game	62	Chancellor 1124
Walk Me Home/Who Will You Hurt	63	Chancellor 1130
Spirals (1)		
Please Be My Love/Forever And A Day	61	Smash 1719
Spirals (2)		
Adios, My Love (a capella)	75	Relic LP 108
Peace Of Mind (a capella)	75	Relic LP 108
Spirals (3)		
My Humble Prayer/Lost My Heart	62	Luxor 1012
Spirits (Doug Sahm & the)		
Crazy, Crazy Feeling/Baby What's On Your Mind	59	Personality 3504
Spitfires (Tony Carmen & the)		
Don't Run To Me/Spitfire	59	Abel 224
Splendors		
Who Can It Be/The Golden Years	59	Taurus 102
Island Called Romance/Puddin' Tain	62	Jano 004
Sportsmen		
Oh Pattie/Please Take My Ring	59	A 103
Dreaming/Sandstorm	59	A 104
Sporttones		
In My Dreams/So Sincere	59	Munich 101
Spotlighters		
It's Cold/Bam, Jingle, Jingle	55	Imperial 5342
Please Be My Girlfriend/Whisper	58	Aladdin 3436
This Is My Story/Preachin'	58	Aladdin 3441
Spotlites		
Travelin'/All Kinds Of Dancin' Going On	59	Catalina 1001

ARTIST/SONG	YEAR	LABEL
Spriggs, Walter (& group)		
I'm Not Your Fool Anymore/Weekend Man	55	Blue Lake 109
Springer, Walter (& group)		
Everytime/One More Chance	59	Kaiser 401
Springers		
I Know My Baby Loves Me So/I Know Why	65	Way Out 2699
Sprouts		
Goodbye She's Gone/Teen Billy Baby	57	RCA 7080/Spangle 2002 (57)
Why Did You Go/Twisting On Bandstand	60	Mercury 71727
Sputniks		
My Love Is Gone/Hey, Maryann	57	Pam Mar 602/Class 217
Johnny's Little Lamb/Wait A Little Longer	58	Class 222
Spy-Dels		
We'll Be Together/Boll Weevil Is Back	62	Crackerjack 4001
Spydells (aka Spydels)		
We're In Love/Big McGoon	60	Addit 1220
Spydels (aka Spydells)		
No More Teasing/Wanted Dead Or Alive	61	MZ 103/MZ 009
Change Your Mind/Peace Of Mind	62	Assault 1860
Squeaks		
Too Young/Oh Yeah	N/A	Gee Clef 077
Squires (1)		
Let's Give Love A Try/Whop	53	Combo 35
Oh, Darling/My Little Girl	53	Combo 42
Squires (2)		
Sayonara/Mia Bella Donna	54	Flair 1030
Squires (3) (aka Blue Jays (4))		
Lucy Lou/A Dream Come True	54	Kicks 1
Sindy/Do-Be-Do-Be-Wop-Wop	55	Mambo 105/Vita 105 (60)
Me And My Deal/Sweet Girl	55	Vita 113
Heavenly Angel/Sweet Girl	56	Vita 116
Guiding Angel/You Ought To Be Ashamed (with Effie Smith)	56	Vita 117
Venus/Breath Of Air	56	Vita 128
Dreamy Eyes/Dangling With My Heart	57	Aladdin 3360
S' Cadillac	73	Relic LP 5007
Squires (4)		
Movin' Out/Our Theme	61	Chan 102/MGM 13044 (61)
Squires (5) (Billy Jones & the)		
Every Word Of The Song/Listen To Your Heart (no group)	58	Deck 478
Squires (6)		
So Many Tears Ago/Don't Accuse Me	62	Gee 1082
Why Should I Suffer/Walkin'	63	Herald 580
Squires (7)		
It's Time/Girls	64	Boss 2120
Shimmy Stomp/Love Me, Leave Me	N/A	Robway 1
Squires (8)		
Joyce/Can't Believe That You've Grown Up	64	Congress 223

ARTIST/SONG	YEAR	LABEL

Staffords
Come Back To Me/Cry Baby Cry — 56 — Decca 29828

Stagehands
Hello Dolly/You Started It — 64 — T.A. 101

Stagg, Tommy (& group)
Memories Of Love/Four In Love — 61 — Bambi 802

Stags
Sailor Boy/Cool Capri — 58 — M&S 502

Standards
Tears Bring Heartaches/No No No — 63 — Debro 3178/Roulette 4487 (63)
Hello Love/My Heart Belongs To Only You — 63 — Magna 1314/Chess 1869 (63)
It Isn't Fair/Everybody Knows — 63 — Magna 1315/Glenden 1315 (63)
When You Wish Upon a Star/When You Wish Upon a Star — 69 — Amos 134
(instrumental)

Standards (Larry & the)
My Lucky Night/Where Is She — 62 — Laurie 3119

Star Drifts
She's Gone/An Eye For An Eye — 62 — Goldisc G3

Star Dusters (Anna Maria With Blinky Allen's)
I'm A Fool To Care/An Angel Cried — 54 — Flair 1047

Star Fires (aka Starfires (3))
Each Night At Night/What Good Is Money — 62 — Haral 777
You Done Me Wrong/Like Socks And Shoes — 66 — Laurie 3332

Star Steppers
The First Signs Of Love/You're Gone — 60 — Amy 801

Stardust
What Did I Do — 81 — Clifton

Stardusters
Love Story/Battle Of Bull Run — 58 — Edison International 404

Stardusters (Bobby Chandler & the)
Serious/If You Loved Me — 56 — O.J. 1000
Me And My Imagination/Shadows Of Love — 57 — O.J. 1005

Starfires (1)
I Have Someone/Three Roses — 58 — Decca 30730
Love Is Here To Stay/Tomorrow — 59 — Decca 30916

Starfires (2) (Wayne Hammond & the)
Can't See Why/Carolyn — 59 — Gala 105

Starfires (3) (aka Star Fires)
Do-Ko-Icki-No/Yearning For You — 58 — Bernice 201
Fender Bender/Camel Walk — 59 — Apt 25030
You're The One/So Much — 61 — Bargain 5001
Love Will Break Your Heart/The Dances — 61 — Bargain 5003/Atomic 1912 (61)
These Foolish Things/Let's Do The Pony — 61 — D&H 200
Chartreuse Caboose/Billy's Blues — 61 — Pama 117
Fools Fall In Love/Under The Stars — 62 — Duel 518
Hand Full Of Blood/Re-Entry — 63 — Sonic 7163
Work Out Fine/Fink — 65 — Triumph 61

Starfires (3) (fb Tom King) (aka Star Fires)
Ring Of Love/Cheating Game — 60 — Pama 115

ARTIST/SONG	YEAR	LABEL
Starfires (4) (Ral Donner & the)		
Girl Of My Best Friend/It's Been A Long Long Time	61	Gone 5102
Starfires (5)		
Go Chattanooga	62	Chip 1010
Starglows (fb Nate Nelson)		
Let's Be Lovers/Walk Softly Away	63	Atco 6272
Starlarks (1)		
Darling, Please Don't Love Me	57	Astra 100
Starlarks (2)		
Fountain Of Love/Send Me A Picture Baby	57	Elm 001/Ember 1013 (57)
Starlarks (2) (Wes Forbes & the)		
Heavenly Father/My Dear	57	Ancho 102/Relic 508 (64)
Starlets (1) (aka Angels (5))		
P.S. I Love You/Where Is My Love Tonight	60	Astro 202/203
Romeo And Juliet/Listen For A Lonely Tambourine	60	Astro 204
Starlets (1) (Jenny Lee & the)		
What I Gotta Do/Show Me A Man	62	Congress 107
Starlets (2) (female)		
I'm So Young/He Got It	60	Lute 5909
Ringo/All Dressed Up	64	Siana 717
Starlets (3) (female)		
Better Tell Him No/You Are The One	61	Pam 1003
My Last Cry/Money Hungry	61	Pam 1004
Starlets (3) (Danetta & the) (female)		
We're Going Steady (You Belong To Me)/Impression	62	Okeh 7155
Starlets (4)		
Multiply By Three/You Won't Even Know Her Name	65	Tower 115
You Don't Love Me/I've Had It	65	Tower 144
Starlets (5) (Ella Thomas & the) (female)		
I'm A Stranger/If You Leave Me	N/A	Gedinson's 101
Starlettes (female)		
Jungle Love/Please Ring My Phone	58	Checker 895
Starlighters (1)		
Love Cry/Last Night	56	Irma 101
Until You Return/Whomp, Whomp!	56	Sun Coast 1001
Slipping Out/Rocking Too Much	57	Lamp 2014
Starlighters (2)		
It's Twelve O'Clock/The Birdland	58	End 1031
I Cried/You're The One To Blame	59	End 1049
A Story Of Love/Let's Take A Stroll (Down Lover's Lane)	60	End 1072
Hot Licks/Creepin'	60	Wheel 1004
Betty Jane	N/A	Minit
Starlighters (3)		
Zoom/Big Feet	60	Hi-Q 5016

ARTIST/SONG	YEAR	LABEL
Starlighters (4) (Joey Dee & the)		
Crazy Love	62	N/A
Peppermint Twist, Pt. 1/Peppermint Twist, Pt. 2	62	Roulette 4401
Starlights (1)		
Ain't Nobodys Business/Who Baby Who	57	RCA 6977
Starlights (2) (Joey & the)		
The Face Of An Angel/Shimmy Baby	60	Scepter 1210
Starlights (3)		
Searching For Love/Count Off Blues	N/A	Premium 101
Starlings		
All I Want/That's Me	59	World Pacific 809
My Plea For Love/Music, Maestro, Please	54	Josie 760
I'm Just A Crying Fool/Hokey-Smokey Mama	55	Dawn 212
A-Loo, A-Loo/I Gotta Go Now	55	Dawn 213
Starliters		
Arline/Sweet Sue	55	Combo 73
Starliters (Joey Dee & the)		
The Face Of An Angel/Shimmy Baby	60	Scepter 1210
Starlites (1)		
Missing You/Give Me A Kiss	57	Peak 5000
My Darling/Sentimental Journey	60	Queen 5000
Bop Diddlie In The Jungle	N/A	Claremont 959
Starlites (1) (Eddie & the)		
To Make A Long Story Short/Pretty Little Girl	59	Scepter 1202
Come On Home/I Need Some Money	63	Aljon 1260/1261
Three Steps To Go/Nobody But You And Me	72	Bim Bam Boom 102
I Can Dream/You Told Me So	73	Vintage 1004
Starlites (1) (Kenny Esquire & the)		
They Call Me A Dreamer/Pretty Brown Eyes	57	Ember 1011
Tears Are Just For Fools/Boom Chica Boom	57	Ember 1021
Starlites (2)		
Valarie/Way Up In The Sky	60	Fury 1034
Ain't Cha Ever Coming Home/Silver Lining	60	Fury 1045
No More Doggin'/Ain't Cha Ever Coming Home	61	Fury 1045
Seven Day Fool/Don't Be Afraid	65	Sphere Sound 705
Starlites (2) (Jackie & the)		
They Laughed At Me/You Put One Over On Me	57	Fire & Fury 1000
I Found Out Too Late/I'm Coming Home	61	Fury 1057
For All We Know/I Heard You	62	Mascot 128
You Keep Telling Me/Sha Pobo Baby	62	Mascot 130
I'll Burn Your Letters/Walking From School	63	Mascot 131
I Still Remember/I Cried My Heart Out	64	Hull 760
Let Him Go	91	Relic LP 5090
No More Heart	91	Relic LP 5090
Starlites (3)		
Merry Christmas Tonight/Xmas In My Heart	62	Goldband 1151
Starlites (4)		
Joanie/My Greatest Thrill	65	Relic 1001
Starnotes		
This Is It/Say The Word	N/A	Caper 101

ARTIST/SONG	YEAR	LABEL
Starr Brothers (ref Donald Jenkins & The Delighters)		
Don Juan/Down On My Knees	63	Cortland 104
Mr. Auctioneer/Beautiful Woman	63	Cortland 106
Starr, Bobby (aka Tony Allen) (& group)		
Please Give Me A Chance/Sweet Man	59	Radio 120
Starr, Suzy (& group)		
Lover's Quarrel/One Day	61	Morgil 711
Stars		
Let's Cuddle Again/When You Love	59	Vega 001
No Letter From You/Night Train	59	Vega 002
Startones (aka Carnations (5))		
Betty/No Time For Tears	54	N/A
I Love You So Dearly/Forever My Love	56	Rainbow 341
Statens		
Summertime Is Time For Love/That Certain Kind	61	Mark-X 8011
Statics (1)		
The Day You Left Me/The Girl In My Dreams	58	Event 4279
Statics (2) (Lynn & the)		
Little Girls Dream/Sunday Kind Of Love	N/A	Mantis 101
Statlers		
Vicky/Gone	62	Little Star 108
Statues		
Love At First Sight/The Commandments Of Love	61	Liberty 55363
Statues (fb Gary Miles)		
Blue Velvet/Keep The Hall Light Burning	60	Liberty 55245
White Christmas/Jeanie With The Light Brown Hair	60	Liberty 55292
Statues (Gary Miles & the)		
Look For A Star/Afraid Of Love	60	Liberty 55261
Wishing Well/Dream Girl	60	Liberty 55279
Steadies		
Rock To The Philadelphia/One Kiss And That's All	58	Josie 837
Two Lovers In Love/Music Goes Round And Round	59	Tad 0711
Steinways		
You've Been Leading Me On/My Heart Is Not	66	Oliver 2002
Don't Wonder Why/Call Me	66	Oliver 2007
Stenotones (Billy James & the)		
Phyllis/My Prayer	61	Rust 5038
Stephens, Jimmy (aka Jimmy Stevens) (bb the Safaris)		
Congratulations/Love Dreams	61	Eldo 112
Stereophonics		
Love Is So Wonderful/No More Heartaches	58	Apt 25003
Stereos		
Echo In My Heart/Tic Tac Toe	62	Columbia 42626
Stereos (1) (aka Tams (1)/aka Hippies)		
Memory Lane/Teenage Kids	59	Mink 022/Parkway 863 (63)

ARTIST/SONG	YEAR	LABEL
Stereos (2)		
A Love For Only You/Sweetpea's In Love	59	Gibraltar 105
I Really Love You/Please Come Back To Me	61	Cub 9095
Sweet Water/The Big Knock	61	Cub 9103
Unless You Mean It/Do You Love Me	62	Cub 9106
Me Heart/You Left Me Forsaken	62	Robins Nest 101
Don't Cry Darling/Run Sinner Run	62	Robins Nest 1588
Mumbling Word/Good News	63	World Artists 1012
Don't Let It Happen To You/The Best Thing To Be Is A Person	64	Val 2
Stereo Freeze, Pt. 1/Stereo Freeze, Pt. 2	67	Cadet 5577
I Can't Stop These Tears/I Feel Soul A'Coming	68	Cadet 5626
Your Memory	N/A	N/A
Stereos (3) (Little Benny & the)		
My Sweetheart/Drinking Wine, Spodee-Odee	59	Spot 106
Stereos (4) (Dave & the)		
This Must Be Love/Roamin' Romeo	61	Pennant 1001
Sterios		
Life	66	Ideal 110
Stevedores (Steve & the)		
Honey Bee	58	Rebel 1314
Stevens, Carol Ann (& group)		
A Heart Is A Toy/Lonely Hearted	61	Carol 4111
Stevens, Jimmy (aka Jimmy Stephens) (bb the Safaris)		
That's Where The Difference Lies/A Funny Thing Happened	63	Valiant 6049
Stevens, Julie (with the Premiers (1))		
I Don't Want To Know/Take My Heart	57	Dig 129
Stevens, Kenny (& group)		
Echo In My Heart/It Was Love At First Sight	64	Old Town 1158
Stevens, Randy (& group)		
All My Love/Sweet Shop	59	Loma 301
Stewart, Sylvester (aka Sly Stone) (& group)		
Long Time Away/Help Me With My Heart	62	G&P 901
Stick Legs (& group)		
The Wedding/Flying Twist	N/A	Hard Times 3002
Stingrays		
Let Them Talk/When You Wish Upon A Star	64	Crazytown 101/102
Stites, Gary (& group)		
Don't Wanna Say Goodbye/Lawdy Miss Clawdy	60	Carlton 525
Stompers		
Foolish One/Quarter To Four Stomp	62	Landa 684
Stone, Lawrence (& group)		
Everytime/Until The Real Thing Comes Along	57	Dig 130
Storey Sisters (aka Twinkles) (female)		
Cha Cha Boom/Which Way Did My Heart Go	58	Baton 255
Bad Motorcycle/Sweet Daddy	58	Cameo 126
Lost Love/Lover How I Miss You	59	Mercury 71457
Stories (Smitty & the)		
Before You Go/Under Your Window	61	Elf 102

RTIST/SONG	YEAR	LABEL

torm, Billy (& group)
Angel Of Mine/The Way To My Heart — 58 — Barbary Coast 1001

torm, Billy (bb the Storms)
Sure As You're Born/In The Chapel In The Moonlight — 60 — Atlantic 2076
Dear One/When You Dance — 61 — Atlantic 2098
Honey Love/A Kiss From Your Lips — 61 — Atlantic 2112

torms (Wally Lee & the)
Eeny Meeny/I Never Felt This Way — 59 — Sundown 123

torytellers (1) (aka Tellers featuring Timmy Lymon)
Hey Baby/You Played Me A Fool — 59 — Stack 500

torytellers (2) (fb Steve Barri)
I Don't Want An Angel/Down In The Valley — 63 — Capitol 5042
Time Will Tell/When Two People — 63 — Dimension 1014/ Ramarca 501 (63)

trands
How Will I Know/Must You Go So Soon — 60 — Firefly 331
Old Man River/Never — 62 — Triode 101

trangers (1)
My Friends/I've Got Eyes — 54 — King 4697
Blue Flowers/Beg And Steal — 54 — King 4709
Hoping You'll Understand/Just Don't Care — 54 — King 4728
Drop Down To My Place/Get It One More Time — 54 — King 4745
Dreams Come True/How Long Must I Wait? — 55 — King 4766
Without A Friend/Think Again — 55 — King 4821
It's Too Bad — N/A — King (unreleased)

trangers (2)
We're In Love/J-U-D-Y — 59 — Christy 107/108

trangers (3)
I'm Feeling Sad/You Ain't Too Cool — 60 — Maske 101
Pa And Billie/Darlin' — 62 — Checker 1010

trangers (4)
Night Winds/These Are The Things I Love — 64 — Warner Bros. 5438

trategics
I Am Looking Too — N/A — Lyndell 773

tratfords (1)
Never Leave Me — 64 — O'Dell 100
Throw Stones — 64 — O'Dell 114

tratfords (2)
Promise Her Anything/Lover's Lullabye — N/A — Universal Artists 1215

trays (Ray & the)
How Will I Know My Love/No, No More — 62 — Larric 101

treet Corner Symphony
Earth Angel/I'm Not Ready — 75 — Bang 719
Nice Guys/That Love Was Magic — 75 — Bang 722

treet Singers
I Was Dreaming/Mambo Love — 55 — Dawn 211
Tonight Was Like A Dream/Caldonia's Mambo — 56 — Tuxedo 899

trickland, Jan (& group)
Come To Me My Little Darling/Let's — 55 — X 0080

ARTIST/SONG	YEAR	LABEL

Striders

Rollin'/Come Back To Me Tomorrow	54	Derby 857
I Wonder/Hesitating Fool	55	Apollo 480

Striders (Betty McLaurin & the)

My Heart Belongs To Only You/I Won't Tell A Soul I Love You	52	Derby 804

Striders (Savannah Churchill & the)

In Spite Of Everything You Do/	51	RCA 4448
Don't Grieve, Don't Sorrow, Don't Cry		
When You Come Back To Me/Once There Lived A Fool	51	Regal 3309/Derby 468

Strikes

Baby I'm Sorry/If You Can't Rock Me	56	Lin 5006/Imperial 5433 (57)
I Don't Want To Cry Over You/Rockin'	57	Imperial 5446

Stringbeans

Starlight/Stop Your Crying	64	Gina 7001

Strings

Love You	N/A	Mellow Town 1006

Strollers (1)

Bitter Dreams	57	States (unreleased)
In Your Dreams/Go Where Baby Lives	57	States 163

Strollers (2)

You're The Only One For Me/Baby Eyes	57	Zebra 22

Strollers (3)

Crowded Classroom/We're Strolling	58	Warner 1018
Summer Love/King Of All Fools	60	20th Fox 226
Dee Dee Brown/Favors	60	Cub 9060
That Look In Your Eye/Nobody But You	60	Dart 1017
Ever Since You Kissed Me/Tangier	63	Jubilee 5449

Strollers (4)

Come On Over/There's No One But You	61	Carlton 546

Strong, Karen (& group)

I Was Made To Love	N/A	N/A

Stuart, Glen (& chorus)

Drip Drop/Ruby Baby	60	Abel 235

Studebaker '"7

Come Go With Me/One Fine Day	N/A	Coulee 142

Students (1) (Beverly Wright & the)

Shake Till I'm Shook/Don't Let The Sun Catch You Cryin'	56	Groove 0153
(no group)		

Students (2)

Jenny Lee	56	Fordham 109
I'm So Young/Every Day Of The Week	58	Note 10012/Argo 5386 (61)/
		Checker 902 (61)
My Vow To You/That's How I Feel	58	Note 10019/Checker 1004 (62)
Mary/Bye Bye Truly	58	Red Top
My Heart Is An Open Door/Mommy And Daddy	58	Red Top 100

Students (3) (Bill Starr & the)

One Heart/Love For A Year	60	Applause 1235

Style Kings

Kissing Behind The Moon/Under The Tropical Sky	59	Sotoplay 0011

ARTIST/SONG	YEAR	LABEL

Stylers

Gentle As A Teardrop/There Were Others	54	Kicks 2
Lost John/Huffin' And Puffin'	56	Jubilee 5246
Confession Of A Sinner/Gonna Tell 'Em	56	Jubilee 5253
You Tell Me/Blues In The Night	57	Golden Crest 1181/1182
Breaker Of Hearts/Miracle In Milan	57	Jubilee 5279
Kiss And Run Lover/Girlie Girlie Girlie	58	Golden Crest 1291
Pushing Up Daisies/Going Steady Anniversary	63	Gordy 7018

Stylers (Dick Thomas & the)

Anytime Is Lovin' Time/	55	Jubilee 5208
When Uncle Joe Plays The Rag On His Old Banjo (no group)		

Styles (1)

Scarlet Angel/Gotta Go, Go, Go	61	Serene 1501
I Love You For Sentimental Reasons/School Bells To Chapel Bells	64	Josie 920

Styles (2) (Chuck Mile & the)

Be Mine Or Be A Fool/Lovin' Daddy	62	Dore 630

Styles (3) (Donnie & the)

Chapel Of Love/Marie	64	Times Square 106

Stylettes

On Fire/Packing Up My Memories	64	Cameo 337
My Boy/You'll Go First	65	Cameo 353

Stylists

Go, Go Daddy Go/Just Don't Sit There	55	Crown 145
Mourning/Move It Over, Baby	59	Jay Wing 5807
One Room/I Wonder	60	Rose 16/17
I've Been Waiting For You/Scarey Harry	60	Sage 317

Suburbans (1)

I Remember/T. V. Baby	56	Baton 227
Leave My Gal Alone/My First And Last Romance	57	Baton 240

Suburbans (1) (Ann Cole & the)

In The Chapel/Each Day	56	Baton 232
Got My Mo-Jo Working (But It Won't Work On You)/	57	Baton 237
I've Got A Little Boy (no group)		

Suburbans (1) (Jimmy Ricks & the)

I'm A Fool To Want You/Bad Man Of Missouri	57	Baton 236

Suburbans (2)

Alphabet Of Love/Sweet Diane Cha Cha	59	Port 70011
Little Bird/King Of Broken Hearts	60	Kip 221
Love Me/Mississippi Mud	61	Flamingo 539
Love Me/Lovin' Hands	61	Gee 1076
Walk Beside Me/Mary Had A Little Lamb	63	Shelley 184

Suddens (1) (aka Safaris)

Childish Ways/Garden Of Love	61	Sudden 103

Suddens (2)

Dream Girl	N/A	N/A

Suedes (1)

I Love You So/Don't Blooper	54	Money 204

Suedes (2)

Don't Be Shy/Please Be Satisfied	59	Dart 117

ARTIST/SONG	YEAR	LABEL
Suedes (3) (Rosie Stevens & the)		
Everybody's Trying To Be My Baby/Wrong Yo Yo	60	Spinning 6011
Sugar Buns		
Pajama Party/Nails And Snails	59	Warner Bros. 5046
Sugar Lumps (Sugar Boy & the)		
So Long, Goodbye/Mama Won't You Turn Me Loose	63	Peacock 1925
Sugar Tones (1) (aka Enchanters (1))		
Wishin'/Today Is Your Birthday	52	Okeh 6877
I Just Want To Dream/I Know You Gotta Go	53	Okeh 6992
Blow The Whistle/Scandal	54	Benida 5021
How Can I Pretend/Hippity Hop	60	Cannon 391
Baby/How Can You Forget So Soon	60	Cannon 392
Sugar Tones (2) (Candy & the)		
Hurtin' All Over/I-Ay-Ou-Lay-Oo-Ya	58	Jackpot 48008
Sugarmints		
You'll Have Everything/I-I-I Could Love You	57	Brunswick 55042
Sugartones (Jimmy Lane & the)		
Constantly/Let Your Conscience Be Your Guide	58	Time 6602
Sultans (1)		
Lemon Squeezing Daddy/You Captured My Heart	51	Jubilee 5054
Don't Be Angry/Blues At Dawn	52	Jubilee 5077
Good Thing, Baby/How Deep Is The Ocean?	54	Duke 125
I Cried My Heart Out/Baby, Don't Put Me Down	54	Duke 133
What Makes Me Feel This Way?/Boppin' With The Mambo	54	Duke 135
If I Could Tell/My Love Is High	57	Duke 178
Sultans (2) (Bob Oakes & the)		
Church Bells My Ring/You Gotta Rock And Roll	56	Regent 7502
Sultans (3)		
It'll Be Easy/You Got Me Goin'	61	Tilt 782
Mary, Mary/How Far Does A Friendship Go	62	Jam 107
Christina/Someone You Can Trust	63	Guyden 2079
Sultans (4) (Wardell & the)		
I Need Your Love/I'm Broke	62	Imperial 5886
Sultans (5)		
Gloria/I Wanna Know	65	Ascot 2228
Sultans (6)		
A Cottage For Sale/Say Hey Girl	61	Knowles 105
Sultans Five		
Life Is Like A River	64	Raynard 1053
Daisy	66	Raynard 843
Summits		
Go Back Where You Came From/Times Square Stomp (instrumental)	61	Times Square 422
He's An Angel/Hanky Panky	63	Harmon 1017/Rust 5072 (63)
Sun-Rays		
The Lonely Hours/Love Is A Stranger	58	Sun 293
Sun-Rays (Cliff & the)		
Lucky Me/No Treason In My Heart	60	Zil 9002

ARTIST/SONG	YEAR	LABEL

Sunbeams (1)

Blue Mountain Waltz/I'm Gonna Come Home To Mama	55	Dot 1271
Tell Me Why/Come Back, Baby	55	Herald 451
How About It/Wrap It Up And Save	56	Dot 1280
Please Say You'll Be Mine/You've Got To Rock And Roll	57	Acme 109

Sunbeams (2) (Donna Rae & the)

| Little Fool/Whisper Your Love | 59 | Satellite 103 |

Sundials

| Whether To Resist/Chapel Of Love | 62 | Guyden 2065 |

Sundowners (1)

| Someone To Care/Such A Lovin' | 60 | Fargo 1051 |

Sundowners (2) (Big Jim & the)

| Poor Little Sad Eyed Sue/Never Let Me Go | 62 | Chip 1008 |

Sunglows (1) (Sunny & the) (fb Sonny Ozuna)

Uptown/Just A Moment	61	Lynn 511
Golly Gee/Touring	62	Sunglow 104/Okeh 7143 (62)
Talk To Me/Every Week Every Month Every Year	63	Tear Drop 3014/Sunglow 110
Rags To Riches/Not Even Judgment Day (by Sunny & the Sunliners)	63	Tear Drop 3022/Sunglow 111
Out Of Sight, Out Of Mind/No One Else Will Do (by Sunny & the Sunliners)	64	Tear Drop 3027
It's Too Late/You Gave Me A True Love	64	Tear Drop 3034
You Send Me/His Greatest Creation	64	Tear Drop 3040
Peanuts (La Cacahuta)/Happy Hippo (instrumentals)	65	Sunglow 107/Disco Grande 1021

Sunglows (2)

| Please Say You Love Me/If You Don't Want My Love | N/A | Carrib 1025 |

Sunliners

| Hully Gully Twist/Sweet Little Girl | N/A | Hercules 182 |
| So In Love/Little Girl Charm | N/A | Hercules 184 |

Sunny Boys

For The Rest Of My Life/My Friend Sam	59	Mr. Maestro 805
Chapel Bells/My Friend Sam	59	Mr. Maestro 806
For The Rest Of My Life/Chapel Bells	59	Take 3 2001

Sunny Lads

| That's My Desire/You're In Love | 59 | Jax 103 |

Suns

| That's My Baby/Dance Girl (by the Camelots) | 64 | Times Square 32/Relic 541 (65) |

Sunsets (1)

| How Will I Remember?/Sittin' And Cryin' | 59 | Rae-Cox 102 |

Sunsets (2)

Lonely Surfer Boy/Playmate Of The Year	63	Challenge 9198
My Little Beach Bunny/My Little Surfin' Woodie	63	Challenge 9208
Lydia/Only You, Only Me	63	Petal 1040

Sunsets (3) (Adrian & the)

| Cherry Pie/Breakthrough | 63 | Sunset 602 |

Sunshine Boys

| If You Still Want Me/My Love, My Love, My Love | 59 | Scottie 1307 |

Superior Angels

| Crying In The Chapel | 64 | Skylark 0023 |

ARTIST/SONG	YEAR	LABEL

Superiors (1)

Lost Love/Don't Say Goodbye	57	Atco 6106/Main Line 104 (58)
Eternal Dream/Happy Days Are Here Again	63	Real Fine 837

Superiors (2)

What Is Love/Flee The Scene	61	Fal 301
I'm Sorry Baby (I Didn't Mean To Do You Wrong)/Dance Of Love	61	Federal 12436

Superiors (3)

Tell Me To Go/What Would I Do	65	Verve 10370
Can't Make It Without You/Let Me Make You Happy	66	MGM 13503
Heavenly Angel/I'd Rather Die	69	Sue 12

Superiors (4) (Tony LaMar & the)

Your Love	65	Go Go 1000

Superlatives

Forget About Tomorrow/Do What You Want To	N/A	Dynamics 1011
Won't You Please	N/A	Dynamics 1012
Don't Walk Away/Lonely In A Crowd	N/A	Dynamics 1016

Superphonics (Dave Kennedy & the)

Me Neither/B-L-U-E	61	Lindy 101

Superphonics

Teen-Age Partner/My Love For You	61	Lindy 102

Supremes (1)

Tonight/She Don't Want Me No More	56	Old Town 1024 (first pressing)
Tonight/My Babe	56	Old Town 1024 (second pressing)
Just For You And I/Honey Honey	57	Ace 530 (unreleased)
Just For You And I/Don't Leave Me Here To Cry	57	Ace 534
You Are Mine/Be My Love	58	Bernice 202
Nobody Can Love You/Snap, Crackle & Pop	58	Mark 129
Little Sally Walker/Just Yell	60	Mascot 126
Zip Boom	85	Murray Hill LP 000083
Glow/You And Me	N/A	Grog 500

Supremes (1) (Ruth McFadden & the) (aka Solitaires)

Darling, Listen To The Words Of This Song/ Since My Baby's Been Gone	56	Old Town 1017

Supremes (2)

Could This Be You?/Margie	56	Kitten 6969

Supremes (3) (fb Diana Ross) (aka Primettes)

I Want A Guy/Never Again	61	Tamla 54038
Buttered Popcorn/Who's Lovin' You?	61	Tamla 54045

Supremes (4) (aka Ruby Nash & the Romantics)

Another Chance To Love/Fidgety	61	Apt 25055

Supremes Four

I Lost My Job/I Love You, Patricia	61	Sara 1032

Surgeons

Don't Tell Me/You Know (by the Electras)	63	Cee-Jam 100

Surprise

Denise/Blue Moon	N/A	Kape 102

Swallows (1)

Will You Be Mine/Dearest	51	King 4458
Wishing For You/Since You've Been Away	51	King 4466
Eternally/It Ain't The Meat	51	King 4501

ARTIST/SONG	YEAR	LABEL
Tell Me Why/Roll, Roll, Pretty Baby	52	King 4515
Beside You/You Left Me	52	King 4525
I Only Have Eyes For You/You Walked In	52	King 4533
Please Baby Please/Where Do I Go From Here	52	King 4579
Laugh (Though You Want To Cry)/Our Love Is Dying	53	King 4612
Bicycle Tillie/Nobody's Loving Me	53	King 4632
Pleading Blues/Trust Me	53	King 4656
My Baby/Good Time Girls	54	After Hours 104/ Chariot 104 (54)
It Feels So Good/I'll Be Waiting	54	King 4676
Angel Baby/Oh Lonesome Me	58	Federal 12319
Rock-A-Bye Baby Rock/We Want To Rock	58	Federal 12328
Beside You/Laughing Boy	58	Federal 12329
Itchy Twitchy Feeling/Who Knows, Do You?	58	Federal 12333

Swallows (2) (aka Guides)
You Must Try/How Long Must A Fool Go On?	59	Guyden 2023 (first pressing, second is by the Guides)

Swanks
Little Angel/Keep Walking	57	Jaguar 3027

Swann, Claudia (with Buddy Griffin & group)
Please Come Back To Me/I Wanna Hug Ya, Kiss Ya (no group)	54	Chess 1586

Swans (1)
For Dreams Come True/Happy	53	Ballad 1000/1001
My True Love/(Ain't Like That) No More	53	Rainbow 233
It's A Must/Night Train	54	Ballad 1003/1006
How Sentimental Can I Be	54	Ballad 1004
Happy/Santa Claus Boogie Song	55	Ballad 1007
I'll Forever Love You/Mr. Cool Breeze	55	Fortune 822
Believe In Me/In The Morning	56	Steamboat 101
Why Must I Cry/Just A Little Bit More (by the Idols)	61	Reveille 1002/Dot 16210 (61)
I Love You So	90	Relic LP 5088
Will You Be Mine	90	Relic LP 5088

Swans (1) (Paul Lewis & the)
Little Senorita/Wedding Bells, Oh Wedding Bells	55	Fortune 813

Swans (2)
If I Could Stop Every Clock/He Wasn't On The Air	59	Roulette 4213

Swans (3)
Daydreamin' Of You/The Promise	63	Parkway 881
He's Mine/You Better Be A Good Girl Now	63	Swan 4151
Please Hurry Home/The Boy With The Beatle Hair	64	Cameo 302

Sweet & Sassy
I Really Love You So/Don't Leave Me	59	Del Pat 207

Sweet Hearts (aka Sweethearts) (female)
My Only You/My Baby	61	D&H 500

Sweet Marquees
You Lied/I Love My Baby	61	Apache 1516

Sweet Nuthins
I Don't Love Him/Nashville, Tennessee	64	Swan 4195

Sweet Sick Teens
The Pretzel/Agnes, The Teenage Russian Spy	61	RCA 7940

Sweet Teens
Forever More/Don't Worry About A Thing	56	Flip 311
My Valentine/With This Ring	57	Gee 1030

ARTIST/SONG	YEAR	LABEL
Sweet Teens (Faith Taylor & the) (female)		
Your Candy Kisses/Won't Someone Tell Me Why?	59	Federal 12334
I Need Him To Love Me/Please Be Mine	60	Bea & Baby 104
I Love You, Darling/Paper Route Baby	60	Bea & Baby 105
Sweet Tymes (aka Tymes)		
I Think I Know Her/You Ought To Belong To Me	67	Epic 10227
Sweethearts (aka Sweet Hearts) (female)		
Just Got The Feeling/Me Heart	58	Terrific 151
Ting-A-Ling-Ling/Sorry Daddy	61	Ray Star 778
(He's My) Superman/In Between Kisses	63	Brunswick 55237
He's A Yankee/What Did I Do	63	Brunswick 55240
Everybody I Know/What Will Mother Say	63	Brunswick 55255
No No/Have You Ever Fell In Love	63	Brunswick 55265
They Talk Too Much/Puppy Love	63	Hi-III 116
Summer Days	63	Hi-III 117
Eddie My Love/Beauty Is Just Skin Deep	65	Kent 428
No More Tears/This Couldn't Be Me	66	Kent 442
Come On, Make Love To Me/Sweetheart, Sweetheart	68	Como 451
Sweeties		
After You/Paul's Love	61	End 1110
Swensons		
Remember Me To My Darling	56	X-Tra 100
Swingin' Bears (Bernadette & the)		
Crazy Yogi/When You're Dancin' With Me	61	Beach 1001
Swingin' Kools		
Forever Dear	59	Harlem 103
Swinging Earls		
All I Do Is Dream Of You/Yum Yum	59	Vega 1001
Swinging Hearts		
Please Say It Isn't So/Something Made Me Stop	60	Lucky Four 1011/ Diamond 162 (64)
How Can I Love You/Spanish Love	61	620 1002/NRM 1002 (61)
I've Got It/You Speak Of Love	64	Magic Touch 2001
Swinging Phillies		
L-O-V-E/Frankenstein's Party	58	DeLuxe 6171
Swinging Reeds (Don Reed & the)		
Why Don't You Believe Me/Western Union	58	United 215
Swinging Rocks (Ruby & Her)		
I Cried A Tear Over You	85	Relic LP 8004
It's Been A Long Time	85	Relic LP 8004
Swingtones		
Geraldine/You Know Baby	58	Rhythm 5001/ABC 9902 (58)
Swordsmen		
Kathi, Please Don't Cry/Lonely Boy, Lonely Girl	N/A	Semac 2114
Sycamores		
I'll Be Waiting/Darling, Is It True?	55	Groove 0121
Sydells		
In The Night/Hokey Pokey	63	Beltone 2032

ARTIST/SONG	YEAR	LABEL
Syllables		
It's You For Me/I've Been Jilted	59	Imperial 5619
Symbols (1) (Marty & the) (aka Devotions)		
You're The One/Rip Van Winkle (by Mr. Bassman)	63	Graphic Arts 1000
Symbols (2)		
Last Year About This Time/Better Get Your Own One Buddy	63	Dore 666
Symbols (3)		
Canadian Sunset/Gentle Art Of Loving	66	President 102
Bye Bye Baby/The Things You Do To Me	67	Laurie 3401
The Best Part Of Breaking Up/Again	68	Laurie 3435
Bye Bye/I Love You	73	Vintage 1007
Symphonics		
Our Love Will Grow/Way Down Low	63	Tru-Lite 116
All Roads Lead To Heartbreak/It Won't Be Long	64	Dee Jon 001
Symphonics (Freddie Scott & the)		
A Blessing To You/Come On Honey	59	Enrica 1002
Syncapates		
Your Tender Lips/Praying For A Miracle	63	Times Square 7
Syndicates		
The Duke/Do What You're Gonna Do	65	Mello 552
Synthetics		
Girl Of My Dreams/My Ol' Lady	N/A	Armour 5577
T-Birds (1)		
Come On, Dance With Me/Green Stamps	61	Chess 1778
T-Birds (2)		
Nobody But You	N/A	Vegas 720
Tabbys (1)		
My Darling/Yes I Do	59	Time 1008
Tabbys (2)		
Hong Kong Baby	63	Metro 2
Tabs (1)		
Will We Meet Again/Still Love You Baby	58	Nasco 6016
First Star/Avenue Of Tears	59	Dot 15887
Rock & Roll Holiday/Never Fo'get	59	Noble 719/Gardena 110 (60)
Oops/My Girl Is Gone	59	Noble 720
Dance All By Myself/Dance Party	61	Vee Jay 418
Mash Dem Taters/But You're My Baby	62	Vee Jay 446
Two Stupid Feet/The Wallop	62	Wand 130
I'm With You/Take My Love Along With You	63	Wand 139
Tabs (2) (Joanie Taylor & the)		
You Lied/Dapper Dan	61	Herald 568
Tads		
Your Reason/The Pink Panther	56	Liberty Bell 9010/Dot 15518 (56)
Wolf Call/She Is My Dream	58	Rev 3513
Taffys		
Key To My Heart/Everybody South Street	63	Fairmount 610
Tags (Johnny Newton & the)		
Sorry, Sorry (I Ran All The Way Home)/A Teenager In Love	59	Bell 114

ARTIST/SONG	YEAR	LABEL
Talents (1) (Julian Barnett & the)		
Don't Walk Away/Come Back To Me	58	Herald 519
Talents (2)		
Rockin' The Tease/New Kind Of Gold	61	Skylark 106
Three Little Fishes/My Favorite Things	61	Twink 1215
Talkabouts		
I Don't Seem To Care Anymore/Sweet Lovin' (by the Visuals)	59	Poplar 117
Tamaneers		
Searching/Be Anything But Be Mine	N/A	Bramley 102
Tamaras (Lee Durell & the)		
You Gave Me Love/Party Time	60	Music City 836
Tamblyn, Larry (& group)		
This Is The Night/Destiny	65	Faro 612
Tamblyn, Larry (bb the Standells)		
This Is The Night/Destiny	60	Faro 612
You'll Be Mine Someday/The Girl In My Heart	64	Linda 112
Tams (1) (aka Hippies/aka Stereos)		
Teenage Kids/Memory Lane	59	Mink 022/Parkway 863 (63)
Tams (2)		
Valley Of Love/Sorry	60	Swan 4055
Vacation Time/If Love Were Like Rivers	61	Heritage 101
Untie Me/Disillusioned	62	Arlen 711
My Baby Loves Me/Find Another Love	62	General American 714
Tangents		
Send Me Something/I Can't Live Alone	60	Fresh 1
That Lucky Old Sun/Never Leave Again	60	Fresh 2274
The Wiggle/The Waddle	60	United Artists 201
Tangerines (1)		
The Answer Is Always You/This Is The Way	61	Wildcat 603
Tangerines (2)		
Jim, That's Him	N/A	Fina 7002
Tangiers (1) (aka Hollywood Flames)		
I Won't Be Around/Tabarin	55	Decca 29603
Remember Me/Oh, Baby!	56	Decca 29973
Don't Try/School Days Will Be Over	58	Class 224
The Plea/The Waddle	62	A-J 905
Tangiers (2)		
Ping Pong/Don't Stop The Music	61	Strand 25039
Tanno, Marc (& group)		
Angel/Dear Baby	61	Whale 501
Tantones (1)		
No Matter/I Love You, Really I Do	56	Lamp 2002
So Afraid/Tell Me	57	Lamp 2008
Tantones (2) (Trade & the)		
Joanne	N/A	Adam & Eve LP 502
Targets		
It Doesn't Matter/Girls Girls Girls	61	King 5538

ARTIST/SONG	YEAR	LABEL
Tartans		
Nothing But Love/I Need You	66	Impact 1010
Tassells (female)		
Since You Went Away/The Twelfth Of Never	63	Goldisc G11
Tassels (female)		
To A Soldier Boy/The Boy For Me	59	Madison 117/Amy 946 (66)
My Guy And I/To A Young Lover	59	Madison 121
Tate, Paul (& group)		
Everybody But Me/Dance On	58	Falcon 1012
Tattletales		
Double Trouble/Magic Wand	59	Warner Bros. 5066
Taylor, Adam (& group)		
Yvonne/I Need Her	N/A	N/A
Taylor, Andrew (& group)		
That's How I Feel About You/	61	Gone 5109
Never Bite Off More Than You Can Chew		
Taylor, Bobby (& group)		
You Are My Heart/Pretty Baby	N/A	Barbara 62640
Taylor, Carmen (& group)		
Why Did You Leave Me Alone/So What	57	King 5085
Taylor, Johnny (& group)		
Never Never/Rome Wasn't Built In A Day	62	Sar 131
Taylor, Mike (& group)		
Mi-A-Suri Talk/He's A Lover	62	Dream
Taylor, Sammy (& group)		
Don't Lie/Your Precious Love	64	Enjoy 2028
Taylor, Ted (& group)		
Be Ever Wonderful/Since You're Home (no group)	59	Duke 304
Anytime, Anyplace, Anywhere/Lost The Best Thing I Ever Had	61	Suncraft 400
Taylortones		
A Star/Poor Little Girl	61	Star Maker 1926
Too Young To Love	85	Relic LP 8004
My Heart Went Zing	N/A	C&T 0001
Team Mates (aka Teamates)		
Sooner Or Later/I Just Might	59	Le Cam 701
Sooner Or Later/If Only I Had Known	59	Le Cam 706
Once There Was A Time/Come On Baby	60	Le Cam 707
Sylvia/Crazy Baby	60	Le Cam 709
Most Of All/Please Believe Me	65	Soft 104/Paula 220 (65)
Teamates (aka Team Mates)		
We've Believed In Love/Once There Was A Time	62	Philips 40029
Calendar Of Love/I Say Goodbye	64	Le Mans 003
Teamates (aka Team Mates) (Tandi & the)		
Trampoline Queen/Week-End Lover	60	Ember 1068
Teardrops (1)		
Come Back To Me/Sweet Lovin' Daddy-O	52	Sampson 634

ARTIST/SONG	YEAR	LABEL
Teardrops (2)		
The Stars Are Out Tonight/Oh, Stop It!	54	Josie 766/Port 70019 (60)
My Heart/Ooh, Baby	54	Josie 771
Al Chiar Di Luna (Porto Fortuna)/We Won't Tell	58	Josie 856
You're My Hollywood Star/Cry No More	59	Josie 862
Daddy's Little Girl/Always You	59	Josie 873
Teardrops (3)		
My Inspiration/I Prayed For love	57	King 5004
Don't Be Afraid To Love/After School	57	King 5037
Teardrops (4)		
Jellyfish/Bridge Of Love	57	Dot 15669
Sugar Baby/Catch Me, I'm Falling Again	58	Rendezvous 102
Teardrops (5) (Billy Taylor & the)		
I'm Young/Wombie Zombie	59	Felco 101
Teardrops (6) (Honey & the)		
You Are The One/Something To Remember You By	59	Val 202
Tears (1) (female)		
Nothing But Love/Until The Day I Die	56	Dig 112
Tears (2) (Linda & the)		
Good Goodbye/Happy Blues	65	Challenge 59317
Tears (3)		
Hurt/She's Mine	N/A	Astronaut 501
Teasers (1)		
How Could You Hurt Me So?/I Was A Fool To Love You	54	Checker 800
Teasers (2) (Jimmy Brinkley & the)		
Why Oh Why/Blue Moon	57	Note 10002
Teasers (3) (Bobby & the)		
She's A Tease/Harry On A Safari	60	Fleetwood 1012
Teasers (4) (Sammy & the)		
As I Remember You/Penny In A Wishing Well	58	Airport 101
Technics		
Because I Really Love You/A Man's Confusion	62	Chex 1012
Hey Girl Don't Leave Me/I Met Her On The First Of September	62	Chex 1013
Technics (Tony & the)		
Ha Ha He Told On You/Work Out With Your Pretty Girl	62	Chex 1010
Techniques		
Hey! Little Girl/In A Round About Way	57	Stars 551/Roulette 4030 (57)
Let Her Go/Marindy	58	Roulette 4048
Moon Tan/The Wisest Man In Town	58	Roulette 4097
Teddy Bears		
To Know Him Is To Love Him/Don't You Worry My Pretty Pet	58	Dore 503
Wonderful Loveable You/Till You'll Be Mine	59	Dore 520
Oh Why/I Don't Need You Anymore	59	Imperial 5562
If You Only Knew/You Said Goodbye	59	Imperial 5581
Don't Go Away/Seven Lonely Days	59	Imperial 5594
Teen Dreams (female) (aka Debbie & the Darnels)		
The Time/Why Why	61	Vernon

ARTIST/SONG	YEAR	LABEL

Teen Five

Darling I Love You/I'll Never Let You Go (by the Gents) (a capella)	63	Times Square 2/
		Times Square 99 (64)
Til The End Of Time/Island Of Love (by the Gents) (a capella)	63	Times Square 4/
		Times Square 98 (64)

Teen Kings (1)

My Greatest Wish/Don't Just Stand There	59	Willett 118

Teen Kings (2)

In The Still Of The Night	N/A	Relic LP 5033
You Are My Love (You)	N/A	Relic LP 5033

Teen Notes

Loco In The Coco/My Precious Jewel	60	Deb 121
Hi-Fi Sweetie/Big Band Polka	61	Deb 127

Teen Tones (1)

Gypsy Boogie/Faded Love	59	Nu-Clear 1

Teen Tones (2)

I'll Never Change/Three Stars	59	Crest 1057
Darling I Love You/My Sweet	59	Dandy Dan 2
Don't Call Me Baby, I'll Call You/Yes You May	59	Decca 30895
My Little Baby/Head Strong Baby	59	Swan 4040
Faded Love/Gypsy Boogie	59	Wynne 107
Susan Ann/Cuckoo	60	Deb 132
I'm So Happy/Shoutin' Twist	61	Tri Disc 102
Do You Wanna Dance/Long Cold Winter ahead	65	T&T 2488

Teen-Kings

That's A Teen-Age Love/Tell Me If You Know	59	Bee 1115

Teenage Moonlighters

Sorry Sorry/I Want To Cry	60	Mark 134

Teenagers (fb by Billy Lobrano)

Everything To Me/ Flip Flop	57	Gee 1046
My Broken Heart/Mama Wanna Rock	58	Roulette 4086
Good Lovin'	86	Murray Hill LP 000148

Teenagers (fb by Frankie Lymon)

Somewhere/Sweet And Lovely	64	Columbia 43094

Teenagers (fb by Joe Negroni)

Jean Of The Ville	61	Columbia (unreleased)
I Hear The Angels Cry	81	Crystal Ball LP 142
Love Me Long	81	Crystal Ball LP 142
The Wild Female	81	Crystal Ball LP 142

Teenagers (fb by Joe Negroni/Kenny Bobo)

Tonight's The Night/Crying	60	End 1071

Teenagers (fb by Johnny Houston)

Can You Tell Me?/A Little Wiser Now	60	End 1076

Teenagers (fb by Sherman Garnes)

He's No Lover	81	Crystal Ball LP 142

Teenagers (Frankie Lymon & the)

Why Do Fools Fall In Love/Please Be Mine	56	Gee 1002
I Want You To Be My Girl/I'm Not A Know It All	56	Gee 1012
I Promise To Remember/Who Can Explain	56	Gee 1018
ABC's Of Love/Share	56	Gee 1022
I'm Not A Juvenile Delinquent/Baby, Baby	56	Gee 1026

ARTIST/SONG	YEAR	LABEL
I Was Alone	57	Gee (unreleased)
Teenage Love/Paper Castles	57	Gee 1032
Love Is A Clown/Am I Fooling Myself Again?	57	Gee 1035
Out In The Cold Again/Miracle In The Rain	57	Gee 1036
Goody Goody/Creation Of Love	57	Gee 1039
Little White Lies	57	Roulette LP 25021/
		Forum LP 9006
Goody Goody Girl/I'm Not Too Young To Dream	59	Gee 1052
Begin The Beguine	86	Murray Hill LP 000148
Fortunate Fellow	86	Murray Hill LP 000148
It Would Be So Nice	86	Murray Hill LP 000148
Love Put Me Out Of My Head	86	Murray Hill LP 000148
Together	86	Murray Hill LP 000148
You	86	Murray Hill LP 000148

Teenagers (Joey & the) (fb by Joe Negroni/Sherman Garnes)
What's On Your Mind/The Draw (with Sherman)	61	Columbia 42054

Teenaires (Harley Davis & the)
My Definition Of You/Mad Lover	61	Wildcat 0064

Teenangels
Tell Me My Love/Ain't Gonna Let You (Break My Heart)	63	Sun 388

Teenbeats
Nightspot/Only The Stars	61	Myrl 407

Teenchords (Lewis Lymon & the)
Too Young/Your Last Chance	57	End 1003
I Found Out Why/Tell Me, Love	57	End 1007/Fury 1007 (57)
I'm So Happy (Tra-La-La-La)/Lydia	57	Fury 1000
Honey Honey/Please Tell The Angels	57	Fury 1003
I'm Not Too Young Too Fall In Love/Falling In Love	57	Fury 1006
Dance Girl/Them There Eyes	58	Juanita 101
Too Young/I Found Out Why	62	End 1113

Teeners (Lulu Reed & the)
Say Hey Pretty Baby/It's Easy Child (by Freddy King)	62	Federal 12477

Teenettes (1) (female)
Too Young To Fall In Love/My Lucky Star	58	Josie 830
From The Word Go/	59	Brunswick 55125
I Want A Boy With A Hi-Fi Supersonic Stereophonic Bloop Bleep		
Let Me Be The One/Bye Bye Baby	63	Sandy 250

Teenettes (2) (Bobby Grabeau & the)
Don't Ever Let Me Go/Back To School, Back To You	59	Crest 1064

Teenettes (3) (Betty Jayne & the)
The Sun Will Rise/Show Your Love	61	Carellen 101
Night Angel/Johnny Preacher	61	Carellen 102
I'm No Longer Jimmy's Girl/Tag Along	61	Carellen 107
Lonely Teenager/Time Will Tell	61	Mona Lee 139
Shoppin' 'Round For Love/I Would Never Dare	61	Net 101

Teenos
Love Only One/Alrightee	58	Dub 2839/Relic 506 (64)

Teens (1) (Little Clyde & the)
A Casual Look/Oh Me	56	RPM 462

Teens (2) (Barbara & the)
Reflections Of You	N/A	Allison

ARTIST/SONG	YEAR	LABEL
Teentones		
Love Is A Vow/Walkie Talkie Baby	56	Rego 1004
Teers (Lancelo & the)		
Whispering Bells/It's Not For Me To Say	N/A	Promenade 12
Tejuns		
Girl/Nobody Knows	N/A	100 Proof 144
Tellers (1) (fb Timmy Lymon) (aka Storytellers (1))		
Hey Baby/You Played Me A Fool	59	Stack 500
Tears Fell From My Eyes/I Wanna Run To You	60	Fire 1038
Tellers (2) (Artie Banks & the)		
Oriental Baby/Spider And The Fly	61	Imperial 5788
Tempests (1)		
Never Let You Go/Falling Like The Rain	59	Williamette 103
Tempests (2)		
My True Story	N/A	Top 6 Hits EP 4
Temples		
Whispering Campaign/I Don't Want To Do A Thing Without You	58	Date 1004
Tempo-Mentals		
Burning Desire/Dearest	57	Ebb 112
Tempo-Tones (fb Richard Lanham)		
Get Yourself Another Fool/Ride Along	57	Acme 713
In My Dreams/My Boy Sleepy Pete	57	Acme 715
Come Into My Heart/Somewhere There Is Someone	57	Acme 718
Tempo-Tones (Nancy Lee & the)		
So They Say/Meet Me At The Crossroads	57	Acme 711
Tempos (1)		
Kingdom Of Love/That's What You Do To Me	57	Kapp 178
The Prettiest Girl In School/Never You Mind	57	Kapp 199
I Got A Job/Strollin' With My Baby	58	Kapp 213
See You In September/Bless You My Love	59	Climax 102
Crossroads Of Love/Whatever Happens	59	Climax 105
Look Homeward Angel/Under Ten Flags	59	Paris 550
Tempos (2) (aka Four Eldorados)		
Promise Me/Never Let Me Go	58	Rhythm 121
Tempos (3)		
It's Tough/Sham-Rock	59	Hi-Q 100
Tempos (4)		
Monkey Do/Oh Play That Thing	63	Fairmount 611
My Dream Island/My Love Goes Deep	64	Vee Jay 580
Tempos (5)		
Why Don't You Write Me/A Thief In The Night	64	U.S.A. 810
My Barbara Ann/When You Loved Me	65	Ascot 2167
My Barbara Ann/I Wish It Were Summer	65	Ascot 2173
It Was You/I Gotta Make A Move	66	Montel 955
Don't Leave Me/I Need You	66	Riley's 8781
Sad Sad Memories	67	Canterbury 504
Temps (Bobby & the)		
Mary Lou, Mary Lou/The Shuffle	63	ABC 10428

ARTIST/SONG	YEAR	LABEL
Temptashuns		
Pretty Ways/Strawberry Man	64	Federal 12530
Temptations (1)		
Standing Alone/Roach's Rock	58	King 5118
Temptation/Pony Tail	58	Savoy (unreleased)
Mad At Love/Mister Juke Box	58	Savoy 1532
I Love You, This I Know/Don't You Know	58	Savoy 1550
Temptations (2)		
Birds 'N Bees/Temptations	59	Parkway 803
Temptations (3)		
Barbara/Someday	60	Goldisc 3001
Letter Of Devotion/Fickle Little Girl	60	Goldisc 3007
Temptations (3) (Neil Stevens & the)		
Ballad Of Love/Tonight My Heart She Is Crying	61	Goldisc 3019
Tempters		
I'll See You Next Fall/I'm Sorry Now	56	Empire 105
Temptones (fb Daryl Hall)		
Girl, I Love You/Good-Bye	66	Arctic 130
Say Those Words Of Love/	67	Arctic 136
This Could Be The Start Of Something Good		
Tenderfoots (ref Rivingtons)		
Watussi Wussi Wo/Kissing Bug	55	Federal 12214
Save Me Some Kisses/My Confession	55	Federal 12219
Those Golden Bells/I'm Yours Anyhow	55	Federal 12225
Sindy/Sugar Ways	55	Federal 12228
Tendertones		
I Love You So/Just For A Little While	59	Ducky 713
Tennyson, Bill (& group)		
Even Now/Slow Down	58	Pet 805
Termites		
Give Me Your Heart/Carrie Lou	64	Bee 1825
Terracetones (ref Monotones)		
Words Of Wisdom/The Ride Of Paul Revere	58	Apt 25016
Terrans (Rene Harris & the)		
Moonrise/Soap 'N Water	63	Graham 801
Terrell, Clyde (& group)		
My One Desire/Poor Folk	59	Excello 2151
Terrifics (1)		
I Don't Care How You Do It/Bump Ti Dee Ump Bump	59	Demon 1516
Terrifics (2)		
Little Star/De Plu De Pinto De Blue	N/A	Bell 88
Terry, Maureen (& group)		
There's A Boy/Whoever You Are	64	Maria 102
Terrytones (Claire Charles & the)		
You're My Ideal/Ah Do Me Kitchie	61	Wye 1002
Terrytones (with Claire Charles & Gayle Fortune)		
Teenage Night Theme/I Cry The Blues	60	Wye 1003
I Beg Your Pardon/Three Steps To The Phone	61	Wye 1010

ARTIST/SONG	YEAR	LABEL
Texas Matadors		
Flower Blossom/I Found Her	N/A	IMA 101
Themes (1)		
The Magic Of You/Yes! That's Love	59	Excello 2152
Themes (1) (Alvin Gaines & the)		
Cross My Heart	59	Fidelity (no #)
Themes (2)		
Marnie/There's No Moon Out Tonight	64	Stork 001
Themes (3)		
Sunday Kind Of Love	N/A	Ideal
Themes (4) (Lanny Hunt & the)		
I Can't Say I Love You	N/A	Sure Star 5001
Thin Men (Dennis Binder & His)		
The Long Man/I'm A Lover	56	United 194
Thomas, Gene (& group)		
Down The Road/Crying Inside	61	Venus 1444
Thomas, Jerry (& group)		
Baby Please/Tell Me	58	Khoury's 708
Thomas, Randy (& group)		
My Heart Cries/Are You Ready	66	Faro 622
Thomas, Vic (bb the Four-Evers)		
Marianne/Napoleon Bonaparte	64	Philips 40183
Village Of Love/Down The Stream To The River	64	Philips 40228
Thor-Ables (fb Aaron Collins)		
Our Love Song/Get That Bread	62	Titanic 1001
My Reckless Heart/Batman And Robin	62	Titanic 1002
Thorne, Roscoe (bb the Caverliers)		
Delores/Peddler Of Dreams	53	Atlas 1033
Thorpe, Lionel (bb the Chords)		
More, More, More/Lover Lover Lover	59	Roulette 4144
Thrashers		
Jeannie/Forever, My Love	57	Masons 0-1
Three (3) Reasons		
No Regrets/Beach Time	N/A	JRE 223/224
Three Beaus And A Peep		
Alibi Baby/The Pal That I Loved Stole The Gal That I Loved	54	Columbia 40344
For Love/Kent Song	57	Aladdin 3382
Three Beaus And A Peep (Rick Vallo & the)		
If That Would Bring You Back To Me/There's No You (no group)	53	MGM 11473
Three Belles (female)		
True Blue Lou/It Makes A Difference To Me	55	Jubilee 5219
Three Cheers		
Broken Dream/Teen Talk	59	Glory 291
Three Chimes		
Tears And Pain/Show Me The Way	64	Crossway 444

ARTIST/SONG	YEAR	LABEL
Three Chuckles (fb Teddy Randazzo)		
Runaround/At Last You Understand	54	Boulevard 100/X 0066 (54)
Foolishly/If You Should Love Again	55	X 0095
So Long/You Should Have Told Me	55	X 0134
Realize/Blue Lover	55	X 0150
Times Two, I Love You/Still Thinking Of You	55	X 0162
Anyway/The Funny Little Things We Used To Do	55	X 0186/Vik 0186 (56)
Midnight Til Dawn/Fallen Out Of Love	56	Vik 0232
Won't You Give Me A Chance/We're Gonna Rock Tonight	56	Vik 0244
As Time Goes By	56	Vik LP 1067
How Deep Is The Ocean	56	Vik LP 1067
I Only Have Eyes For You	56	Vik LP 1067
In The Still Of The Night	56	Vik LP 1067
It's Been A Long Long Time	56	Vik LP 1067
Marta	56	Vik LP 1067
Maybe You'll Be There	56	Vik LP 1067
Red Sails In The Sunset	56	Vik LP 1067
Solitude	56	Vik LP 1067
These Foolish Things	56	Vik LP 1067
To Each His Own	56	Vik LP 1067
Where Or When	56	Vik LP 1067
And The Angels Sing/Tell Me	56	X 0194/Vik 0194 (56)
Gypsy In My Soul/We're Still Holding Hands	56	X 0216/Vik 0216 (56)
Runaround/Lonely Traveller (by the Chuckles)	61	ABC 10276
Runaround/You Lied	66	Cloud 507
Three Coquettes (female)		
I Wonder/Snooty Poo	60	Hope 1002
Three D's		
Tell Me That You Love Me/Broken Dreams	56	Pilgrim 719
Let Me Know/Little Billy Boy	57	Paris 503
Birth Of An Angel/Never Let You Go	57	Paris 508
Crazy Little Woman/Baby Doll	58	Paris 511
I Never See My Baby Alone/Jumpin' Jack	58	Paris 514
Nothin' To Wear/Happiest Boy And Girl	59	Brunswick 55152
Broken Hearted/I Love You So	61	Dean 521
My Fraternity Dance/	N/A	Lowell 212
Summertime Sweetheart (by Henry Pinard & the Three D's)		
Squeeze/Graveyard Cha-Cha	N/A	Square 502
Three Dolls (1) (Larry Stevens & the)		
Wait For Me/A Girl Named Marie	60	Epic 9358
Three Dolls (2) (L. Succeed & the)		
Aftereffect Of Love	60	Magnificent 111
Three Dots		
Window Of Love/Tip Toe	59	Buzz 104
White Silver Sands/Snow Dreams	60	Rich 1003
Three Dots And A Dash (fb Jesse Belvin)		
I'll Never Love Again/Let's Do It	51	Imperial 5164
Three Emotions		
The Night We Met/The Girl I Left Behind	59	Fury 1026
Three Friends (1) (aka Heartbeats (2))		
Blanche/Baby I'll Cry	56	Lido 500/Relic 1021 (73)
I'm Only A Boy/Jinx	56	Lido 502
Chinese Tea Room/Jinx	57	Brunswick 55032
Now That You're Gone/Chinese Tea Room	57	Lido 504
Three Friends (2)		
Walkin' Shoes/Blue Ribbon Baby	61	Cal Gold 169
Dedicated (To The Songs I Love)/Happy As A Man Can Be	61	Imperial 5763
Go On To School/You're A Square	61	Imperial 5773

The Three Friends

Three G's

Let's Go Steady For The Summer/Wild Man	58	Columbia 41175
Sweet Thing/I'd Wait Forever	58	Columbia 41256
These Are The Little Things/Wonder	58	Columbia 41292
Oh, Suzette/When It's Summer Again	59	Columbia 41383
Barbara/Don't Cry Katy	59	Columbia 41513
Take That Step/Eeny-Meeny-Miny-Moe	60	Columbia 41584
Love Call/Let's Go Steady For The Summer	60	Columbia 41678
Take My Love/She's Mine	60	Columbia 41868
Foolish Tears/Blueberry Hill	61	Columbia 41955

Three Graces (female)

X Equals Kiss/Jimmy Joe	59	Golden Crest 515
Lonesome And Sorry/Billy Boy's Tune	59	Golden Crest 528
Missed/7-L	60	Golden Crest 534
My Hero/Larry Applebaum	60	Golden Crest 546

Three Honeydrops

Honeydrop/In The Summer	57	Music City 813
Rockin' Satellite/You're The One For Me	57	Music City 814

Three J's

Always Stay In Love With Me/Oh There She Goes	57	Glory 253

Three Jays (Vera & the)

Fire In Your Heart/Be Bop Baby Sitter	57	El-Bee 162

Three Moods

Stop, Look And Listen (For The Heart You Save)/Never Again	55	Sarg 124

Three Naturals

Bad Boy/Hang On Baby	N/A	Sin 725

Three Notes

Bertha/Lucy Lucy	58	Tee Gee 106

Three Pals (Roc La Rue & the)

I'm Not Ashamed/Baby Take Me Back	57	Rama 226

Three Pennies

Why Am I So Shy/A Penny For Your Thoughts	64	B.T. Puppy 501

Little Joe & Thrillers

Three Playmates

Sugah Woogah/Lovey Dovey Pair	58	Savoy 1528
I Dreamed/Give Your Love To Me	58	Savoy 1537

Three Queens (gm Eddie King)

Love You Baby/Shakin' Inside	60	J.O.B. 1122

Three Reasons

No Regrets/Kangaroo Twist	N/A	JRE 224

Three Vales

Blue Lights Down Low/Ay Ay Ay	57	Cindy 3007

Three Wishes

Guiding Light/It's All Said And Done	63	Dolton 72

Threeteens (female)

X Plus Y Equals Z/For The Love Of Mike	58	Rev 3522/Todd 1021 (59)
Dear 53310769 (Elvis' U.S. Army Serial #)/Doowaddie	59	Rev 3516

Thrillers (1)

The Drunkard/Mattie, Leave Me Alone	53	Big Town 109
Lessie Mae/I'm Going To Live My Life Alone	53	Thriller 3530
'Lizabeth/Please Talk To Me	54	Herald 432
If You Ever Need A Friend	N/A	Herald (unreleased)
Long Lasting Love	N/A	Herald (unreleased)
Take That	N/A	Herald (unreleased)
Woman Was Made For Love	N/A	Herald (unreleased)

Thrillers (2) (Little Joe & the)

This I Know/Let's Do The Slop	56	Okeh 7075
Peanuts/Lily Lou	57	Okeh 7088
The Echoes Keep Calling Me/Lonesome	57	Okeh 7094
What Happened To Your Halo?/Don't Leave Me Alone	58	Okeh 7099

ARTIST/SONG	YEAR	LABEL
Mine/It's Too Bad We Had To Say Goodbye	58	Okeh 7107/Epic 9293 (58)
Cheery Pt. 1/Cheery Pt. 2	59	Okeh 7116
I Need Somebody/It's Been A Long Time	59	Okeh 7121
I'll Never Let You Go/Give Me All Your Love	59	Okeh 7127
Ev'ry Now And Then/Goodnight, Little Girl	59	Okeh 7134
Stay/Please Don't Go	60	Okeh 7136
Run Little Girl/Public Opinion	60	Okeh 7140/Epic 9431 (61)
For Sentimental Reasons/One More Time	61	20th Century 1214
Peanuts/No, No, I Can't Stop	63	Reprise 20142
How Am I Doing/I'll Do Anything	63	Rose 835
Peanuts And Popcorn/Chicken Little Boo Boo	64	Enjoy 2011
Come What May/This I Know, Little Girl	65	Uptown 715
Someone For Me/Love Me	N/A	Peanut (no #)

Thrillettes (Bette Renne & the)
Your Kinda Love/You Ain't So Such A Much	64	Lawn 246

Thrills (George Zimmerman & the)
I Ain't Got The Money To Pay For This Drink/Whose Baby Are You	56	Jab 103

Thunderbirds (1)
Baby, Let's Play House/Pledging My Love	55	DeLuxe 6075
Love Is A Problem/Rock Boom Boom	55	G.G. 518

Thunderbirds (2)
Blueberries/Ayuh, Ayuh	55	Era 1000
I'd Be A Fool To Let You Go/Buguino	55	Era 1004

Thunderbirds (2) (Bert Convy & the)
Hoo Bop De Bow/C'Mon Back	55	Era 1001

Thunderbirds (3)
In My Thunderbird/Mary	57	Holiday 2609

Thunderbirds (4) (Billy Ford & the)
Billy Boy Blow/How Can I Be Sure	57	Vik 0263

Thunderbirds (5) (Ron Holden & the)
Love You So/My Babe	59	Donna 1315/Nite Owl 10 (59)
Gee But I'm Lonesome/Susie Jane	60	Donna 1324
True Love Can Be/Everything's Gonna Be Alright	60	Donna 1328
Your Line Is Busy/Who Says There Ain't No Santa Claus?	60	Donna 1331
Let No One Tell You/The Big Shoe	61	Donna 1335
So Dearly/Bring Me Happiness (Rosie & Ron)	61	Donna 1338
I'll Be Happy/I'll Always Have You	61	Eldo 117

Thunderbirds (6) (Rudy Grayzell & the)
You'll Be Mine/F.B.I. Story	59	Award 130

Thunderbirds (7) (Chris Farlow & the)
Just A Dream/What You Gonna Do	65	General American 718

Thunderbirds (8) (Johnny & the)
They Say/You Are My Sunshine	59	Clover 1001

Thunderbolts
Blending	N/A	Rondak

Tiaras (1) (Roy Milton & the)
Bless Your Heart/Early In The Morning	60	Lou Wa 1002/Warwick 549 (60)

Tiaras (2) (female)
You Told Me/I'm Gonna Forget You	63	Valiant 6027
Don't Believe A Word/Hey Senor	63	Valiant 6030

ARTIST/SONG	YEAR	LABEL
Tibbs, Kenneth (& group)		
Darling I Want Your Love/No More Tears	58	Federal 12335
Tic Tocs		
Zola/Walking Alone	57	Back Beat 502
Stop/True By You	57	Rush 1042
Tick Tocks (Bobby Marchan & the)		
Snoopin' And Accusin'/This Is The Life	60	Fire 1014
Tidal Waves		
Booma Shooma Rock/The Clock (Is Ticking My Life Away)	61	Tide 0020
You Name It/So I Guess	N/A	Strafford 6503
Tides (1)		
Rock Me Gently/Stoned	59	Dore 529
Say You're Mine/Follow Me	61	Dore 579
Ring A Ding Ding/Dear Mr. President	61	Dore 611
Ring A Ding Ding/Chicken Spaceman	61	Dore 618
Limbo Rock/Midnight Limbo	62	Mercury 71990
Banana Boat Song/Patricia	62	Mercury 72045
Tides (2)		
Bring It Home To Me/Who Told You	61	620 1007
Stranger/Would I Still Be Loving You	61	Warwick 653
Tiers (Jimmy Kemper & the)		
I'm Free To Choose/Lonely For Kathy	64	Le Mans 002
Tifanos		
It's Raining/Louisiana	60	Tifco 822
Tiffanies (aka Tiffanys (2)) (female)		
He's Good For Me/It's Got To Be A Great Song	67	KR 120
Tiffanys (1) (male)		
The Pleasure Of Love/Atlanta	62	Swan 4104
Tiffanys (2) (aka Tiffanies) (female)		
I've Got A Girl/I Don't Dig (Western Movies)	63	Rockin Robin 1
Love Me/Happiest Girl In The World	64	Arctic 101
Please Tell Me/Gossip	64	MRS 777/Atlantic 2240 (64)
I Feel The Same Way Too/I Just Wanna Boy Or Girl	65	Josie 942
Take Another Look At Me/Heaven On Earth	66	Josie 952
He's Good For Me/It's Got To Be A Great Song	67	RKO 120
Tigers (1) (Little Julian Herrera & the)		
Lonely, Lonely Nights/In Exchange For Your Love	56	Dig 118
Symbol Of Heaven/Here In My Arms	57	Dig 137
I Remember Linda/True Fine Mama	57	Starla 6
Tigers (2) (Danny Peil & the)		
Jingle Jump	N/A	Raynard 602
Tigers (3) (Al Tigro & the)		
Yvonne/Do The Zombie	N/A	Cuppy 112
Tigre Lilies		
Love That Melody/Great Mistake	59	Gone 5047
Tillis, Clyde (& group)		
It Makes No Difference Now/Just Dreaming	56	Cash 1054
Tillman, Bertha (& group)		
Oh My Angel/Lovin' Time	62	Brent 7029
I Wish/(I Believe) Something Funny Is Going On	62	Brent 7032

ARTIST/SONG	YEAR	LABEL

Tilman, Mickey (& group)
Dear Mom And Dad/I Have Chosen You — 58 — Vee Jay 296

Timberlanes (1) (Dino & the) (Dion DiMucci before the Belmonts)
The Chosen Few/Out In Colorado — 57 — Mohawk 105/Jubilee 5294 (58)

Timberlanes (2)
Wedding Bells/Sweet Dreams — 58 — Dragon 101

Timbers (1) (Ronnie Martin & the)
Hey Doc/I'm Thankful — 56 — Pilgrim 721

Timbers (2) (aka Nobles (2))
Oops Oh Lawdy/Stop Crying — 58 — Tee Gee 101/Cupid 1002 (58)

Time-Tones (aka Timetones)
Here In My Heart/My Love — 61 — Times Square 421 (first pressing)/Relic 538 (65)
In My Heart/My Love — 61 — Times Square 421 (second pressing)

Timetones (aka Time-Tones)
Pretty, Pretty Girl (The New Beat)/I've Got A Feeling — 61 — Atco 6201 (Times Square Productions)/Relic 539 (65)
Sunday Kind Of Love/Angels In The Sky — 63 — Times Square 26/Relic 543 (66)
House Where Lovers Dream/Get A Hold Of Yourself — 63 — Times Square 34/Relic 526 (65)

Tindley, George (& group)
Close Your Eyes/Heart Of Gold — 61 — Herald 558

Tingles
Tell Me Now/Rain Rain — 61 — Era 3040

Tiny Tim (& group)
Face To Face/By My Side — 59 — DeLuxe 6184

Tip Tops
Oo-Kook-A-Boo/He's A Braggin' — 63 — Parkway 868

Tip Tops (David Lastie & the)
Jack The Ripper, Pt. 1/Jack The Ripper, Pt. 2 (with Little Sonny) — 62 — Chess 1800

Tip Tops (Tiny Tip & the)
Say It/Matrimony — 62 — Chess 1822
I Said A Prayer/I Found My Love — 62 — Scarlet 4129

Titans (aka Vitamins)
Sweet Peach/Free And Easy — 57 — Specialty 614
So Hard To Laugh, So Easy To Cry/Rhythm And Blues — 57 — Vita 148
G'Wan Home Calypso/Look What You're Doing Baby — 57 — Vita 158
Don't You Just Know It?/Can It Be? — 58 — Specialty 625
Arlene/Love Is a Wonderful Thing — 58 — Specialty 632
No Time/Tootin' Tutor — 59 — Class 244
Everybody Happy/What Have I Done? — 60 — Fidelity 3016
A-Rab/Marquette — 61 — Nolta 351

Titans (aka Vitamins) (Don & Dewey & the)
Just A Little Lovin'/When The Sun Has Begun To Shine — 57 — Specialty 617

Titones
Symbol Of Love/The Movies — 59 — Scepter 1206
Symbol Of Love/My Movie Queen (The Movies) — 60 — Wand 105

Tokays (1)
Fatty-Boom Bi Laddy/Lost And Found — 52 — Bonnie 102

ARTIST/SONG	YEAR	LABEL
Tokays (2)		
Hey Senorita/Baby Baby Baby	67	Brute 001
Tokens (1)		
Doom-Lang/Come Dance With Me	57	Gary 1006/Musictone 1113 (59)
Oh What A Night/(Hey Hey) Juanita	61	Date 2737
Tokens (2)		
When I Go To Sleep At Night/Dry Your Eyes	61	RCA 7896
Sincerely/When The Summer Is Through	61	RCA 7925
The Lion Sleeps Tonight/Tina	61	RCA 7954
Tonight I Fell In Love/I'll Always Love You	61	Warwick 615
B'wa Nina/Weeping River	62	RCA 7991
The Riddle/The Big Boat	62	RCA 8018
La Bamba/A Token Of Love	62	RCA 8052
The Fly Swatter/Bee Side	62	RCA 8064
Dream Angel Goodnight/I'll Do My Crying Tomorrow	62	RCA 8089
A Bird Flies Out Of Sight/Wishing	62	RCA 8114
Please Write/I'll Always Love You	63	Laurie 3180
Tonight I Met An Angel/Hindu Lullaby	63	RCA 8148
Hear The Bells/ABC-1-2-3	63	RCA 8210
A Girl Named Arlene/Swing	64	B.T. Puppy 500/
		Music Makers 110
He's In Town/Oh Kathy	64	B.T. Puppy 502
You're My Girl/Havin' Fun	64	B.T. Puppy 504
Let's Go To The Drag Strip/Two Cars	64	RCA 8309
Nobody But You/Mr. Cupid	65	B.T. Puppy 505
A Message To The World/Sylvie Sleepin'	65	B.T. Puppy 507
Only My Friend/Cattle Call	65	B.T. Puppy 512
The Bells Of St. Mary/Just One Smile	65	B.T. Puppy 513
The Three Bells/A Message To The World	66	B.T. Puppy 516
I Hear The Trumpets Blow/Don't Cry, Sing Along With The Music	66	B.T. Puppy 518
Breezy/The Greatest Moments Of A Girl's Life	66	B.T. Puppy 519
Life Is Groovy/Split	66	B.T. Puppy 524
Please Say You Want Me/Get A Job	66	B.T. Puppy 525
Green Plant/Saloogy	67	B.T. Puppy 552
Portrait Of My Love/She Comes And Goes	67	Warner Bros. 5900
It's A Happening World/How Nice	67	Warner Bros. 7056
Ain't That Peculiar/Bye, Bye, Bye	67	Warner Bros. 7099
Till/Poor Man	68	Warner Bros. 7169
Animal/Bathroom Wall	68	Warner Bros. 7202
Banana Boat Song/Grandfather	68	Warner Bros. 7233
The World Is Full Of Wonderful Things/Some People Sleep	68	Warner Bros. 7255
She Lets Her Hair Down/Oh To Get Away	69	Buddah 151
Go Away Little Girl-Young Girl/I Want To Love You	69	Warner Bros. 7280
I Could Be/End Of The World	69	Warner Bros. 7323
Don't Worry Baby/Some People Sleep	70	Buddah 159
Both Sides Now/I Can See You Dancing With Me	70	Buddah 174
Groovin' To The Music-Sesame Street/	70	Buddah 187
Listen To The Words,Listen To The Music		
You And Me/I Like To Throw My Head Back And Sing	72	Bell 190
Penny Whistle Band/The Lord Can't Do A Solo	74	Atco 7009
Tokens (2) (aka Margo, Margo, Medress & Siegel)		
Needles Of Evergreen/Mr. Snail	68	Warner Bros. 7183
Tokens (2) (with Neil Sedaka)		
While I Dream/I Love My Baby	58	Melba 104
Tokens (3) (Johnny & the)		
The Taste Of A Tear/Never Till Now	61	Warwick 658
Toledos		
This Is Our Night/John Smith's Body	61	Down 2003/End 1094 (61)

ARTIST/SONG	YEAR	LABEL

one Deafs (Dean Barlow & the)
| Night Before Last | N/A | Beltone |

ones (1)
| Paula Is Mine/A Love Such As You | 62 | Elmar 6001 |

ones (2) (Little Sammy & the) (aka Little Sammy Rozzi & the Guys)
| Christine/Over The Rainbow | 62 | Pelham 722/Jaclyn 1161 (62) |

ones (3) (W. Williams & the)
| A Star | N/A | Kennedy 5146 |

onettes (aka Claremonts) (female)
Tonight You Belong To Me/Don't Fall In Love Too Soon	56	Modern 997
Oh What A Baby/Howie	58	Doe 101/ABC 9905 (58)
He Loves Me, He Loves Me Not/Uh-Oh	58	Doe 103
Please Don't Go/No Tears	62	Volt 101
Stolen Angel/Teardrop Sea	63	Volt 104
Rockabye Baby	89	Relic LP 5081

op Hands (Joe Dee & His)
| Honky-Tonk Guitar/Blind Heart | 62 | Pat Riccio 105 |
| Some Of These Nights/I Thought I Heard You Calling My Name | 62 | Pat Riccio 1107 |

Top Hands (Joe Dee & His) (with the Tremonts)
| Believe My Heart/Legend Of Love | 62 | Pat Riccio 101 |

Top Hits
| Thum-A-Lum-A/Love No One | 61 | Norman 504 |

Top Kicks
| Don't Break The Heart That Loves You/Boodylya Botten Baby | 54 | Guyden 706 |

Top Notes
Wonderful Time/Walkin' With Love	60	Atlantic 2066
Say Man/Warm Your Heart	60	Atlantic 2080
Hearts Of Stone/The Basic Things	61	Atlantic 2097
Always Late (Why Lead Me On)/Twist And Shout	61	Atlantic 2115
Come Back, Cleopatra	62	Festival 1021
It's Alright/I Love You So Much	63	ABC 10399

Top Overs
| What's Your Name | N/A | N/A |

Topics (aka Frankie Valli & the Four Seasons)
| The Girl In My Dreams | 62 | Perri 1007 |

Topics (Billy Dixon & the) (aka Frankie Valli & the Four Seasons)
| I Am All Alone/Trance | 60 | Topix 6002 |
| Lost Lullabye/Trance | 61 | Topix 6008 |

Toppers (1) (Bobby Mitchell & the)
I'm Crying/Rack'Em Back	53	Imperial 5236
One Friday Morning/4 X 11 = 44	53	Imperial 5250
Baby's Gone/Sister Lucy	54	Imperial 5270
Angel Child/School Boy Blues	54	Imperial 5282
Wedding Bells Are Ringing/Meant For Me	54	Imperial 5295
I'm A Young Man/She Couldn't Be Found	54	Imperial 5309
I Wish I Knew/Nothing Sweet As You	55	Imperial 5326
I Cried/I'm In Love	55	Imperial 5346
I Tried So Hard/Goin' Round In Circles	56	Imperial 5392

Toppers (2)
I Love You, I Love You/Bow-Legged Boy	54	Avalon 63707
Baby Let Me Bang Your Box/You're Laughing 'Cause I'm Crying	54	Jubilee 5136
Honey, Honey/George Washington	56	ABC 9667
Lonely/Three Roads	56	ABC 9759

ARTIST/SONG	YEAR	LABEL
Toppers (3)		
Tell Me Why/All Around	62	Stacy 927
Toppiks		
Give It A Chance To Grow	N/A	Larsam
Topps		
What Do You Do? (To Make Me Love You So)/Tippin'	54	Red Robin 126
I've Got A Feeling/Won't You Come Home, Baby?	54	Red Robin 131
Ain't It Good (Mmm, Baby I Love You So)	N/A	Red Robin (unreleased)
Young Girls	N/A	Red Robin (unreleased)
Tops (1)		
An Innocent Kiss/Walkin' With My Baby	57	Singular 712
Tops (2) (Little Jimmy Rivers & the)		
Puppy Love/Say You Love Me	61	Len 1011/Swan 4091 (61)/ V-Tone 102 (61)
Topsy, Tiny (bb the Five Chances)		
Aw! Shucks Baby/Miss You So	57	Federal 12303
Torches		
Darn Your Love/No I Won't	65	Ring-O 302
Toreadors		
Do You Remember/Do You Remember	N/A	Midas 1001
Torkeys		
She's Everybody's Darling	N/A	Perri 2
Tormentors		
Didn't It Rain	N/A	Kerwood 712
Tornados (1) (Stanley Mitchell & the)		
Four O'Clock In The Morning/Would You, Could You	56	Chess 1649
Tornados (2)		
Genie In The Jug/Love In Your Life	59	Bumble Bee 503
Clap Your Hands And Skate	N/A	Winley 2017
Tornados (2) (Johnny Mann & the)		
Breaker Of Dreams/Chick-A-Lou	58	Donnie 27746
Tornados (3) (Aaron McNeil & the)		
Without Romance/Carolyn	60	C.J. 615
Tots (Barry & the)		
I'm A Happy Little Christmas Tree/ Listen To The Words,Listen To The Music	61	Fury 1058
Toughtones (Bobby Sanders & the)		
It Was You/I'm On My Way	61	Kaybo 60618
Towers (Jimmy & the)		
One More Chance/The Meaning Of Love	N/A	Debann 102
Townsmen (1)		
It's Time/Little Jeanie	60	Vanity 579/580
Townsmen (2) (fb Louie Lymon)		
Moonlight Was Made For Lovers/I'm In The Mood For Love	62	Joey 6202
Is It All Over/Just A Little Bit	63	Herald 585
I Can't Go/That's All I'll Ever Need	63	PJ 1341
Please Don't Say Goodbye/Gotta Get Moving	64	Columbia 43207

ARTIST/SONG	YEAR	LABEL

TR 4
Never Too Young — 66 Velvet Tone

Tra-Velles (female)
Can't Go For That/Little Bad Wolf — N/A Debonair 101

Tradewinds (Rudy & the)
Careless Love/Unemployed — 62 Angle Tone 543

Trailblazers (Shirlee Hunter & the)
Hot Blood/Allentown Jail — 59 Tip Top 720

Trains
We Two/The Plan — 64 Swan 4196
Fourteen And Getting Older/The Beware Song — 64 Swan 4203

Trammell, Bobby Lee (& group)
You Mostest Girl/Uh Oh — 58 Radio 102

Tramps
Ride On/You're a Square — 59 Arvee 548
Your Love/Midnight Flyer — 59 Arvee 570

Tranells
Come On And Tell Me/The Music Swayed — 56 Chelten 090

Travelers (1)
Go Away/Why Darling Why — 53 Okeh 6959

Travelers (2) (fb Frank Lopez)
Lenora/Betty Jean — 57 Atlas 1086
Love Is All I Crave — 73 Relic LP 5012

Travelers (3)
I'll Be Home For Christmas/Katie The Kangaroo — 58 Andex 2011
Why/Teen Age Machine Age — 58 Andex 3-4006
He's Got The Whole World In His Hands/Green Town Girl — 58 Andex 4012
I'll Always Be In Love With You/I Go For You — 59 Andex 4033
Rock Me Baby/Girl In The Bikini — 59 MGM 928
June, July, August And September/What A Weekend — 60 ABC 10119
Ivy On The Old School Wall/Cadwallader — 61 Decca 31215
Oh My Love (Love Me)/White Rose — 61 Decca 31282
Seven Minutes Till Four/Traveler — 62 Don Ray 5965
Tie Me Surfer Board Down, Sport/In The Pines — 63 Gass 1000
She's Got The Blues/Spanish Moon — 63 Princess 52/Vault 911
Windy And Warm/Last Date — 63 Yellow Sand 2
Malibu Sunset/Hang On — 65 Yellow Sand 452

Travelers (4) (Roger & the) (aka Premiers (4))
You're Daddy's Little Girl/Just Gotta Be That Way — 61 Ember 1079

Travelers (5)
Too Young/Twist In School — 61 World Wide 8511

Travellers (1) (Frankie Valley & the) (featuring Frankie Valli)
Somebody Else Took Her Home/Forgive And Forget — 54 Mercury 70381

Travellers (2) (Ronnie Cates & the)
Old Man River/Long Time — 62 Terrace 7501

Travis, Danny (& group)
Ever Since/Bye-Bye-Baby — 62 Benn-X 54

Treasurers
The Story Of Love/I Walk With An Angel — 61 Crown 005

ARTIST/SONG	YEAR	LABEL
Treasures (1) (Pete Anders & the) (aka Videls)		
Hold Me Tight/Pete Meets Vinnie	64	Shirley 500
Treasures (2) (Bonnie & the)		
Home Of The Brave/Our Song	65	Phi-Dan 5005
Trebelaires (female)		
I Gotta/There Goes The Train	55	Nestor 16
Trebels		
Oh Darlin'/My Little Girl	63	Viking 1021
Treble Chords		
Theresa/My Little Girl	59	Decca 31015
Treckles (aka Trickels)		
With Each Step A Tear/Outside The Chapel Door	59	Gone 5078
Trells		
I'm Sorry/Bad Weather	N/A	Port City 1112
Trem-Los		
Walkin' Along/Silly Affair	61	Nolta 350
Tremaines		
Jingle, Jingle/Moon Shining Bright	58	Cash 100/101/Val 100/101 (58)/ Old Town 1051 (58)
Wonderful, Marvelous/Heavenly	59	Kane 008/V-Tone 507 (60)
Tremonts (1) (with Joey Dee)		
Believe My Heart/Legend Of Love	61	Pat Riccio 101/ Brunswick 55217 (61)
Tremonts (2)		
I Hear The Wind (a capella)	75	Relic LP 104
Merry-Go-Round Love (a capella)	75	Relic LP 104
Tren-Dells (aka Trend-Els)		
Hully Gully Jones/Nite Owl	62	Jam 1100/Capitol 4852 (62)
Ain't That Funny/Mr. Doughnut Man	63	Sound Stage 7 2508
Everyday/I'll Be There	64	Southtown 22001
That's My Desire/Let's Go Steady For The Summer	N/A	Boss 9921
Tren-Teens		
My Baby's Gone/Your Yah Yah Is Gone	64	Carnival 501
Trend-Els (aka Tren-Dells)		
I'm So Young/Don't You Hear Me Calling, Baby	61	Tilt 779
I Miss You So/Moments Like This	62	Tilt 788
Trend-Tones		
This Is Love/Never Again	N/A	Superb 100
Trends		
I'll Be True/Class Ring	59	Argo 5341/Clover 1002
Silly Grin/Once Again	59	Scope 102
Chug-A-Lug/The Beard	60	RCA 7733
Treney, Joey (& group)		
Why Walk Alone/This I Declare	61	Magenta 05
Trentons (aka Shy-Tones/aka Hi-Tones)		
All Alone/Star Bright	62	Shepherd 2204

RTIST/SONG	YEAR	LABEL
retones		
Blind Date/Cool Baby	60	B-W 604
reys		
Come To Me/Sugar Baby	59	Bella 16
reys (Wes Griffin & the)		
It Hurts So Bad/Rockin' Mary	59	Bella 17
reytones		
Dreamlover	N/A	Sunliner
ri-Dells		
Baby I Love You So/Little Do I Know	60	Eldo 104
ri-Five (John Lythgoe & the)		
Jeannie, Joanie, Shirley/Oh Baby	61	Varbee 2002
ri-Lads		
Cherry Pie/Always Be True	58	Bullseye 1003
ri-Tones (1) (Al Barkle & the)		
Teenage Angel/The Signal	57	Vita 171
With This Ring/Sputnik II	57	Vita 173
ri-Tones (2)		
Teardrops/Everytime I Think Of You	64	Miss Julie 6501
riads		
One More Kiss/Nickelodian Tango	56	Encino 1002
riangle		
Jacqueline/Your Love Comes Shinin' Through	70	Paramount 0055
riangles		
Savin' My Love/'Tis A Pity	60	Herald 549
Dance The Magoo/Step Up And Go	62	Fargo 1023
My Oh My/Really I Do	64	Fifo 107
ribunes		
The Code Of Love/Now That You're Gone	62	Derrick 502
rickels (aka Treckles)		
With Each Step A Tear/When I Fall In Love	58	Gone 5075/Power 250 (58)
ricks		
My One Desire/Someone Like You	59	Jane 108
ridels		
Land Of Love/Image Of Love	64	San-Dee 1009
rilons		
I'm The One/Forever	61	Tag 449
rinidads		
Don't Say Goodbye/On My Happy Way	59	Formal 1005
One Lonely Night/When We're Together	59	Formal 1006
rinities (Kayo & the)		
Kathy Jo/Walking To School With My Love	60	Souvenir 1004
rinkets (1)		
Little Boy/You Can't Be Trusted	58	Imperial 5497

ARTIST/SONG	YEAR	LABEL
Trinkets (2) (aka Versalettes) (female)		
Fisherman/Nobody But You	63	Cortland 111
Triotones		
Valerie Jo/Tired Of Being A Little Boy	59	Intrastate 43
Triplets		
Gently My Love/Bagdad Beat	60	Dore 574
Trippers		
Charlena/Taking Care Of Business	67	Ruby-Doo 5
Tritones (1)		
Sweet And Lovely/Blues In The Closet	55	Grand 126/Jamie 1035 (57)
Tritones (2) (Terry & the)		
Patty	N/A	Kaybee
Triumphs (Tico & the) (fb Paul Simon)		
I'm Lonely/I Wish I Weren't In Love (by Jerry Landis)	61	Canadian American 130
Motorcycle/I Don't Believe Them	61	Madison 169/Amy 835 (61)
Express Train/Wildflower	62	Amy 845
Cry, Little Boy, Cry/Get Up And Do The Wonder	62	Amy 860
Cards Of Love/Noise	63	Amy 876
Trojans (1) (aka Five Trojans)		
As Long As I Have You/I Wanna Make Love To You	56	RPM 466
Make It Up/The Man I'm Gonna Be	58	Felsted 8534
Don't Ask Me To Be Lonely/Alone In This World	58	Tender 516
Trojans (2)		
All Night Long/I Wanted You So Long	60	Triangle 51317
Just About Daybreak/Just Got Up	61	Dodge 804
Medley (Cherry Pie/What's Your Name/A Thousand Miles Away/ We Belong Together/Talk To Me/Diamonds & Pearls)	66	Air Town 003/Air Town 70971
Trojans (3) (fb Henry Clement)		
I'll Be Waiting/Trojan's Walls	61	Zynn 1006
Troopers		
My Resolution/Get Out	57	Lamp 2009
Troopers (George Powell & the)		
My Choice For A Mate/In That Order	59	Lummtone 101
Trophies		
Desire/Doggone It	61	Challenge 9133
Peg O' My Heart/I Laughed So Hard I Cried	62	Challenge 9149
Felicia/That's All I Want From You	62	Challenge 9170
Walkin' The Dog/Somethin' Else	N/A	Nork 79907
Tropicals		
Sweet Sixteen	N/A	Specialty
Tropics (Eddie & the)		
We've Got Something/Don't Monkey With Another Monkeys Monkey	65	Josie 930
Troupers		
Peter, Peter, Pumpkin Eater/Non Support	59	Red Top 118
Troy, Ricky (& group)		
Linda	63	Cavetone 511
Troys		
Ding-A-Ling-A-Ling/Cling	59	Okeh 7120

RTIST/SONG	YEAR	LABEL
ru Tones		
Darling I'm Sorry/Surfin' Here We Go	N/A	Tree
ru-Tones		
Tears In My Eyes/Magic	57	Chart 634
ru-Tones (Terry Clement & the)		
Teenage Rock/Sugar G	59	Rocko 517
rue Loves (aka Lovenotes (1))		
A Love Like Ours/Never Look Behind	57	Premium 411
rue Tones		
Never Had A Chance/Lovin' From My Baby	64	Spot 1115
Little Hit And Run Darling	64	Spot 1121
That's Love/He's Got The Nerve	65	Soulville/Josie 950 (65)/ Josie 1003 (69)
rueleers		
Forget About Him/Waiting For You	63	Checker 1026
ruetones		
Honey, Honey/Whirlwind	58	Monument 4501
Blushing Bride/Singing Waters	61	Felsted 8625
rutones		
Trouble In Paradise	N/A	N/A
u-Tones		
Saccharin Sally/Still In Love With You	59	Lin 5021
ucker, Frank (& group)		
Nobody But Me/Hey Hester	56	Baton 234
uggle, Bobby (& group)		
I Wonder/I Know She Loves Me	56	Checker 840
une Blenders		
Oh, Yes, I Know/Shoo-Shoo	54	Federal 12201
une Drops		
Rosie Lee/Speak For Yourself	57	Gone 5003
Smoothie/Jumpin' Jellybeans (instrumental)	59	Gone 5072
une Drops (Malcolm Dodds & the)		
It Took A Long Time/Beauty And The Beast	57	End 1000
Fools Rush In/Can't You See	57	End 1004
Tonight/Unspoken Love	57	End 1010
Your Voice/The Swingin' Platoon	58	Decca 30653
une Tailors		
Beverly/My First Love	58	Century 4158
une Timers		
Thinking/What Have I Got To Dream About	55	Okeh 7081
une Tones (1)		
Little Sandy/Please Baby, Please	58	Herald 524
She's Right With Me/Lonesome Soul	59	Herald 539
une Tones (2) (fb Terry Clement)		
Jacqueline/French Blues	61	Zynn 1007

ARTIST/SONG	YEAR	LABEL

Tune Weavers
My Congratulations, Baby/This Can't Be Love	57	Casa Grande 3038
Happy Happy Birthday Baby/Ol' Man River	57	Casa Grande 4037/ Checker 872 (57)
Happy Happy Birthday Baby/Yo Yo Walk (instrumental by Paul Gayten)	57	Checker 872
Ol' Man River/Tough Enough (instrumental by Paul Gayten)	57	Checker 880
Little Boy/Look Down That Lonesome Road	58	Casa Grande 101
There Stands My Love/I'm Cold	58	Casa Grande 4040
I Remember Dear/Pamela Jean	60	Casa Grande 4038
Your Skies Of Blue/Congratulations On Your Birthday	62	Checker 1007
I Hear Mission Bells	N/A	Casa Grande (unreleased)
Think And Cry	N/A	Casa Grande (unreleased)

Tune Weavers (Margo Sylvia & the)
Come Back To Me/I've Tried	88	Classic Artists 104
Merry Merry Christmas Baby/What Are You Doing New Years	88	Classic Artists 107

Tunemasters (aka Chantels)
Sending This Letter/It's All Over	57	Mark 7002

Tunemasters (Willie Wilson & Arlene Smith & the) (aka Chantels)
Sending You This Letter/I've Lied	58	End 1011

Tunerockers
No Stoppin' This Boppin'	58	Pet 804

Tunes
The Lie/Only Time Will Tell	59	Pel 101/Pel 345 (59)
My Heart/Close The Door	59	Swade 102

Tunesters
Casually/Wykiup	59	Tiara 6129

Tunisians (Terry & the)
The Street/Tom-Tom	63	Seville 131

Turbans (1)
When You Dance/Let Me Show You (Around My Heart)	55	Herald 458
Sister Sookey/I'll Always Watch Over You	56	Herald 469
I'm Nobody's/B.I.N.G.O. (Bingo)	56	Herald 478
It Was A Night Like This/All Of My Love	56	Herald 486
Valley Of Tears/Bye And Bye	57	Herald 495
Congratulations/The Wadda Doo	57	Herald 510
I Promise You Love/Curfew Time	59	Red Top 115
Diamonds And Pearls/Bad Man	60	Roulette 4281
Six Questions/The Lament Of Silver Gulch	61	Imperial 5807
When You Dance/Golden Rings	61	Parkway 820
I'm Not Your Fool Anymore/Three Friends (Two Lovers)	61	Roulette 4326
This Is My Story/Clicky Clicky Clack	62	Imperial 5828
I Wonder/The Damage Is Done	62	Imperial 5847

Turbans (2)
No No Cherry/Tick Tock A-Woo	55	Money 209
The Nest Is Warm/Tick Tock A-Woo	55	Money 209
When I Return/Emily (by the Turks)	55	Money 211

Turbo Jets (Cliff Davis & the)
Rock & Roll/Back Mountain Rock	59	Federal 12366

Turks (aka Hollywood Flames)
Emily/When I Return (by the Turbans)	55	Money 211
It Can't Be True/Wagon Wheels (by the Hollywood Flames)	56	Cash 1042
I'm A Fool/I've Been Accused	56	Money 215
This Heart Of Mine/Why Did You?	58	Bally 1017

ARTIST/SONG	YEAR	LABEL
Fathertime/Okay	58	Keen 4016
It Can't Be True/I'm A Fool	58	Knight 2005/Imperial 5783 (61)
Emily/My Soul (by the Seniors)	59	Ball 001
Hully Gully/Rockville, U.S.A.	59	Class 256
Emily/Going Back Home	60	Ball 101
Dianne/Baja	N/A	P.B.D. 112

Turn Ons (Tim Tam & the)

Wait A Minute/Opelia	66	Palmer 5002
Cheryl Ann/Seal It With A Kiss	66	Palmer 5003
Kimberly/I Leave You In Tears	66	Palmer 5006
Don't Say Hi/Don't Say Hi (instrumental)	67	Palmer 5014

Turner, Bennie (& group)

I Want To Know	N/A	Skyline 1005

Turner, Ike (& group)

My Love/That's All I Need	59	Sue 722

Tuxedo Sleepers

I Want To Love You	60	Tuxedo 938

Tuxedos

Yes It's True/Trouble, Trouble	60	Forte 1414

Twains (Tommy Sawyer & the)

How Deep Is The Ocean/15th Row Down	62	Diamond 112

Twi-Lighters (aka Twiliters (1))

Sittin' In A Corner/It's A Cold, Cold, Rainy Day	56	Groove 0154

Twi-Lites

Just Can't Let Her Go	N/A	Spenada 101

Twigs (Sonny Woods & the)

Chapel Of Memories/Song Of India	54	Hollywood 1015
Wonderful World/Lover Boy	54	Hollywood 1026

Twilighters (1) (Buddy Milton & the)

Please Understand/Say Another Word	54	RPM 418/Cadet
O-O-Wah/I'm The Child	54	RPM 419

Twilighters (2)

I Believe/Eternally	55	Caddy 103/Dot 15526 (56)/ Pla-Bac 1113
Little Did I Dream/Gotta Get On The Train	55	MGM 55011
Lovely Lady/Half Angel	55	MGM 55014
It's True/Wah-Bop-Sh-Wah	55	Specialty 548
Pride And Joy/Live Like A King	57	Ebb 117
How Many Times?/Water-Water	57	J.V.B. 83
Let There Be Love/Eternally	58	Cholly 712
Yes You Are/A Possibility	60	Spin 0001
Helene	60	Spin-It 202
Sit Right Down And Cry/Please Come Home	60	Super 1003
Nothin'/Do You Believe	61	Eldo 115
To Love In Vain/The Beginning Of Love	61	Fraternity 889
Help Me/Rockin' Mule	61	Ricki 907
My Silent Prayer/Little Bitty Bed Bug	62	Bubble 1334
She Needs A Guy/Scratchin'	62	Chess 1803
Sweet Lips/My Beatle Haircut	64	Roulette 4546
I Need Your Lovin'/Out Of My Mind	68	Vanco 204

Twilighters (2) (Tony Allen & the)

Just Like Before/Come-A, Come-A, Baby	61	Bethlehem 3002
It Hurts Me So/The Trakey-Doo	62	Bethlehem 3004

ARTIST/SONG	YEAR	LABEL

Twilighters (3)

Please Tell Me You're Mine/Wondering — 56 — Marshall 702

Twilighters (4) (Tony & the) (aka Anthony & the Sophomores)

Be My Girl/Did You Make Up Your Mind	60	Jalynne 106/Red Top
Key To My Heart/Yes Or No	60	Red Top 127
Gee, But I'd Give The World	60	Red Top
I Promise To Remember	60	Red Top

Twilights (1) (James Carter & the)

| I'm Falling For You/Wild Hog | 56 | Tuxedo 917 |
| Get Hep Little Girl/Wild Hog Baby | 59 | Tuxedo 932 |

Twilights (1) (Phyllis Branch & the)

Calypso Fever/Babalu — 57 — Tuxedo 919

Twilights (2)

| Oh Baby Love/My Heart Belongs To Only You | 59 | Finesse 1717 |
| It's Been So Long/For The First Time | 64 | Harthon 135 |

Twilights (3) (Tony Richards & the)

| Please Believe In Me/Paper Boy | 61 | Colpix 178 |
| Summer's Coming/Shout My Name | 61 | Colpix 199 |

Twilights (4) (Teddy & the)

Woman Is A Man's Best Friend/Goodbye To Love	62	Swan 4102
You Gotta Be Alone To Cry/Running Around Town	62	Swan 4115
I'm Just Your Clown/Bimini Bimbo	62	Swan 4126

Twilights (5)

It Could Be True/Sum'pin Else	62	Twilight 1028
Bohemian/Little Richard	63	6 Star 1001/1002
Shipwreck/For The First Time	67	Parkway 128

Twilights (5) (Helen Simon & the)

Believe It Or Not/Living Letter — 63 — Felice 713

Twiliters (1) (aka Twi-Lighters)

Sittin' In A Corner/It's A Cold, Cold, Rainy Day — 61 — Groove 0154

Twiliters (2)

Infatuation/Til I Waltz Again With You	61	Flippin' 106
Hey There/Caused By You	61	Nix 102
Love Bandit/Back To School	61	Nix 103
Sweet Lips/You Better Make It	64	Paloma 100

Twiliters (3) (Ron Holden & the)

Ya Got That Lovin' Touch/Things Don't Happen That Way — 62 — Baronet 3

Twin Tones

| He Pretty Girl/How Can I Win Your Love | 55 | Atlantic 1064 |
| The Flip-Skip/My Dear | 58 | RCA 7148 |

Twin Tones (aka Twins)

Joanne's Sister/Who Knows The Secret — 58 — RCA 7235

Twin Tunes

I'll Make You Mine/Japanese Rhumba — 55 — Sound 115

Twinettes

Let The People Talk/I'm So Glad — 58 — Vee Jay 284

Twinkle Tones (Jimmie Hombs & the)

Ask The Stars/Voo Doo Dolly — 59 — Jack Bee 1004
(by the Invictas & Hollywood Rebels with Jimmie Hombs)

ARTIST/SONG	YEAR	LABEL
Twinkles (female) (aka Storey Sisters)		
Bad Motorcycle/Sweet Daddy	58	Peak 5001
Fairy Tales/Oh, Little Star	63	Musicor 1031
Twinkletones (Rocky Storm & the)		
Should I/My Baby Left Me Swingin'	58	Josie 847
Twintones		
Most Of All/Bumpity Road To Love	60	Banner 60203
Twisters (1) (Sammy Turner & the)		
Thunderbolt/Sweet Annie Laurie	58	Big Top 3007
Twisters (2)		
Count Down 1-2-3/Speed Limit	59	Felco 103
Come Go With Me/Pretty Little Girl Next Door	60	Apt 25045
Dancing Little Clown/Turn The Page	60	Capitol 4451
Elvis Leaves Sorrento/Street Dance	61	Campus 125
Please Come Back/This Is The End	61	Sunset 501
Twisters (3) (Joey & the)		
Peppermint Twist/Silly Chili	61	Dual 502
Bony Moronie/Mumblin'	62	Dual 505
Do You Want To Dance/Last Dance	62	Dual 509
Two Jays (Jimmy Allen &)		
My Girl Is A Pearl/Forgive Me, My Darling	59	Al-Brite 1200
Twylights		
Darling Let's Fall In Love/I'm Gonna Try	N/A	Rockin 102
Tyce, Napoleon (& group)		
Sitting Here/Paper Doll	60	Norwood 105
Tyler, Gladys (& group)		
I'm In The Mood For Love	N/A	N/A
Tymes		
Alone	63	Parkway LP 7032
Autumn Leaves	63	Parkway LP 7032
Goodnight My Love	63	Parkway LP 7032
Let's Make Love Tonight	63	Parkway LP 7032
Summer Day	63	Parkway LP 7032
That Old Black Magic	63	Parkway LP 7032
Way Beyond Today	63	Parkway LP 7032
You Asked Me To Be Yours	63	Parkway LP 7032
So In Love/Roscoe James McClain	63	Parkway 871A (first pressing)
So Much In Love/Roscoe James McClain	63	Parkway 871C (second pressing)
Wonderful! Wonderful!/Come With Me To The Sea	63	Parkway 884
Somewhere/View From My Window	63	Parkway 891
To Each His Own/Wonderland Of Love	64	Parkway 908
The Magic Of Our Summer Love/With All My Heart	64	Parkway 919
Here She Comes/Malibu	64	Parkway 924
The Twelfth Of Never/Here She Comes	64	Parkway 933
I'm Always Chasing Rainbows/Isle Of Love	64	Parkway 7039
Tyrants (Terry & the)		
Weep No More/Yea, Yea, Yea, Yea, Yea, Yea	61	Kent 399
Tyrones		
Year Round Love/My Rock 'N' Roll Baby	56	Mercury 70939
The Campus Rock/(She Wants) Candy And Flowers	56	Wing 90072
Street Of Memories/Pink Champagne	57	Mercury 71104
Giggles/Broke Down, Baby	58	Decca 30559
I'm Shook/Blast Off	58	Decca 30643

ARTIST/SONG	YEAR	LABEL
Tyson, Roy (& group)		
Oh What A Night For Love/Not Too Young To Sing The Blues	63	Double L 723
The Girl I Love/I Want To Be Your Boyfriend	63	Double L 733
U.S. Four		
Make Up Your Mind/Please Don't Stay Away Too Long	62	Heritage 110
Ubans		
Gloria/On The Bridge	64	Radiant 102
Ultimates (1)		
Lonely Night/I Can Tell You Love Me Too	61	Envoy 2302
Ultimates (2)		
Lost Romance	N/A	Kama
Ultratones		
Restless/Chain Reaction	60	San Tana 101
Locomotion/Sister Of The Girl I Once Loved	62	Cary 2001
Underbeats		
Foot Stompin'/Route 66	64	Garret 4004
Book Of Love/Darling Lorraine	66	Soma 1449
Shake It For Me/I Can't Stand It	66	Soma 1458
Uneeks		
Look At Me (flip is instrumental)	N/A	Toledo 1501
Unforgettables		
Was It All Right/It Hurts	61	Colpix 192
Oh Wishing Well/Daddy Must Be A Man	61	Pamela 204
He'll Be Sorry/Oh There He Goes	63	Titanic 5012
Unforgettables (Little John & the)		
Funny What A Little Kiss Can Do/Little Mary	62	Alan-K 6901
Unique Echos		
Zoom/Italian Twist	61	Southern Sound 108
Unique Teens		
Watcha Know New?/Run Fast	57	Dynamic 110/Relic 518 (64)
Jeannie/At The Ball	58	Ivy 112/Hanover 4510 (58)
Uniques (1) (gm Earl King)		
Somewhere/Right Now	57	Peacock 1677
Mysterious/Picture Of My Baby	60	Peacock 1695
Uniques (2)		
Tell The Angels/Hey, Little Cupid	58	End 1012
Do You Remember?/Come Marry Me	59	Flippin' 202
I'm So Unhappy/I'm Confessin'	60	Bliss 1004/Gone 5113 (61)
I'm So Unhappy/It's Got To Come From Your Heart	60	Pride 1018/Gone 5113 (61)/ Pride 4
One Million Miles Away/All At Once	62	Tee Kay 112
Uniques (2) (Sabby Lewis & the)		
Bwana/Sabby	59	Gone 5074
Uniques (3)		
That's Love	59	World Pacific 808
Uniques (4)		
Silvery Moon/Chocolate Bar	62	Lucky Four 1024

ARTIST/SONG	YEAR	LABEL
niques (5)		
Blue Skies/Loving You	63	Capitol 4949
Times Change/Allright Okay You Win	63	Demand 2490
Merry Christmas Darling/Rockin' Rudolph	63	Demand 2936
Merry Christmas Darling/Times Change	63	Dot 16533
Send Him To Me/This Little Boy Of Mine	63	Roulette 4528
niques (6)		
It Was The Night (a capella)	75	Relic LP 105
Senorita (a capella)	75	Relic LP 105
Speedoo (a capella)	75	Relic LP 105
The New Beat (a capella)	75	Relic LP 108
Dance (a capella)	75	Relic LP 109
niques (7)		
Let Me Weep, Let Me Cry/I've Got A Secret	59	C-Way 2676
niques (8)		
Look At Me/Bossa Nova Cha Cha	60	Mr. Cee 100
nisons (George Jackson & the)		
Watching The Rainbow/Miss Frankenstein	61	Lescay 3006
nitones		
Judy/The Sound	59	Candy 005
niversals		
Again/Teenage Love	57	Mark-X 7004
The Picture/He's So Right	58	Cora-Lee 501
Dreaming/Love Bound	61	Festival 1601
I'll Just Have To Go On (Dreaming)/Love Bound	61	Festival 1601/ Festival 25001 (62)
A Love Only You Can Give/I'm In Love	62	Shepherd 2200
In My Heart You'll Always Remain/You'll Always Remain	62	V-Tone 236
Dear Ruth/Prayer Of Love	63	Southern 102
Dear Lord (acappella)	73	Relic LP 5006
Don't Leave Me This Way (acappella)	73	Relic LP 5006
Ebb Tide (acappella)	73	Relic LP 5006
Good Loving (acappella)	73	Relic LP 5006
Have Mercy Baby (acappella)	73	Relic LP 5006
I'll Be Satisfied (acappella)	73	Relic LP 5006
Love Is A River (acappella)	73	Relic LP 5006
Money Honey (acappella)	73	Relic LP 5006
Tears In My Eyes (acappella)	73	Relic LP 5006
That's My Baby (acappella)	73	Relic LP 5006
The Love I Long For (acappella)	73	Relic LP 5006
Think	85	Murray Hill LP 000083
niversals (Sis Watkins & the)		
Dear Ruth/Gotta Little Girl	63	Ascot 2124
Only You Can Give/Here I Stand	62	Diplomacy
nknowns		
One More Chance/You And Me	57	Shield 7101/X-Tra 102 (57)
Oh Summer Love/Cool Wool	58	Felsted 8535
ntouchables (aka Chavelles) (fb Billy Jones/aka Billy Storm)		
Poor Boy Needs A Preacher/New Fad	60	Madison 128
Vicki Lee/Goodnight Sweetheart, Goodnight	60	Madison 134
60 Minute Man/Everybody's Laughing	60	Madison 139
Lovely Dee/You're On Top	61	Liberty 55335
Do Your Best/Raisin' Sugar Cane	61	Madison 147
Little Mary/Funny What A Little Kiss Can Do	62	Alan K 6901
Medicine Man/Papa	62	Liberty 55423

ARTIST/SONG	YEAR	LABEL
Upbeats (1)		
I Don't Know/Never In My Life	57	Prep 119
The Night We Both Said Goodbye/Oh What It Seemed To Be	58	Joy 223
My Last Frontier/Will You Be Mine	58	Prep 131
Just Like In The Movies/My Foolish Heart	58	Swan 4010
Keep Cool Crazy Heart/You're The One I Care For	59	Joy 227
Teenie Weenie Bikini/Satin Shoes	59	Joy 229
To Me You're A Song/Unbelievable Love	59	Joy 233
Upbeats (2) (Ray Allen & the)		
Let Them Talk/Sweet Lorraine	61	Sinclair 1004
Peggy Sue/La Bamba	62	Blast 204
Upfronts		
When You Kiss Me/Little Girl	61	Lummtone 106
Send Me Someone To Love Who Will Love Me/Baby, For Your Love	61	Lummtone 107
I Stopped The Duke Of Earl/Baby, For Your Love	62	Lummtone 107
Baby, For Your Love/It Took Time	62	Lummtone 108
Most Of The Pretty Young Girls/Do The Beatle	64	Lummtone 114
Upfronts (fb Davie "Little Caesar" Johnson)		
Betty Lou And The Lion/It Took Time	60	Lummtone 103
Too Far To Turn Around/Married Jive	60	Lummtone 104
Upnilons (female)		
Grow Up Romeo/He Fell For Me	64	Lummtone 115
Upsets (Eddy & the)		
Cry Cry Cry/I Got News	N/A	Dektr 41668
Upstarts (1)		
Feed Me Baby/Open The Door Baby	54	Apollo 468
Upstarts (2) (Jerry McCain & the)		
Courtin' In A Cadillac/That's What They Want	56	Excello 2068
If It Wasn't For My Baby/You Don't Love Me No More	56	Excello 2079
Run Uncle John Run/Things Ain't Right	56	Excello 2081
My Next Door Neighbor/Trying To Please	57	Excello 2103
Listen! Young Girls/Bad Credit	57	Excello 2111
Upstarts (3)		
Lovely Dream/Get It Together	N/A	Top Ten 7000
Upstarts (3) (Don Dell & the)		
Time/May It Be My Fortune	61	East Coast 101/102
A Special Love/Someone For Me	62	East Coast 105/106
Make Believe Love/I Want You, I Need You, I Love You (by Don Dell & the Montereys)	64	Roman 2963
Uptones		
Lil Blue Tears	65	Genie 103
Uptones (aka Swallows (3))		
I'll Be There/No More	62	Lute 6225
Be Mine/Dreamin'	62	Lute 6229
Dreaming/Wear My Ring	63	Watts 1080/Magnum 714 (63)
Uptowners		
Vicki/You're A Habit	64	Le Cam 126
Utmosts		
I Need You/Big Man	62	Pan Or 1123
Utopians (1) (Mike (Lasman) & the)		
Erlene/I Wish	58	Cee Jay 574 (first pressing)
Erlene/I Found A Penny (And I Made A Wish)	58	Cee Jay 574 (second pressing)

ARTIST/SONG	YEAR	LABEL
Utopians (2)		
Dutch Treat/Ain't No Such Thing	62	Imperial 5861
Along My Lonely Way/Hurry To Your Date	62	Imperial 5876
Let Love Come Later/Opera Vs. The Blues	63	Imperial 5921
Utopias		
Welcome Back To My Heart/Sally Bad	63	Fortune 568
Maybe/Good Friends Forever	N/A	Fortune 102X
V-8s (aka V-Eights)		
Pretty Girl/Please Come Back	59	Most 711/713
V-Eights (aka V-8s)		
My Heart/Papa's Yellow Tie	60	Vibro 4005/ABC 10201 (61)
Guess What/Everything That You Said	61	Vibro 4006
V-Eights (Stoney Jackson & the)		
Let's Take A Chance/Hot Water	61	Vibro 4007
V-Notes		
Get A Baby Like Mine/Smashed	58	Volk 102
V.I.P.s (1)		
Strange Little Girl/My Girl Friend	61	Congress 211
V.I.P.s (2)		
Fall Guy/Long John	63	Carmel 44
Vacels		
You're My Baby/Hey Girl, Stop Leading Me On	65	Kama Sutra 200
Can You Please Crawl Out Your Window/I'm Just A Poor Boy	65	Kama Sutra 204
Vacels (Ricky & the)		
His Girl/Don't Want Your Love No More	60	Fargo 1050
Lorraine/Bubble Gum	62	Express 711
Vails		
Great Somewhere/Buy Now, Pay Later	60	Belmont 4002
There'll Come A Time/She's Back	60	Belmont 4004
Val-Aires		
Launie, My Love/Which One Will It Be	59	Willette 114/Coral 62119 (59)/ Coral 62177 (59)
Val-Chords		
Candy Store Love/You're Laughing At Me	57	Gametime 104
Val-Tones		
Tender Darling/Siam Sam	55	DeLuxe 6084
Valadiers		
Greetings (This Is Uncle Sam)/Take A Chance	61	Miracle 6
While I'm Away/Because I Love Her	62	Gordy 7003
I Found A Girl/You'll Be Sorry Someday	63	Gordy 7013
Valaquons		
Teardrops/Madelaine	64	Laguna 102
Diddy Bop/Jolly Green Giant	64	Rayco 516
I Wanna Woman/Window Shopping On Girls Avenue	65	Tangerine 951
Valcounts (Tommy Sena & the)		
I Can't Get Up/Choo Choo Train	61	Adore 903
Valdoros		
Don't Open The Grave/A Woman, A Man	57	Silhouette 518

ARTIST/SONG	YEAR	LABEL
Valentines (1)		
Tonight Kathleen/Summer Love	54	Old Town 1009
Lily Maebelle/Falling For You	55	Rama 171
I Love You, Darling/Hand Me Down Love	55	Rama 181
A Christmas Prayer/K-I-S-S Me	55	Rama 186
Woo Woo Train/Why?	55	Rama 196
Twenty Minutes (Before The Hour)/I'll Never Let You Go	56	Rama 201
Nature's Creation/My Story Of Love	56	Rama 208
Don't Say Goodnight/I Cried Oh, Oh	57	Rama 228
If You Love Me, Pretty Baby	86	Murray Hill LP 000202
Sweetheart Of Mine	86	Murray Hill LP 000202
The Joe Smith Theme	86	Murray Hill LP 000202
Valentines (2)		
That's It Man/Please Don't Leave, Please Don't Go	60	King 5338
That's How I Feel/Hey Ruby	60	King 5433
I'll Forget You/Yes, You Made It That Way	62	Bethlehem 3055
I Have Two Loves/Camping Out (instrumental)	63	King 5830
Alone In The Night/Mink Coat And Sneakers	64	United Artists 764
Valentines (3) (Little Tom & the)		
School Girl/Letter From My Darling	61	Mr. Big 222
Valentines (4) (female)		
Johnny One Heart/Mama I Have Come Home	62	Ludix 102
Valentines (5)		
Beautiful/You're Everthin'	63	Lee 5465
Valentinos (female)		
Let Me Be Your Girl/A Kiss From Your Lips	60	Brunswick 55171
Valets		
I Need Someone/When I Met You	58	Jon 4025
Sherry/You And You Alone	59	Vulcan/Jon 4219 (59)
Valiant Trio		
You Left Me	N/A	EV
Valiants (1)		
This Is The Night/Good Golly, Miss Molly	57	Keen 34004
Lover, Lover/Walkin' Girl	57	Keen 34007
Frieda, Frieda/Please Wait, My Love	58	Keen 4026/Andex 4026 (59)
That's The Way To My Heart	59	N/A
Dear Cindy/Surprise	59	Shar-Dee 703
This Is The Night/Walkin' Girl	61	Keen 82120
Valiants (1) (Billy Storm & the)		
We Knew/Walkin' Girl	59	Ensign 4035
Valiants (2) (Sandy Vale & the)		
Boppin' On The Beach/Suntan Tattoo	59	Decca 30941
Valiants (3) (aka Du Droppers/aka Dixieaires)		
Let Me Go Lover/Let Me Ride	59	Joy 235
Valiants (4) (Norman Sands & the)		
Don't Wanna Leave The Congo/Rockin' With Joe	60	Warwick 598
Valiants (5)		
Honky Tonk Joe/Calcutta	61	Columbia 41931
Valiants (6)		
The Wedding/Velma	58	Speck 1001
See-Saw/Blue Jeans And A Pony-Tail	61	Fairlane 21007

ARTIST/SONG	YEAR	LABEL
You Are Sweeter Than Wine/Love Comes In Many Ways	62	Imperial 5843
Are You Ready/Frankie's Angel	62	KC 108
Living In Paradise/I'm In A World Of My Own	63	Imperial 5915
Johnny Lonely/Eternal Triangle	63	Roulette 4510/ Roulette 4551 (64)
Lonely Hours/Come On Let's Go	64	Cortland 114

aliants (7) (Phil DeMarco & the)

Lonely Guy/Be On Your Way	64	Debby 065

alids

Blue Moon (a capella)/Hey Senorita (a capella)	66	Amber 853
Barbara Ann (a capella)/Congratulations (a capella)	66	Amber 855

alleyites (Nathan McKinney & the)

Weep No More/Oh How I Love You	64	Rayco 526

alor, Tony (& group)

Story In My Heart/So Tenderly	63	Musictone 1119

alquins

My Dear/Falling Star	59	Gaity 161/162

alrays

Yo Me Pregunto/Get Aboard	63	Parkway
Get Aboard/Pee Wee	63	Parkway 880
I Ask Myself/Honky Tonk	64	Parkway 904
I'm Walkin' Proud/It Hurts, Doesn't It Girl	67	United Artists 50145

als

The Song Of A Lover/Compensation Blues	62	Unique Laboratories (no #)
Too Late/I'm Stepping Out With My Memories	64	Ascot 2163

altairs

Soul/Strangers Away	64	Selsom 101
The Ko Ko Mo/Moonlight In Vermont	65	Selsom 106

altones

Have You Ever Met An Angel?/You Belong To My Heart	56	Gee 1004

alues

That's The Way/Return To Me	62	Invicta 1002

alumes (aka Volumes (3))

I Love You/Dreams	62	Chex 1000.2 (correct!) (first pressing, second is by Volumes)

ampires

Why Didn't I Listen To Mother/Did Anybody Lose A Tear	64	Carroll 104

an Delles

Time After Time/I Got The Blues	62	Bolo 731

an Dellos

I Need You/Bring Back	61	Card 558

an Dyke Five (aka Van Dykes (4))

Only If I Had Your Love/Bring Back My Life	67	Corner Closet 101

an Dykes (1)

Run Betty Run/The Fixer	58	Decca 30654
Come On, Baby/Lambie Baby	58	Decca 30762
I Don't Know What To Do/Better Come Back To Me	60	Decca 31036

ARTIST/SONG	YEAR	LABEL
Van Dykes (2)		
The Bells Are Ringing/Meaning Of Love	58	King 5158/DeLuxe 6193 (61)
Once Upon A Dream/Dame Tu Corazon	59	Felsted 8565
Gift Of Love/Guardian Angel	60	Spring 1113/Donna 1333 (60)
Van Dykes (3)		
King Of Fools/Stupidity	62	Atlantic 2161
Van Dykes (4) (aka Van Dyke Five)		
Again And Again/Rich Girl	65	Green Sea 101
Miracle After Miracle/How Can I Forget Her	66	Green Sea 108
Rich Girl/Miracle After Miracle	67	Co-Op 515
Rock-A-Bye Girl/I'll Be By	67	Co-Op 516
Van Loan Quartet, Joe		
Until I Fell For You/Trust In Me	54	Carver 1402
Van-Dells (Myron & the)		
Heartaches/Crazy Little Mama	63	Flo-Roe 15
Vance, Sammy (& group)		
Run Run Run/Guilty Of Love	58	Ebb 134
Vandells		
A Small Silver Ring/Bumble Bee	64	USA 758
Vandells (Johnny Greco & the)		
Gloria/I Dunno	63	Far-Mel 1
Vanguards (1)		
So Live/Don't Let It Happen Again	54	Derby 854
Baby Doll/My Friend Mary Ann	58	Dot 15791
Moonlight/I'm Movin'	58	Ivy 103
Vanguards (1) (Buddy Gibson & the)		
Just A Game/The Session	59	Swingin' 615
Vanguards (2)		
I Love You Darling/Tears Fall	N/A	Regency 743
Vann, Joey (& group)		
Try To Remember/My Love, My Love	65	Coed 606
Varnells (aka Vernalls)		
Raindrops/Why Can't You Be True (by the Vernalls)	58	Rulu 6753
Who Created Love/Strut Time	61	Arnold 1003
Day In Court/All Because	61	Arnold 1006
Vectors		
One Day/Slow, But Sure	58	Standord 700
Vel-Aires (Donald Woods & the) (aka Donald Woods & the Bel-Aires (3))		
This Paradise/Let's Party Awhile	55	Flip 303 (second pressing, first is by the Bel-Aires)
Death Of An Angel (My Baby's Gone)/Man From Utopia	55	Flip 306/Happy Tiger Era 5065
Stay With Me, Always/My Very Own	55	Flip 309
Heaven In My Arms/Mighty Joe	56	Flip 312
You Won't Be Satisfied	N/A	N/A
Vel-Tones		
Broken Heart/Please Say You'll Be True	60	Vel 9178
Now/I Need You So	60	Zara 901/Lost Nite 103 (65)
I Want To Know/My Dear	64	Wedge 1013
A Fool Was I	N/A	Collectables LP 5037

ARTIST/SONG	YEAR	LABEL
Velaires (1)		
Roll Over Beethoven/Brazil	61	Jamie 1198
Roll Over Beethoven/Frankie And Johnny	61	Jamie 1198
Dream/Sticks And Stones	61	Jamie 1203
Ubangi Stomp/It's Almost Tomorrow	62	Jamie 1211
Memory Tree/Don't Wake Me Up	62	Jamie 1223
Yes, It Was Me/I Could Have Cried	65	Hi-Mar 9173
Velaires (2) (Danny & the)		
What Am I Livin' For/Shaggy Dog	67	Brent 7072
I Found A Love/It's Over	67	Ramco 1983
Velairs		
A Prom And A Promise/Don't Tell Tales Out Of School	58	MGM 12667
Vells (1) (Little Butchie & the)		
Sometimes Little Girl/Over The Rainbow	59	Angle Tone 535
(by Little Butchie Saunders & His Buddies)		
Vells (2) (aka Vandellas) (female)		
There He Is At My Door/You'll Never Cherish A Love So True	62	Mel-O-Dy 103
Velons		
Shelly/From The Chapel	64	Blast 216
Summer Love/Why Don't You Write	N/A	BJM 6568
What Love Can Do	N/A	BJM 6569
Velours		
My Love Come Back/Honey Drop	56	Onyx 501/Relic 503 (64)
Romeo/What You Do To Me	57	Onyx 508/Relic 502 (64)
Can I Come Over Tonight?/Where There's A Will (There's A Way)	57	Onyx 512/Gone 5092 (60)/ Relic 504 (64)
This Could Be The Night/Hands Across The Table	57	Onyx 515/Relic 516 (64)
I'll Never Smile Again/Crazy Love	58	Cub 9014
Can I Walk You Home?/Remember	58	Onyx 520/Orbit 9001 (58)/ Cub 9001 (58)
Blue Velvet/Tired Of Your Rock & Rolling	59	Cub 9029
I Promise/Little Sweetheart	59	Studio 9902
Sweet Sixteen/Daddy Warbucks	60	Goldisc 3012
Lover, Come Back To Me/The Lonely One	61	End 1090
Don't Pity Me/I'm Gonna Change	67	MGM 13780
Vels (1)		
In-Laws/Do The Walk	63	Amy 881
Vels (2)		
Please Be Mine/Mysterious Teenage	57	Trebco 16/Trebco 702 (57)
Veltones		
Playboy/Cal's Tune	59	Coy 101/Kapp 268 (59)
Take A Ride/Lover's Blues	59	Jin 107
I'm Your Fool/Jail Bird	59	Jin 115
Someday/Fool In Love	59	Satellite 100/ Mercury 71526 (59)
Darling/I Do	66	Goldwax 301
Velvateens		
Please Don't Let Me Go	N/A	Velvet 1001
Velvatones		
Real Gone Baby/Feeling Kinda Lonely	57	Meteor 5042
Impossible/My Lonely Friend (by the Continentals)	74	Candlelite 412
Velvatones (bb Li'l Walter's Band)		
Impossible/I'm Leaving Home	59	Nu Kat 110

ARTIST/SONG	YEAR	LABEL
Velvet Angels (aka Diablos)		
I'm In Love/Let Me Come Back	64	Medieval 201
Since You've Been Gone (a capella)/Baby I Wanna Know	64	Medieval 207
I'm In Love (a capella)/Baby I Wanna Know	65	Co-Op 201
For Sentimental Reasons (acappella)	72	Relic LP 5004
I Want To Know Baby (acappella)	72	Relic LP 5004
Jungle Fever (acappella)	72	Relic LP 5004
Mary (Let It All Out) (acappella)	72	Relic LP 5004
Old MacDonald (acappella)	72	Relic LP 5004
When You're Smiling (acappella)	72	Relic LP 5004
Your Love (acappella)	72	Relic LP 5004
Lola (acappella)	72	Relic LP 5004/Relic LP 102 (75)
Mary (acappella)	72	Relic LP 5004/Relic LP 102 (75)
Be Ever Wonderful (acappella)	72	Relic LP 5004/Relic LP 108 (75)
It's Too Soon To Know (acappella)	72	Relic LP 5004/Relic LP 108 (75)
Johnny Johnny (acappella)	72	Relic LP 5004/Relic LP 109 (75)
Blue Moon	75	Relic LP 101
Fools Rush In	75	Relic LP 101
Velvet Keys		
Let's Stay After School/My Baby's Gone	57	King 5090
Don't Take My Picture, Take Me/The Truth About Youth	58	King 5109
Velvet Satins		
Heading For The Rooftop/Angel Adorable	64	General American 720
Up To The Rooftop/Nothing Can Compare To You	65	General American 006
Cherry/An Angel Like You	65	General American 716
Velvet Satins (Bobby Capri & the)		
Charm Bracelet/One Sided Love	60	Ariste 101/Jason Scott 17447
You And I/Cleopatra	63	Johnson 124
The Night/I'm Gonna Be Another Man	63	Johnson 126
Velvet Sounds		
Silver Star/Devil And The Stocker	N/A	Cosmopolitan 100/101
Pretty Darling/Who'll Take My Place	N/A	Cosmopolitan 105/106
Velvet Tones		
Good Lovin'	65	Velvet Tone 104
Velvet, Jimmy (& group)		
Young Hearts/It's Almost Tomorrow	65	Velvet Tone 102
Velveteens (1)		
I Feel Sorry For You Baby/Ching Bam Bah	65	Golden Artist 614
Velveteens (1) (female)		
Baby Baby/Teen Prayer	61	Stark 101
Please Holy Father/Baby Baby	61	Stark 101
I Thank You/Meant To Be	62	Stark 105/Laurie 3126 (62)
Velveteens (2) (Terri & the)		
Bells Of Love/You've Broken My Heart	62	Kerwood 711
Velveteers		
Tell Me You're Mine/Boo Wacka Boo	56	Spitfire 15
Velvetiers		
Oh, Baby/Feelin' Right Saturday Night	58	Ric 958
Velvetones (1)		
Glory Of Love/I Love Her So	57	Aladdin 3372/Imperial 5878 (6?
Melody Of Love/I Found A Love	57	Aladdin 3391
Happy Days Are Here Again/If I Could Be With You	59	20th Fox 165
Come Back/Penalty Of Love	59	D 1049/Glad

ARTIST/SONG	YEAR	LABEL
Worried Over You/Space Men	59	D 1072
Who Took My Girl/Stars Of Wonder	59	Deb 1008
My Every Thought/Little Girl, I Love You So	60	Aladdin 3463
The Glory Of Love/I Found My Love	64	Imperial 66020

Velvetones (2) (female)

Yes I Will/I Want Him So Bad	62	Ascot 2117
Starry Eyes/I'm Ashamed	63	Ascot 2126

Velvetones (3) (Bingo Miller & the)

Martha Sue/I Know A Valley	N/A	Young Artists 103

Velvetones (4)

Reaching For A Rainbow	N/A	Vanda 0001

Velvets (1)

They Tried/She's Gotta Grin	53	Red Robin 120
I/At Last	53	Red Robin 122/Pilgrim 706 (55)/ Event 4285 (55)
I Cried/Tell Her	54	Red Robin 127/Pilgrim 710 (55)
I-I-I/Dance Honey Dance	57	Fury 1012

Velvets (2)

Happy Days Are Here Again/If I Could Be With You	59	20th Century Fox 165
Everybody Knows/Hand Jivin' Baby	59	Plaid 101
That Lucky Old Sun/Time And Again	61	Monument 435
Tonight (Could Be The Night)/Spring Fever	61	Monument 441
Laugh/Lana	61	Monument 448
The Love Express/Don't Let Him Take My Baby	62	Monument 458
Let The Good Times Roll/The Lights Go On, The Lights Go Off	62	Monument 464
Crying In The Chapel/Dawn	63	Monument 810
Here Comes That Song Again/Nightmare	64	Monument 836
If/Let The Fool Kiss You	64	Monument 861
Baby, The Magic Is Gone/Let The Fool Kiss You	66	Monument 961

Velvets (3) (Bobby & the)

I Promise/Now We Know	59	Rason 501

Velvets (4) (Ronnie Price & the)

White Bucks/Look At Me	N/A	Carousel 1001

Velvettones (Lee Martin & the)

Lover's Plea/Born To Be A Loser	62	Jin 159

Velvitones

Little Girl I Love You/A Prayer At Gettysburg	59	Milmart 113

Vendors

Steppin' Stones/Public Lover No. 1	63	MGM 13133
Where All Lovers Meet/That's All Right	63	Victorio 128

Veneers (female) (aka Chantels)

Believe Me (My Angel)/I	60	Princeton 102

Venetians (Nick Marco & the)

Little Boy Lost/Would It Hurt You	60	Dwain 813

Ventrills

Alone In The Night/Confusion	67	Ivanhoe 5000/Parkway 141 (67)

Verdicts (1)

My Life's Desire/The Mummy's Ball	61	East Coast 103/104/ Relic 507 (64)

ARTIST/SONG	YEAR	LABEL
Verdicts (2)		
Never Let Me Go/Now You Did It	73	Vintage 1009
Verity (Lady Jane &)		
A Junior At The Senior Prom/Slow Rock	59	Palette 5031
Vernalls (aka Varnells)		
Raindrops/Why Can't You Be True	58	Rulu 6753
Versa-Tones		
How Long/Cobra	61	Kenco 5015
Versailles		
Little Girl Of Mine/Teenager's Dream	57	Harlequin 401
I'm In The Mood For Love (a capella)/Lorraine (a capella)	65	Old Timer 607
Versalettes (aka Trinkets (2)) (female)		
True Love Is A Treasure/Shining Armor	63	Witch 116
Don Juan In Town	63	Witch 120
Versatiles (1) (Sonny Day & the)		
Speedilac/Half Moon	58	Checker 886
Versatiles (2) (aka Majors/aka Performers)		
Crying/Passing By	58	Atlantic 2004
I'll Whisper In Your Ear/Lundee Dundee (by the Majors	60	Rocal 1002
White Cliffs Of Dover/Just Words	62	Peacock 1910
Versatiles (3) (Dee Thomas & the)		
In The Garden Of Love/Don't Know Where I'm Going	60	Coaster 800
Versatiles (4)		
Blue Feeling/Just Pretending	62	Ramco 3717
Versatiles (5)		
Lonely Boy	64	Sea Crest 6001
Versatiles (6)		
Easy To Say	67	Richtone 186
Versatiles (7)		
Blue Feeling/Just Pretending	N/A	Marie 101
Versatiles (8)		
Lonely Man	N/A	Staff 210
Versatiles (9) (Jerry Shelly & the)		
Love Only Me/It's All Over	N/A	Star 220
Versatiles (10) (Tootsie & the)		
I've Got A Feeling/Nobody But You	62	Elmar 6000
Versatones (1)		
Wait For Me/De Obeah Man	57	RCA 6917
Bikini Baby/Lovely Teenage Girl	57	RCA 6976
All Around The Bush	57	RCA LPM-1538/RCA EP 1538
Hold Me Lover/Will She Return	63	Richie 4081
Versatones (2)		
Tight Skirt And Sweater/Bila	58	All Star 501/Fenway 7001 (60)/ Atlantic 2211 (63)/Bruce
So Good	N/A	N/A
Versitiles		
Love Me/Don't Go	62	Amaker 417

ARTIST/SONG	YEAR	LABEL
Vespers (aka Four Epics)		
Mr. Cupid/When I Walk With My Angel	63	Swan 4156
Vestee, Russ (& group)		
Teardrops/Well Alright	62	Amy 833
Vestelles (female)		
Come Home/Ditta-Wa-Do	58	Decca 30733
Vets		
Wipe The Tears From Your Eyes/Natural Born Lover	61	Swami 551/552
Vi-Kings		
Rock A Little Bit/Desert Boots	60	Del-Mann 545
Vi-Tones		
The Storm (So Blue) (a capella)/Fall In Love (a capella)	64	Times Square 105
Vibes (1) (aka Vibranaires)		
Stop Torturing Me!/Stop Jibing, Baby	54	After Hours 105/ Chariot 105 (54)
Vibes (2)		
Darling/Come Back, Baby	57	ABC 9810
Vibes (3)		
What's Her Name?/You Are	58	Allied 10006
Misunderstood/Let The Old Folks Talk	59	Allied 10007
Vibes (4)		
In The Middle Of The Night	87	Relic LP 8011
Love Me Too	87	Relic LP 8011
Won't You Marry Me	87	Relic LP 8011
Vibes (5)		
A Killer Comes To Town/You Got Me Crying	N/A	Rayna 103
Vibra-Tones		
I'm Begging You Baby	62	Candi 1025
Vibra-Tones (Sabby Lewis & the)		
Forgive Me, My Love/Regretting	56	ABC 9687
Vibraharps (1) (aka Vibra-Harps)		
Walk Beside Me/Cosy With Rosy	56	Beech 713
It Must Be Magic/Nosey Neighbors	59	Atco 6134
The Only Love Of Mine/Be My Dancing Partner	59	Fury 1022
Vibraharps (2)		
A Friend (a capella)	75	Relic LP 108
I Hear Bells (a capella)	75	Relic LP 108
Secret Love (a capella)	75	Relic LP 108
Talking To My Heart (a capella)	75	Relic LP 109
Vibranaires (aka Vibes (1))		
Doll Face/Ooh, I Feel So Good	54	After Hours 103/ Chariot 103 (54)
Vibrations (aka Jayhawks/aka Marathons)		
So Blue/Love Me Like You Should	61	Bet 001/Checker 954 (60)
Feel So Bad/Cave Man	60	Checker 961
Doing The Slop/So Little Time	60	Checker 967
The Watusi/Wallflower	60	Checker 969
Continental With Me Baby/The Junkeroo	60	Checker 974
Stranded In The Jungle/Don't Say Goodbye	60	Checker 982

ARTIST/SONG	YEAR	LABEL
Peanut Butter/Talkin' Trash	59	Argo 5349
All My Love Belongs To You/Stop Right Now	61	Checker 987
Let's Pony Again/What Made You Change Your Mind	61	Checker 990
I Had A Dream	61	Checker LP 2978
People Say	61	Checker LP 2978
Serenade Of The Bells	61	Checker LP 2978
Sweet Slumber	61	Checker LP 2978
Time After Time	61	Checker LP 2978
Oh Cindy/Over The Rainbow	62	Checker 1002
The New Hully Gully/Anytime	62	Checker 1011
If He Don't/Hamburgers On A Bun	62	Checker 1022
Between Hello And Goodbye/Lonesome Little Lonely Girl	63	Atlantic 2204
Since I Fell For You/May The Best Man Win	63	Checker 1038
Dancing Danny/Dancing Danny (instrumental)	63	Checker 1061
My Girl Sloopy/Daddy Woo-Woo	64	Atlantic 2221
Everlasting Love	N/A	Checker (unreleased)
I Still Love You	N/A	Checker (unreleased)
Talk That Talk	N/A	Checker (unreleased)

Vibrations (Evelyn Dell & the)

Sincerely/Please Tell Me Why	61	ABC 10218

Vice-Roys

Please, Baby, Please/I'm Yours As Long As I Live	55	Aladdin 3273

Viceroys (1)

I'm So Sorry (It's Ending With You)/Uncle Sam Needs You	61	Little Star 107/Smash 1716 (6
Dreamy Eyes/Ball N' Chain	61	Original Sound 15
I Need Your Love So Bad/My Heart	62	Ramco 3715

Viceroys (1) (Jimmy Norman & the)

You Crack Me Up/I Know I'm In Love	63	Little Star 121

Viceroys (2)

Until/Bacon Fat	63	Bolo 750

Viceroys (3)

Tears On My Pillow/Not Too Much Twist	64	Bethlehem 3088
Earth Angel/Death Of An Angel	64	Imperial 66058

Victones

Two Sides Of Love/Somebody Really Loves You	59	Front Page 2302
I Need You So/My Baby Changes	N/A	Front Page 1001

Victorials

I Get That Feeling/Prettiest Girl In The World	56	Imperial 5398

Victorians (1)

Heartbreaking Moon/I'm Rollin'	56	Saxony 103
Wedding Bells/Please Say You Do	56	Selma 1002

Victorians (2)

Move In A Little Closer/Lovin'	63	Arnold 571
Climb Every Mountain/What Makes Little Girls Cry	63	Liberty 55574
You're Invited To A Party/The Monkey Stroll	63	Liberty 55656
Happy Birthday Blue/Oh What A Night For Love	64	Liberty 55693
If I Love You/Monkey Stroll	64	Liberty 55728

Victorians (3)

C'Mon Dream/Catrina	N/A	Hercules 101

Victors (1)

Slow But Sure	58	N/A
It Will Happen By And By/Mi Amor	59	Jackpot 48015

ARTIST/SONG	YEAR	LABEL
Victors (2) (Little Man & the)		
I Need An Angel/King Of The Mountain	63	Tarheel 064
Smile/My Funny Way Of Looking At You	64	Roulette 4576
Victory Five		
I Never Knew/Swing Low	58	Terp 101
Vidaltones		
Forever/Someone To Love	61	Josie 900
Videls		
I Wish/Blow Winds Blow	60	Dusty Disc 473/Early 702 (60)
I'll Keep On Waiting/Streets Of Love	60	Kapp 361
Walking Down The Street/Ya Ya	64	Fargo 1062
Be My Girl/A Place In My Heart	59	Rhody 2000/Medieval 203 (61)
Mr. Lonely/I'll Forget You	60	JDS 5004
Now That Summer Is Here/She's Not Coming Home	60	Tic Tac Toe 5005/JDS 5005 (60)
A Letter From Anne/This Year's Mister New	61	Kapp 405
We Belong Together/It's All Over	63	Musicnote 117
Videos		
Trickle Trickle/Moonglow, You Know	58	Casino 102
Love Or Infatuation/Shoo-Bee-Doo-Bee Cha Cha Cha	59	Casino 105
Vidletts (female)		
He's Gone For Good/What Makes The World Go Round	64	Herald 594
Vikings (1) (Lee Martin & the)		
I Lost Again/Change Of Heart	60	Jin 149
Vikings (2) (Barry & the)		
I Love You, Yes I Do/Last Night	64	Jamie 1281
Vikings (3) (Erik & the)		
Step By Step/Heaven And Paradise	65	Karate 503
Villa, Joey (with the Original Three Friends)		
Blanche/The Oriental	62	Chevron 500
Blanche/Mona Lisa	62	MF 101
Vilons		
What Kind Of Fool Am I?/Let Me In Your Life	61	Lake 713
Mother Nature/Lone Stranger	63	Aljon 1259/1260/Relic 524 (64)
Angel Darling/Wish She Was Mine	72	Bim Bam Boom 104
Tears On My Pillow/Sweetest One	73	Vintage 1011
Vincente, Vin (& group)		
I'm In Your Corner All The Way/Little Cutie	62	Swingin' 644
Vines		
I Must See You Again/Love So Sweet	61	Cee Jay 582
Violinaires		
Another Soldier Gone/Joy In The Beulah Land	54	Drummond 4000
Vipers		
Same Old Valarie/Little Miss Sweetness	N/A	Duchess 102
Viriations		
A Shot Of Love/Tra La La La La	68	Amy 11006
Viscaynes		
I Guess I'll Be/Stop What You're Doing	58	Tropo 101
Yellow Moon/Heavenly Angel	61	VPM 1006

ARTIST/SONG	YEAR	LABEL
Viscount V		
My Angel/She Doesn't Know	N/A	Lavette 5009
Viscounts (1) (Sammy Hagen & the)		
Out Of Your Heart/Smoochie, Poochie	57	Capitol 3772
Don't Cry/Wild Bird	57	Capitol 3818
Tail Light/Snuggle Bunny	58	Capitol 3885
Viscounts (2)		
Raindrop/My Girl	57	Mercury 71073
Saki Laki Waki	59	Vega 103/
		Vega 1003 (unreleased)
Visions		
Marlene/Darling Dear	59	Warwick 108
Teenager's Life/Little Moon	60	Elgey 1003/Lost Nite 102 (61)
All Through The Night/Tell Me You're Mine	61	Big Top 3092
There'll Be No Next Time/So Close	61	Brunswick 55206
Swingin' Wedding/Secret World (Of Tears)	62	Big Top 3119
Tommy's Girl/Oh Boy, What A Girl	63	Mercury 72188
Cigarette/Look At Me Now	63	Original Sound 32
Down In My Heart/Tell Her Now	65	Co-Ed 598
Visions (Connie McGill & the)		
A Million Years/For That Great Day	63	Toy 107
I Wanna Be Yours/Peace Of Mind	63	Triode 115
No I Won't Believe It/He Created You For Me	63	United International 1009
My Love Will Never Change/Take It Like A Man	64	Edge 502
Vistas (Little Victor & the)		
No More/Love Marches On	62	Rendezvous 183
No More/Weeping Eyes	62	Rendezvous 183
Visuals		
The Submarine Race/Maybe You	62	Poplar 115
My Juanita/A Boy, A Girl And A Dream	63	Poplar 117
Please Don't Be Mad At Me/Blue (Enough To Cry)	63	Poplar 121
Vitells		
Shirley/The Dip	62	Decca 31362
Vitones		
Fall In Love	89	Relic LP 5079
The Storm (So Blue)	89	Relic LP 5079
Vocal Lords		
Girl Of Mine/At Seventeen	59	Able (no #)/Taurus (no #)
Vocal-Teens		
Till Then/Be A Slave	72	Downstairs 1000
Vocal-Tones		
Walkin' With My Baby/Wanna Lee	57	Juanita 100
Vocalaires		
Dance Dance/These Empty Arms	62	Herald 573
Dream Ship/We Build A Nest (by the Actuals)	76	Ronnie 200
Vocaleers		
Chittlin Switch/Get Together Blues (by Little Esther)	51	Savoy 824
Be True/Oh! Where	52	Red Robin 113
Is It A Dream?/Hurry Home	52	Red Robin 114
I Walk Alone/How Soon?	53	Red Robin 119
Will You Be True?/Love You	54	Red Robin 125
Angel Face/Lovin' Baby	54	Red Robin 132

TIST/SONG	YEAR	LABEL
I Need Your Love So Bad/Have You Ever Loved Someone?	59	Paradise 113
Love And Devotion/This Is The Night	60	Old Town 1089
The Night Is Quiet/Hear My Plea	60	Vest 832
Cootie Snap/A Golden Tear	62	Twistime 11
Oh Where (flip by Mango Jones)	64	Oldies 45 166

caltones

I'm Gonna Get That Gal/My Girl	56	Apollo 488
Three Kinds Of People/Darling (You Know I Love You)	56	Apollo 492
I'll Never Let You Go/My Version Of Love	56	Apollo 497
Answer To My Dreams	57	N/A
Come Dance With Me	57	N/A
Hawaiian Rock 'N Roll/Walkin' My Baby	57	Cindy 3004
I Ain't Gonna Give Nobody	89	Relic LP 5082
My Last Goodbye To You	89	Relic LP 5082
Please Don't Leave Me	89	Relic LP 5082

caltones (Bobby Harris & the)

Don't Do It Baby/Crazy Crazy Crazy	55	Wen-Dee 1933

gues

Love Is A Funny Little Game/Which Witch Doctor	58	Dot 15798
Try Baby Try/Falling Star	58	Dot 15859

ice Masters

Oops I'm Sorry/Hope And Pray	59	Anna 101
Needed/Needed (For Lovers Only)	59	Anna 102
Hit And Runaway Love/Advertising For Love	59	Anna 103

ice Masters (Ty Hunter & the)

Everything About You/Orphan Boy	60	Anna 1114
Everytime/Free	60	Anna 1123

icemasters

In Love In Vain/Two Lovers	60	Frisco 15235

ices (1) (aka Bobby Bird & the Birds)

Two Things I Love/Why?	55	Cash 1011
Hey, Now/My Love Grows Stronger	55	Cash 1014
Takes Two To Make A Home/I Want To Be Ready	55	Cash 1015
Santa Claus Boogie/Santa Claus Baby	55	Cash 1016

ices (2) (Ravon Darnell & the)

I'll Be Back/One Of These Mornings	56	Million 2015

ices (3) (Frankie Bearse & the)

I Cry/No End To Love	64	Olimpic 247

ices Five (Bud Johnson & the) (aka Chanters (2))

For Sentimental Reasons/All Alone	59	Craft 116

l-Tones

If She Should Call/Don't Monkey With A Donkey	57	Dynamic 108

lcanos

Gotta Be A False Alarm	64	Harthon 138
Take Me Back Again	65	Harthon 146

lchords

Bongo Love/Peek-A-Boo Love	61	Regatta 2004

lumes (1)

I Won't Tell A Soul/Gotta Feed The Ol' Horse Lotta Hay	54	Jaguar 3004

ARTIST/SONG	YEAR	LABEL
Volumes (1) (Lucille Watkins & the)		
You Left Me Lonely/So Disappointed With Love	54	Jaguar 3006
Volumes (2) (Jimmie Lewis & the)		
In My Heart/I Saw A Cottage In My Dreams	58	Ivy 104
Volumes (3)		
I Love You/Dreams	62	Chex 1002 (second pressing, first is by Valumes)
Come Back Into My Heart/The Bell	62	Chex 1005
Sandra/Teenage Paradise	63	Jubilee 5446
Oh, My Mother-In-Law/Our Song	63	Jubilee 5454
Ink Dries Quicker Than Tears/Why Must We Go To School (by the Nutmegs)	63	Times Square 22
Gotta Give Her Love/I Can't Live Without You	64	American Arts 6
I Just Can't Help Myself/One Way Lover	65	American Arts 18
Trouble I've Seen/That Same Old Feeling	66	Impact 1017
A Way To Love You/You Got It Baby	67	Inferno 2001
My Road Is The Right Road/My Kind Of Girl	67	Inferno 2004
Ain't That Lovin' You/I Love You Baby	68	Inferno 5001
Angel	N/A	Chex
County Jail	N/A	Chex
I Wanna Be Your Man	N/A	Chex
La La La Song	N/A	Chex
Miss Silhouette	N/A	Chex
Roly Poly	N/A	Chex
You Put A Spell On Me	N/A	Chex
Volumes (4)		
Why/Monkey Hop	64	Old Town 1154
Von Carl, Jimmy (bb the June Voices)		
Lonely Night/This Doesn't Seem Real	59	Flick 002
Von Gayels		
The Twirl/Crazy Dance	60	Dore 544
The Twirl/Loneliness	N/A	USA 1221
Vondells		
Valentino/Errand Boy	64	Marvello 5003
Errand Boy/Then I Know	64	Marvello 5005
Lenora/Valentino	64	Marvello 5006
Vonns		
Leave Us Alone/So Many Days/So Many Days	63	King 5793
Vowels		
Your Lovin' Kisses	N/A	Lebam 157
Vows		
Have You Heard/I Wanna Chance	62	Markay 103
Say You'll Be Mine/When A Boy Loves A Girl	63	Sta-Set 402
Dottie/The Things You Do To Me	63	Tamara 760
Buttered Popcorn/Tell Me	65	V.I.P. 25016
Voxpoppers (1)		
Wishing For Your Love/The Last Drag	58	Amp-3 1004/Mercury 71282 (58
Pony Tail/Ping Pong Baby	58	Mercury 71315
Love To Last A Lifetime/Come Back Little Girl	58	Poplar 107
Can't Understand It/Blessing After All	59	Versailles 200
Voxpoppers (2) (Freddie & the)		
Lonely For You/Helen Isn't Tellin'	60	Warwick 589

RTIST/SONG	YEAR	LABEL
yagers		
I Never Loved Anyone/Farewell	60	Titan 1712
de, Earl (& group)		
You're Still My Baby/Feel So Bad	61	Seville 111
de, Morris (bb the Four Pharaohs)		
It Was A Night Like This/Is It Too Late (by the Four Pharaohs)	58	Ransom 102
gner, Cliff (& group)		
When You're Dancin'/Something's Got A Hold On Me	64	Jolum 2509
ilers		
Hot Love/Stop The Clock	54	Columbia 40288
lker, Charles (with the Daffodils)		
Slave To Love	59	Champion 1014
lker, Wayne (& group)		
Whatever You Desire/A Teenage Love Affair	57	Columbia 40905
llace, Jerry (& group)		
Gloria/On A Night When Flowers Were Dancing	56	Mercury 70812
llace, Jerry (bb the Jewels)		
How The Time Flies/With This Ring	58	Challenge 59013
anderers (1)		
We Could Find Happiness/Hey, Mae Ethel	53	Savoy 1109
How Can I Get Along Without You/Don't Do Nothing I Wouldn't Do	54	Savoy 1098 (unreleased)
My First, Last and Only Girl/What Do I Do	54	Savoy 1099 (unreleased)
Thinking Of You/Great Jumping Catfish	57	Onyx 518
Two Hearts On A Window Pane/Collecting Hearts	58	Cub 9019
A Teenage Quarrel/My Shining Hour	58	Orbit 9003/Cub 9003 (58)
Please/Shadrach Meshack And Abednego	59	Cub 9023
I'm Not Ashamed/Only When You're Lonely	59	Cub 9035
I'm Waiting In Green Pastures/I Walked Through A Forest	59	Cub 9054
If I Could Make You Mine/I Need You More	60	Cub 9075
For Your Love/Sally Goodheart	61	Cub 9089
I'll Never Smile Again/A Little Too Long	61	Cub 9094
Somebody Else's Sweetheart/She Wears My Ring	61	Cub 9099
As Time Goes By/There Is No Greater Love	62	Cub 9109/MGM 13082 (62)
After He Breaks Your Heart/Run Run Senorita	62	United Artists 570
I'll Know/You Can't Run Away From Me	63	United Artists 648
My Sweetie Pie	N/A	UGHA LP 001
anderers (1) (Dolly Cooper & the)		
Love Can Be Blind/Be Good To Yourself	54	Savoy 1121
anderers (1) (Pearl Woods & the)		
I Can't Wait	N/A	UGHA LP 001
anderers (2)		
Mask Off/My Lady Chocaonine	57	Gone 5005
anderers (3)		
Quiet Night/One Look	60	Panama 3900
anderers (4) (Tony Allen & the)		
Everybody's Somebody's Fool/If Love Was Money	61	Kent 356
anderers (5) (Dion & the)		
Time In My Heart For You/Wake Up Baby	66	Columbia 43483
Two Ton Feather/So Much Younger	66	Columbia 43692

592 Wans (Larry Burns & the)

ARTIST/SONG	YEAR	LABEL
Wans (Larry Burns & the)		
Back To School	N/A	Voom 17
Warblers		
Is This The Real Thing/It's Wrong (by the Ontarios)	73	Baron 101
Scheming/Love Me Baby (by the Ontarios)	73	Baron 106
Ward, Lee (& group)		
The Defense Rests/You Are My Sunshine	61	Gait 407
Ware, Curtis (bb the Four-Do-Matics)		
Flame In My Heart/Am I In Love	61	Kaybee 101
Warner, Little Sonny (& group)		
Oh What A Fool/I Love You, Oh Darling	60	Swingin' 627
Warner, Merrill (& group)		
Don't Let Me Dream Tonight/Sit, Hope And Cry	N/A	Travel 505
Washington, Baby (& group)		
The Bells/Why Did My Baby Put Me Down	59	Neptune 104
Let's Love In The Moonlight/Work Out	59	Neptune 107
Washington, Baby (bb the Hearts)		
I Hate To See You Go/Knock Yourself Out	59	J&S 1632/1633
Washington, Dinah (bb the Dells)		
Am I Blue	62	N/A
Waters, Larry (& group)		
I Wonder, Wonder/Wish I Didn't Love You So	56	Dig 121
Watesians		
I'll Find Myself A Guy/I Told You Baby	62	Donna 1371
Watkins, Billy (& group)		
Sandman Of Love/Spade Love	54	Allied 10000
Where Is My Love/I Wanna Know	61	Chess 1786
Beverly/Just For You	64	Kent 411
Watts (Jimmy Mack &)		
I Believe I Love You/True Lover Girl	60	Gee 1056
Watts, Bette (& male group)		
Do Me A Favor/Let It Be Me	60	Wand 104
Watts, Maymie (& group)		
Quicksand/There Goes That Train	55	Groove 0103
Waymates		
Once In A Lifetime	N/A	Skyland
Wayne, Art (& group)		
Let Me Make My Own Mistakes/Try And Try Again	61	Xavier 8890
Wayne, James (& female group)		
It's You/Please Be Mine	57	Peacock 1672
Wayne, Wee Willie (bb the Kidds)		
I Remember/Traveling Mood (no group)	55	Imperial 5355
Weber, Lewis (& group)		
Judy/Queen Of Rock And Roll	59	Scottie 1304

RTIST/SONG	YEAR	LABEL
ebs		
Let Me Take You Home/Do I Have A Chance	58	Sotoplay 006
Question/Steamboat	63	Guyden 2090
People Sure Act Funny/You Pretty Fool	66	MGM 13602
Tomorrow/This Thing Called Love	67	Popside 4593
We Belong Together/I Want You Back	68	Verve 10610
ebtones		
My Lost Love/Walk, Talk And Kiss	58	MGM 12724
elch, Lenny (& group)		
My One Sincere/Rocket To The Moon	58	Decca 30637
Ebb Tide/Congratulations, Baby	62	Cadence 1422
est Rudy (& group)		
Just To Be With You (with male group)/You Were Mine (with female group)	59	King 5276
est Siders		
No Tears Left For Crying/Don't You Know	63	Leopard 5004/ United Artists 600 (63)
est Winds		
You Know I'll Miss You/What A Kiss That Was	64	Enith International 1269
You're Lookin' At My Guy/Oowee, Oowee, Oowee, Oowee	64	Kapp 588
eston, Billy (& group)		
It Won't Be This Way/I Need You	N/A	Ep-Som 1002
halers (1) (Hal Paige & the)		
Don't Have To Cry No More/Pour The Corn	57	Fury 1002/Checker 873 (57)
Sugar Bird/Thunderbird	57	J&S 1601
Going Back To My Hometown/After Hour Blues	59	Fury 1024
halers (2) (Kenny & the) (aka Donny & the Dreamers)		
Life Is But A Dream	61	Whale 504
heeler, Art (& group)		
Jo Jo/Too Late For Tears	62	Swingin' 642
heelers		
Once I Had A Girl/Shine 'Em On	N/A	Cenco 107
heels (1)		
My Heart's Desire/Let's Have A Ball	56	Premium 405
Teasin' Heart/Loco	56	Premium 408
I Can't Forget/How Could I Ever Leave You?	57	Premium 410
So Young And So In Love/Where Were You	58	Time 1003
Clap Your Hands, Pt. 1/Clap Your Hands, Pt. 2	59	Folly 800
No One But You/I've Waited For A Lifetime	60	Roulette 4271
I Can't Go On Without You	N/A	Premium
heels (1) (Arthur Lake & the)		
May I Count On You?/The Good Earth	56	Premium 406
heels (1) (Rudy & the)		
Copy Cat/It's Not For Me	59	Curtis 751
heels (2) (Ferris & the)		
Chop Chop/I Want To Dance (Every Night)	61	Bambi 801
Moments Like This/He Was A Fortune Teller	62	United Artists 458
heels (3) (Midge Olinde & the)		
Precious Love/Driving Wheel	62	Viking 1011

ARTIST/SONG	YEAR	LABEL
Whelletts (Sammy & the)		
Goodbye My Love	N/A	Rip Cor 6001
Whipoorwills		
I Want My Love/Kiss A Fool Goodbye	53	Dooto 1201
Deep Within/Going To A Party	61	Josie 892
Whippets		
I Want To Talk With You/Go Go With Ringo	64	Josie 921
Whips (1) (aka Flairs (1))		
Pleadin' Heart/She Done Me Wrong	54	Flair 1025
Whips (2)		
Yes Master/Rosie's Blues	58	Dore 502
Whirlers		
Magic Mirror/Tonight And Forever	56	Whirlin' Disc 108/ Port 70025 (60)
Whirlwinds (1) (Joe Welden & the)		
Someone/Answer Soon	59	Khoury's 714
Whirlwinds (2)		
Angel Love/The Mountain	61	Guyden 2052
Heartbeat/After The Party	63	Philips 40139
Heartbeat/That's My Girl (by De Jan & the Elgins)	67	Times Square 112
Whirlwinds (3) (James Loyd & the)		
I Can't Stand Another Broken Heart/ I Know About The Boy Next Door	63	Empala 117
Whispers (1)		
Ever Lovin' Slick/I've Got No Time	50	Apollo 1156
Don't Fool With Lizzie/Fool Heart	54	Gotham 309
Are You Sorry?/We're Getting Married	55	Gotham 312
Whispers (2)		
If You Don't Care/Here Comes Summer	66	Laurie 3344
Whispers (3)		
Tomorrow Is On Your Side	N/A	N/A
White, Floyd (& group)		
Pains Of Love/Hey Theresa	58	Tee Vee 302
White, Ruth (& group)		
Give Us Your Blessings	N/A	Candi 1029
Whooping Cranes		
Heart And Soul/Tears And Dreams	N/A	El Rey 1000
Wig Twisters		
Wheel Of Love/Baby Wanna Rock	57	A-Ron 1001
Wigs		
You're Sweeter Than Wine/Chicken Switch	64	Golden Crest 592
Wil-Ettes		
Summertime Is Gone/One Love Is Lost	62	Jamie 1234
Wil-Sons		
Let Me Help You/Come On Mama	61	Highland 1020

ARTIST/SONG	YEAR	LABEL
Wilco, Roger (& group)		
So Lonely/I Won't Love Nobody	61	Milestone 2007
Wildcats		
Keep Talkin'/Beatin' On A Rug	55	RCA 6386
Wilde, Jimmy (& group)		
Crazy Eyes For You/Bonnie Bonnie	62	Chelsea 1006
Wilder Brothers		
Party Line/Sick, Sick, Sick	59	Leeds 781
Wildtones		
King Cobra/Mendelsohn Rock	58	Tee Gee 105
Wildwoods (fb Fred Parris)		
When The Swallows Come Back To Capistrano/Heart Of Mine	60	Caprice 101/102
Golden Sunset/Here Comes Big Ed	61	May 106
Williams, Andre (& group)		
Don't Touch/Please Pass The Biscuits (by Gino Parks)	57	Fortune 839X
Williams, Bernie (& group)		
Don't Tease Me/Why Fool Yourself	55	Imperial 5360
Williams, Billy (& group)		
Ask Me No Questions/I've Got An Invitation To A Dance	57	Mercury 71187
Williams, Bobby (& group)		
Chapel Of Love/You	58	Deck 142
Just A Fool/So Many Women	60	Swingin' 619
Williams, Clarence (& group)		
Royal Queen/Love Me	62	Chancellor
Williams, Curley (& group)		
This Heart Of Mine/Be Mine	56	Modern 1004
Williams, Dicky (& group)		
Te Na Na/What Makes You Think You're In Love	60	Vin 1021
Williams, Eddie (& group)		
Never Too Late/Just One More	60	R-Dell 114
Should Pretending End/Tears Had Fallen	64	Corsair 402
Have A Heart/Dancing Shoes	N/A	Alcor 2013
Williams, Fletcher (& group)		
Stop, Look And Love Me/Mary Lou	57	Bullseye 1001
Williams, Jimmy (& group)		
I Knew/Love Only Me	56	Neil 104
Williams, Johnny (& group)		
Don't Call For Me/My Foolish Pride	61	Cy 001
Williams, Kae (& group)		
Everyday Blues/Old Man Mose	56	Kaiser 385
Williams, Kenny (& group)		
Old Fashioned Christmas, Pt. 1/Old Fashioned Christmas, Pt. 2	N/A	Ben Mor 100
Williams, Marie (& group)		
Cat Scratching/Come Back To Me	61	Smart 324

ARTIST/SONG	YEAR	LABEL
Williams, Maurice (bb the Zodiacs)		
Lollipop/May I	65	Vee Jay 678
Williams, Mel (& group)		
Lonely Heart/Soldier Boy	55	Federal 12236
Here At My Phone/Talk To Me	56	Dig 107
All Through The Night/I Cried A Million Tears	56	Dig 128
Stand There, Mountain/I Don't Care If The Sun Don't Shine	57	Dig 140
Williams, Mel (bb the Montclairs)		
Eternal Love/Roses Never Fade	55	Decca 29499
You're Alright Baby	56	Decca EP 2400
Williams, Otis (& group)		
It'll Never Happen Again/It Just Ain't Right	64	King 5816
Williams, Tony (& group)		
The Miracle/My Prayer	61	Reprise 20030
Williams, Verna (& group)		
Mine All Mine	N/A	Versailles 865
Willis, Robert (Chick)		
Pleading/Yes I Do (no group)	60	Bay-Tone 104
Willows (1) (aka Five Willows)		
This Is The End/Don't Pull, Don't Push, Don't Shove	56	Club 1014/Michelle 501
Church Bells Are Ringing/Baby Tell Me	56	Melba 102 (first pressing)
Church Bells May Ring/Baby Tell Me	56	Melba 102 (second pressing)
Do You Love Me?/My Angel	56	Melba 106
Little Darlin'/My Angel	57	Melba 115
Fooled By Her Kisses/Lazy Daisy	N/A	Mercury
Willows (1) (fb Dotty Martin)		
My Dear, Dearest Darling/You	60	Warwick 2025/Warwick 524 (6
Willows (1) (Tony Middleton & the)		
The First Taste Of Love/Only My Heart	57	Eldorado 508
Let's Fall In Love/Say Yeah	58	Gone 5015
Willows (2)		
Now That I Have You/There's A Dance Goin' On	61	Four Star 1753
Willows (3)		
It's Such A Shame/Tears In My Eyes	64	Heidi 103
Such A Night/Sit By The Fire	64	Heidi 107
Wilson, Faye (& group)		
I Miss You So/Playing Me For A Fool	57	Hip 401
Wilson, Robin (& group)		
Close To Me/Nervous Auctioneer	60	Monument 426
Wilson, Sonny (& group)		
Lonely Nights/Troubled Times	61	Plaza 1
Wilson, Steve (& group)		
Written In The Stars/Oh-Be-Dum	61	Pamela 205
Wilson, Wally (& group)		
If You Don't Love Me/The Hunt	54	Sabre 106
Winchell, Danny (& group)		
I Do, I Do/My Little Tree-House	57	MGM 12577

TIST/SONG	YEAR	LABEL

nchell, Danny (bb Nino & the Ebbtides)

Jeannie/Beware You're Falling In Love	59	Recorte 406
We're Gonna Have A Rockin' Party/Don't Say You're Sorry	59	Recorte 410
Come Back Baby/I've Chosen You	59	Recorte 415

indsors (1) (Lee Scott & the)

My Gloria/Cool Sea Breeze	58	Back Beat 506

indsors (2)

Carol Ann/Keep Me From Crying	N/A	Wig Wag 203

inn, Ricky (& group)

Till Eternity	N/A	Campbell 1001

inners (1)

My Sin/To Think We're Only Friends	52	Derby 802

inners (2)

Can This Be Love?/Rockin' And Rollin'	56	Rainbow 331

inners (3)

Dance Romeo Dance/Lucky Guy	62	Vee Jay 494

instons

Hey Little School Girl/To The Aisle	N/A	Cinemascope 8705

inters, David (& group)

Sunday Kind Of Love/Princess	59	Addison 15004
Dori Anne/Bye Bye	62	Rori 703

isdoms

Two Hearts Make One Love/Lost In Dreams	59	Gaity 169

ombats (Gary & the)

Summer's Over/Squidgy Bod	63	Regina 291
So Tough/Winter Dream	63	Regina 297

onderlettes

How Soon/So Wonderful	N/A	Baja 4506

onders (1)

Well Now/Cuttin' Out	57	Reserve 122

onders (1) (Tony Allen & the)

By My Love, Be My Love/Tell Me	58	Forward 601/Tampa 157 (58)
Looking For My Baby/Loving You	59	Jamie 1119
God Gave Me You/Train Of Love	59	Jamie 1143

onders (2)

I'll Write A Book/Hey Senorita	59	Ember 1051
I Wonder/Summer Love	61	Chesapeake 604
What's The World Comin' To/One Day At A Time	61	Manco 1024
Please Don't Cry/With These Hands	62	Bamboo 523
Marilyn/Say There	63	Colpix 699

ood, Lori (bb the Belmonts)

But That Was Long Ago/The End Of The World For Me	62	Amy 842

oods, Cora (& group)

I Don't Want To Cry/Rock In Your Head	55	Federal 12223

oods, Sonny (& group)

Together	N/A	Lu Pine

ARTIST/SONG	YEAR	LABEL
Worth, Bob (& group)		
All In The Game	N/A	N/A
Wrens		
Love's Something That's Made For Two/Beggin' For Love	54	Rama 53/Rama 157 (55)
Eleven Roses (And The Twelfth Is You)/	55	Rama 110
Love's Something That's Made For Two		
Serenade Of The Bells/Hey, Girl	55	Rama 174
Serenade Of The Bells/Love's Something That's Made For Two	55	Rama 174
Betty Jean/She's My Everything	55	Rama 175
I Won't Come To Your Wedding/	55	Rama 184
What Makes You Do The Things That You Do?		
Come Back My Love/Beggin' For Love	55	Rama 65
Come Back My Love/Eleven Roses (And The Twelfth Is You)	55	Rama 65
C'Est La Vie/C'Est La Vie (instrumental by Jimmy Wright Orch.)	56	Rama 194
House Of Cards	86	Rama (unreleased)
Wreckless	86	Rama (unreleased)
I Love You Baby	N/A	Casa Grande
Wright, Beverly (bb the Four Students)		
Shake Till I'm Shook/Don't Let The Sun Catch You Cryin'	56	Groove 0153
(no group)		
Wright, Leo (& group)		
I Pretend And Cry/Bops-A-Bops Love	65	Perico 1257
Wright, Mary (& group)		
One Guy/I Was A Fool	60	Kim 101
Wright, Rubin (& group)		
To You/Bye Bye	59	Lancer 101
Wright, Willie (bb the Sparklers)		
Your Letter/Slowly Losing My Mind	60	Federal 12372
I'm Gonna Leave You Baby/Just Let Me Love You	61	Federal 12406
Wyatt, Don (& group)		
I'm In Love/Reason To Love	61	Brent 7026
Wyatt, Johnny (& group)		
Once Upon A Time/Bottom Of The Top	65	Magnum 736
Wyatt, Johnny (bb the Candles)		
One Night With You/Goodnight	61	Swingin' 643
Yachtsmen		
It's So Hard To Be Young/Now	58	Destiny 402
Our Future/Strut And Stroll	61	Har-Glo 420
Yellow Jackets (Walter & the)		
Mine Forever More/I Was Wrong	57	Goldband 1033
Yeomans		
I'm The Guy/Unlucky	64	Heidi 113
Yo Yo's (Delma Goggins & the)		
I Thank My Lucky Star/Leave Me If You Want to	61	Vibro 4008
Young Hearts		
Do Not Forsake Me/Unwelcome Guest	61	Infinity 006
Young Ideas		
Touchdown/Dream	59	Swan 4044

ARTIST/SONG	YEAR	LABEL
Young Jessie (& group)		
Make Believe/Shuffle In The Gravel	57	Atco 6101
Young Jessie (bb the Flairs (1))		
I Smell A Rat/Lonesome Desert	54	Modern 921
Young Jessie (bb the Jacks)		
Mary Lou/Don't Think I Will	55	Modern 961
Young Lads (1)		
Moonlight/I'm In Love	56	Neil 100
Young Lads (2)		
Night After Night/Graduation Kiss	63	Felice 712
Young Lions		
Oh Dolly/How Can You Be	58	Tampa 158
Summertime With You/Maybe Someday	59	United Artists 177
Little Girl/It Would Be	60	Dot 16172
Young Ones (aka Youngones)		
Marie/Those Precious Love Letters	63	Yussels 7701
I'm In The Mood For Love/No No Don't Cry	63	Yussels 7703
Diamonds And Pearls/Three Coins In The Fountain	63	Yussels 7704
I Only Want You (a capella)/Over The Rainbow (a capella)	64	Times Square 104
Sweeter Than/Picture Of Love (by the El Sierros)	64	Times Square 36/Relic 527 (65)
To Make A Long Story Short (a capella)	75	Relic LP 102
Mary Ann (a capella)	75	Relic LP 102/Relic LP 5079 (89)
Shining Star (a capella)	75	Relic LP 102/Relic LP 5079 (89)
Young Sisters		
My Guy/Casanova Brown	60	Twirl 2001
Playgirl/Hello Baby	61	Twirl 2008
Jerry Boy/She Took His Love Away	63	Mala 467
Young, Billy (& group)		
Are You For Me/Glendora	63	Original Sound 29
Young, Bobby (with Rick & the Masters)		
Only Girl For Me/To Each His Own	68	Guyden 2087
Young, Cecil (& quartette)		
Ooh-Diga-Gow	54	King
Young, Donny (& group)		
From Twelve To Seven	64	Amcan 407
Young, George (& group)		
You Know I Wanna Love You/Wow Wow Wow	57	Chord 1301
Youngones (aka Young Ones)		
Gloria (a capella)/Just Two Kinds Of People (a capella)	62	Times Square 28/Relic 540 (65)
Youngsters (1)		
Shattered Dreams/Rock'n Roll'n Cowboy	56	Empire 104
Counterfeit Heart/You're An Angel (With The Devil In Your Eyes)	56	Empire 107
Dreamy Eyes/Christmas In Jail	56	Empire 109
Dreamy Eyes/I'm Sorry Now	56	Empire 109
Youngsters (2)		
Sweet Talk/Teenager Susan	58	Apt 25021
Lucky Sixteen/Piel Canela (by Cinnamon Skin)	59	Checker 917
Youngsters (3) (fb Sue Black)		
Take Me/It Doesn't Matter Anymore	61	Candix 313

ARTIST/SONG	YEAR	LABEL
Youngsters (4) (Little Pete & the)		
You Told Another Lie/I'll Never Leave You Again	62	Lesley 1925
Youngtones (1)		
Come On Baby/O, Tell Me	58	Brunswick 55089
Youngtones (2)		
It's Over Now/You I Adore	58	X-Tra 104
Patricia/By The Candleglow (with the Dolls)	58	X-Tra 110/Times Square 13 (6
Can I Come Over?/Gonna Get Together Again	59	X-Tra 120/121
I Do/Day Train (by the Blasters)	64	Times Square 31
Z-Debs		
Changing My Life For You/I Would If I Could	64	Roulette 4544
Zane, Herb (& group)		
By You, By You/Let Me In Your Heart	56	DeLuxe 6099
Zanies		
The Blob/Do You Dig Me, Mr. Pygmy	58	Era 1080/Dore 509 (58)
She's A Winner/The Mad Scientist	59	Dore 515
It's Love/Saxaphone Safari	61	Dore 597
Frustration/Rockin' Chopin	62	Dore 632
London Rock/Stalled	62	Dore 638
Sleepwalker/Alexanders Ragtime Band	62	Dore 647
Hello Jackie/Comin' Down The Track	62	Dore 655
Caught In A Ringer/Russian Roulette	62	Dore 658
Chicken Surfer/London Rock	63	Dore 683
Get Your Good Good Lovin' From Me/I Wish I'd Stayed In Bed	64	Dore
Bless'Em All/Last Dance At The Prom	65	Dore
Frankenstein's Laboratory/	71	Dore 653
Will The Real Dr. Frankenstein Please Stand Up		
Do The 1-2-3/Mr. President-To-Be	72	Dore 875
Let Out A Scream/Lost Angeles, Los Angeles	74	Dore
Zebulons		
Falling Water/Wo-Ho-La-Tee-Da	60	Cub 9069
Zee, Ginny (& group)		
You Can't Imagine/Bobby Baby	61	Atco 6218
Zel, Rita (& group)		
Need You To Help Me/I Don't Understand You No More	60	J&S 1685
Zell Rocks (Danny Zella & His)		
Wicked Ruby/Black Sax	59	Fox 10057
Zella, Danny (with the Laredos)		
Sapphire/You Made Me Blue	59	Dial 100
Zephers (Ben Zeppa & the)		
Baby, I Need (Ting-A-Ling)/A Foolish Fool	56	Specialty 577
Zephyrs		
There's Something About You/She's Lost You	65	Rotate 5006
Let Me Love You Baby	65	Rotate 5009
Zeppa, Ben (bb the Four Jacks)		
Why Do Fools Fall In Love	56	Tops 278
Young Heartaches/Ridin' Herd	58	Hush 1000
Zeppers		
Let's Forget The Past	63	Long Fiber 202
Zeroes		
Flossie Mae/Twisting With Crazee Babee	63	Ty-Tex 105

ARTIST/SONG	YEAR	LABEL
Zeu Review (Ziggy & the) (gm Ena Anka)		
Come Go With Me/Little Star	N/A	Zeu 5011
Da Doo Run Run/Sherry	N/A	Zeu 5011
Zip, Danny (& group)		
Hey, Hey, Girl/Please Listen To Me	64	MGM 13254
Zippers (Zip & the)		
Where You Goin', Little Boy/Gig (no group)	63	Pageant 607
Zircons (1)		
Only One Love/I Need It	57	Winston 1020/Dot 15724 (58)
No Twistin' On Sunday/Mama Wants To Drive	62	Federal 12452
Get Up And Go To School/Mr. Jones	62	Federal 12478
Zircons (2)		
Lonely Way (a capella)/Your Way (a capella)	63	Mellomood 1000/Relic 1008 (65)
(I Hear) Silver Bells/You Are My Sunshine	64	Cool Sound 1030
Stormy Weather (a capella)/Sincerely (a capella)	64	Siamese 403/Old Timer 603 (64)
One Summer Night (a capella)/The Lone Stranger (a capella)	66	Amber 851
Zircons (3)		
Surfin' In The Sunset/Going Places	63	Bagdad 1007
Zircons (4)		
Where There' A Will/Don't Put Off For Tomorrow	67	Heigh Ho 607
I Couldn't Stop Crying/Sit Down Girl	67	Heigh Ho 608/609
Go On And Cry, Cry/Was It Meant To Be This Way	67	Heigh Ho 645/646
Zirkons (Johnny Parker & the)		
Oongawa/T.V. Commercial	N/A	C T 302
Zodiacs (Johnny Ballad & the)		
Another Day/My Song	59	Wildcat 0016
Search For Love/I'll Gamble	59	Wildcat 0017
Zodiacs (Maurice Williams & the)		
Say Yeah/College Girl	59	Selwyn 5121
Stay/Do You Remember	60	Herald 552
I Remember/Always	61	Herald 556
Come Along/Do I	61	Herald 559
Come And Get It/Someday	61	Herald 563
Here I Stand/It's All Right (by Maurice Williams)	62	Herald 572
Funny/Loneliness	63	Atlantic 2199
Golly Gee/"T" Town	63	Cole 100
Lover (Where Are You?)/She's Mine	63	Cole 101
Another Little Darling/Lita	64	Soma 1410
Little Sally Walker/Anything	64	Soma 1418
May I/Lollipop	64	Vee Jay 678
Nobody Knows/I Know	65	Scepter 12113
So Fine/The Winds	65	Sphere Sound 700
May I/This Feeling	67	Dee-Su 304
The Four Corners/My Reason For Livin'	68	Veep 1294
But Not For Me	74	Relic LP 5017
I Got A Woman	74	Relic LP 5017
I Love You Baby	74	Relic LP 5017
The Nearness Of You	74	Relic LP 5017
We're Lovers	74	Relic LP 5017/ Collectables LP 5021
Surely/Don't Ever Leave Me	N/A	Dee-Su 309
How To Pick A Winner/Don't Be Half Safe	N/A	Dee-Su 311
Stay/Dance, Dance, Dance	N/A	Dee-Su 318
Try/I'd Rather Have A Memory Than A Dream	N/A	Plus 4401
Return/My Baby's Gone	N/A	Sea-Horn 503
Always	N/A	Sphere Sound LP 7007
Do You Believe	N/A	Sphere Sound LP 7007
Little Mama	N/A	Sphere Sound LP 7007
Running Around	N/A	Sphere Sound LP 7007

Notes

Chapter 1: A Doo-wop In The Bucket

8   "Page through. . . rock 'n' roll." Santelli, Robert. "Rhino Records remembers doo-wop." *Asbury Park Press*, Asbury Park, N.J.: Feb. 9, 1990, p.12.

9   "Some of the most beautiful. . . rock and soul." Marsh, Dave. *The Heart Of Rock and Soul: The 1001 Greatest Singles Ever Made.*" New York: New American Library, 1989.

14   "A real doo-wop. . . Chi-town..." Davis, Chuck. "Platters." *Chicago Defender*, March 18, 1961.

Chapter 2: What Is Doo-Wop Music?

19   ...lyrics were. . . upstate New York. Groia, Phil. *They All Sang On The Corner.* Port Jefferson, N.Y.: Phillie Dee Enterprises, 1983.

21   According to. . . at the Apollo. Groia, Phil. *They All Sang On The Corner.* Port Jefferson, N.Y.: Phillie Dee Enterprises, 1983.

21   "'In The Still Of The Nite'. . . of the time." Ward, Ed, et al. *Rock Of Ages: The Rolling Stone History Of Rock & Roll.* New York: Summit Books, 1986.

Chapter 3: The Evolution Of Doo-Wop

23   He asserts... Gillett, Charlie. *The Sound Of The City: The Rise Of Rock And Roll.* New York: Pantheon Books, 1983.

23   He defines three eras... McCutcheon, Lynn Ellis. *Rhythm And Blues.* Arlington, VA: Beatty, 1971.

35   ...further narrows down... Groia, Phil. *They All Sang On The Corner.* Port Jefferson, N.Y.: Phillie Dee Enterprises, 1983.

38   Bobby Jay (Robert Jeffers)... From an interview on "Don K. Reed's 'Doo Wop Shop' "(audiotape), WCBS-FM Radio, New York, June 24, 1990.

Chapter 4: The Teen Subculture

48   When Alan Freed... Jackson, John A. *Big Beat Heat: Alan Freed and the Early Years of Rock & Roll.*" New York: Schirmer Books, 1991.

48   "...disguised the blackness..." George, Nelson. *The Death Of Rhythm & Blues.* New York: E. P. Dutton, 1988.

49   "Since the 1920s. . . teen hormones." Smith, Wes. *The Pied Pipers of Rock 'n' Roll.* Marietta, GA: Longstreet Press, 1989.

49   "poor white kids. . . chance to be somebody." Ward, Ed, et al. *Rock of Ages: The Rolling Stone History Of Rock & Roll.* New York: Summit Books, 1986.

49   "The jocks. . . listeners' taste." Smith, Wes. *The Pied Pipers of Rock 'n' Roll.* Marietta, GA: Longstreet Press, 1989.

50   "The Vocaleers. . . folk heroes." Groia, Phil. *They All Sang On The Corner.* Port Jefferson, N.Y.: Phillie Dee Enterprises, 1983.

52   "...the artist. . . today's teenagers." Gart, Galen. *The History Of Rhythm & Blues, Vol 4. (1954).* Milford, NH: Big Nickel Publications, 1990.

2 "...obscene. . . radio broadcast." Gart, Galen. *The History Of Rhythm & Blues, Vol 4.* Milford, NH: Big Nickel Publications, 1990.

2 "I hope. . . rhythm and blues." Gart, Galen. *The History Of Rhythm & Blues, Vol 4.* Milford, NH: Big Nickel Publications, 1990.

2 Freberg later. . . in jest. Gart, Galen. *The History Of Rhythm & Blues, Vol 4.* Milford, NH: Big Nickel Publications, 1990.

3 "...[mental health professionals]. . . cultural expression." Smith, Wes. *The Pied Pipers of Rock 'n' Roll.* Marietta, GA: Longstreet Press, 1989.

Chapter 6: The Personality Deejays

2 "Going to. . . Brooklyn Paramount." "Rock 'n' Roll Pied Piper: Alan Freed." *New York Times,* May 20, 1960, p.62.

3 "Soon after. . . a teen-ager." "Rock 'n' Roll Pied Piper: Alan Freed." *New York Times,* May 20, 1960, p.62.

3 In 1952 . . . into the action. Smith, Wes. *The Pied Pipers of Rock 'n' Roll.* Marietta, GA: Longstreet Press, 1989.

3 "Four or five singers . . . heads shake no." Greenfield, Jeff. *No Peace, No Place.* Garden City, NY: Doubleday & Co., 1973.

3 "...solid mass . . . revival meeting." Gart, Galen: *The History Of Rhythm & Blues, Vol. 5 (1955).* Milford, N.H.: Big Nickel Publications, 1990.

4 "...the entire troupe . . . went wild." Gart, Galen: *The History Of Rhythm & Blues, Vol. 5 (1955).* Milford, N.H.: Big Nickel Publications, 1990.

5 Unfortunately . . . camera. Smith, Wes. *The Pied Pipers of Rock 'n' Roll.* Marietta, GA: Longstreet Press, 1989.

5 ...pressure . . . outings. Jackson, John A. *Big Beat Heat: Alan Freed and the Early Years of Rock & Roll."* New York: Schirmer Books, 1991.

6 WOV offered . . . 8 P.M. Gart, Galen: *The History Of Rhythm & Blues, Vol. 5 (1955).* Milford, N.H.: Big Nickel Publications, 1990.

6 'He was . . . one or two.' Fox, Ted. *Showtime At The Apollo.* New York: Holt, Rinehart & Winston, 1983.

7 "He got away . . . might come cup.' " Smith, Wes. The *Pied Pipers of Rock 'n' Roll.* Marietta, GA: Longstreet Press, 1989.

0 "The whole economic . . . with success." Ward, Ed, et al. *Rock of Ages: The Rolling Stone History Of Rock & Roll.* New York: Summit Books, 1986.

1 Johnny . . . recourse. Keyes, Johnny. *Du-Wop.* Chicago: Vesti Press, 1987.

Chapter 7: Indies Versus The Establishment

9 "[He] could never . . . he was saying." Groia, Phil. "The Paul Winley Story." *Bim Bam Boom,* Vol. 2, No. 3.

Chapter 8: The Streetcorner Singers

4 "...I was a runaway . . . set of relatives." Pollock, Bruce. *When Rock Was Young,* New York: Holt, Reinhardt and Winston, 1981.

4 "Pitt came . . . important help." Stierle, Wayne. "The Jive Five: A True New York Story" *Goldmine,* Aug. 12, 1988.

5 "Those four chords . . . of the future." Pollock, Bruce. *When Rock Was Young,* New York: Holt, Reinhardt and Winston, 1981.

6 "The men's room . . . similar reasons." Keyes, Johnny. *Du-Wop.* Chicago: Vesti Press, 1987.

86   "Picture five . . . and harmonize." Horner, Charlie and Applebaum, Steve "The Castelles." *Bim Bam Boom*, Vol.2, No. 6, 1974.

86   "We were just . . . High School together." Jones, Wayne "The Five Satins featuring Fred Parris." *Goldmine*, May 1979.

86   " 'We used to sit . . . being a star...' " Weinger, Harry. "The Platters' Glory Days" *Goldmine*, Feb. 21, 1992.

86   "The Hodge house . . . each other's records.' " Weinger, Harry. "The Platters' Glory Days" *Goldmine*, Feb. 21, 1992.

86   "There were very . . . within a fraternity." Keyes, Johnny. *Du-Wop*. Chicago: Vesti Press, 1987.

86   " 'They weren't social clubs . . . fell right into." Pollock, Bruce. *When Rock Was Young*, New York: Holt, Reinhardt and Winston, 1981.

87   "There were several . . . lead singer on that song." Stierle, Wayne. "The Monotones: They Wrote The Book Of Love" *Goldmine*, Aug. 12, 1988.

87   "A Group singer . . . get hit in the head." Keyes, Johnny. *Du-Wop*. Chicago: Vesti Press, 1987.

88   William "Pete" Johnson . . . Dreamlovers." Jancik, Wayne. "The Dreamlovers: Keeping The Dream Alive" *Goldmine*, Dec. 28, 1990.

88   "It was an easy . . .when you sang." From an interview on "Don K. Reed's 'Doo Wop Shop'" (audiotape), WCBS-FM Radio, New York, May 19, 1991.

88   "...[they] were just . . . manual labor." Beckman, Jeff and Feigenbaum, Hank. "Gee, It's The Crows." *Big Town Review*, Vol. 1, No.2, 1972.

88   "In [Harlem's] one high school . . . academic diplomas." Schoener, Allon (ed.) *Harlem On My Mind: Cultural Capitol Of Black America 1900-1968*. New York: Random House, 1968.

88   "...a kid who never . . . I could do was sing." Turco, Art. "Interview: 'Little' Anthony Gourdine" *Record Exchanger*, April 1973.

88   "Captivated . . . knew his name." Aita, Frank. "The Rivieras" *Record Exchanger*, Vol. 4, No. 3.

89   "I started . . . Absolutely!" From an interview on "Don K. Reed's 'Doo Wop Shop'" (audiotape), WCBS-FM Radio, New York, June 24, 1990.

89   " 'As the years . . . to The Teardrops.' " Anderson, Will. "The Carnations" *Bim Bam Boom*, Issue 8, December 1972.

89   The changes within . . . on to the Vocaleers. Goldberg, Marv and Redmond, Mike. "The Life And Times Of The Solitaires" *Record Exchanger*, Fall 1973.

90   "Well, when you're arranging . . . in the background." From an interview on "Don K. Reed's 'Doo Wop Shop'" (audiotape), WCBS-FM Radio, New York, July 29, 1990.

90   Phil Spector . . . member Eddie Brian. Mennie, Don. "Ducanes Chart With 'I'm So Happy,' Phil Spector Discovers Doo-wop" *Record Collector's Monthly* #39, December 1987-January 1988.

90   "Fortunately . . . Old Town Records." Goldberg, Marv and Redmond, Mike. "The Life And Times Of The Solitaires" *Record Exchanger*, Fall 1973.

90   " '...used to stand around . . . first record...' " Jones, Wayne. "The Five Satins Featuring Fred Parris" *Goldmine*, May 1979.

90 "...used to sing . . . Singular Records." Vance, Marcia. "Danny & the Juniors" *Bim Bam Boom*, Vol. 2, No. 6, 1974.

91 " 'We went down . . . we sang for him.' " Horner, Charlie. "Lee Andrews And The Hearts" *Goldmine*, Dec. 28, 1990.

91 According to Paul Albano . . . of the country. Dunne, Richard W. "The Five Discs" *Goldmine*, Feb. 8, 1991.

91 " '...had them come down . . . worked it out.' " Turco, Art et al. "An Interview With Bobby Robinson" *Record Exchanger*, May 1972.

91 " 'a certain street charm . . . circumstances.' " Tamarkin, Jeff. "The Laddins: A New York Story" *Goldmine*, April 6, 1990.

91 "A hallmark of the early days . . . all-night affairs..." Cox, Herb & West, Steve. "The Heart And Soul Of The Cleftones" *Goldmine*, Feb. 21, 1992.

92 Eddie Brian . . . record of the week. Mennie, Don. "Ducanes Chart With 'I'm So Happy,' Phil Spector Discovers Doo-wop" *Record Collector's Monthly* #39, December 1987-January 1988.

92 " 'We used to rehearse . . . shows we were on...' " Pruter, Robert. "The Five Chances And Their World Of Chicago R & B" *Goldmine*, April 6, 1990.

92 " 'The Five Chances . . . have great choreography.' " Pruter, Robert. "The Five Chances And Their World Of Chicago R & B" *Goldmine*, April 6, 1990.

92 "Nolan Strong . . . and white tie..." Grendysa, Peter. "The Diablos" *Goldmine*, Jan. 3, 1986.

92 " 'jumped up and ripped our nightgowns right off.' " Gagnon, Rick & Gnerre, Dave. "Little Caesar & the Romans: Still Singin' Those Oldies But Goodies" *Goldmine*, Aug. 12, 1988.

92 "You sing two . . . serious adrenalin flowing." Keyes, Johnny. *Du-Wop*. Chicago: Vesti Press, 1987.

93 " 'You'd hang out . . . a lot of parties.' " Pollock, Bruce. *When Rock Was Young*, New York: Holt, Reinhardt and Winston, 1981.

94 "[Our] first big . . . Apollo Theater too." From an interview on "Don K. Reed's 'Doo Wop Shop'" (audiotape), WCBS-FM Radio, New York, July 8, 1990.

94 " 'You try to remain calm . . . do afterward.' " Bosco, Robert. "Joey/Flips From Bandstand To Obscurity" *Record Collector's Monthly* #50, November-December 1991.

94 " 'If they didn't . . . bottles at you.' " Horner, Charlie. "Lee Andrews And The Hearts" *Goldmine*, Dec. 28, 1990.

94 " 'Frankie Lymon . . . a hard place.' " Horner, Charlie. "Lee Andrews And The Hearts" *Goldmine*, Dec. 28, 1990.

94 "There was only one . . . on stage." Cox, Herb & West, Steve. "The Heart And Soul Of The Cleftones" *Goldmine*, Feb. 21, 1992.

94 "Traveling in the South . . . black entertainers." Horner, Charlie. "Lee Andrews And The Hearts" *Goldmine*, Dec. 28, 1990.

94 "Since much . . . for jaywalking." Horner, Charlie. "Lee Andrews And The Hearts" *Goldmine*, Dec. 28, 1990.

95 " 'One night . . . from the tree.' " Garvey, Dennis. "The Bobbettes: Mister Lee's Star Pupils" *Goldmine*, Feb. 21, 1992.

95 " 'Leonard Chess . . . about copyrighting.' " Pruter, Robert. "The Flamingos: The Chicago Years" *Goldmine*, April 6, 1990.

95   Peter . . . fair with their artists. Grendysa, Peter. "Fifties (50s) R & B Stars Helped Cheat Themselves By Signing Poorly Negotiated Contracts" *Record Collector's Monthly* #17, February 1984.

95   "...maintaining a piece . . . I had to apply for it." Pollock, Bruce. *When Rock Was Young*, New York: Holt, Reinhardt and Winston, 1981.

96   " 'He tied us up . . . out of that contract...' " Pollock, Bruce. *When Rock Was Young*, New York: Holt, Reinhardt and Winston, 1981.

96   "...In those days . . . six months to a year." Pollock, Bruce. *When Rock Was Young*, New York: Holt, Reinhardt and Winston, 1981.

96   "Although 'Church Bells' . . . And on a million seller!!" Vance, Marcia & Groia, Phil. "The Willows" *Bim Bam Boom*, Vol. 1, No. 6, 1972.

96   "Although 'Be Fair' . . . 'sessions and traveling.' " Whitesell, Rick. "The Pipes" *Goldmine*, April 1979.

96   " 'People may not . . . had any recourse.' " Jancik, Wayne. "Down The Aisle With The Quin-Tones" *Goldmine*, Dec. 28, 1990.

96   "Tony maintains . . .they would receive after!" Newman, Ralph. "Tony Passalacqua and the Fascinators" *Bim Bam Boom*, Vol. 1, No. 7, 1972.

96   " 'We did the Clay Cole Show . . . did what you had to do.' " Garvey, Dennis. "Randy and the Rainbows: What's In A Name?" *Goldmine*, Feb. 8, 1991.

96   The Bay Bops... Diskin, Bobby. "Brooklyn's Bay Bops Launch White-Group Harmony And Pave The Way For '60s Doowop Hitmakers" *Record Collector's Monthly* #33, November-December 1985.

96   ...Little Joey & the Flips... Bosco, Robert. "Joey/Flips From Bandstand To Obscurity" *Record Collector's Monthly* #50, November-December 1991.

98   " 'made a lot of money . . . or lawyers.' " Sicurelli, Joe. "(I Found Out Why) The Lymon Brothers" *Big Town Review*, Vol. 1, No. 3, July-August 1972.

98   " 'a combination of the urban ghetto struggle, plus some personal hang-ups.' " Sicurelli, Joe. "(I Found Out Why) The Lymon Brothers" *Big Town Review*, Vol. 1, No. 3, July-August 1972.

98   " 'super-stardom, attained before maturity...' " Sicurelli, Joe. "(I Found Out Why) The Lymon Brothers" *Big Town Review*, Vol. 1, No. 3, July-August 1972.

98   " 'Frankie's desire to please . . . he was exposed to.' " Sicurelli, Joe. "(I Found Out Why) The Lymon Brothers" *Big Town Review*, Vol. 1, No. 3, July-August 1972.

98   Clyde McPhatter . . . according to Hank Ballard... Pollock, Bruce. *When Rock Was Young*, New York: Holt, Reinhardt and Winston, 1981.

98   " 'The next thing . . . enjoying ourselves.' " Pollock, Bruce. *When Rock Was Young*, New York: Holt, Reinhardt and Winston, 1981.

99   " 'We stayed together . . . I became a cop.' " Flam, Steve. "The Classics" *Bim Bam Boom*, Vol. 1, No. 6, 1972.

99   Danny Zipfel . . . to get lost. Diskin, Bobby. "Brooklyn's Bay Bops Launch White-Group Harmony And Pave The Way For '60s Doowop Hitmakers" *Record Collector's Monthly* #33, November-December 1985.

100   " 'I just didn't have . . . we all did.' " Pruter, Robert. "The Early Dells" *Record Collector's Monthly* #50, November-December 1991.

100   " 'My son was eight months . . . over there?' " Garvey, Dennis. "The Tune Weavers: One-Hit Wonderfuls" *Goldmine*, Feb. 8, 1991.

00 For the (Chicago) Pastels . . . never recorded again. Pruter, Robert. "Pastels' Promise Eclipsed By Manager's Marital Problems" *Record Collector's Monthly* #45, December 1989.

00 " 'That much touring . . . started in the studio.' " Pollock, Bruce. *When Rock Was Young*, New York: Holt, Reinhardt and Winston, 1981.

00 "Attempting to unravel . . . even singing together." Grendysa, Peter. "The Coming And Going Of The Del Vikings" *Goldmine*, Feb. 21, 1992.

01 "...In 1959 the group . . . and the group disbanded." Goldberg, Marv. "Toppers, Hurricanes, Memos Are Same Brooklyn R&B Group On Wax" *Record Collector's Monthly* #43, March-April 1989.

01 " 'People just don't get along . . . too close to each other.' " Wasserman, Steve. "Buck Ram And The Platters" *Bim Bam Boom*, Vol. 1, No. 6, 1972.

01 " 'By early 1961 . . . had families.' " Heather, Bruce and Dawson, Jim. "The Pearls: Anatomy of a Doo-Wop Group" *Goldmine*, Feb. 8, 1991.

01 " 'This was a pretty unhappy time . . . at the wrong time.' " Heather, Bruce and Dawson, Jim. "The Pearls: Anatomy of a Doo-Wop Group" *Goldmine*, Feb. 8, 1991.

101 The co-manager . . . at the age of 32. Bosco, Robert. "Joey/Flips From Bandstand To Obscurity" *Record Collector's Monthly* #50, November-December 1991.

103 Tony Middleton . . . split among five guys. Phone interview conducted with Tony Middleton on Feb. 24, 1992.

103 "Another difference . . . Nobody could ever break us up. ' " Garvey, Dennis. "The Bobbettes: Mister Lee's Star Pupils" *Goldmine*, Feb. 21, 1992.

Chapter 9: The Death Knell(s)

105 ...the legal battles . . . forty-three. Smith, Wes. *The Pied Pipers of Rock 'n' Roll*. Marietta, GA: Longstreet Press, 1989.

Chapter 10: Some Idiosycrasies Of Doo-Wop

112 Esther Navarro . . . pass by the window. Mondrone, Sal et al. "The Cadillacs". *Bim Bam Boom*, Vol. 1, Issue 5, April-May 1972.

112 Cadillacs' member . . . impress the ladies. Mondrone, Sal et al. "The Cadillacs". *Bim Bam Boom*, Vol. 1, Issue 5, April-May 1972.

116 "Gloria" has the most interesting history... Gonzales, Ferdie and Turco, Art. "It's Not Cherie..." *Record Exchanger*, June 1973.

117 Navarro wrote the song... Mondrone, Sal et al. "The Cadillacs". *Bim Bam Boom*, Vol. 1, Issue 5, April-May 1972.

Bibliography

Aita, Frank. "The Rivieras." *Record Exchanger*, Vol. 4, No. 3.

"Alan Freed and 7 Others Arrested in Payola Here." *New York Times*, May 20,1960, 1:2.

Anderson, Will. "The Carnations." *Bim Bam Boom*, Issue 8, December 1972.

Ball, Aimee Lee. "Rock Of Ages: WCBS-FM Rides The Crest Of An Oldies Revival." New York: *New York Magazine*, Aug. 6, 1990.

Beckman, Jeff and Feigenbaum, Hank. "Gee, It's The Crows." *Big Town Review*, Vol. 1, No.2, 1972.

Bosco, Robert. "Joey/Flips From Bandstand To Obscurity." *Record Collector's Monthly* #50, November-December 1991.

Bronson, Fred. *Billboard Book of Number One Hits*. New York: Billboard Books, 1985.

Brown, Charles T. *The Rock & Roll Story*. Englewood Cliffs, CA: Prentice-Hall, 1983.

Chapman, Robert L. (ed.) *New Dictionary Of American Slang*. New York: Harper & Row, 1986.

Chapple, Steve & Garofalo, Reebee. *Rock 'n' Roll is Here to Pay*. Chicago, IL: Nelson-Hall, 1977.

Clarke, Donald (ed.). *The Penguin Encyclopedia Of Pop Music*. London: Viking Press, 1989.

Clee, Ken. *The Directory of American 45 R.P.M. Records (4 Vols)*. Philadelphia: Stak-O-Wax, 1989.

Cox, Herb & West, Steve. "The Heart And Soul Of The Cleftones." *Goldmine*, Feb. 21,1992.

Davis, Chuck. "Platters." *Chicago Defender*, March 18, 1961.

Davis, Clive. *Clive: Inside the Record Business*. New York: William Morrow, 1975.

Diskin, Bobby. "Brooklyn's Bay Bops Launch White-Group Harmony And Pave The Way For 60s Doowop Hitmakers." *Record Collector's Monthly* #33, November-December 1985.

"Don K. Reed's 'Doo Wop Shop' "(audiotape), WCBS-FM Radio, New York, June 24, 1990.

"Don K. Reed's 'Doo Wop Shop' "(audiotape), WCBS-FM Radio, New York, July 8, 1990.

"Don K. Reed's 'Doo Wop Shop' "(audiotape), WCBS-FM Radio, New York, July 29, 1990.

"Don K. Reed's 'Doo Wop Shop' "(audiotape), WCBS-FM Radio, New York, May 19, 1991.

Dunne, Richard W. "The Five Discs." *Goldmine*, Feb. 8, 1991.

Engel, Edward R. *White And Still All Right! (2nd ed.)*. Edward R. Engel, 1980.

Ferlingere, Robert. *A Discography Of Rhythm & Blues And Rock 'N Roll Vocal Groups, 1945 To 1965*. Hayward, CA: California Trade School, 1976.

Flam, Steve. "The Classics." *Bim Bam Boom*, Vol. 1, No. 6, 1972.

Fox, Ted. *Showtime At The Apollo*. New York: Holt, Rinehart & Winston, 1983.

Gagnon, Rick & Gnerre, Dave. "Little Caesar & the Romans: Still Singin' Those Oldies But Goodies." *Goldmine*, Aug. 12, 1988.

Gaines, Steven. *Heroes & Villains: The True Story of the Beach Boys*. New York: New American Library, 1986.

Gart, Galen. *American Record Label Directory And Dating Guide (4th ed.)*. Milford, NH: BigNickel Publications, 1990.

Gart, Galen, ed. *First Pressings: The History Of Rhythm & Blues, Vol. 3: 1953*. Milford, NH: Big Nickel Publications, 1989.

Gart, Galen, ed. *First Pressings: The History Of Rhythm & Blues, Vol. 4: 1954*. Milford, NH: Big Nickel Publications, 1990.

Gart, Galen, ed. *First Pressings: The History Of Rhythm & Blues, Vol. 5: 1955*. Milford, NH: Big Nickel Publications, 1990.

Garvey, Dennis. "Randy and the Rainbows: What's In A Name?" *Goldmine*, February 8, 1991.

Garvey, Dennis. "The Tune Weavers: One-Hit Wonderfuls." *Goldmine*, Feb. 8, 1991.

Garvey, Dennis. "The Bobbettes: Mister Lee's Star Pupils." *Goldmine*, Feb. 21, 1992.

George, Nelson. *The Death Of Rhythm & Blues*. New York: E.P. Dutton, 1988.

Gilbert, Bob & Theroux, Gary. *The Top Ten: 1956-Present*. New York: Simon & Schuster,1982.

Gillett, Charlie. *The Sound Of The City: The Rise Of Rock And Roll*. New York: Pantheon Books, 1983.

Goldberg, Marv. "Toppers, Hurricanes, Memos Are Same Brooklyn R&B Group On Wax." *Record Collector's Monthly* #43, March-April 1989.

Goldberg, Marv and Redmond, Mike. "The Life And Times Of The Solitaires." *Record Exchanger*, Fall 1973.

Goldstein, S. & Jacobson, A. Oldies But Goodies: The Rock & Roll Years. New York: Mason-Charter, 1977.

Gonzales, Fernando L. *Disco-File (2nd ed.)*. Flushing, N.Y.: Fernando L. Gonzales, 1977.

Gonzales, Ferdie and Turco, Art. "It's Not Cherie..." *Record Exchanger*, June 1973.

Greenfield, Jeff. *No Peace, No Place*. Garden City, N.Y.: Doubleday & Co., 1973.

Greig, Charlotte. *Will You Still Love Me Tomorrow?* London: Virago Press,1989.

Grendysa, Peter. "Fifties (50s) R & B Stars Helped Cheat Themselves By Signing Poorly Negotiated Contracts." *Record Collector's Monthly* #17, February 1984.

Grendysa, Peter. "The Diablos." *Goldmine*, Jan. 3, 1986.

Grendysa, Peter. "The Coming And Going Of The Del Vikings." *Goldmine*, Feb. 21, 1992.

Groia, Phil. "The Paul Winley Story." *Bim Bam Boom*, Vol. 2, No. 3, 1972.

Groia, Phil. *They All Sang On The Corner*. Port Jefferson, N.Y.: Phillie Dee Enterprises,1983.

Guralnick, Peter. *Sweet Soul Music*. New York: Harper & Row,1986.

610

Hardy, Phil & Laing, Dave. *Encyclopedia of Rock*. New York: Schirmer Books, 1988.

Heather, Bruce and Dawson, Jim. "The Pearls: Anatomy of a Doo-Wop Group." *Goldmine*, Feb. 8, 1991.

Helander, Brock. *The Rock Who's Who: A Complete Guide to the Great Artists...* New York: Schirmer Books, 1982.

Hibbard, Don J. & Kaleialoha, C. *The Role of Rock*. Englewood Cliffs, CA: Prentice-Hall, 1983.

Hill, Randall C. *The Official Price Guide To Collectible Rock Records, 2nd ed.* House Of Collectibles, 1980.

Hitchcock, H.W. & Sadie, S. (eds.) *The New Grove Dictionary Of American Music*. New York: MacMillan, 1986.

Horner, Charlie. "Lee Andrews And The Hearts." *Goldmine*, Dec. 28, 1990.

Horner, Charlie and Applebaum, Steve. "The Castelles." *Bim Bam Boom*, Vol.2, No. 6, 1974.

Jackson, John, A. *Big Beat Heat: Alan Freed and the Early Years of Rock & Roll*. New York: Schirmer Books, 1991.

Jancik, Wayne. "Down The Aisle With The Quin-Tones." *Goldmine*, Dec. 28, 1990.

Jancik, Wayne. "The Dreamlovers: Keeping The Dream Alive." *Goldmine*, Dec. 28, 1990.

Jones, Wayne "The Five Satins featuring Fred Parris." *Goldmine*, May 1979.

Keyes, Johnny. *Du-Wop*. Chicago: Vesti Press, 1987.

Kreiter, Jeff. *45 R.P.M. Group Collector's Record Guide, 4th ed.* Bridgeport, OH: Boyd Press, 1992.

Leibowitz, Alan. *The Record Collector's Handbook*. New York: Everest House, 1980.

Logan, Nick & Woffinden, Bob. *The Illustrated Encyclopedia of Rock*. New York: Harmony Books, 1979.

Manchester, William. *The Glory And The Dream, Vol. 1*. Boston, MA: Little, Brown & Co., 1973.

Manchester, William. *The Glory And The Dream, Vol. 2*. Boston, MA: Little, Brown & Co., 1974.

Marsh, Dave. *The Heart Of Rock And Soul: The 1001 Greatest Singles Ever Made*. New York: New American Library, 1989.

Mawhinney, Paul C. *The Music Master: The 45 RPM Record Directory By Artist (V. I)*. Pittsburgh, PA: Record-Rama Sound Archives, 1983.

Mawhinney, Paul C. *The Music Master: The 45 RPM Record Directory By Title (V. II)*. Pittsburgh, PA: Record-Rama Sound Archives, 1983.

McCutcheon, Lynn Ellis. *Rhythm and Blues*. Arlington, VA.: Beatty, 1971.

Mennie, Don. "Ducanes Chart With 'I'm So Happy,' Phil Spector Discovers Doo-wop." *Record Collector's Monthly* #39, December 1987-January 1988.

Miller, Don Ethan. *The Book Of Jargon*. New York: Macmillan, 1981.

Miller, Jim (ed.) *The Rolling Stone Illustrated History Of Rock & Roll*. New York: Rolling Stone Press, 1980.

Mondrone, Sal et al. "The Cadillacs." *Bim Bam Boom*, Vol. l, Issue 5, April-May 1972.

Morrow, Bruce & Baudo, Laura. *Cousin Brucie: My Life In Rock 'n' Roll Radio.* New York: William Morrow, 1987.

Newman, Ralph. "Tony Passalacqua and the Fascinators." *Bim Bam Boom,* Vol. 1, No. 7, 1972.

Nite, Norm N. *Rock On, Vol. I.* New York: Thomas Y. Crowell Co., 1974.

Nite, Norm N. *Rock On Almanac.* New York: Harper & Row, 1989.

Osborne, Jerry. *Record Collector's Price Guide, 1st ed.* O'Sullivan, Wardside, 1976.

Osborne, Jerry. *Blues, R&B And Soul Price Guide, 1st ed.* O'Sullivan, Wardside, 1980.

Osborne, Jerry. *The Complete Library Of Amer. Phonograph Recordings, 1959.* Tempe, AR: Osborne Enterprises, 1987.

Osborne, Jerry. *The Complete Library Of Amer. Phonograph Recordings, 1960.* Tempe, AR: Osborne Enterprises, 1987.

Osborne, Jerry. *The Complete Library Of Amer. Phonograph Recordings, 1961.* Tempe, AR: Osborne Enterprises, 1987.

Osborne, Jerry. *Rockin' Records: Buyers & Sellers Ref. Book And Price Guide.* Port Townsend, WA: Osborne Enterprises, 1989.

Oxford English Dict., 2nd ed. "Doo-Wop." Oxford, GB: Clarendon Press, 1989.

Pollock, Bruce. *When Rock Was Young.* New York: Holt, Rinehart and Winston, 1981.

Propes, Steve. *Those Oldies But Goodies: A Guide To 50s Record Collecting.* New York: MacMillan, 1973.

Propes, Steve. *Golden Oldies: A Guide To 60s Record Collecting.* New York: Chilton, 1974.

Pruter, Robert. "Pastels' Promise Eclipsed By Manager's Marital Problems." *Record Collector's Monthly* #45, December 1989.

Pruter, Robert. "The Five Chances And Their World Of Chicago R & B." *Goldmine,* April 6, 1990.

Pruter, Robert. "The Flamingos: The Chicago Years." *Goldmine,* April 6, 1990.

Pruter, Robert. "The Early Dells." *Record Collector's Monthly* #50, November-December 1991.

Random House Dictionary, 2nd ed. "Doo-Wop." New York: Random House, 1987.

Robinson, Smokey & Ritz, David. *Smokey: Inside My Life.* New York: McGraw-Hill, 1989.

"Rock 'n' Roll Pied Piper: Alan Freed." *New York Times,* May 20, 1960, p. 62.

Santelli, Robert. "Rhino Records remembers doo-wop." *Asbury Park Press,* Asbury Park, NJ, Feb. 9, 1990, p. 12.

Schoener, Allon (ed.) *Harlem On My Mind: Cultural Capitol Of Black America 1900-1968.* New York: Random House, 1968.

Shaw, Arnold. *Honkers And Shouters: The Golden Years Of Rhythm & Blues.* New York: MacMillan, 1978.

Shemel, Sidney & Krasilovsky, M. William. *This Business Of Music, 6th Ed.* New York: Billboard Books, 1990.

Shore, Michael. *The History of American Bandstand.* New York: Ballantine, 1985.

Sicurelli, Joe. "(I Found Out Why) The Lymon Brothers." *Big Town Review*, Vol. 1, No. 3, July- August 1972.

Smith, Wes. *The Pied Pipers of Rock 'n' Roll*. Marietta, GA: Longstreet Press, 1989.

Stambler, Irwin. *The Encyclopedia Of Pop, Rock And Soul (revised edition)*. New York: St. Martin's Press, 1989.

Stierle, Wayne. "The Jive Five: A True New York Story." *Goldmine*, Aug. 12, 1988.

Stierle, Wayne. "The Monotones: They Wrote The Book Of Love." *Goldmine*, Aug. 12, 1988.

Tamarkin, Jeff. "The Laddins: A New York Story." *Goldmine*, April 6, 1990.

Tobler, John, ed. *The Rock 'N' Roll Years*. New York: Crescent Books, 1990.

Turco, Art, et al. "An Interview With Bobby Robinson." *Record Exchanger*, May 1972.

Turco, Art. "Interview: 'Little' Anthony Gourdine." *Record Exchanger*, April 1973.

Umphred, Neal. *Goldmine's Rock 'n Roll 45 RPM Record Price Guide*. Iola, WI: Krause Publications, 1990.

Vance, Marcia. "Danny & the Juniors." *Bim Bam Boom*, Vol. 2, No. 6, 1974.

Vance, Marcia & Groia, Phil. "The Willows." *Bim Bam Boom*, Vol. 1, No. 6, 1972.

Ward, Ed, et al. *Rock of Ages: The Rolling Stone History Of Rock & Roll*. New York: Summit Books, 1986.

Wasserman, Steve. "Buck Ram And The Platters." *Bim Bam Boom*, Vol. 1, No. 6, 1972.

Weinger, Harry. "The Platters' Glory Days." *Goldmine*, Feb. 21, 1992.

Whitburn, Joel. *Billboard Top 1000 Singles: 1955-1987*. Milwaukee, WI: Hal Leonard Books, 1988.

Whitburn, Joel. *The Billboard Book Of Top 40 Hits: 1955-1987*. New York: Billboard Books, 1989.

Whitesell, Rick. "The Pipes." *Goldmine*, April 1979.

"Willie Bryant, Entertainer, Dies; Was Once 'Mayor Of Harlem.' "*New York Times*, Feb. 15, 1964.

World Book Encyclopedia. "Transistors." Chicago, IL: World Books, 1987.

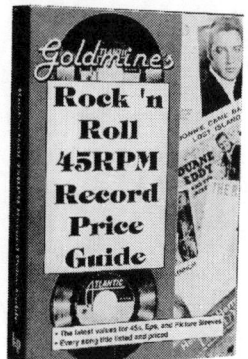